T.O. 1F-86D-1
FLIGHT HANDBOOK
USAF Series
F-86D & TF-86D
AIRCRAFT

Schiffer Military/Aviation History
Atglen, PA

The USAF F-86D & TF-86D flight handbook used to print this book is from the collection of John M. Campbell.

The information in this book is true and complete to the best of our knowledge. All recommendations are made without any guarantee on the part of the author or publisher, who also disclaim any liability incurred in connection with the use of this data or specific details.

We recognize that some words, model names and designations, for example, mentioned herein are the property of the trademark holder. We use them for identification purposes only. This is not an official publication.

Cover photography from the John M. Campbell collection.

Copyright © 1995 by John M. Campbell.
Library of Congress Catalog Number: 95-67633

All rights reserved. No part of this work may be reproduced or used in any forms or by any means – graphic, electronic or mechanical, including photocopying or information storage and retrieval systems – without written permission from the copyright holder.

Printed in China.
ISBN: 0-88740-822-2

We are interested in hearing from authors with book ideas on related topics.

Published by Schiffer Publishing Ltd.
77 Lower Valley Road
Atglen, PA 19310
Please write for a free catalog.
This book may be purchased from the publisher.
Please include $2.95 postage.
Try your bookstore first.

T. O. 1F-86D-1

FLIGHT HANDBOOK

USAF SERIES
F-86D & TF-86D AIRCRAFT

Commanders are responsible for bringing this handbook to the attention of all personnel cleared for operation of affected aircraft.

Published under the authority of the Secretary of the Air Force.

This reissue replaces T. O. 1F-86D-1, dated 29 August 1955, and Safety of Flight Supplements thereto: -1CH through -1CV. Only supplements issued subsequent to -1CV remain active.

Kerr Lithographers—Culver City, Calif.—11,105—6-20-56

18 MAY 1956

TABLE OF CONTENTS

SECTION	I	DESCRIPTION	1-1
SECTION	II	NORMAL PROCEDURES	2-1
SECTION	III	EMERGENCY PROCEDURES	3-1
SECTION	IV	Description and Operation of AUXILIARY EQUIPMENT	4-1
SECTION	V	OPERATING LIMITATIONS	5-1
SECTION	VI	FLIGHT CHARACTERISTICS	6-1
SECTION	VII	SYSTEMS OPERATION	7-1
SECTION	VIII	CREW DUTIES	(not applicable)
SECTION	IX	ALL-WEATHER OPERATION	9-1
APPENDIX	I	PERFORMANCE DATA	A-1
		ALPHABETICAL INDEX	Index-1

It is the intent of Air Force Regulation 5-13, dated 11 August 1953, that each pilot (except those attached to an administrative base) is entitled to his own copy of the Flight Handbook for his airplane. However, since the Flight Handbook is Government property and subject to specific controls, distribution responsibility rests wtih the Base Commander.

SCOPE. This handbook contains all the information necessary for safe and efficient operation of the F-86D Airplane. These instructions do not teach basic flight principles, but are designed to provide you with a general knowledge of the airplane, its flight characteristics, and specific normal and emergency operating procedures. Your flying experience is recognized, and elementary instructions have been avoided.

SOUND JUDGMENT. The instructions in this handbook are designed to provide for the needs of a pilot inexperienced in the operation of this airplane. This book provides the best possible operating instructions under most circumstances, but it is a poor substitute for sound judgment. Multiple emergencies, adverse weather, terrain, etc, may require modification of the procedures contained herein.

PERMISSIBLE OPERATIONS. The Flight Handbook takes a "positive approach," and normally tells you only what you can do. Any unusual operation or configuration (such as asymmetrical loading) is prohibited unless specifically covered in the Flight Handbook. Clearance must be obtained from ARDC before any questionable operation is attempted which is not specifically covered in the Flight Handbook.

STANDARDIZATION. Once you have learned to use one Flight Handbook, you will know how to use them all—closely guarded standardization ensures that the scope and arrangement of all Flight Handbooks are identical.

ARRANGEMENT. The handbook has been divided into 10 sections, each with its own table of contents. The objective of this subdivision is to make it easy both to read the book straight through when it is first received and thereafter to use it as a reference manual. The independence of these sections also makes it possible for the user to rearrange the book to satisfy his personal taste and requirements. The first three sections cover the minimum information required to safely get the airplane into the air and back down again. Before flying any new airplane, you must read and fully understand these three sections. Section IV covers all equipment not essential to flight but which permits the airplane to perform special functions. The contents of Sections V, VI, and the Appendix are obvious from their titles. Section VII covers lengthy discussions on any technique or theory of operation which may apply to the particular airplane in question. The experienced pilot will probably not need to read this section, but he should check it for any possible new information. The contents of the remaining sections are fairly obvious from their titles.

YOUR RESPONSIBILITY. These Flight Handbooks are constantly maintained current through an extremely active revision program. Frequent conferences with operating personnel and constant review of UR's, accident reports, flight test reports, etc, ensure inclusion of the latest data in these handbooks. In this regard, it is essential that you do your part! If you find anything you don't like about the book, let us know right away. We cannot correct errors whose existence is unknown to us.

BINDERS AND TABS. Flexible loose-leaf binders and tabs have been provided to hold your personal copy of the Flight Handbook. These good-looking, simulated-leather binders will make it much easier for you to revise your handbook as well as to keep it in good shape. These binders and tabs are secured through your local contracting officer.

HOW TO GET COPIES. If you want to be sure of getting your handbooks on time, order them before you need them. Early ordering will ensure that enough copies are printed to cover your requirements. Technical Order 0-5-2 explains how to order Flight Handbooks so that you automatically will get all revisions, reissues, and Safety of Flight Supplements. Basically, all you have to do is order the required quantities in the Publication Requirements Table (T. O. 0-3-1). Talk to your base supply officer—it is his job to fulfill your Technical Order requests. Establish some system that will rapidly get the books and Safety of Flight Supplement to the pilots once the books are received on the base.

SAFETY OF FLIGHT SUPPLEMENTS. Safety of Flight Supplements are used to get information to you in a hurry. Safety of Flight Supplements use the same number as your Flight Handbook, except for the addition of a suffix letter. Supplements covering loss of life will get to you in 48 hours; those concerning serious damage to equipment will make it in 6 days. You can determine the status of Safety of Flight Supplements by referring to the Index of Technical Publications (T. O. 0-1-1) and the Weekly Supplemental Index (T. O. 0-1-1A). The title page of the Flight Handbook and title block of each Safety of Flight Supplement should also be checked to determine the effect that these publications may have on existing Safety of Flight Supplements. If you have ordered your Flight Handbook on the Publication Requirements Table, you automatically will receive all supplements pertaining to your airplane. Technical Order 0-5-1 covers some additional information regarding these supplements.

WARNINGS, CAUTIONS, AND NOTES. For your information, the following definitions apply to the "Warnings," "Cautions," and "Notes" found throughout the handbook.

 Operating procedures, practices, etc, which will result in personal injury or loss of life if not carefully followed.

 Operating procedures, practices, etc, which if not strictly observed will result in damage to equipment.

Note   An operating procedure, condition, etc, which it is essential to emphasize.

MAINTENANCE HANDBOOKS. One more thing. If you desire more detailed information on the various airplane systems and components than is provided within the scope of the Flight Handbook, refer to the Systems Maintenance Handbooks (T. O. 1F-86D-2 Series) for your airplane.

COMMENTS AND QUESTIONS. Comments and questions regarding any phase of the Flight Handbook program are invited and should be addressed to the Directorate of Systems Management, HQ Air Research and Development Command, Wright-Patterson AF Base, Ohio, Attention: RDZSTH.

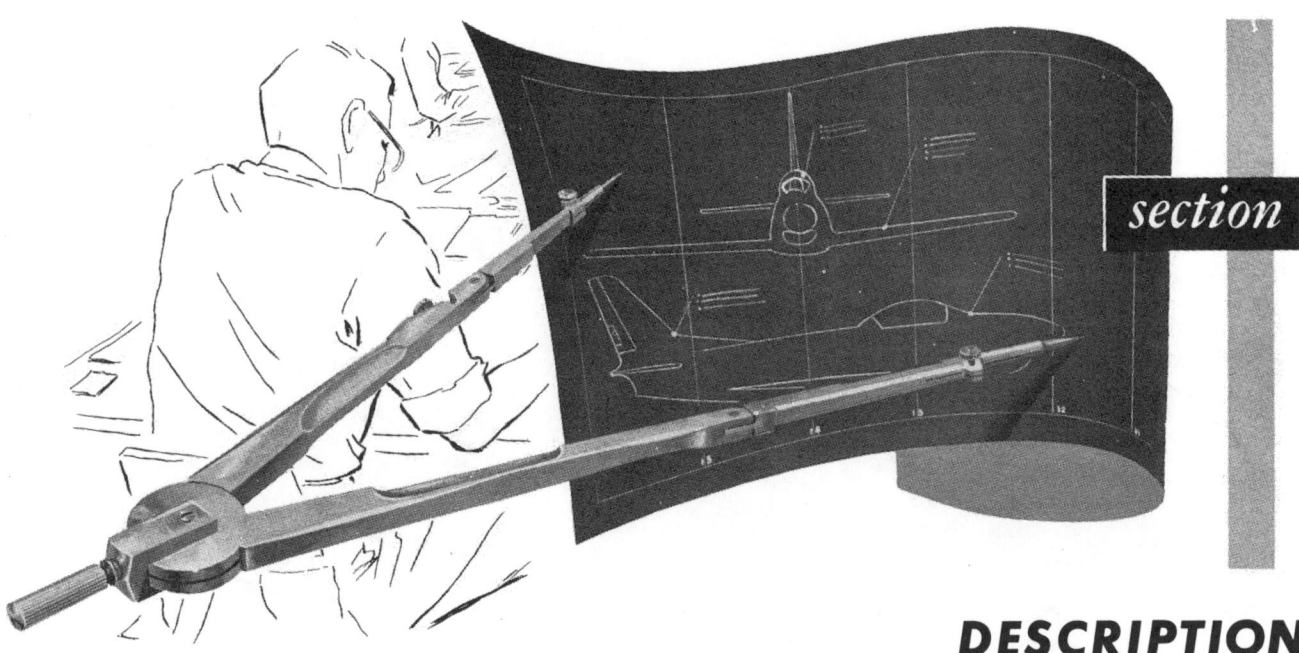

section I

DESCRIPTION

TABLE OF CONTENTS	PAGE
Airplane	1-1
Engine	1-5
Afterburner System	1-24
Oil System	1-26
Fuel System	1-26
Electrical Power Supply System	1-30
Utility Hydraulic Power Supply System	1-36
Flight Control System	1-38
Wing Slats	1-44
Wing Flap System	1-45

	PAGE
Speed Brake System	1-45
Landing Gear System	1-46
Nose Wheel Steering System	1-48
Brake System	1-49
Drag Chute System	1-49
Instruments	1-50
Emergency Equipment	1-52
Canopy	1-52
Ejection Seat	1-55
Auxiliary Equipment	1-60

AIRPLANE.

The North American F-86D is a single-place, all-weather fighter-interceptor. Principal recognition features are its swept-back low wing and empennage and the radome, similar in appearance to a propeller spinner, on the nose above the air intake duct. The engine is an axial-flow, turbojet unit equipped with an afterburner. Other noteworthy features include electronic engine control, leading edge wing slats, fuselage speed brakes, the combination of elevators and horizontal stabilizer into a single surface known as the controllable horizontal tail, and a drag chute on late airplanes* and those changed by T. O. Designed chiefly as a high-altitude fighter-interceptor, the airplane is equipped with the latest and most advanced equipment (a large part of which is electronic) to accurately and effectively launch the rockets with which the airplane is armed. The rocket-firing control system computer tracks the target and tells the pilot the course to follow. This system requires precision flying in order to work with a minimum amount of error, as it will more accurately compute the true rocket interception course if abrupt maneuvers, high G, rapid rates of roll or pitch, or steep angles of bank are avoided. For better use of the full abilities of the rocket-firing control system and for longer service life of the equipment, smooth, organized precision flying should be practiced. However, it must be stressed that whenever evasive action is necessary, high-G turns and abrupt maneuvers within the structural limits of the airplane are permissible.

*F-86D-45 and later airplanes

GENERAL ARRANGEMENT

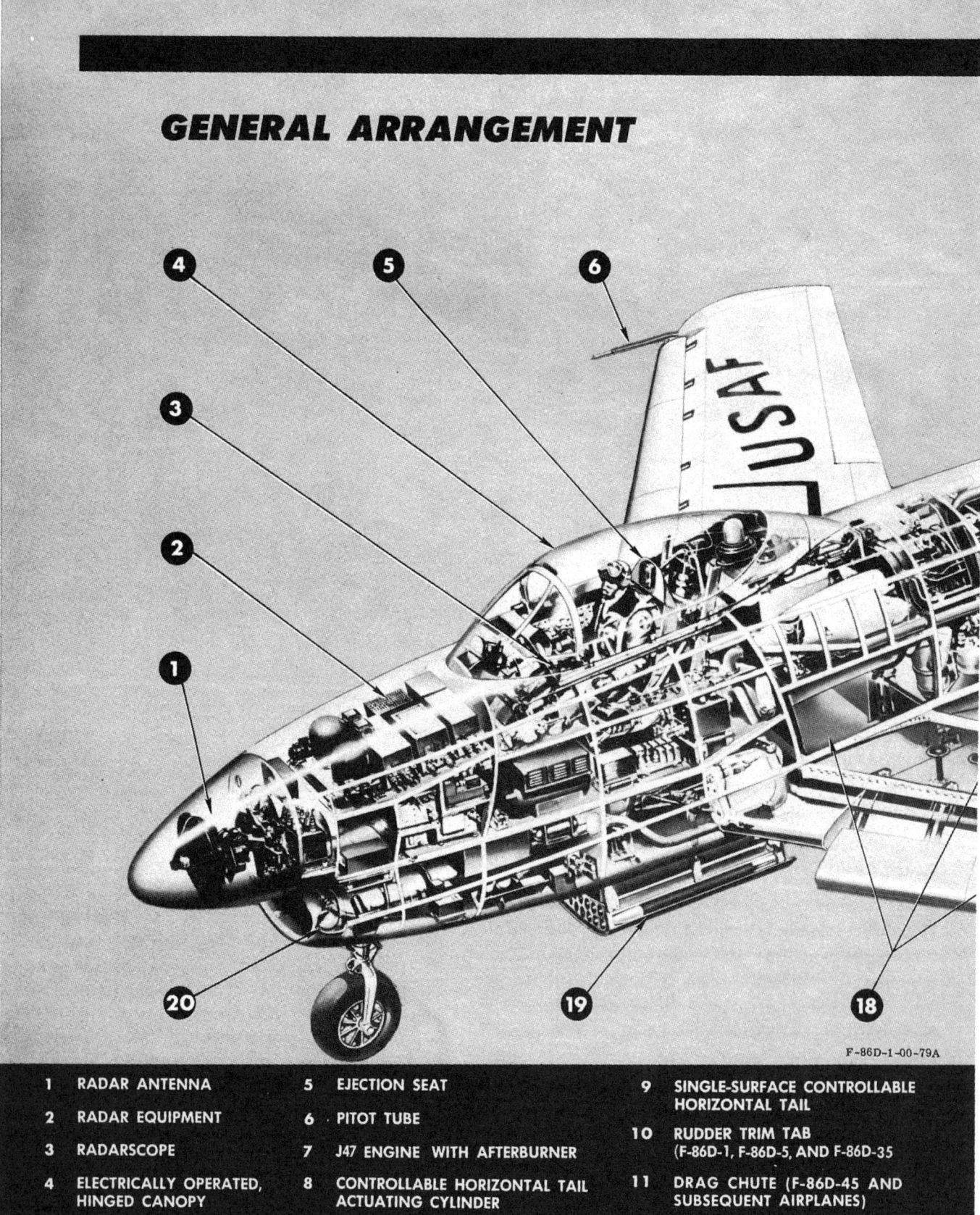

1	RADAR ANTENNA	5	EJECTION SEAT	9	SINGLE-SURFACE CONTROLLABLE HORIZONTAL TAIL
2	RADAR EQUIPMENT	6	PITOT TUBE	10	RUDDER TRIM TAB (F-86D-1, F-86D-5, AND F-86D-35)
3	RADARSCOPE	7	J47 ENGINE WITH AFTERBURNER		
4	ELECTRICALLY OPERATED, HINGED CANOPY	8	CONTROLLABLE HORIZONTAL TAIL ACTUATING CYLINDER	11	DRAG CHUTE (F-86D-45 AND SUBSEQUENT AIRPLANES)

Figure 1-1

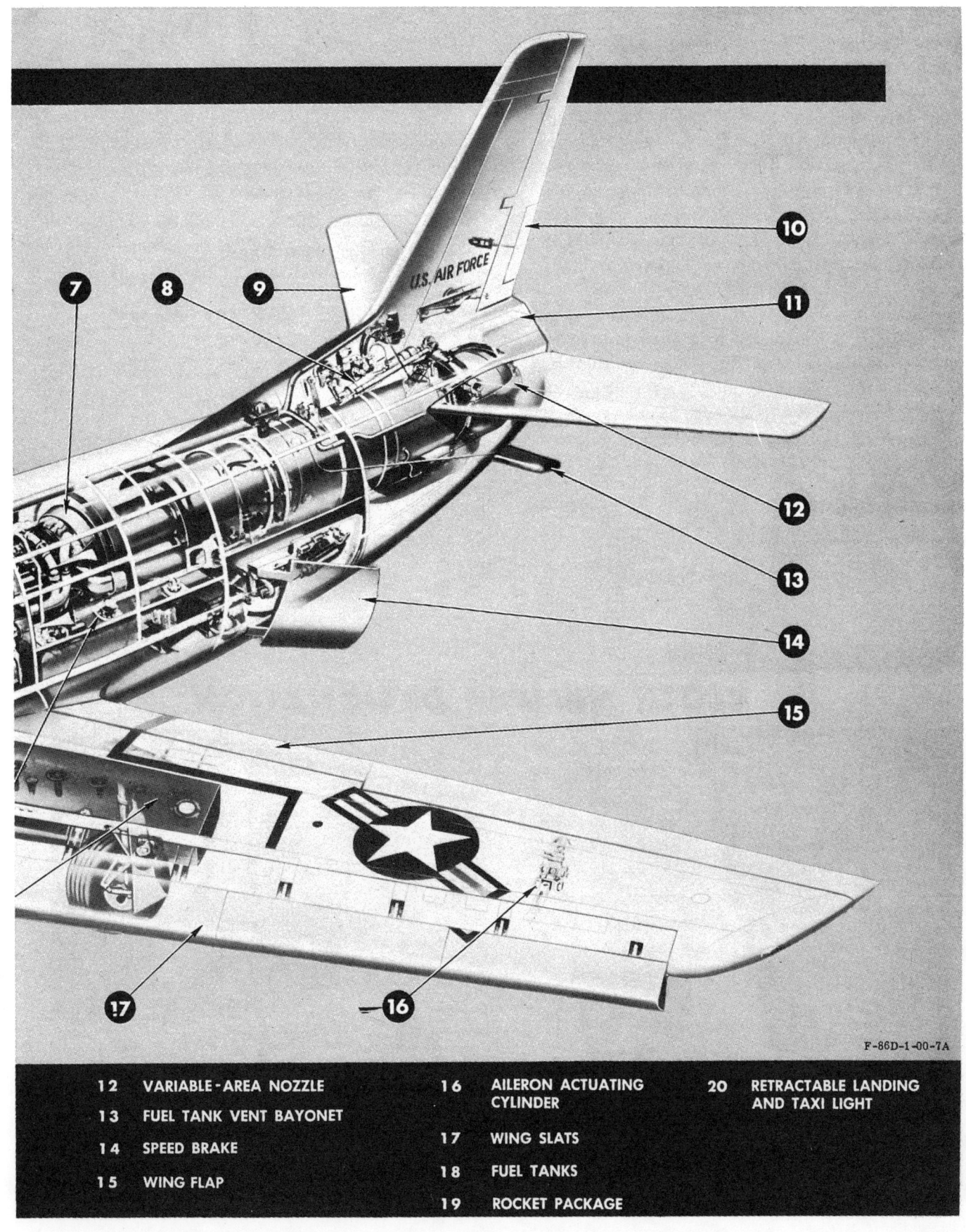

12	VARIABLE-AREA NOZZLE	16	AILERON ACTUATING CYLINDER
13	FUEL TANK VENT BAYONET	17	WING SLATS
14	SPEED BRAKE	18	FUEL TANKS
15	WING FLAP	19	ROCKET PACKAGE
		20	RETRACTABLE LANDING AND TAXI LIGHT

TF-86D (CHASE) AIRPLANES.

Some F-86D-1 and F-86D-5 Airplanes were changed and redesignated as TF-86D Airplanes. The modification consists of the following: the radome is replaced with a metal nose; the rocket package and hydraulic equipment for operating the package is removed and the exposed opening covered with metal skin; and the E-3 or E-4 fire control system, automatic pilot, engine-driven alternator, the glide path, localizer, and marker beacon radio equipment (AN/ARN-14, AN/ARN-5B, RC-103D, and AN/ARN-12) are removed. Ballast is added to provide a satisfactory center-of-gravity location because of the removal of equipment from the forward section. The flight handling characteristics are basically the same as for the F-86D Airplane. However, because of the decrease in gross weight (about 750 pounds), performance is generally improved. The flight limitations are the same as for the F-86D Airplane.

AIRPLANE DIMENSIONS.

Over-all dimensions of the airplane are as follows:

Wing span	37.1 feet
Length	40.3 feet
Height	15.0 feet

AIRPLANE GROSS WEIGHT.

The approximate normal take-off gross weight of the airplane, including pilot (230 pounds), full internal fuel, and rockets, is as follows:

Clean airplane	18,760 pounds
With two 120-gallon drop tanks	20,550 pounds

The TF-86D Airplane is about 750 pounds lighter than the F-86D Airplane.

ARMAMENT.

Armament consists of twenty-four 2.75-inch, folding-fin rockets. The rockets are suspended in a package, located in the under portion of the fuselage, which extends for firing and then retracts when the firing is completed. The rockets can be fired either automatically or manually.

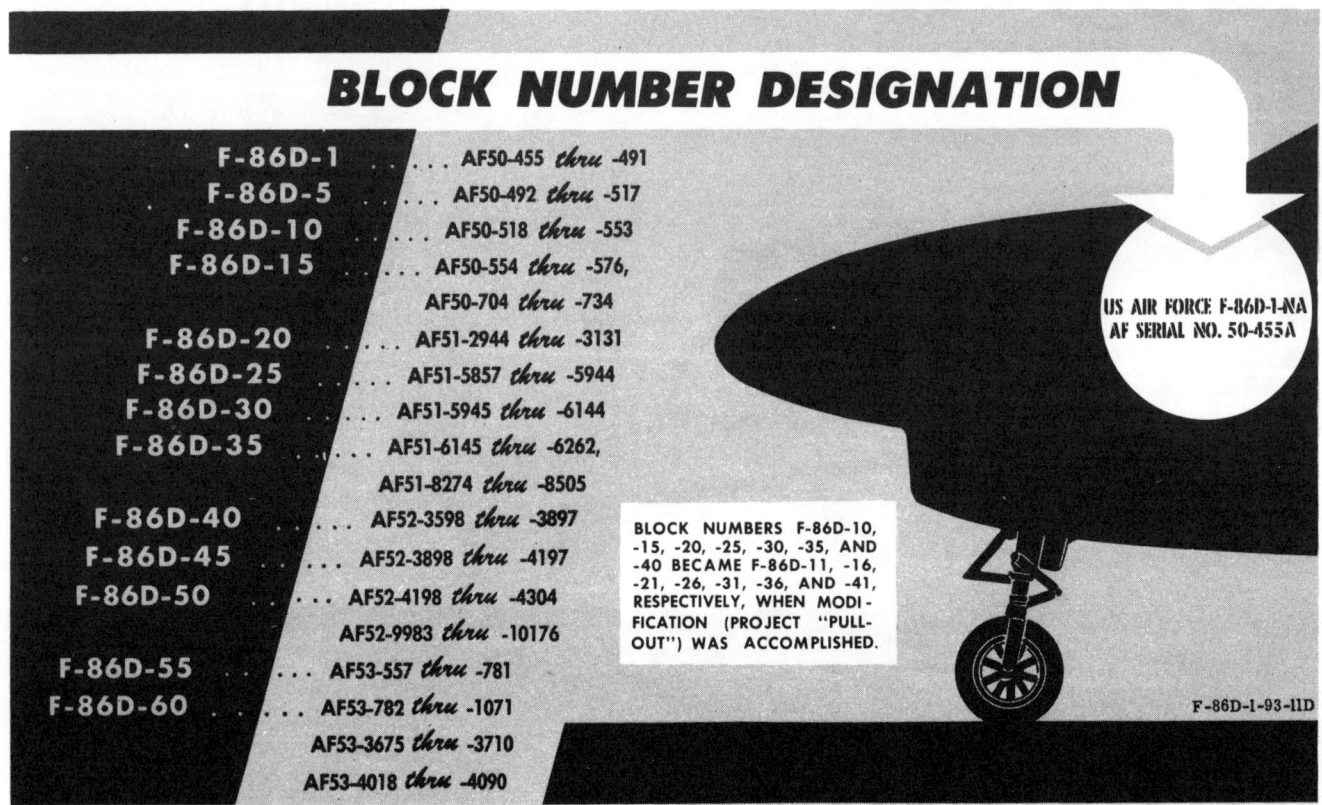

Figure 1-2

MAIN DIFFERENCES TABLE

ITEM	F-86A	F-86D	F-86E	F-86F	F-86H	F-86K
ENGINE	J47-GE-7 OR -13	J47-GE-17, -17B, OR -33	J47-GE-13	J47-GE-27	J73-GE-3	J47-GE-17B
ENGINE AIR INTAKE DUCT	IN NOSE	BELOW RADOME IN NOSE	IN NOSE	IN NOSE	IN NOSE	BELOW RADOME IN NOSE
DRAG CHUTE	NO	IN EMPENNAGE ABOVE EXHAUST NOZZLE AND BELOW RUDDER*	NO	NO	NO	IN EMPENNAGE ABOVE EXHAUST NOZZLE AND BELOW RUDDER
CANOPY	SLIDING	CLAMSHELL	SLIDING	SLIDING	CLAMSHELL	CLAMSHELL
HORIZONTAL TAIL ACTION	CONVENTIONAL	STABILIZER AND ELEVATOR COMBINED INTO ONE MOVABLE SURFACE	CONTROLLABLE STABILIZER AND ELEVATOR	CONTROLLABLE STABILIZER AND ELEVATOR	CONTROLLABLE STABILIZER AND ELEVATOR	STABILIZER AND ELEVATOR COMBINED INTO ONE MOVABLE SURFACE
SURFACE CONTROLS	CONVENTIONAL WITH HYDRAULIC BOOST	COMPLETELY HYDRAULIC IRREVERSIBLE CONTROL	COMPLETELY HYDRAULIC IRREVERSIBLE CONTROL	COMPLETELY HYDRAULIC IRREVERSIBLE CONTROL	COMPLETELY HYDRAULIC IRREVERSIBLE CONTROL	COMPLETELY HYDRAULIC IRREVERSIBLE CONTROL
ENGINE CONTROLS	CONVENTIONAL (MECHANICAL LINKAGE)	ELECTRONIC	CONVENTIONAL (MECHANICAL LINKAGE)	CONVENTIONAL (MECHANICAL LINKAGE)	HYDROMECHANICAL	ELECTRONIC
AUTOMATIC PILOT	NO	YES	NO	NO	NO	YES
ARTIFICIAL FEEL	NO	YES	YES	YES	YES	YES
SIGHT	A-1B, A-1CM, OR MARK 18	E-3 FIRE CONTROL† E-4 FIRE CONTROL‡ N-9-1 (STAND-BY)	A-1CM OR A-4	A-1CM OR A-4	A-4	MG-4 FIRE CONTROL (WITH A-4 SIGHT)
ARMAMENT	GUNS AND EXTERNALLY MOUNTED BOMBS, ROCKETS, OR CHEMICAL TANKS	ROCKETS MOUNTED IN RETRACTABLE PACKAGE	GUNS AND EXTERNALLY MOUNTED BOMBS, ROCKETS, OR CHEMICAL TANKS	GUNS AND EXTERNALLY MOUNTED BOMBS, ROCKETS, OR CHEMICAL TANKS	MACHINE GUNS, BOMBS, ROCKETS, OR SPECIAL STORES	20 MM RAPID-FIRE GUNS

*F-86D-45 and later airplanes and those changed by T. O. 1F-86D-251
†F-86D-1 Airplanes
‡F-86D-5 and later airplanes

Figure 1-3

MAIN DIFFERENCES TABLE.

The main differences between the F-86D Airplane and the other models of the F-86 Series are shown in figure 1-3. Under a modification program ("Project Pull-out"), all airplanes of the F-86D-10, -15, -20, -25, -30, -35, and -40 block number designations were changed. These airplanes have been redesignated as F-86D-11, -16, -21, -26, -31, -36, and -41, respectively. Instructions in this handbook that are coded for F-86D-10 through F-86D-40 Airplanes also apply to F-86D-11 through F-86D-41 Airplanes. A major identifying feature of the modification program is the installation of the drag chute on these airplanes. Upon completion of this program, all applicable forms, historical records, and reports were changed.

ENGINE.

The Model J47-GE-17, -17B,* or -33† turbojet engine is characterized by an afterburner and a variable-area jet nozzle. (See figure 1-11.) The -17 and -17B engines have a rated sea-level static thrust of about 5425 pounds at Military Thrust and 7500 pounds at Maximum Thrust; the -33 engine has about 5550 pounds at Military Thrust and 7650 pounds at Maximum Thrust. During engine operation, air enters the intake duct below the nose of the airplane and is routed to an axial-flow compressor, where it is compressed progressively in 12 stages. The compressed air then flows to the combustion chambers, where atomized fuel is injected and combustion occurs. From the combustion chambers, the hot exhaust gas passes through a turbine and out the tail

---

*F-86D-45 Airplanes AF52-3898 through -4135
†F-86D-45 Airplane AF52-4136 and all later airplanes

Section I
T. O. 1F-86D-1

1. ENGINE CONTROL PANEL
2. ACCELEROMETER
3. MACHMETER
4. OXYGEN SYSTEM WARNING LIGHT
5. LANDING GEAR UNSAFE WARNING LIGHT*
6. ALTIMETER
7. SLAVED GYRO MAGNETIC COMPASS FAST SLAVE SWITCH*
8. APPROACH INDICATOR
9. MARKER BEACON INDICATOR LIGHT
10. AIRSPEED INDICATOR
11. CLOCK
12. ZERO READER
13. VOLTMETER
14. LOADMETER (GENERATOR NO. 1)
15. GENERATOR WARNING LIGHTS
16. VOLTMETER SELECTOR SWITCH
17. LOADMETER (GENERATOR NO. 2)
18. ATTITUDE INDICATOR

19. LOCKUP INDICATOR LIGHT
20. PITCH TRIM INDICATOR
21. TACHOMETER
22. EXHAUST TEMPERATURE GAGE
23. RIGHT INSTRUMENT SUBPANEL
24. STAND-BY COMPASS
25. VARIABLE-NOZZLE POSITION INDICATOR
26. FUEL PRESSURE GAGE
27. RATE-OF-CLIMB INDICATOR
28. FUEL QUANTITY GAGE
29. OIL PRESSURE GAGE
30. RADARSCOPE
31. FLIGHT CONTROL ALTERNATE SYSTEM INDICATOR LIGHT
32. HYDRAULIC PRESSURE GAGE
33. HYDRAULIC PRESSURE GAGE SELECTOR
34. TURN-AND-BANK INDICATOR
35. RADAR ANTENNA HANDLE
36. SCOPE PRESENTATION INTENSITY CONTROL PANEL
37. FLIGHT CONTROL EMERGENCY HANDLE
38. RADIO COMPASS

F-86D-1 AIRPLANES

COCKPIT

*Some airplanes, see applicable text.

F-86D-1-00-27D

Figure 1-4

1-6

1. ACCELEROMETER
2. ENGINE CONTROL PANEL
3. DRAG CHUTE HANDLE*
4. APPROACH INDICATOR*—COURSE INDICATOR*
5. LANDING GEAR UNSAFE WARNING LIGHT*
6. MARKER BEACON INDICATOR LIGHT
7. CLOCK
8. AIRSPEED INDICATOR
9. PITCH TRIM INDICATOR*
10. OXYGEN SYSTEM WARNING LIGHT*
11. ALTIMETER
12. ZERO READER*— SLAVED GYRO MAGNETIC COMPASS*
13. RATE-OF-CLIMB INDICATOR
14. ATTITUDE INDICATOR
15. FIRE-WARNING LIGHTS*
16. FUEL PRESSURE GAGE* VARIABLE-NOZZLE POSITION INDICATOR*
17. TACHOMETER
18. SLAVED GYRO MAGNETIC COMPASS FAST SLAVING SWITCH
19. EXHAUST TEMPERATURE GAGE
20. LOCKUP INDICATOR LIGHT*
21. RIGHT INSTRUMENT SUBPANEL
22. STAND-BY COMPASS
23. FUEL FLOWMETER* VARIABLE-NOZZLE POSITION INDICATOR*
24. LOCKUP INDICATOR LIGHT*
25. CANOPY LOCK HANDLE*
26. FUEL QUANTITY GAGE TEST SWITCH*
27. FUEL QUANTITY GAGE
28. RADARSCOPE
29. GENERATOR WARNING LIGHTS
30. OIL PRESSURE GAGE
31. HYDRAULIC PRESSURE GAGE
32. FLIGHT CONTROL ALTERNATE SYSTEM INDICATOR LIGHT
33. HYDRAULIC PRESSURE GAGE SELECTOR SWITCH
34. DROP TANK EMERGENCY JETTISON HANDLE*
35. TURN-AND-BANK INDICATOR
36. RADIO COMPASS*— COURSE BEARING INDICATOR*
37. FLIGHT CONTROL EMERGENCY HANDLE
38. MACHMETER

*Some airplanes, see applicable text.

F-86D-5 AND SUBSEQUENT AIRPLANES

FORWARD VIEW

Figure 1-5

Section I T. O. 1F-86D-1

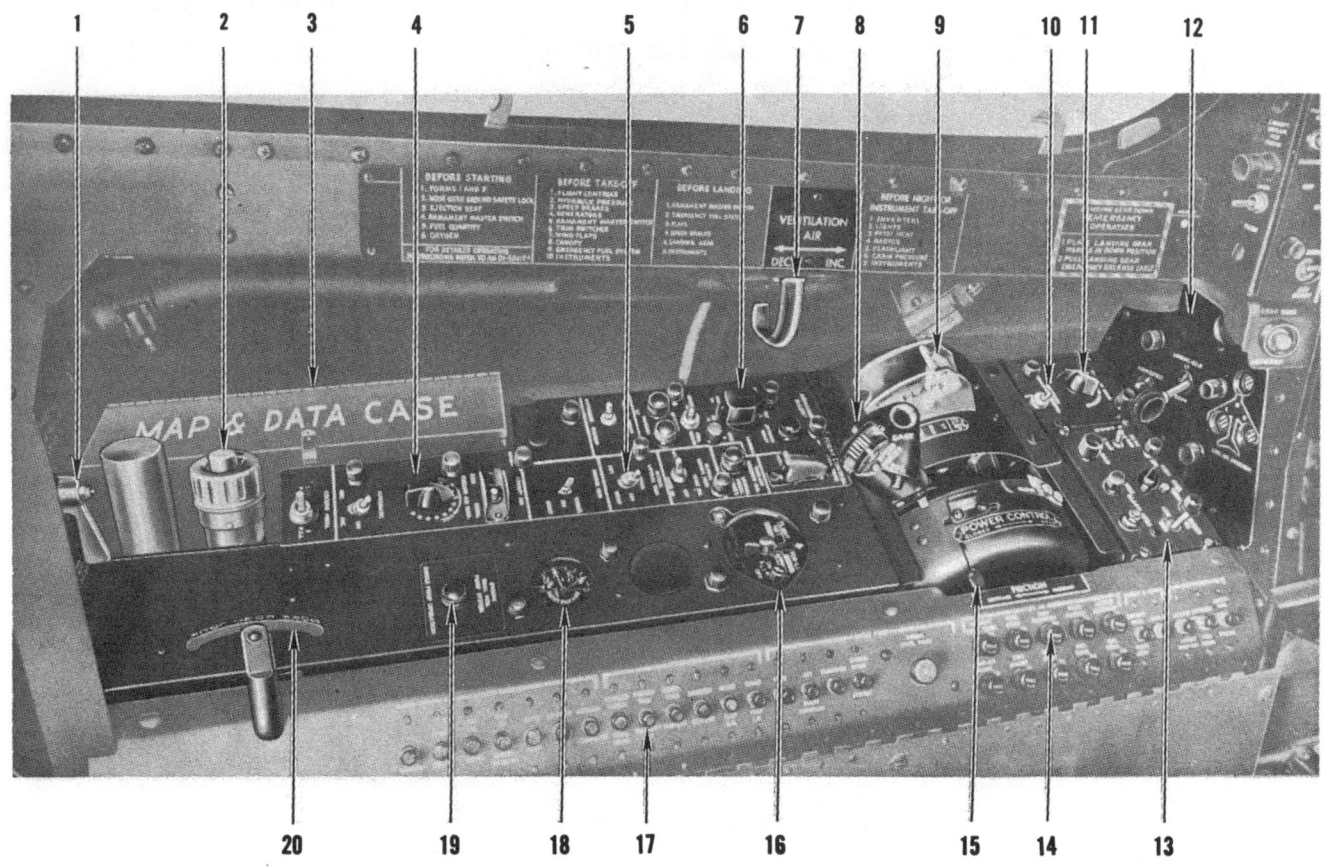

1. DROP TANK AIR PRESSURE SHUTOFF VALVE
2. ANTI-G SUIT PRESSURE REGULATOR VALVE
3. MAP CASE
4. COCKPIT AIR CONTROL PANEL
5. FLIGHT CONTROL PANEL
6. ARMAMENT CONTROL PANEL
7. VENTILATION AIR LEVER
8. THROTTLE GRIP
9. WING FLAP LEVER
10. STAND-BY SIGHT ALTERNATE FILAMENT SELECTOR SWITCH
11. STAND-BY SIGHT RHEOSTAT
12. LANDING GEAR CONTROL PANEL
13. E-3 ROCKET-FIRING CONTROL PANEL
14. FUSE PANEL
15. THROTTLE FRICTION LEVER
16. ZERO READER SELECTOR SWITCH UNIT
17. CIRCUIT-BREAKER PANEL
18. CABIN ALTIMETER
19. DUAL FUEL PUMP WARNING LIGHT
20. RUDDER LOCK HANDLE

F-86D-1 AIRPLANES

COCKPIT

Figure 1-6

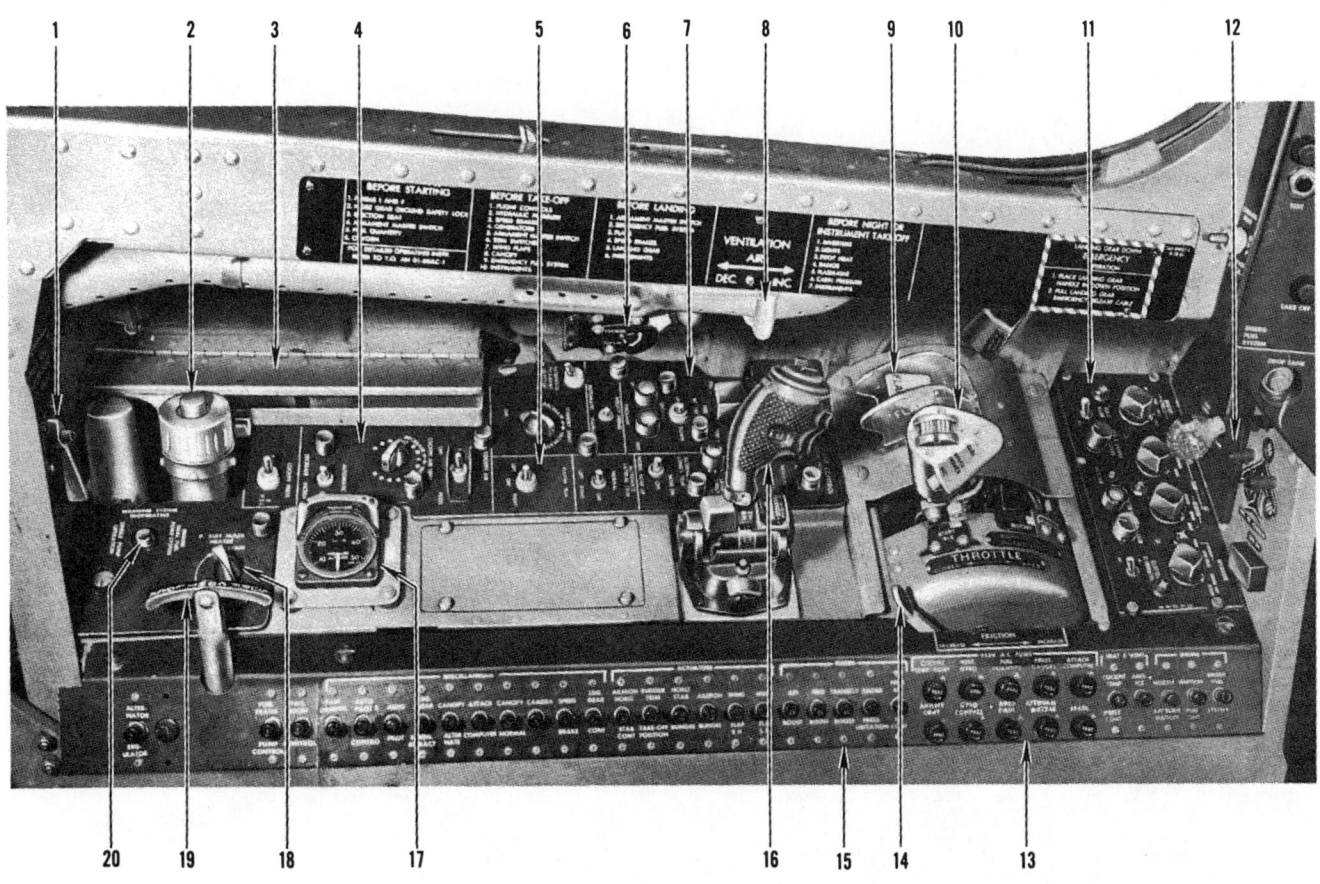

1. DROP TANK AIR PRESSURE SHUTOFF VALVE
2. ANTI-G SUIT PRESSURE REGULATOR VALVE
3. MAP CASE
4. COCKPIT AIR CONTROL PANEL
5. FLIGHT CONTROL PANEL
6. MANUAL RAM-AIR LEVER*
7. ARMAMENT CONTROL PANEL
8. VENTILATION AIR LEVER
9. WING FLAP LEVER
10. THROTTLE GRIP
11. E-4 ROCKET-FIRING CONTROL PANEL
12. LANDING GEAR CONTROL PANEL
13. FUSE PANEL
14. THROTTLE FRICTION LEVER
15. CIRCUIT-BREAKER PANEL
16. ANTENNA HAND CONTROL
17. COCKPIT ALTIMETER
18. PRESSURE SUIT MASK HEATER RHEOSTAT*
19. RUDDER LOCK HANDLE*
20. DUAL FUEL PUMP WARNING LIGHT*

LEFT SIDE

F-86D-5 AND SUBSEQUENT AIRPLANES

*Some airplanes (see applicable text)

Figure 1-7

Section I T. O. 1F-86D-1

1. YAW DAMPER SWITCH
2. CONSOLE PANEL AND FLOODLIGHT SELECTOR SWITCH
3. WINDSHIELD AND CANOPY DEFROST LEVER
4. CONSOLE PANEL AND FLOODLIGHT RHEOSTAT
5. RADIO CONTROL PANEL
6. VOLTAGE RHEOSTATS *

    *Some airplanes (see applicable text).

7. FUSE PANEL
8. CIRCUIT-BREAKER PANEL
9. LIGHTING CONTROL PANEL
10. AUTOMATIC PILOT FLIGHT CONTROLLER
11. OXYGEN REGULATOR
12. CANOPY LOCK HANDLE
13. LANDING GEAR EMERGENCY RELEASE HANDLE

F-86D-1 AIRPLANES

COCKPIT •

Figure 1-8

1. YAW DAMPER SWITCH
2. AUTOMATIC APPROACH COUPLER CONTROLLER*
3. CONSOLE PANEL AND FLOODLIGHT SELECTOR SWITCH
4. WINDSHIELD AND CANOPY DEFROST LEVER
5. CONSOLE PANEL AND FLOODLIGHT RHEOSTAT
6. RADIO CONTROL PANEL
7. VOLTMETER SELECTOR SWITCH
8. VOLTAGE RHEOSTATS*
9. THUNDERSTORM LIGHT RHEOSTAT*
10. AUTOMATIC PILOT POWER SWITCH*
11. LOADMETER (GENERATOR NO. 2)
12. VOLTMETER
13. LOADMETER (GENERATOR NO. 1)
14. FUSE PANEL
15. LIGHTING CONTROL PANEL
16. RADARSCOPE PRESENTATION INTENSITY CONTROL PANEL
17. AUTOMATIC PILOT FLIGHT CONTROLLER
18. CIRCUIT-BREAKER PANEL
19. OXYGEN REGULATOR
20. CANOPY LOCK HANDLE*
21. LANDING GEAR EMERGENCY RELEASE HANDLE

*Some airplanes (see applicable text)

RIGHT SIDE

F-86D-5 AND SUBSEQUENT AIRPLANES

Figure 1-9

Section I T. O. 1F-86D-1

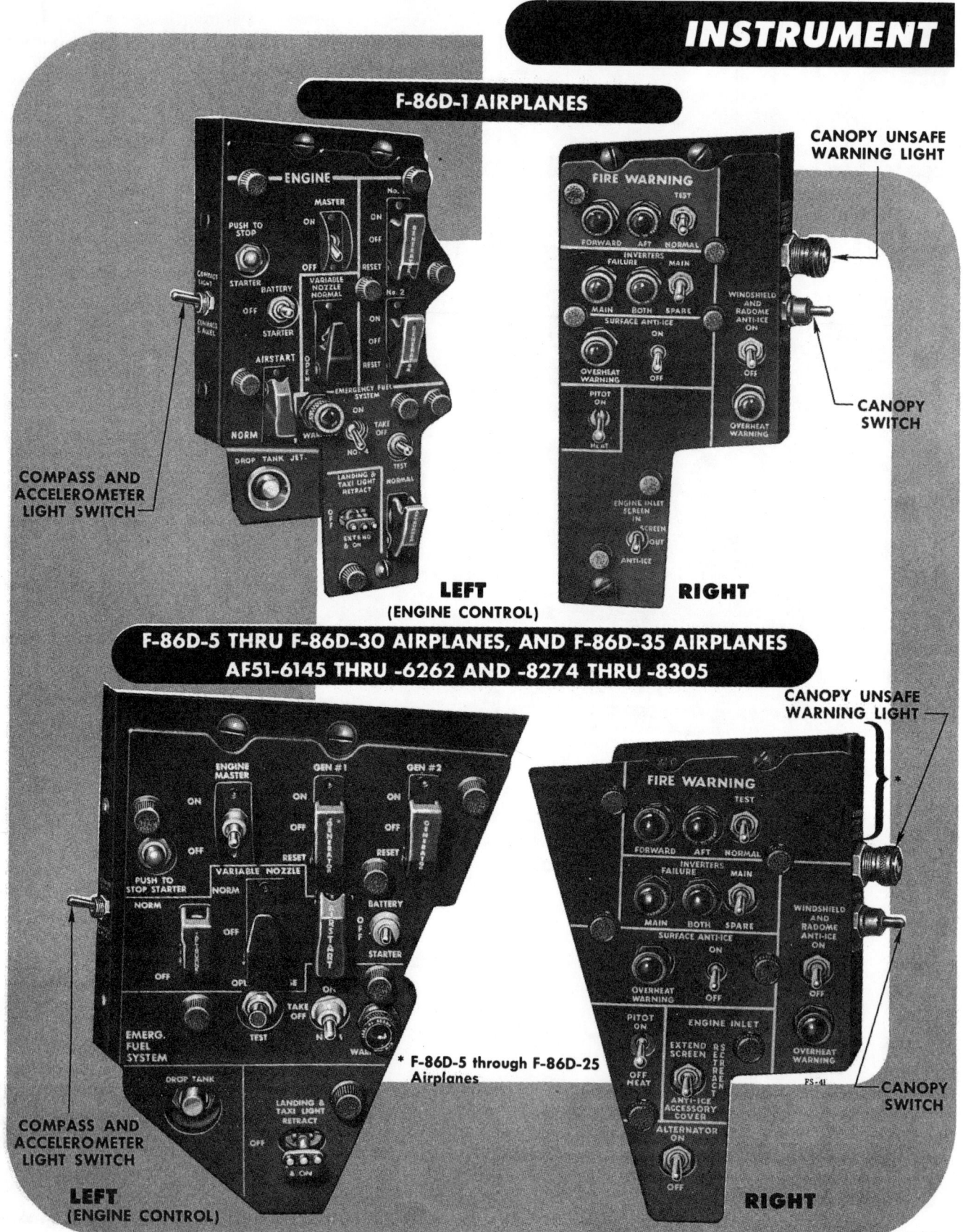

Figure 1-10

SUBPANELS

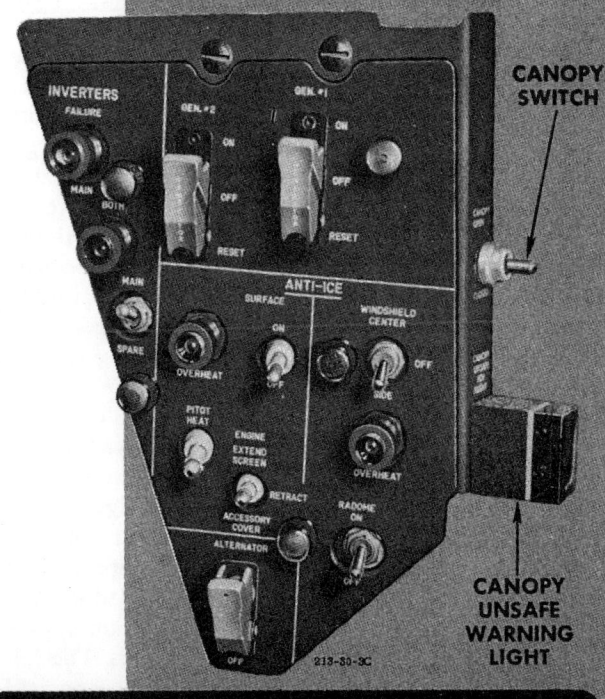

F-86D-35 AIRPLANES AF51-8306 THRU -8505, AND F-86D-40 AND SUBSEQUENT AIRPLANES

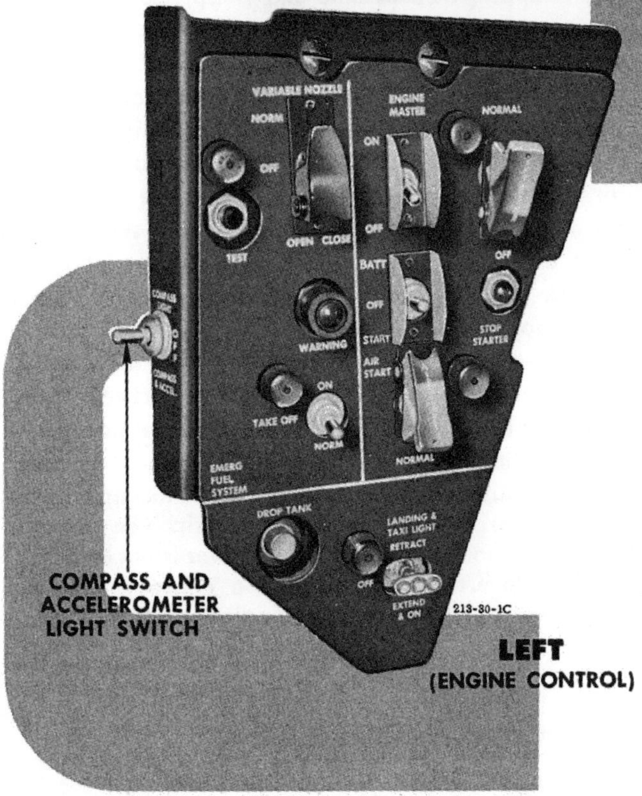

LEFT (ENGINE CONTROL)

RIGHT

F-86D-55 AND SUBSEQUENT AIRPLANES

pipe in gradually expanding form to provide the high-velocity jet and reaction thrust. The turbine, which is rotated by the exhaust gas passing through it, is directly connected to, and drives, the compressor. When maximum performance for short periods is desired, the exhaust gas may be reheated by the injection of fuel into the tail pipe aft of the turbine. The burning of this injected fuel, providing added thrust, is called afterburning. An automatically controlled, variable-area nozzle on the end of the tail pipe provides correct nozzle conditions for most favorable performance, with or without afterburner operating. A ceramic-coated inner liner is installed in the exhaust nozzle to prevent the high temperatures from damaging the exhaust nozzle and aft fuselage section. On late airplanes* and those on which T. O. 2J-J47-293 and -311 have been accomplished, increased engine performance is provided by

---

*F-86D-35 Airplanes AF51-8397 through -8406 and -8419 through -8505, and F-86D-40 and later airplanes

the installation of a new-type amplifier or a modified old-type amplifier in the afterburner system. This change increases afterburner fuel flow, which increases engine thrust. This new fuel schedule is sometimes referred to as the "flattop" fuel schedule. For increased thrust in afterburner, the J47-GE-33 engine has a higher "flattop" fuel schedule than that used on the -17 or -17B engines.

Most "Project Pull-out" airplanes and some F-86D-45 Airplanes* are equipped with a J47-GE-17B engine. This engine is an improved version of the basic -17 engine, and subsequently all -17 engines now in service will be converted to the -17B configuration. The main features of this improved engine include a later-type emergency fuel system regulator that incorporates a new altitude schedule setting that reduces the possibility of overspeed on climb-out; a new main fuel valve and main amplifier that allows for better altitude performance, faster engine acceleration, better recovery from push-to-test emergency operation, and a lower rpm for initiation of afterburning; an improved flame holder and flame dome in the afterburning section to give more rigidity and strength; and a ceramic liner in the exhaust nozzle for better insulation of exhaust temperatures.

On late airplanes,† the J47-GE-33 engine is installed. Operating procedures for this engine are the same as for the basic -17 or -17B engine. The main features changed are as follows: The inlet air guide vanes are changed from a 3-degree pitch angle to 6 degrees to allow a greater amount of intake air and increase the thrust about 200 pounds. The variable-position exhaust nozzle is capable of a 4 percent larger opening. A floating turbine shroud ring is installed to aid in keeping a more even and constant clearance between the turbine blades and shroud ring. It is designed to eliminate shroud ring warpage and seizures caused by abrupt temperature changes. Semiannular transition liners have been used to reduce structural failures in the transition liner section and given longer service life. To reduce failures of turbine wheels and turbine buckets, the turbine bucket mounting and the method of fastening the blade to the wheel have been improved to provide a more positive locking in place. The vibrator-type engine ignition system is replaced by a lightweight capacitor discharge type and improves ground and high-altitude starting characteristics. The dual spark plug installation is replaced by single plugs installed in combustion chambers 3 and 7. This new ignition system results in a weight saving of about 20 pounds. The following changes are in common with those incorporated on the -17B engine. For afterburner ignition, the "hot streak" ignition system is used. The exhaust nozzle incorporates an improved flame dome and flame holder to give rigidity and strength, and a ceramic-coated inner liner for better insulation of exhaust temperatures.

ELECTRONIC ENGINE CONTROL.

The airplane is equipped with an electronic engine control, the main advantage of which is the extremely rapid response of the engine to changes in throttle setting. Also, starting and operating technique is considerably simplified. Flame-outs and compressor stalls due to excessively rapid throttle movement are eliminated because the controls will always respond at the correct rate, regardless of how fast the throttle is moved. Control of the engine is tied in with the control of the variable-area nozzle, thereby automatically maintaining correct tail-pipe temperature. When the throttle is moved, an electronically amplified signal energizes the main and afterburner fuel control valves and the variable-area nozzle. If the electrical inverters do not work properly when external power is applied for a start, the electronic power control will be inoperative. Inverter failure warning lights should be checked and all circuit breakers pushed in when external power has been applied before an engine start is attempted. Before an automatic start, check that the lockup light is out. Otherwise, a hot start may result. The starting circuit will not be energized if ac power is not available from the inverters. Refer to Section VII for further information on the electronic engine control and its characteristics.

ENGINE FUEL CONTROL SYSTEM.

Engine fuel control is provided by a main fuel control valve and an emergency fuel regulator, controlled by a three-position emergency fuel switch. (See figure 1-12.) On airplanes changed by T. O., a two-position (NORM and ON) emergency fuel switch is installed. The emergency fuel system has been changed to eliminate the chance of interaction between the main and emergency fuel control systems during take-off. It also eliminates confusion caused by two engine control systems being in use at the same time. This change *removes* the TAKE-OFF position of the emergency fuel switch and removes the emergency fuel system test button. A throttle-actuated, spring-loaded idle detent plunger and switch (replacing the 72-degree thrust selector switch) are added to the throttle quadrant to allow the pilot to abort take-off if the electronic engine control locks up during take-off roll.

Engine-driven pumps, a booster pump‡ (on airplanes changed by T. O., the booster pump has been removed), and a dual pump supply fuel to the main control valve, which meters the amount of fuel required by the engine.

---

*F-86D-45 Airplanes AF52-3898 through -4135
†F-86D-45 Airplanes AF52-4136 and all later airplanes
‡F-86D-1 through F-86D-40 Airplanes

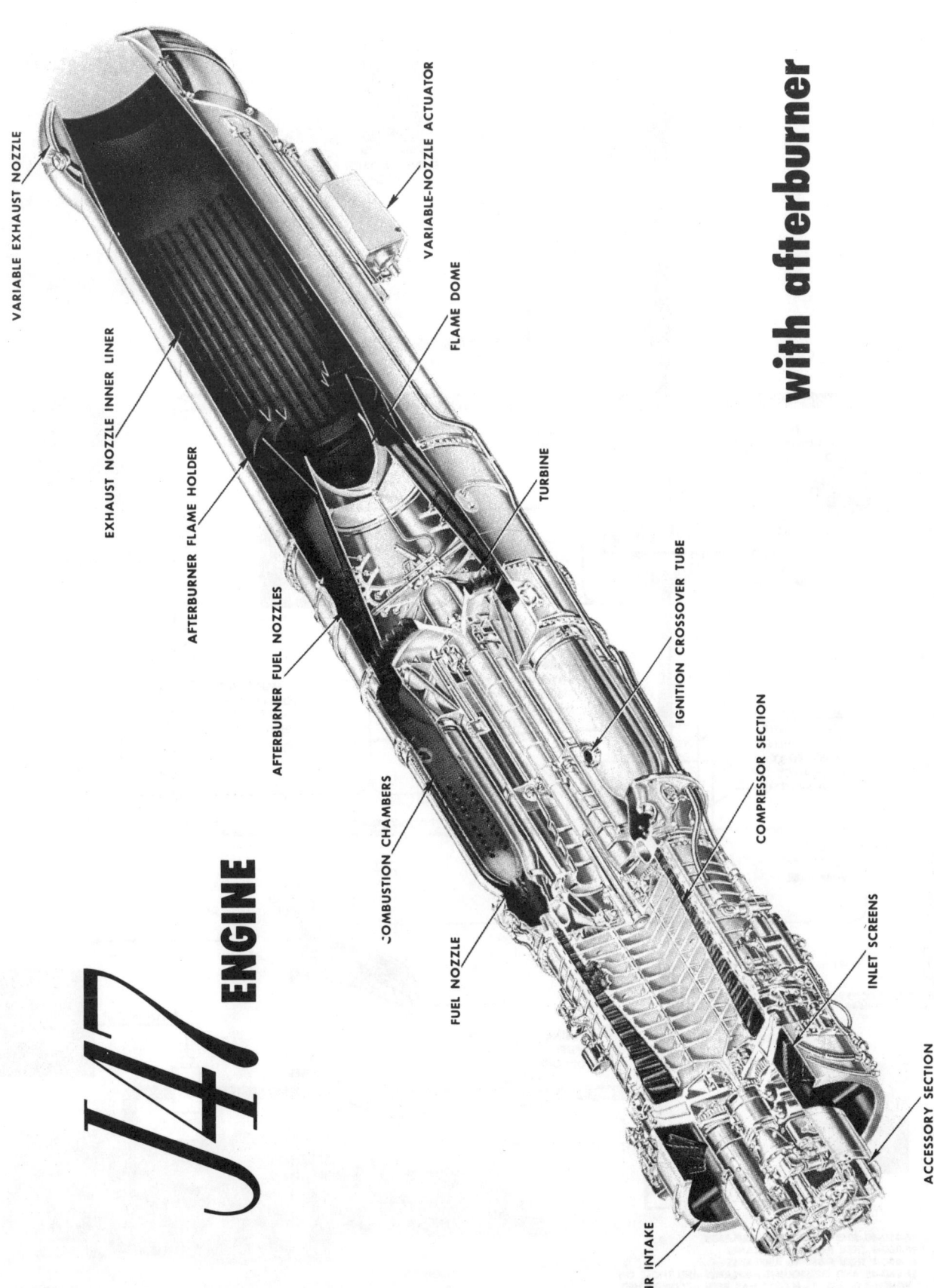

Figure 1-11

Section I
T. O. 1F-86D-1

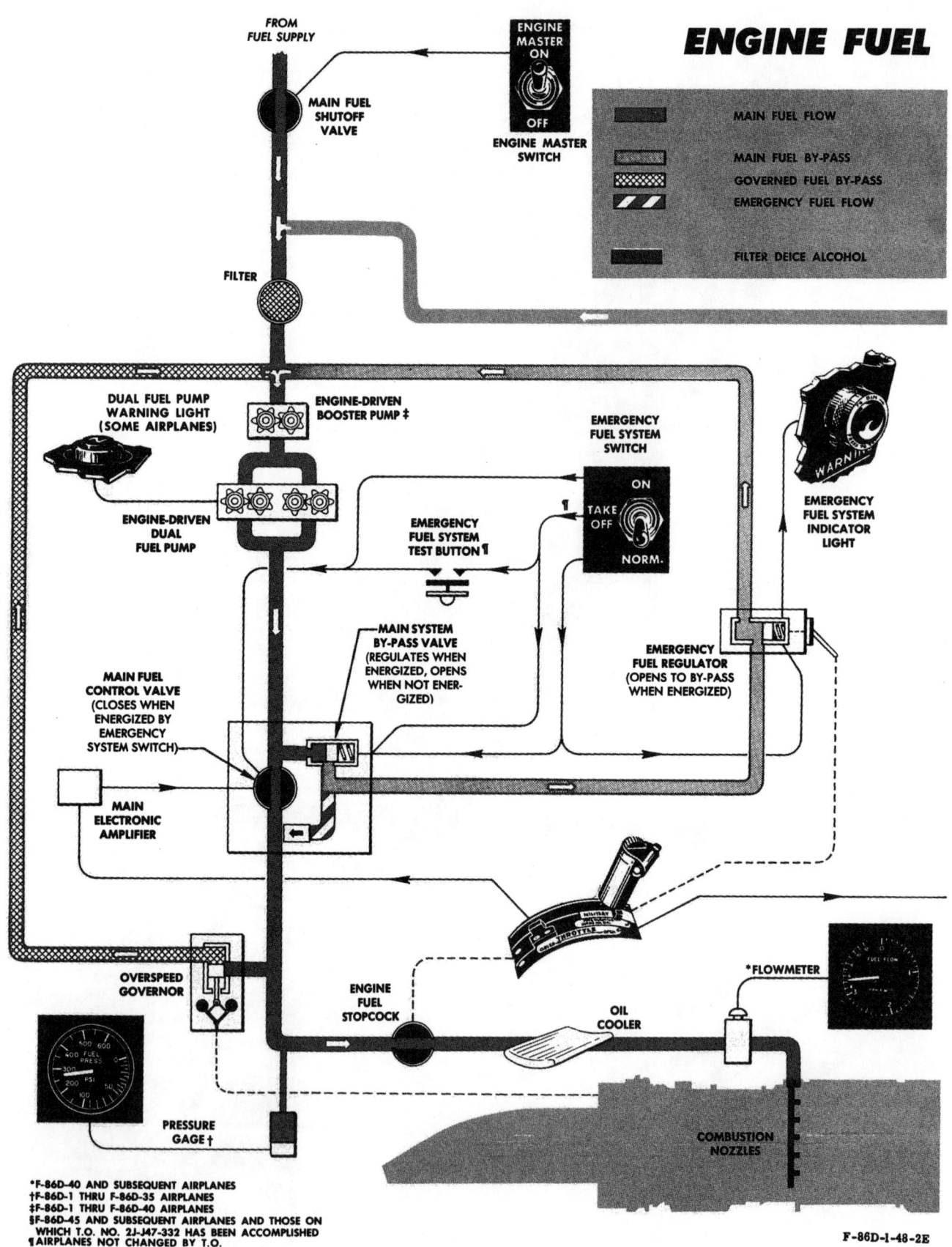

*F-86D-40 AND SUBSEQUENT AIRPLANES
†F-86D-1 THRU F-86D-35 AIRPLANES
‡F-86D-1 THRU F-86D-40 AIRPLANES
§F-86D-45 AND SUBSEQUENT AIRPLANES AND THOSE ON WHICH T.O. NO. 2J-J47-332 HAS BEEN ACCOMPLISHED
¶AIRPLANES NOT CHANGED BY T.O.

F-86D-1-48-2E

Figure 1-12

CONTROL SYSTEM

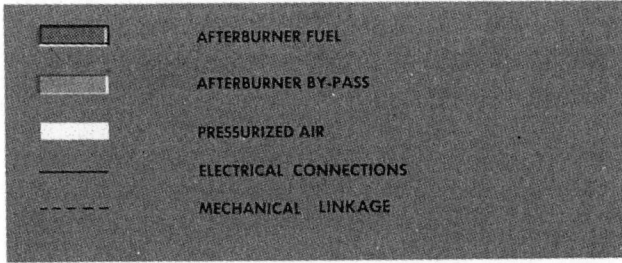

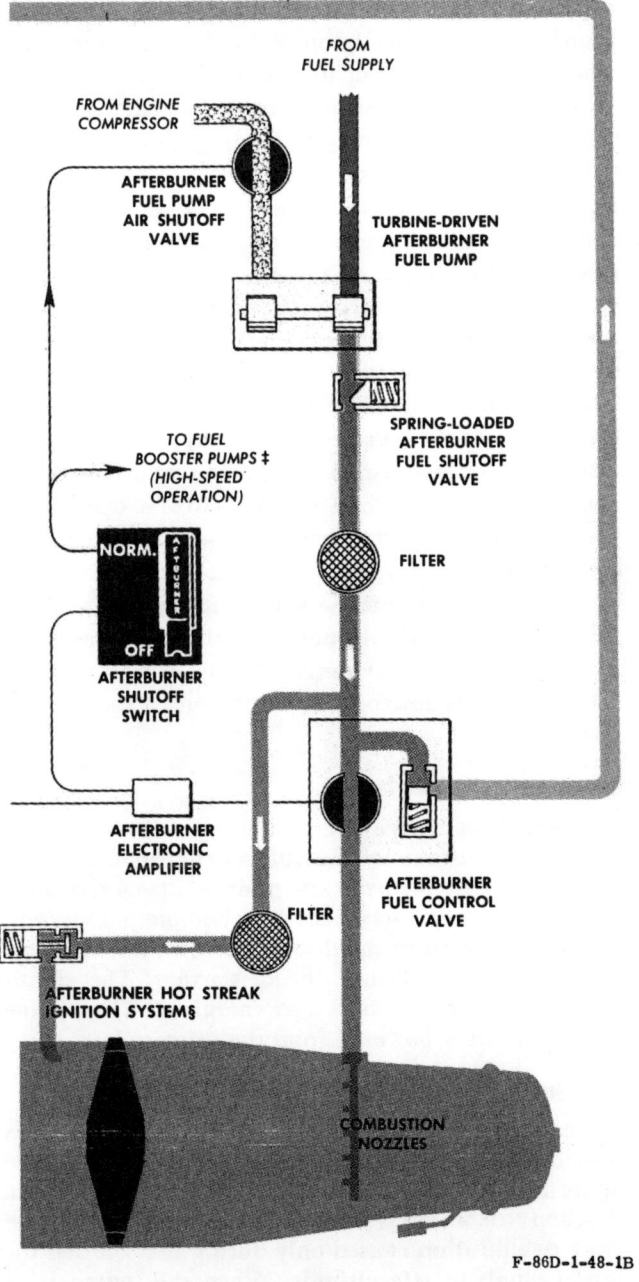

The engine-driven booster pump provides enough fuel boost pressure if the tank-mounted electrical booster pumps fail. Excess fuel is by-passed through the open emergency fuel regulator back to the booster fuel pump inlet. Metered fuel from the control valve passes through a throttle-actuated engine fuel stop-cock to the engine combustion chambers. The setting of the fuel control valves is determined electronically by throttle position, airspeed, exhaust temperature, engine rpm, altitude, and outside air temperature. The main fuel control valve automatically regulates fuel flow to the engine during starting; the correct fuel flow is provided for ignition and then for acceleration to the speed previously selected by the throttle. In case of failure of the electronically controlled main control valve, the throttle-controlled emergency fuel regulator takes over engine fuel control when the emergency fuel system switch is positioned at TAKE OFF or ON (at the ON position on airplanes with the two-position emergency fuel switch). The emergency regulator limits the amount of by-passed fuel in accordance with throttle setting, airspeed, and altitude. In normal operation, the emergency regulator is held in a full by-pass position by an energized holdout solenoid. The solenoid may be de-energized by positioning the emergency fuel system switch to TAKE OFF or ON (ON position for airplanes with two-position emergency fuel switch), enabling the throttle to mechanically control the emergency regulator. On airplanes with three-position emergency fuel switch, with the switch at TAKE OFF (the emergency regulator holdout solenoid is de-energized, alerting the emergency regulator to a stand-by condition) during 100% rpm operation, a drop in fuel pressure causes the emergency regulator to take over control of fuel flow at a pressure slightly below normal (depending on outside air temperature). The emergency regulator, at a position determined by the throttle, forces fuel around the main control valve to the combustion chambers. When control by the emergency regulator is selected, a main system by-pass valve is opened and the main fuel control valve is closed to enable the emergency regulator to control fuel flow. A throttle-actuated switch (72-degree switch incorporated in the thrust selector on airplanes with the three-position emergency fuel switch, or the idle detent switch on airplanes incorporating the two-position emergency fuel switch) also allows engine control to be converted to the emergency fuel system (with three-position emergency fuel switch at TAKE OFF) if the engine controls lock up at Take-off Thrust on main fuel system and it is desired to abort the take-off. The 72-degree switch (about ¾ throttle position) or idle detent switch is actuated by rapidly retarding the throttle to START IDLE. This switch, when actuated, electrically opens the main fuel system by-pass valve and permits the emergency fuel system to assume engine control; however, it does not unlock the electronic engine controls. A complete loss of electrical power to the primary bus, or movement of the battery-starter and generator switches to OFF during engine operation will also cause the holdout solenoid to be de-energized and the main system by-pass valve to open. This will allow the emergency fuel system to take over fuel control, regardless of the position of the emergency fuel system switch and without the emergency fuel system indicator light coming on. The emergency regulator is set to deliver normally a slightly lower fuel pressure than the main fuel control valve. The emergency regulator does not provide automatic fuel control in starts, accelerations, and decelerations; therefore, with engine operating below 85% rpm, any rapid throttle movement with the emergency regulator operating would supply too much fuel to the engine, causing flame-out, stall, or excess temperatures. A mechanical overspeed governor is installed downstream of the main control valve and emergency regulator. The governor by-passes excess fuel if the engine tends to overspeed. Refer to Section VII for additional information on the emergency fuel system.

Throttle (Power Control).

The throttle quadrant on the left console is labeled "CLOSED" and "OPEN." Immediately adjacent to the throttle, the markings are "START IDLE," "MILITARY," and "AFTERBURNER." There are three stops on the quadrant: one at the CLOSED position, one at START IDLE to prevent shutting off the fuel supply inadvertently, and one at MILITARY. Outboard movement of the throttle, which is spring-loaded inboard, allows the stops to be by-passed. Throttle movement during engine starting has been simplified; the throttle is simply moved outboard and forward to the desired power setting when 6% rpm is obtained. With the engine master switch at ON, the initial outboard movement of the throttle actuates a microswitch that energizes the ignition system; the later movement of the throttle to START IDLE opens the engine fuel stopcock. Ignition is automatically cut off by a starter cutout relay when engine speed reaches about 23% rpm. Since the mixture in the combustion chambers will burn continuously after once being ignited, ignition is required only during the starting procedure. When the engine is running, movement of the throttle in the normal operating range changes engine rpm by electronically changing the setting of the main fuel control valve. The throttle setting in conjunction with the temperature limiting control circuitry determines the position of the variable-area nozzle which maintains the most favorable exhaust temperatures. When the throttle is moved past the stop at MILITARY, compressor air is supplied for afterburner fuel pump turbine operation and the afterburner fuel shutoff valve is opened. In the afterburner operating range, the afterburner fuel control valve is electronically controlled by movement of the throttle to obtain various afterburner settings. Afterburning continues until the throttle is retarded from the AFTERBURNER range. The throttle grip (figure 1-13) contains a microphone button and a speed brake switch.

Engine Master Switch.

An engine master switch is on the engine control panel (figure 1-10) on the left instrument subpanel. Turning the master switch to the ON position opens the main fuel shutoff valve, starts the fuel booster pumps, and completes circuits to the throttle-actuated microswitch, which provides ignition during starting. The circuit to the air start switch is also energized. The engine master switch is powered from the primary bus.

Emergency Fuel System Switch (Three-position.)

A means of selecting the proper engine fuel control is provided by a switch on the engine control panel. (See figure 1-10.) The switch has three positions, ON, TAKE OFF, and NORM, and is powered by the primary bus. The TAKE OFF position is used only during take-off and for initial climb to safe altitude. When the switch is at TAKE OFF at 100% rpm, fuel flow to the engine is electronically controlled by the main control valve, with

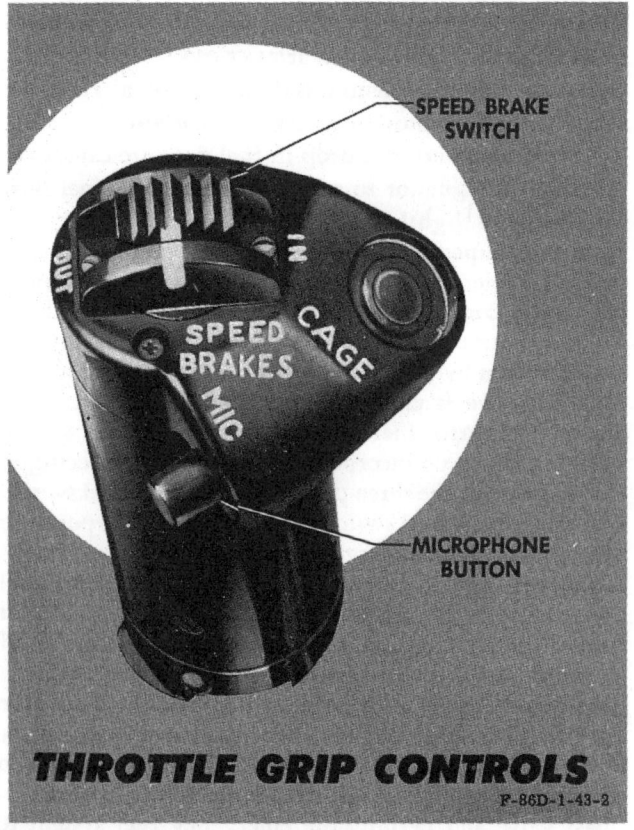

THROTTLE GRIP CONTROLS

Figure 1-13

the emergency regulator serving as a stand-by. With the switch in this position, the emergency fuel system indicator light is on to serve as a warning that rapid throttle movements should not be made when engine rpm is below 85%; otherwise a compressor stall or flame-out may result. If the main fuel system pressure drops while the switch is at TAKE OFF, the emergency fuel regulator automatically takes over fuel control. However, if the main fuel control valve again becomes operative, it will serve as the primary control and the emergency fuel regulator will return to stand-by.

CAUTION

If it becomes necessary to reduce power with emergency fuel system switch at TAKE OFF, the switch should be moved to ON, then back to NORM without hesitating at TAKE OFF before throttle is readvanced, to avoid undesirable power surges, possible compressor stall, or overtemperature condition.

When the emergency fuel system switch is at NORM, the main control valve controls fuel flow without the emergency regulator serving as a stand-by. The switch should normally be in this position for all flight conditions except take-off and initial climb. When the switch is moved to ON, the emergency regulator takes over fuel control, the main system by-pass valve is opened, and the main fuel control valve is closed. If loss of electrical power to the primary bus occurs, or if the battery-starter and generator switches are moved to OFF during engine operation, the emergency fuel system will take over fuel control, regardless of the position of the emergency fuel system switch and without the emergency fuel system indicator light coming on.

Emergency Fuel System Switch (Two-position).

A means of selecting the proper engine fuel control is provided by a switch on the engine control panel. The switch has two positions, ON and NORM, and is powered by the primary bus. With the switch in the ON position, engine control is provided by the emergency fuel system and the emergency fuel system indicator light comes on to provide a warning that rapid throttle movements should not be made when engine rpm is below 85%; otherwise, a compressor stall or flame-out may result. The switch is to be set at the NORM position for take-off and all normal operation. If automatic lock-up occurs during take-off and it is desired to abort the take-off, the throttle is moved to the START IDLE position with enough effort to push in the idle detent plunger. This actuates the idle detent switch and immediately switches control from the main fuel system to the emergency fuel system. The emergency fuel system should be selected only when actual failure of the main fuel control system occurs. If loss of electrical power to the primary bus occurs or if the battery-starter and generator switches are moved to OFF during engine operation, the emergency fuel system will take over fuel control, regardless of the position of the emergency fuel system switch and without the emergency fuel system indicator light coming on.

Emergency Fuel System Test Button (Airplanes With Three-position Emergency Fuel System Switch).

Operation of the emergency fuel system may be checked by means of a test button to the right of the emergency fuel system switch on the engine control panel. (See figure 1-10.) The emergency fuel system switch must be at TAKE OFF during the test. When the test button is pressed, completing the circuit from the primary bus, the main fuel control system is shut off by electrical closing of the main fuel control valve. A decrease in engine rpm to a lower stabilized value (figure 2-4) will show that the emergency fuel regulator has taken over fuel control. When the test button is released, the main fuel control valve is allowed to regain fuel control, and the emergency fuel regulator is again at stand-by.

Emergency Fuel System Indicator Light.

An amber emergency fuel system indicator light, labeled "WARNING," is on the engine control panel. (See figure 1-10.) On airplanes with three-position emergency fuel switch, the light will come on when the emergency fuel system switch is moved to ON or TAKE OFF. The light coming on serves as a warning that the emergency regulator is in control or in stand-by. With the emergency fuel switch in the ON position, any accelerations from below 85% rpm engine speed must be made very cautiously. With the selector switch in TAKE OFF, the throttle should not be advanced. On airplanes with the two-position emergency fuel switch, the light will come on when the switch is moved to the ON position or when the idle detent switch is actuated during a lockup condition. Throttle movements should be made cautiously, if rpm is below 85% when the light is on. The light is powered from the primary bus.

Dual Fuel Pump Warning Light.

A warning light on the left console (19, figure 1-6; 20, figure 1-7) comes on when either element of the engine-driven dual fuel pump has failed. Although failure of one pump element will result in negligible change in engine performance under most operating conditions, failure of both elements will cause engine failure. Therefore, the warning light coming on shows that flight should be discontinued as soon as practical. The warning light operates on power from the primary bus when the engine master switch is ON. On some airplanes, the dual fuel pump warning light has been made inoperative and a decal, "WARNING SYSTEM INOPERATIVE," is placed by the light. However, if a new type pressure differential switch is installed, the light is operable. Refer to "Dual Fuel Pump Warning Light Characteristics" in Section VII.

ELECTRONIC ENGINE CONTROL AUTOMATIC LOCKUP SYSTEM (AIRPLANES WITH THREE-POSITION EMERGENCY FUEL SYSTEM SWITCH).

An engine control automatic lockup system is installed in this airplane. It gives protection against possible loss of power should the electronic engine control be deprived of ac power. The lockup system is used in conjunction with the electronic engine control and permits full engine control to be maintained until an ac power supply failure is actually encountered. When the ac power supply to the electronic engine control falls below 92 volts, the main and afterburner fuel control valves and the variable exhaust nozzle are automatically locked in position. This locked power setting is then maintained until about 15 seconds after the ac power supply rises above about 98 volts. The lockup is then automatically removed, and the electronic engine control resumes operation. The 15-second interval following inverter change-over is required so that the electronic engine control components can be rewarmed after a main inverter failure. If the ac power supply is not re-established above about 98 volts, the engine controls will stay in automatic lockup. Engine control is accomplished by converting to operation on the emergency fuel system. Power settings should not be changed when engine controls are in lockup, since engine overtemperature or surging may result when lockup is removed. *During an engine start, the automatic lockup system is made ineffective when the battery-starter switch is momentarily set at START.* After the engine is operating, positioning the emergency fuel system switch to ON then back to NORM without hesitating at TAKE OFF will again make the automatic lockup system operable. It will then remain operable during normal operation if the emergency fuel system switch is moved to ON, then back to NORM without hesitating at TAKE OFF. If automatic lockup occurs during take-off roll with the emergency fuel system switch at TAKE OFF, the take-off can be aborted by rapidly retarding the throttle to START IDLE. (The throttle is retarded rapidly to prevent engine overspeed, because back pressure on the turbine wheel is released as afterburner operation ceases.) This action actuates the 72-degree switch in the thrust selector, which transfers engine operation to the emergency fuel system. For taxiing after take-off is aborted, before the throttle is readvanced, positioning the emergency fuel system switch to ON will eliminate any power surges that may occur when the throttle is readvanced. A lockup indicator light, labeled "ENG. CONT. LOCKUP," is provided to show when engine controls are in lockup. Refer to Section VII for added information on characteristics of the automatic lockup system.

ELECTRONIC ENGINE CONTROL AUTOMATIC LOCKUP SYSTEM (AIRPLANES WITH TWO-POSITION EMERGENCY FUEL SYSTEM SWITCH).

When ac power to the electronic engine control drops below 92 volts, the main and afterburner fuel control valves and the variable exhaust nozzle are automatically locked in position. This locked power setting is then maintained until about 15 seconds after the ac power rises above about 98 volts. The lockup is then automatically removed, and the electronic engine control resumes operation. The 15-second interval following inverter change-over (automatic or manual) is required so that the electronic engine control parts can be rewarmed after a main inverter failure. If the ac power is not re-established above about 98 volts, the engine controls will stay in automatic lockup.

With the installation of the two-position emergency fuel switch, the automatic lockup system is capable of locking engine controls during an automatic start. (Refer to "Automatic Start" in Section II.) After the engine is operating, the automatic lockup system will remain operable during normal operation with the emergency fuel system in the NORM position. If automatic lockup occurs during take-off roll, with the emergency fuel switch at NORM, the take-off can be aborted if desired, by rapidly retarding the throttle to START IDLE. The throttle is retarded rapidly to prevent engine overspeed because back pressure on the turbine wheel is decreased as afterburner operation ceases. This throttle action actuates the idle detent switch, which transfers engine operation to the emergency fuel system during a lockup condition only. The emergency fuel system will remain in control until the engine control lockup light goes out and until the emergency fuel switch is cycled to ON and returned to NORM. For taxiing after take-off is aborted and before the throttle is readvanced, position the emergency fuel system switch to ON. If it is desired, the take-off can be continued in the lockup condition. After a safe altitude is reached, (if engine controls do not unlock automatically, or if engine controls do not unlock within 30 seconds after manually selecting the secondary inverter) the emergency fuel system should be manually selected, by moving emergency fuel switch to ON, and a landing made using the emergency fuel system for engine operation.

Engine Control Lockup Indicator Light.

An amber engine control indicator light (19, figure 1-4; 20 and 24, figure 1-5), labeled "ENG. CONT. LOCKUP," is on the upper right side of the instrument panel on early airplanes* and on the instrument panel on late airplanes.† The light shows when the electronic engine controls are in lockup. The light is powered by the primary bus. When ac power loss occurs, causing the electronic engine controls to be locked in position, this light will come on. This light will remain on until ac power is restored and the electronic engine controls have been automatically released from auto-

---

*F-86D-1 through F-86D-30 Airplanes
†F-86D-35 and later airplanes

matic lockup. Therefore, during operation of the main fuel control system, this light serves as a warning that power settings should not be changed as long as the light remains on. If it is necessary to operate on the emergency fuel system, engine operation on the emergency fuel system will have no effect on the illumination of the light. The light will remain on as long as ac power is not available. Switching the emergency fuel system switch from the ON position to the NORM position must not be attempted while the lockup indicator light is on. For example, if lockup occurs when operating at Military Thrust and throttle reductions are made while transferred to the emergency fuel system, and then the emergency fuel system switch is moved back to NORM, the sudden surge of fuel fed through the locked-up open main fuel control valve will cause a dangerous overtemperature condition.

VARIABLE-AREA NOZZLE.

Two clamshell-type doors form the variable nozzle at the end of the tail pipe. The electrically actuated nozzle is electronically controlled by throttle position and exhaust temperature to maintain correct nozzle temperature for most favorable performance. The nozzle may also be manually actuated. When the variable-area nozzle is full open, its area is about 160 percent that of a fixed nozzle (Military Thrust area on a standard NACA day); when variable-area nozzle is fully closed, its area is 95 percent that of a fixed nozzle. When automatically controlled, the nozzle is scheduled to close from about $\frac{1}{2}$ position on some airplanes at idle rpm ($\frac{3}{4}$ position on others) to about $\frac{1}{8}$ position at Military Thrust. The nozzle will gradually close to follow the scheduled throttle position if the throttle is slowly advanced. On a throttle burst, the nozzle will lock at the lower power position until the engine rpm is within 2% to 7% of the higher power rpm. The nozzle will then rapidly close to the scheduled position. If this scheduled nozzle position, at steady-state operation, is such that it will cause the exhaust temperature to exceed 685°C, the nozzle will be driven open to the position necessary to maintain 685°C by the exhaust temperature control circuitry. During normal afterburner operation, the nozzle position is decided mainly by exhaust temperature; that is, the nozzle is moved to whatever position is necessary to maintain 685°C. If, in an effort to maintain the correct exhaust temperature, the nozzle is driven full open and exhaust temperature still tends to exceed 685°C, the electronic engine control will automatically decrease afterburner fuel flow to prevent excessive exhaust temperatures. The afterburner fuel flow is also cut back in case the nozzle jams at a position which would normally result in overtemperature operation; or if the nozzle is manually jogged closed during afterburner operation, the afterburner fuel flow will be automatically decreased as nozzle area is decreased.

Figure 1-14

WARNING

It is recommended that the variable-nozzle switch be left in the NORM (automatic) position during landing approach and ground run. If the nozzle has been jogged open, enough thrust will not be available for a go-around unless the nozzle is jogged closed or the switch is returned to NORM position.

Note

With the variable-nozzle switch in the NORM position, the nozzle is automatically controlled to give most favorable engine performance. Opening the nozzle has a negligible effect on the landing roll, because thrust loss is a very small percentage of the total available braking force during a landing. This force is about 4000 pounds, and idle thrust is reduced only 100 pounds by opening the nozzle.

Variable-nozzle Switch.

For automatic operation of the variable nozzle through the electronic engine control, a variable-nozzle switch on the engine control panel (figure 1-10) is placed in the guarded NORM position. When the switch is turned OFF, automatic control is cut off and, if the switch is left at OFF during normal operation, engine control will be limited, allowing possible overspeed and/or overtemperature to occur. If the automatic controls fail or are to be overridden, the nozzle may be actuated by movement of the switch from OFF to either of the spring-loaded positions, OPEN or CLOSE. The nozzle will move more slowly when actuated by means of the switch than when automatically controlled. The switch is powered from the primary bus. However, when switch is at NORM, ac power must be available for automatic operation of the variable nozzle.

Variable-nozzle Position Indicator.

A position indicator (25, figure 1-4; 16 and 23, figure 1-5) for the variable nozzle is on the main instrument panel. The indicator dial is calibrated in quarters from minimum to maximum nozzle area. On engines with an early-type thrust selector, the indicator will show about ½ position at idle rpm; on engines with a late-type thrust selector, it will show about ¾ position at idle rpm. Power for operation of the position indicator is supplied from the primary bus. On early airplanes* and those not changed by T. O. 2J-J47-293 and -311, the position indicator is marked with a red limit radial, located 10 degrees past the ¾ position. On all other airplanes, there is no limit radial, because of installation of a new-type afterburner amplifier or a modified afterburner amplifier which schedules a higher fuel flow; also, a ceramic-coated inner liner must be installed in the exhaust nozzle to aid in controlling the higher temperatures resulting from the increased fuel flow and, therefore, full range of nozzle operation is required for temperature control.

IGNITION SYSTEM.

The ignition system, providing ignition through two spark plugs, functions only during ground starts and windmilling air starts. For ground starts, with the engine master switch ON and the battery-starter switch in the momentary STARTER position, the initial outboard movement of the throttle (to pass the START IDLE stop) actuates a microswitch that supplies dc power to the ignition vibrator units. This dc power is converted by the ignition vibrator unit into high-voltage alternating current and is fed to the spark plugs in the No. 3 and No. 7 burners. After ignition occurs and the engine has accelerated to about 23% rpm, the ignition system is de-energized by the action of the automatic starter drop-out relay. During windmilling air starts, the main ignition system is energized through the AIR START (up) position of the air start switch and the throttle microswitch as in ground starts. After an air start, it is necessary to return the air start switch to NORMAL (down) to de-energize the main ignition system. Afterburner ignition is accomplished by spontaneous combustion, the temperature of the gases from the engine being used to ignite the fuel discharged from the afterburner combustion nozzles. On late airplanes† and those changed by T. O. 2J-J47-332, afterburner ignition is accomplished by a hot-streak ignition system. Fuel is bled from the inlet side of the afterburner fuel control valve through the hot-streak ignition valve, which permits a metered amount of fuel to flow through the turbine wheel. The metered fuel is ignited aft of the turbine wheel by hot gases or spontaneous combustion and streaks down to ignite fuel discharged from the afterburner fuel nozzle. The hot-streak ignition system is automatically cut off after a short time interval and will be recharged automatically only when the throttle is moved from AFTERBURNER range.

Engine Master Switch.

Refer to "Engine Fuel Control System."

Air Start Switch.

To provide ignition for restarting the engine in flight, a two-position switch is installed on the engine control panel. (See figure 1-10.) On early airplanes‡ when the switch is moved from the guarded NORMAL (down) position to the AIR START (up) position, current is supplied for engine ignition. On all later airplanes, the throttle also must be moved outboard to complete the ignition circuit. At the same time, an inverter for the fuel pressure gage is energized and all electrical equipment powered by the secondary bus, monitored bus No. 1, monitored bus No. 2, monitored bus No. 3, and the ac bus is automatically turned off to temporarily decrease the load on the battery. The air start switch is powered from the primary bus. (See figure 1-19.) When the air start switch is returned to the NORMAL (down) position, after the start is completed and the generators are again operating, ignition shuts off and electrical equipment returns to normal operation. If the emergency fuel system switch is returned to NORM before engine control lockup light goes out and after the generator warning lights go out, the inverters and electronic engine controls will not have enough time to warm up to proper operating temperatures.

CAUTION

Continuous operation of the air start ignition circuit is limited to a maximum of 3 minutes per start. Longer periods of use will damage the ignition vibrator units.

---

*F-86D-1 through F-86D-30 Airplanes and F-86D-35 Airplanes AF51-6145 through -6262, -8274 through -8396, and -8407 through -8418
†F-86D-45 and later airplanes
‡F-86D-1 Airplanes AF50-455 through -464

EQUIPMENT AFFECTED BY AIR START SWITCH

WARNING ▶ PLACING AIR START SWITCH AT **AIR START** (UP) POSITION TURNS OFF MOST ELECTRICALLY POWERED EQUIPMENT.

NOT OPERABLE

EQUIPMENT POWERED BY

SECONDARY BUS
MONITORED NO. 1 BUS
MONITORED NO. 2 BUS
MONITORED NO. 3 BUS
A-C BUS

WHICH INCLUDES....

ELECTRONIC ENGINE CONTROLS

WING FLAP CONTROLS

LANDING GEAR CONTROLS AND INDICATORS*

RADIO EQUIPMENT

*F-86D-1 THROUGH F-86D-5 AIRPLANES

Figure 1-15

STARTER SYSTEM.

A combination starter-generator works as a starter until engine speed reaches about 23% rpm, and thereafter works as a generator. The starter can be energized only when an external power source is connected to the airplane, as the airplane batteries are automatically disconnected from the electrical system during ground starts. Starter operation is entirely automatic after the battery-starter switch is momentarily moved to the STARTER or START position. Should the engine fail to start, the starter is de-energized if the stop-starter button is pressed.

Note

An external power source capable of 28 volts, 1200 amperes surge and a continuous operating current of 500 amperes must be connected to both external power receptacles for starting.

Battery-Starter Switch.

A battery-starter switch on the engine control panel (figure 1-10) has two maintained positions, BATTERY and OFF, and a spring-loaded STARTER or START position for ground use only. When the switch is moved momentarily to STARTER, power from the primary bus is supplied to the starter-generator when an external power source is connected. The starter-generator and ignition is automatically disconnected from the circuit at about 23% rpm. The engine will automatically accelerate to the speed previously selected with the throttle. The switch will return to OFF from the STARTER position and should be returned to BATTERY for all normal operation. With the battery-starter switch at BATTERY, battery power is supplied to the primary bus when external or generator power is not available. When battery-starter switch is OFF, battery power is supplied only to the battery bus. (See figure 1-19.)

Stop-starter Button.

A stop-starter button, on the engine control panel (figure 1-10), is for use in the event of a false start. When the button is pressed, current to the starter-generator and to the ignition system is cut off. Since the starter-generator is automatically disconnected from the circuit during starts, it is unnecessary to use the stop-starter button except in case of a false start.

ENGINE AIR INLET.

The engine inlet air is routed from the air inlet opening, at the nose of the airplane, under the radome, to the engine by a duct designed to provide maximum airflow to the engine under all flight conditions. Foreign objects entering the duct during take-off or landing are prevented from entering the engine by a retractable engine inlet screen. Position of this screen is manually controlled by movement of an inlet switch to the desired position, if the surface anti-ice switch is OFF. (Refer to "Anti-icing Systems" in Section IV.) A glide path antenna is on the leading edge of the lower part of the air inlet opening.

Engine Inlet Switch.

The movable engine inlet screen, which protects the engine from foreign objects, is controlled by a three-position switch on the right instrument subpanel. (See figure 1-10.) The switch is normally at EXTEND SCREEN (SCREEN IN on F-86D-1 Airplanes) on the ground and during take-off and landing, so that the screen covers the inlet. To maintain maximum airflow and to prevent icing of the screen, the switch is moved to RETRACT (SCREEN OUT on F-86D-1 Airplanes) in flight to retract the screens. The third position, ACCESSORY COVER (ANTI-ICE on F-86D-1 Airplanes) provides for anti-icing the accessory cover and retracting the screens. (Refer to "Anti-icing and Defrosting Systems" Section IV.) The engine inlet switch receives power from the primary bus, but is operable only when the surface anti-ice switch is in the OFF position.

ENGINE INDICATORS.

Exhaust Temperature Gage.

An exhaust temperature gage, calibrated in 25-degree increments from 0 to 1000°C (22, figure 1-4; 19, figure 1-5), is on the instrument panel. It provides a visual indication of engine operating condition, so that accurate power settings can be obtained. The gage is a self-generated electrical unit. It does not require power from the electrical system of the airplane for operation.

Tachometer.

The tachometer, calibrated from 0% to 110% rpm (21, figure 1-4; 17, figure 1-5), is on the instrument panel. It indicates engine speed in percentage of maximum rated rpm (7950). This indicator, used in conjunction with the exhaust temperature gage, enables engine power to be accurately set without exceeding engine limitations. The tachometer is not powered from the electrical system of the airplane. It is supplied by the tachometer generator, which generates a voltage proportional to engine speed.

Fuel Pressure Gage (F-86D-1 Through F-86D-25 Airplanes).

The fuel pressure gage (26, figure 1-4; 16, figure 1-5) is on the instrument panel. It shows pressure of fuel to the engine. On F-86D-1 Airplanes, the gage is calibrated from 0 to 500 psi; on F-86D-5 through F-86D-35 Airplanes, the gage is calibrated from 0 to 600 psi. The gage is normally powered from the ac bus of the airplane. However, during air starts, when no power can be derived from the ac bus, a special inverter only for fuel pressure gage power is energized from the primary bus.

Fuel Flowmeter (F-86D-40 and Later Airplanes).

A fuel flowmeter, calibrated from 0 to 12,000 pounds per hour fuel flow (23, figure 1-5), is on the lower right side of the instrument panel. It gives the rate of fuel flow in pounds per hour. The indicator dial has the 0- to 3000-pound-per-hour position expanded, thus enabling more accurate readings within this range. The fuel flowmeter does not show rate of afterburner fuel flow. The flowmeter is powered from the ac bus; however, in case normal ac power is not available (when air start switch is actuated), a special inverter, powered by the primary bus, supplies ac power only for the flowmeter.

Oil Pressure Gage.

The oil pressure gage, calibrated from 0 to 100 psi (29, figure 1-4; 30, figure 1-5) and mounted on the instrument panel, shows the pressure of oil within the engine. The gage is an electrical instrument powered from the ac bus of the airplane.

AFTERBURNER SYSTEM.

For Maximum Thrust for short periods, fuel discharged from combustion nozzles aft of the turbine wheel is burned in the tail pipe. In this manner, the engine exhaust gas is reheated and provides added thrust. Fuel to the afterburner combustion nozzles is controlled by an afterburner fuel control valve. (See figure 1-12.) Throttle position, altitude, airspeed, engine rpm, and exhaust temperature electronically determine the afterburner fuel control valve setting. An afterburner fuel pump, driven by engine compressor air, supplies fuel to the afterburner fuel control valve. On some

Note
Extensive use of afterburner materially reduces flight range and operational time.

airplanes,* the afterburner fuel pump is a line-mounted unit, and excess fuel is by-passed through the control valve back to the main system engine-driven booster pump inlet. On these airplanes, the booster pumps in the forward fuselage tank operate at high speed during afterburner operation to provide constant fuel flow to the afterburner fuel pump. On the remaining airplanes, the afterburner fuel pump is tank-mounted and will discharge enough fuel for afterburning operation without using the booster pumps. By-pass fuel from the tank-mounted unit is routed back to the forward fuselage tank.

CAUTION

- If afterburner blowout occurs with less than 1300 pounds of fuel remaining, do not attempt further afterburner operation unless dictated by emergency or combat conditions.
- This precaution does not form an operating limitation, but rather a measure for protection of the afterburner turbine-driven pump if the aft fuselage tank transfer pump fails.

*F-86D-1 through F-86D-40 Airplanes

Afterburning can be obtained by further advancing the throttle past the MILITARY stop to the AFTERBURNER range. This action causes an afterburner fuel pump air shutoff valve to be opened. The fuel pump air shutoff valve supplies compressor air to the afterburner fuel pump turbine, which begins operating. The fuel pressure of the pump output then opens the afterburner fuel shutoff valve and allows flow to the afterburner fuel control valve. As afterburner fuel flow is increased, the variable nozzle is automatically opened to prevent excessive exhaust temperatures. When the variable nozzle is fully open, afterburner fuel flow is limited by control valve position as required to prevent excessive exhaust temperatures, regardless of throttle position. The afterburner is shut off when the throttle is retarded from the AFTERBURNER range. It has been found that the afterburner fuel control valve could function improperly and cause excessive fuel flow to the afterburner, resulting in dangerously high exhaust temperatures, which cause failure of the tail pipe and aft fuselage. To eliminate this dangerous condition, certain changes are being made to airplanes in production, and Technical Order changes are being made on those airplanes already in service. On late airplanes† and those changed by T. O. 2J-J47-293, the afterburner fuel control valve has a mechanical stop to prevent the fuel flow from exceeding desired maximum limit.

WARNING

Afterburner operation is not permitted on airplanes that have not had the mechanical stop included in the afterburner fuel control valve. Refer to DD Form 781 for accomplishment of T. O. 2J-J47-293.

A ceramic-coated inner liner is installed in the tail pipe to prevent high temperatures from damaging the tail pipe and aft fuselage. The inner liner, made of corrugated metal sprayed with heat-resistant ceramic compound, fits around the inner circumference of the tail pipe. The tail pipe should be checked for the inner-liner installation before flight.

WARNING

Afterburner operation is prohibited above 15,000 feet unless the tail pipe has the ceramic-coated inner liner.

†F-86D-35 Airplanes AF51-8397 through -8406 and -8419 through -8505, and F-86D-40 and later airplanes

Afterburner operation is unlimited with regard to altitude on those airplanes equipped with an afterburner fuel control valve having the mechanical stop and the ceramic-coated inner liner. On these late airplanes* and on those changed by T. O. 2J-J47-311, the afterburner fuel amplifier has been changed to increase the fuel schedule (sometimes referred to as the "flattop" fuel schedule) to provide added engine performance. Refer to Section VII for additional information on the afterburner system.

WARNING

Engines that have this amplifier change must have the ceramic-coated inner liner installed in the tail pipe to prevent high temperatures, caused from the increased fuel flow, from damaging the tail pipe and aft fuselage.

Afterburner Shutoff Switch.

A guarded switch (figure 1-10), is on the left engine subpanel and is powered by the primary bus. It provides an emergency means of cutting off afterburner operation. The switch has two positions: NORMAL and OFF. For afterburner operation, the switch must be in the NORMAL position. Movement of the switch to OFF will close the air valve to the air-turbine-driven afterburner fuel pump, thus shutting off afterburner operation.

OIL SYSTEM.

Lubrication of the various gears and bearings of the engine is accomplished by means of a pressure-type oil system and a scavenge pump return. The oil serves both for lubricating and cooling and is a completely automatic system requiring no control action by the pilot. Oil is routed to the different sections of the engine, where it lubricates and cools, and then through a scavenge pump that transfers the oil back to the oil supply tank. If the oil has been heated above the preset temperature of the oil temperature control valve, it is automatically routed through the oil cooler before being returned to the oil supply tank. The oil system uses 3 US gallons of oil in a 4½ US gallon tank (1½ gallons expansion space). The tank is located high on the right side of the fuselage, aft and above the trailing edge of the wing. Inverted operation is limited because of inability of scavenge pumps to return oil from sumps to oil supply tank. (See figure 1-33 for oil specifications.)

---

*F-86D-35 Airplanes AF51-8397 through -8406 and -8419 through -8505, and F-86D-40 and later airplanes.

FUEL SYSTEM.

Four fuel tanks are installed in the airplane: two in the fuselage, and one in each wing outer panel. (See figure 1-16.) Fuel is supplied to the engine from the forward fuselage tank by electric booster pumps. On early airplanes, during afterburner operation, the pumps automatically operate at a higher speed to provide added fuel flow. On late airplanes,† the afterburner fuel pump is tank-mounted with its own integral boost pump unit and supplies enough afterburner fuel without using the other existing booster pumps for afterburner operation. (See figure 1-17.) The forward fuselage tank consists of two cells. The lower one, in the wing center section, receives fuel by gravity feed from the upper cell and from the outer wing tanks. Fuel is transferred from the aft fuselage tank to the forward fuselage tank (lower cell) under pressure by an electric transfer pump that operates automatically when the fuel quantity in the forward tank drops below a preset value. On F-86D-1 and F-86D-5 Airplanes, fuel transfer is possible only after about 115 gallons has been consumed from the forward fuselage tank. On F-86D-10 and later airplanes, fuel transfer is made when about 30 gallons has been consumed from the forward fuselage tank. If drop tanks are carried, aft fuselage tank fuel transfer is made after all the drop tank fuel is consumed. The transfer pump is powered by monitored bus No. 2 and automatically operates at a higher speed during afterburner operation. Also fuel flow to the engine is obtainable from the forward fuselage tank and from the aft fuselage tank by suction flow, if the electric booster pumps fail. There are individual filler points for each tank. Also, a single-point refueling nozzle receptacle and line system are provided on F-86D-15 and later airplanes. The nozzle receptacle is in the left side of the fuselage, next to the aft fuselage fuel tank. Single-point refueling time is about 3 minutes. The refueling equipment should be capable of delivering fuel at the rate of about 200 gpm with a refueling nozzle pressure of 40 to 60 psi (50 psi is recommended for maximum filling). If a nozzle pressure of less than 40 psi is used, incomplete filling of the system will result, and a nozzle pressure greater than 60 psi may be detrimental to the equipment. The refueling flow is automatically shut off when the airplane system is full; this is shown by a rise on the nozzle pressure gage and a zero flow indication. When the airplane is refueled by means of the individual filler points, the forward fuselage tank must be filled first in order to use full fuel capacity; if the wing tanks or aft fuselage tank is filled first, fuel from these tanks will drain into the forward fuselage tank lower cell while the forward fuselage tank is being serviced. (See figure 1-33 for fuel specification.) Refer to Section VII for additional information on the fuel system.

---

†F-86D-45 and later airplanes

DROP TANKS.

The main fuel supply can be increased by installation of a 120-gallon (US) external drop tank under each wing. Four types of drop tanks can be carried. Type I and II tanks are of knockdown construction and are designed so that final assembly can be accomplished in the field by maintenance personnel. Type III and IV tanks are completely assembled for installation. Only Type II and IV tanks will have identifying markings stenciled on the inboard side of the tank nose section because of the tank restrictions. The identification mark is visible from the cockpit. Fuel in the drop tanks can be transferred into the main wing outer tanks by directing engine compressor air to the drop tanks. On F-86D-1 and F-86D-5 Airplanes, transfer of the fuel is possible only when fuel quantity in the forward fuselage tank drops about 60 gallons. On F-86D-10 and later airplanes, transfer of fuel is possible when fuel quantity in the forward fuselage tank drops about 5 gallons.

FUEL BOOSTER PUMPS (EARLY AIRPLANES*).

The forward fuselage tank lower cell contains three electrical booster pumps: a forward pump, an aft pump, and a dual pump. The pumps (figure 1-16) are energized and operate at low speed when the engine master switch is set at ON. To provide the added fuel flow required for afterburner operation, the booster pumps automatically operate at a higher speed when the throttle is advanced past the MILITARY stop into AFTERBURNER range. The aft and dual booster pumps are powered by the primary bus, while the forward booster pump is powered by the monitored bus No. 2.

FUEL BOOSTER PUMPS (LATE AIRPLANES†).

Two constant-speed booster pumps, a forward and an aft pump, are in the lower cell of the forward fuselage tank. These pumps supply fuel to the engine when the engine master switch is set at ON. The forward booster pump is powered by the monitored bus No. 2, while the aft booster pump is powered by primary bus. (See figure 1-17.)

FUEL SYSTEM CONTROLS AND INDICATORS.

Throttle.

Refer to "Engine Fuel Control System" in this section.

Engine Master Switch.

Refer to "Engine Fuel Control System" in this section.

Drop Tank Air Pressure Shutoff Valve.

A drop tank air pressure shutoff valve (1, figure 1-6; 1, figure 1-7) is aft of the left console. When the valve is turned ON, both drop tanks are pressurized by engine compressor air, which has been cooled in the heat exchanger. Drop tank pressurization is almost immediate after engine start is made and engine rpm is increased above idle. The valve must be at ON whenever fuel is to be transferred from the drop tanks. Since no drop tank fuel quantity gage is provided, fuel transfer from the drop tanks during operation at high-altitude cruise is shown by a constant aircraft fuel quantity gage reading during the transfer. On F-86D-1 and F-86D-5 Airplanes, the fuel quantity gage will maintain a reading of about 3560 pounds during the transfer. On F-86D-10 and later airplanes, because of a change in fuel tank sequencing, the fuel quantity gage will show about full during the transfer. During afterburner operation (high fuel consumption rate), fuel transfer from the drop tanks may be insufficient to maintain a constant reading on the fuel quantity gage. In this case, fuel transfer is indicated by a relatively low rate of fuel quantity reduction. The valve should be set at ON at all times in flight, when drop tanks are installed, to prevent possible drop tank collapse during rapid descents. Uneven feeding from the drop tanks does not affect the flying qualities of the airplane.

Drop Tank Jettison Button.

Tanks can be jettisoned by pressing the drop tank jettison button on the engine control panel. (See figure 1-10.) Power for jettisoning the tanks is supplied by the battery bus.

WARNING

To prevent accidental explosion of drop tanks while on ground, they must not be installed, removed, or given an operational drop test (either manually or electrically) unless the airplane and drop tanks are electrostatically grounded.

Note

Drop tanks and rockets can also be jettisoned by pressing the tank-rocket jettison button on the control stick grip when the armament master switch is at JETTISON READY. (Refer to "Armament Controls" in Section IV.)

Drop Tank Emergency Jettison Handle.

On F-86D-25 and later airplanes and those changed by T.O., a manual drop tank emergency jettison handle (34, figure 1-5), located below and to the left of the radarscope, provides a means of jettisoning the drop

---

*F-86D-1 through F-86D-40 Airplanes
†F-86D-45 and later airplanes

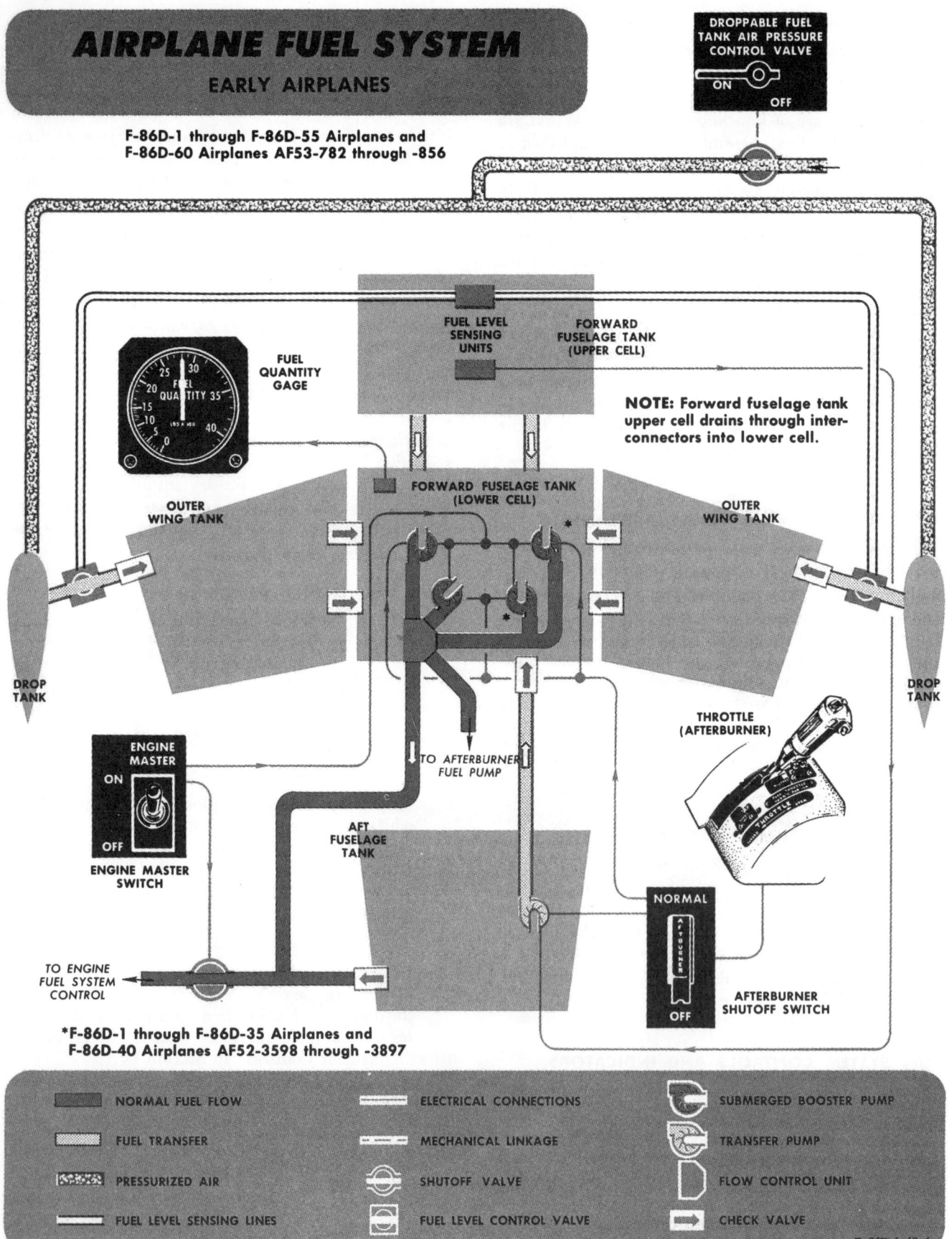

Figure 1-16

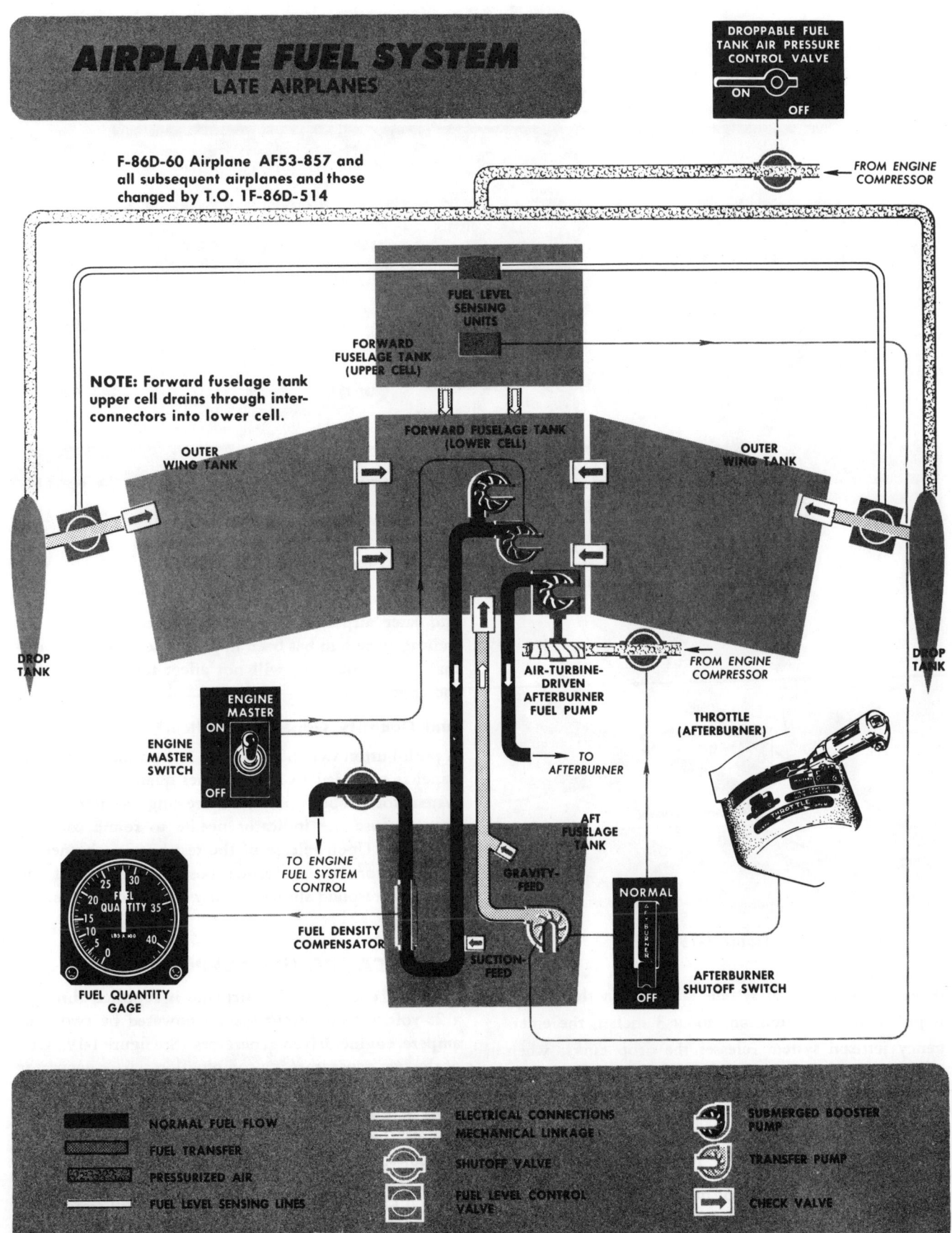

Figure 1-17

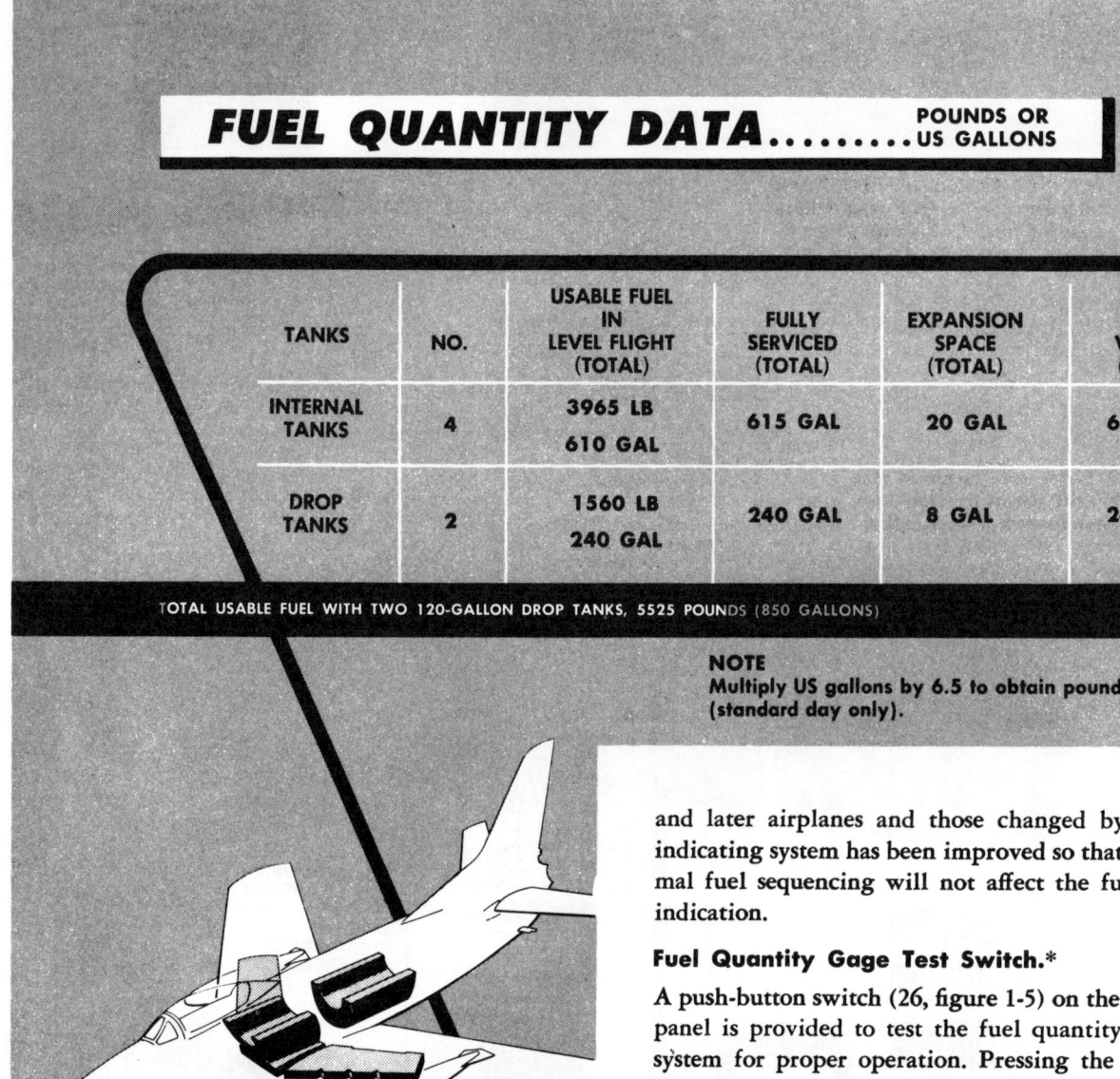

Figure 1-18

FUEL QUANTITY DATA .... POUNDS OR US GALLONS

TANKS	NO.	USABLE FUEL IN LEVEL FLIGHT (TOTAL)	FULLY SERVICED (TOTAL)	EXPANSION SPACE (TOTAL)	TANK VOLUME (TOTAL)
INTERNAL TANKS	4	3965 LB / 610 GAL	615 GAL	20 GAL	635 GAL
DROP TANKS	2	1560 LB / 240 GAL	240 GAL	8 GAL	248 GAL

TOTAL USABLE FUEL WITH TWO 120-GALLON DROP TANKS, 5525 POUNDS (850 GALLONS)

NOTE
Multiply US gallons by 6.5 to obtain pounds (standard day only).

tanks if the electrical system fails. When the handle is pulled to full extension, about 3 inches, the emergency jettison system releases the drop tanks; when the handle is released, it returns to its normal position.

Fuel Quantity Gage.

A fuel quantity gage (28, figure 1-4; 27, figure 1-5) is on the lower right side of the instrument panel. It shows total actual pounds of internal fuel regardless of temperature or type of fuel. The fuel quantity gage is powered from the ac bus of the airplane. No fuel quantity gage is provided for the drop tanks. On F-86D-25 and later airplanes and those changed by T.O., the indicating system has been improved so that any abnormal fuel sequencing will not affect the fuel quantity indication.

Fuel Quantity Gage Test Switch.*

A push-button switch (26, figure 1-5) on the instrument panel is provided to test the fuel quantity indicating system for proper operation. Pressing the test switch should cause the indicator needle to rotate counterclockwise. Upon release of the test button, the needle should return to its former position. Failure of the needle to respond shows a faulty indicating system.

ELECTRICAL POWER SUPPLY SYSTEM.

Electrical energy in this airplane is supplied through a 28-volt, direct-current system powered by two 400-ampere, engine-driven generators. (See figure 1-19.) One of the two generators is a combination starter-generator unit, acting as a starter up to about 23% rpm, and thereafter acting as a generator. On F-86D-1 Airplanes, a 24-volt, 36-ampere-hour storage battery is used. On later airplanes, two 24-volt, 24-ampere-hour storage batteries serve as a stand-by to supply current to the essential units if both generators fail. All ac operated equipment

---

*F-86D-30 and later airplanes

(except radar) is powered by a main inverter (single-phase). Power for the radar equipment is supplied by a secondary inverter (single-phase) and, on F-86D-5 and later airplanes, a single-phase engine-driven alternator. The secondary inverter supplies the radar with a regulated frequency and will automatically disconnect from the radar and assume the ac load of the airplane if the main inverter fails (or when inverter selector switch is positioned at SPARE). On all but the earliest airplanes, the alternator supplies the radar with an unregulated frequency. On early airplanes,* loss of the unregulated frequency will cause all ac and dc power to the radar to be shut off, and on late airplanes,† and those changed by T. O., the radar will function improperly. Three-phase power is provided for the automatic pilot, vertical gyro, yaw damper, zero reader,* and gyro magnetic compass† by four power converters which are normally powered by the main inverter.

ELECTRICALLY OPERATED EQUIPMENT.

See figure 1-19.

If the electrical equipment (including radar equipment) is to be ground-operated, such operation must not exceed 30 minutes unless a special cooling supply is attached to the in-flight cooling system or the fuselage access panels covering the electrical equipment are removed. Heat generated in the electrical compartments will cause a serious reduction in life or immediate failure of equipment if adequate ventilation is not provided.

DC ELECTRICAL POWER DISTRIBUTION.

The dc electrical power necessary for operation of the electrical units in the airplane is distributed by a group of six busses: a battery bus, a primary bus, a secondary bus, and monitored busses No. 1, 2, and 3. The battery bus is hot at all times, so that essential equipment, powered from the battery bus, is operable regardless of the position of the battery-starter switch. When external power is supplied through either No. 1 or No. 2 receptacle (oval receptacle on F-86D-35 and later airplanes) or when both generators are operating, all busses are energized through the primary bus. If one generator fails, monitored bus No. 3 is disconnected from the system. If both generators fail, monitored busses No. 2 and 3 are disconnected, and, with the battery-starter switch at BATTERY, the remaining busses are powered by the battery. On F-86D-35 and later airplanes, external power supplied through the rectangular receptacle is used only to supply power to the starter during ground starts. During an air start, with the air start switch in AIR START (up), the secondary bus, the gyro bus, and the monitored busses No. 1, 2, and 3 are automatically disconnected to conserve battery power. The fuel pressure gage or fuel flowmeter, as applicable, remains energized during an air start by means of an auxiliary inverter which is turned on when the air start switch is energized.

External Power Receptacles.

Two dc external power receptacles (No. 1 and 2) are on the right side of the fuselage, forward of the wing leading edge. On F-86D-20 and later airplanes, the external power receptacles (oval and rectangular) are on the bottom of the fuselage at the wing trailing edge to permit forward movement of the airplane to disconnect the external power source. On F-86D-1 through F-86D-30 Airplanes, all equipment is operable when external power is connected to either dc power receptacle. On F-86D-35 and later airplanes, one dc receptacle is oval-shaped and the other is rectangular-shaped. All equipment except the starter is operable when external power is connected to the oval (left) receptacle; power supplied through the rectangular (right) receptacle powers only the starter. *An external power source must be connected to both receptacles for ground starts on all airplanes.*

Circuit Breakers.

Most of the dc electrical circuits are protected by push-pull circuit breakers on panels on each side of the cockpit.

Circuit breakers should not be pulled or reset without a thorough understanding of all the effects and results. Use of the circuit breakers can eliminate from the system some related warning system, interlocking circuit, or cancelling signal, which could result in an undesirable reaction.

Battery-Starter Switch.

Refer to "Starter System" in this section.

*F-86D-1 through F-86D-30 Airplanes
†F-86D-35 and later airplanes

Section I   T. O. 1F-86D-1

ELECTRICAL POWER
NORMAL-FLIGHT FUNCTIONAL FLOW

BATTERIES (ONLY ONE BATTERY ON F-86D-1 AIRPLANES)

BATTERY BUS
Energized by battery. Energized by generators or external power when battery switch is at *BATT*.

- Canopy switches
- Emergency jettison
- Flight control alternate hydraulic system
- Flight control hydraulic system automatic change-over
- IFF destructor
- Landing gear emergency retract button

PRIMARY BUS
Energized by generators, by external power, or by battery power when battery switch is at *BATT*.

- Afterburner shutoff switch
- Air start switch
- Alternator warning light
- Cockpit pressurization (F-86D-30 Airplanes AF51-6020 thru -6144, and F-86D-35 and subsequent airplanes)
- Dual and aft fuel booster pumps
- Dual fuel pump warning light
- Emergency fuel system
- Engine inlet switch
- Flight control alternate hydraulic system
- Fire-warning system
- Fuel pressure gage inverter (energized during air start)
- Generator warning lights and switches
- Ignition (main and air start)
- Instrument panel and console lights
- Inverter warning lights
- Landing gear system (F-86D-10 and subsequent airplanes)
- Main fuel shutoff valve
- Navigation lights
- Nose wheel steering
- Oxygen regulator warning light and switch
- Pitch correction
- Position lights
- Pressure suit mask heater
- Purging system (some airplanes)
- Single-point refueling
- Speed brake switch
- Turn-and-bank indicator
- Variable-nozzle position indicator
- Variable-nozzle switch and indicator
- Voltmeter (F-86D-5 and subsequent airplanes)
- Windshield and surface overheat warning lights (F-86D-5 and subsequent airplanes)

SECONDARY BUS
Energized by primary bus when air start switch is at *NORMAL*.

- Aileron and horizontal tail trim controls and bungee actuators
- Camera (F-86D-5 and subsequent airplanes)
- Command radio
- Landing gear system (F-86D-1 and F-86D-5 Airplanes)
- Radio compass
- Rocket control
- Rocket fire
- Rocket fire stand-by sight
- Rudder trim
- Take-off trim indicator light

MONITORED BUS NO. 1
Energized by primary bus when air start switch is at *NORMAL*.

- Instrument panel vibrator
- Landing and taxi lights
- Pitot heater
- Voltmeter (F-86D-1 Airplanes)
- Wing flap system

MONITORED BUS NO. 2
Energized by primary bus when air start switch is at *NORMAL*.

- Anti-ice control
- Camera (F-86D-1 Airplanes)
- Canopy switches
- Canopy unsafe warning light
- Cockpit pressurization (F-86D-1 thru F-86D-25 Airplanes and F-86D-30 Airplanes AF51-5945 thru -6019)
- Forward fuel booster pump
- Fuel transfer pump
- Glide path receiver
- Localizer receiver
- Marker beacon radio
- Omnidirectional receiver
- Radar pressurization (F-86D-5 and subsequent airplanes)
- Windshield and surface overheat warning lights (F-86D-1 Airplanes)

MONITORED BUS NO. 3
Energized by primary bus when air start switch is at *NORMAL*.

- Alternator regulator
- Radar pressurization (F-86D-1 Airplanes)
- DC power to fire control system

* With switch at *START*, power is supplied to starter when external power is applied. With switch at *BATT*, battery power is supplied to primary, secondary, and monitored No. 1 busses when external power is not available and engine is inoperative.

† When main inverter fails and inverter switch is positioned to *SPARE*, the spare inverter is no longer controlled from monitored bus No. 3. Control of the spare inverter is assumed by monitored bus No. 2.

F-86D-1-54-7B

Figure 1-19

1-32

DISTRIBUTION

FLIGHT EMERGENCIES

EMERGENCY CONDITIONS	AIR START SWITCH AT AIR START (UP)	BOTH GENERATORS INOPERATIVE	ONE GENERATOR INOPERATIVE	BOTH INVERTERS INOPERATIVE	MAIN INVERTER INOPERATIVE (SECONDARY AUTOMATICALLY DROPS RADAR AND TAKES OVER AC LOAD)*
COLORED BUSSES OPERATIVE	BATTERY BUS	BATTERY BUS	BATTERY BUS	BATTERY BUS	BATTERY BUS
	PRIMARY BUS	PRIMARY BUS	PRIMARY BUS	PRIMARY BUS	PRIMARY BUS
	SECONDARY BUS	SECONDARY BUS	SECONDARY BUS	SECONDARY BUS	SECONDARY BUS
	MONITORED BUS NO. 1	MONITORED BUS NO. 1	MONITORED BUS NO. 1	MONITORED BUS NO. 1	MONITORED BUS NO. 1
	MONITORED BUS NO. 2	MONITORED BUS NO. 2	MONITORED BUS NO. 2	MONITORED BUS NO. 2	MONITORED BUS NO. 2
	MONITORED BUS NO. 3	MONITORED BUS NO. 3	MONITORED BUS NO. 3	MONITORED BUS NO. 3	MONITORED BUS NO. 3
	AC BUS	AC BUS	AC BUS	AC BUS	AC BUS

* Secondary inverter must be manually selected on F-86D-55 and subsequent airplanes and those changed by T. O.

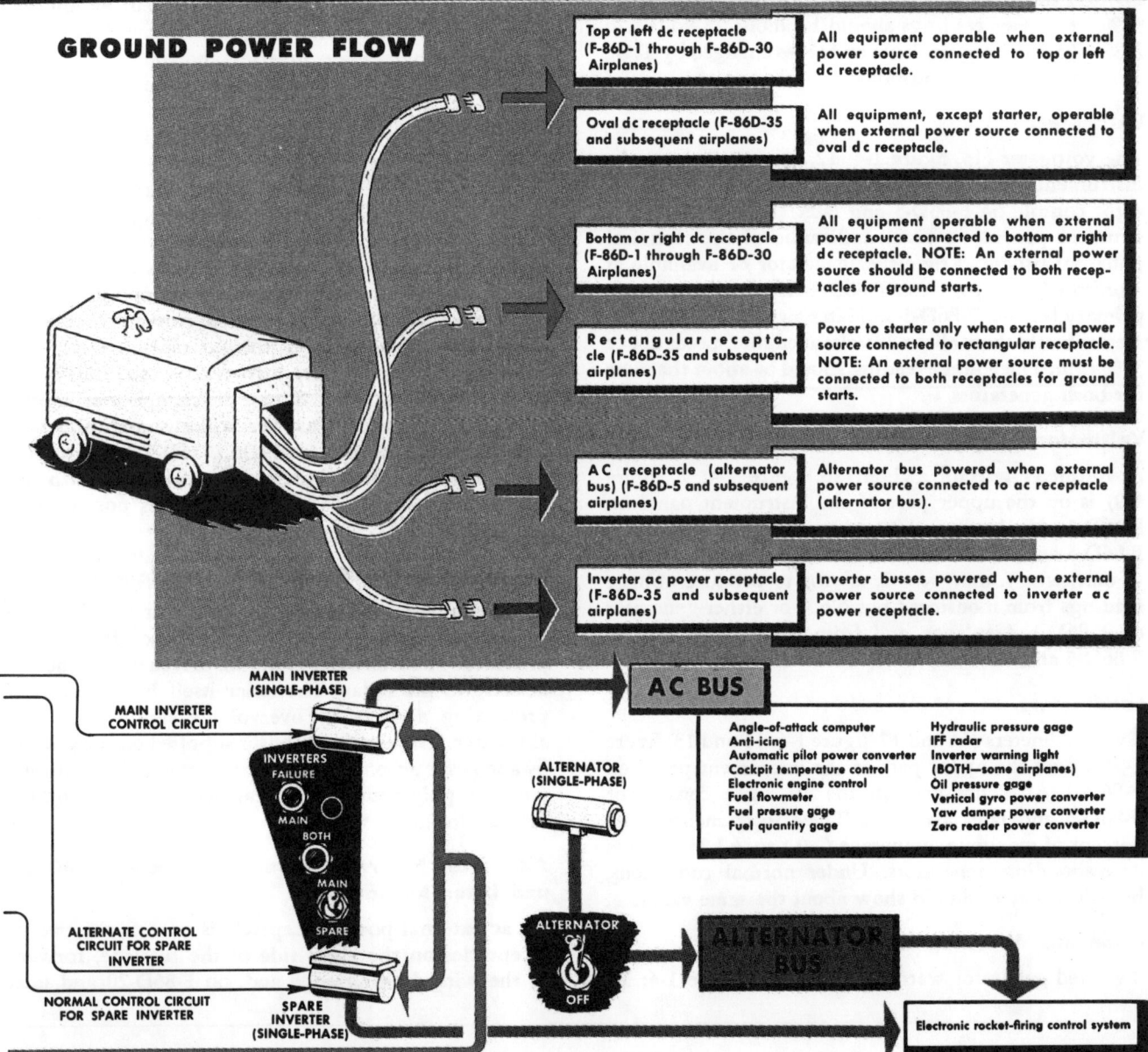

F-86D-1-54-1D

Section I   T. O. 1F-86D-1

Generator Switches.

Two generator switches on the engine control panel on early airplanes,* and on the right instrument subpanel on late airplanes† (figure 1-10), are guarded in the ON position and have two other positions, OFF and RESET. If the generator voltage becomes excessive (over 31 volts), an overvoltage relay automatically cuts the affected generator out of the electrical circuit. The spring-loaded RESET position is used to bring the generator back into the circuit. The generator switches operate on power from the primary bus.

Generator Voltage Regulator Rheostats.

The voltage regulator is preset on the ground, but in an extreme emergency may be adjusted in flight by means of a guarded rheostat (6, figure 1-8; 8, figure 1-9), on the right aft console. With engine rpm above 37%, voltmeter readings should be about 28 volts. On F-86D-55 and later airplanes and those changed by T.O., the rheostats are not installed.

Voltmeter.

The voltmeter (13, figure 1-4; 12, figure 1-9) is on the instrument panel on F-86D-1 Airplanes and on the aft right console on F-86D-5 and later airplanes. This instrument provides a visual indication of the electrical potential produced by either generator or available at monitored bus No. 1 (on F-86D-1 Airplanes) or at the primary bus (on F-86D-5 and later airplanes). The voltmeter should show about 28 volts at engine speeds above 37% rpm. The voltage reading should be about the same for both generators.

Voltmeter Selector Switch.

A voltmeter selector switch (16, figure 1-4; 7, figure 1-9) is on the upper part of the instrument panel on F-86D-1 Airplanes and on the aft right console on F-86D-5 and later airplanes. This switch may be moved to GEN. NO. 1, GEN. NO. 2, or BUS to produce voltage readings from monitored bus No. 1 or either generator on F-86D-1 Airplanes, and from the primary bus on F-86D-5 and later airplanes.

Loadmeters.

Two loadmeters (14 and 17, figure 1-4; 11 and 13, figure 1-9) are on the upper part of the instrument panel on F-86D-1 Airplanes and on the aft right console of F-86D-5 and later airplanes. These instruments show percent of maximum amperage (−0.1 to +1.25) for the corresponding generators. Under normal conditions, both loadmeters should show about the same value.

Generator Warning Lights.

Two red generator warning lights (15, figure 1-4; 29, figure 1-5), one for each generator, are on the instrument panel. On F-86D-1 Airplanes, these lights are on the top right corner of the main instrument panel; on F-86D-5 and later airplanes, they are on the small subpanel below the main instrument panel. Illumination of either warning light shows that the respective generator has failed or has been disconnected because of overvoltage. Both lights are powered by the primary bus and come on during air starts.

AC ELECTRICAL POWER DISTRIBUTION.

The ac electrical power is distributed to the ac electrical equipment throughout the airplane by two busses: the ac bus and the alternator bus. The ac bus is powered by the main single-phase inverter and supplies power to all ac operated equipment except the radar. Power to the radar equipment is supplied by the secondary single-phase inverter and, on F-86D-5 and later airplanes, by an engine-driven alternator. Both inverters are powered by the primary bus. Control of the main inverter is powered from monitored bus No. 2; the main inverter will be cut out if power from monitored bus No. 2 is not available. Likewise, control of the secondary inverter is powered from monitored bus No. 3; the secondary inverter will not operate if monitored bus No. 3 fails. If the main inverter fails during any flight with only one generator operating (monitored bus No. 3 and secondary inverter rendered inoperative), the control of the secondary inverter will automatically be transferred from monitored bus No. 3 to monitored bus No. 2. When the change-over is completed, the secondary inverter will automatically take over the main inverter load. On F-86D-5 and later airplanes, the alternator bus supplies the radar with unregulated frequency. The alternator bus powers only the radar.

Alternator (F-86D-5 and Later Airplanes).

For unregulated frequency ac power for the radar, an 8-kilovolt-ampere, 115-volt, single-phase alternator is provided. The alternator is engine-driven and connected directly to the radar. The radar itself has a means of preventing damage by overvoltage supply from the alternator. The alternator bus is supplied on the ground by a separate ac external power receptacle. The external power supply cannot be paralleled with the engine-driven alternator supply.

Alternator External Power Receptacle (F-86D-5 and Later Airplanes).

An ac external power receptacle is next to the two dc receptacles on the right side of the fuselage, forward of the wing leading edge and, on F-86D-20 and later

---

*F-86D-1 through F-86D-30 Airplanes and F-86D-35 Airplanes AF51-6145 through -6262 and -8274 through -8305
†F-86D-35 Airplane AF51-8306 and all later airplanes

A-C EXTERNAL POWER RECEPTACLES

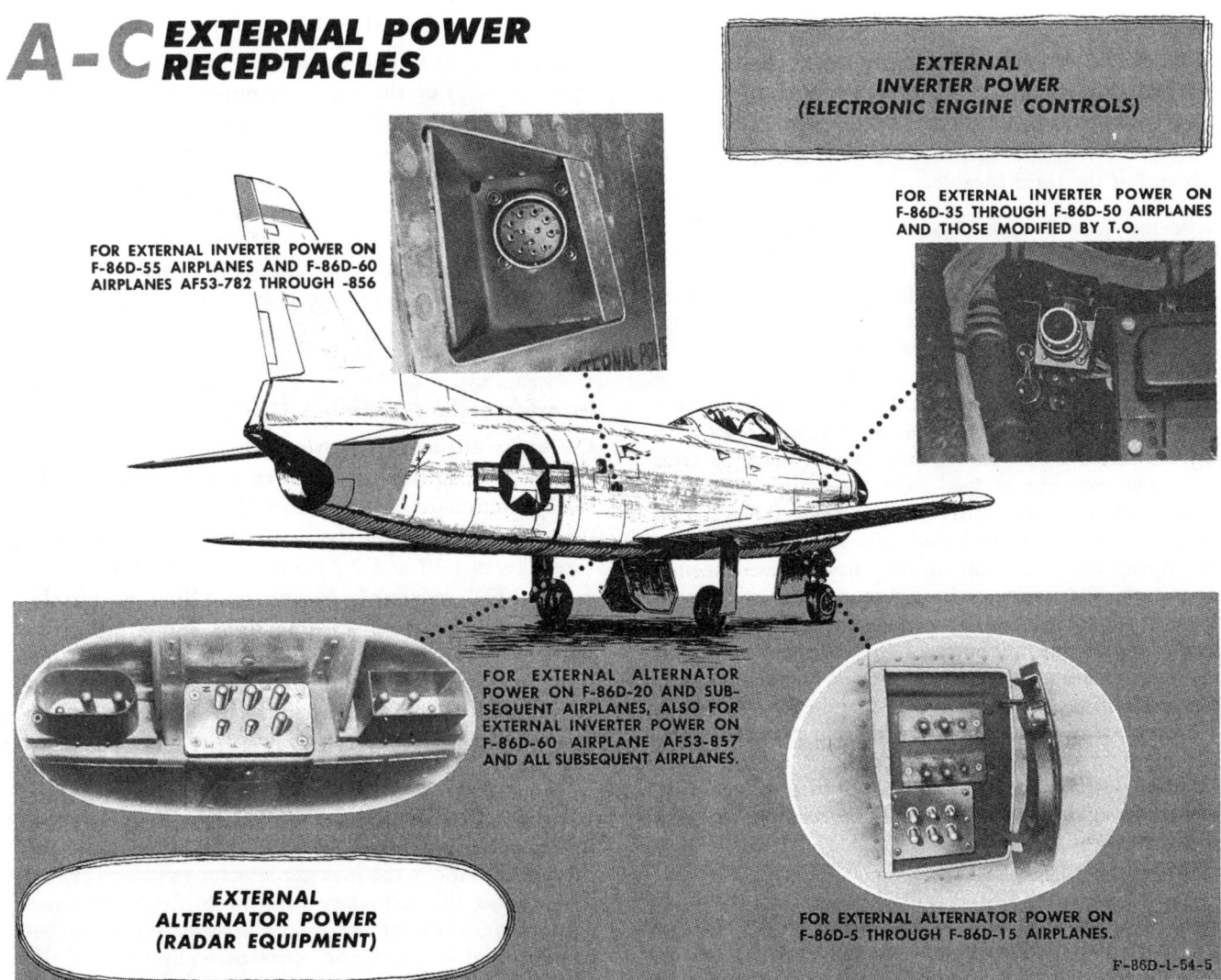

Figure 1-20

airplanes, on the bottom of the fuselage at the wing trailing edge. (See figure 1-20.) The ac receptacle may be used to furnish power for ground operation of the radar; the power is furnished between 380 and 770 cycles per second.

Inverter External Power Receptacle (F-86D-35 and Later Airplanes).

An electrical receptacle is provided to allow inverter power to be supplied by means of an external power source for ground operational purposes only. (See figure 1-20.) On some airplanes,* the receptacle is within the nose section, on the right side. A jumper plug covers the receptacle and must be removed (disconnects the airplane inverters) to allow the external power source to be used. On late airplanes,† the receptacle is on the fuselage side, aft of the right wing; on later airplanes,‡ the receptacle is on the bottom of the fuselage. The center receptacle has been changed so that external power for the radar and electronic equipment can be supplied at the same time. The airplane inverters are disconnected when the external power source is connected and the engine master switch is OFF, allowing for extended ground operation and to provide alert power for those units requiring ac power. If the engine master switch is ON, the external power source is automatically disconnected. To prevent damage occurring to the plug connection upon disconnecting, the engine master switch should be turned ON before the plug is removed.

*F-86D-1 through F-86D-50 Airplanes
†F-86D-55 Airplanes and F-86D-60 Airplanes AF53-782 through -856
‡F-86D-60 Airplane AF53-857 and all later airplanes

AC Fuses.

Most of the ac circuits are protected by fuses which are replaceable in flight. The fuses are grouped together on panels on each side of the cockpit. One group is on the panel next to the throttle; the other group is on the left end of the right console.

Inverter Test Switch (F-86D-1 Through F-86D-50 Airplanes).

An inverter test switch on the right instrument subpanel (figure 1-10) has a NORMAL position and a spring-loaded TEST position. This switch is used to test the inverter change-over circuit and to ensure that the secondary inverter is operable. When the switch is held at TEST for about 4 seconds, the main inverter warning light comes on. This shows that the secondary inverter has taken over the ac load from the main inverter. If the switch is continuously held at TEST, the warning light will go out after an additional 5 to 35 seconds, indicating that the main inverter has resumed normal operation. The entire cycle will require about 10 to 40 seconds for completion. The actual amount of time will depend upon the tolerance of the change-over circuit time-delay temperature, time allowed for change-over circuit cooling after previous test, and other variables. However, if the switch is released from TEST as soon as the main inverter warning light comes on, the main inverter will remain disconnected; to turn the main inverter on again, the switch must be returned to TEST until the light goes out.

Note

The warning light that shows failure of both inverters will come on momentarily as the test switch is actuated. This is considered normal and should not be taken as a malfunction of both inverters.

Inverter Selector Switch.

On F-86D-55 and later airplanes and those changed by T. O., the inverter selector switch replaces the inverter test switch and automatic change-over relay (figure 1-10) and is used for manually selecting the main or secondary inverter as power sources for the ac operated equipment. The switch has two fixed positions: MAIN, which is the position for all normal operation; and SPARE, for manually selecting the secondary inverter as a power source if the main inverter fails. Normally, the main inverter supplies power for all ac operated equipment except radar, which is supplied by the secondary inverter and alternator. If the main inverter fails, the inverter selector switch must be placed at SPARE, causing the secondary inverter to drop the radar equipment, and allowing secondary inverter power to become available for the ac operated equipment.

Alternator Switch (F-86D-5 and Later Airplanes).

A two-position switch for control of the alternator is at the bottom of the right instrument subpanel. (See figure 1-10.) When the switch is in the ON position, the alternator bus is provided with ac voltage from the engine-driven alternator or from an external power source. When an external source is supplying power to the alternator bus, it alone supplies the power until disconnected. The switch is powered by the monitored Bus No. 3 and should be ON at all times unless an alternator failure is shown by failure of the radarscope picture.

Inverter Failure Warning Lights.

On early airplanes* having the automatic inverter change-over, failure of the main inverter is shown by steady illumination of an amber "MAIN" inverter failure warning light on the right instrument subpanel. (See figures 1-10 and 7-3.) Steady illumination of the red "BOTH" inverter failure warning light, next to the main inverter failure warning light, shows failure of both inverters. Both of the inverter failure warning lights receive their power from the primary bus. On late airplanes† and those changed by T. O. having the manual inverter change-over, failure of the inverter in use causes both the amber "MAIN" inverter failure warning light and the red "BOTH" inverter failure warning light to come on. This, however, does not show failure of both inverters. When both lights come on, the pilot should move the inverter selector switch to SPARE. This causes the secondary inverter to drop the radar equipment, allowing secondary inverter power to become available for the ac operated equipment. If the secondary inverter is operative, the amber "MAIN" inverter failure warning light will remain on, but the red "BOTH" inverter failure warning light will go out when the switch is set at SPARE. If both lights remain on when the switch is moved, the secondary inverter also has failed.

UTILITY HYDRAULIC POWER SUPPLY SYSTEM.

The utility hydraulic power supply system is a closed-center, constant-pressure type system with an engine-driven, variable-output pump. (See figure 1-21.) This system is completely independent of the flight control hydraulic systems. A pressure storage accumulator is provided for nose gear emergency extension. This system supplies power for operation of the rudder, landing gear, speed brakes, nose wheel steering, wheel brakes, and rocket package operation. (See figure 1-33 for hydraulic fluid specification.)

---

*F-86D-1 through F-86D-50 Airplanes
†F-86D-55 and later airplanes

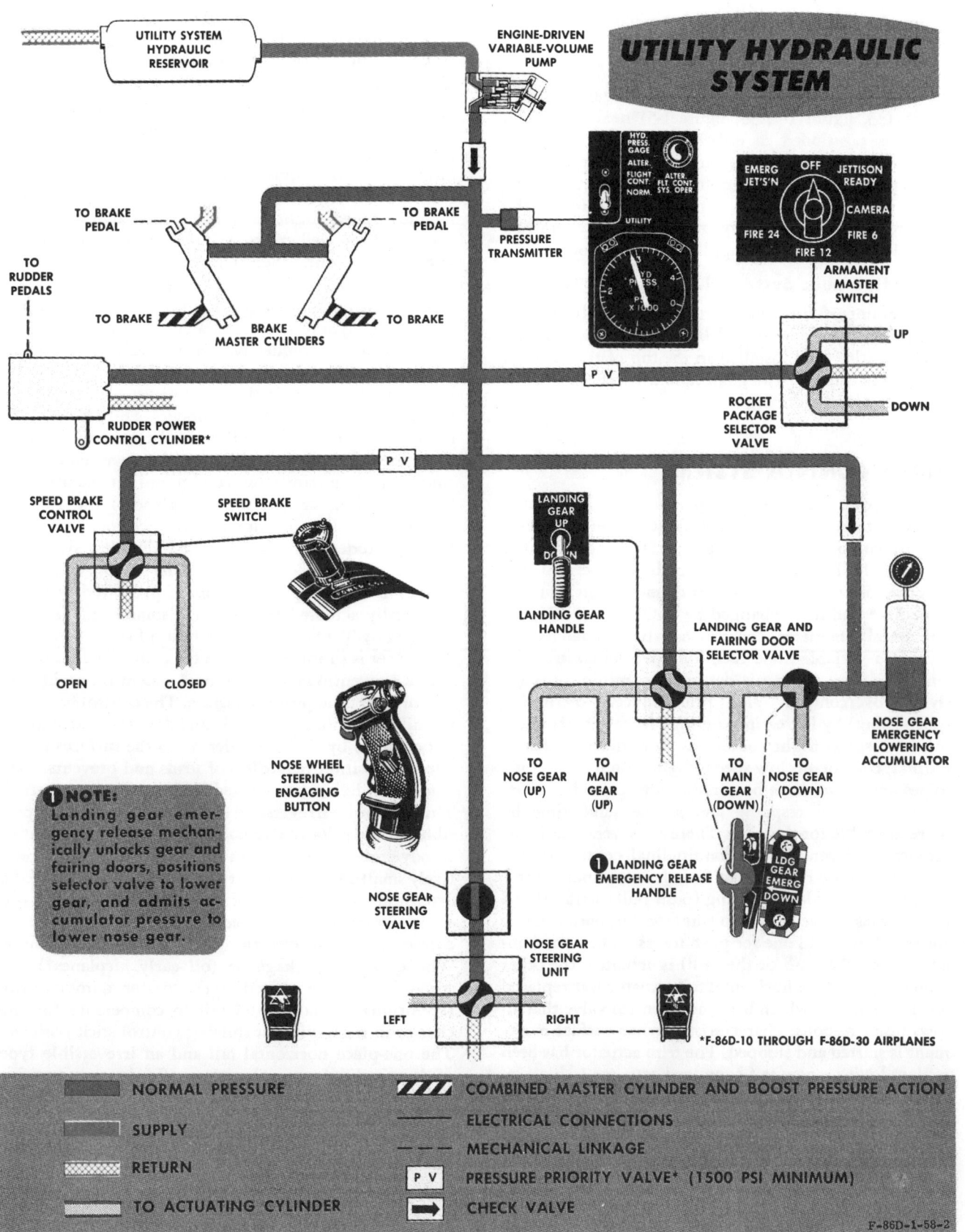

Figure 1-21

UTILITY HYDRAULIC SYSTEM INDICATORS.

Hydraulic Pressure Gage and Pressure Gage Selector Switch.

A pressure gage (32, figure 1-4; 31, figure 1-5) is beneath the instrument panel, with a pressure gage selector switch (33, figure 1-4; 33, figure 1-5) next to it. The switch is positioned to either UTILITY, NORMAL, or ALTER (FLT. CONT. EMERG. on F-86D-1 Airplanes) to obtain pressure gage readings for the respective systems. As the pressure gage is an ac powered instrument, the pressure gage and pressure gage selector switch will be operable when power is supplied by the ac bus.

Utility Hydraulic System Fluid Quantity Gage.

The amount of fluid in the utility hydraulic system reservoir can be determined by the indication of the fluid quantity gage installed in the top of the fuselage behind the canopy. The gage should be checked for a full indication before flight.

FLIGHT CONTROL SYSTEM.

Four unique features are incorporated in control surface action. First, the horizontal stabilizer and elevators are combined into a single surface known as the controllable horizontal tail, which is operated for longitudinal control through stick movement. On late airplanes* and those changed by T. O. 1F-86D-236, the horizontal stabilizer control has been changed to include a variable-slope feel, longitudinal control system. This new feature is designed to minimize sensitivity, overcontrol, and pilot-induced oscillation (porpoising) by increasing the stick force gradient during high-speed flight conditions. For increased longitudinal control at low-speed flight conditions, stick forces and travel have been reduced to provide a more positive control response and at the same time be more desirable for the pilot. There are several main differences between the old longitudinal control system and the new (variable-slope feel) longitudinal control system. The one double-acting (push-pull) artificial feel bungee was replaced by two single-acting bungees, one for pull forces and one for push forces. When one bungee (either the push or the pull) is actuated, the other bungee is idle. The horizontal tail actuator was replaced with an actuator which has a new control valve that allows faster response characteristics when surface movement is started and stopped. The trim actuator has been replaced with a new self-contained actuator (which increases the rate of trim) rather than the screw-jack type that was driven by a remote power unit through a flexible drive. The ratio of the stick throw (movement) and stabilizer displacement is varied by a mechanical linkage in the follow-up system. For high-speed flight, the stick-to-stabilizer ratio has been increased 60 percent over the old system; for low-speed flight conditions, the ratio has been reduced to 75 percent of the old system. *The trimmed position of the horizontal tail determines the stick force rate by varying the mechanical advantage of the stick to the artificial feel bungees.* For example, during straight-and-level flight and with the airplane trimmed for cruising speed, the stick-movement-to-stabilizer ratio is about equal (for a given amount of stick movement, the stabilizer moves about the same). When trimmed for high-speed flight condition (airplane trimmed nose-down), the stick must be moved farther than for normal cruise trimmed position to get a small amount of surface deflection. The reverse is true for slow-speed flight (airplane trimmed nose-up), as the stabilizer deflection will be larger for a small stick movement. (See figure 1-22.) Second, the ailerons, horizontal tail, and (on some airplanes,† except on airplanes changed by T. O.) the rudder are completely hydraulically operated. On these airplanes, the conventional rudder system is installed; movement of the control stick and rudder pedals positions only the hydraulic control valves that direct pressure to the respective surface actuating cylinders. Third, to provide normal stick feel to the pilot at all times, an artificial feel system is built into the control system. Fourth, no control surface trim tabs are required on the ailerons, horizontal tail, or (on some airplanes†) the rudder; trim is effected by positioning the stick for the desired flight attitude and then operating the trim switch to remove the stick loads. The rudder on all other airplanes is cable-operated and is provided with an electrically actuated trim tab. On some airplanes† not changed by T. O., hydraulic pressure for the control of the rudder is supplied through the utility hydraulic system; a conventional cable control system is provided in case of hydraulic pressure failure. The control system of the ailerons, horizontal tail, and (on some airplanes† not changed by T. O.) rudder holds the surfaces in the selected position regardless of loads and prevents these loads from being transmitted back to the control stick. This hydraulic irreversible control system makes it possible for the pilot to overcome a tremendous amount of aerodynamic force through the control stick with relatively small effort on his part. Changes in trim due to the extension and retraction of the rocket package and (on early airplanes‡) the speed brakes are automatically corrected by an electric pitch correction actuator. Whenever the package or (on early airplanes‡) the speed brakes are moved, the actuator automatically repositions the horizontal tail to compensate for the change in trim, without shifting control stick position. The one-piece horizontal tail and an irreversible type of longitudinal control system afford more positive action with less control surface movement, eliminating or reducing many of the undesirable effects of compressibility, such as loss of control effectiveness at high Mach numbers.

---

*F-86D-50 and later airplanes
†F-86D-10 through F-86D-30 Airplanes
‡F-86D-1 through F-86D-25 Airplanes

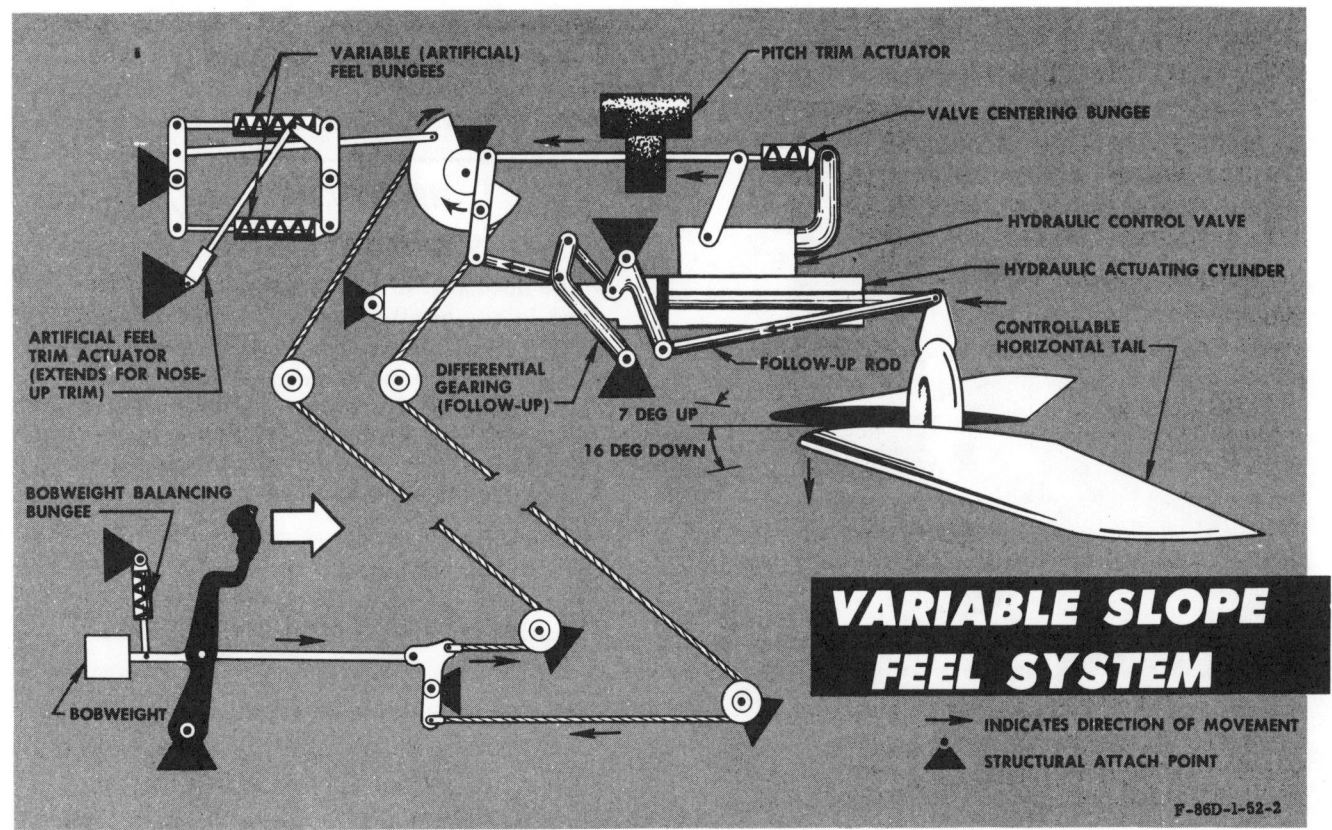

Figure 1-22

YAW DAMPER.

A yaw damper is installed to increase the directional stability of the airplane. The yaw damper senses rate of directional changes and electrically varies rudder position to dampen out the change. It should be on during the search and attack phase of the mission, to provide the necessary directional stability, and at any time that yawing oscillation becomes pronounced.

FLIGHT CONTROL ARTIFICIAL FEEL SYSTEM.

Because no feel of air loads can be transmitted through the flight control hydraulic system, no conventional stick feel is present. Therefore, to supply the usual stick feel under all flight conditions, an artificial feel system is installed. (See figure 1-22.) Normal stick forces resulting from G are provided through a bob-weight, while stick forces resulting from control surface air loads are simulated through spring bungees. The normal and alternate trim switches control the position of the bungees so that the control stick no-load position is changed and desired trim is obtained.

FLIGHT CONTROLS AND INDICATOR.

Control Stick.

The control stick grip (figure 1-23) has an aileron and horizontal tail normal trim switch, a camera and rocket-firing trigger, a nose wheel steering engaging button, a microphone button, a tank-rocket jettison button (this button has been removed on TF-86D Airplanes), and an automatic pilot release switch.

Rudder Pedals.

The angle of the rudder pedals is adjustable on the ground. The pedals can also be individually adjusted fore and aft by adjustment levers outboard of each pedal. When the lever is held out with the foot, the pedal can be moved to one of five neutral positions; the pedal position will lock as selected when the lever is released.

On F-86D-1 through F-86D-35 Airplanes, marginal clearance between top of left rudder pedal and airspeed static block, above pedal, can cause binding and catching of pilot's shoe during braking and/or hard-over rudder action. Pilot's foot should be placed low enough on pedal to prevent this from occurring.

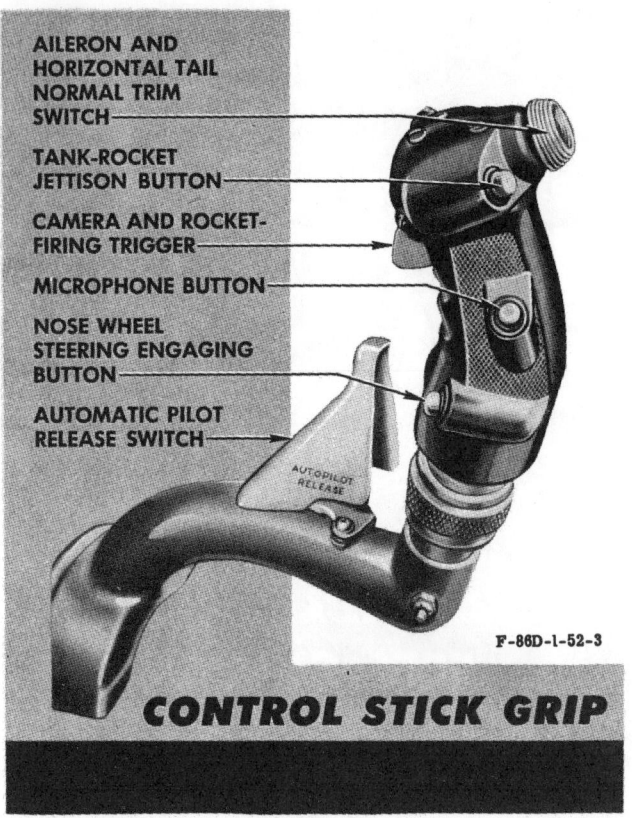

Figure 1-23

Control Lock.

The control surfaces and the rudder on some airplanes* not changed by T. O., are locked against external loads at all times because of the irreversible hydraulic system. On some airplanes,† the rudder lock handle (20, figure 1-6; 19, figure 1-7) is on the left aft console. When the handle is pulled up, a mechanical lock is set to engage when the rudder pedals are neutralized. To unlock the rudder, the lock handle is pivoted to release an incorporated catch, then pushed down.

Do not twist the rudder lock handle. This could cause the locking system to function incorrectly.

Normal Trim Switch.

Normal trim of the horizontal tail or of the ailerons is provided through a five-position switch on top of control stick grip. (See figure 1-23.) This switch is powered by the secondary bus and is spring-loaded to the center position. Trim is effected by setting the stick for the desired flight attitude and then operating the normal trim switch to remove the stick loads. Holding the normal trim switch to either side causes the corresponding wing to be trimmed down. Holding the normal trim switch forward trims the nose down; holding it aft trims the nose up. When the switch is released, it automatically returns to the center OFF position and trim action stops.

WARNING

- The normal trim switch is subject to sticking in any or all of the actuated positions, resulting in application of extreme trim. If this condition occurs during preflight check and the switch does not return automatically to the center OFF position, enter this fact in the DD Form 781 with red cross and do not fly the airplane.

- If the normal trim switch sticks in any actuated position during flight, the switch must be returned manually to the center OFF position after the desired amount of trim is obtained.

Alternate Longitudinal Trim Switch.

A four-position switch, on the flight control panel (figure 1-24) on the left console, provides an alternate trim circuit for the horizontal tail. Use of this switch accomplishes longitudinal trim at the same speed obtained through use of the normal trim switch. The alternate longitudinal trim switch must be kept at NORM. to provide power for the normal trim switch (on the stick grip) to be used for trimming. Moving the alternate longitudinal trim switch to OFF disconnects both the alternate and the normal trim circuits for the stabilizer and prevents operation of the stabilizer automatic trim by the autopilot. Holding the switch at NOSE UP or NOSE DN. overrides any malfunction of the normal trim switch and trims the airplane accordingly. The switch is powered by the secondary bus and is spring-loaded from NOSE UP or NOSE DN. to OFF.

Alternate Lateral Trim Switch.

A four-position switch, on the flight control panel (figure 1-24), provides an alternate means of lateral trim. Trim by the use of this switch is accomplished at the same speed as with the normal trim switch. Ordinarily, this switch is kept at NORMAL, which allows use of the normal trim switch on the control stick. Placing the switch at OFF disconnects both normal and alternate aileron trim circuits; holding the switch at either LEFT or RIGHT overrides any malfunction of the normal trim switch and trims the corresponding wing down. The switch is powered by the secondary bus and is spring-loaded from LEFT or RIGHT to OFF.

---

*F-86D-10 through F-86D-30 Airplanes
†F-86D-1, F-86D-5, and F-86D-35 and later airplanes

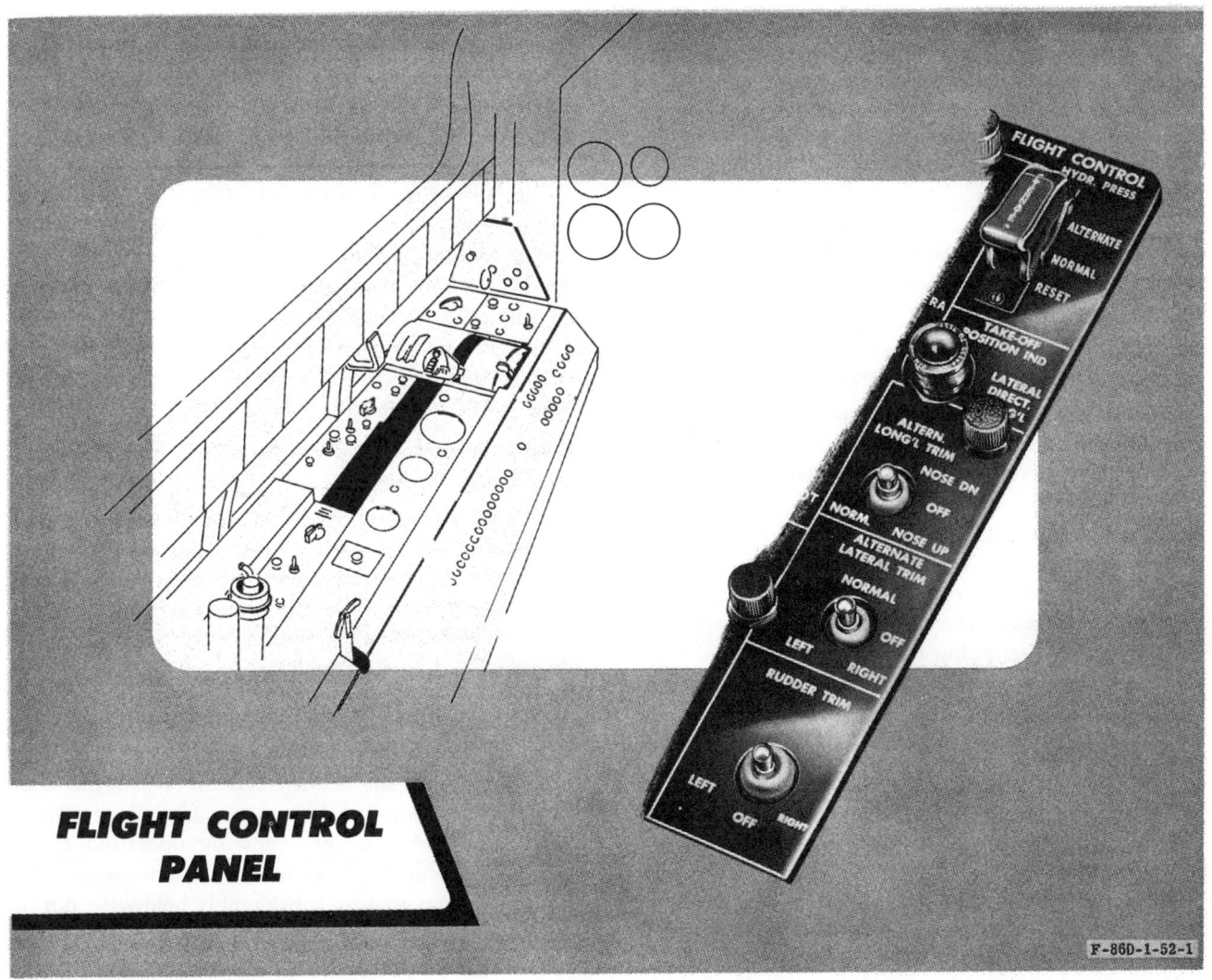

Figure 1-24

Rudder Trim Switch.

Rudder trim is electrically controlled through a spring-loaded switch on the flight control panel. (See figure 1-24.) The switch is held to LEFT or RIGHT for corresponding rudder trim and is spring-loaded to the OFF position. The switch should be in the OFF position (NORM'L on F-86D-1 Airplanes, NORM on F-86D-5 through F-86D-20 Airplanes) at all times after desired rudder trim is obtained. The rudder trim switch receives its power from the secondary bus.

Yaw Damper Switch.

A two-position switch (1, figure 1-8; 1, figure 1-9), on the vertical panel forward of the right console, controls the yaw damper. Placing the switch in the ON position puts the yaw damper into operation whenever the monitored bus No. 2 is energized, if the automatic pilot is not engaged.

Note

To fully utilize the advantages of the yaw damper, it is recommended that the damper be turned on during climb-out and turned off during pre-traffic-pattern check.

Take-off (Trim) Position Indicator Light.

An amber light, on the flight control panel (figure 1-24), shows take-off trim position for ailerons, horizontal tail, and rudder. The light is powered by the secondary bus; it will come on when any one of these surfaces is trimmed to take-off position and will go out when the trim switch is released; it will come on again when the next surface is trimmed for take-off, etc. On F-86D-1 Airplanes, trim by use of the alternate lateral trim switch will not cause the light to come on. Aileron and rudder take-off trim positions are neutral; horizontal tail take-off trim position is set for an airplane nose-up condition.

1-41

Note

On F-86D-25 and later airplanes, the take-off trim position indicator light will not come on when surfaces are being trimmed if the automatic pilot master switch is ON.

FLIGHT CONTROL HYDRAULIC SYSTEMS.

A constant-pressure hydraulic system supplies power for operation of ailerons and horizontal tail. (See figure 1-25.) An alternate constant-pressure hydraulic system is provided in case the normal system fails. Change-over from the normal to the alternate system is usually accomplished automatically when normal system pressure fails. A manual method of change-over, however, is provided by a control handle in the cockpit. A flight control switch is provided to test the alternate system by simulating a failure of the normal system. When normal system pressure falls below 650 psi, two pressure switches close (one of which serves as stand-by for the other), energizing two solenoid-operated shut-off valves. One valve shuts off the pressure supply in the normal system; the other opens to allow operation of the alternate system. However, if alternate system pressure is also below 650 psi, a second pair of pressure switches, in the alternate system lines, will remain open; the circuits to the solenoid valves will not be completed, and the valves will remain in the positions to use normal system pressure. Therefore, automatic transfer to the alternate system is prevented if alternate pressure is below a usable amount. (See figure 1-33 for fluid specification.) Refer to "Hydraulic Systems" in Section VII for additional information.

Flight Control Normal Hydraulic System.

The system is pressurized by a variable-volume, engine-driven pump which receives fluid from the normal system reservoir. The pump is supplemented by an accumulator for instantaneous high rates of demand. The accumulator air pressure gage, behind the same access door as the oil filler point, should be checked before flight for 600 to 650 psi air precharge when hydraulic pressure is depleted. The pressure is applied to three hydraulically operated dual actuating cylinders; one for the horizontal tail and one for each aileron. Each actuating cylinder is, in effect, two independent actuating cylinders and contains one normal and one alternate control valve. The normal and the alternate control valves on the actuating cylinder operate entirely independent of each other; malfunction or loss of fluid in one valve or cylinder will not affect operation of the other in any way. The amount of fluid in the system can be determined by the fluid quantity indicator pin which protrudes from the compensator. The pin is seen by removal of the access door just forward of the flight control normal hydraulic system filling point. The pin should protrude a minimum of 1/4 inch to 1 1/4 inches maximum and should be checked before flight. Movement of the control stick, which is mechanically linked to the control valves, directs system pressure through the valves to the actuating cylinders, which cause movement of the corresponding control surface. As the control system for the ailerons is designed to hold against air loads up to the structural design limits of the airplane, and the control system for the horizontal tail is designed to hold against any amount of outside force, air loads on the control surfaces are not transmitted to the pilot through the control stick.

Flight Control Alternate Hydraulic System.

The system is pressurized by an electric-motor-driven pump, which receives fluid from an alternate reservoir. When the alternate system is operating, pressure is supplied through separate hydraulic lines to a hydraulic control valve on each of the three actuating cylinders. Two pressure storage accumulators are included in the system. The pump is automatically turned on by two pressure switches (one of which serves as a stand-by for the other) whenever accumulator pressure drops below 2700 psi. The operation of the alternate system is the same as that of the normal system. When the alternate system shutoff valve opens, an indicator light comes on in the cockpit, showing operation of the alternate system. Rapid control stick movement causes system pressure to drop considerably below the normal 3000 psi. The amount of fluid in the alternate system can be determined by checking the alternate compensator shaft extension length. The compensator is forward of the alternate system accumulators on the front spar and is visible when the access panel at the right wing root lower fairing is removed. *The shaft should extend a minimum of 1/4 inch to 1 1/4 inches maximum.*

Rudder Flight Control System.

On F-86D-10 through F-86D-30 Airplanes, hydraulic pressure for control of the rudder is supplied through the utility hydraulic system. This rudder control system, together with the separate hydraulic flight control systems for ailerons and horizontal tail, provides complete hydraulic operation of all flight controls. If utility hydraulic system pressure momentarily falls below 1500 psi, two priority valves cut out the portions of the system supplying the speed brakes and the rocket package in an effort to sustain a system pressure of 1500 psi or more for rudder control. If utility hydraulic system pressure falls below 200 to 250 psi, the hydraulic rudder control valve automatically by-passes hydraulic power, and rudder control is taken over by a conventional cable control system. On airplanes changed by T. O. 1F-86D-250, the power-operated rudder is changed to a conventional rudder system.

FLIGHT CONTROL HYDRAULIC SYSTEM

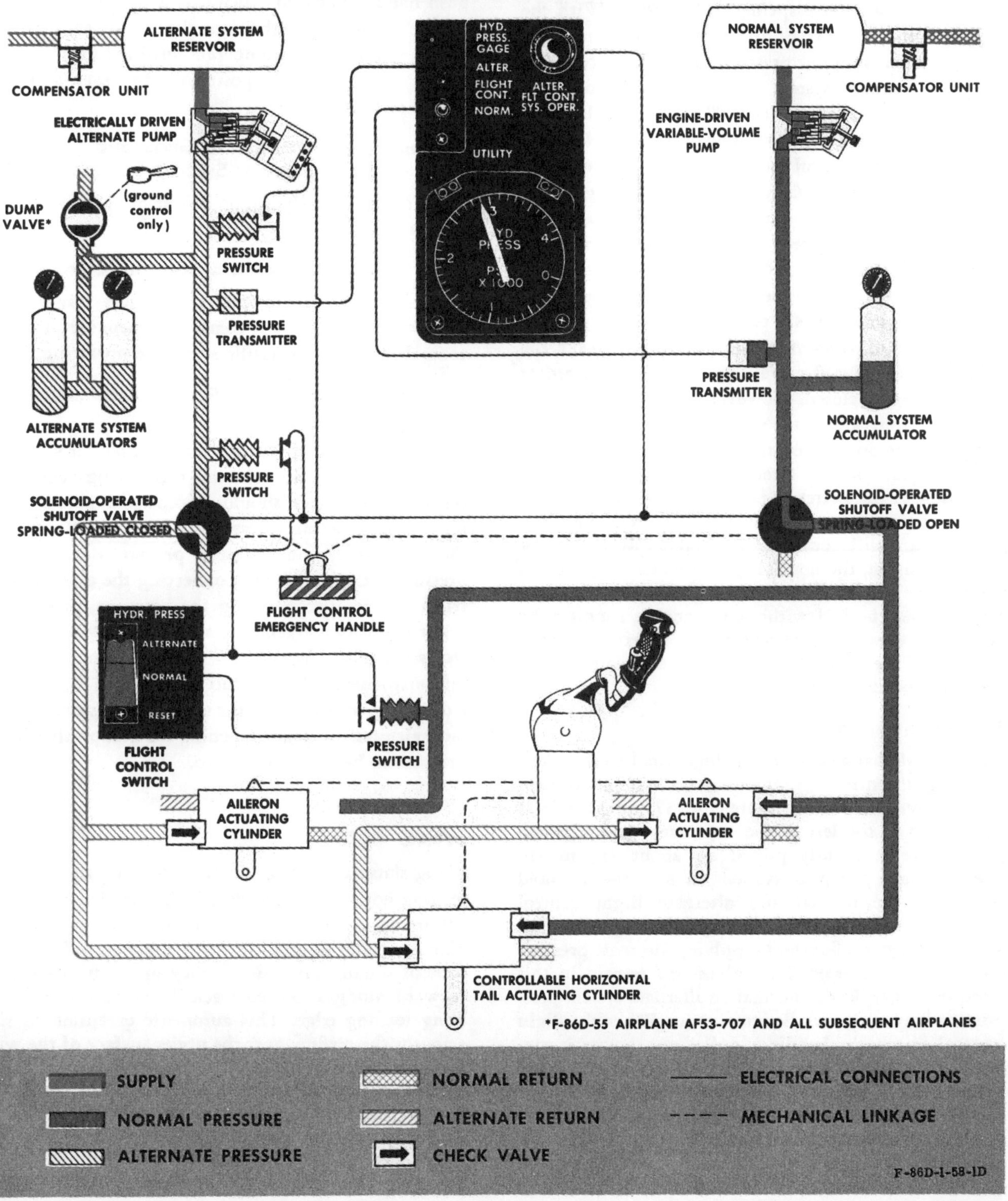

Figure 1-25

Flight Control Switch.

A three-position flight control switch is on the flight control panel (figure 1-24) aft of the throttle. It provides a selective means of changing from the normal to the alternate flight control hydraulic system for test purposes. The three positions are ON or ALTERNATE, guarded NORMAL, and spring-loaded RESET. With the switch in the NORMAL position (engine running), the normal system supplies pressure to the flight controls, and the alternate system will cut in automatically should the normal system fail. With the switch in the ON or ALTERNATE position, two solenoid valves are energized, shutting off normal system pressure and supplying alternate system pressure to the flight controls. If alternate system pressure is below 650 psi, however, the alternate system valve will not be energized even though the switch is ON or ALTERNATE. To return control to the normal system, the switch must be moved to the spring-loaded RESET position momentarily before it is returned to NORMAL. With the switch at RESET, the normal system shutoff valve is opened and the alternate system valve is closed. However, when the switch is returned from RESET to NORMAL, if normal system pressure is below 650 psi, the valves will automatically transfer again and the alternate system will return to operation. If the switch is positioned at NORMAL without first being moved to the RESET position, the alternate system will continue to operate. Regardless of switch position, the normal system will not operate as long as the engine is not running. The alternate system may be checked without the engine running, by use of an external electrical power source; to check transfer of the normal system to the alternate system, the engine must be running.

Flight Control Emergency Handle.

For manual change-over from the normal to the alternate flight control hydraulic system, a flight control emergency handle (37, figure 1-4; 37, figure 1-5) is below and to the left of the instrument panel. When the handle is rapidly pulled aft about 2½ inches, the alternate pump is turned on and the solenoid valves in the normal and alternate flight control hydraulic systems are manually actuated, shutting off normal system flow and supplying alternate pressure to the flight controls. The valves will remain in this position, regardless of normal or alternate system pressure, as long as the handle remains out. When the flight control emergency handle is pulled out, power is supplied from the battery bus to the alternate system pump, which operates continuously as long as the handle remains extended. This will result in pressure indications above the maximum marked on the hydraulic pressure gage, ranging as high as 4000 psi, the pressure at which the relief valve automatically functions. No damage to the hydraulic system is likely to result, but such high pressures should be reported at the conclusion of flight. A detent is provided on the handle shaft for locking the handle in the emergency position. To release handle from emergency position, push handle down and forward. When the emergency handle is returned to the normal position, the alternate system will continue to operate until the flight control switch is momentarily positioned to RESET and then placed at NORMAL.

Hydraulic System Pressure Gage and Pressure Gage Selector Switch.

Refer to "Utility Hydraulic Power Supply System" in this section.

Flight Control Alternate System Indicator Light.

An amber light (31, figure 1-4; 32, figure 1-5) is below the instrument panel. It comes on whenever the flight control alternate hydraulic system is operating.

Flight Control Alternate System Accumulator Air Pressure Gages.

Two accumulator air pressure gages and filler valves are behind an access door in the right wing root lower fairing. The gages should be checked before flight for a precharge air pressure of 600 to 650 psi with the alternate system hydraulic pressure depleted. The pressure is depleted by disconnecting the external electrical power, disconnecting the batteries, pulling the flight control emergency handle, and moving the control stick until the controls will no longer move. On late airplanes,* the pressure is depleted by opening a dump valve, located in the same recess as the accumulator air pressure gages. Opening the dump valve allows pressure to be routed to return.

WING SLATS.

Wing slats extend from fuselage to wing tip along the leading edge of each wing panel. Aerodynamic forces acting upon the slats cause them to open and close automatically, depending upon the airspeed and attitude of the airplane. When they open, the slats move forward along a curved track, forming a slot in the wing leading edge. This automatic extension of slats smooths the airflow over the upper surface of the wing and allows the wing to go to higher angles of attack before stalling, resulting in lower stalling speeds. At higher speed, in unaccelerated flight, the slats automatically close to provide minimum drag for maximum performance in flight.

---

*F-86D-55 Airplane AF53-707 and all later airplanes

WING FLAP SYSTEM.

Electrically operated, slotted-type wing flaps extend from the aileron to the fuselage on each wing panel. Each flap is operated by an individual electrical actuator through an individual electric circuit. The actuators are mechanically interconnected by a flexible shaft to synchronize the flap travel. Each actuator is capable of driving the opposite flap through the synchronizing shaft along with the flap to which it is attached. Therefore, in case of a power failure to one actuator, flap positioning (at a reduced speed) is still obtainable. The actuators are of the screw-jack type, and are mechanically irreversible, thus preventing air loads from moving the flaps. No emergency system is provided, as there is enough protection present in the normal system through the mechanical interconnection, the individual electric motors, and the individual electric circuits.

WING FLAP LEVER.

The wing flap lever (9, figure 1-6; 9, figure 1-7) is outboard of the throttle. It moves on a quadrant marked "UP," "HOLD," and "DOWN." The wing flap lever receives its power from the monitored bus No. 1. To position the flaps full up or down, the flap lever is moved to the corresponding position and left there. (Power is automatically removed from the actuators when the flaps reach the extreme position.) If "sink" occurs during flap retraction immediately after take-off (at high gross weights), the flap lever can be temporarily positioned to HOLD to maintain an intermediate flap position.

SPEED BRAKE SYSTEM.

Hydraulically operated speed brakes are on each side of the fuselage, below the dorsal fin. Each of the two brakes consists of a hinged panel which, when open, extends down and forward into the air stream. On F-86D-1 through F-86D-25 Airplanes, the speed brakes will open in about 2 seconds with the engine at high or medium rpm and will close in about one second. On these airplanes, the changes in trim, due to the opening or closing of the speed brakes, are automatically corrected, with no shift in control stick position. On F-86D-30 and later airplanes, the speed brakes will open or close in about 2 seconds; on these airplanes, a slight nose-up pitch will be noticed when speed brakes are opened and, correspondingly, a slight nose-down pitch will be noticed when the brakes are closed. Speed brakes can be positioned as desired.

Note

If utility hydraulic system pressure on F-86D-10 and later airplanes is momentarily reduced to less than 1500 psi, a pressure priority valve

Warning

Before operating speed brakes, be sure aft fuselage area around speed brakes is clear, as brakes operate rapidly and forcefully and could injure any personnel near the brakes.

F-86D-1-0-5

will cut out the part of the system supplying the speed brakes.

SPEED BRAKE SWITCH.

A serrated toggle switch, on top of the throttle grip (figure 1-13), controls the speed brake hydraulic control valve. The switch is powered by the primary bus and has three fixed positions: IN, OUT, and a neutral position, which is shown by a white mark on the switch guide. The brakes can be stopped in any position by movement of the switch to neutral. After the brakes have been opened or closed, the switch is normally returned to neutral (center position).

CAUTION

- Since the speed brake hydraulic lines are routed near the engine, it is important that the speed brake switch be kept in the neutral position to cut off pump pressure to the lines and minimize the fire hazard in case of a damaged line.
- If the speed brakes do not open when the control switch is set to OUT, return switch to neutral position. The switch should not be cycled to IN and OUT, as additional fluid will be lost with each cycle if the malfunction is caused by a broken line.

NOSE GEAR GROUND SAFETY LOCK

Figure 1-26

LANDING GEAR SYSTEM.

The landing gear and wheel fairing doors are hydraulically actuated and electrically (dc power) controlled and sequenced. An accumulator supplies pressure for emergency lowering of the nose gear. The accumulator air pressure may be checked by operating the nose gear accumulator dump valve in the nose wheel well. The air pressure should be 1200 ($\pm$50) psi with hydraulic pressure exhausted. The steerable nose gear retracts aft into the fuselage, pivoting to lie parallel with the bottom of the airplane. The main gear retracts inboard into the wing panels and fuselage. Hydraulic brakes are provided on the main wheels.

NOSE GEAR GROUND SAFETY LOCK.

A mechanical ground safety lock (figure 1-26) may be installed to prevent accidental retraction of the nose gear during ground maintenance and towing. A red streamer is attached so that installation of the lock is apparent. Main gear ground safety locks are unnecessary, as the weight on the main gear downlocks prevents accidental release while the airplane is motionless.

LANDING GEAR HANDLE.

A handle, on the landing gear control panel (figure 1-27) above the left forward console, electrically controls the landing gear and gear door selector valves. The gear handle has two positions, UP and DOWN. On F-86D-1 and F-86D-5 Airplanes, the gear handle is powered by the secondary bus; on F-86D-10 and later airplanes, it receives its power from the primary bus. When the gear is down and locked and the weight of the airplane is on the gear, a ground safety switch prevents gear retraction if the gear handle is inadvertently moved to UP. The fairing doors are not controlled by this switch and will follow their normal sequence, opening when the gear handle is moved to UP. Gear retraction time is about 7 seconds; extension time is about 10 seconds.

LANDING GEAR EMERGENCY RETRACT BUTTON.

If it is necessary to collapse the gear during take-off or landing, the landing gear ground safety switch can be overridden by use of a guarded emergency retract push-button switch, above the gear handle on the landing gear control panel. (See figure 1-27.) The landing gear emergency retract button is powered by the battery bus and is operable only when the landing gear handle is positioned at UP. When the gear handle is at UP and the emergency retract button is pressed and held, the ground safety switch is by-passed and the gear is retracted hydraulically; however, the fairing doors may not have enough time to fully open, and the gear may collapse on the doors. Utility hydraulic pressure must be available for emergency retraction of the gear.

CAUTION

Do not use the landing gear emergency retract button in flight to raise the gear. Damage to gear doors and gear lowering mechanism may result.

CAUTION

Although the ground safety switch will not allow the gear to retract even though the gear handle is moved to UP while the weight of the airplane is on the gear, subsequent taxiing on rough ground might allow enough strut extension to open the safety switch and allow the gear to retract.

F-86D-1-0-6

LANDING GEAR EMERGENCY RELEASE HANDLE.

Should failure of the utility hydraulic system or electrical system occur, the gear may be lowered by use of the landing gear emergency release handle. When the landing gear emergency release handle (13, figure 1-8; 21, figure 1-9), below the instrument panel on the right, is pulled to full extension (to about 14 inches and with a force of about 65 pounds), all fairing doors and the main gear uplocks are mechanically unlocked, gear and door hydraulic selector valves are set to lower the gear, and a special nose gear accumulator provides pressure to extend the nose gear. The main gear will fall by gravity to the down-and-locked position. Once the gear has been lowered by the emergency release handle, the nose gear cannot be retracted until the nose gear portion of the emergency release system has been reset on the ground. Late airplanes* and those changed by T. O. have a red rod that protrudes through the right side of the fuselage, just above the nose gear door, when the landing gear emergency release handle is pulled. On these airplanes, the nose gear portion of the emergency release system is reset when this rod is pushed until it is again flush with the fuselage. On early airplanes,† it is reset when the emergency nose gear selector valve reset button, on the right wall of the nose gear well, is pulled to full extension (about 1½ inches) and then released.

CAUTION

- The emergency release handle must be pulled to full extension to ensure release of all uplocks and proper positioning of hydraulic selector valves. The handle should be held in the full extended position until landing gear indicators show a safe landing gear position.

- Do not release handle to allow it to snap back into place, because handle can damage the surrounding equipment.

LANDING GEAR DOOR GROUND CONTROL SWITCH.

A switch is in the recess well for the retractable step on the left forward fuselage, to open the landing gear wheel well doors for ground maintenance. The switch has two positions, OPEN and CLOSE. The switch should be checked before flight to ensure that it has been placed in the CLOSE position. The only safe method for opening the landing gear doors for ground maintenance is by operation of this switch. Any other method of opening the doors for maintenance is unsafe, with the exception that if after the switch has been moved to OPEN, but because of lack of hydraulic pressure the doors will not open. Then, with the switch in the OPEN position, the landing gear emergency release handle can be pulled to open the doors. If the emergency release is used to open the doors, the nose gear valve must be reset before the next flight.

LANDING GEAR SYSTEM INDICATORS.

Three landing gear position indicators and one unsafe warning light, on the landing gear control panel (figure 1-27), provide constant visual indication of gear and fairing door position. The unsafe warning light is in

---

*F-86D-35 and later airplanes
†F-86D-1 through F-86D-30 Airplanes

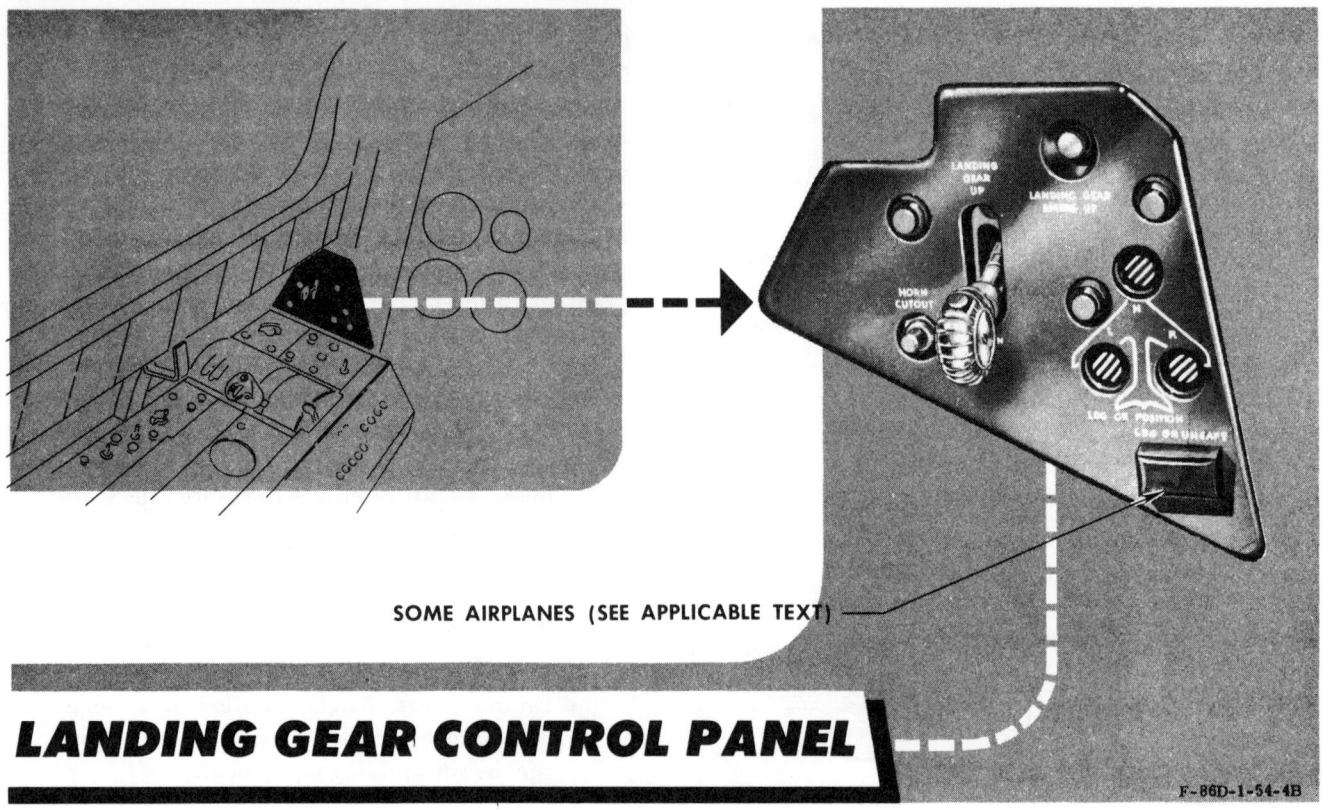

Figure 1-27

the landing gear handle knob. On some airplanes,* an added unsafe warning light is on the landing gear control panel; on late airplanes† and those changed by T. O., the light is on the left side of the instrument shroud. Each indicator shows red crosshatching if the related gear is in an unlocked condition, the word "UP" if the gear is up and locked, or a miniature wheel if the gear is down and locked. Red crosshatching will also appear if the electrical system is inoperative. The warning light comes on any time landing gear or door position does not correspond with the position of the gear handle or when the throttle is retarded below minimum cruising rpm and gear is not down and locked. A warning horn in the cockpit sounds when the gear is in any position other than down and locked if the throttle is at less than cruising power. A warning horn cutout button (figure 1-27), beside the gear handle, is provided to silence the horn. Advancing the throttle silences the horn and resets the horn circuit. Both the unsafe warning light and the warning horn operate either in the air or on the ground whenever power is available. Power for the landing gear position indicators, unsafe warning light, and warning horn is supplied by the secondary bus on F-86D-1 and F-86D-5 Airplanes. On F-86D-10 and later airplanes, power to operate these indicators is received from the primary bus. On F-86D-40 and later airplanes, and those changed by T. O., the landing gear unsafe warning light is automatically dimmed when the instrument panel lights are turned on.

NOSE WHEEL STEERING SYSTEM.

Utility hydraulic system pressure is supplied to the nose wheel steering unit through a shutoff valve actuated by a push-button switch on the control stick grip. (See figure 1-23.) The nose wheel may be turned about 27 degrees either side of center by pressure on the corresponding rudder pedal while the steering system is engaged. The nose wheel steering unit acts as a shimmy damper when not being used for steering.

NOSE WHEEL STEERING RELEASE PIN.

A nose wheel steering release pin is on the left side of the nose gear assembly just above the wheel. It is

---

*F-86D-55 Airplanes and F-86D-60 Airplanes AF53-782 through -931
†F-86D-60 Airplane AF53-932 and all later airplanes

disengaged to disconnect the nose wheel steering unit from the nose wheel for towing the airplane. It is held disengaged by inserting a tow-pin wedge in the release pin.

CAUTION

It is important to check before flight to make sure the safety cap is on and tight; this will ensure that the release pin is engaged and that nose gear will retract properly.

NOSE WHEEL STEERING ENGAGING BUTTON.

An engaging button, on the control stick grip (figure 1-23), is pressed to operate the nose wheel steering system. To engage the nose wheel steering unit, the switch must be pressed and the rudder pedals aligned in the direction the nose wheel is turned. When the nose wheel and the rudder pedals are coordinated in this manner, the nose wheel steering unit will remain engaged as long as the switch is pressed. The nose wheel steering engaging button is powered by the primary bus and is operable only when the airplane is on the ground.

BRAKE SYSTEM.

The hydraulic brake system is of the segmented rotor-disk type unit, incorporating boost-type brake master cylinders. The braking units, on each main landing gear wheel, consist of rotor and stator plate assemblies. Braking effect is obtained by metered hydraulic pressure pushing the stationary stator plates against the rotor plates. Multiple plates are used to increase braking efficiency, aid in heat dissipation, and prevent brake seizure because of disk warpage caused from high temperatures. The brakes are operated by toe action on the rudder pedals. Brake pressure is supplied from brake master cylinder supplemented by power boost from the utility hydraulic system. However, if no pressure is available from the utility hydraulic system, the brakes work through conventional action of the brake master cylinders when enough toe pressure is applied to the rudder pedals. Excessive use of the brakes can cause them to overheat and in turn cause damaging effects upon the tires. If the heat is great enough, it can cause the tires to weaken and later blow out. Best braking results are effected by applying the brakes below 100 knots IAS, intermittently and hard, but not hard enough to slide the wheels.

Note
This airplane is not equipped with parking brakes.

DRAG CHUTE SYSTEM.

On late airplanes* and airplanes changed by T. O., a drag chute is provided to reduce landing distances. The 16-foot, ring-slot type drag chute, packaged in a deployment bag, is stowed in a compartment below the rudder and above the exhaust nozzle. In order to accommodate the drag chute, the aft fuselage section is changed. This change enables easy recognition of airplanes with the drag chute. The extreme aft part of the tail cone is squared off and a door, hinged vertically, is installed. The fairing below the rudder has been spread and refaired to allow for drag chute stowage. The door is held closed by a roller latch assembly. The latch is controlled from the cockpit. A door latch safe indicator is provided for visual and touch inspection. A riser joins

---

*F-86D-45 and later airplanes

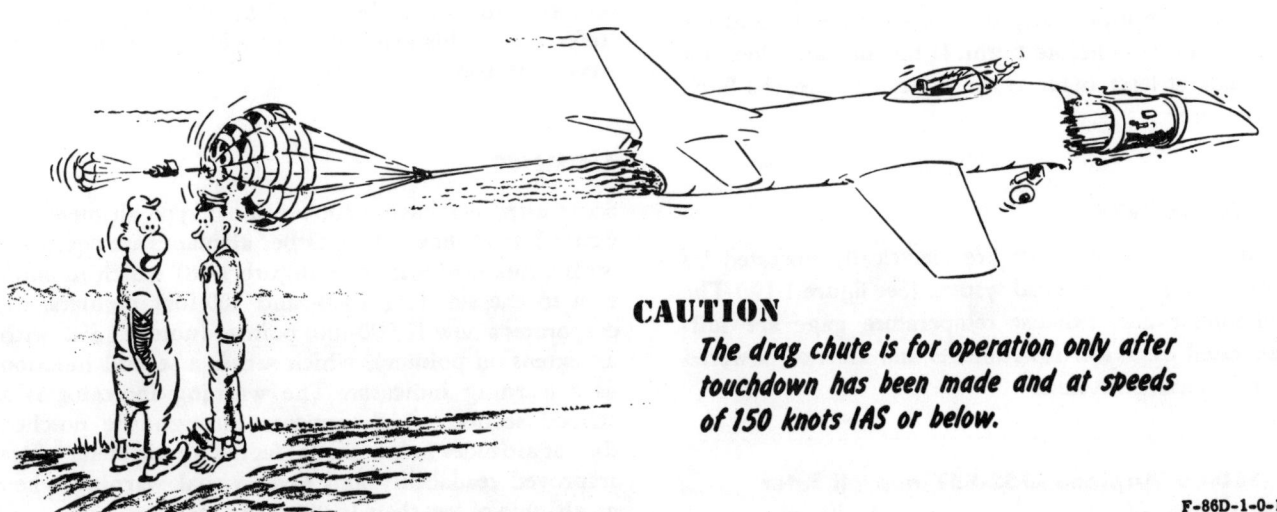

CAUTION
The drag chute is for operation only after touchdown has been made and at speeds of 150 knots IAS or below.

the chute to a release mechanism, enclosed in the tail-cone assembly. On late airplanes* and those changed by T. O., mechanical linkage of riser assembly to the release mechanism is not accomplished until the initial movement of the drag chute handle is made to deploy the drag chute. With this method of installation, accidental opening of the drag chute compartment door will allow the complete drag chute assembly to jettison without affecting the airplane flight attitude. Normal operation (deployment) and jettisoning of the chute is manually controlled from the cockpit. The riser has a breakaway fitting designed to permit the chute to be automatically jettisoned, if it is opened above about 160 knots IAS. The chute is designed for operation after touchdown, and at speeds of 150 knots IAS or below.

DRAG CHUTE HANDLE.

The drag shute handle (3, figure 1-5) is in a bracket directly above the upper left corner of the instrument panel. Pulling the drag chute handle aft to the first stop position (about 2 inches) releases the compartment door, allowing the pilot chute to be deployed and in turn open the drag chute. For controlled jettisoning of the chute after deployment, the handle must be rotated 90 degrees counterclockwise and pulled full aft (about 3 additional inches). This releases the locking assembly and allows the chute to be jettisoned.

DRAG CHUTE DOOR LATCH SAFE INDICATOR.

The latch indicator is directly below the drag chute compartment door and to the left of the door latch. The indicator is a square pin that protrudes from a hole next to the latch to show that the latch is securely locked. The indicator pin must extend at least 1⅜ inches (as determined by a latch indicator gage, riveted alongside the indicator pin), and must be checked for a safe indication before flight. If the indicator does not protrude at least as far as the indicator gage, the latch is insecure.

INSTRUMENTS.

Most of the instruments are electrically operated by power from the electrical system. (See figure 1-19.) The tachometer and exhaust temperature gage are self-generated electrical instruments and are not powered by the electrical system.

---

*F-86D-60 Airplane AF53-857 and all later airplanes

Note

For information regarding instruments that are an integral part of a particular system; refer to applicable paragraphs in this section and Section IV.

PITOT-STATIC BOOM.

Pitot and static pressures for various flight instruments are obtained from the pitot-static boom, which extends from the right wing tip. Boom anti-icing protection is afforded by electrical heating elements. (Refer to "Anti-icing and Defrosting Systems" in Section IV.)

AIRSPEED INDICATOR.

The airspeed indicator (10, figure 1-4; 8, figure 1-5; and 5-1) is essentially a conventional airspeed indicator with the addition of a maximum allowable airspeed pointer which shows airspeed for the airplane when it is equipped with drop tanks. The fluorescent pointer registers indicated airspeed. The striped pointer is used as a limit only when drop tanks are carried. This pointer is preset for the limit Mach number of the airplane with drop tanks, and it moves to show the airspeed corresponding to the limit Mach number or limit airspeed, whichever is less, during flight at 15,000 feet or below. Clockwise movement of the striped pointer will stop at the limiting airspeed at low altitude.

MACHMETER.

A Machmeter (3, figure 1-4; 38, figure 1-5) is provided for use in conjunction with the airspeed indicator.

ACCELEROMETER.

An accelerometer (2, figure 1-4; 1, figure 1-5), installed on the bottom of the left wiindshield bow, indicates G. Reference to this instrument provides an indication of structural loads.

ALTIMETER.

Some airplanes have a conventional type altimeter (6, figure 1-4; 11, figure 1-5). Other airplanes are equipped with a modified altimeter (figure 1-28) which in addition to the standard 1000- and 100-foot pointers, incorporates a new 10,000-foot pointer (notched disk with an extension pointer), which serves a second function as a warning indicator. The warning indicator is a striped section which appears through the notched disk at altitudes below 16,000 feet. This altimeter offers improved readability and gives visual warning when an altitude of less than 16,000 feet is entered.

Figure 1-28

SLAVED GYRO MAGNETIC COMPASS.

Refer to "Navigation Equipment" in Section IV.

STAND-BY COMPASS.

A conventional magnetic compass (24, figure 1-4; 22, figure 1-5), on the windshield bow to the right of the instrument panel, is furnished for navigation if the instrument or electrical system fails. Lighting of the stand-by compass is controlled by a switch on the aft edge of the right or left instrument subpanel.

ATTITUDE INDICATOR.

The Type B-1A attitude indicator (18, figure 1-4; 14, figure 1-5), on the instrument panel, shows the attitude of the airplane in relation to the horizon. The gyro is electrically driven and receives its power from the ac electrical bus. Erection of the gyro requires about 2½ minutes after application of power and can be observed by disappearance of the "OFF" power failure flag visible through the cover glass of the indicator. The "OFF" flag will appear in case of a complete ac or dc power failure. However, a slight reduction in ac or dc power, or failure of certain electrical components within the system, *will not* cause the "OFF" flag to appear, even though the system is not operating properly.

WARNING

It is possible that a malfunction of the attitude indicator might be determined *only* by checking it with the slaved gyro magnetic compass and the turn-and-bank indicator.

The instrument is operative through 360 degrees of roll, 82 degrees of climb, and 82 degrees of dive, and is not likely to tumble even during extreme maneuvers. However, should the gyro tumble, it will erect in about 2½ minutes if the circuit breaker labeled "VERTICAL GYRO," on the right console circuit-breaker panel, is momentarily pulled out and then pushed back in. If the circuit breaker is not used, the gyro will require about 15 minutes to erect. Indication error is less than ½ degree in level flight, and, up to a turn rate of 40 degrees per minute, the indication error compares to that of the conventional indicator. In turns of 40 degrees or more per minute a compensating mechanism in the instrument limits turn error indication to 2 degrees.

WARNING

A slight amount of pitch error in the indication of the Type B-1A attitude indicator will result from accelerations or decelerations. It will appear as a slight climb indication after a forward acceleration and as a slight dive indication after deceleration when the airplane is flying straight and level. This error will be most noticeable at the time the airplane breaks ground during the take-off run. At this time, a climb indication error of about 1½ bar widths will normally be noticed; however, the exact amount of error will depend upon the acceleration and elapsed time of each individual take-off. The erection system will automatically remove the error after the acceleration ceases.

The indicator does not have a manual caging handle. When power is turned off, a snubber automatically grips the gimbal and keeps it from tumbling. When power is turned on, the snubber is released after a 15-second time delay. As level-flight pitch attitude of the airplane varies with different loadings and speeds, a pitch trim knob is provided on the indicator for the pilot to center the horizon bar after the airplane has been trimmed for level flight.

Section I   T. O. 1F-86D-1

TURN-AND-BANK INDICATOR.

The conventional turn-and-bank indicator (34, figure 1-4; 35, figure 1-5) is on the instrument panel. It is electrically driven by power from the primary bus. The instrument is calibrated so that one standard needle-width turn will accomplish a 360-degree turn in 4 minutes (1½-degree-per-second rate of turn). Because of the excessive tilt of the turn-and-bank indicator required on the present installation, the indicator will show a turn in the opposite direction to that of actual airplane attitude during a high rate of roll. When the attitude indicator is inoperative and the turn-and-bank indicator is being used as a primary flight instrument, observe the following instructions:

1. Avoid excessive rate of roll. The turn needle indicates a turn in the opposite direction during all entries into turns, and the error increases as rate of roll increases. The turn needle indicates correctly only when no movement occurs around the longitudinal axis.

2. Maintain a constant bank angle during turn, then the indicator will show correct direction and rate of turn.

EMERGENCY EQUIPMENT.

ENGINE FIRE-WARNING SYSTEM.

Two fire detector systems are provided to detect and show fire in the forward section of the engine compartment and an overtemperature condition or fire in the aft section. A stainless-steel fire wall divides the engine compartment immediately aft of the compressor. Therefore, the forward section includes the compressor and the accessory section, and on some airplanes,* the main wheel wells; the aft section, the combustion chambers and tail pipe. Each system consists of fire detector units throughout the engine compartments and a warning light in the cockpit. On F-86D-1 through F-86D-25 Airplanes, the warning lights are on the right instrument subpanel (figure 1-10); on F-86D-30 and later airplanes and airplanes changed by T.O., they are on the right side of the main instrument panel (15, figure 1-5). Illumination of the red warning light, marked "FORWARD," shows that fire has occurred in the forward section of the engine compartment. Illumination of the amber warning light, marked "AFT," shows that an excessive overtemperature condition or fire exists in the aft engine section. Operation of the warning system and lights can be checked by the system test switch next to the lights. When the switch is moved from NORM to the spring-loaded TEST position, the entire fire-warning circuit is energized and both warning lights should come on. The lights are powered by the primary bus and are of the push-to-test type, permitting check of bulb lighting independent of system operation.

CANOPY.

The electrically actuated, clamshell-type canopy opens and closes by rotating about a hinge point at the rear. The airplane may be taxied at speeds up to 50 knots IAS with the canopy in any position from fully closed to fully open. The canopy is closed by an electrically powered actuator and is locked by manually operated latches on the canopy rails. When the landing gear leaves the ground, a hook at the canopy hinge point automatically disengages, releasing the canopy from the actuator. The canopy is then secured by the mechanical latches in readiness for emergency ejection. When the landing gear again touches the ground, the hook engages, and, when the mechanical latches are released, the canopy may be opened by the actuator. Emergency ejection of the canopy during flight in F-86D-1 through F-86D-35 Airplanes is accomplished when the ejection seat right armrest is raised to full up position. This releases the latches and fires a canopy ejector by means of a gas charge from the canopy initiator. When the canopy is ejected, it pulls a safety pin from the seat catapult firing mechanism. The purpose of the safety pin is to prevent seat ejection until after the canopy leaves the airplane. On F-86D-40 and later airplanes, emergency ejection of the canopy during flight is made when either the right or left ejection seat armrest is raised, which fires the canopy initiator and its gas charge fires the canopy ejector. The ejection seat armrests are interconnected. Raising either armrest raises the opposite armrest. On these airplanes, actuation of the ejection seat catapult firing mechanism is not dependent upon canopy jettisoning or operation, as there is no seat catapult firing mechanism safety pin to be pulled by the canopy as it leaves the airplane. Thus, if canopy fails to leave the airplane, the ejection seat may be ejected through the canopy as a last resort. However, either armrest must be raised to the full up position in order to squeeze its trigger and eject through the canopy.

GROUND AND MAINTENANCE SAFETY PINS.

The canopy jettison system is safetied by inserting a ground safety pin (figures 1-29 and 1-30) through a block on the front of the seat and across the trigger in the right seat armrest. This pin will prevent raising the seat armrest and inadvertently firing the canopy. This ground safety pin is to be removed before flight and replaced immediately after flight. When the safety pin is removed, the canopy and seat catapults are armed. A maintenance safety pin for the canopy initiator is also provided.

---

*F-86D-60 Airplane AF53-1007 and all later airplanes

WARNING

The canopy initiator may be safetied during ground maintenance by a safety pin. This maintenance safety pin should not be inserted in the initiator for normal ground operations, but if installed must be removed before flight.

CANOPY SEAL.

An inflatable canopy seal is provided to seal the canopy in the closed position. Pressure for inflation of the seal is provided by the engine compressor and is automatically controlled by a pressure regulator when the engine is operating. The seal is automatically inflated whenever the canopy is fully latched and is deflated whenever the canopy is unlatched.

CANOPY OPERATING BUTTONS (EXTERNAL).

The canopy is operated externally by means of two electrical spring-loaded push buttons, on the left side of the fuselage, about 2 feet below and in line with the windshield. One button is marked "OPEN"; the other, "CLOSE." These operating buttons receive their power from monitored bus No. 2 when this bus is energized. If this bus is not energized, the battery bus supplies these buttons with power.

EXTERNAL CANOPY EMERGENCY RELEASE HANDLE.

An external canopy emergency release handle can be reached through an access door on the left side of the fuselage, about 3½ feet below the canopy frame and slightly forward of the windshield bow line, below the canopy frame. When the door is opened, the canopy hook is electrically released. Pulling the external emergency release handle unlocks the canopy latches so that the canopy can be lifted. On F-86D-5 and later airplanes, if electrical power is not available, the canopy hook may be disengaged by a handle beneath a small access door directly behind the canopy in the top of the fuselage.

CANOPY SWITCH.

From within the cockpit, the canopy is controlled by a three-position toggle switch on the right instrument subpanel. (See figure 1-10.) To operate the canopy, the switch must be held at either of the spring-loaded positions, OPEN or CLOSED. When the canopy has fully opened or closed, power to the canopy actuator is automatically cut off. When the switch is released, it returns to the center OFF position and the canopy remains in the selected position. The canopy switch is powered by monitored bus No. 2 when this bus is energized and from the battery bus when monitored bus No. 2 is not energized. The circuit to the switch is opened whenever the canopy latches are in the locked position.

CAUTION

When the canopy is being closed, the canopy switch should be held at CLOSED until the canopy actuator automatically cuts off. If the switch is released before the actuator cuts off, the hook at the canopy hinge point may not disengage. Emergency canopy ejection is still possible if the hook fails to disengage, but structural damage to the fuselage may result.

Note

Operation of either external button overrides the selection of the cockpit switch.

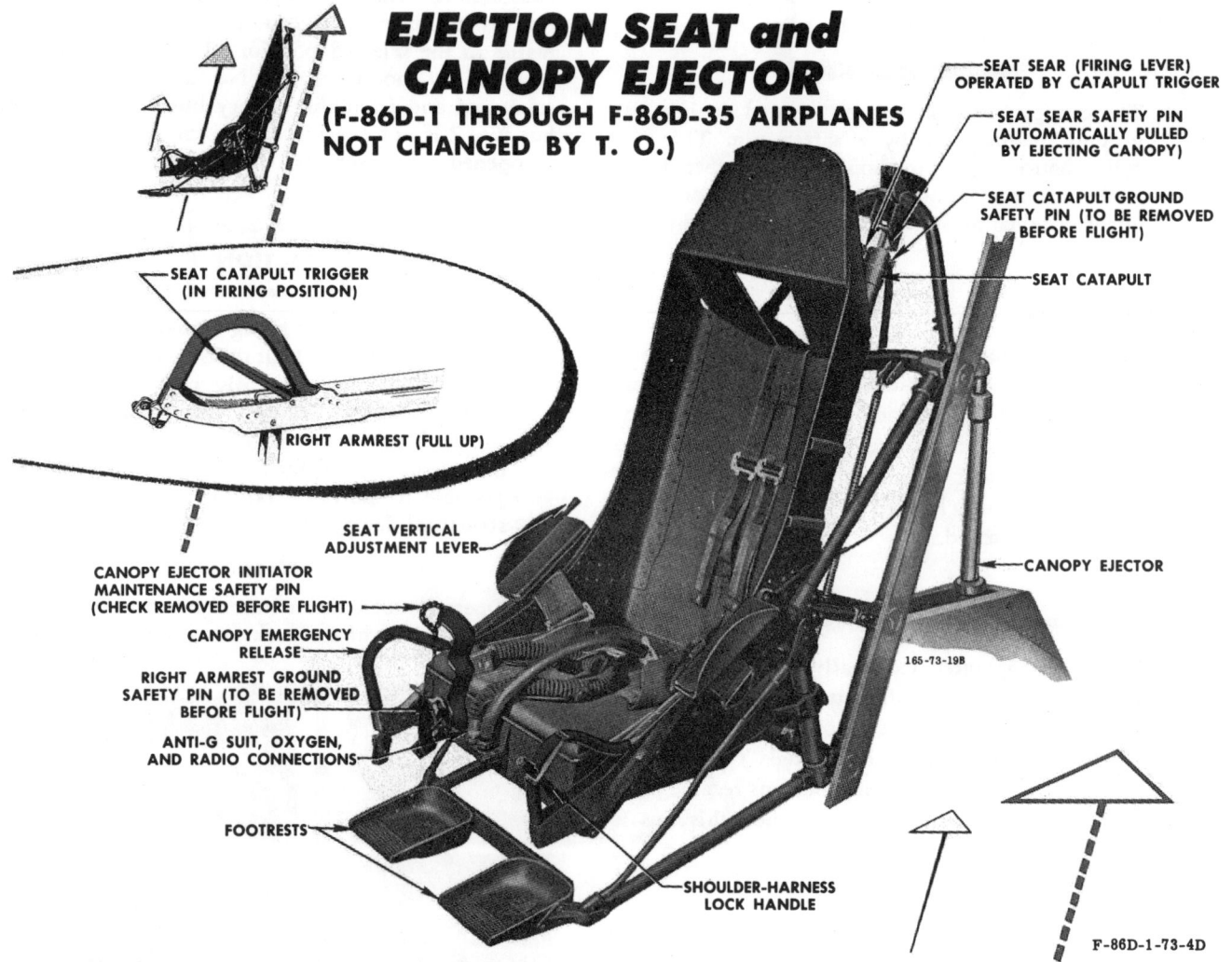

Figure 1-29

CANOPY LOCK HANDLE (F-86D-1 THROUGH F-86D-35 AIRPLANES NOT CHANGED BY T. O.).

The canopy, when closed, is locked or unlocked by means of a canopy lock handle (25, figure 1-5; 12, figure 1-8), forward of the right side of the seat. When the handle is pulled full aft, the latches are engaged and the canopy is locked. At the same time, the canopy switch circuit automatically opens and the canopy unsafe warning light goes out. When the handle is moved forward, the latches are unlocked, the canopy switch circuit is activated, and the unsafe warning light comes on.

CANOPY LOCK HANDLE (F-86D-40 AND LATER AIRPLANES, AND THOSE CHANGED BY T. O.).

The canopy, when closed, is locked or unlocked by means of a push-pull type canopy lock handle (20, figure 1-9), extending through the vertical panel forward of the right console. When the handle is pushed full forward, the latches are engaged and the canopy is locked. When the canopy is fully locked, the canopy switch circuit is opened and the canopy unsafe warning light goes out. Pulling the handle aft unlocks the latches and activates the canopy switch circuit, and the canopy unsafe warning light comes on.

CANOPY EMERGENCY RELEASE (SEAT ARMREST).

The latches are released and the canopy ejector is fired when the right armrest* (late airplanes, either armrest†) on the ejection seat (figures 1-29 and 1-30) is pulled full up in preparation for seat ejection.

---

*F-86D-1 through F-86D-35 Airplanes
†F-86D-40 and later airplanes

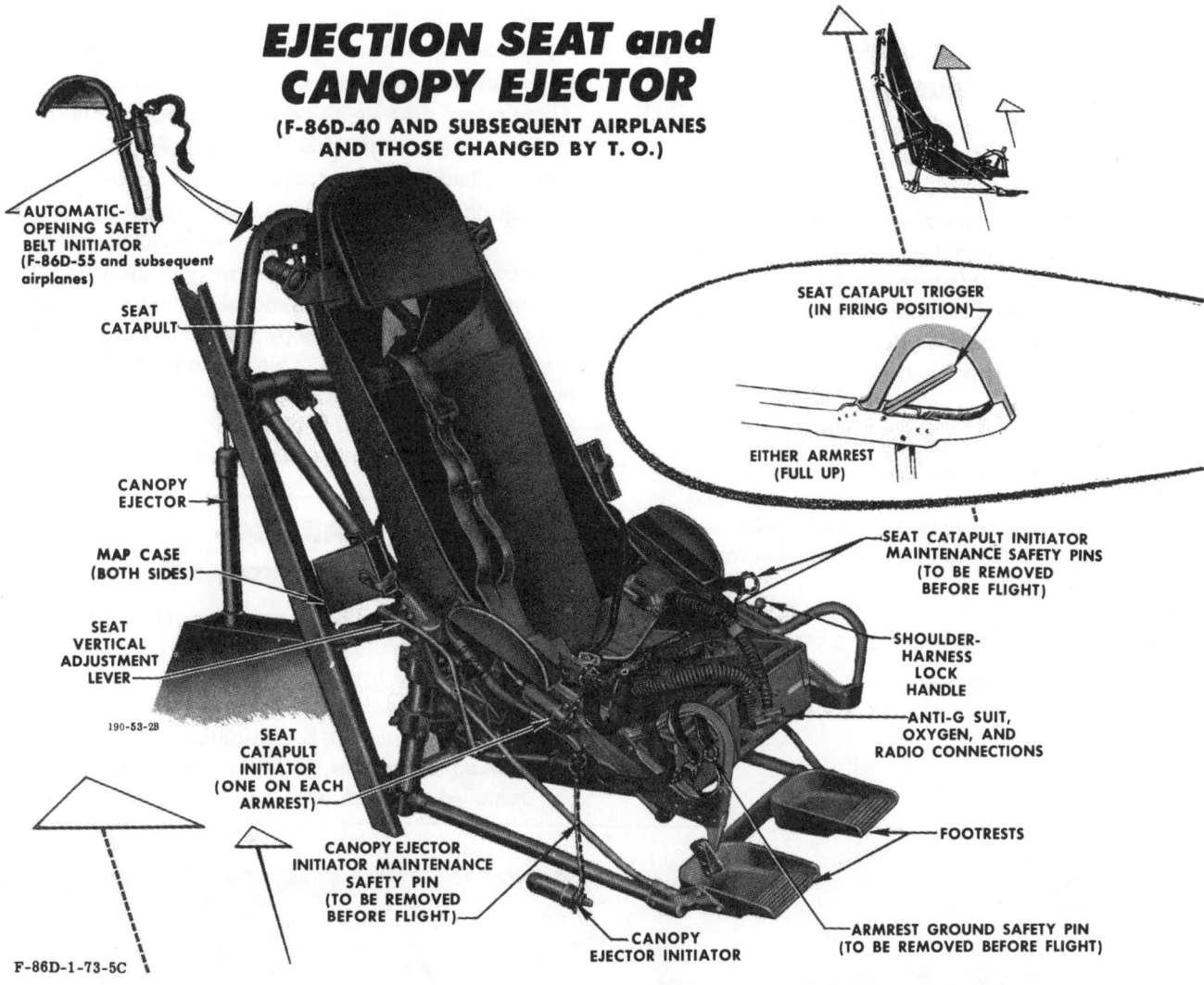

Figure 1-30

CANOPY UNSAFE WARNING LIGHT.

A canopy unsafe warning light (figure 1-10) is on the right instrument subpanel. The light is powered by the monitored bus No. 2 and will come on and remain on as long as the canopy latches are unlocked. The light goes out when the latches are locked. A yellow stripe is painted on the forward canopy latches so that a visual check may be made to ensure, when the canopy unsafe warning light is out, that the canopy latches are in the fully locked position. This added visual check can be made by leaning forward and looking, right or left, through the forward latch rig pin hole. If the yellow stripe is not readily visible, repeat locking procedure until yellow stripe is apparent, to ensure that latches are fully locked.

EJECTION SEAT.

An ejection seat (figures 1-29 and 1-30) is provided which will catapult the seat clear of the tail surfaces, thus making ejection possible at any speed. A catapult (explosive cartridge with telescoping tubes) aft of the seat supplies the propelling force to eject seat and pilot from the cockpit. F-86D-1 through F-86D-35 Airplanes not changed by T.O. use mechanical linkage to fire the seat catapult. On F-86D-40 and later airplanes and those changed by T.O., a gas initiator system is used to fire the seat catapult. The seat may be adjusted up and forward, but the footrests will remain in a fixed position. If added height in seat is needed, use a solid filler block, if the frontal height does not exceed 5 inches. When a C-2A raft is carried, *a filler block should not be used.* The armrests are hinged to actuate the ejection sequence. When the seat is ejected, the anti-G suit, oxygen hose, and microphone and headset connections automatically disconnect at a single fitting attached to the seat between the footrests. On airplanes changed by T.O. 1F-86-530, the radio headset plug-in is just above the left armrest of the seat.

WARNING

- Do not use the A-5 seat cushion, or any similar sponge rubber cushion, when equipped with a one-man life raft or survival kit. If ejection is necessary, serious spinal injuries can result when the ejection force compresses the cushion and enables the seat to gain considerable momentum before exerting a direct force on the pilot. The chance of injury during a crash landing is also increased.

- No cushion, life raft pack, or survival kit should be used that has a frontal height greater than 5 inches; otherwise, there may be interference between control stick and kit when seat is raised to its top position.

GROUND AND MAINTENANCE SAFETY PINS.

To prevent inadvertent firing of the ejection seat catapult while on the ground, early airplanes* have provisions for inserting a maintenance safety pin in the top of the seat catapult and a ground safety pin at the seat right armrest (across the trigger). (See figure 1-29.) These safety pins are to be removed before flight and replaced immediately after the flight. On F-86D-40 and later airplanes, a ground safety pin is inserted through a block on the front of the seat and across the trigger in the right seat armrest. (On these airplanes, there is no provision for a safety pin at the catapult head.) The ground safety pin will prevent raising the seat armrest, and prevent firing the canopy and positioning the ejection seat firing triggers. This ground safety pin is to be removed before flight and replaced immediately after flight. (See figure 1-30.) When the safety pin is removed, the canopy and seat catapults are armed.

WARNING

On F-86D-40 and later airplanes, the seat catapult initiators may be safetied during ground maintenance by initiator safety pins at each armrest. These maintenance safety pins should not be inserted in the initiators for normal ground operations, but if installed must be removed before flight.

*F-86D-1 through F-86D-35 Airplanes

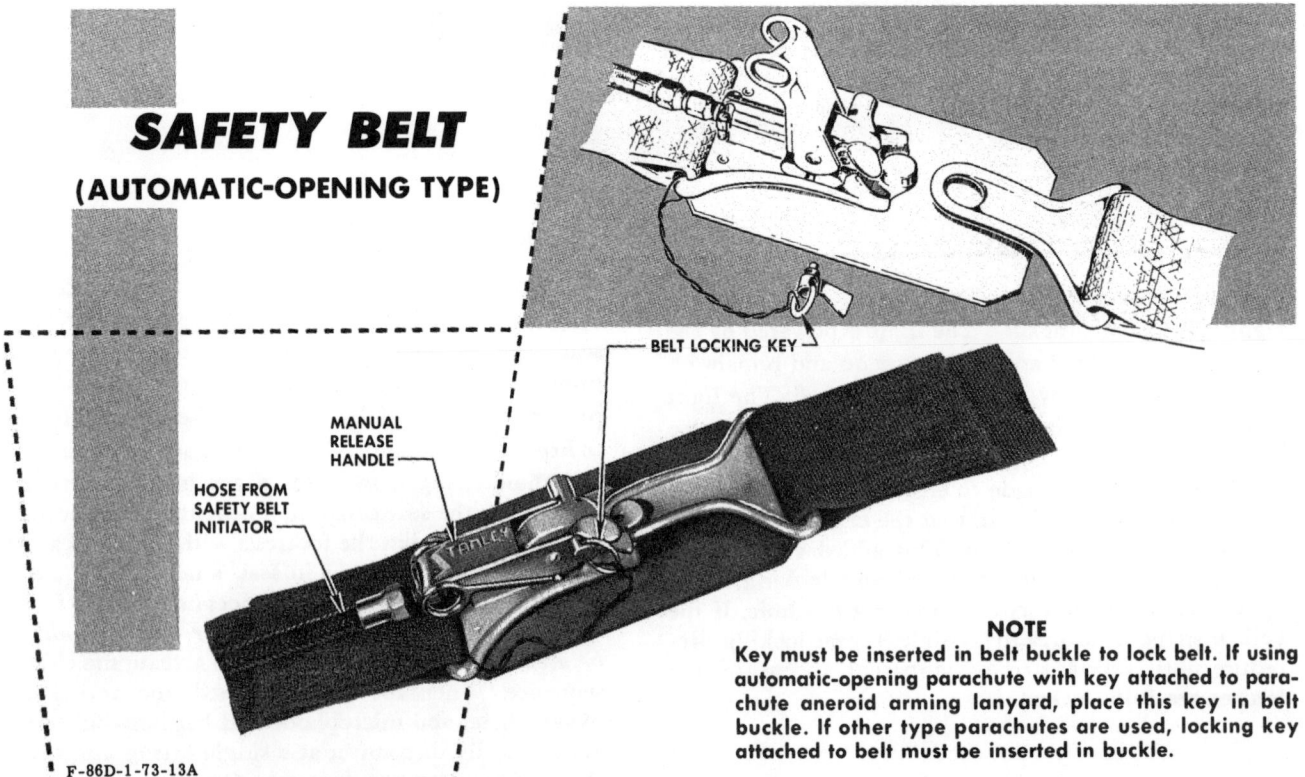

SAFETY BELT (AUTOMATIC-OPENING TYPE)

- BELT LOCKING KEY
- MANUAL RELEASE HANDLE
- HOSE FROM SAFETY BELT INITIATOR

NOTE
Key must be inserted in belt buckle to lock belt. If using automatic-opening parachute with key attached to parachute aneroid arming lanyard, place this key in belt buckle. If other type parachutes are used, locking key attached to belt must be inserted in buckle.

Figure 1-31

AUTOMATIC-OPENING SAFETY BELT.

On F-86D-55 and later airplanes and those changed by T.O., the ejection seat is equipped with an automatic-opening safety belt (figure 1-31) which facilitates pilot separation from the seat following ejection. Belt opening is accomplished as part of the ejection sequence and requires no added effort on the part of the pilot. As the seat is ejected, a mechanical linkage fires a cartridge in the safety belt initiator on the upper left side of the seat. The firing of the initiator cartridge produces a gas pressure, which is directed to the belt buckle through a flexible hose. Pressure of the gases opens the buckle about 2 seconds after the seat fires.

WARNING

The initiator unit may be safetied for servicing by a maintenance safety pin; however, this pin is not necessary for normal on-the-ground operations. If pin is installed, it must be removed before flight.

To lock the belt, it is necessary to insert a key into the buckle of the safety belt. If the pilot has an automatic-opening aneroid-type parachute with a key attached to the lanyard (figure 1-32) from the automatic ball-handle control, this key must be inserted into the belt buckle. As the pilot separates from the seat, the lanyard, which is locked to the belt by the key, serves as a static line to arm the chute-opening device. The parachute will then open after the preset time lapse or at the preset altitude. When a conventional chute or an automatic-opening aneroid-type parachute without a lanyard key is used, the key that is attached to the belt must be inserted into the belt buckle. The automatic-opening safety belt is unlocked in the same manner as a conventional safety belt, and can be opened manually if desired.

WARNING

If the belt is opened manually after ejection, the chute (either manual or automatic-opening type) must be opened by manually pulling the "D" ring or automatic ball-handle control, since the key is released when the belt is opened manually.

SEAT ARMRESTS.

The ejection seat armrests are hinged to actuate the ejection sequence. Lifting the right armrest to the full up position fires the canopy ejector and raises the seat catapult trigger into firing position. Lifting the left armrest locks the shoulder harness. (See figure 1-29.)

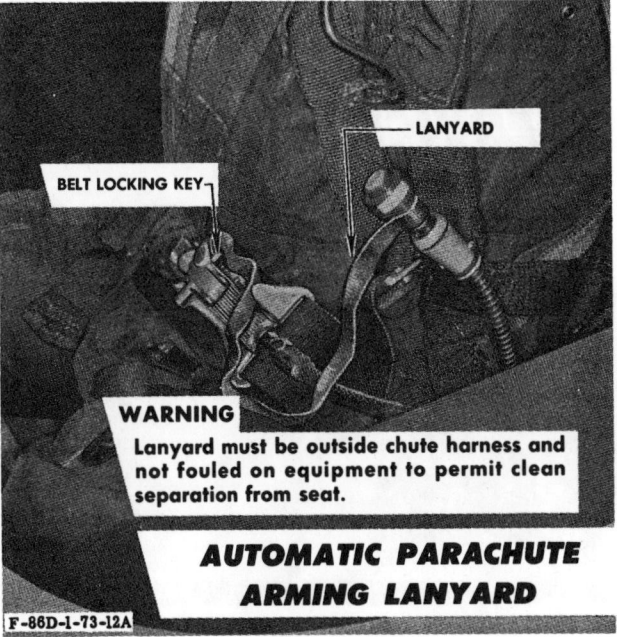

Figure 1-32

On later airplanes,* the left armrest is so interconnected to the right armrest that lifting either armrest raises the opposite armrest at the same time. A seat catapult trigger is provided on each armrest. (See figure 1-30.) On these airplanes, lifting either the right or left armrest raises the opposite armrest, fires the canopy ejector, locks the shoulder harness, and raises both triggers into firing position.

SEAT CATAPULT TRIGGER (F-86D-1 THROUGH F-86D-35 AIRPLANES).

The seat catapult trigger, beneath the handgrip at the forward end of the right armrest of the ejection seat (figure 1-29), is protected by a guard. As the right armrest is pulled up in preparation for seat ejection, the trigger is raised out of the guard. Pulling the right armrest of the ejection seat to the full up position fires the canopy from the airplane. At its full up position, the armrest locks and the trigger is within reach of the fingers. Two safety pins in the seat catapult firing mechanism render the trigger ineffective. One must be removed before flight, and the other is removed when the canopy is ejected by raising of the seat right armrest. With the right armrest raised, squeezing the trigger will fire the seat catapult. Pulling up the left seat armrest locks the shoulder harness in preparation for ejection. This step may be omitted if time is a critical item.

*F-86D-40 and later airplanes

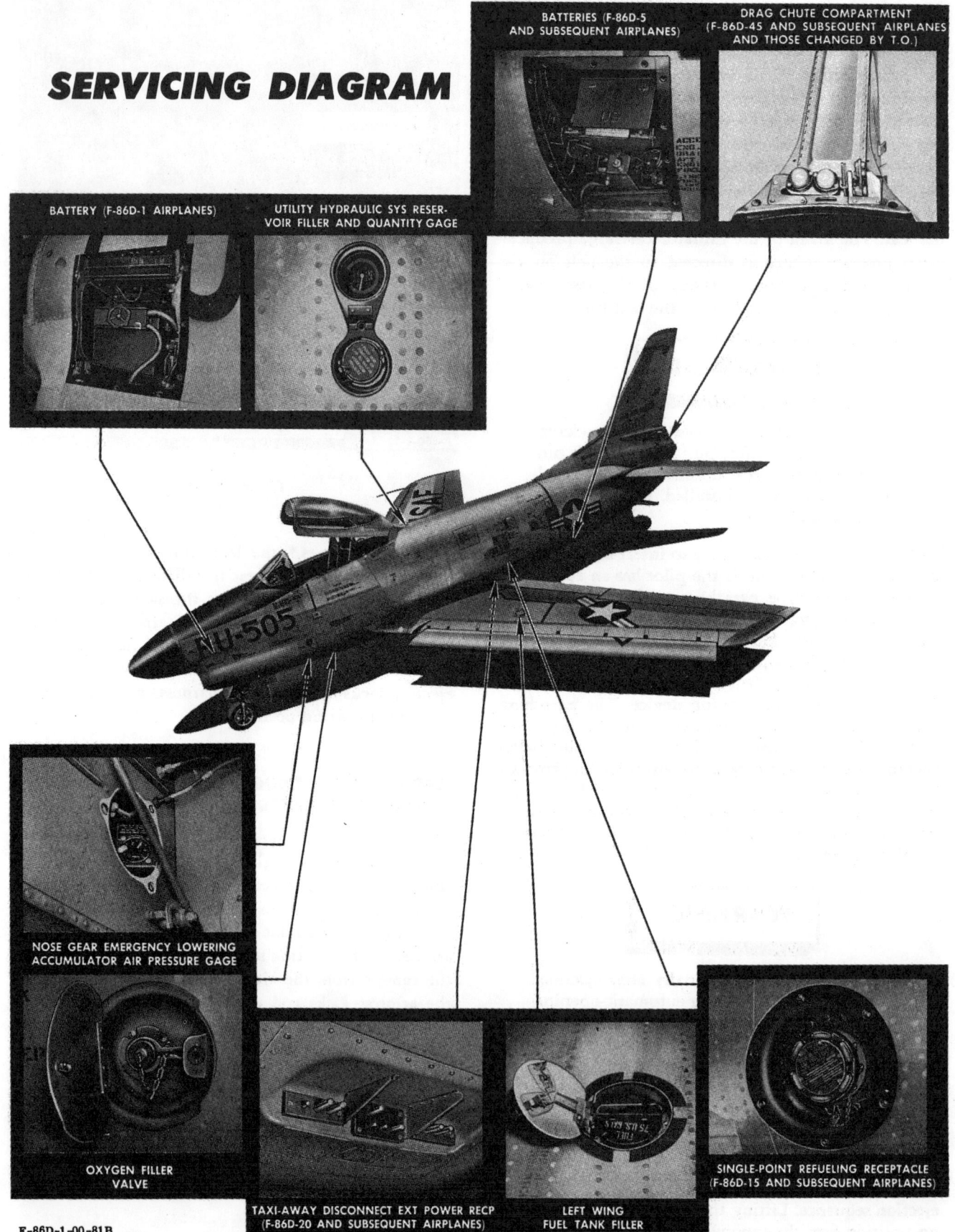

Figure 1-33

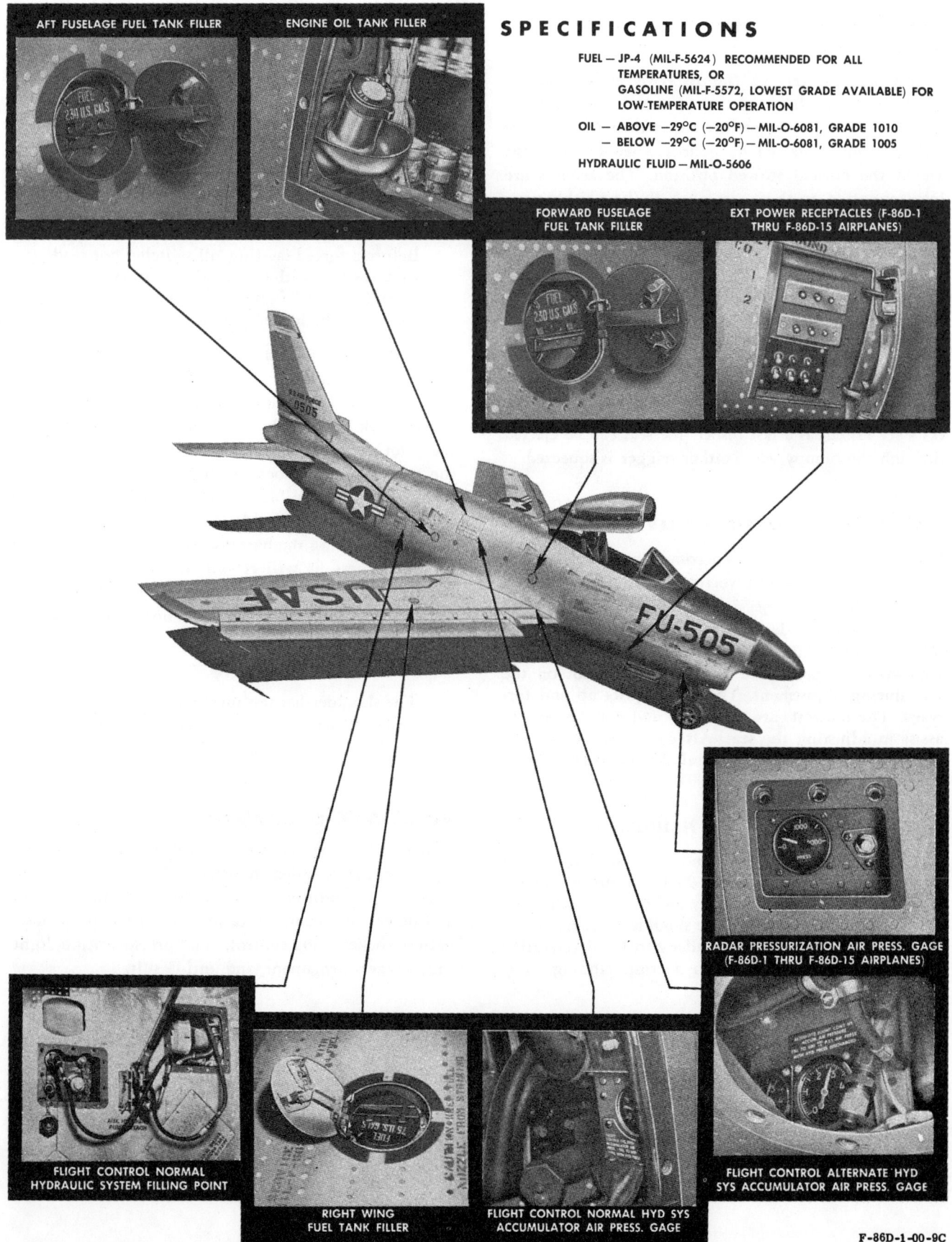

SEAT CATAPULT TRIGGERS (F-86D-40 AND LATER AIRPLANES).

A seat catapult trigger (figure 1-30) is beneath the handgrip at the forward end of each armrest of the ejection seat; the triggers are recessed in the armrests and are thus protected by guards when the armrests are in the normal stowed position. The armsets are interconnected on these airplanes. Pulling either armrest to its full up position also raises the opposite armrest to its full up position, which raises both triggers out of their guards to within reach of the fingers, fires the canopy from the airplane, and locks the shoulder harness. With armrests raised, squeezing either trigger will fire the seat catapult. On these airplanes, actuation of the ejection seat catapult firing mechanism is not dependent upon canopy jettisoning or operation. Thus, if the canopy fails to leave the airplane when the armrests are raised, as a last resort the seat can be ejected through the canopy when either trigger is squeezed.

SEAT VERTICAL ADJUSTMENT LEVER.

Vertical seat adjustment is accomplished mechanically by operation of the seat vertical adjustment lever, on the right side of the ejection seat. (See figures 1-29 and 1-30.) Pulling the lever forward and up releases the seat for adjustment. A handle on the left bow of the windshield helps relieve weight of the pilot on the seat during adjustment. The seat adjusts up and forward. The footrests are stationary and may be used to assist in adjusting the seat. After any seat adjustment is made, make sure seat is securely locked in position.

SHOULDER-HARNESS LOCK HANDLE.

The shoulder-harness lock handle, on the left armrest of the ejection seat (figures 1-29 and 1-30), is conventionally operated for manually locking and unlocking the shoulder harness. Also, the shoulder-harness inertia reel will automatically lock under 2 to 3 G deceleration in a forward direction, as in a crash landing. It is recommended that the shoulder harness be manually locked during maneuvers and flight in rough air, or as a safety precaution in event of a forced landing. The shoulder harness is automatically locked before seat ejection when the left armrest on the seat is in the full up position.

CAUTION

Before a forced landing, all switches not readily accessible with the shoulder harness locked should be "cut" before harness lock handle is moved to the locked position.

If the harness is locked while the pilot is leaning forward, as he straightens up, the harness will retract with him, moving into successive locked positions as he moves back against the seat. To unlock the harness, the pilot must be able to lean back enough to relieve the tension on the lock. Therefore, if the harness is locked while the pilot is leaning back hard against the seat, he may not be able to unlock the harness without first loosening the harness. After automatic locking of the harness, it will remain locked until the lock handle is moved to the locked position and then back to the unlocked position while tension on the shoulder harness cable is released.

Note

The shoulder-harness inertia reel is locked and unlocked when the handle is moved fore and aft. Forward is LOCKED, and aft is UNLOCKED.

AUXILIARY EQUIPMENT.

Information concerning the following operational equipment is supplied in Section IV of his handbook: cockpit air conditioning and pressurization, anti-icing and defrosting, communication, automatic pilot, navigation, rocket-firing control, radar pressurization, lighting, oxygen, armament, and anti-G suit.

T. O. 1F-86D-1 Section II

NORMAL PROCEDURES

TABLE OF CONTENTS	PAGE		PAGE
Status of Airplane	2-1	Flight Characteristics	2-20
Preflight Check	2-2	Systems Operation	2-20
Starting Engine	2-6	Descent	2-20
Engine Ground Operation	2-10	Pre-traffic-pattern Check	2-20
Ground Tests	2-10	Traffic-pattern Check	2-21
Taxiing	2-12	Landing	2-21
Before Take-off	2-14	Go-around	2-24
Take-off	2-16	After Landing	2-24
After Take-off	2-18	Stopping Engine	2-24
Climb	2-19	Before Leaving Airplane	2-26
Afterburner Operation During Flight	2-19	Condensed Check List	2-26

STATUS OF THE AIRPLANE.

FLIGHT RESTRICTIONS.

Refer to Section V for detailed airplane and engine limitations.

FLIGHT PLANNING.

The performance data in Appendix I is provided to determine fuel consumption and correct airspeed, power setting, and altitude for the intended flight and mission.

WEIGHT AND BALANCE.

Refer to Section V for weight and balance limitations. For loading information, refer to Handbook of Weight and Balance Data, T.O. 1-1B-40. Before each flight, check the following:

1. Check take-off and anticipated landing gross weight and balance.

2. Check that weight and balance clearance DD Form 365F (formerly Form F) is satisfactory. If no rockets are installed, check for proper ballast installation.

3. Make sure total amount of fuel, oil, rockets, oxygen, and special equipment is enough for the mission to be performed.

ENTRANCE.

Cockpit entry is gained from the left side of the airplane (figure 2-1), after the canopy is opened by use of the external switch. A telescoping step (released by a push latch) and two combination handhold and kick-in steps facilitate entrance to the cockpit.

2-1

Section II
T. O. 1F-86D-1

ENTERING COCKPIT

Figure 2-1

Note

The telescoping step is stored manually from outside the airplane.

PREFLIGHT CHECK.

BEFORE EXTERIOR INSPECTION.

Check DD Form 781 for engineering status, and make sure airplane has been serviced with required amounts of fuel, oil, hydraulic fluid in utility and flight control hydraulic systems (by extension of compensator shafts), correct precharge air pressure in flight control normal and alternate system accumulators, radar pressurization air or nitrogen, and oxygen. For servicing points, see figure 1-33.

EXTERIOR INSPECTION.

Perform exterior inspection as outlined in figure 2-2.

CANOPY AND EJECTION SEAT CHECK.

Before entering cockpit, check the canopy ejector and ejection seat as follows:

1. Open canopy fully to visually check canopy ejector.

2. Make sure shoulder-harness straps are over upper horizontal tube of seat supporting structure behind seat.

3. Check that both armrests are full down and latched.

4. Check that ground safety pin is installed in right seat armrest across the trigger.

5. On some airplanes,* make sure seat catapult sear safety pin (no red streamer attached) is connected to canopy release bell crank at top of seat and that safety wire retains bell crank to catapult attachment fitting on seat.

---

*F-86D-1 through F-86D-35 Airplanes

T. O. 1F-86D-1 Section II

EXTERIOR INSPECTION

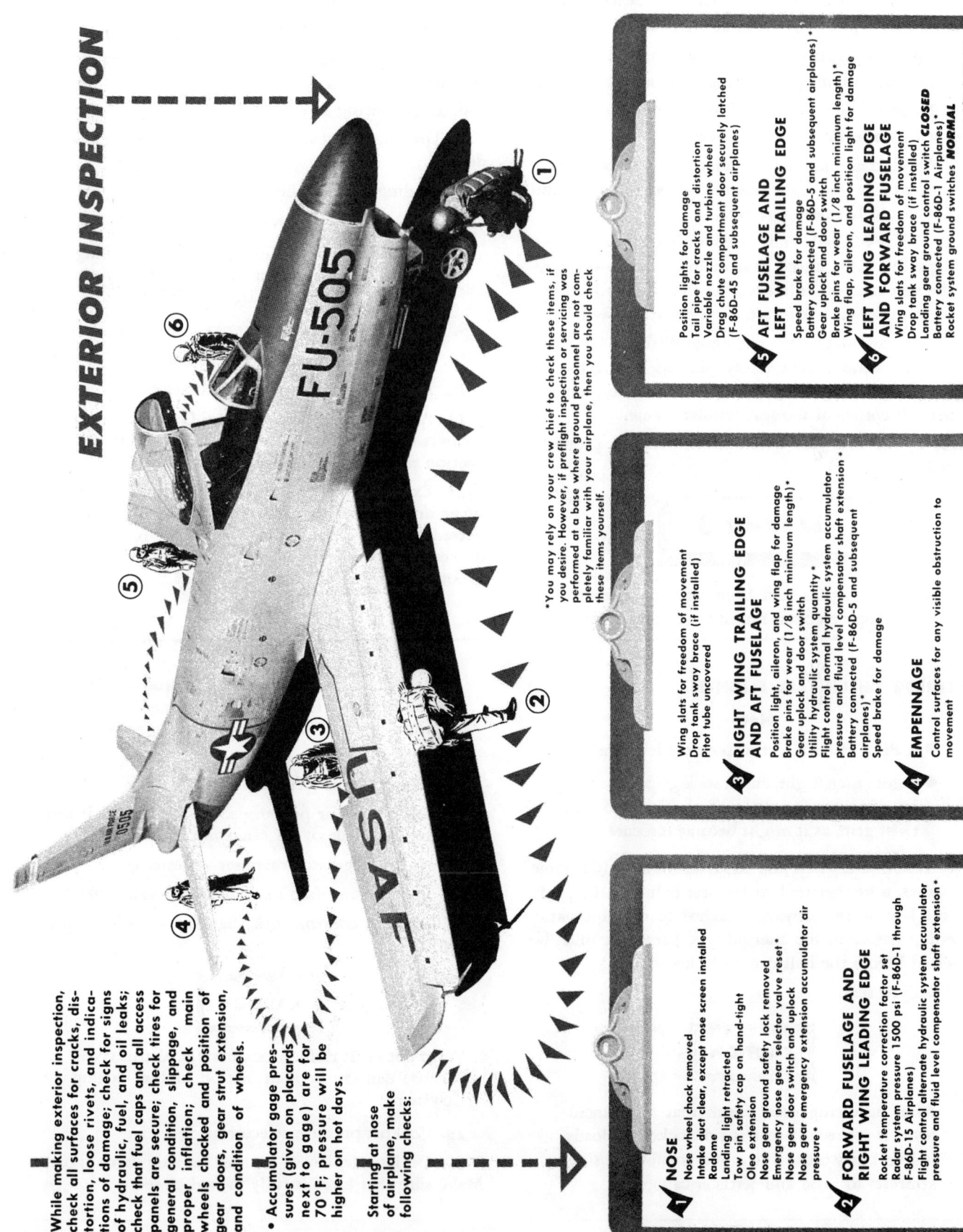

While making exterior inspection, check all surfaces for cracks, distortion, loose rivets, and indications of damage; check for signs of hydraulic, fuel, and oil leaks; check that fuel caps and all access panels are secure; check tires for general condition, slippage, and proper inflation; check main wheels chocked and position of gear doors, gear strut extension, and condition of wheels.

- Accumulator gage pressures (given on placards next to gage) are for 70°F; pressure will be higher on hot days.

Starting at nose of airplane, make the following checks:

▶ **1 NOSE**
Nose wheel chock removed
Intake duct clear, except nose screen installed
Radome
Landing light retracted
Tow pin safety cap on hand-tight
Oleo extension
Nose gear ground safety lock removed
Emergency nose gear selector valve reset*
Nose gear door switch and uplock
Nose gear emergency extension accumulator air pressure*

▶ **2 FORWARD FUSELAGE AND RIGHT WING LEADING EDGE**
Rocket temperature correction factor set
Radar system pressure 1500 psi (F-86D-1 through F-86D-15 Airplanes)
Flight control alternate hydraulic system accumulator pressure and fluid level compensator shaft extension*

▶ **3 RIGHT WING TRAILING EDGE AND AFT FUSELAGE**
Wing slats for freedom of movement
Drop tank sway brace (if installed)
Pitot tube uncovered
Position light, aileron, and wing flap for damage
Brake pins for wear (1/8 inch minimum length)*
Gear uplock and door switch
Utility hydraulic system quantity*
Flight control normal hydraulic system accumulator pressure and fluid level compensator shaft extension*
Battery connected (F-86D-5 and subsequent airplanes)*
Speed brake for damage

▶ **4 EMPENNAGE**
Control surfaces for any visible obstruction to movement

*You may rely on your crew chief to check these items, if you desire. However, if preflight inspection or servicing was performed at a base where ground personnel are not completely familiar with your airplane, then you should check these items yourself.

▶ **5 AFT FUSELAGE AND LEFT WING TRAILING EDGE**
Position lights for damage
Tail pipe for cracks and distortion
Variable nozzle and turbine wheel
Drag chute compartment door securely latched (F-86D-45 and subsequent airplanes)
Speed brake for damage
Battery connected (F-86D-5 and subsequent airplanes)*
Gear uplock and door switch
Brake pins for wear (1/8 inch minimum length)*
Wing flap, aileron, and position light for damage

▶ **6 LEFT WING LEADING EDGE AND FORWARD FUSELAGE**
Wing slats for freedom of movement
Drop tank sway brace (if installed)
Landing gear ground control switch *CLOSED*
Battery connected (F-86D-1 Airplanes)*
Rocket system ground switches *NORMAL*

Figure 2-2

6. On some airplanes,* check that seat catapult ground safety pin (red streamer attached) is removed.

7. On some airplanes,* check connection of linkage from seat catapult trigger to firing lever on seat catapult.

8. Be sure neither lead seal on canopy ejector nor lead seal* on seat catapult is broken.

9. Check that maintenance safety pin of canopy ejector initiator, on the right side of the cockpit below the right console, has been removed.

10. On F-86D-40 and later airplanes and those changed by T.O., check that maintenance safety pins of the seat catapult initiators, on the outboard side of the seat under each armrest, have been removed.

11. On late airplanes† and those changed by T.O., check that maintenance safety pin has been removed from automatic-opening safety belt initiator, on aft upper left corner of the seat tubular frame.

12. Check that seat quick-disconnects are properly mated.

WARNING

After safety pins have been removed, the seat and canopy ejection systems are fully armed.

INTERIOR CHECK (ALL FLIGHTS).

Note

- A Pilot's Check List is above the left console.
- Before each flight, check stick grip for security of mounting on control stick. Do not twist grip, as it might become insecure.

1. Fasten safety belt and shoulder harness. (On some airplanes, a key secured to the seat belt by a lanyard† or the key on the lanyard attached to the automatic-opening device of the aneroid-type parachute must be inserted before the belt can be locked closed.)

2. Adjust seat.

CAUTION

After adjusting seat, check that adjustment lever is locked. If seat is not locked, G-loads in flight may cause it to move, possibly causing armrests to raise and jettison canopy.

3. Adjust the rudder pedals.

4. Armament master switch OFF.

5. Rocket package override switch in center OFF position.

6. Rocket-firing switch AUTOMATIC.

7. Throttle CLOSED, and adjust throttle friction as desired.

8. Landing gear handle DOWN.

Note

Test operation of landing gear unsafe warning light by pressing horn cutout button while throttle is CLOSED. The light should come on.

9. Speed brake switch at NEUTRAL position.

10. Engine master and battery switches OFF.

11. Radio and radar master switches OFF.

12. Attach radio leads and anti-G suit hose to disconnect block leads on seat. Check bail-out bottle connection to oxygen mask hose.

13. External power source (28-volt, 1200-ampere surge and a continuous current of 500 amperes) connected to both dc receptacles for starting or to both dc receptacles and the ac receptacles for starting and ground operation of radar equipment.

Note

External power units suitable for use on this airplane are the A3, A4, C-22, C-26, and V-1 (if they have been maintained to produce their rated output). However, the A4 and V-1 require a separate source for supplying ac power to the airplane.

14. Check circuit breakers in.

15. Drop tank air pressure shutoff valve ON if drop tanks are installed; OFF if tanks not installed.

16. Anti-G regulator valve set as desired.

17. Pressure suit face mask heater rheostat OFF.

18. Rudder control lock handle unlocked (push down).

CAUTION

Do not twist rudder lock handle, as this could cause damage or malfunction of the locking system.

19. Cockpit pressure selector as desired.

20. On late airplanes,‡ manual ram-air valve CLOSED. Make sure that lever is fully locked closed.

---

*F-86D-1 through F-86D-35 Airplanes
†F-86D-55 and later airplanes

‡F-86D-45 Airplane AF52-4048 and all later airplanes

21. Cockpit air temperature control switch AUTOMATIC.

22. Cockpit temperature rheostat controls as desired.

23. Cockpit air pressure switch, PRESS.

24. Zero reader selector switch unit*; selector knob FLIGHT INST., altitude knob OFF.

25. Check alternate longitudinal and lateral trim switches and rudder trim switch for operation, and return switches to NORMAL.

Note

Movement of the rudder trim tab on some airplanes† must be checked visually. As the rudder artificial feel spring bungee is repositioned on F-86D-10 through F-86D-30 Airplanes (except those changed by T.O.), the rudder pedals will move, resulting in corresponding movement of the rudder.

26. Flight control switch NORMAL.

27. Stand-by sight rheostat as desired.

28. Ventilation air control as desired.

29. Wing flap lever UP.

30. Flight control emergency handle fully in.

31. Check generator switches ON.‡

32. Check afterburner shutoff switch NORMAL.

33. Check variable-nozzle switch through operating range and then back to NORM.

34. Check air start switch NORM (guard cover down).

35. Emergency fuel system switch NORM.

36. Landing and taxi light switch OFF.

37. Drag chute handle stowed (full in).

38. Stand-by compass light switch OFF.

39. Set clock, altimeter, and accelerometer.

40. Hydraulic pressure gage selector switch NORMAL.

41. Inverter test switch NORMAL§ (switch spring-loaded to NORMAL). Inverter selector switch MAIN.¶

42. Surface anti-ice switch OFF.

43. Windshield and radome anti-ice switch OFF.

44. Pitot heat switch OFF.

45. Alternator switch ON (F-86D-5 and later airplanes).

46. Check generator switches ON (F-86D-40 and later airplanes).

47. Engine inlet switch SCREEN IN (F-86D-1 Airplanes); EXTEND SCREEN (F-86D-5 and later airplanes).

48. Yaw damper switch OFF.

49. Automatic approach coupler controls OFF (F-86D-30 and later airplanes and airplanes changed by T.O.).

50. Landing gear emergency release handle stowed.

51. Oxygen regulator diluter lever NORMAL OXYGEN.

WARNING

If airplane is to be operated on the ground under possible conditions of carbon monoxide contamination, such as taxiing directly behind another operating jet airplane or during operation with tail into wind, use oxygen with regulator diluter lever at 100% OXYGEN.

52. Oxygen regulator emergency toggle lever in center position.

53. Oxygen regulator warning light switch ON.

54. Check oxygen regulator supply lever safety-wired to ON and pressure at 400 psi.

55. Check oxygen system operation. (Refer to "Oxygen System Preflight Check" in Section IV.)

56. Automatic pilot engaging switch OFF.

57. Voltmeter selector switch BUS.

58. Windshield and canopy defrost lever OFF.

59. Check rocket package up and locked. To check, turn armament master switch to JETTISON READY. If rocket package is up and locked, the rocket-package-up light (green) will come on. Return armament master switch to OFF.

CAUTION

With armament master switch at JETTISON READY, drop tanks will be jettisoned if stick grip tank-rocket jettison button is pressed. (With the weight of the airplane on the gear, a ground safety switch keeps the rocket package from being jettisoned when the stick button is pressed.)

60. Check all warning lights, warning systems, and indicators for operation.

61. Light switches OFF.

62. Check automatic pilot power switch** ON. Check CSTI and autopilot power switch at CSTI & AUTOPILOT position on F-86D-55 and later airplanes. With autopilot engaging switch ON, set autopilot roll trim wheel

---

*F-86D-1 through F-86D-30 Airplanes
†F-86D-1, F-86D-5, and F-86D-35 and later airplanes
‡F-86D-1 through F-86D-35 Airplanes

§F-86D-1 through F-86D-50 Airplanes
¶F-86D-55 and later airplanes
**F-86D-20 Airplanes AF51-3044 through -3131, and F-86D-25 through F-86D-50 Airplanes

at neutral position by rotating the wheel as required to streamline the ailerons.

CAUTION

Failure to take this precaution could cause the airplane to suddenly roll to an extreme of 10 degrees when the autopilot is first turned ON.

63. Release rudder lock handle, if installed, and check rudder, ailerons, and horizontal tail for proper response to control action.

Note

Only the flight control alternate hydraulic system will operate until after the engine has been started and the flight control switch momentarily placed at RESET and released to NORMAL.

64. Check horizontal tail and ailerons for normal operation, using the normal trim switches. As the aileron or horizontal tail artificial feel spring bungees are repositioned, the control stick will move, resulting in corresponding movement of the ailerons or horizontal tail.

WARNING

The normal trim switch is subject to sticking in an actuated position, resulting in application of extreme trim; therefore, operate the normal trim switch in all four trim positions and check that it automatically returns to the center OFF position when released. If the switch sticks in any of the actuated positions, enter this fact with a red cross in the DD Form 781 and do not fly the airplane.

65. Check operation of stand-by sight.

66. Check operation of radar and communication equipment.

Note

For ground operation of radar on F-86D-5 and later airplanes, provide power from external ac source at 400 cycles per second or more. In place of external power provisions, the alternator will power the radar when the engine is operating.

67. Check operation of fuel quantity test button.

68. Check fuel quantity.

69. Check operation of all interior and exterior lighting.

70. Check that flashlight has been included in personal gear.

STARTING ENGINE.

CAUTION

Before starting engine, make sure nose intake duct screen is installed, to prevent engine damage caused by foreign objects being sucked into the engine.

Before starting engine, hold toe brakes on if wheel chocks have been removed, and make sure that danger areas fore and aft of airplane are clear of personnel, airplanes, and vehicles.

Warning
Suction at the intake duct is sufficient to kill or severly injure personnel drawn into or pulled suddenly against the duct.

WARNING

Danger aft of the airplane is created by the high exhaust temperature and blast from the tailpipe. (See figure 2-3.)

Whenever practicable, start and run up engine on a paved surface to minimize the possibility of dirt and foreign objects being drawn into the compressor and damaging the engine. Start engine with airplane heading into, or at right angles to, the wind whenever possible, as exhaust temperatures may be increased or an engine fire during starting may be aggravated by a tail wind.

CAUTION

- Before every engine start, the tail pipe should be visually checked to ensure that there are no puddles of fuel. If fuel puddles are allowed to remain in the tail pipe during starting, fire may occur in the fuselage rear section.
- When operating within the jet blast of another airplane, maintain a minimum distance of 80 feet, to prevent damage to the canopy. When jet blast is from afterburner operation, maintain a minimum of 150 feet distance.

AUTOMATIC START.

Note

The automatic start procedure will normally be used for all operational and training missions.

Start engine as follows:

1. Recheck throttle CLOSED.
2. Check inverter circuit breakers in and inverter warning lights off. The starting circuit will be held open if inverter power is not available.
3. Turn engine master switch ON.

CAUTION

After external power is connected, check that engine control lockup light is out, showing that electronic engine control amplifiers are warmed up enough to permit a safe automatic start.

4. Hold battery-starter switch momentarily at the STARTER position; then return switch to BATTERY.

CAUTION

The high current required for starting will burn out the starter in a matter of seconds if the engine doesn't "turn over" as soon as the starter is energized. If there are no audible indications of engine rotation, or if there is no response on the tachometer within a few seconds, press stop-starter button immediately.

*F-86D-1 through F-86D-35 Airplanes

Note

It is not necessary to position battery-starter switch at OFF during engine start, as battery is automatically cut out when starter is in operation.

5. At 5% rpm, check for minimum of 18 volts.

6. When engine cranking speed is 6% rpm, advance throttle rapidly and directly to START IDLE. The fuel flow will rise to about 900 to 1000 pounds per hour and stabilize at about 600 pounds per hour. (Fuel pressure* holds at about 50 psi.) Exhaust temperature will rise and stabilize at about 600°C (700°C on -33 engine).

Warning

If ignition does not occur within 5 seconds, close throttle and depress stop-starter button. Wait 3 minutes, to allow drainage of fuel accumulation from combustion chamber and tail pipe, before attempting restart.

Note

During automatic starts, the fuel flow or fuel pressure indications in the cockpit will precede the exhaust gas temperature indications by about 3 seconds. For this reason, the fuel flow or fuel pressure indications will give a more rapid indication of the engine start than will the exhaust temperature. Using the fuel flow gage or fuel pressure gage as a primary instrument and observing the exhaust temperature will allow a start to be aborted before an overtemperature condition can take place.

7. Observe that exhaust temperature declines slightly at about 12% rpm. The fuel flow or fuel pressure will remain steady.

Section II — T. O. 1F-86D-1

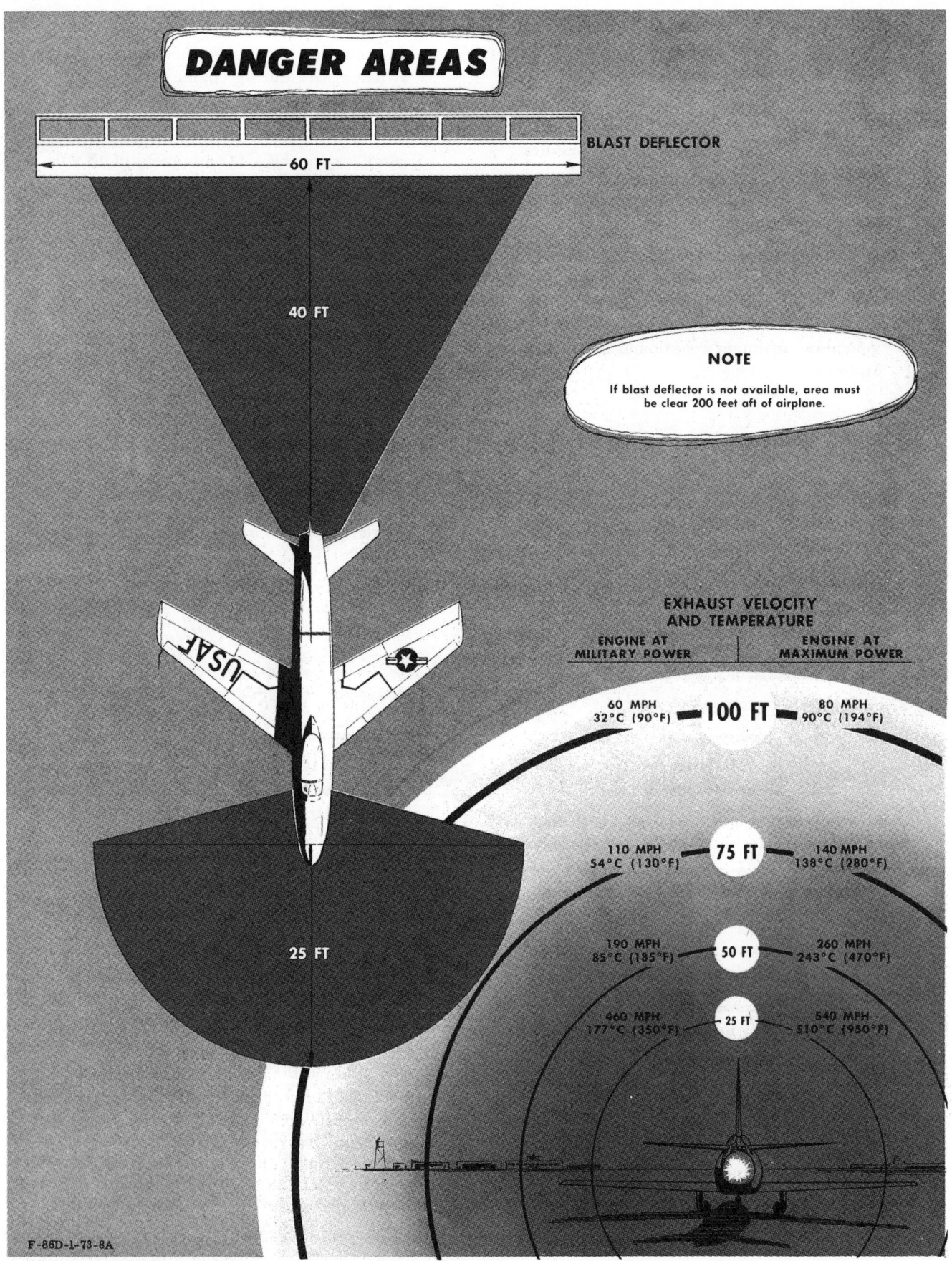

Figure 2-3

8. At approximately 14% rpm, observe that the fuel flow starts to rise to about 950 pounds per hour, fuel pressure starts to rise to about 100 psi, and exhaust temperature starts to rise and will peak at about 815°C.

9. Check that from 14% to 40% rpm, the fuel flow continues to rise slowly to about 1500 pounds per hour, fuel pressure slowly climbs to about 150 psi, and exhaust temperature remains at about 815°C.

The rise to 815°C exhaust temperature should occur before 18% rpm is reached; if it does not, chop throttle to CLOSED immediately and investigate before flight.

10. As 40% rpm is reached, observe that fuel flow, fuel pressure, and exhaust temperature decline to a lower reading of about 1000 pounds per hour fuel flow (100 psi fuel pressure) and about 500°C exhaust temperature. (Refer to "Automatic Start Characteristics," Section VII. Complete knowledge of such characteristics is very important if engine overtemperature operation during starting is to be prevented in the event of an electronic engine control malfunction.) Idle rpm should be about 40% on the main fuel system.

WARNING

- If cockpit indications depart from these normal trends (and continue to rise), retard throttle to CLOSED position, press stop-starter button, and investigate. Failure to accomplish a satisfactory automatic start shows a control system malfunction, and the airplane should not be flown until an investigation is made to isolate and replace the faulty component. The inability to accomplish an automatic start does not necessarily mean that the faulty component is used only during the starting cycle, nor does it mean a "hot start" need occur.

- During *engine starts* up to idle rpm (within 2 minutes), exhaust temperatures of 950°C or above for 2 seconds or more constitute overtemperature operation.

- For all engine operation (except starting), exhaust temperatures of 600°C to 750°C for 40 seconds or more, temperatures of 750°C to 800°C for 10 seconds or more, and temperatures above 800°C for 2 seconds or more constitute overtemperature operation.

- The duration and degree of all overtemperature must be entered in the DD Form 781.

CAUTION

If exhaust temperature of 1000°C is reached, such overtemperature operation requires engine removal.

Note

On throttle bursts from about 90% rpm to Military Thrust, exhaust gas temperature encountered during the transient condition may be higher than that experienced during throttle bursts from lower power settings. However, it should be noted that existing exhaust gas temperature limits are not exceeded.

WARNING

- The starter is limited to three consecutive starts of one minute duration per start, with a 3-minute cooling period between starts. If more than three starts are required, allow starter to cool 30 minutes before using again.

- If engine speed does not reach 25% rpm in one minute, shut down and investigate the cause. Excessive operation below 25% engine rpm can cause extensive damage to starter and engine.

- If the starter should become de-energized before the engine reaches about 20% rpm, shut down engine immediately. No attempt to accelerate the engine should be made.

Note

It is unnecessary to use the stop-starter button to disengage the starter after starts, since the starter relay is designed to cut out automatically at about 25% rpm.

11. Check oil pressure. If there is no sign of oil pressure within 30 seconds, shut down engine and investigate.

12. Check dual fuel pump warning light off. If warning light is on, showing single-pump operation, discontinue engine run and investigate. On some airplanes, the dual fuel pump warning light has been made inoperative.

13. Check engine instruments for desired readings.

14. Have external power source disconnected.

15. Check that generator warning lights are out.

START ON EMERGENCY FUEL SYSTEM.

When it is necessary to use the emergency fuel system for engine start, observe same cautions and warnings as during an automatic start. Start engine as follows:

1. Recheck throttle CLOSED.

2. Turn engine master switch ON.

3. Check inverter circuit breakers in and inverter warning lights off.

4. Check variable-nozzle switch NORMAL.

5. Emergency fuel system switch ON.

6. Hold battery-starter switch momentarily at the STARTER position; then return switch to BATTERY.

7. At 6% rpm, advance throttle about halfway to START IDLE.

8. As fuel pressure (fuel flow) rises, regulate throttle to maintain 35 to 40 pounds fuel pressure (400 to 500 pounds per hour fuel flow) until ignition occurs, as shown by a rise in exhaust temperature.

9. When ignition occurs, use both hands to regulate throttle to maintain 700°C to 750°C exhaust temperature; then move throttle to START IDLE as rapidly as possible without exceeding 750°C.

CAUTION

- Do not make excessively cool starts; try to maintain recommended temperatures. Cold starts prolong the starting period, put excessive loads on the starter-generator unit, and give a poor airflow through the combustion chambers at low rpm.

- When a hot start occurs, shut down engine immediately. If smoking or fire persists, engage starter with throttle closed for about 20 to 30 seconds, to clear engine of excess fuel.

10. Check engine instruments for desired readings.

11. Have external power source removed.

CAUTION

After start is made, check that engine control lockup light is out, showing that electronic engine control amplifiers are warmed up enough to permit operation on main fuel system.

12. Move emergency fuel system switch to NORM. Engine should stabilize at about 40% rpm.

CAUTION

If abnormal engine operation is evidenced with emergency fuel system switch at NORM, return switch to the ON position and check for correct position of power switches and circuit breakers.

ENGINE GROUND OPERATION.

No engine warm-up is necessary. As soon as the engine stabilizes at idling speed with normal gage readings, the throttle may be opened to full power. Idle rpm should be about 40% on the main fuel system, but will vary slightly with the setting of each individual airplane.

Note

Be sure wheels are firmly chocked and, also, hold toe brakes on. This airplane is not equipped with parking brakes.

GROUND TESTS.

At idle rpm, perform the following checks:

Note

The following checks of the flight control and utility hydraulic systems are necessary to ensure proper operation of the systems.

1. Hydraulic pressure gage selector switch at NORMAL.

2. Hold flight control switch at RESET momentarily and then release. Check that flight control alternate system indicator light is out.

3. Check flight control normal hydraulic system as follows: With flight control switch at NORMAL, visually check control surface for proper movement. With hydraulic pressure gage selector switch at NORMAL, check that pressure returns to normal range (control stick not in motion).

4. Check flight control alternate hydraulic system as follows: With flight control switch at ON or ALTERNATE, check that flight control alternate system indicator light comes on and visually check for proper movement of control surfaces.

5. With hydraulic pressure gage selector switch at ALTER. (FLT. CONT. EMERG. on F-86D-1 Airplanes), check that pressure returns to normal range (control stick not in motion).

Note

The alternate system pressure should slowly fluctuate between the maximum limits of 2550 and 3200 psi because of the designed leakage in the flight control actuators causing the alternate system hydraulic pump to cycle on and off.

6. Momentarily hold flight control switch at RESET and then release. Check that flight control alternate system indicator light is out.

CAUTION

When checking control surface movement on both normal and alternate systems, check rate of travel of control stick by rapid, full-travel movements of the stick. If rate is slower than normal, as determined by experience, have ground personnel check systems to determine malfunction. (Refer to "Hydraulic Systems," Section VII.)

7. Check operation of the flight control system manual emergency (override) control as follows: Position hydraulic pressure gage switch to ALTER. (FLT. CONT. EMERG. on F-86D-1 Airplanes).

8. Hold flight control switch at RESET, and pull out flight control emergency handle to its full extension (about 2½ inches). Holding flight control switch at the RESET position opens the electrical circuit to the flight control system transfer valves. This ensures that the normal system transfer is held in the closed position and the alternate system transfer valve is held in the open position by the mechanical flight control manual emergency control only. The alternate system indicator light should not be on. Continue holding flight control switch at RESET, and move control stick. Visually check for proper control surface movement.

9. Release flight control switch to NORMAL position. The alternate system indicator light should come on, showing that the electrical circuit is complete. Check that pressure remains constant at a value between the maximum limits of 3050 and 4000 psi (control stick not in motion).

10. Return emergency handle to its normal (stowed) position. Check that alternate pressure returns to normal range (2550 to 3200 psi).

Note

Because of the tolerances of the alternate system relief valves and the pressure indicating system, the pressure may exceed the red limit value (3200 psi) and may even reach 4000 psi when manual emergency handle is actuated. These pressures are considered normal for this part of the alternate system operation.

11. Check that flight control systems will automatically return to normal system operation. Leave flight control switch in NORMAL and move control stick rapidly to deplete alternate system pressure below about 650 psi. Check that flight control alternate system indicator light goes out, showing that normal system is in control again. Return hydraulic pressure gage selector switch to NORM. (NORMAL on F-86D-1 Airplanes) and check that pressure is in normal range (2550 to 3200 psi).

12. Check utility hydraulic system as follows: Run speed brakes through one complete cycle. Close speed brakes and return switch to neutral. With hydraulic pressure gage selector switch at UTILITY, check pressure shown on the gage (about 3000 psi).

WARNING

Before operating speed brakes, be sure fuselage rear section around speed brakes is clear, as brakes operate rapidly and forcefully and could injure any personnel near the brakes.

13. Before the first flight of the day, the operational check of inverter change-over and electronic engine control automatic lockup system may be made, using the following procedures:

a. On airplanes with the three-position emergency fuel switch, move switch to ON then back to NORM without hesitating at TAKE OFF position, to make the automatic lockup system operable. On airplanes with two-position switch, the lockup system remains operable at all times.

CAUTION

- The interruption of the ac power to the electronic engine controls during the inverter change-over may cause an overtemperature condition, if the lockup system is not operable.

- On airplanes with three-position emergency fuel switch, do not hesitate in TAKE OFF position when switching from ON back to NORM. This could cause an overtemperature condition due to the main fuel valve going to an excessively open position when switch is in TAKE OFF.

b. With variable-nozzle switch, jog the exhaust nozzle full open. Leave switch in OFF position.

c. Advance throttle to 50% rpm. Hold inverter test switch at TEST until main inverter failure light (amber) comes on and then goes out, and the lockup indicator light comes on. On F-86D-55 and later airplanes and those changed by T.O., move inverter selector switch to SPARE. Lockup indicator light should come on. Then return switch to MAIN.

Note

On early airplanes,* holding test switch at TEST fails the primary inverter and transfers operation to the secondary inverter. If switch remains at TEST, the inverters will recycle and power to the engine controls will again be supplied by the primary inverter. Inverter failure light will go out (about 10 to 40 seconds).

d. Retard throttle to START IDLE and move variable-nozzle switch to NORM. Note that rpm and variable-nozzle position remain constant, indicating engine controls are in lockup condition.

e. With throttle at START IDLE, note time required for recovery of engine controls. When the lockup indicator light goes out, an abrupt reduction to idle rpm (about 40%) and the automatic closing of the variable-nozzle to one-half position (about the three-quarter position on some airplanes) takes place. This should occur within 10 to 25 seconds after the inverter failure light goes out. Engine control is restored by automatic lockup system when the primary inverter again supplies power to the electronic engine controls.

Note

The exhaust nozzle should close from full open to one-half position (or three-quarter position on some airplanes) within 3 seconds after lockup indicator light goes out.

14. At 55% rpm, check that generator loadmeter differentials do not vary more than 10 percent from each other and that voltmeter shows about 28 volts. (Generators will not generate below about 37% rpm.)

15. Trim settings: horizontal tail, rudder, and aileron trimmed individually until take-off position indicator light comes on.

Note

- On F-86D-1 through F-86D-45 Airplanes not changed by T.O. 1F-86D-236 (variable-slope feel control system), a different horizontal tail trim setting should be used. With rockets (or ballast), trim the airplane nose-up until the take-off position indicator light comes on; then retrim airplane nose-down until top of stick moves about one inch forward. For flights when rockets (or ballast) are not carried, retrim airplane nose-down until top of stick moves about 2 inches forward after trimming to the take-off indicator light.

- Under any load configuration, trimming to the light on airplanes with the variable-slope feel control ensures a more comfortable feel for lifting the nose off during take-off and for holding the nose down during the transition phase of retracting gear and flaps after take-off.

16. Wing flaps full down for take-off with or without drop tanks.

TAXIING.

Observe the following instructions for taxiing:

1. Remove ground safety pin from right seat armrest.

WARNING

After ground safety pins have been removed, the seat and canopy ejection systems are fully armed.

2. Have main wheel chocks removed.

3. Once the airplane is moving, it can be taxied with the throttle in the START IDLE position (about 40% rpm) on a hard surface. This setting will provide enough cooling air for the generators.

CAUTION

Do not exceed canopy-open speed limit of 50 knots IAS while taxiing; otherwise, damage to canopy and canopy mechanism may result.

4. Maintain directional control through steerable nose wheel by use of rudder pedals; press steering switch continuously while taxiing. Remember that nose wheel and rudder pedal positions must be coordinated before steering mechanism will engage.

5. Minimize taxi time, as airplane range is considerably decreased by high fuel consumption during taxiing. Fuel consumption during taxiing is about 3 gallons per minute (20 pounds per minute) with engine at 40% rpm.

6. If airplane is to be operated on the ground under possible conditions of carbon monoxide contamination, such as taxiing directly behind another jet airplane or

---

*F-86D-1 through F-86D-50 Airplanes

T. O. 1F-86D-1   Section II

EMERGENCY FUEL REGULATOR CHECK

SUMMER OPERATION +40°F TO +100°F

OUTSIDE AIR TEMPERATURE °F	% RPM	EXHAUST TEMPERATURE °C
100	96.0	685 (+5, −15)
90	94.0	685 (+5, −15)
80	92.5	680 (+10, −15)
70	91.5	665 (±15)
60	91.0	655 (±15)
50	90.5	645 (±15)
40	90.0	635 (±15)

WINTER OPERATION 0°F TO +60°F

OUTSIDE AIR TEMPERATURE °F	% RPM	EXHAUST TEMPERATURE °C
60	96.0	685 (+5, −15)
50	94.0	685 (+5, −15)
40	92.5	680 (+10, −15)
30	91.5	665 (±15)
20	91.0	655 (±15)
10	90.5	645 (±15)
0	90.0	635 (±15)

EXTREME WINTER OPERATION −60°F TO +20°F

OUTSIDE AIR TEMPERATURE °F	% RPM	EXHAUST TEMPERATURE °C
20	96.0	685 (+5, −15)
10	94.0	685 (+5, −15)
0	92.5	680 (+10, −15)
−10	91.5	665 (±15)
−20	91.0	655 (±15)
−30	90.5	645 (±15)
−40	90.0	635 (±15)
−50	89.5	620 (±15)
−60	89.0	610 (±15)

ALLOWABLE VARIATIONS

1. RPM ±2%

Select correct table for emergency fuel schedule setting temperature range. The exhaust temperature and rpm should read, within the allowable variations as shown. If reading is other than given in table, the scheduled emergency fuel system performance will not be realized, and a check of the emergency fuel regulator is desirable.

Figure 2-4

2-13

during operation with tail into the wind, use oxygen with diluter lever at 100% OXYGEN.

7. Perform operational check of all gyro indicators during taxiing.

BEFORE TAKE-OFF.

PREFLIGHT AIRPLANE CHECK.

After taxiing to take-off position, complete the following checks:

1. Intake duct nose screen removed.

WARNING

The intake duct nose screen must be removed before preflight engine check and with engine at idle rpm. Ground personnel removing screen must not wear articles of loose clothing or carry equipment likely to be drawn into the intake duct.

2. Safety belt tightened and shoulder harness fitted snugly; shoulder-harness lock handle unlocked.

3. Check rocket package up and locked. To check, turn armament master switch to JETTISON READY. If rocket package is up and locked, the rocket-package-up light (green) will come on. Return armament master switch to OFF.

4. Check flight controls for correct operation and freedom of movement.

5. Canopy switch CLOSE. Check canopy unsafe warning light out and canopy latches visually (yellow stripe visible) after canopy lock handle is pulled aft. (On F-86D-40 and later airplanes and those changed by T. O., push handle full forward.)

CAUTION

When the canopy is being closed, the canopy switch should be held at CLOSE until the canopy actuator automatically cuts off. If the switch is released before the actuator cuts off, the hook at the canopy hinge point may not disengage. Emergency canopy ejection is still possible if the hook fails to disengage, but structural damage to the fuselage may result.

6. Check automatic pilot engaging switch OFF.

7. Check oxygen regulator diluter lever at NORMAL OXYGEN. If contamination is suspected, use 100% OXYGEN.

8. Roll into take-off position, airplane straight down the runway, nose wheel centered. Hold airplane with brakes.

PREFLIGHT ENGINE CHECK.

Perform preflight engine check as follows:

CAUTION

The engine inlet screens should not be cycled if foreign objects are believed to be present. Instead, the airplane should be returned and the preflight inspection for foreign objects repeated.

1. With engine power at idle rpm, operate engine inlet screens through one-half cycle; then return engine inlet switch to EXTEND SCREEN (SCREEN IN on F-86D-1 Airplanes).

Note

This check allows any foreign matter caught on the edge of the engine screens to be dumped into the engine while airplane is on the ground, before flight safety is involved.

2. On airplanes with the three-position emergency fuel switch, follow this procedure for emergency fuel system check:

a. Advance throttle rapidly from START IDLE to MILITARY stop and allow engine to stabilize. Normal stabilized exhaust temperature should be 685°C (±5°C) at 100% rpm. Check engine instruments for desired readings.

CAUTION

When operating within the jet blast of another airplane, maintain a minimum of 80 feet distance, to prevent damage to the canopy. When jet blast is from afterburner operation, maintain a minimum of 150 feet distance.

b. Move emergency fuel system switch to TAKE OFF.

CAUTION

- When moving emergency fuel system switch to TAKE OFF, be prepared to retard throttle immediately to minimize engine overspeed in case of maladjustment or malfunction of emergency fuel regulator.

- If it becomes necessary to reduce power, retard throttle to START IDLE and move the emergency fuel system switch to ON for about 2 seconds; then, without hesitating at TAKE OFF, return the switch to NORM before readvancing throttle. This action is necessary to avoid undesirable power surges, possible compressor stall, or overtemperature conditions.

Note

Placing the emergency fuel system switch at TAKE OFF, when the throttle is above three-quarter-open position, places the emergency fuel system in stand-by condition. When the throttle is below the three-quarter-open position, the engine is operating on the emergency fuel system. (Refer to "Automatic Lockup System Characteristics," Section VII.)

c. With variable-nozzle switch at NORMAL, press emergency fuel system test button. Stabilized rpm and exhaust temperature should be in accordance with chart in figure 2-4.

d. Release test button. If recovery is slow or if rpm fails to recover to 100%, move emergency fuel switch to NORM. Retard throttle as necessary to assist rpm recovery. (Refer to "Nonrecovery Characteristic Following An Emergency Fuel System Test," Section VII.)

e. With emergency fuel switch at TAKE OFF, advance throttle steadily and rapidly past MILITARY stop to full forward position. It is not necessary to stabilize at Military Thrust before advancing the throttle into the afterburner range.

3. On airplanes with the two-position emergency fuel switch, follow this procedure for emergency fuel system check:

a. Advance throttle rapidly from START IDLE to MILITARY stop and allow engine to stabilize. Normal stabilized exhaust temperature should be 685°C (±5°C) at 100% rpm. Check engine instruments for desired readings.

CAUTION

When operating within the jet blast of another airplane, maintain a minimum of 80 feet distance, to prevent damage to the canopy. When jet blast is from afterburner operation, maintain a minimum of 150 feet distance.

b. Move emergency fuel switch to ON. RPM and exhaust temperature should be in accordance with chart in figure 2-4.

---

*F-86D-35 Airplanes AF51-8397 through -8406 and -8419 through -8505, and F-86D-40 and later airplanes

CAUTION

When moving emergency fuel system switch to ON, be prepared to retard throttle immediately to minimize engine overspeed in case of maladjustment or malfunction of emergency fuel regulator.

c. Move emergency fuel switch to NORM.

CAUTION

- Engine rpm will drop momentarily to about 70% rpm. Do not return switch to emergency ON during this rpm drop unless throttle is first retarded to idle, as overtemperature condition or compressor stall could result.
- Be prepared to retard throttle to IDLE when moving the emergency fuel switch to NORM, as compressor stall could result if main fuel system is maladjusted. If stall occurs, corrective maintenance must be accomplished before flight.

d. With emergency fuel switch at NORM, advance throttle steadily and rapidly past MILITARY stop to full forward position. It is not necessary to stabilize at Military Thrust before advancing the throttle into the afterburner range.

On all airplanes, complete the rest of preflight engine check as follows:

WARNING

- Afterburner operation is prohibited until T.O. 1F-86D-519 is accomplished. Nonaccomplishment of subject T.O. should be indicated in DD Form 781.
- Afterburner operation is permitted only on those airplanes* that have the mechanical stop included in the afterburner fuel control valve and those on which T.O. 2J-J47-293 has been accomplished. (DD Form 781 should show if noncompliance of the T.O. exists.)

4. Observe that afterburner ignition occurs within 5 seconds, shown by definite increase in thrust and an increase in variable-nozzle area. Exhaust temperature should not exceed afterburner ignition temperature limits. Normal stabilized temperature should be 685°C (±5°C). Engine speed should stabilize between 98% and 100% rpm. Variable-nozzle position indicator should not exceed red radial limit (there is no red radial limit on airplanes that have the "flattop" fuel schedule).

CAUTION

- The temperature and duration of any afterburner lightup during which an exhaust temperature of 870°C is exceeded for 2 seconds or more, or an exhaust temperature of 950°C is exceeded momentarily, shall be entered in DD Form 781. However, if 1000°C is reached, shut down engine; such overtemperature operation requires engine removal.

- Before retarding throttle from afterburner range, move emergency fuel switch to NORM to prevent engine overspeed.

- Should the engine overspeed exceed 104% rpm, either with or without an overtemperature condition, shut down engine; the engine must be removed for overhaul.

5. After stabilizing, check for proper afterburner fuel valve control by retarding the throttle slowly and carefully about one half the afterburner range and noting a decrease in exhaust nozzle area and holding a constant exhaust temperature. Readvance throttle.

CAUTION

If exhaust nozzle area does not decrease as throttle is retarded, the afterburner fuel control valve is not operating properly. Shut down afterburner operation by retarding throttle to MILITARY position or below. Electronic engine controls should be checked before throttle is readvanced to afterburner range.

6. Check engine instruments for desired readings.

TAKE-OFF.

NORMAL TAKE-OFF.

The procedure set forth will produce results shown in the take-off charts (figures A-3 and A-4).

For normal take-off, proceed as follows:

CAUTION

- Before take-off roll is started, check to see that exhaust temperature and variable-nozzle position are stabilized. Take-off should not be attempted if the variable-nozzle position indicator pointer goes beyond the red radial limit (there is no red radial limit on air-

Use of afterburner is recommended for take-off. However, take-off at Military Power (without afterburner) is satisfactory although the take-off run is approximately 50 percent greater under standard conditions.

F-86D-1-0-19

planes that have the "flattop" fuel schedule). In this instance, the throttle should be immediately retarded and the engine shut down. The tail cone and electronic engine controls should be inspected for damage before flight.

- During flight, the throttle should be immediately retarded to MILITARY position whenever the variable-nozzle position indicator pointer goes beyond the red radial limit (there is no red radial limit on airplanes that have the "flattop" fuel schedule). Upon completion of the flight, appropriate entry should be made in the DD Form 781 and the tail cone and electronic engine controls should be inspected for damage before the next flight.

WARNING

After an aborted take-off, for any reason, the airplane must be taxied back to the line, the engine shut down, and the brakes allowed to cool enough that they can be touched by hand before further flight.

Note

The three-position emergency fuel switch should be in the TAKE OFF position for take-off. The two-position emergency fuel switch should be in the NORM position for all normal operation.

1. Release brakes and begin take-off run, using nose wheel steering to maintain directional control. Use of brakes will increase ground roll. Rudder control becomes effective at about 60 knots IAS.

2. At about 95 knots IAS, lift nose wheel only slightly.

3. As speed reaches 115 knots IAS with no external load (120 knots IAS with drop tanks installed), pull stick back firmly to lift airplane nose to take-off attitude.

Note

On rough runways where it is advisable to get the nose wheel off the ground as soon as possible to minimize shock loads, hold nose wheel just off the runway until the preceding speeds are attained; then lift airplane nose to take-off attitude.

4. Maintain very nose-high attitude. (After take-off, the airplane will assume a more normal attitude as airspeed increases and wing flaps are raised.)

Note

- Take-off speed is 125 knots IAS at normal take-off gross weight (with rockets) of about 18,250 pounds with no external load. With full 120-gallon drop tanks installed at 20,000 pounds gross weight, take-off speed is 130 knots IAS. (See figure 2-5.)
- Refer to take-off charts (figures A-3 and A-4) for take-off distances required.

MINIMUM-RUN TAKE-OFF.

A minimum-run take-off is a maximum-performance maneuver, with the airplane lifting off near the stalling speed, and should be attempted only when using afterburner. It is closely related to slow flying with the airplane in a high angle-of-attack attitude. Therefore, you should be familiar with the characteristics of this maneuver to be able to maintain the necessary safe margin above the stall. The same trim settings should be used as for a normal take-off, and the initial take-off run is the same. As the take-off run progresses, the stick should be pulled back firmly at about 105 knots IAS (with no external load); at about 110 knots IAS (with drop tanks). As the nose wheel lifts off, a steady rotation of the airplane to take-off attitude will occur, with airplane lifting off at about 120 knots IAS (with no external load) and at about 125 knots IAS (with drop tanks). See figure 2-5 for ground roll distances. As the

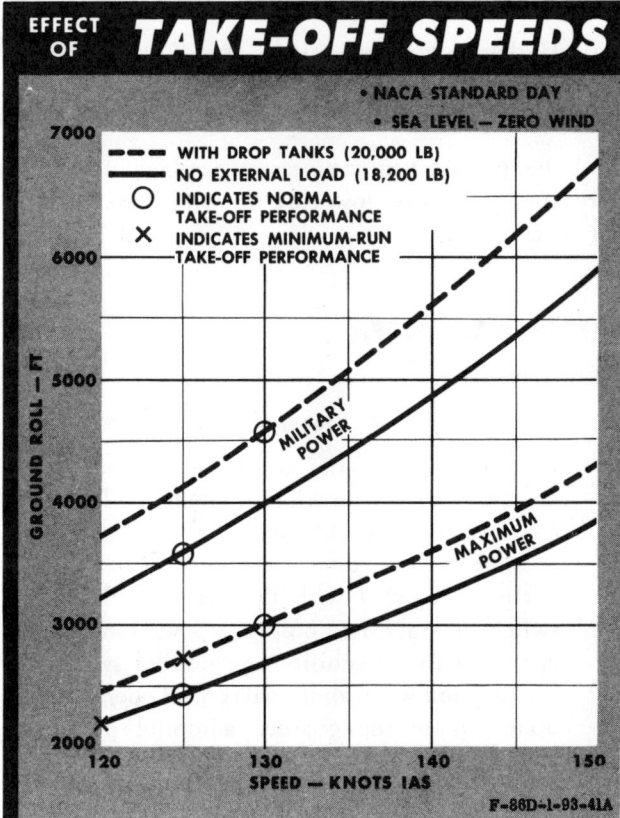

Figure 2-5

airplane lifts off, reduce back pressure enough to maintain minimum airspeed buildup and maximum climb angle, to effect the shortest air run that will clear all obstacles. The landing gear should not be retracted until the airplane accelerates to the normal take-off speeds; i.e., at least 5 knots faster than minimum-run take-off speeds. After all obstacles are cleared, retrim the airplane and accelerate to best climb speed.

When the airplane is very close to stall speed, retracting the gear may cause a nose-up pitch sufficient to cause a stall. Waiting until normal take-off speeds are reached or exceeded eliminates this hazard.

CROSS-WIND TAKE-OFF.

In addition to the procedures used in a normal take-off, the following steps should be observed:

1. Be prepared to exert rudder pressure after nose wheel lift-off to keep the airplane on a straight path down the runway until air-borne.

Note

Higher nose wheel lift-off speeds are necessary to improve the controllability normally decreased by loss of lift on the upwind wing.

2. Be prepared to counteract airplane drift after breaking ground by lowering the wing into the wind or by crabbing.

AFTER TAKE-OFF.

When airplane is definitely air-borne:

Note

Binding and/or jerky control operation can be caused by malfunction of either the flight control system or the autopilot system. It is possible for the autopilot system to become partially engaged with the flight controller switch in the OFF position. Therefore, to eliminate the possibility of autopilot system malfunction when abnormal control operation occurs, place the guarded autopilot power switch in the OFF position, pull the autopilot circuit breaker, or remove the autopilot ac fuse.

CAUTION

During flight, the throttle should be immediately retarded to MILITARY position whenever the variable-nozzle position indicator pointer goes beyond the red radial limit (there is no red radial limit on airplanes that have the "flattop" fuel schedule). Upon completion of the flight, appropriate entry should be made in the DD Form 781, and the tail cone and electronic engine controls should be inspected for damage before the next flight.

1. Landing gear handle UP. Check position indicators.

2. Wing flap lever UP above 155 knots IAS. Normally, no "sink" will occur because of the rapid acceleration of the airplane. However, if "sink" does occur (at high gross weights), the flap control can be temporarily set to HOLD to maintain intermediate flap position. After flaps are fully retracted, leave wing flap lever at UP.

CAUTION

- Do not retract landing gear while yawing or slipping, as damage to gear doors may result.

- Raise landing gear and flaps below limit airspeeds; otherwise, excessive air loads may damage gear doors or flap operating mechanism and prevent later operation.

- Wing flaps must be fully retracted to avoid failure of the flap actuating mechanism that may occur if the flaps are not supported against the up-stop (fully retracted) during accelerated maneuvers at high speed.

3. Engine inlet switch SCREEN OUT (F-86D-1 Airplanes); RETRACT SCREEN (F-86D-5 and later airplanes).

4. Trim longitudinally as required.

Note

Slats will close at about 180 to 200 knots IAS.

5. On airplanes with the three-position emergency fuel switch, when a safe altitude is reached, position emergency fuel system switch at NORM. The switch should be at NORM for all normal operation except take-off and initial climb.

Note

- If loss of engine power occurs when the emergency fuel system switch is set at NORM, it is merely necessary to move the switch to ON. If rpm decreases below 90%, shut off afterburner to prevent engine damage due to overheating the tail pipe.

- If engine speed is inadvertently allowed to drop below 85% rpm before the switch is moved back to the ON position, the throttle should be retarded to START IDLE before the emergency fuel switch is placed ON.

- Any time outside air temperature causes the emergency fuel regulator setting to approach that of the main fuel system and the emergency fuel switch is at TAKE OFF, it is possible for the emergency fuel system to take over engine control and result in engine overspeed. Engine overspeeding during climb after take-off with emergency fuel system switch at TAKE OFF shows that the emergency fuel system has taken over engine control. When such an engine overspeed exists, an apparent loss of engine power will result when emergency fuel system switch is set at NORM. For further information, refer to "Emergency Fuel System Overriding Main Fuel System," Section VII.

6. Increase speed, holding constant altitude. Start climb about 20 knots IAS before reaching best climb speed for that particular altitude to stabilize on desired climb schedule as quickly as possible. Maintain best

climb speeds for minimum time to altitude. Refer to Appendix I for further information.

7. Move armament master switch to desired position and radar power or radar master switch to STBY position. Maintain wing-level flight during 4½-minute warm-up period.

8. Yaw damper switch ON.

9. As soon as added thrust is no longer needed, shut off afterburner by retarding throttle past MILITARY stop to desired setting.

Note

- To prevent engine overspeeding when afterburner is shut off, the emergency fuel system switch must first be set at NORM.
- A momentary surge of 101% rpm is often experienced when coming out of afterburner operating range. These momentary surges are not harmful to the engine.

10. If 100% OXYGEN was used for take-off, return oxygen regulator diluter lever to NORMAL OXYGEN, unless carbon monoxide contamination is suspected. If such is the case, continue use of 100 percent oxygen as long as considered necessary.

WARNING

Oxygen diluter lever must be returned to NORMAL OXYGEN as soon as possible, because use of 100% oxygen will so deplete the oxygen supply as to be hazardous.

CLIMB.

Military Thrust is recommended for climb for maximum range conditions when minimum time to altitude is not important. (Time limit for continuous operation at Military Thrust is 30 minutes.) For minimum time to altitude, such as in a point interception mission, Maximum Thrust is required. (Time limit for continuous operation at Maximum Thrust is 20 minutes.) Refer to climb charts in Appendix I for recommended indicated airspeeds to be used during climb and for estimated rates of climb and fuel consumption.

CAUTION

If in-flight seat adjustment is made, check that seat vertical adjustment lever is locked and seat is locked in position. If seat is not locked, G-loads may cause it to move and possibly cause armrests to raise and jettison the canopy.

AFTERBURNER OPERATION DURING FLIGHT.

Note
Afterburner should be used only when maximum thrust is essential and should be turned off when this need has passed, because of the greatly increased fuel consumption.

CAUTION

- If afterburner blowout occurs with less than 1300 pounds of fuel remaining, do not attempt further afterburner operation unless dictated by emergency or combat conditions.
- This precaution does not constitute an operating limitation, but rather a measure to reduce the possibility of afterburner fuel pump overspeed if the fuselage rear tank transfer pump fails.
- No attempt is to be made to ignite the afterburner whenever engine is operating on the emergency fuel system.

Follow this procedure for afterburner operation while in flight:

1. Variable-nozzle switch at NORMAL.

2. From any intermediate power setting, advance throttle steadily and rapidly past MILITARY stop to full forward position. When engine is operating at Military Thrust, throttle should first be momentarily retarded to obtain an engine speed of 95% rpm before the throttle is advanced to the full forward position. (On late airplanes* incorporating the "hot streak" ignition and

---

*F-86D-45 and later airplanes

on airplanes modified by T. O. 2J-J47-332, it is not necessary to use this throttle technique, as afterburner ignition is possible by movement to afterburner range from any throttle position.) Ignition will be shown by an increase in thrust and variable-nozzle area. Variable-nozzle position indicator should not exceed the red radial limit (there is no red radial limit on airplanes that have the "flattop" fuel schedule).

CAUTION

- To prevent engine damage due to overheating the tail pipe, do not operate continuously in afterburning with engine rpm below 90%.
- During flight, the throttle should be immediately retarded to MILITARY position whenever the variable-nozzle position indicator pointer goes beyond the red radial limit (there is no red radial limit on airplanes that have the "flattop" fuel schedule). Upon completion of the flight, appropriate entry should be made in the DD Form 781 and the tail cone and electronic engine controls should be inspected for damage before the next flight.

Note

- Limit continuous operation of afterburner to duration of 20 minutes.
- Ten seconds may be required to effect afterburner light-up in flight. Time necessary for afterburner light-up will normally increase as altitude is increased.
- During periods of prolonged afterburner operation at high altitudes and high Mach, the aft fire-warning light may come on in airplanes using the J47-GE-33 engine and having drop tanks installed. Flight tests have shown that this can be overcome by slowing down (by raising the nose of the airplane or opening the speed brakes).

3. When added thrust is no longer needed, shut off afterburner by retarding throttle past MILITARY stop to desired setting.

Note

Limit continuous operation at Military Thrust to duration of 30 minutes.

FLIGHT CHARACTERISTICS.

Refer to Section VI for information regarding flight characteristics.

SYSTEMS OPERATION.

Refer to Section VII for information regarding systems operation.

DESCENT.

Circumstances may arise which require a descent from high altitude in the shortest possible time. Rates of descent as high as 55,000 feet per minute can be obtained with this airplane. For a typical descent, refer to descent chart (figures A-21 and A-22).

Note

The windshield and canopy defrost system provides enough heating of the transparent surfaces to effectively eliminate the formation of frost or fog during descent.

On airplanes equipped with J47-GE-17 or -17B engine, the following procedures are recommended to minimize shroud ring rub when the throttle is retarded during a descent or letdown from altitude:

1. At any altitude, when operating at Normal Rated Thrust or below, make descents by chopping power to obtain a minimum of 300°C.

2. At altitudes above 25,000 feet, when using Maximum or Military Thrust, reduce power to maintain 600°C exhaust temperature for about 2 minutes. After about 2 minutes of operation at 600°C, or when descending through 25,000 feet altitude, the throttle may be further retarded to maintain a minimum of 300°C for the remainder of the letdown.

3. On descents from altitudes at or below 25,000 feet, retard throttle to maintain a minimum of 300°C throughout the letdown.

PRE-TRAFFIC-PATTERN CHECK.

During approach to the field, make the following checks:

1. Armament master switch OFF.

CAUTION

To prevent landing shock loads from damaging the fire control system gyro, wait until landing has been made and taxiing is completed before turning radar off.

2. Utility hydraulic pressure normal.

3. Safety belt tightened and shoulder harness fitted snugly.

4. Shoulder-harness lock handle unlocked.

5. Engine inlet switch SCREEN IN (F-86D-1 Airplanes) or EXTEND SCREEN (F-86D-5 and later airplanes).

6. Yaw damper switch OFF.

7. Turn windshield anti-icing switch ON if vision is impaired by rain during landing approach.

Note

- Enough anti-icing airflow is available over windshield to improve vision effectively, if a minimum of 75% engine rpm is maintained. If rain is still encountered as power is reduced for landing, vision through windshield side panels may be necessary. Turn anti-icing switch OFF after touchdown, if warning light has not come on. If light comes on, leave switch on; reduced engine power on the ground or selecting ram air will allow gradual cooling of windshield, and thus prevent cracking of the glass by sudden temperature changes.

- Illumination of the light shows that the design limit of the air supply in the system has been reached, but does not necessarily mean that the windshield has reached the same temperature. In addition to reducing engine power to lower anti-ice air temperature, selecting ram air will reduce the amount of air to be cooled in the heat exchanger, thus reducing the temperature.

- It is recommended that ram air be used in conjunction with anti-ice system only during taxiing, take-off, or landings, as unsatisfactory cockpit temperatures could result if windshield anti-icing is used extensively during flight.

TRAFFIC-PATTERN CHECK.

While following the procedure outlined in figure 2-6 for making a normal approach and landing, observe the following precautions.

CAUTION

- Do not lower landing gear in accelerated turns or pull-ups, as the G encountered may damage the landing gear operating mechanism. Also, if the gear is lowered above the gear down limit airspeed of 185 knots IAS, the air loads may damage the landing gear doors or fairings.

- To prevent possible damage to gear doors, the landing gear should not be extended or retracted while the airplane is in a slipping or yawing attitude.

In addition to improving deceleration and shortening ground roll, extending the speed brakes will permit the use of higher engine rpm during a normal approach. This is a definite advantage if a go-round is required.

Note

On F-86D-10 and later airplanes, the speed brakes will be rendered inoperative automatically if utility hydraulic system pressure falls below 1500 psi.

Flying the landing pattern at 160 to 185 knots IAS, using power for level flight, results in about the same amount of thrust as that produced at much lower rpm in airplanes with fixed nozzles. Rapid increases in thrust are possible only above about 75% rpm, Military Thrust being reached in 3.5 seconds from this setting. Therefore, to ensure adequate acceleration, use full flaps, speed brakes, and high engine rpm on the approach, if required.

LANDING.

NORMAL LANDING.

The procedure set forth will produce results shown in the landing chart in the Appendix.

While following the procedure outlined in figure 2-6 for completing a normal landing, observe the following precautions:

Note

The full length of the runway should be used during the landing roll, so that the brakes can be used as little and as lightly as possible for stopping.

Speed brakes may be used optionally in the traffic pattern although the recommended approach procedure is to have the speed brakes open to allow carrying a higher power setting in the event of a go-around. To avoid high rate of sink, a power setting of 75% to 85% rpm will be necessary to hold the rate of descent to the most favorable of 1000 to 1200 feet per minute during the final approach.

WARNING

It is recommended that the variable-nozzle switch be left in the NORMAL (automatic) position during the landing approach and ground run. If the nozzle has been jogged open, enough thrust will not be available for a go-around unless the nozzle is jogged closed or the switch is returned to the NORMAL position.

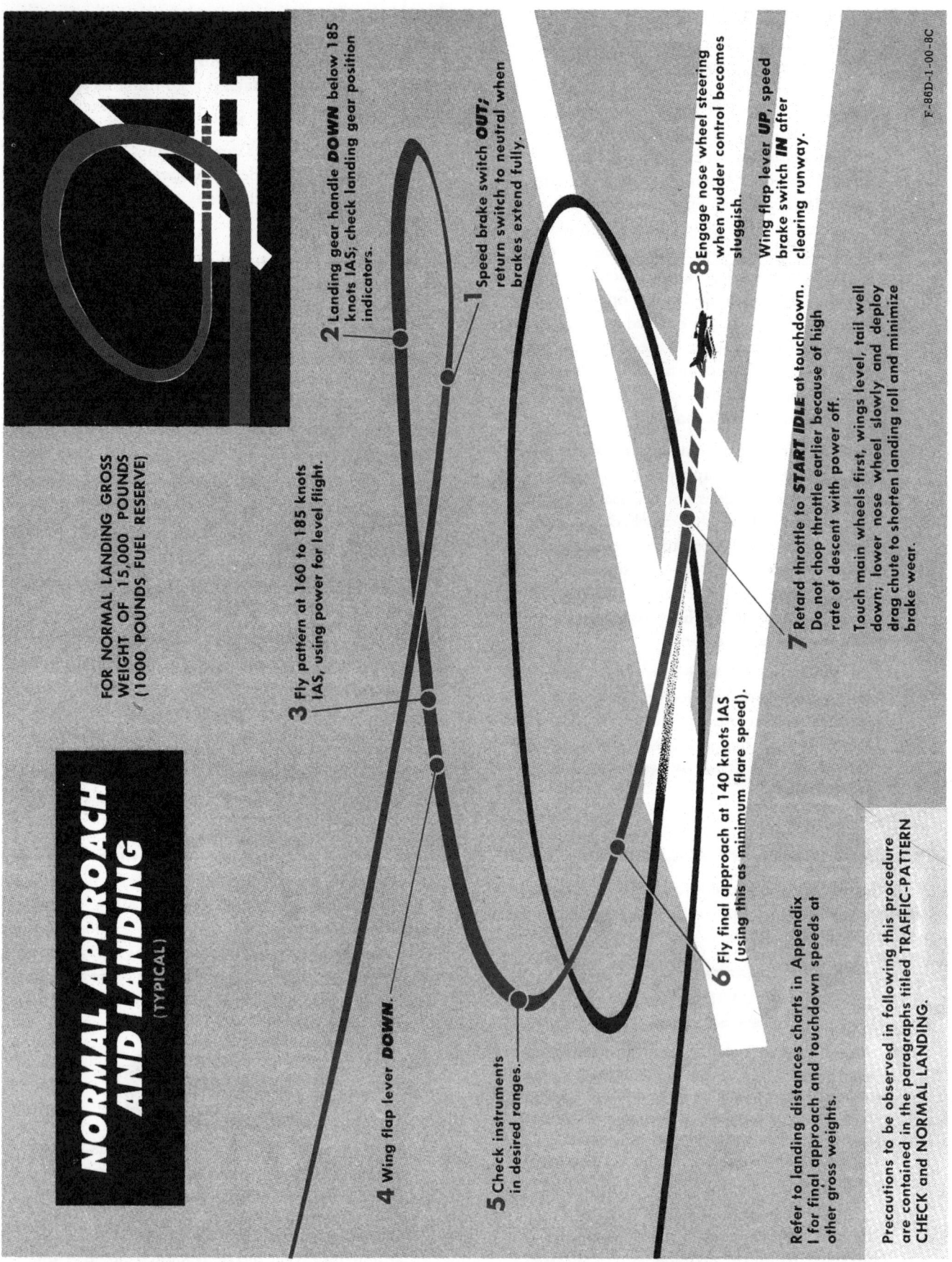

Figure 2-6

Note

With the variable-nozzle switch in the NORMAL position, the nozzle is automatically controlled to give the most favorable engine performance. Opening the nozzle has a negligible effect on the landing ground roll, because the thrust loss is a very small percentage of the total available braking force during a landing. The total available braking force is about 4000 pounds, and idle thrust is reduced only 100 pounds by opening the nozzle.

Do not attempt a full-stall landing, since the angle of attack at the stall is so high the tail will drag the ground.

CROSS-WIND LANDING.

1. Maintain 160 knots IAS in turn onto final approach.

2. On final approach, crab or drop wing to keep lined up with runway.

3. Use normal approach speed for flare. If crabbing, align airplane with runway just before touchdown; if using wing-down approach, lift wing before touchdown.

4. At touchdown, lower nose wheel smoothly to runway as soon as practical.

5. Deploy drag chute, if necessary, only after nose wheel is on the ground.

CAUTION

- The drag chute should not be deployed in 90-degree cross winds exceeding 20 knots or in 45-degree cross winds exceeding 30 knots, because of weathercocking tendencies of the airplane with the chute deployed.

- However, in an emergency, the drag chute may be deployed during strong cross winds to provide fast deceleration but only after the nose wheel is on the ground; then jettison the chute as soon as practical if excessive yaw develops. Be prepared to use brakes, rudder, and/or nose wheel steering to maintain directional control.

- If possible, be sure that drag chute will clear following airplanes if it becomes necessary to jettison the chute to maintain control.

MINIMUM-RUN LANDING.

1. Maintain 160 knots IAS in turn onto final approach.

2. On final approach, maintain 120 to 130 knots IAS, using power as necessary, and shoot for end of runway.

3. Chop throttle when landing is ensured.

4. Deploy drag chute after touchdown.

Note

Although the drag chute is not designed for in-flight use, it will not adversely affect the airplane's flight characteristics if it is inadvertently opened just before touchdown and the proper flareout has been initiated.

5. Get nose wheel down smoothly and quickly after touchdown (after drag chute opens) to permit braking below 100 knots IAS. Use brakes intermittently and hard, but not hard enough to slide wheels. (Apply brakes for about 2 to 3 seconds; allow one-second release intervals between applications.)

CAUTION

- Braking is permissible above 100 knots IAS; however, caution should be used to prevent wheels from sliding, because brake action is extremely difficult to feel above this speed.

- Excessive use of the brakes can cause them to overheat, causing damaging effects on the tires. If the heat is great enough, it can cause the tires to weaken and later blow out. If the brakes are used excessively during taxiing, landings, or aborted take-offs, for any reason, the airplane must be taxied back to the line, engine shut down, and the brakes allowed to cool enough to touch by hand before starting another flight.

- The drag chute should be jettisoned before taxiing downwind in winds exceeding 15 knots, because of the possibility of the chute collapsing and risers burning by contact on hot areas of exhaust nozzle.

HEAVY-WEIGHT LANDING.

The same technique for normal landing applies for the heavy-weight landing (near maximum take-off gross weight), except for necessary increases in power settings. As gross weight increases, approach and touchdown speed should be increased accordingly. For example, if the take-off is made with full internal fuel, full 120-gallon drop tanks, and full rocket load, and a landing has to be made before any excess fuel and the rocket load can be expended, the landing weight will be about 19,500 pounds. With this landing weight, the recommended final approach speed is 160 knots IAS, to provide adequate flare characteristics. A stall landing should be avoided, if at all possible, in an attempt to keep the G to a minimum at point of touchdown.

Note

- If necessary, the drag chute may be deployed to provide maximum deceleration after touchdown.
- If a heavy-weight landing is made, the airplane should be checked for signs of overstress before the next flight.

GO-AROUND.

While following the procedure outlined in figure 2-7 for making a go-around from an aborted landing approach, observe the following precautions:

WARNING

- Make decision to go around as early as possible. The low-altitude acceleration characteristics of a jet-propelled airplane are definitely inferior to those of a propeller-driven airplane.
- During a go-around, if engine does not respond to throttle advancement on the first attempt, as shown by engine instruments, retard throttle to START IDLE (if rpm drops below 85%), position emergency fuel system switch to ON, and cautiously readvance throttle.
- If the main fuel system has failed during flight, the emergency fuel system switch should be ON, and if the variable nozzle is inoperative, the variable-nozzle switch OFF (nozzle closed). Under these conditions, the acceleration characteristics of the airplane are extremely poor. Also, advancement of the throttle must be done with caution to prevent flame-out or dangerous overtemperature.

Afterburning should not be used if the emergency regulator is controlling fuel flow, since the emergency regulator does not have the safety features of the main fuel control valve.

AFTER LANDING.

Maintain directional control during the landing roll by use of rudder and differential braking. After completion of landing roll:

1. Move windshield and canopy defrost lever to OFF.
2. Return speed brake switch to NEUTRAL.
3. Engage nose wheel steering when slow taxiing becomes necessary.

CAUTION

- To obtain the best drag chute service life, it is recommended that the drag chute be jettisoned, at the lowest possible taxi speed, immediately after taxiing off the runway onto the taxiway while drag chute is still inflated.
- Do not stop during taxiing, or the nylon riser will be severely damaged by exhaust heat. Use extreme care when taxiing for long distances with the drag chute deployed, to prevent it from dragging on the ground or touching the hot exhaust nozzle area.
- Do not make sharp turns during taxiing with the drag chute deployed, to prevent chute from collapsing, and resultant damage to chute and chute compartment.

STOPPING ENGINE.

To stop engine, proceed as follows:

1. Hold brakes.
2. Before engine shutdown, operate engine between 65% and 70% rpm for 2 minutes.

Note

This permits engine stabilization at the lowest temperature, which minimizes the possibility of shroud ring rub. If required by emergency conditions, engine may be shut down immediately.

3. Close throttle sharply.

Note

When ac power stops during engine shutdown as rpm decreases, the ac powered fuel pressure or fuel flow, oil pressure, and hydraulic pressure gages may deceptively change indications. Therefore, during this period, no reliance should be placed upon these indicators.

4. Turn engine master switch to OFF below 10% rpm.
5. Wait a few seconds before turning battery-starter switch OFF.

Note

If operation at idling speed is performed for more than 3 minutes, advance throttle to

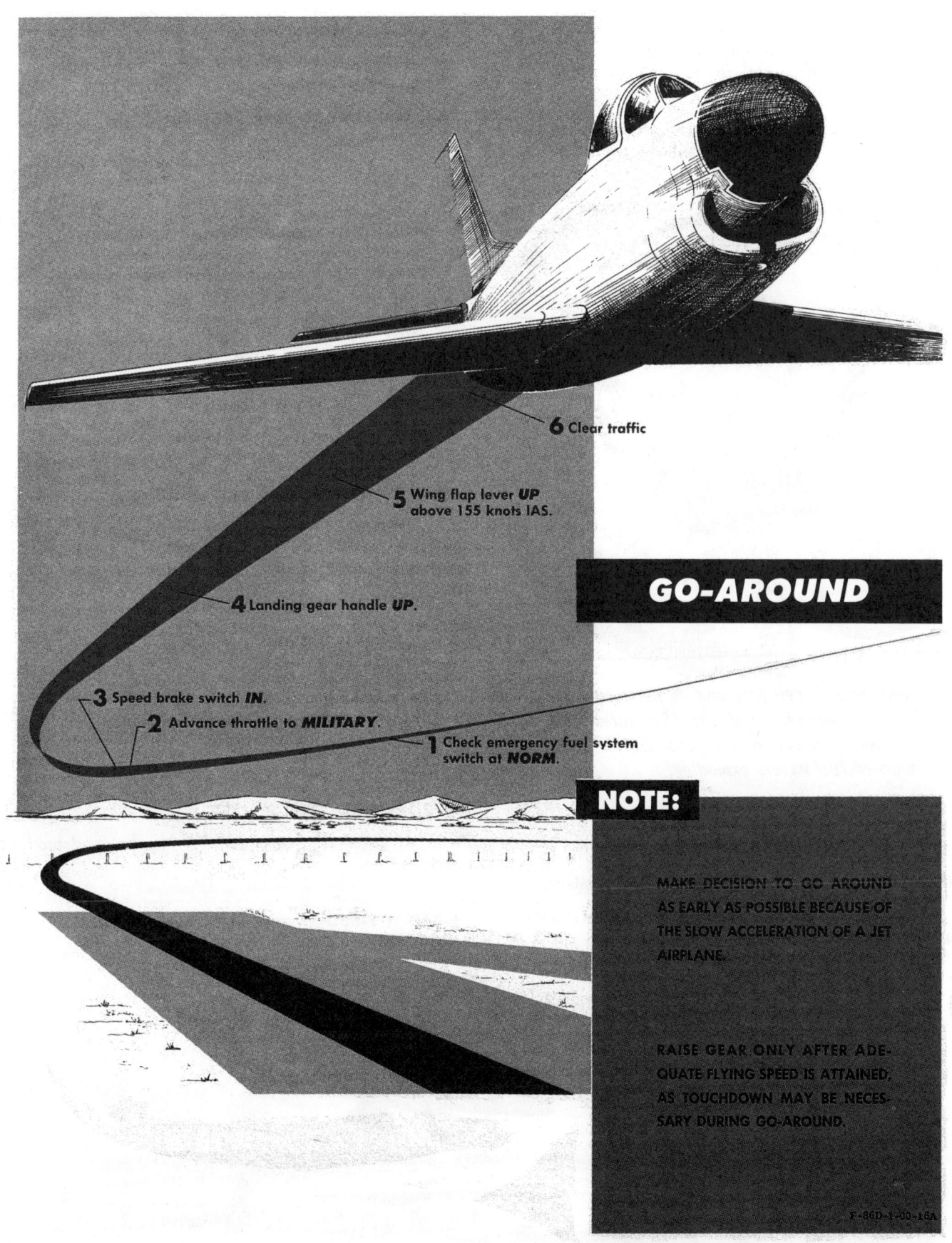

Figure 2-7

Military Thrust for 30 seconds to reduce carbon accumulation on spark plugs. Then operate engine at 65% to 70% rpm for 2 minutes and shut down engine.

6. Turn off all switches except generator switches (and on F-86D-5 and later airplanes, the alternator switch).

Warning

Keep clear of tail pipe and do not move airplane into hangar for at least 15 minutes after shutdown, because of the possibility of accumulated fuel vapors exploding.

BEFORE LEAVING AIRPLANE.

Make following checks before leaving the airplane:

1. Install ground safety pin in ejection seat right armrest (across the trigger).
2. Check that armrests are full down and latched.
3. Check drop tank air pressure shutoff valve OFF.
4. Complete DD Form 781.
5. Lock rudder on some airplanes.*

CAUTION

If wearing an automatic-opening, aneroid-type parachute that has a key attached to the aneroid arming lanyard, make sure key does not foul when leaving cockpit, to prevent chute from being opened inadvertently.

6. Close canopy and have cover installed, if necessary.
7. Have main wheels chocked.
8. Nose gear ground safety lock installed.
9. Check installation of nose wheel tow pin wedge.
10. Check installation of pitot head cover.
11. Check installation of intake duct plug and tail-pipe cover if needed. Wait at least 15 minutes after shutdown before installing intake duct plug and tail-pipe cover.

Note

The pilot may rely on the crew chief to chock wheels, install tow pin wedge, pitot boom cover, and duct plugs. However, the responsibility of having these duties performed still remains with the pilot.

CONDENSED CHECK LIST.

Refer to pages 2-27 through 2-38 for the condensed check list.

*F-86D-1, F-86D-5, and F-86D-35 and later airplanes

CUT ON SOLID LINE

F-86D CONDENSED CHECK LIST

NOTE

The following check lists are condensed versions of the procedures presented in Section II. These condensed check lists are arranged so that you may remove them from your Flight Handbook and insert them into a flip pad for convenient use. They are arranged so that each action is in sequence with the expanded procedure given in Section II. Presentation of these condensed check lists does not imply that you need not read and thoroughly understand the expanded versions. To fly the airplane safely and efficiently, you must know the reason why each step is performed and why the steps occur in certain sequence.

T. O. 1F-86D-1
18 May 1956

PREFLIGHT CHECK.

BEFORE EXTERIOR INSPECTION.

DD Form 781—Check.

EXTERIOR INSPECTION.

Check all surfaces for cracks, distortion, loose rivets, and signs of damage; check for signs of hydraulic, fuel, and oil leaks; check that all access doors and panels and fuel filler caps are secured; check tries for general condition, slippage, and proper inflation; check position of gear doors, gear strut extension, and condition of wheels.

1. Nose:

Nose wheel chock removed.
Intake duct clear, except nose screen installed.
Radome.
Landing light retracted.
Tow pin safety cap on hand-tight.
Oleo extension.
Nose gear ground safety lock removed.
Nose gear emergency selector valve reset.
Nose gear door switch and uplock.
Nose gear emergency extension accumulator air pressure.

2. Forward Fuselage and Right Wing Leading Edge.

Rocket temperature correction factor set.
Radar system pressure 1500 psi (F-86D-1 through F-86D-15 Airplanes).
Flight control alternate hydraulic system accumulator air pressure and fluid level compensator shaft extension.
Wing slats for freedom of movement.
Drop tank sway brace (if installed).
Pitot tube uncovered.

3. Right Wing Trailing Edge and Aft Fuselage.

Position light, aileron, and wing flap for damage.
Brake pins for wear (⅛-inch minimum length).
Gear uplock and door switch.
Utility hydraulic system quantity.
Flight control normal hydraulic system accumulator air pressure and fluid level compensator shaft extension.
Battery connected (F-86D-5 and later airplanes).
Speed brake for damage.

T. O. 1F-86D-1
18 May 1956

2

4. **Empennage.**

   Control surfaces for any visible obstruction to movement.
   Position lights for damage.
   Tail pipe for cracks, distortion, and clearance.
   Variable nozzle and turbine wheel.
   Drag chute compartment door securely latched.

5. **Aft Fuselage and Left Wing Trailing Edge.**

   Speed brake for damage.
   Battery connected (F-86D-5 and later airplanes).
   Gear uplock and door switch.
   Brake pins for wear (1/8-inch minimum length).
   Wing flap, aileron, and position light for damage.

6. **Left Wing Leading Edge and Forward Fuselage.**

   Wing slats for freedom of movement.
   Drop tank sway brace (if installed).
   Landing gear ground control switch CLOSED.
   Battery connected (F-86D-1 Airplanes).
   Rocket system ground switches NORMAL.

CANOPY AND EJECTION SEAT CHECK.

1. Canopy—OPEN.
2. Shoulder-harness routing—Check.
3. Both seat armrests—Full down and latched.
4. Ground safety pin—Installed in right seat armrest.
5. F-86D-1 through F-86D-35 Airplanes, seat catapult sear safety pin—Installed in catapult and connected to canopy.
6. F-86D-1 through F-86D-35 Airplanes, seat catapult ground safety pin—Removed.
7. F-86D-1 through F-86D-35 Airplanes, linkage from trigger to catapult firing lever—Check.
8. Lead seal on canopy remover and seat catapult—Check.
9. Canopy ejector initiator maintenance safety pin—Removed.
10. Seat catapult initiator maintenance safety pins—Removed.
11. Safety belt initiator maintenance safety pin—Removed.
12. Seat quick-disconnects—Properly mated.

T. O. 1F-86D-1

18 May 1956

3

CUT ON SOLID LINE

ON ENTERING COCKPIT.
INTERIOR CHECK.

1. Safety belt and shoulder harness—Fastened.
2. Seat—Adjusted.
3. Rudder pedals—Adjusted.
4. Armament master switch—OFF.
5. Rocket package override switch—OFF.
6. Rocket-firing switch—AUTOMATIC.
7. Throttle—CLOSED and adjust friction as desired.
8. Landing gear handle—DOWN.
9. Speed brake switch—Neutral.
10. Engine master and battery switches—OFF.
11. Radio and radar master switches—OFF.
12. Radio leads, anti-G suit, and bail-out bottle—Connected.
13. External power—Connected.
14. Circuit breakers—In.
15. Drop tank pressure shutoff valve—ON if tanks installed, OFF if tanks not installed.
16. Anti-G suit regulator valve—As desired.
17. Pressure suit face mask heater rheostat—OFF.
18. Rudder control lock handle—Unlocked (push down).
19. Cockpit pressure selector—As desired.
20. Manual ram-air valve—CLOSED.
21. Cockpit air temperature control switch—AUTOMATIC.
22. Cockpit temperature rheostat control—As desired.
23. Cockpit air pressure switch—PRESS.
24. Zero reader selector switch unit—Selector knob, FLIGHT INST; altitude knob, OFF.
25. Rudder, alternate longitudinal, and lateral trim switches—NORMAL.
26. Flight control switch—NORMAL.
27. Stand-by sight rheostat—As desired.
28. Ventilation air control—As desired.
29. Wing flap lever—DOWN.
30. Flight control emergency handle—In.
31. Generator switch—ON.
32. Afterburner shutoff switch—NORMAL.
33. Variable-nozzle switch—NORMAL.
34. Air start switch—NORM.
35. Emergency fuel system switch—NORM.

T. O. 1F-86D-1
18 May 1956

CUT ON SOLID LINE

36. Landing and taxi light switch—OFF.
37. Drag chute handle—Stowed.
38. Stand-by compass light switch—OFF.
39. Clock, altimeter, and accelerometer—Set.
40. Hydraulic pressure gage selector switch—NORMAL.
41. Inverter test switch—NORMAL; inverter selector switch—MAIN.
42. Surface anti-ice switch—OFF.
43. Windshield and radome anti-ice switch—OFF.
44. Pitot heat switch—OFF.
45. Alternator switch—ON.
46. Generator switches—ON.
47. Engine inlet switch—EXTEND SCREEN.
48. Yaw damper switch—OFF.
49. Automatic approach coupler controls—OFF.
50. Landing gear emergency release handle—Stowed.
51. Oxygen regulator diluter lever—NORMAL OXYGEN.
52. Oxygen regulator emergency toggle lever—Center.
53. Oxygen regulator warning light switch—ON.
54. Oxygen regulator supply lever—Safetied ON.
55. Oxygen system operation—Check.
56. Automatic pilot engaging switch—OFF.
57. Voltmeter selector switch—BUS.
58. Windshield and canopy defrost lever—DEC.
59. Rocket package—Up and locked.
60. All warning lights and indicators—Check operation.
61. Light switches—OFF.
62. Automatic pilot power switch—ON; CSTI and automatic pilot power switch—ON (if installed).
63. Rudder, ailerons, and horizontal tail—Check operation.
64. Normal trim switch—Check operation.
65. Stand-by sight—Check operation.
66. Radar and communication—Check operation.
67. Fuel quantity gage test button—Press and observe movement of fuel quantity gage needle.
68. Fuel quantity—Check.
69. Interior and exterior lights—Check operation.
70. Flashlight—Check operation.

T. O. 1F-86D-1

18 May 1956

5

CUT ON SOLID LINE

STARTING ENGINE.
AUTOMATIC START.

1. Throttle—CLOSED.
2. Inverter circuit breakers—In; inverter warning lights—Out.
3. Engine master switch—ON.
4. Battery-starter switch—START; then—BATTERY.
5. At 5% rpm, 18 volts minimum.
6. At 6% rpm, advance throttle—START IDLE.
7. At 12% rpm, exhaust temperature will decline slightly.
8. At 14% rpm, fuel flow rise to 950 pounds per hour (fuel pressure to 100 psi); exhaust temperature peak at 815°C.
9. From 14% to 40% rpm, fuel flow rise to 1500 pounds per hour (fuel pressure to 150 psi); exhaust temperature—815°C.
10. As 40% rpm is reached, fuel flow declines to 1000 pounds per hour (fuel pressure to 100 psi); exhaust temperature to 500°C.
11. Oil pressure—Check.
12. Dual fuel pump warning light—Out.
13. Engine instruments—Desired readings.
14. External power source—Disconnected.
15. Generator warning lights—Out.

EMERGENCY FUEL SYSTEM START.

1. Throttle—CLOSED.
2. Engine master switch—ON.
3. Inverter circuit breakers—In; inverter warning lights—Out.
4. Variable-nozzle switch—NORMAL.
5. Emergency fuel system switch—ON.
6. Battery-starter switch—START; then—BATTERY.
7. At 6% rpm, throttle halfway to START IDLE.
8. As fuel flow (fuel pressure) starts to rise, regulate throttle to maintain 400 to 500 pounds per hour fuel flow (fuel pressure 35 to 40 psi) until ignition occurs.
9. When ignition occurs, use both hands to regulate throttle to maintain 700°C to 750°C exhaust temperature; then move throttle rapidly to START IDLE.
10. Engine instruments—Desired readings.
11. External power source—Disconnected.
12. Emergency fuel switch—NORM; rpm stabilized at about 40%.

T. O. 1F-86D-1

18 May 1956

6

GROUND TESTS.

1. Hydraulic pressure gage selector switch—NORMAL.
2. Flight control switch—RESET (alternate system light out).
3. Flight control switch—NORMAL. Move control stick and visually check control surface movement. Check that pressure returns to normal range (control stick not in motion).
4. Flight control switch—ALTERNATE (alternate system light on). Move control stick and visually check control surface movement.
5. Hydraulic pressure gage selector switch—ALTER and check pressure returns to normal range (control stick not in motion).
6. Flight control switch—RESET momentarily (alternate system light out).
7. Hydraulic pressure gage selector switch—ALTER.
8. Hold flight control switch—RESET and pull emergency override handle to full extension, alternate system light out. Move control stick and visually check control surface movement.
9. Flight control switch—NORMAL. Alternate system light on. Alternate system pressure constant value between 3050 and 4000 psi (control stick not in motion).
10. Emergency override handle—Stowed. Alternate system pressure returns to normal range (control stick not in motion).
11. Move control stick to deplete alternate system pressure below 650 psi, alternate system light out. Hydraulic pressure gage selector switch—NORMAL, check pressure for normal range (control stick not in motion).
12. Open and close speed brakes; then return switch to Neutral. Hydraulic pressure gage selector switch—UTILITY, pressure about 3000 psi.

CUT ON SOLID LINE

13. Before first flight of day, make check of inverter change-over and automatic lockup systems as follows:
    a. Three-position emergency fuel switch—Move to ON then back to NORM; two-position emergency fuel switch—Leave at NORM.
    b. Variable-nozzle switch—Jog nozzle full open, leave switch at OFF.
    c. At 50% rpm—Hold inverter test switch at TEST (inverter selector switch to SPARE). Inverter failure warning lights and engine control lockup light come on; return switch to MAIN.
    d. Retard throttle—START IDLE; move variable-nozzle switch—NORM (rpm and nozzle position remain constant).
    e. When lockup indicator light goes out—RPM reduces to idle and nozzle closes to one-half or three-quarter position.
14. Generators—Check at 55% rpm.
15. Horizontal tail, rudder, and ailerons trimmed individually until take-off indicator light comes on (or as required).
16. Wing flaps—Full down.

TAXIING.

1. Right armrest ground safety pin—Removed and stowed.
2. Wheel chocks—Removed.
3. Taxi at lowest practical rpm.
4. Nose wheel steering switch—Pressed continuously.
5. Minimize taxi time.
6. Oxygen regulator diluter lever—NORMAL OXYGEN. (100% OXYGEN if carbon monoxide suspected).
7. Gyro indicators—Check operation.

T. O. 1F-86D-1
18 May 1956

8

BEFORE TAKE-OFF.

PREFLIGHT AIRPLANE CHECK.

1. Nose screen—Removed.
2. Safety belt—Tightened; shoulder harness—Fitted snugly; and shoulder-harness lock handle—Unlocked.
3. Rocket package—Up and locked.
4. Flight controls—Operation and free movement.
5. Canopy switch—CLOSE, canopy unsafe warning light out.
6. Automatic pilot engaging switch—OFF.
7. Oxygen regulator diluter lever—NORMAL OXYGEN (100% OXYGEN if carbon monoxide suspected).
8. Toe brakes—Hold.

PREFLIGHT ENGINE CHECK.

1. Engine inlet screens—Operate through one complete cycle.
2. On airplanes with the three-position emergency fuel switch:
    a. Throttle—Advance from START IDLE to MILITARY.
    b. Emergency fuel system switch—TAKE OFF (emergency fuel system warning light on).
    c. Emergency fuel system test button—Press (stabilized rpm and exhaust temperature within allowable limits).
    d. Test button—Release.
    e. Advance throttle steadily and rapidly from MILITARY to full AFTERBURNER.
3. On airplanes with the two-position emergency fuel switch:
    a. Throttle—Advance from START IDLE to MILITARY.
    b. Emergency fuel system switch—ON (emergency fuel system warning light on). Stabilized rpm and exhaust temperature within allowable limits.
    c. Emergency fuel system switch—NORM.
    d. Throttle—Advance steadily and rapidly from MILITARY to full AFTERBURNER.
4. Afterburner ignition—Should occur within 5 seconds.
5. Retard throttle one-half afterburner range—Note decrease in exhaust nozzle area; readvance throttle.
6. Engine instruments—Check for desired readings.

T. O. 1F-86D-1
18 May 1956

TAKE-OFF.

1. Release brakes and begin take-off run, using nose wheel steering to maintain directional control.
2. At about 95 knots IAS, lift nose wheel slightly.
3. At 115 knots IAS, no external load (120 knots IAS with drop tanks installed), pull stick back firmly to obtain take-off attitude.
4. Maintain a nose-high attitude.

AFTER TAKE-OFF.

1. Landing gear handle—UP. (Check position indicators.)
2. Wing flap lever—UP.
3. Engine inlet switch—SCREEN OUT or RETRACT SCREEN.
4. Horizontal tail—Trim as required.
5. Three-position emergency fuel switch—NORM when safe altitude is reached.
6. Start climb 20 knots IAS before reaching best climb speed.
7. Armament master switch—Desired position; radar power or radar master switch—STBY.
8. Yaw damper switch—ON.
9. Throttle—Retard from AFTERBURNER when need is passed.
10. Oxygen regulator diluter lever—NORMAL OXYGEN (100% OXYGEN if carbon monoxide suspected).

PRE-TRAFFIC-PATTERN CHECK.

1. Armament master switch—OFF.
2. Utility hydraulic pressure—Normal.
3. Safety belt—Tightened; shoulder harness—Fitted snugly.
4. Shoulder-harness lock handle—Unlocked.
5. Engine inlet screen switch—SCREEN IN or EXTEND SCREEN.
6. Yaw damper switch—OFF.
7. Anti-icing (windshield rain and ice removal) switch—ON if vision impaired by rain.

T. O. 1F-86D-1
18 May 1956

TRAFFIC-PATTERN CHECK AND LANDING.

1. Speed brake switch—OUT.
2. Landing gear handle—DOWN.
3. Fly pattern at 160 to 185 knots IAS.
4. Wing flap lever—DOWN.
5. Engine instruments—Check for desired readings.
6. Fly final approach at 140 knots IAS.
7. Throttle—START IDLE at touchdown and deploy drag chute.
8. Nose wheel steering—Engage.
9. After clearing runway—Wing flap lever—UP; speed brake switch—IN.

GO-AROUND.

1. Emergency fuel system switch—NORM.
2. Throttle—MILITARY.
3. Speed brake switch—IN.
4. Landing gear handle—UP.
5. Wing flap lever—UP.
6. Clear traffic.

AFTER LANDING.

1. Windshield and canopy defrost lever—DEC.
2. Speed brake switch—Neutral.
3. Maintain directional control for taxiing with nose wheel steering.

STOPPING ENGINE.

1. Brakes—Hold.
2. Engine—65% to 70% rpm for 2 minutes.
3. Throttle—CLOSED.
4. Engine master switch—OFF.
5. Battery switch—OFF.
6. All switches—OFF (except generator and alternator switches).

T. O. 1F-86D-1

18 May 1956

CUT ON SOLID LINE

T. O. 1F-86D-1
18 May 1956

12

BEFORE LEAVING AIRPLANE.

1. Ground safety pin—Installed in ejection right seat armrest (across trigger).
2. Both armrests—Full down and latched.
3. Drop tank pressure shutoff valve—OFF.
4. DD Form 781—Complete.
5. Rudder—Locked.
6. Canopy—Closed.
7. Main wheels—Chocked.
8. Nose gear ground safety lock—Installed.
9. Nose wheel towing release pin—Disengaged.
10. Pitot head cover—Installed.
11. Intake duct plug and tail-pipe cover—Installed.

EMERGENCY PROCEDURES

F-86D-1-00-37A

TABLE OF CONTENTS

	PAGE
Engine Failure	3-1
Fire	3-8
Elimination of Smoke or Fumes	3-10
Landing Emergencies	3-10
Loss of Canopy	3-12
Emergency Entrance	3-12
Ditching	3-14
Ejection	3-14
Afterburner Failure	3-15

	PAGE
Variable-area Nozzle Automatic Control Failure	3-18
Main Fuel Control System Failure	3-18
Electrical System Emergency Operation	3-19
Landing Gear Emergency Operation	3-22
Flight Control Hydraulic System Failure	3-22
Flight Control Artificial Feel System Failure	3-23
Horizontal Tail Normal Trim Failure	3-23
Aileron Normal Trim Failure	3-23
Drop Tank and Rocket Package Emergency Jettison in Flight	3-23

ENGINE FAILURE.

Complete engine failures are rarely experienced on this airplane. Engine flame-outs and malfunctions of various types do, however, occur from time to time. These malfunctions are usually the result of improper fuel scheduling caused by a malfunction of the integrated electronic engine control or of one of its components, or by incorrect techniques during critical flight conditions. (Refer to "Main Fuel Control System Failure.") When time and altitude permit, air starts can usually be accomplished if engine failure is due to malfunction of the main fuel control system. Signs of failure of the main fuel control system are often shown by the engine instruments. Air starts should never be attempted if engine failure can be attributed to some obvious mechanical failure within the engine proper.

ENGINE OVERSPEED DURING TAKE-OFF.

On airplanes with the three-position emergency fuel switch installed, any time outside air temperature causes the emergency fuel regulator setting to approach that of the main fuel system, it is possible for the emergency fuel system to take over engine control and result in engine overspeed during the climb after take-off. This overspeed is gradual and is a result of the emergency fuel system overriding the main fuel system, when the emergency fuel system switch is in the TAKE OFF position. If the emergency fuel system switch is set at NORM, with the overspeed condition present, what appears to be a complete power loss will occur. (Refer to Section VII for further information.) If engine overspeed stabilizes at about 102% rpm, the climb may be continued without any power change being made. As altitude is increased, the engine speed will return to 100% rpm. However, before the emergency fuel system switch is set to NORM, the engine must be allowed to remain stabilized at 100% rpm for about 15 seconds. If engine overspeed tends to exceed 104% rpm during climb after take-off, while operating in afterburner range with the emergency fuel system switch at TAKE OFF, perform the following:

1. Move emergency fuel system switch to NORM.

2. Immediately and rapidly retard throttle to below MILITARY stop.

Note

When emergency fuel system switch is positioned to NORM, a loss in power results. For this reason, the throttle must be retarded from the AFTERBURNER range.

3. Readvance throttle to desired setting. Engine will respond on the main fuel system.

Note

This condition does not occur on airplanes incorporating the two-position emergency fuel switch, as the switch is in NORM position for take-off.

ENGINE FAILURE DURING TAKE-OFF BEFORE LEAVING GROUND.

If complete engine failure occurs before leaving ground, or if take-off is aborted for any other reason and runway is equipped with a runway barrier (refer to "Engaging Runway Barrier," in this section), accomplish as much of the following as possible before engaging the barrier:

1. Throttle CLOSED.

2. Apply brakes as necessary.

3. Deploy drag chute, if necessary.

WARNING

- The heat generated in the brake during an aborted take-off continues to build up during taxiing operation back to take-off position. This heat is transmitted to the wheel and into the tire itself. This heat in the tire melts the rubber and weakens the cords until the casing blows out.

- After an aborted take-off, for any reason, the airplane must be taxied back to the line. Shut down engine. Make sure brake assembly is cool enough to touch by hand before further flight.

CAUTION

Use care after deploying drag chute in cross winds of 45 to 90 degrees because of weathercocking tendencies of airplane with chute deployed. Be ready to use brakes, rudder, and/or nose wheel steering to maintain directional control.

If landing gear must be retracted because of insufficient remaining runway, proceed as follows:

CAUTION

Do not retract gear if barrier is present.

1. Press drop tank jettison button if drop tanks are installed.

Note

Rockets cannot be jettisoned when weight of airplane is on the landing gear.

2. Deploy drag chute.

3. Landing gear handle UP. Press landing gear emergency retract button and hold it down until landing gear retracts.

4. Raise both armrests to jettison canopy, and lock shoulder harness before coming to a complete stop.

WARNING

If armrests have not been raised and if spilled fuel is in the vicinity of the airplane, use the mechanical or electrical means to remove the canopy, if time permits. If these systems fail, the canopy jettison mechanism may be used; however, a fire may result from a hot powder spark when the canopy catapult is actuated.

5. Turn engine master switch OFF.

6. Wait one second to allow fuel shutoff valve to close; then move battery-starter switch to OFF. If time permits, turn OFF generator switches.

ENGINE FAILURE DURING TAKE-OFF AFTER LEAVING GROUND.

If complete engine failure occurs after airplane is airborne, prepare for an emergency landing, accomplishing as much as possible of the following:

1. Throttle CLOSED.

2. Press drop tank jettison button if drop tanks are installed. If time permits, move armament master switch to EMERG. JET'S'N to jettison rocket package if rockets are installed.

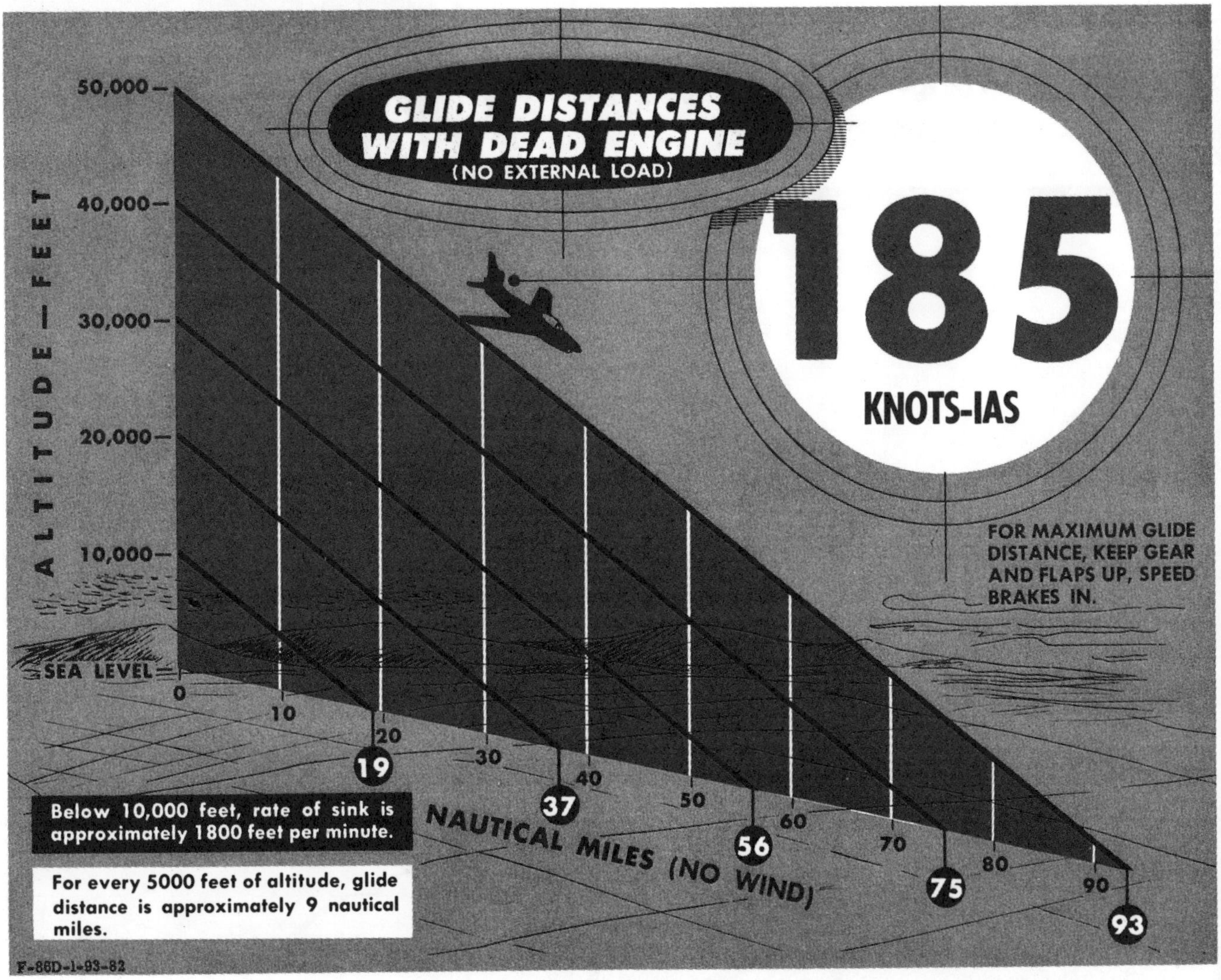

Figure 3-1

3. Unlock canopy latches manually to allow air stream to break canopy away from fuselage.

WARNING

If canopy has not been released and if spilled fuel is in the vicinity of the airplane, use the mechanical or electrical means to remove the canopy, if time permits. If these systems fail, the canopy jettison mechanism may be used; however, a fire may result from a hot powder spark when the canopy catapult is actuated.

4. If landing gear has been retracted, move landing gear handle DOWN.

5. If wing flaps have been raised, move wing flap lever to DOWN.

6. Turn engine master switch OFF.

7. Wait one second to allow fuel shutoff valve to close; then move battery-starter switch to OFF. If time permits, turn OFF generator switches.

8. Shoulder harness locked.

9. Land straight ahead, changing course only enough to miss obstacles.

10. Deploy drag chute immediately after airplane contacts ground.

CAUTION

If drag chute is deployed at speeds in excess of about 160 knots IAS, it will automatically jettison.

ENGINE FAILURE DURING FLIGHT.

If engine failure occurs during flight, follow this procedure:

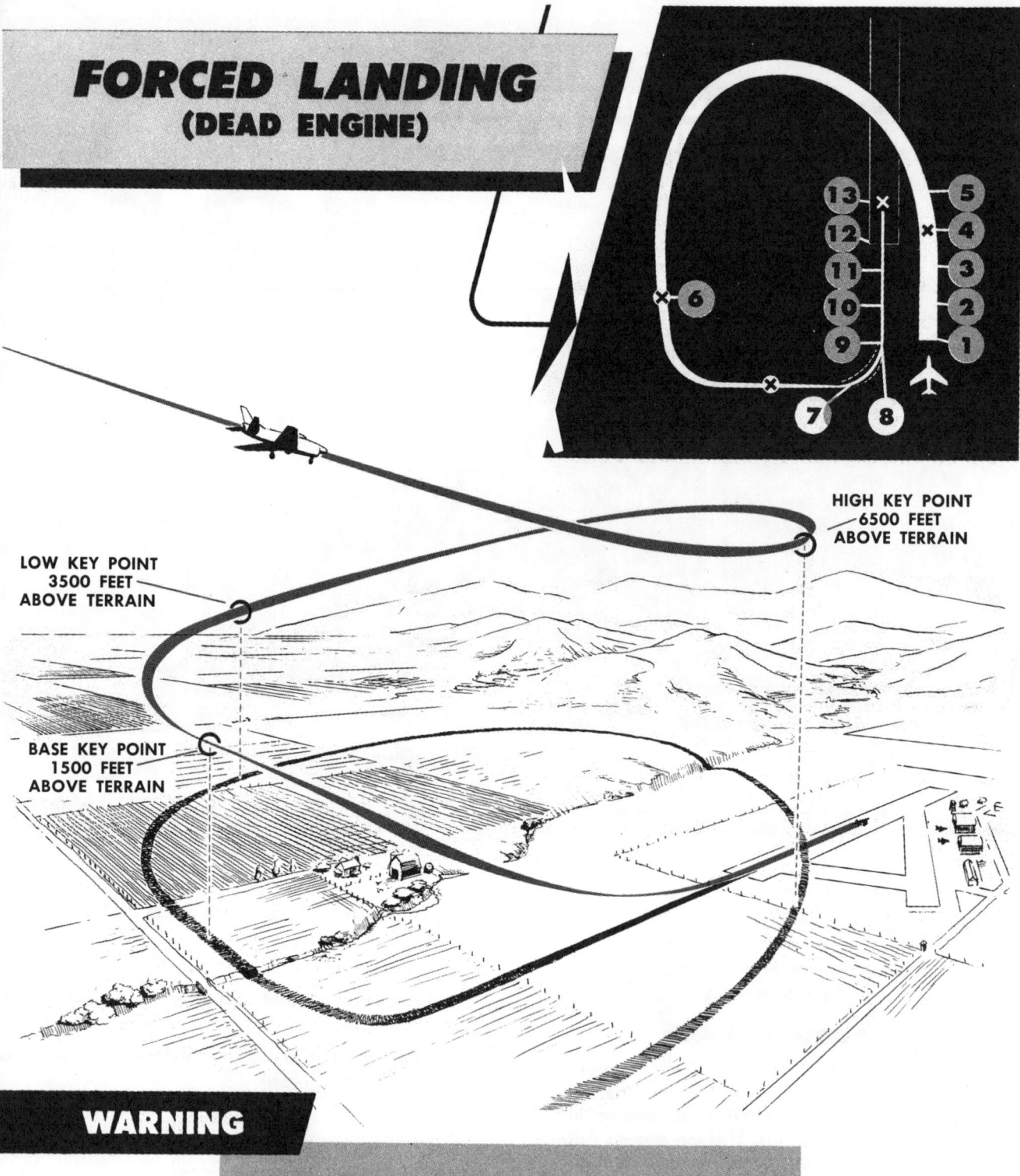

Figure 3-2

1. Throttle CLOSED.

2. Immediately attempt an air start if a mechanical malfunction is not apparent. (Refer to "Engine Air Start.")

Note

The actuation of the air start switch automatically shuts off electrical equipment not essential when making an air start. However, after the air start is made, turn off any electrical equipment not required.

3. If engine does not start before airspeed decreases to about 185 knots IAS, establish glide at 185 knots IAS, with landing gear and wing flaps up and speed brakes closed for maximum glide distance. (See figure 3-1.)

4. Repeat air start procedure.

If engine failure necessitates a forced landing, maximum gliding distance can be obtained by establishment of a glide of 185 knots IAS, with landing gear and wing flaps up, speed brakes closed. Unless engine is damaged, it will windmill at enough speed to operate all hydraulic controls, including the flight control normal hydraulic system. However, engine windmilling will be inadequate to provide generator power at any normal gliding speed. Operation of landing gear, wing flaps, and speed brakes will be considerably slower than normal. Since electrical power is being derived only from the battery, such power will be available for about 25 to 28 minutes with all unnecessary electrical equipment turned off, unless a failure of the flight control normal hydraulic system accompanies the engine failure. If this is the case, electrical power will be available for about 20 minutes only, and alternate system hydraulic accumulator pressure should be conserved by minimum movement of control surfaces. Operation from localities with low prevailing outside temperature causes more rapid loss of battery power. (See figure 1-19 for list of equipment powered by battery when battery-starter switch is at BATTERY and both generators are inoperative.)

ENGINE AIR START.

Although engine starts during flight (figure 3-3) are more readily obtainable below 40,000 feet, the air start should be attempted as soon as possible after flame-out. During the restart, if ignition does not occur within 20 seconds after throttle is opened, slowly retard throttle to CLOSED and then readvance throttle until a higher fuel pressure or fuel flow is reached. Repeat this procedure until ignition occurs or until one minute has elapsed, as a 5-second fuel accumulation drainage period should be allowed after each one-minute restart attempt. On some altitude restarts, the engine may be on the verge of compressor stall with throttle at START IDLE, and any

---

1 — Jettison external load (rocket package if loaded).

2 — Place engine master and generator switches OFF.

3 — Lower landing gear above 12,000 feet (field made).
If altitude is too low to enter pattern at HIGH KEY point, leave gear up until a later key point can be reached.

WARNING

Do not leave landing gear up for landing. Investigation has shown that emergency landings with gear down minimize pilot injury and damage to airplane.

NOTE

If engine is "frozen," lower gear by means of landing gear emergency lowering handle, because utility hydraulic pressure will not be available (gear cannot be retracted).

4 — Hold pattern speed of 170 knots IAS.

5 — Fly rectangular pattern, varying flight path to make key points. Aim for one-third point on runway.

6 — If landing on an unprepared surface, unlock canopy latches to allow air stream to carry canopy away.

7 — Fly turn "long" or "short" for accurate touchdown.

8 — Hold 150 knots IAS on final and use straight-in approach.

9 — Use flaps as necessary on final when sure of reaching landing spot.

10 — If overshooting, "S" turn, slip, or fishtail. Use speed brakes as necessary.

11 — Battery switch OFF only after speed brake operation is no longer necessary, then shoulder-harness lock handle LOCKED.

12 — Over end of runway at 140 knots IAS.

13 — Deploy drag chute only after touchdown and below 150 knots IAS.

ENGINE AIR START PROCEDURE

WHEN FLAMEOUT OCCURS

1 Throttle **CLOSED**.
To prevent flooding the engine with fuel.

2 Emergency fuel system switch **ON**.
The electronic engine control is inoperative with air start switch in **AIR START** (up).

3 Variable nozzle closed.
To aid in making an easier air start.

4 Air start switch to **AIR START** (up).
To reduce electrical load, providing maximum battery life.

5 Hold airplane as level as possible for at least 5 seconds to drain any fuel that may have accumulated in the engine. Attempt air start as soon as possible. However, starts are more readily obtained below 40,000 feet.

WARNING

WHEN AIR START SWITCH IS IN **AIR START** (UP) POSITION, EQUIPMENT POWERED BY THESE BUSSES IS INOPERATIVE:

SECONDARY BUS
MONITORED NO. 1 BUS
MONITORED NO. 2 BUS
MONITORED NO. 3 BUS
AC BUS
    WHICH
    INCLUDES

RADAR EQUIPMENT
RADIO EQUIPMENT
WING FLAP CONTROL
LANDING GEAR CONTROLS*
LANDING GEAR INDICATORS*
ELECTRONIC ENGINE CONTROLS

CAUTION

With air start switch at **AIR START** (up), do not move the battery-starter switch out of **BATTERY**, as a complete loss of fuel pump and ignition power could result.

*F-86D-1 and F-86D-5 Airplanes

F-86D-1-73-3B

attempt to advance the throttle will cause a complete stall. If this occurs, retard the throttle below initial position and then readvance it slowly, keeping exhaust temperature well within limits. If, after several attempts have been made, ignition does not occur before airplane has descended to an altitude of 10,000 feet above the ground and a forced landing is to be made, return air start switch to NORM (down) to re-establish radio communication and landing gear, landing light, and flap operation for landing. Refer to "Ejection," if engine failure necessitates bail-out.

MAXIMUM GLIDE.

For maximum glide distance, the most favorable gliding speed is 185 knots IAS with gear and flaps up, 160 knots IAS with gear down, and 140 knots IAS with gear and flaps down. These speeds apply with speed brakes closed and no external load. (See figure 3-1.)

LANDING WITH ENGINE INOPERATIVE.

If engine failure during flight necessitates a forced landing, a maximum gliding distance can be obtained by

RESTARTING

1. At 40,000 feet or below, air starts are readily obtained at engine speeds of 20% to 40% rpm.

2. Advance throttle until 25 pounds (at high altitudes) to 75 pounds (at low altitudes) fuel pressure or 250 pounds per hour (at high altitudes) to 750 pounds per hour (at low altitudes) fuel flow is indicated.

3. When ignition is indicated by rising exhaust temperature, very cautiously regulate throttle to maintain exhaust temperature of approximately 400°C until engine speed begins to stabilize.

4. When this stable range is reached, cautiously advance throttle to desired power setting, keeping exhaust temperature below 750°C.

5. Upon reaching 37% rpm or above, so that generators are again operating, return air start switch to **NORM** (down).

6. Wait until lockup indicator light is extinguished; then return variable-nozzle switch to **NORM**.

7. Then move the emergency fuel system switch to **NORM**.

> **CAUTION**
>
> If a sufficient warm-up period is not allowed before the emergency fuel system switch is moved to **NORM**, another flame-out may result. However, if main fuel system failure is suspected, leave emergency fuel system switch at **ON** and land as soon as practicable.

Figure 3-3

establishment of a glide of 185 knots IAS, with landing gear and wing flaps up, speed brakes closed.

Note

Braking action is difficult to feel between normal recommended touchdown airspeed of 120 knots IAS and when decelerating to 100 knots IAS. Maximum braking technique should be used immediately after touchdown by rapid on-off applications on brake pedals (about one second on, one second off), this pressure being applied very lightly at higher indicated airspeeds, with heavier pressure being applied as airplane decelerates under 100 knots IAS. With the utility hydraulic system pressure low or inoperative, brake boost pressures will drop with continued brake application. Braking action is still possible, but pedal pressures are extremely high.

The procedure outlined in figure 3-2 is recommended for a forced landing.

SIMULATED FORCED LANDING.

The normal concept of retarding the throttle to idle to practice flame-out forced landings does not apply with jet airplanes. With the throttle at START IDLE, the engine produces about 400 pounds of thrust, whereas a flame-out and windmilling engine create drag. Thus, with the engine at idle power, the rate of descent would be less and the glide distance would be greater than during an actual flame-out forced landing. To simulate the drag of a flame-out and windmilling engine, extended speed brakes are used. However, as the drag produced when the speed brakes are extended is greater than that of a windmilling engine, certain engine power has to be maintained. In the final approach, under actual forced landing conditions, it may be desired to extend speed brakes to prevent possible overshooting. This increased drag effect of speed brake extension can be simulated during a practice forced landing by removing engine power, by retarding throttle to START IDLE. As the idling engine still produces some thrust, touchdown will be slightly farther down the runway than during an actual flame-out landing. Familiarization with forced-landing techniques and procedures, as shown in figure 3-2, can be attained by accurately practicing forced landings, using the recommended engine power (established by extensive flight tests) and extended speed brakes to simulate a flame-out engine condition. Rate of descent, glide distance, and flight characteristics with the engine windmilling can be simulated above 12,000 feet by reducing the engine rpm to 74% (78% rpm for airplanes incorporating the new-type thrust selector), opening speed brakes, and establishing a glide speed of 185 knots IAS. Landing gear should be lowered at 12,000 feet, and a glide speed of 170 knots IAS initiated. If approach during practice forced landing is not as desired, make a normal go-around and repeat forced landing until desired efficiency is attained. If the engine seizes (rotor locked), the airplane characteristics in actual forced landings are not noticeably changed. Actually, the drag of the airplane with the engine rotor locked is slightly less than with a windmilling engine. Although the decreased drag results in a decreased rate of descent, the difference will not be easily discerned. Thus, the techniques developed for forced landings with a windmilling engine are also applicable for forced landings with engine in the rotor-locked condition.

FIRE.

FIRE-WARNING CIRCUITS.

The fire-warning system consists of two detector circuits, each circuit controlling a cockpit warning light. The forward circuit (a red indicating light) senses fire in the forward engine compartment and main wheel wells.* The aft circuit (an amber indicating light) senses overheat or fire in the afterburner compartment. The afterburner compartment is substantially more resistant to immediate fire damage than the forward engine compartment. This permits less drastic action in case the amber warning light comes on, as indicated in the following procedures.

Note
There is **no** fire extinguishing system on this airplane.

*F-86D-60 Airplane AF53-1007 and all later airplanes

ENGINE FIRE DURING STARTING.

If there is indication of fire:

1. Throttle CLOSED.

2. Engine master switch OFF.

3. Keep engine turning; however, if fire presists, press stop-starter button.

4. Battery-starter and generator switches OFF.

5. Leave airplane as quickly as possible.

ENGINE FIRE DURING TAKE-OFF.

Forward Fire-warning Light.

Illumination of the forward fire-warning light during take-off shows a fire in the forward engine section, necessitating immediate action. The exact procedure to follow will vary with each set of circumstances, and will depend upon altitude, airspeed, length of runway and overrun clearance remaining, location of populated areas, etc. The decision you make will depend on these factors. To help you decide, the following procedures are presented for your information.

Before Becoming Air-borne. If light comes on during ground roll, and enough runway or overrun area is available to allow for aborting the take-off, chop the throttle to OFF and jettison external load. Deploy drag chute and retract gear, if necessary. Abandon airplane immediately upon stopping, if fire is apparent.

After Becoming Air-borne. If light comes on after airplane is air-borne, and if enough runway is not available and overrun area is congested, preventing aborting take-off, the following is recommended if altitude is too low for a safe ejection.

1. Jettison external load.

2. Maintain power and immediately climb to a minimum safe ejection altitude; then eject. (See figure 3-5 for minimum safe ejection altitudes.)

Aft Fire-warning Light.

Illumination of the aft fire-warning light shows an overheat condition or possible fire in the aft section, necessitating action as follows:

Before Becoming Air-borne. If light comes on during ground roll, and enough runway and overrun area is available to abort the take-off:

1. Chop throttle to CLOSED.

2. Jettison external load.

3. Use maximum braking, and deploy drag chute, if necessary.

4. Abandon airplane immediately, if warning light is still on after stopping.

5. Turn engine master switch OFF, and then turn battery-starter switch OFF, if light is out.

After Becoming Air-borne. If light comes on and take-off cannot be aborted safely:

1. Retard throttle from AFTERBURNER range to Military Thrust and continue climb-out.

   a. If light is out, continue flight at reduced power, landing as soon as possible. It is remotely possible that fire may have damaged the fire detector circuit. To test the circuit, hold fire warning system test switch at TEST. If light comes on while the switch is at TEST, circuit is still operative.

   b. If light is not out with reduced power, maintain climb at reduced power and check for other signs of fire, such as trailing smoke, long exhaust flames, etc.

   c. If no fire is apparent, continue flight at reduced power, landing as soon as possible.

   d. If positive signs of fire exist, maintain power, immediately climb to a minimum safe ejection altitude, and eject. (See figure 3-5 for minimum safe ejection altitudes.)

ENGINE FIRE DURING FLIGHT.

Forward Fire-warning Light.

Illumination of the forward fire-warning light shows a fire in the forward engine section, necessitating immediate action as follows:

1. Chop throttle to the CLOSED position and place engine master switch at OFF.

2. If light is off and there is no other sign of continuing fire, such as smoke in cockpit, engine roughness, trailing smoke, verification from another airplane, etc, make a power-off emergency landing or eject. It is remotely possible that fire may have damaged the fire detector circuit. To test the circuit, hold fire-warning system test switch at TEST. If light comes on while the switch is at TEST, circuit is still operative.

3. If light remains on, or if light does not come on while fire-warning system test switch is at TEST, eject.

Aft Fire-warning Light.

Illumination of the aft fire-warning light shows an overheat condition or possible fire in the aft section, necessitating action as follows:

1. Reduce power in attempt to put out light.

   a. If light is out, continue flight at reduced power, landing as soon as possible. It is remotely possible that fire may have damaged the fire detector circuit. To test the circuit, hold fire-warning system test switch at TEST. If light comes on while the switch is at TEST, circuit is still operative.

   b. If light cannot be put out with throttle retarded to START IDLE, showing possible fire rather than overheat, or if light does not come on while fire-warning system test switch is at TEST, proceed to step 2.

2. Check for other signs of fire, such as trailing smoke, engine noise, verification from another airplane, etc.

   a. If no fire is apparent, continue flight at minimum power, landing as soon as possible.

   b. If positive signs of fire exist, proceed to step 3.

3. Chop throttle to CLOSED position and place engine master switch at OFF.

   a. If fire continues, eject.

   b. If fire ceases, make a power-off emergency landing or eject.

Note

During periods of prolonged afterburner operation at high altitudes and high airspeed, the aft fire-warning light may illuminate on airplanes using the J47-GE-33 engine and having drop tanks installed. Flight tests have shown that this can be prevented by maintaining airspeed at or below .90 Mach number and 35,000-foot altitude or below.

ENGINE FIRE AFTER SHUTDOWN.

If there is sign of fire in the engine or tail pipe after shutdown:

1. External power source connected to both receptacles.

2. Throttle CLOSED.

3. Battery-starter switch momentarily at STARTER.

4. Audibly check that engine begins to turn as starter is engaged, or note tachometer indication.

5. Allow engine to crank to about 9% rpm (one minute maximum); then press stop-starter button.

ELECTRICAL FIRE.

Circuit breakers and fuses protect most of the electrical circuits, to minimize the probability of electrical fires. However, if an electrical fire does occur, turn battery-starter and generator switches OFF, and land as soon as possible. Battery power will last from 25 to 28 minutes unless the flight control normal hydraulic system goes out. If the flight control alternate hydraulic system must be used, battery power will last only about 20 minutes and alternate hydraulic accumulator pressure should be conserved by minimum movement of control surfaces. Operation from bases with low prevailing outside temperatures will make loss of battery power even more rapid.

If it becomes necessary to move battery-starter and generator switches to OFF, the emergency fuel system will take over fuel control, regardless of the position of the emergency fuel system switch and without illuminating the emergency fuel system indicator light. Thus, all later throttle movements must be made cautiously to prevent compressor stall or flameout.

ELIMINATION OF SMOKE OR FUMES.

If smoke or fuel fumes enter the cockpit, proceed as follows:

Note

When necessary to depressurize cockpit at high altitude, first descend to 20,000 feet or less; then depressurize.

1. Cockpit air switch RAM (on F-86D-45 and later airplanes, move manual ram-air valve to OPEN).

2. Oxygen regulator diluter lever 100% OXYGEN.

3. Push oxygen regulator emergency toggle lever either way from center.

LANDING EMERGENCIES.

BELLY LANDING.

If a belly landing is unavoidable, proceed as follows:

1. After turning final approach, unlock canopy latches manually to allow air stream to break canopy away from fuselage.

WARNING

- Canopy should be released before landing, to prevent the possibility of being trapped in the cockpit if the fuselage warps and canopy jams in the closed position.
- Jettisoning the canopy after a belly landing during which the fuel tanks have ruptured can cause spilled fuel to ignite.

2. Jettison rocket package, if loaded; retain, if empty.

3. Jettison drop tanks if they contain fuel, or when landing on an unprepared surface.

WARNING

Empty drop tanks should be retained if landing on a prepared surface, to reduce possible pilot injury, impact damage, and fire hazard.

4. Make normal approach with flaps down, speed brakes open, and landing gear up.

5. Just before touchdown, close throttle and turn engine master switch OFF. Wait one second to allow fuel shutoff valve to close; then move battery-starter switch to OFF. If time permits, turn generator switches OFF.

6. Shoulder harness locked.

7. Touch down in normal landing attitude.

8. Deploy drag chute immediately after touchdown.

CAUTION

If drag chute is deployed at speeds in excess of approximately 160 knots IAS, it will automatically jettison.

F-86D-1-0-10A

Note

Flight tests have shown that a properly packed chute has the least compartment pull-out resistance and will deploy at speeds as low as 60 knots IAS in about 4 seconds. However, to ensure consistent and proper operation, it is recommended that the chute be deployed above 75 knots IAS.

9. Abandon airplane immediately after it stops.

ANY ONE GEAR UP OR UNLOCKED.

If any one gear will not extend or lock down, leave remaining gear down and proceed as follows:

1. After turning final approach, unlock canopy latches manually to allow air stream to break canopy away from fuselage.

WARNING

- Canopy should be released before landing, to prevent the possibility of being trapped in the cockpit if the fuselage warps and canopy jams in the closed position.
- Jettisoning the canopy after a belly landing during which the fuel tanks have ruptured can cause spilled fuel to ignite from a hot powder spark when canopy catapult is actuated.

2. Jettison rocket package, if loaded; retain, if empty.

3. Jettison drop tanks if they contain fuel, or when landing on an unprepared surface.

WARNING

Empty drop tanks should be retained if landing on a prepared surface, to reduce possible pilot injury, impact damage, and fire hazard.

4. Plan approach to touch down as near end of runway as possible.

5. Make normal approach with wing flaps down, speed brakes open.

6. Just before touchdown, close throttle and turn engine master switch OFF. Wait one second to allow fuel shutoff valve to close; then move battery-starter switch to OFF. If time permits, turn generator switches OFF.

7. Shoulder harness locked.

8. After touchdown, hold unlocked gear off as long as possible, easing it down to runway before flight controls become ineffective.

9. Deploy drag chute immediately after touchdown.

If chute is deployed at speeds in excess of about 160 knots IAS, the chute will automatically jettison.

10. Do not use brakes if you can stop without them.

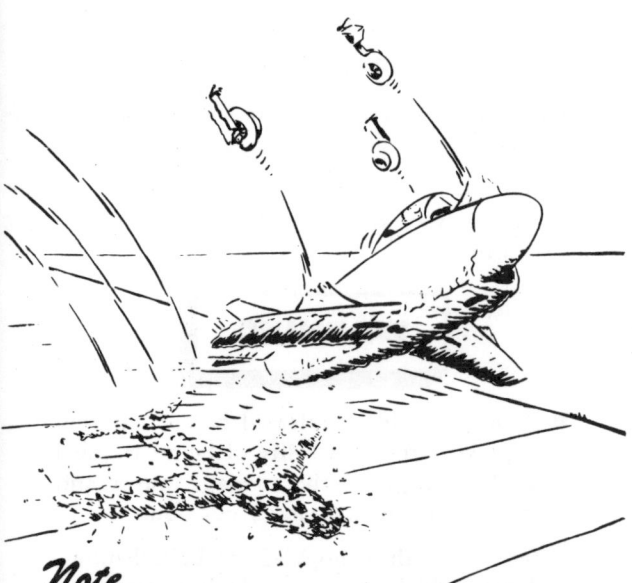

Note

If nose gear is down but unlocked and other emergency procedures have failed, you can attempt to snap it locked by making a touch-and-go landing. Make a power approach and touch the main gear to the runway with a slight bounce; then go around.

F-86D-1-0-16

ENGAGING RUNWAY BARRIER.

Successful engagements have been made with the nylon net overrun barrier in this airplane up to 130 knots ground speed. However, minimum speeds have been established which must be exceeded to ensure successful engagements. When the overrun barrier is to be engaged, you should engage it as close to the recommended minimum speeds as possible. Off-center engagements can be made successfully, but the airplane will swerve as a result of the webbing pulling unevenly on the nose wheel. This momentary swerve is not dangerous and therefore should be disregarded. If for any reason you are unable to bring the airplane to a stop or to a safe taxiing speed after a landing before reaching the end of the runway and if the runway is equipped with a nylon net overrun barrier, observe the following:

1. Avoid excessive braking during barrier engagement, to prevent tire blowouts.

2. With no external load installed, exceed minimum engagement speed of 17 knots ground speed.

3. With drop tanks installed, exceed minimum engagement speed of 40 knots ground speed.

4. Retract rocket package to make engagement.

Note

In cases of known emergency, jettison drop tanks before landing.

LANDING WITH FLAT TIRE.

When a landing is to be made with the nose gear tire flat, extend the gear in the normal manner and proceed as follows:

1. Hold nose wheel off runway as long as possible after main gear has touched down.

2. Use a combination of braking and nose wheel steering to maintain directional control.

When landing with a main gear tire flat, extend the gear in the normal manner and proceed as follows:

1. Land on the side of the runway away from the flat tire.

Note

This is necessary to minimize the requirement necessary for differential braking should the airplane pull toward the low tire.

2. Use a combination of braking and nose wheel steering to maintain directional control.

LOSS OF CANOPY.

The flight characteristics with or without the canopy are the same. Stall speeds with or without canopy remain unchanged, and the stall warning of general airframe buffet remains unchanged. At about 5 to 10 knots IAS above stall, turbulence around the empennage causes a directional oscillation with accompanying roll. Without the canopy, the noise level caused from airflow over the open cockpit is extremely disturbing, but not considered dangerous. If the canopy should come off during the take-off roll and there is not enough runway remaining to abort the take-off, it is recommended that the take-off be completed. Use higher power settings and maintain normal approach speed during landing. The normal approach speed is 30 knots IAS above stall speed; however, it should be remembered that, if a landing is made immediately after take-off, the airplane weight will be higher than normal and therefore the approach and touchdown speeds will be higher. The stall speeds and the recommended approach and touchdown speeds for various conditions are shown in figure 6-2.

EMERGENCY ENTRANCE.

See figure 3-4.

EMERGENCY ENTRANCE

NOTE:
On F-86D-1 Airplanes, if canopy cannot be readily lifted off, emergency entrance must be made forcibly.

WARNING

When canopy is removed, the ejection seat is armed.

1 Pull canopy emergency release handle to release canopy latches. Then, to complete canopy opening electrical circuit, close access door or hold switch depressed with finger while opening canopy electrically by pushing external control button marked "OPEN." Hold button fully depressed until canopy is completely open.

2 If the canopy will not open, lift canopy with handholds in canopy frame and remove canopy from airplane. It may be necessary to pull and hold extended (or secure in extended position) the canopy hook release in order to free canopy.

WARNING

Avoid unnecessary handling of any portion of seat and canopy firing mechanisms at all times and stay clear of line of canopy ejection.

3 Determine position of seat armrests.

If both seat armrests are in normal down or stowed position, complete rescue operation, being sure to keep clear of armrests at all times.

If either armrest is raised:
A. On airplanes that have mechanically actuated seat catapults, insert a safety pin in the fore-and-aft hole in seat catapult. The seat catapult sear lever may be moved *up* slightly in order to align the hole for insertion of the safety pin. Then complete rescue operation.

WARNING

- If original safety pin is in seat catapult, DO NOT REMOVE IT.
- Do not move sear lever *down* to align hole, since such movement will set off seat catapult charge and eject seat.

B. On airplanes that have gas-actuated seat catapults, disarm catapult by cutting or disconnecting* hose leading from seat catapult to "T" fitting on back of seat. Cut hose as close to seat catapult as possible. Make sure that loose hose ends are not aligned; otherwise, if seat initiators fire accidentally, expanding gases still may actuate catapult exactor and cause seat to fire.

*Use 9/16-inch open-end wrench.

Figure 3-4

Warning

If the airplane is ditched in a near-level attitude, it will dive violently after contact.

DITCHING.

Note

Inspect emergency equipment, parachute, life vest, and raft pack before each overwater flight.

Ditch only as a last resort. All emergency survival equipment is carried by the pilot; therefore, there is no advantage in riding the airplane down. However, if altitude is not sufficient for emergency exit, and ditching is unavoidable, proceed as follows:

1. Follow radio distress procedure.

2. Jettison drop tanks and rocket package.

3. See that no personal equipment will foul when you leave the cockpit. Disconnect anti-G suit and radio leads. Leave oxygen hose connected until ready to leave cockpit. Remove oxygen mask as you leave the cockpit.

Note

In the event of ditching and sinking in water where you find yourself unable to immediately escape because of any number of factors, it is possible for you to survive under water with your oxygen equipment until you can free yourself and escape. It is essential that the mask be in place and tightly strapped, and that the regulator be set at 100% OXYGEN, but remember the bail-out bottle cannot be used under water.

4. Make sure safety belt is tight.

5. Check landing gear up and speed brakes closed.

6. Unlock canopy latches to allow air stream to carry canopy away.

7. Throttle CLOSED.

8. Wing flap lever DOWN. Flaps collapse on impact and do not tend to make airplane dive.

9. Turn engine master switch OFF.

10. Wait one second to allow fuel shutoff valve to close; then move battery-starter switch to OFF. If time permits, turn generator switches OFF.

11. Shoulder harness locked.

12. Unless wind is high or sea is rough, plan approach heading parallel to any uniform swell pattern and try to touch down along wave crest or just after crest passes. If wind is as high as 25 knots or surface is irregular, the best procedure is to approach into the wind and touch down on the falling side of a wave.

13. Make normal approach and flare out to normal landing attitude, being careful to keep the nose high.

EJECTION.

In all cases of ejection, escape must be made by means of seat ejection. For ejection seat operation, see figure 3-5.

Manual opening of the automatic safety belt is considered unnecessary and undesirable for the following reasons: Normal operation of the automatic-opening safety belt requires about 2 seconds for the safety belt to open after ejection. This time element is faster than manual operation and is considered sufficient to assist in deceleration, since deceleration of the pilot alone, without the seat, is considerably greater. Immediate separation from the seat could result in serious injury from deceleration or the parachute blowing open accidentally, as well as possible damage to the parachute due to opening shock. Manual opening of the automatic safety belt requires one more step before ejection, and creates a hazard during uncontrollable flight, as the pilot cannot stay in the seat before ejection if negative G is incurred. The automatic arming feature of the parachute is eliminated unless the pilot arms his parachute by pulling the arming lanyard. Except for failure of the safety belt automatic-opening device, manual opening should not be made at any altitude or speed.

WARNING

- Should the automatic-opening safety belt fail to open in about 2 seconds after ejection, the belt may be opened manually in the same manner as a conventional safety belt. However, when the belt is opened manually, the chute (either manual or automatic-opening type) must then be opened by pulling the "D" ring.

- When overwater ejection is made, remove oxygen mask before hitting water, to prevent sucking water into the mask.

FAILURE OF SEAT TO EJECT.

If the seat does not eject when the triggers are squeezed, proceed as follows:

1. Unfasten safety belt, actuate bail-out bottle (if necessary), and disconnect personal leads (oxygen, radio, face mask antifrost lead, and anti-G suit).

2. If you have control of the airplane, trim nose down and pull stick back to slow airplane as much as possible; then invert airplane. Maintain positive G-load until inverted; then sharply release stick and push free of seat. If you do not have control of the airplane, slow airplane as much as possible, then bail out over the side.

3. Pull automatic parachute arming lanyard or, if at low altitude, pull "D" ring.

Note

If you lose your oxygen mask and you do not have an automatic parachute, you should "free-fall" to as low an altitude as possible, then pull "D" ring. The length of time you can "free-fall" before anoxia prevents you from pulling the "D" ring depends on your physical condition and bail-out altitude.

AFTERBURNER FAILURE.

LOSS OF AFTERBURNING DURING TAKE-OFF.

If afterburner failure occurs during ground roll, abort take-off by immediately closing throttle, applying brakes as necessary, and deploying drag chute if required.

LOSS OF AFTERBURNING DURING CLIMB-OUT.

If afterburner fails after airplane is air-borne and take-off is to be continued, automatic closing of the variable nozzle should restore operation to Military Thrust in about 2 seconds. (If proper response to automatic closing of nozzle is not obtained, manually close nozzle to desired position.) The throttle should be rapidly retarded from AFTERBURNER range upon afterburner failure. If afterburner failure occurs and engine controls are in lockup, move emergency fuel system switch to ON and retard throttle to mid-throttle position, jog nozzle closed, and cautiously readvance throttle to desired power setting. In addition, retract landing gear immediately, and flaps as soon as a safe airspeed is reached; leave wing flap lever at UP. Remember, with the emergency fuel system switch ON, the emergency fuel system is in control, and all throttle advancements must be slow, smooth, and gradual to prevent compressor stall or flame-out. When a safe altitude is reached, the inverter selector switch should be moved to SPARE, on airplanes equipped with manual inverter change-over; on airplanes equipped with automatic inverter change-over, the secondary inverter will be automatically selected. After lockup indicator light is out, move emergency fuel system switch to NORM.

CAUTION

When switching from ON to NORM, a momentary drop in rpm to about 70% will occur because the main fuel valve has not had time to open to a Military Thrust setting. As the main fuel control assumes engine control, rpm will return to the required setting. Do not return switch to ON during this transition, as a compressor stall may result.

LOSS OF AFTERBURNING DURING FLIGHT.

When loss of afterburning occurs during flight, the automatic closing of the variable nozzle will restore full Military Thrust in about 2 seconds. The throttle should immediately be retarded from the AFTERBURNER range. An attempt should be made to relight the afterburner, watching for any signs of abnormal operation. If all cockpit indications of afterburner operation are normal on the relight, continue afterburner operation.

AFTERBURNER SHUTOFF FAILURE.

If retarding the throttle below the MILITARY stop does not shut off the afterburner, move the afterburner shutoff switch to OFF. This will change the forward and

EJECTION SEAT

1 RAISE RIGHT ARMREST TO FULL UP POSITION TO JETTISON CANOPY. RAISE LEFT ARMREST TO LOCK SHOULDER HARNESS.
   F-86D-1 THROUGH F-86D-35 AIRPLANES

RAISE EITHER ARMREST TO FULL UP POSITION TO JETTISON CANOPY AND TO LOCK SHOULDER HARNESS (ARMRESTS INTERCONNECTED).
   F-86D-40 AND SUBSEQUENT AIRPLANES

WARNING

BEFORE EJECTION BELOW 2000 FEET ABOVE THE TERRAIN (AIRPLANE IN AN UPRIGHT POSITION), UNFASTEN SAFETY BELT MANUALLY (ONLY IF EQUIPPED WITH A MANUAL-TYPE SAFETY BELT) TO AID IN SEPARATING FROM THE SEAT. AFTER SEPARATION, PULL PARACHUTE "D" RING IMMEDIATELY TO OPEN EITHER CONVENTIONAL OR AUTOMATIC-TYPE PARACHUTE.

IN A DIVE, MANUALLY OPEN SAFETY BELT (MANUAL BELT ONLY) _BEFORE_ EJECTION AT ALTITUDES BELOW 5000 FEET. FOR ALTITUDES ABOVE 5000 FEET, DO NOT OPEN THE MANUAL SAFETY BELT UNTIL _AFTER_ EJECTION, ESPECIALLY AT EXTREMELY HIGH AIRSPEEDS.

AT ALTITUDE, ACTUATE BAIL-OUT BOTTLE.

Figure 3-5

OPERATION

2 SQUEEZE TRIGGER TO EJECT SEAT (EITHER TRIGGER ON F-86D-40 AND SUBSEQUENT AIRPLANES).

IF CANOPY FAILS TO EJECT...

F-86D-1 THROUGH F-86D-35 AIRPLANES, THE SEAT CANNOT BE EJECTED.

F-86D-40 AND SUBSEQUENT AIRPLANES, SQUEEZE EITHER TRIGGER TO EJECT SEAT THROUGH CANOPY.

IF TIME AND CONDITIONS PERMIT BEFORE EJECTION

OBSERVE THE FOLLOWING:

1. Hook heels in footrests, and brace arms in armrests. Sit erect, head hard back against headrest, chin tucked in.
2. Stow all loose equipment.

AFTER EJECTION

- Release safety belt; then kick free of seat.*
- *If safety belt fails to open automatically after 2 seconds*, manually unfasten belt and kick free of seat. Then pull parachute arming lanyard.
- *If pilot is wearing automatic parachute WITH lanyard key inserted into safety belt buckle*, parachute opens at a preset altitude after pilot kicks free of seat. (Parachute opens 2 seconds after seat separation if below a preset altitude.)
- *If wearing automatic parachute WITHOUT lanyard key*, kick free of seat and pull parachute arming lanyard.
- *If wearing manually operated parachute*, kick free of seat; pull "D" ring at altitude where normal breathing is possible.

*For use on airplanes that have a manually operated safety belt

MINIMUM SAFE EJECTION ALTITUDES ABOVE THE TERRAIN ARE AS FOLLOWS:

1. WITH MANUAL SAFETY BELT AND MANUAL-TYPE PARACHUTE ..... 2000 FEET
2. WITH AUTOMATIC SAFETY BELT AND MANUAL-TYPE PARACHUTE ..... 1000 FEET
3. WITH AUTOMATIC SAFETY BELT AND AUTOMATIC-TYPE PARACHUTE (IF PARACHUTE-ATTACHED LANYARD KEY IS INSERTED INTO SAFETY BELT BUCKLE) ..... 500 FEET

WARNING
After leaving seat, manually pull "D" ring for all ejections below 2000 feet, to open parachute immediately.

aft fuel booster pumps and dual pumps to low speed* and shut off the afterburner turbine-driven fuel pump, which allows the afterburner fuel shutoff valve to close.

VARIABLE-AREA NOZZLE AUTOMATIC CONTROL FAILURE.

A malfunction of the automatic control of the variable-area nozzle will be shown by improper response of the nozzle to throttle movement, or inability to hold engine exhaust temperature near the Military Thrust limit. Control the nozzle opening by moving the variable-nozzle switch to OPEN or CLOSE, as necessary. The switch will return to OFF when released. Do not attempt to light the afterburner with variable-nozzle switch at OFF. Do not move the variable-nozzle switch from NORMAL unless failure of the nozzle automatic control is shown, or unless emergency fuel switch is moved to ON during a lockup condition. The nozzle will move more slowly when actuated by means of the nozzle switch than when automatically controlled.

MAIN FUEL CONTROL SYSTEM FAILURE.

MAIN FUEL CONTROL SYSTEM FAILURE DURING TAKE-OFF AND CLIMB.

On airplanes equipped with the three-position emergency fuel system switch, a main fuel control system failure during take-off and climb will not be shown, except for a slight drop in rpm down to the emergency fuel system setting, when the emergency fuel system switch is at TAKE OFF position. However, when the emergency fuel system switch is moved out of TAKE OFF, a failure will be evidenced by rapid decrease in engine speed or by no response when throttle is retarded. In either case, immediately move emergency fuel system switch to ON. One type of failure that may occur in the main fuel control system during take-off and climb will result in full or partial closing of the main fuel control valve. If the emergency fuel system switch is at TAKE OFF when such a failure occurs, the emergency fuel regulator will take over automatically, and the only sign of the failure will be a drop of 4% to 10% in engine rpm. (The emergency fuel system indicator light will be on whenever the emergency fuel system switch is at TAKE OFF or ON.)

CAUTION

- A drop in rpm may result from causes other than failure of the main fuel control system and automatic take-over by the emergency fuel regulator. Leave emergency fuel system switch at TAKE OFF during take-off if a slight rpm decrease is noticed. Wait until safe altitude is reached, and then move emergency fuel system switch to NORM. If any decrease in rpm is evident, showing failure of the main fuel control system, immediately move switch to ON.

- If engine speed is inadvertently allowed to drop below 85% rpm before switch is moved to the ON position, the throttle should be retarded to START IDLE before the emergency fuel system switch is placed ON, to prevent an overtemperature condition.

On those airplanes with the two-position emergency fuel switch installed, the switch will be in the NORM position for take-off and climb, and the emergency fuel regulator will not be in the "stand-by condition." Therefore, it will be necessary for the pilot to recognize a main fuel control failure (shown by rpm drop and decrease in exhaust temperature) and immediately move the emergency fuel switch to ON. If main fuel control system failure occurs:

1. On airplanes with the three-position emergency fuel switch, move switch to ON when a safe altitude is reached. On airplanes with the two-position emergency fuel switch, move switch to ON as soon as failure is detected.

CAUTION

If engine speed is allowed to drop below 85% rpm before switch is moved to the ON position, retard throttle to START IDLE; then move switch to ON to prevent an overtemperature condition.

2. Retard throttle from AFTERBURNER to MILITARY. If the automatic control of the nozzle does not work properly, the nozzle can be closed manually by movement of the variable-nozzle switch to CLOSE and then OFF. If the nozzle works automatically, it will move toward a closed position as the throttle is moved to MILITARY, even if the emergency fuel system is controlling the engine. Failure of the main fuel control system during take-off and climb to altitude, which results in locking of the main fuel control valve, may not be detected until the lower fuel requirements of increased altitude produce a gradual increase in engine rpm or until the throttle is retarded after take-off and there is no response. Such a failure necessitates operation through the emergency fuel system, and the emergency fuel system switch should be moved to ON.

---

*F-86D-1 through F-86D-40 Airplanes

MAIN FUEL CONTROL SYSTEM FAILURE DURING FLIGHT.

If the main fuel control system fails during flight, a landing must be made using the emergency fuel system. The throttle should not be retarded to START IDLE during a landing approach if the emergency fuel system is used, since the time required to accelerate the engine from speeds below 40% rpm may be excessive if a go-around is necessary. Therefore, caution must be exercised to maintain the rpm above 40% when operating on the emergency fuel system during an approach.

Failure of the main fuel control system, with a resulting excessively open position of the main fuel control valve, will be evidenced by engine overspeeding to the overspeed governor setting and/or stalling. Should such a failure occur, the emergency fuel system switch should be moved immediately to ON.

Sudden loss of fuel pressure, or fuel flow, and any decrease in engine rpm during flight show failure of the main fuel control system (unless fuel starvation has occurred) and necessitate operation on the emergency fuel regulator. To recover power following failure of the main fuel control system:

1. Retard throttle to START IDLE (if rpm drops below 85%).

2. Move emergency fuel system switch ON.

3. Slowly readvance throttle.

When the emergency fuel system is in operation, throttle movement must be slow and smooth to avoid flame-out or engine overtemperature, particularly at high altitudes.

4. With variable-nozzle switch, jog nozzle to desired position. Return nozzle switch to OFF to lock nozzle in position.

5. If engine flame-out occurs before throttle is readvanced, attempt an air start. (Refer to "Engine Air Start.")

FUEL SYSTEM TRANSFER PUMP FAILURE.

Service tests have shown that erratic engine operation may occur with airplane in high angles of attack (during landing approaches) with low fuel supply, if the aft fuselage tank transfer pump fails during flight. If evidence of fuel starvation (fuel pressure or fuel flow fluctuation and rpm drop-off on both the main and emergency fuel systems) occurs, attempt to regain rpm by lowering the nose of the airplane. If altitude permits, plan a power-off approach and landing pattern. Make sure to allow for the increase in rate of descent during final approach. However, if emergency conditions dictate and power must be used, fly at the minimum angle of attack, which permits a minimum rate of descent at approach airspeeds. Use power (and if necessary, speed brakes) to give any one of the following conditions. These conditions permit use of all fuel except 14 gallons that is trapped in the aft fuselage tank.

APPROACH SPEED (Knots IAS)	MINIMUM RATE OF DESCENT (FPM)
140	1500
150	1200
160	1000

On late airplanes,* and airplanes changed by T. O. 1F-86D-514, the aft fuselage fuel tank feeding characteristics have been improved. The added features of this system prevent the possibility of trapping fuel in the aft tank, regardless of airplane attitude, thereby allowing all fuel to be available to the engine.

ELECTRICAL SYSTEM EMERGENCY OPERATION.

FAILURE OF ONE GENERATOR.

If a generator warning light comes on, showing that one generator has failed or has been disconnected because of overvoltage, equipment powered by the monitored bus No. 3 and the secondary inverter will be automatically shut off. Attempt to bring the generator back into the circuit as follows:

1. Move voltmeter selector switch to related generator position.

2. Hold related generator switch at RESET momentarily; then turn switch ON. If warning light remains out and the voltmeter shows normal system voltage, it shows that the overvoltage was temporary; leave generator switch ON.

3. If warning light comes on again, turn generator switch OFF.

FAILURE OF BOTH GENERATORS.

If both generator warning lights come on, showing that both generators are out, equipment powered by monitored busses No. 2 and 3 and dc gyro power will

*F-86D-60 Airplane AF53-857 and all later airplanes

be shut off. This will result in loss of power from the primary inverter to the ac bus.

> **CAUTION**
>
> The electronic engine control is inoperative when ac power is cut off. To provide later engine control on the emergency fuel system, the emergency fuel system switch should be immediately placed to ON. All later throttle movements must be made cautiously to prevent compressor stall or flame-out.

With ac power removed, the fuel flowmeter, fuel quantity, fuel pressure, oil pressure, and hydraulic pressure gages will be inoperative. These instruments, while inoperative, will deceptively continue to show the condition that existed at the time of power failure. Attempt to bring the generators back into the circuit as follows:

1. Immediately set emergency fuel system switch at ON.

2. Immediately shut off all nonessential electrical equipment to reduce load on battery.

Note

Failure of both generators does not automatically turn off all nonessential equipment. In order to effectively prolong battery life, you must turn off equipment you don't absolutely need.

3. Move voltmeter selector switch to related position and momentarily hold one generator switch at RESET.

4. If related warning light does not go out, turn generator switch OFF and attempt to reset other generator.

5. If related warning light does go out, make a single attempt to reset other generator.

> **CAUTION**
>
> Repeated attempts to reset the inoperative generator may result in disconnecting the operative generator. If this occurs, leave the inoperable generator switch OFF and again reset the operable generator.

6. When at least one generator is operating, wait 2 minutes to allow electronic engine control to warm up; then move emergency fuel system switch to NORM.

On F-86D-1 through F-86D-50 Airplanes, if neither generator can be turned on, attempt to reset one generator as follows:

1. Attempt to bring voltage to 28 volts by adjusting the voltage regulator rheostat with generator switches OFF. A maximum of 31 volts is allowable in an emergency if voltage cannot be decreased to 28 volts. Hold one generator switch momentarily at RESET again, and then turn switch ON. If corresponding generator warning light remains out, check voltage and readjust regulator rheostat as necessary to obtain normal system voltage.

2. If one generator cannot be turned on in this manner, move the related generator switch to OFF and attempt to turn on the other one in the same way.

> **CAUTION**
>
> If one generator is operating, do not use the voltage regulator rheostat in an attempt to turn on the other one, as this may result in both generators becoming inoperative.

If a complete electrical failure should occur, or if for any reason it becomes necessary to move both battery-starter and generator switches to OFF, remember that most equipment and controls will be inoperative without electrical power. See figure 1-19 for equipment powered by battery bus.

> **CAUTION**
>
> If a complete electrical power failure occurs, or if it becomes necessary to move the battery-starter and generator switches to OFF, the emergency fuel system will take over fuel control, regardless of the position of the emergency fuel system switch and without illuminating the emergency fuel system indicator light. Thus, all later throttle movements must be made cautiously to prevent compressor stall or flame-out.

Flight under these conditions will be limited, and the following precautionary measures should be observed:

1. If possible, reduce airspeed and readjust trim before turning off electrical power, as trim is not available with the loss of electrical power.

2. If necessary, reduce altitude and engine rpm to maintain satisfactory engine operation, as the fuel booster and transfer pump are inoperative when electrical power is shut off.

3. Land as soon as possible.

Note

Use landing gear emergency lowering system to ensure that gear lowers and locks (refer to "Landing Gear Emergency Lowering" in this section). When electrical power is not available to the primary bus, landing gear position indicators will be inoperative and will continuously show an unsafe condition.

INVERTER FAILURE (AUTOMATIC LOCKUP SYSTEM).

When failures of the main inverter or both inverters occur, such failures are shown by the inverter warning lights coming on. Should inverters fail while operating under electronic engine control, no manual emergency procedures are mandatory until power changes are required. The automatic lockup system automatically locks the electronic engine controls in position and illuminates the amber engine control lockup indicator light. (Refer to "Automatic Lockup System Characteristics" in Section VII.) On F-86D-1 through F-86D-50 Airplanes, failure of the main inverter causes the "MAIN" inverter failure warning light to come on; the secondary inverter is automatically selected to assume the load of the failed main inverter. On F-86D-55 and later airplanes and those changed by T.O., failure of the main inverter (with inverter selector switch at MAIN) causes both the "MAIN" and "BOTH" inverter failure warning lights to come on. The inverter selector switch must then be moved to SPARE; this will allow the secondary inverter to assume the load of the failed main inverter and extinguish the "BOTH" inverter failure warning light.

Inverter Failure During Take-off Roll.

If during the take-off roll, the main inverter fails (shown by inverter failure warning light or lights coming on) and the engine controls automatically lock up (shown by the engine control lockup light coming on) and it is desired to continue the take-off in a locked up condition, follow this procedure:

1. Continue take-off and climb to a safe altitude, leaving throttle set at Maximum Thrust.

2. On airplanes equipped with manual inverter change-over, move inverter selector switch to SPARE. On airplanes equipped with the automatic inverter change-over, the secondary inverter is automatically selected.

Note

The engine controls will automatically unlock when ac power is restored (above about 98 volts) and the electronic engine control will then govern engine operation.

3. If lockup light does not go out within 30 seconds, move emergency fuel switch to ON, rapidly retard throttle to START IDLE, jog nozzle closed, and cautiously readvance throttle to desired power setting.

4. Land as soon as practical.

If during the take-off roll, the main inverter fails (shown by inverter failure warning light or lights coming on) and the engine controls automatically lock up (shown by the engine control lockup light coming on) and it is desired to abort the take-off, perform the following:

1. Rapidly retard throttle to START IDLE.

Note

On airplanes with the three-position emergency fuel switch, this action automatically converts engine control to the emergency fuel system by actuation of the 72-degree thrust selector switch. On airplanes with the two-position emergency fuel switch, the throttle has to be retarded with enough force to actuate the idle detent switch.

2. Apply brakes as necessary.

WARNING

- The heat generated in the brake during an aborted take-off continues to build up during taxiing operation back to take-off position. This heat is transmitted to the wheel and into the tire itself. This heat in the tire melts the rubber and weakens the cords until the casing blows out.

- After an aborted take-off, for any reason, the airplane must be taxied back to the line. Shut down engine. Make sure brake assembly is cool enough to touch by hand before flight.

3. Position emergency fuel system switch to ON before readvancing the throttle.

4. On airplanes equipped with inverter selector switch, place switch at SPARE.

5. Readvance throttle as desired for taxiing, keeping in mind that all throttle movements must be made cautiously during operation on emergency fuel system.

6. When it is certain that the electronic engine control lockup is removed (engine control lockup light and inverter failure warning lights are no longer on), the emergency fuel system switch may be set to NORM.

Inverter Failure During Flight.

If during flight, the amber engine control lockup indicator light comes on (showing that ac power has failed and the electronic engine control is in automatic lockup), maintain altitude and power settings. If conditions arise that require power readjustment before automatic unlocking of the engine electronic controls, it will be necessary to change to the emergency fuel system to restore engine control. The switch-over to the emergency fuel system is accomplished as follows:

1. Move emergency fuel system switch to ON and rapidly retard throttle to START IDLE.

2. Manually close variable nozzle as desired; then return variable-nozzle switch to OFF to lock nozzle in desired position.

3. Advance throttle cautiously to desired power setting.

4. On airplanes equipped with automatic inverter change-over, if engine control lockup indicator light goes out (showing ac voltage is restored), engine control may be returned to the electronic engine control system as desired. On airplanes equipped with manual inverter change-over, the inverter selector switch must be placed at SPARE before the lockup indicator light will go out. Placing the switch at SPARE selects the secondary inverter as the electronic engine control power source. When power is restored, the lockup system requires about 15 seconds to release the lockup condition.

Note

On F-86D-1 through F-86D-50 Airplanes, the lockup indicator light should go out in about 10 to 25 seconds, and the electronic engine control will be restored automatically. On F-86D-55 and later airplanes, it will be necessary to switch to SPARE (secondary inverter) manually.

If automatic electronic engine control lockup occurs during approach or landing, position throttle at about mid-throttle position before moving emergency fuel system switch to ON.

LANDING GEAR EMERGENCY OPERATION.

LANDING GEAR EMERGENCY RETRACTION.

If it is necessary to retract gear during take-off, move landing gear handle UP, press emergency retract button, and hold button down until landing gear retracts.

Note

- Use of the emergency retract button is effective only if hydraulic pressure and battery power are available.
- The nose gear will not retract if the landing gear has been lowered by means of the emergency lowering system.

Landing Gear Retraction Emergency.

During flight, the following condition may be encountered. The landing gear red unsafe warning light may remain on after landing gear handle is placed at UP. This does not necessarily constitute an emergency condition, but under certain conditions, air loads on the landing gear doors can prevent the gear from retracting. This would be shown by a safe "down" indication on all three gear, with the unsafe warning light on and the handle at UP. If such a condition occurs, proceed as follows: Leave landing gear handle at UP, maintain a straight flight path to minimize G and eliminate yaw, and reduce speed to below 185 knots IAS (155 to 160 knots IAS is recommended to minimize air load on doors). If a safe indication is obtained from this procedure, continue flight. However, if unsafe condition still exists, extend the gear, and when a safe indication is obtained, return for landing. If mission is of importance, maintain straight flight path to minimize G and eliminate yaw, hold airspeed below 185 knots IAS (155 to 160 knots IAS is recommended) and cycle gear down and up. If unsafe warning light goes out, continue mission; if unsafe light remains on, extend gear and land as soon as practicable.

LANDING GEAR EMERGENCY LOWERING.

See figure 3-6.

FLIGHT CONTROL HYDRAULIC SYSTEM FAILURE.

If flight control normal hydraulic system pressure drops below a set value (about 650 psi), the flight control alternate system is automatically engaged, if alternate system pressure is available. The alternate system will supply pressure for all normal flight requirements. If the flight control normal system fails, use the following procedure:

1. Check that flight control alternate system indicator light is on, showing that alternate system is in control.

2. Move hydraulic pressure gage selector switch to ALTER (FLT. CONT. EMERG. on F-86D-1 Airplanes) and constantly check alternate system pressure.

3. Do not continue prolonged flight; land as soon as practicable.

4. If the flight control normal hydraulic system fails, and even though the alternate system is engaged automatically, pull the flight control emergency handle just before entering the traffic pattern, to ensure positive, continuous engagement of the alternate system during the landing phase.

Note

This action will prevent cycling from the alternate system to the failed normal system and a possible momentary "freezing" of the controls.

5. If automatic transfer to flight control alternate system does not occur and flight controls remain inoperative, pull flight control emergency handle to full extension (about 2½ inches) to manually engage flight control alternate system.

Pull emergency handle only if automatic transfer to alternate system does not occur; otherwise, the alternate system pump will operate continuously and drain the battery power (if generators are inoperative).

LANDING GEAR EMERGENCY LOWERING

1 REDUCE AIRSPEED TO LESS THAN 175 KNOTS IAS.

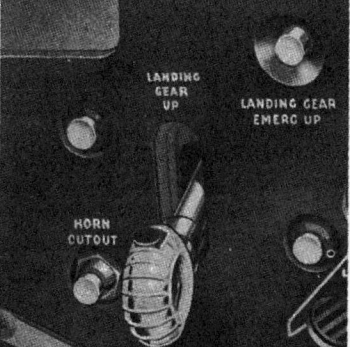

2 LANDING GEAR HANDLE *DOWN.*

3 LANDING GEAR EMERGENCY RELEASE HANDLE FULLY EXTENDED, APPROXIMATELY 14 INCHES, AND HOLD.

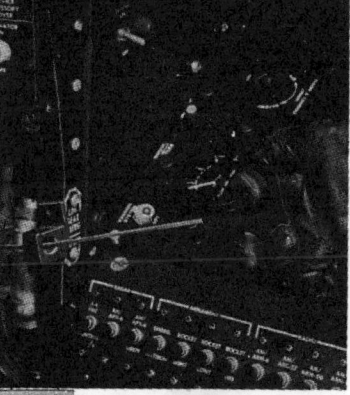

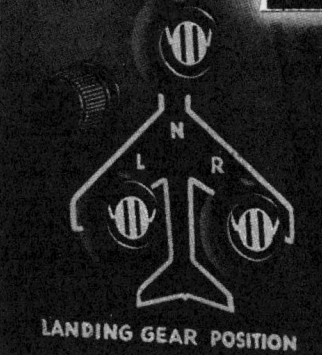

4 CHECK GEAR POSITION INDICATOR FOR SAFE GEAR INDICATION. IF NECESSARY, YAW AIRPLANE TO LOCK MAIN GEAR. RELEASE EMERGENCY RELEASE HANDLE AND CHECK GEAR UNSAFE WARNING LIGHT OUT.

F-86D-1-33-1A

Figure 3-6

WARNING

If the flight control normal and alternate hydraulic systems fail, control stick forces will be extremely high. Reduce airspeed to about 200 knots IAS and attempt to maintain control by varying the power settings and applying steady push and pull forces on the stick, allowing the air loads to streamline the control surfaces. If control cannot be maintained, eject. If some control is possible, however, and if altitude permits, attempt to effect recovery and return to a suitable area; then eject, as landing with these high stick forces should not be attempted under any circumstances.

FLIGHT CONTROL ARTIFICIAL FEEL SYSTEM FAILURE.

Artificial feel system failure can be indicated by a lightening of stick forces (resulting in overcontrol), lack of trim response, and poor stick centering characteristics. Failure of the flight control artificial feel control system will result in loss of adequate control. Reduction of engine power may relieve severe oscillation of the airplane; however, when such a failure occurs, ejection is recommended.

HORIZONTAL TAIL NORMAL TRIM FAILURE.

If a failure of the normal trim control for the controllable horizontal tail occurs, the controllable horizontal tail can be trimmed through use of the alternate longitudinal trim switch on the left side of the cockpit.

AILERON NORMAL TRIM FAILURE.

If the normal aileron trim control fails, the ailerons can be trimmed through use of the alternate lateral trim switch on the left console, aft of the throttle.

DROP TANK AND ROCKET PACKAGE EMERGENCY JETTISON IN FLIGHT.

To release drop tanks, press drop tank jettison button on left instrument subpanel. On F-86D-25 and later airplanes, and airplanes changed by T.O., the drop tanks can also be released manually when the drop tank emergency jettison handle is pulled to full extension (about 3 inches). To release rocket package, turn armament master switch to EMERG. JET'S'N. To release drop tanks and rocket package at the same time, turn armament master switch to JETTISON READY and press tank-rocket jettison button on control stick (this button has been removed on TF-86D Airplanes). After rocket package has been jettisoned, leave armament master switch at JETTISON READY.

Note

Refer to "Drop Tank Release Speed" in Section V for release speeds with various types of drop tanks. (See figure 5-1.)

Section IV

description and operation of AUXILIARY EQUIPMENT

TABLE OF CONTENTS

	PAGE
Cockpit Air Conditioning and Pressurization System	4-1
Radar Pressurization	4-6
Anti-icing and Defrosting Systems	4-6
Communication and Associated Electronic Equipment	4-10
Lighting Equipment	4-17
Oxygen System	4-19
Automatic Pilot	4-23
Navigation Equipment	4-29
Armament	4-30
Fire Control System	4-33
Control Surface Tie-in System (CSTI)	4-46
Miscellaneous Equipment	4-47

COCKPIT AIR CONDITIONING AND PRESSURIZATION SYSTEM.

The air conditioning system is designed to supply air for pressurization and heating or cooling of the cockpit. (See figure 4-1.) Hot air taken from the engine compressor section is passed through an air-cooling radiator. A by-pass valve diverts an automatically selected amount of this air through a cooling turbine. This refrigerated air then mixes with by-pass warm air and enters the cockpit at a preselected temperature. Air outlets are provided along each side of the cockpit above the consoles and in the area just forward of the pilot's feet. The cockpit is nonpressurized from sea level to 12,500 feet. Above this altitude, a cockpit altitude of 12,500 feet is maintained until the selected cockpit pressure is reached. Pressure schedules for either 2.75 psi or 5.00 psi differential may be selected. A pressure dump valve releases all cockpit pressure when operated by the pilot or automatically relieves any excess pressure if the pressure regulator fails. All air conditioning and pressurization controls are powered from monitored bus No. 2 on early airplanes.* On all later airplanes, power is supplied from the primary bus.

COCKPIT AIR CONDITIONING AND PRESSURIZATION SYSTEM CONTROLS AND INDICATOR.

Cockpit Air Switch.

The cockpit air switch is at the front of the cockpit air control panel (figure 4-2) on the left aft console. With the switch in the PRESS position, the main system shut-off valve in the air supply line from the engine is open and enough air flows into the cockpit to maintain the selected pressure schedule. When the switch is moved to

---

*F-86D-1 through F-86D-25 Airplanes and F-86D-30 Airplanes AF51-5945 through -6019

4-1

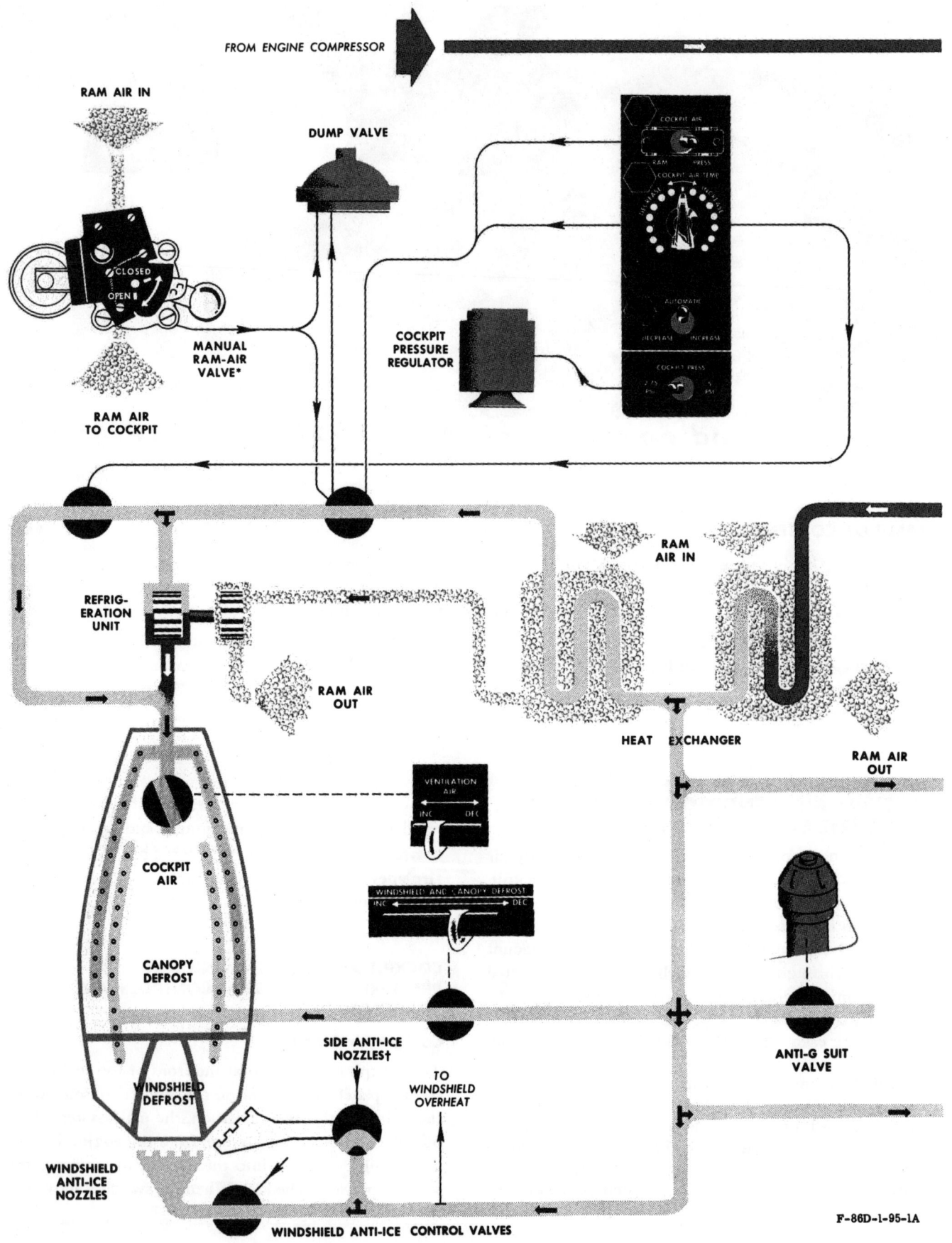

Figure 4-1

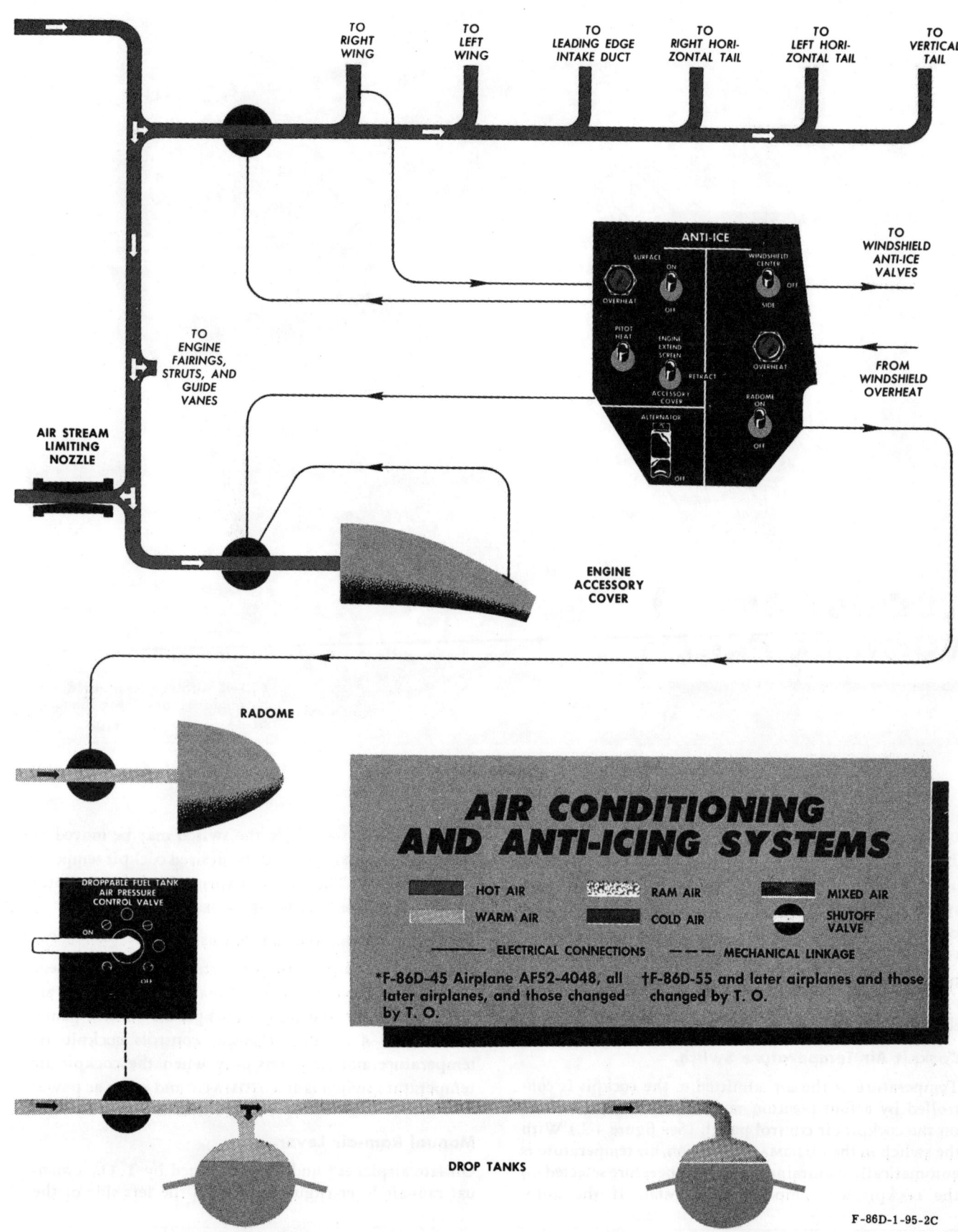

Section IV
T. O. 1F-86D-1

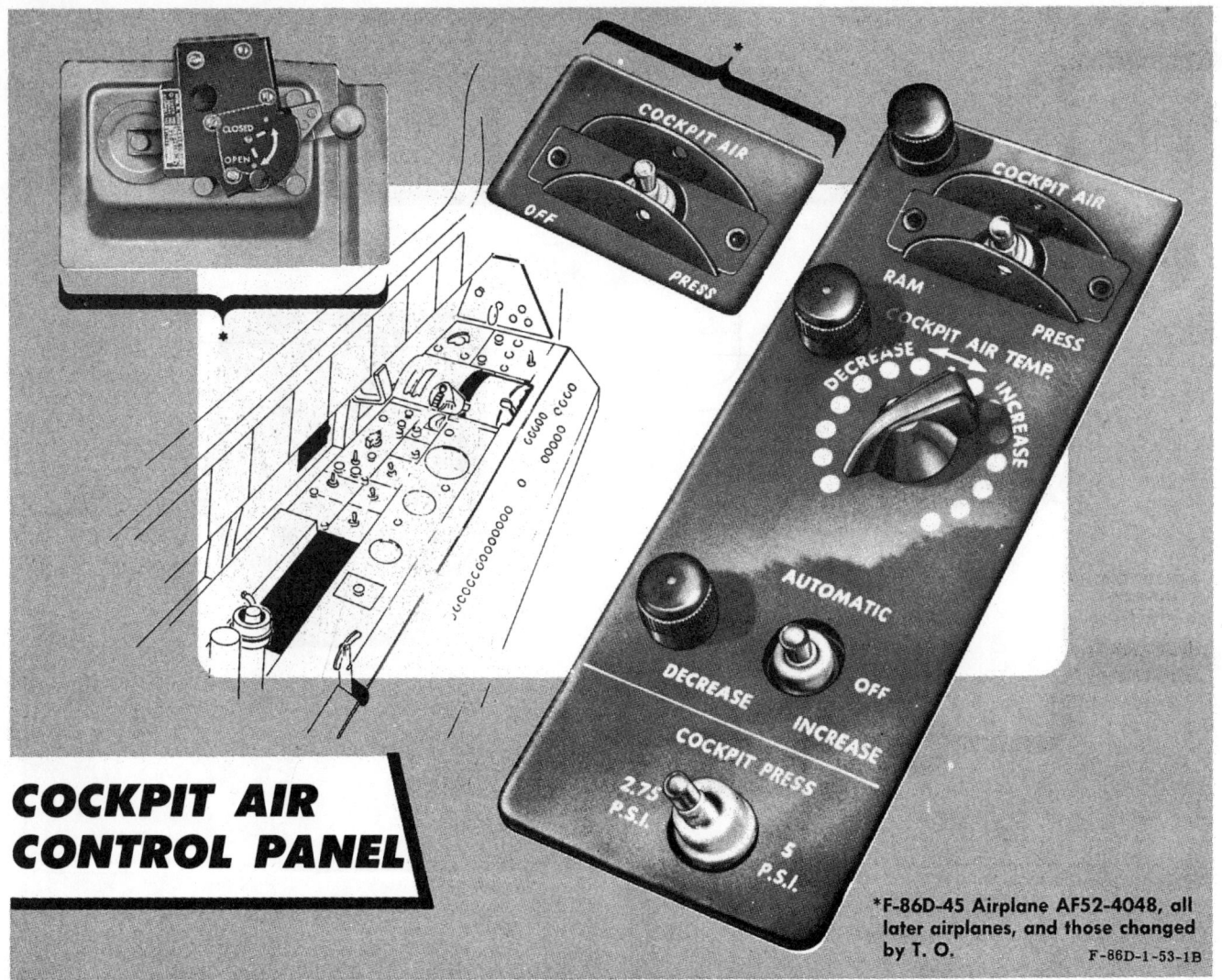

COCKPIT AIR CONTROL PANEL

*F-86D-45 Airplane AF52-4048, all later airplanes, and those changed by T. O.

Figure 4-2

OFF, the main system shutoff valve is closed and the dump valve is opened. Ram air will not be introduced, however, until the switch is moved to RAM. With the switch in this position, the main system shutoff valve is closed, the dump valve held open, and the ram-air valve opened. On later airplanes* and those changed by T.O., the switch has just two positions, OFF and PRESS. (See figure 4-2.) A manual ram-air lever replaces the ram function of the cockpit air switch.

Cockpit Air Temperature Switch.

Temperature of the air admitted to the cockpit is controlled by a four-position temperature control switch, on the cockpit air control panel. (See figure 4-2.) With the switch in the AUTOMATIC position, air temperature is automatically maintained at the temperature selected on the cockpit air temperature rheostat. If the auto-matic control system fails, the switch may be moved to INCREASE or DECREASE until the desired cockpit temperature is reached. The switch is spring-loaded to a center OFF position from INCREASE or DECREASE.

Cockpit Air Temperature Rheostat.

Cockpit air temperature is selected by an adjustment toward either INCREASE or DECREASE of the cockpit air temperature rheostat on the cockpit air control panel. (See figure 4-2.) This rheostat controls cockpit air temperature and functions only when the cockpit air temperature switch is at AUTOMATIC and when ac power is available at the cockpit temperature control unit.

Manual Ram-air Lever.

On late airplanes* and those changed by T. O., a manual ram-air lever (figure 4-1) is on the left side of the

---

*F-86D-45 Airplane AF52-4048 and all later airplanes

4-4

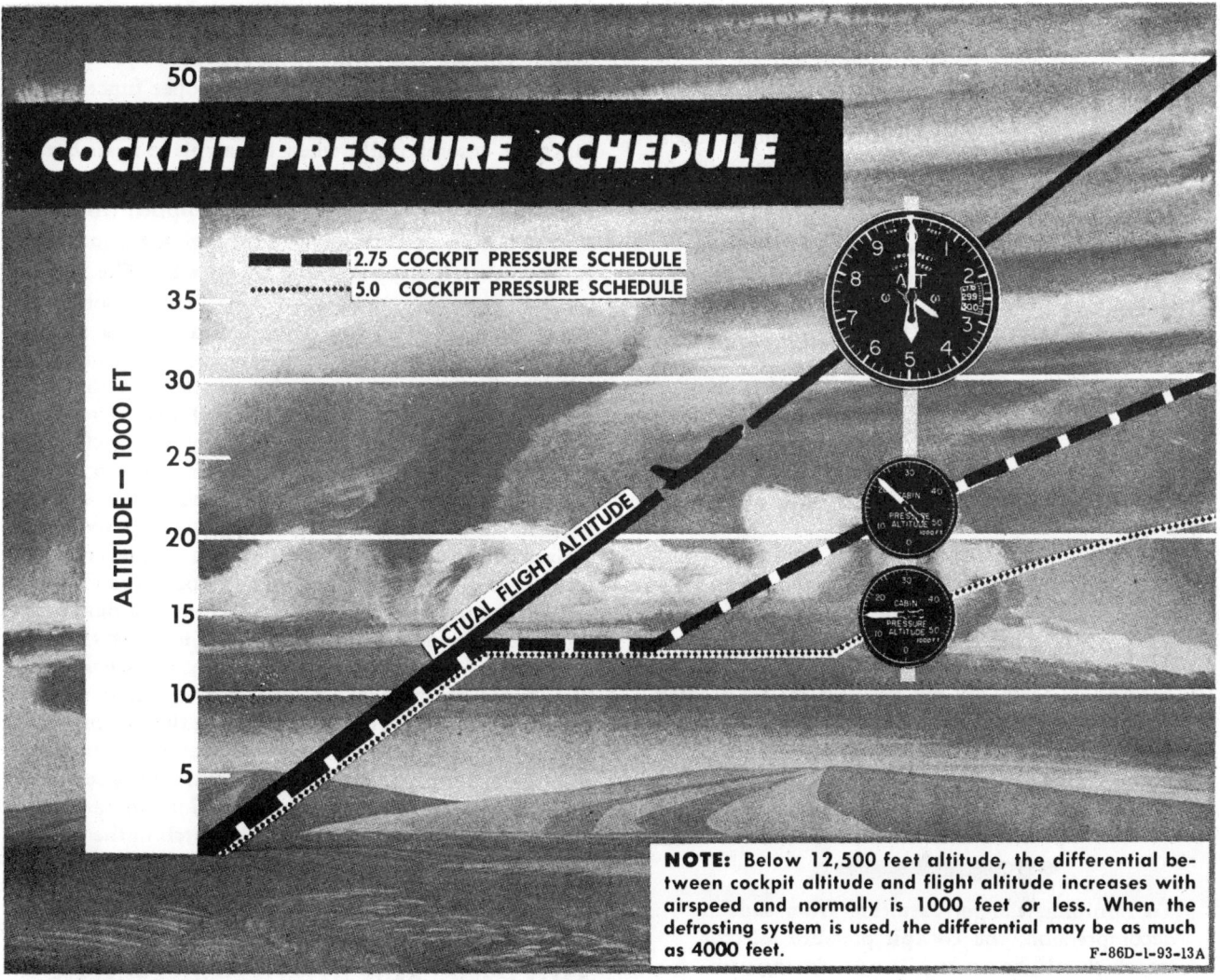

Figure 4-3

cockpit, under the canopy rail. When the lever is moved to the OPEN position, an electric switch operates to open the dump valve and close the main system shutoff. At the same time, this lever mechanically opens a small ram-air inlet door, on the left fuselage side below the canopy skirt, and allows ram air to enter the cockpit. With the manual ram-air lever in the CLOSED position and the cockpit air switch in the PRESS position, this inlet door and the dump valve are closed and the system shutoff valve is opened.

Ventilation Air Lever.

A manually operated ventilation air lever (7, figure 1-6; 8, figure 1-7) is on the underside of the left canopy rail. Moving this lever from INC. toward DEC. discharges a large part of the air from the air conditioning system at a point aft of the seat rather than through the tubes that supply the forward part of the cockpit. This provides for less air circulation, with subsequent less heating or cooling, while maintaining the same pressurization.

Cockpit Pressure Selector Switch.

The cockpit pressure selector switch, at the bottom of the cockpit air control panel (figure 4-2), selects one of two available cockpit pressure schedules. When the switch is at 2.75 P.S.I., the cockpit pressure regulator maintains a cockpit altitude of 12,500 feet until a flight altitude of 21,200 feet is reached. Above 21,200 feet, the regulator maintains a constant cockpit pressure of 2.75 psi greater than the corresponding outside air pressure. Moving the switch to 5 P.S.I. causes a cockpit altitude of 12,500 feet to be maintained up to a flight altitude of 31,000 feet, with a 5.00 psi pressure differential maintained above that altitude. At altitudes above either 21,200 feet or 31,000 feet, depending on the pressure schedule selected, the cabin altimeter will rise above 12,500 feet on a scale proportional to the flight altitude. See figure 4-3 for comparison of flight altitude to cockpit altitude and for cockpit altitude tolerances.

Cockpit Altimeter.

This airplane is provided with a cockpit altimeter (18, figure 1-6; 17, figure 1-7), on the left console. A few airplanes* have a Type A-1 cockpit altimeter. The dial of this instrument is equipped with two pointers and a scale window. Each pointer travels over a separate arc of calibrations. One pointer shows cockpit pressure altitude; the other shows flight pressure altitude. Visual reference to the actual pressure differential between flight and cockpit pressure altitudes is shown in psi by the figures seen through the scale window. All other airplanes are equipped with a Specification MIL-I-5099 cockpit altimeter. This instrument has one pointer and shows cockpit pressure altitude.

NORMAL OPERATION OF COCKPIT AIR CONDITIONING AND PRESSURIZATION SYSTEM.

1. Cockpit air switch PRESS.
2. Cockpit pressure selector switch at either 2.75 P.S.I. or 5 P.S.I.
3. Cockpit air temperature switch AUTOMATIC.
4. Cockpit air temperature rheostat set for desired temperature.
5. Ventilation air lever adjusted as desired.

To minimize danger resulting from sudden decompression, the cockpit pressure selector switch should be set at 2.75 P.S.I. during combat.

EMERGENCY OPERATION OF PRESSURIZATION SYSTEM.

Should sudden depressurization of the cockpit be necessary:

1. If at high altitude, and if circumstances permit, immediately descend to 20,000 feet or less.

Note

Following sudden cockpit depressurization at altitude, check oxygen mask for proper fit and oxygen flow.

2. To dump pressure without admitting ram air, move cockpit air switch to OFF. If introduction of ram air is desired, move cockpit air switch to RAM. On later airplanes,† position manual ram-air lever to OPEN.

---

*F-86D-1 Airplanes AF50-455 through -466
†F-86D-45 Airplane AF52-4048 and all later airplanes

RADAR PRESSURIZATION‡

Certain components of the radar system are pressurized to near sea-level pressure to ensure proper functioning at high altitude. The independent pressurization system functions automatically when the airplane is air-borne and the radar is turned on. On F-86D-1 through F-86D-15 Airplanes, the pressure is supplied from two storage bottles that are serviced through a ground filler valve to the right of the nose wheel well. The system pressure gage, mounted behind a small access door in the lower right forward fuselage, should show a charge of 1500 psi before flight. Whenever the supply pressure falls too low, a pressure switch automatically shuts off the radar equipment. On F-86D-20 and later airplanes, pressurization is supplied by an electrically driven air pump system. The air pump system, using air from the cockpit pressurized area, automatically regulates and maintains correct pressure in the pressurized components of the radar system whenever monitored bus No. 2 is energized. F-86D-40 and later airplanes and those changed by T.O. have a dual-pressurization system installed. In addition to pressurization of the radar components of the system with low pressure, a tunable magnetron unit is pressurized with a higher pressure. If pressure in either of the two pressure sections drops below a predetermined level, the air pump is automatically energized to repressurize the sections. Relief valves prevent overpressurization. In case of a pressurization failure, an interlock switch in the system prevents radar operation by opening the power circuits to the radar equipment.

ANTI-ICING AND DEFROSTING SYSTEMS.

COCKPIT DEFROSTING SYSTEM.

Part of the hot air from the engine compressor section that conditions cockpit air is also used for cockpit enclosure defrosting. This air is released from duct apertures along the canopy rail on either side and along either side of the windshield in such a way that the inner surfaces of the canopy and windshield are warmed and defrosted. This interior defrosting system can be operated independently or in conjunction with the exterior anti-icing system. On late airplanes,§ an electrical anti-frost system is included for the pilot's pressure suit face mask.

Windshield and Canopy Defrost Lever.

The windshield and canopy defrost lever (3, figure 1-8; 4, figure 1-9) is on the underside of the right canopy rail. This lever, when moved toward INC. from DEC., lets hot air pass to the windshield and canopy inside surface for defrosting.

---

‡Removed from TF-86D Airplanes
§F-86D-40 and later airplanes

Pressure Suit Face Mask Heater Rheostat.*

The pressure suit face mask defrosting heater rheostat (18, figure 1-7) is on the aft end of the left console. The face mask antifrost heater elements are energized when the rheostat is rotated clockwise from its OFF position. Heat is increased by continued clockwise rotation of the rheostat. This rheostat is powered from the primary bus.

ANTI-ICING SYSTEMS.

The anti-icing systems prevent the formation of ice, rather than dispose of ice already formed. Hot air is drawn from the engine compressor section and passed through ducts in the interior of exposed surfaces. (See figure 4-1.) The surface anti-icing system provides hot air for the interior areas of the leading edges of wings, tail, and engine air inlet duct. The engine accessory cover and engine compressor inlet receive hot air from the engine accessory cover anti-icing system. This system always operates simultaneously with the surface anti-icing system when the surface anti-ice switch is turned ON. The engine accessory cover anti-icing system does, however, have its own individual control by which it can be set in operation without actuating the surface anti-icing system. The interior windshield defrosting system and radome anti-icing system can operate simultaneously or independently of each other. In the windshield and radome anti-icing system, hot air is injected into the radome and is also discharged at the outside base of the windshield. The only unit that is electrically heated to prevent icing is the pitot head on the right wing tip.

*F-86D-40 and later airplanes

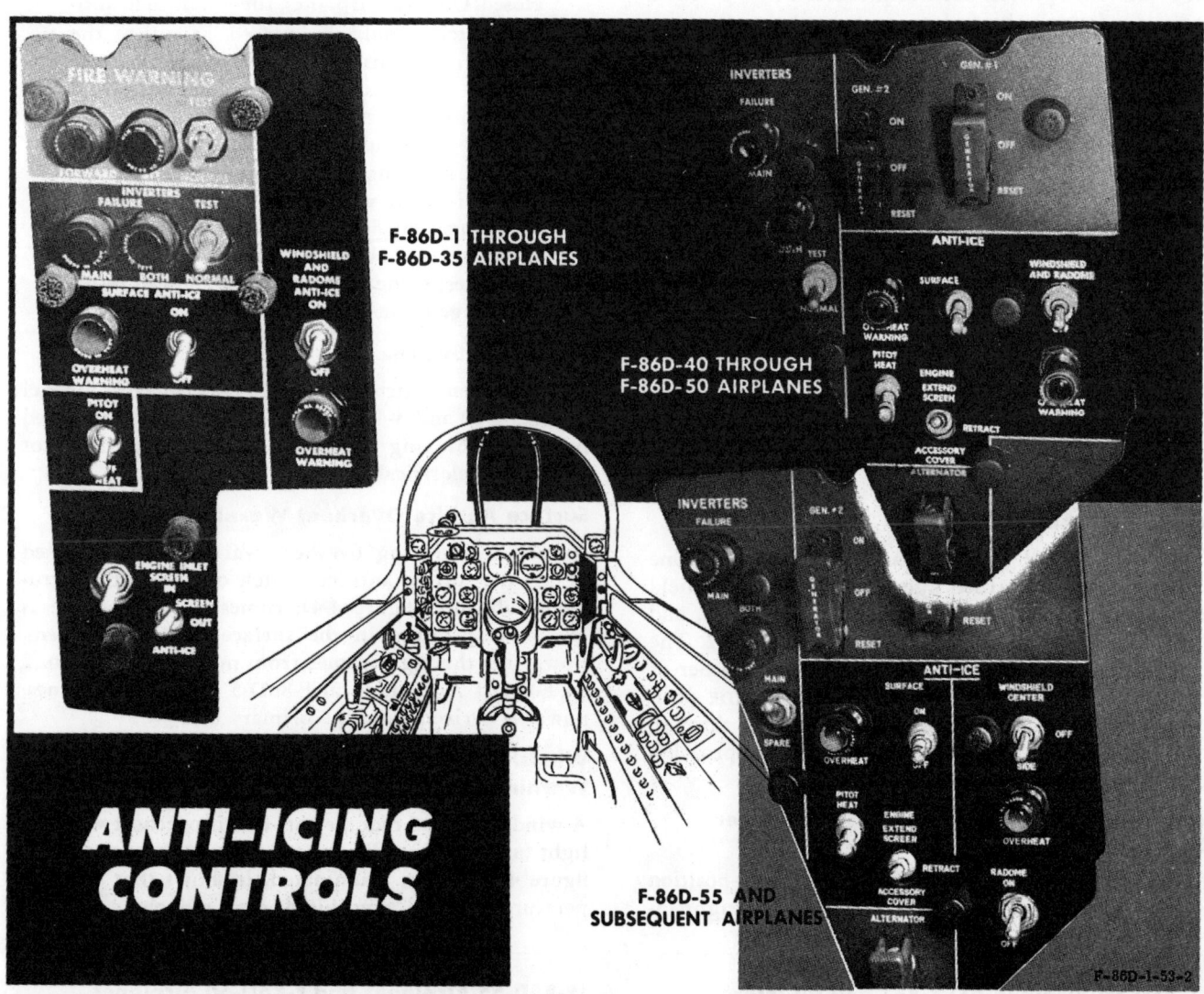

Figure 4-4

Section IV

T. O. 1F-86D-1

Surface Anti-ice Switch.

The two-position surface anti-ice switch is mounted on the right instrument subpanel. (See figure 4-4.) This switch is powered from monitored bus No. 2, provided ac power is available. When the switch is placed in the ON position, hot air is made available for both the surface anti-icing and the engine accessory cover anti-icing systems, and the engine inlet screen is automatically retracted.

Engine Inlet Switch.

The engine inlet switch, on the right instrument subpanel (figure 4-4), controls both the engine inlet screen and the engine accessory cover anti-icing system. Power for the engine inlet screen actuator reaches this switch from the primary bus, provided the surface anti-ice switch is in the OFF position. Power for the engine accessory cover anti-icing system reaches the engine inlet switch from monitored bus No. 2, provided the surface anti-ice switch is in the OFF position. Placing the engine inlet switch at EXTEND SCREEN (SCREEN IN on F-86D-1 Airplanes) extends the screen into position to prevent foreign objects from entering the engine compressor section. Moving the switch to RETRACT (SCREEN OUT on F-86D-1 Airplanes) retracts the screen to allow maximum airflow and to prevent ice accumulation. (Refer to "Engine Inlet Switch," Section I.) When the switch is moved to ACCESSORY COVER (ANTI-ICE on F-86D-1 Airplanes), the screen is retracted, and a thermal sensing unit controls anti-icing air for the engine accessory cover and forward compressor section as required.

Windshield and Radome Anti-ice Switch.

On F-86D-1 through F-86D-50 Airplanes, a two-position windshield and radome anti-ice switch, on the right instrument subpanel (figure 4-4) and powered by monitored bus No. 2, lets hot air pass to the windshield and radome for anti-icing when the switch is placed in the ON position.

Windshield Anti-ice Switch.

On F-86D-55 and later airplanes, a separate radome switch is provided. (See figure 4-1.) The windshield anti-ice switch has three positions, CENTER, OFF, and SIDE, and is powered from monitored bus No. 2. The CENTER and SIDE positions allow selection of either of two windshield areas to be anti-iced. The SIDE position is provided to give improved visibility through the left windshield panel during landing approaches in rain or icing conditions.

Radome Anti-ice Switch (F-86D-55 and Later Airplanes).

Powered by monitored bus No. 2, the two-position radome anti-ice switch (figure 4-4) is on the right instrument subpanel. Selecting the ON position* allows engine compressor air to be directed to the radome and the center area of the windshield for anti-icing. The radome anti-ice switch controls windshield anti-ice airflow *if* the windshield anti-ice switch is in the SIDE or OFF position. Hot air for the side windshield can be furnished only when the radome anti-ice switch is in the OFF position; therefore, if the windshield anti-ice switch has been positioned at SIDE, and the radome anti-ice switch is turned ON, the windshield side panel air will be cut off and the windshield center panel air will be turned on automatically.

CAUTION

On some airplanes,† with the radome anti-ice switch in the ON position, engine compressor air is allowed to pass to the radome only. With the switch OFF, the shutoff valve is closed. On these airplanes, the windshield anti-ice switch should be placed at either the CENTER or the SIDE position *before* the radome anti-ice switch is placed ON. Thus, the high static pressure trapped within the anti-ice ducting as a result of valve sequencing is dissipated, allowing the radome to receive normal anti-ice air when it is turned on. Placing the radome anti-ice switch ON before the windshield anti-ice switch is placed at CENTER or SIDE releases the static pressure and can result in damage to the radome.

Pitot Heat Switch.

The pitot heat switch, on the right instrument subpanel (figures 1-10 and 4-4), receives power from monitored bus No. 1. Moving the switch to ON causes the pitot head to be electrically heated.

Surface Anti-ice Overheat Warning Light.

A surface anti-icing overheat warning light, located beside the surface anti-ice switch on the right instrument subpanel (figure 4-4), comes on when there is excess temperature in the surface anti-icing system. Power for this light comes from monitored bus No. 2 on F-86D-1 Airplanes; on F-86D-5 and later airplanes, power is derived from the primary bus.

Windshield and Radome Anti-ice Overheat Warning Light.

A windshield and radome anti-ice air overheat warning light (amber) is on the right instrument subpanel. (See figure 4-4.) When illuminated, it shows that air temperature in the windshield and radome anti-icing

---

*F-86D-60 Airplane AF53-857 and all later airplanes

†F-86D-55 Airplanes and F-86D-60 Airplanes AF53-782 through -856

4-8

system has reached or exceeded the design limit of 135°C (275°F); it does not necessarily mean an immediate overheat condition, as windshield temperature depends largely on outside air temperature. On F-86D-1 Airplanes, this light is powered from monitored bus No. 2; on F-86D-5 and later airplanes, it receives power from the primary bus.

NORMAL OPERATION OF ANTI-ICING AND DEFROSTING SYSTEMS.

1. Surface anti-ice switch ON.

2. Windshield and radome anti-ice switch ON. On some airplanes,* the windshield anti-ice switch must be placed in either the CENTER or the SIDE position, and then the separate radome switch turned ON. On these airplanes, radome anti-icing should not be used unless windshield anti-icing is used also.

Note

The windshield and canopy defrost system provides enough heating of the transparent surfaces to effectively eliminate the formation of frost or fog during descent.

3. Adjust windshield and canopy defrost lever toward INC. as desired.

4. Pitot heat switch ON.

5. On some airplanes,* when turning anti-ice systems off, first turn radome anti-ice switch to OFF, wait 6 seconds, and then turn windshield anti-ice switch OFF. On other airplanes, turn systems off as desired.

Rain Removal System.

The air blast from the windshield anti-icing system can be used for rain removal. As the windshield anti-ice system in F-86D-55 and later airplanes was designed for rain removal, it will be more effective in clearing the windshield of rain than the earlier system. The anti-ice system of all airplanes, however, may be used to remove rain encountered in light to moderate rainstorms. On F-86D-1 through F-86D-50 Airplanes, the radome and windshield anti-ice system is controlled by a single cockpit control; therefore, the windshield and radome anti-ice switch must be turned on for rain removal. On F-86D-55 and later airplanes, the windshield anti-ice control should be placed at CENTER or SIDE as desired, and the radome anti-ice switch should be turned OFF. Turning off the radome anti-ice system and other systems using engine bleed air reduces the likelihood of windshield glass cracking due to overheat. A windshield overheat warning indication may be observed during some landing approaches, take-offs, and low-speed flight

---

*F-86D-55 Airplanes and F-86D-60 Airplanes AF53-782 through -856

conditions. This condition should not be considered an immediate overheat of the windshield, since the indicator senses the temperature of the anti-ice air (design limit 275°F) in the windshield nozzle. The actual temperature of the glass is less than that of the nozzle air because of the conditions of rain, ice, outside air temperature, and airflow over the windshield. Therefore, the system need not be shut off during flight requiring maximum available visibility, since windshield cracking would not necessarily result for at least 30 seconds. Flight safety considerations are more important than the prevention of windshield cracking. The following procedures prevent, or reduce the severity of, windshield overheat if flight conditions preclude turning the system off.

Landing and Take-off.

1. Place cockpit air switch on RAM (or OFF and manual ram-air lever to OPEN).

2. Reduce cockpit defrost airflow to minimum practicable. During landing or take-off, if the overheat warning light comes on, the windshield anti-ice system should not be shut off.

Ground Run.

1. With warning light on, leave windshield anti-ice switch at CENTER.

2. Place cockpit air switch on RAM (or OFF and manual ram-air lever to OPEN).

3. Reduce cockpit defrost airflow to minimum practicable.

4. Reduce engine rpm until light goes off (about 80% rpm).

Level Flight.

1. Increase or decrease airspeed about 30 to 50 knots.

2. Reduce cockpit defrost airflow to minimum practicable.

It is recommended that the OPEN position of the manual ram-air lever be used in conjunction with the anti-ice system only during landing, take-off, or taxiing, because unsatisfactory cockpit temperatures could result if it were used extensively during flight. The rain removal feature of the windshield anti-ice system is limited by engine power and the intensity of the rain.

EMERGENCY OPERATION OF ANTI-ICING SYSTEMS.

Overheating of Windshield and Radome Anti-icing System.

If the windshield and radome anti-ice overheat warning light comes on, indicating an overheated condition in the windshield and radome anti-icing system, proceed as follows:

During Ground Run.

1. With warning light on, leave windshield anti-ice switch ON.

2. Place cockpit air switch on RAM (or OFF and manual ram-air lever to OPEN).

3. Reduce cockpit defrost airflow to minimum practicable.

4. Reduce engine rpm until light goes off (about 80% rpm).

During Landing and Take-off.

1. Place cockpit air switch on RAM (or OFF and manual ram-air lever to OPEN).

2. Reduce cockpit defrost airflow to minimum practicable.

During Level Flight.

1. Increase or decrease airspeed about 30 to 50 knots.

2. Reduce cockpit defrost airflow to minimum practicable.

It is recommended that the OPEN position of the manual ram-air lever be used in conjunction with the anti-ice system only during landing, take-off, or taxiing, because unsatisfactory cockpit temperatures could result if it were used extensively during flight. The rain removal feature of the windshield anti-ice system is limited by engine power and the intensity of the rain.

Overheating of Surface Anti-icing System.

If the surface anti-ice overheat warning light illuminates, indicating an overheated condition in the surface anti-icing system, proceed as follows:

1. Cycle surface anti-ice switch OFF and ON to try to maintain a temperature below maximum necessary to illuminate warning light. Any momentary malfunction may be eliminated during this switch cycling.

Note

If the surface anti-ice overheat warning light remains on after the switch has been cycled, it may be necessary to reduce engine power to lower the temperature of the air supply.

2. If a power reduction is impractical or if it fails to lower air supply temperature below the maximum necessary to illuminate the warning light, place surface anti-ice switch at OFF.

COMMUNICATION AND ASSOCIATED ELECTRONIC EQUIPMENT.

UHF COMMAND RADIO—AN/ARC-27.*

The AN/ARC-27 radio equipment provides two-way AM radiotelephone communication in the frequency range of 225 to 399.9 megacycles between aircraft and ground stations or between aircraft. Remote selection of 18 preset frequencies may be made; also, a guard frequency that can be operated alone or with the selected frequency may be selected. The radio set control (figure 4-7), which is a pilot's remote-control panel, contains three control devices: a power switch, a channel selector, and an audio volume control. The power switch is powered from the secondary bus.

Operation of Command Radio—AN/ARC-27.

1. Rotate power switch on command radio control panel (figure 4-7) from OFF to T/R and allow about one minute for warm-up.

2. Rotate power switch to T/R + G REC. This allows monitoring of an additional independent receiver preset to a frequency that is guarded continuously throughout scheduled periods.

3. Rotate frequency selector on command radio control panel to desired preset frequency. Reception and transmission will now be on this frequency.

4. Adjust volume control on command radio control panel for desired output.

5. To transmit, press push-to-talk button either on the throttle or on the control stick grip.

6. To operate with separate guard receiver off, rotate power switch to T/R. For operation of both receivers, rotate power switch to T/R + G REC. To transmit on guard frequency, rotate power switch to T/R and frequency selector to G.

7. To turn radio off, rotate power switch to OFF.

UHF COMMAND RADIO—AN/ARC-34.†

The AN/ARC-34 command radio equipment (figure 4-7) provides two-way AM radiotelephone communications on 1750 different channels in the radio-frequency range of 225.0 through 399.9 megacycles on frequencies spaced 0.1 megacycle apart. It has provisions for presetting 20 channels on the receiver unit at any one time, and any of the preset channels may be selected as desired. The guard channel receiver (a separate integral component) is capable of covering the frequency range of 238.0 through 248.0 megacycles. The normal guard channel frequency is 243.0 megacycles. The controls for the unit are the main control switch, which has four po-

---

*F-86D-1 through F-86D-50 Airplanes
†F-86D-55 and later airplanes

WARNING: RADAR GROUND CHECKS MUST NOT BE MADE WITHIN 50 FEET OF OPERATIONS INVOLVING FUEL.

COMMUNICATION AND ASSOCIATED ELECTRONIC EQUIPMENT

TYPE	DESIGNATION	USE	RANGE
UHF COMMAND	AN/ARC-27 * AN/ARC-34†	TWO-WAY VOICE COMMUNICATION	LINE OF SIGHT
GLIDE PATH RECEIVER	AN/ARN-5B‡ AN/ARN-18§	INSTRUMENT APPROACH	15 MILES
LOCALIZER RECEIVER	RC-103-D¶	INSTRUMENT APPROACH	25-50 MILES
ZERO READER¶		FLIGHT PLAN INDICATOR AND INSTRUMENT APPROACH	
OMNIDIRECTIONAL RECEIVER	AN/ARN-14**	RECEPTION OF VOICE AND CODE COMMUNICATIONS, INSTRUMENT APPROACH, AND OMNIDIRECTIONAL VHF RADIO RANGE	LINE OF SIGHT
RADIO COMPASS	AN/ARN-6	RECEPTION OF VOICE AND CODE COMMUNICATION POSITION FINDING; HOMING	20-200 MILES
IFF	AN/APX-6†† AN/APX-25‡‡	AUTOMATIC IDENTIFICATION	LINE OF SIGHT
MARKER BEACON	AN/ARN-12	VISUAL AND AURAL RECEPTION OF MARKER BEACON SIGNALS	VERTICAL

*F86D-1 Airplanes AF50-464 through -491, and F-86D-5 through F-86D-50 Airplanes
†F-86D-55 and subsequent airplanes
‡F-86D-1 through F-86D-35 Airplanes
§F-86D-40 and subsequent airplanes
¶F-86D-1 through F-86D-30 Airplanes
**F-86D-35 and subsequent airplanes
††F-86D-1 through F-86D-55 Airplanes
‡‡F-86D-60 and subsequent airplanes

Figure 4-5

sitions, OFF (turns set off), MAIN (allows transmission and reception on main selected channels only), BOTH (allows transmission and reception on main selected channels and reception only on the guard frequency), and ADF (which has no function at the present time); the channel selector (a rotary selector switch for selection of the preset channels); the "MANUAL-PRESET-GUARD" selector control (MANUAL position for manual selection of a desired frequency from 225.0 to 399.9 megacycles by use of the four frequency selection knobs at the top of the control panel, PRESET position for use with the channel selector and the 20 preset frequencies, and GUARD position for monitoring the emergency guard frequency); a volume control for manual adjustment of volume; and a tone button for sending a continuous tone to aid in obtaining a direction finding bearing. A placard, at the bottom of the control panel, is used to list the frequencies selected for the 20 preset channels.

Operation of Command Radio—AN/ARC-34.

1. Select PRESET position with the selector control ("MANUAL-PRESET-GUARD" control).

2. Rotate main control switch to BOTH position and allow about 2 minutes for warm-up of main and guard receiver units.

3. Place channel selector control to a channel other than desired channel. Allow tuning cycle to be completed; then return to desired channel.

Note

An inherent characteristic of the radio set will reduce the reception and transmission qualities of the set if step 3 is not observed. If the first selection is retained, full power for reception and transmission will not be obtainable.

4. Adjust volume control for desired audio level.

5. For manual selection of a frequency not included in preset channels, set selector control to MANUAL. The

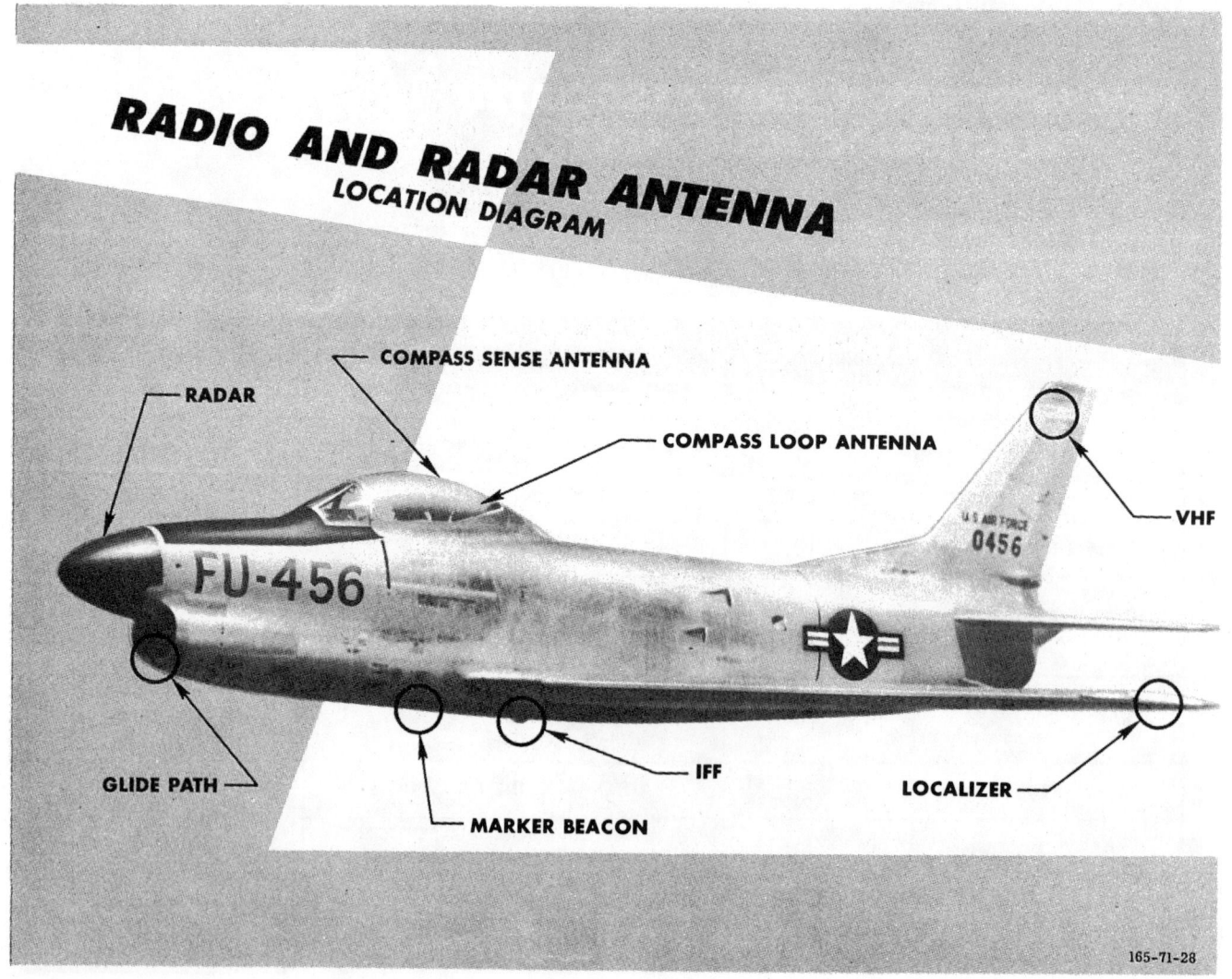

Figure 4-6

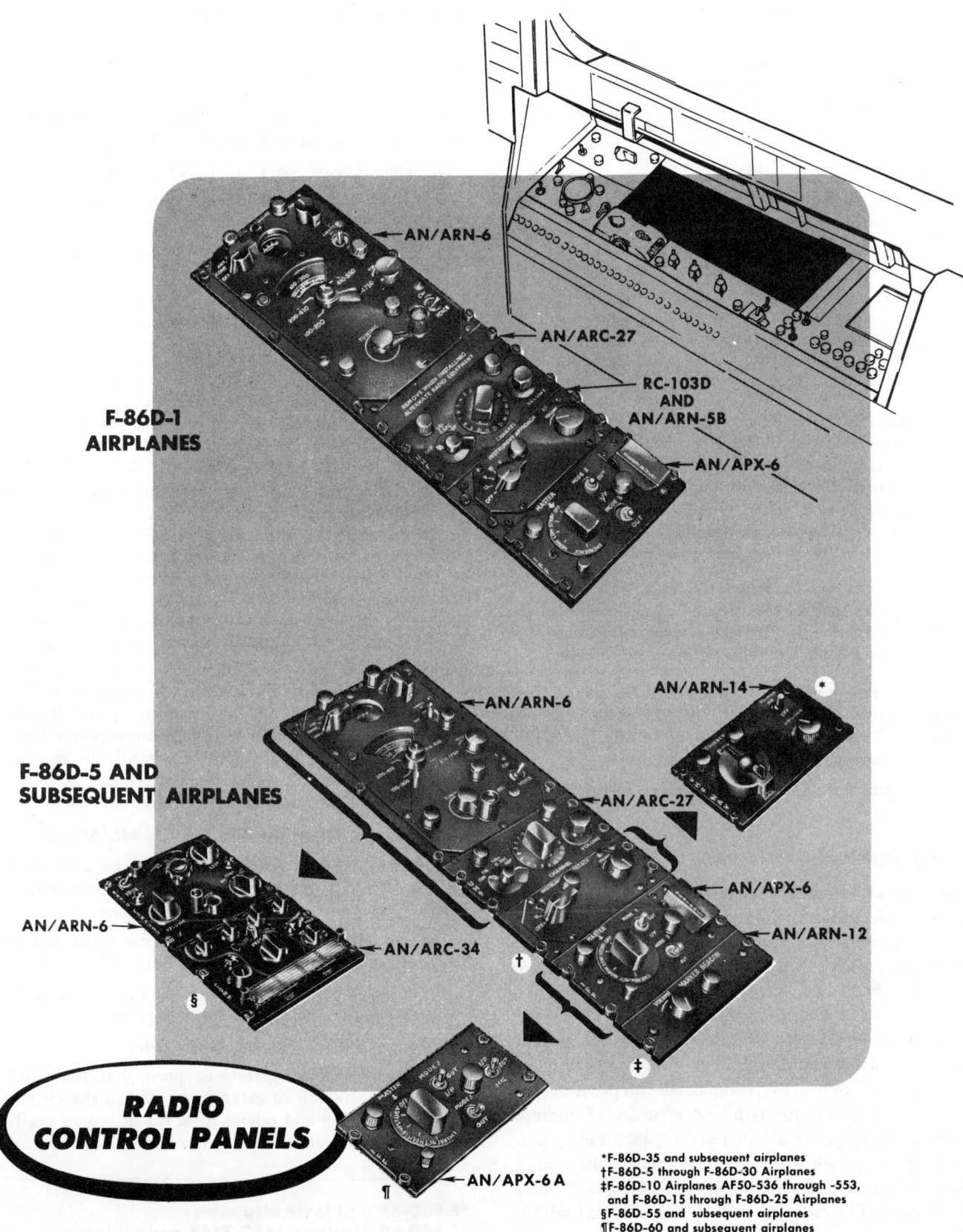

Figure 4-7

four windows across the top of the panel should now be open. Use the four knobs across top of panel to select desired frequency. The digits that appear in the windows indicate the operating frequency. (The main control switch must be at MAIN or BOTH for manual operation.)

Note

- This procedure places the equipment in the "receive" condition. Tranmission of the same frequency is obtained by depressing the microphone button; however, if it is desired to change the transmitter frequency, the microphone button should be released before the frequency is changed. About 4 seconds should elapse before transmission is begun on the new frequency.

- A thermal time-delay relay cuts out and stops the drive motor after 50 to 125 seconds of continuous operation (switching from one channel to another without stopping). If this occurs, place main control switch to OFF and allow a 30-second cooling period. Then switch to BOTH and select desired channel.

- Do not try to tune receiver to any frequency below 225 megacycles, as set will not operate in this range and continuous operation of channeling drive motor results.

6. For transmission and reception on guard frequency, move "MANUAL-PRESET-GUARD" selector to GUARD. This tunes the receiver and transmitter to the guard frequency and cuts out the main units.

7. To turn set off, rotate main control switch to OFF.

RADIO COMPASS—AN/ARN-6.

The AN/ARN-6 radio compass set is a visual and navigational aid used in conjunction with the radio compass indicator (38, figure 1-4; 36, figure 1-5) on the instrument panel. Four separate frequency bands are provided: band one, 100 to 200 kilocycles; band two, 200 to 410 kilocycles; band three, 410 to 850 kilocycles; and band four, 850 to 1750 kilocycles. Controls permit selection of automatic or manual direction finding. A tuning meter, on the radio compass control panel (figure 4-7), shows signal strength and accuracy of tuning. Late airplanes* have a miniature 4½-inch radio compass control panel, which does not include the tuning meter. This panel is used when the AN/ARC-34 radio is installed. The radio compass loop is installed within the aft portion of the canopy, and the sense antenna is in the upper arc of the canopy enclosure. (See figure 4-6.) The control switch on the radio compass control panel is powered from the secondary bus.

Operation of Radio Compass—AN/ARN-6.

1. Turn radio compass control switch on radio compass control panel (figure 4-7) to ANT.

2. Select desired frequency band with frequency selector switch on radio compass control panel and tune desired station with tuning crank.

3. Select type of operation, COMP. or LOOP.

4. Adjust volume control on radio compass control panel for desired output.

5. To turn radio off, rotate power switch to OFF.

IDENTIFICATION RADAR—AN/APX-6.

The AN/APX-6 identification radar set is used to automatically identify the airplane as friendly whenever it is properly challenged by suitably equipped friendly air or surface forces. The set also has provisions for identifying specific friendly airplanes within a group and means for transmitting a special distress code. Functionally, the AN/APX-6 set receives challenges and transmits replies to the source of the challenges, where the replies are displayed, together with the associated radar targets, on radar indicators. When a radar target is accompanied by a proper reply from the IFF set, the target is considered friendly. Three destructors, mounted in the AN/APX-6 transpondor, may be fired manually by the pilot, or automatically by an impact switch if enough impact force is applied. On some airplanes,† the impact destructor switch is not incorporated. The master switch on the IFF radio control panel (figure 4-7), mounted on the right console, receives power from monitored bus No. 2 if ac power is available; the destructors are powered from the battery bus. On late airplanes,‡ the destructors are not installed.

Operation of Identification Radar—AN/APX-6.

1. Rotate master switch on IFF radio control panel (figure 4-7) to NORM (full sensitivity and maximum performance) or to STDBY or LOW as required.

2. Set mode 2 switch on IFF radio control panel to required position. Normally, this will be OUT.

3. Set mode 3 switch on IFF radio control panel to required position. Normally, this will be OUT.

4. Set "I/P-MIC." switch as desired.§

5. For emergency operation, press dial stop and rotate master switch to EMERGENCY. When the switch is in this position and power from the ac bus in available, the equipment will automatically transmit a

---

*F-86D-55 and later airplanes
†F-86D-40 Airplane AF52-3748 and all later airplanes
‡F-86D-45 Airplane AF52-4055 and all later airplanes
§F-86D-60 and later airplanes

Section IV

IDENTIFICATION RADAR—AN/APX-25.

Provisions for the installation of the AN/APX-25 identification radar are incorporated on late airplanes.† The AN/APX-6 radar is still used.

OMNIDIRECTIONAL RECEIVER—AN/ARN-14‡ (F-86D-35 AND LATER AIRPLANES).

The AN/ARN-14 omnidirectional receiver is a vhf navigation receiver, with associated indicators, that provides reception of all vhf omnirange, localizer, and voice facilities (which include both military and commercial communications) in 108- to 135.9-megacycle channels. Reception of vhf omnirange facilities provides a display of on-course information, indication of the magnetic bearing of the vhf omnirange from the airplane, indication of angular difference between selected course and the magnetic heading of the airplane, and to-station, from-station indications. Reception of localizer facilities provides on-course information for the instrument landing approach system. Voice facilities are received on communication channels or are superimposed on navigation signals in localizer or omnirange bands for station identification. The AN/ARN-14 receiver control panel (figure 4-7) is on the right console. The panel, marked "VHF NAV," contains a power switch, an audio volume control, and a frequency selector switch. Display of the information selected by the positioning of the frequency selector will appear on either the course indicator or the course bearing indicator, or both. This receiver is powered by monitored bus No. 2.

Operation of Omnidirectional Receiver—AN/ARN-14.

1. Turn power switch to ON.
2. Position frequency selector to desired frequency setting. Identify station from coded signal in headset.

CAUTION

The destructor switch should be operated only when the AN/APX-6 equipment is in danger of falling into enemy hands.

F-86D-1-0-14

distress signal, indicating that the airplane requires immediate assistance.

6. An impact switch to fire the destructors and destroy the IFF transpondor is incorporated as a security measure. On some airplanes,* the impact destructor switch is not incorporated. However, the destructors may be fired manually by a destructor switch on the IFF radio control panel. (See figure 4-7.) To manually fire destructors, lift destructor switch guard by breaking safety wire, and place switch to ON position.

7. To turn off equipment, rotate IFF master switch to OFF. If AN/APX-6 transpondor is destroyed during flight, report this information immediately upon landing.

CAUTION

Before take-off, make sure that AN/APX-6 IFF frequency counters have been set to the proper frequency channels and that the three destructors and an AN. connector have been inserted in the face of the IFF transpondor. (IFF units are accessible through radio access door on right forward fuselage.)

CAUTION

The flag alarm for the vertical needle on the course indicator must be out of sight before the vertical needle can be relied upon.

3. Set desired magnetic course heading in course window of course indicator.
4. Adjust volume as desired.

GLIDE PATH AND LOCALIZER RECEIVERS.‡

AN/ARN-5B and RC-103-D (F-86D-1 Through F-86D-30 Airplanes).

The AN/ARN-5B glide path receiver and the RC-103-D localizer receiver are the main components of the

---

*F-86D-40 Airplane AF52-3748 and all later airplanes
†F-86D-60 and later airplanes
‡Removed from TF-86D Airplanes

4-15

instrument landing system radio. The two sets operate at the same time, and each shows the flight path of the airplane on the same approach indicator (8, figure 1-4; 4, figure 1-7) by means of two needles crossed perpendicularly. The AN/ARN-5B receiver gives the position of the airplane vertically in relation to a radio beam projected at an angle from the ground, and the RC-103-D receiver registers the position of the airplane laterally in relation to a radio beam projected down the approach runway. Both receivers are controlled from a single panel on the right console (figure 4-7), marked "INSTRUMENT APPROACH," and are powered from monitored bus No. 2. The AN/ARN-5B receiver operates on 332.6, 333.8, and 335 megacycles, while the RC-103-D receiver can be tuned to 108.1, 108.3, 109.5, 109.9, 110.1, and 110.3 megacycles.

AN/ARN-5B* (AN/ARN-18†) and AN/ARN-14 (F-86D-35 and Later Airplanes).

The AN/ARN-5B* (AN/ARN-18 on late airplanes†) glide path receiver and the localizer portion of the AN/ARN-14 omnidirectional receiver operate at the same time and show the flight path of the airplane on the course indicator (4, figure 1-5) by means of two needles crossed perpendicularly. The AN/ARN-5B* (AN/ARN-18 on late airplanes†) receiver shows the position of the airplane vertically in relation to a radio beam projected at an angle from the ground; the localizer portion of the AN/ARN-14 receiver shows the position of the airplane laterally in relation to a radio beam projected down the approach runway. Both receivers are controlled from a single panel on the right console (figure 4-7), marked "VHF NAV," and are powered from monitored bus No. 2. Tuning the omnidirectional receiver as shown in the following table automatically tunes the glide path receiver to the required frequency.

OMNIDIRECTIONAL RECEIVER	GLIDE PATH RECEIVER
108.1 mc	334.4 mc
108.3 mc	335.0 mc
109.5 mc	332.6 mc
109.9 mc	333.8 mc
110.1 mc	334.4 mc
110.3 mc	335.0 mc
111.5 mc	332.6 mc
111.9 mc	333.8 mc

Operation of Glide Path and Localizer Receivers.

1. About 20 minutes before arrival at destination, rotate frequency selector on vhf navigational control panel (instrument approach control panel on F-86D-1 through F-86D-30 Airplanes) to desired channel.

2. Adjust localizer volume control on vhf navigational control panel (instrument approach control panel on F-86D-1 through F-86D-30 Airplanes) for desired audio level.

3. Observe approach indicator on instrument panel for course indications.

4. On F-86D-1 through F-86D-30 Airplanes, with zero reader selector switch at FLIGHT INST., begin instrument approach. (Refer to "Manual ILAS Approaches With Zero Reader," Section IX.)

5. After completion of landing, turn instrument approach frequency selector OFF.

MARKER BEACON RADIO—AN/ARN-12.‡

The marker beacon radio is automatically turned on when power is supplied to the electrical system of the airplane. The marker beacon indicator light (9, figure 1-4; 6, figure 1-5) is on the approach indicator. This radio is powered through monitored bus No. 2.

ZERO READER (F-86D-1 THROUGH F-86D-30 AIRPLANES).

The zero reader (12, figure 1-4; 12, figure 1-5) is a gyroscopic flight and navigation instrument which electronically combines attitude, heading, altitude, and radio information and presents it on a single indicator. The indicator is mounted on the center of the instrument panel, directly above the radarscope. The indication is presented by means of a vertical bar, a horizontal bar, and a heading pointer. Deflection of the vertical bar is controlled by the directional signal from the slaved gyro magnetic compass, the bank signal from a vertical gyro, and radio track signals from the glide path and localizer receivers. The horizontal bar is actuated by a pitch signal from the vertical gyro and by deviation from a preselected altitude or from the glide path. The heading pointer shows the azimuth heading and, while the airplane is flying, the localizer beam shows the drift angle. The drift can be compensated for by adjustment of the course set knob on the indicator while a zero indication is maintained on both bars of the zero reader. The selector switch unit is on the left aft console. The automatic control unit, which is under the right console, contains the signal amplifier, the bellows-actuated altitude control, and the pitch-roll vertical gyro. The zero reader also uses the slaved gyro magnetic compass to provide azimuth heading signals. Attitude signals from the glide path receiver and directional signals from the localizer receiver are presented on the zero reader during instrument approach. (Refer to Section

---

*F-86D-35 Airplanes
†F-86D-40 and later airplanes

‡Removed from TF-86D Airplanes

IX for instrument letdown instructions.) The zero reader is powered from the primary bus, and its operation depends upon the availability of ac power.

Zero Reader Indicator Controls.

The zero reader indicator incorporates a course set knob used to "zero in" a new directional heading and a pitch trim adjustment knob to compensate for changes in pitch with changes in airspeed at a constant attitude.

Zero Reader Selector Switch Unit.

The selector switch unit (16, figure 1-6) contains an altitude knob to turn the altitude control signal on or off and a selector knob to switch radio signals. A mechanical interlock automatically turns the altitude knob OFF when the selector knob is placed at APPROACH so that the glide path signal can control the horizontal bar. Whenever the altitude knob is OFF, a green light at the lower left corner of the selector switch unit comes on. The selector knob, which controls reception of radio signals, has four positions: FLIGHT INST., RIGHT, LEFT, and APPROACH. The selector knob is placed at FLIGHT INST. when it is desired to have the zero reader function as a gyro-controlled flight instrument independent of radio signals. When knob is in the RIGHT position, the indicator bars are affected by the signals as when knob is in the FLIGHT INST. position, but a radio navigation signal also controls the vertical bar. This position is selected for flight on a localizer beam with the blue sector on the right of the flight path (normal approach heading). The RIGHT position is always used for flight on a visual omnirange so that "to and from" signals can be discriminated without reversing indication on zero reader vertical bar. The LEFT position of the selector knob is used when the blue sector is on the left of the flight path so that the zero reader vertical bar response is not reversed. With selector knob in the APPROACH position, all signals present with knob in the RIGHT position remain in effect, except that the altitude control signal to the horizontal bar is replaced by the glide path signal.

LIGHTING EQUIPMENT.
EXTERIOR LIGHTING.

Exterior lighting consists of four position lights on wing tips and tail, two fuselage lights, and a combination landing and taxi light. One fuselage light is in the top of the fuselage, just aft of the cockpit; the other is in the bottom of the fuselage, directly below. On F-86D-1 Airplanes and F-86D-10 and later airplanes, each fuselage light contains one large lamp and one small lamp; on F-86D-5 Airplanes, only one lamp is employed. The retractable landing and taxi light, mounted on the bottom of the engine air intake duct just forward of the nose wheel strut, extends downward. The landing light beam is directed forward and down from the nose of the airplane for illumination during approach and landing. In the landing position, the light beam extends downward 12.5 degrees below the longitudinal axis of the airplane. When the weight of the airplane is on the nose gear, the light extends further, until the angle of the beam is one degree above the longitudinal axis of the airplane, for taxiing. When used during night take-off, the beam is high until the airplane "breaks ground"; then it returns to the beam-low position, where it remains until retracted manually. All exterior lighting controls are powered from the primary bus except the landing and taxi light switch; it is powered from monitored bus No. 1.

Exterior Lighting Flasher Switch.

The flasher switch, mounted on the instrument and position light control panel (figure 4-8) on the right aft console, controls the position lights. From the OFF position, the switch can be moved to STEADY, which will cause all four position lights to burn steadily, or it can be moved to FLASH, effecting a repeated regular-interval flashing.

Position Light Dimmer Switch.

The position light dimmer switch, on the instrument and position light control panel (figure 4-8), regulates the brilliance of the wing tip and tail position lights, and on F-86D-5 and later airplanes, controls the brilliance of the fuselage lights. Its two positions are DIM and BRIGHT.

Fuselage Light Dimmer Switch (F-86D-1 Airplanes).

The fuselage light dimmer switch, on the instrument and position light control panel (figure 4-8) on the right aft console, controls the small lamp in each fuselage light. When this switch is moved from OFF to DIM or BRIGHT, these lamps come on and burn steadily at the selected degree of brilliance.

Landing and Taxi Light Switch.

The switch for the combination landing and taxi light is on the engine control panel. (See figure 1-10.) It has three positions: RETRACT, OFF, and EXTEND & ON. The light is automatically turned on when extended and turned off when retracted.

Master Code Switch and Code Selector Switch (F-86D-1 Airplanes).

The two-position master code switch and the code selector switch are on the instrument and position light control panel. (See figure 4-8.) When the master code switch is turned ON and the code selector switch is moved from OFF to one of the 12 letter selections, the large lamps in the fuselage lights will repeatedly flash the selected letter in Morse code.

Section IV

T. O. 1F-86D-1

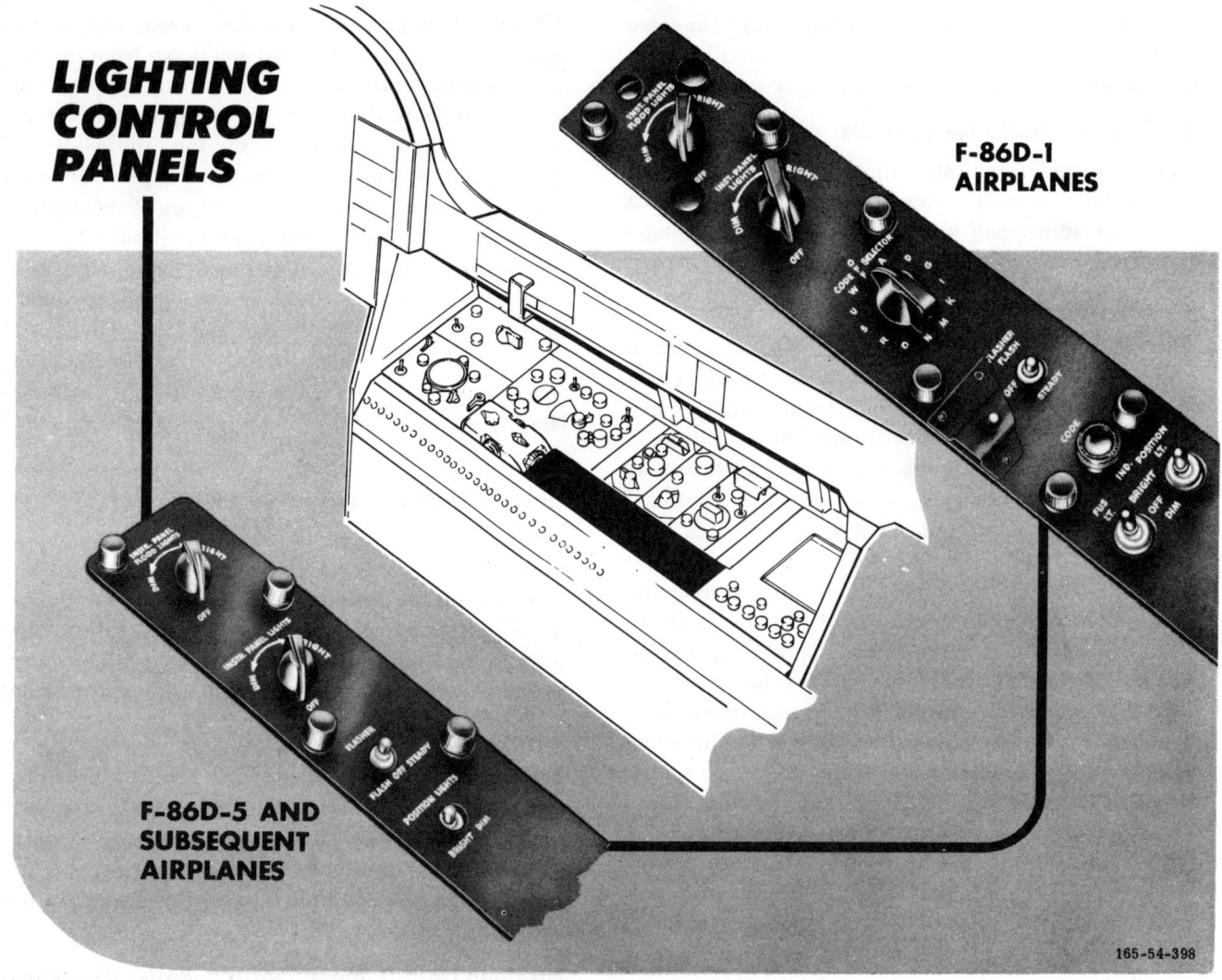

Figure 4-8

Note

On F-86D-1 Airplanes, the master code switch, code selector switch, code indicator light, and the large lamp in each fuselage light are inoperative.

Code Indicator Light (F-86D-1 Airplanes).

A code indicator light, mounted between the dimmer switches and the flasher and master code switches on the instrument and position light control panel (figure 4-8), flashes simultaneously with the large lamps in the fuselage lights, showing that the selected letter is being flashed. The light is a push-to-test type, permitting check of bulb illumination when the master code switch is OFF.

INTERIOR LIGHTING.

On F-86D-1 Airplanes, the instrument panel and the console panels, with the exception of the oxygen regulator panel, are lighted indirectly. On F-86D-5 and later airplanes, the instruments are individually lighted. In addition, two auxiliary floodlights for each console and one auxiliary floodlight for the instrument panel are provided on each side of the cockpit. The console auxiliary floodlights are directed down upon the consoles, while the instrument panel auxiliary floodlights are directed forward from mountings on either side of the lower forward canopy frame. The oxygen regulator panel is lighted by a small hooded utility light just above the regulator. The stand-by compass and the accelerometer, mounted at the base of the windshield bow on each side of the main instrument panel, are individually lighted. The stand-by compass light is built into the instrument, while the accelerometer lights are enclosed in an instrument lighting fixture attached to the face of the instrument. An extension light on the right aft side of the cockpit has a spring-coiled cord; the light can be disengaged and held by hand, or it can be remounted in another socket-type mounting on the

4-18

lower right forward canopy frame for maximum flexibility. On F-86D-25 and later airplanes, two thunderstorm lights (one on either side of the seat headrest) are provided to supply a constant white light so that vision is protected against lightning flashes during any thunderstorm operation. All interior lighting controls are powered from the primary bus. When no external power is being supplied and generators are inoperative, all lighting is made operable when the battery-starter switch is turned to BATTERY.

Instrument Panel Floodlight Rheostat.

An instrument panel floodlight rheostat is mounted at the top of the instrument and position light control panel (figure 4-8) on the right aft console. When moved from OFF to DIM or BRIGHT, this rheostat turns on and controls the brilliance of the two auxiliary instrument panel floodlights.

Instrument Panel Light Rheostat.

The instrument panel light rheostat is aft of the instrument panel floodlight rheostat on the instrument and position light control panel. (See figure 4-8.) This rheostat, with OFF, DIM, and BRIGHT positions, controls the lighting and brilliance of the instrument panel lights.

Console Panel and Floodlight Rheostat and Selector Switch.

A console panel and floodlight rheostat (4, figure 1-8; 5, figure 1-9), on the console light control panel, is outboard of the oxygen regulator on the right console. This rheostat, when moved from OFF toward DIM and BRIGHT, simultaneously turns on and regulates the degree of brilliance of the console panel lights, auxiliary console floodlights, and oxygen regulator utility light. The console panel and floodlight selector switch (2, figure 1-8; 3, figure 1-9), also on the console light control panel, allows the selection of either CONSOLE or FLOOD & CONSOLE or turns OFF all console panel and floodlights. Both the rheostat and the selector switch must be moved from the OFF position for the console panel lights and floodlights to be illuminated. On late airplanes,* three lights which illuminate the landing gear control panel are also controlled from the rheostat.

Compass and Accelerometer Light Switch.

A switch, mounted on a panel below the stand-by compass (figure 1-10), controls the lights for both the stand-by compass and the accelerometer. When moved from the neutral OFF position to COMPASS & ACCEL, the switch causes the lights for both instruments to come on. When the switch is moved to COMPASS LIGHT, only the light for the stand-by compass is turned on. The brilliance of the compass and accelerometer lights is controlled by the instrument panel light rheostat.

---

*F-86D-45 and later airplanes

Thunderstorm Light Rheostat (F-86D-25 and Later Airplanes).

The thunderstorm light rheostat (9, figure 1-9) is on the vertical panel, aft of the right console. This rheostat, when moved from OFF to DIM or BRIGHT, turns on and controls the brilliance of the two thunderstorm lights.

OXYGEN SYSTEM.

The airplane is equipped with a gaseous oxygen system in two different supply configurations. On F-86D-1 Airplanes, oxygen is supplied by two Type D-2 cylinders on each side of the upper fuselage behind the cockpit. These may be supplemented by temporary installation of a third Type D-2 cylinder to increase the oxygen supply for ferrying. On F-86D-5 and later airplanes, a permanent installation of two Type D-2 cylinders and a smaller Type B-3 cylinder is incorporated, with no provisions for temporary installation of additional cylinders. The system has an operating pressure of 400 psi. For combat safety, the cylinders supply the regulator through two distribution lines joined at a check valve near the regulator. The complete oxygen system can be serviced at a single filler valve accessible through an access door on the lower left side of the fuselage forward of the wing. (See figure 1-32.) On F-86D-1 through F-86D-30 Airplanes, a Type D-1 automatic pressure-breathing diluter-demand oxygen regulator, mounted on the right forward console, controls the system. On F-86D-35 and later airplanes, a D-2 oxygen regulator is installed. Operation of the D-2 regulator is identical to that of the D-1 regulator. A pressure gage and flow indicator is incorporated in the regulator. This regulator automatically supplies a proper mixture of oxygen and air at all altitudes. At high altitudes, the regulator automatically supplies positive pressure breathing. The delivery pressure varies automatically with changes in altitude. Regardless of how much oxygen is being used, the pressure will always be the amount required for any specific altitude. A red warning light is mounted on the instrument panel to warn the pilot of any malfunction or abnormal operating condition of the oxygen regulator. A pressure relief valve on the outlet side of the regulator relieves excess pressures. Only a pressure-demand oxygen mask should be used. The approximate duration of the oxygen supply is given in figures 4-9 and 4-10. To prevent damage to oxygen hose when it is not in use, the hose may be clipped to the webbing provided below the right side of the instrument panel.

OXYGEN SYSTEM CONTROLS.

Regulator Diluter Lever.

An oxygen regulator diluter lever is provided in the top right corner of the oxygen regulator panel (figure

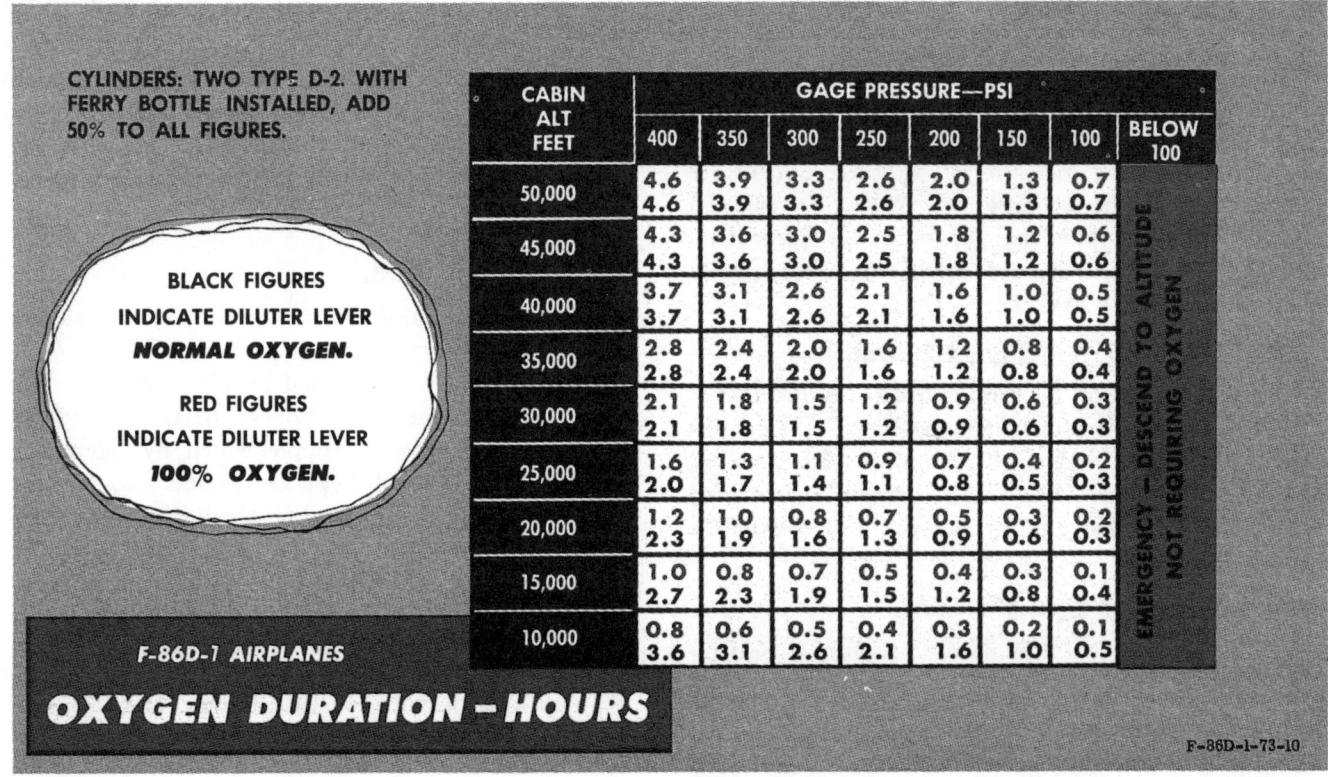

Figure 4-9

4-11), to select NORMAL OXYGEN for all normal usage or 100% OXYGEN for emergency use.

Regulator Supply Lever.

The oxygen regulator supply lever, at the bottom of the oxygen regulator panel (figure 4-11), should be safety-wired to the ON position at all times during normal operation, to prevent inadvertent closing off of the oxygen supply. If desired, because of regulator malfunction or emergency conditions, the safety wire can easily be broken and the supply lever can be positioned at OFF.

Regulator Emergency Toggle Lever.

The oxygen regulator emergency toggle lever, above the supply lever on the oxygen regulator panel (figure 4-11), should be in the center position at all times unless an unscheduled pressure increase is desired. Moving the toggle lever either way from its unmarked center OFF position provides continuous positive pressure to the oxygen mask. When the toggle lever is in the center position, it may be pressed to momentarily release enough pressure to test the oxygen mask for leaks.

Regulator Warning Light Switch.

The oxygen regulator warning light switch, in the top left corner of the oxygen regulator panel (figure 4-11), derives its power from the primary bus and turns on the red warning light circuit. The switch should be ON at all times when the regulator is in use.

OXYGEN SYSTEM INDICATORS.

Pressure Gage and Flow Indicator.

The pressure gage and flow indicator on the oxygen regulator panel (figure 4-11) combines the oxygen pressure gage and the oxygen flow indicator in a single instrument. The pressure gage shows the amount of oxygen in the cylinders. The oxygen flow indicator consists of four small slots arranged symmetrically around the lower half of the gage dial face. These slots show alternately black and white with each breath of the user.

Note

As the airplane ascends to high altitudes and low temperatures, the oxygen cylinders become chilled. As the cylinders become cooled, the oxygen gage pressure indication is reduced, sometimes rather rapidly. With a 100°F decrease in temperature in the cylinders, the gage pressure can be expected to drop 20 percent. This rapid fall in pressure is occasionally a cause for unnecessary alarm. All the oxygen is still there, and as the airplane descends to warmer altitudes, the pressure will tend to rise

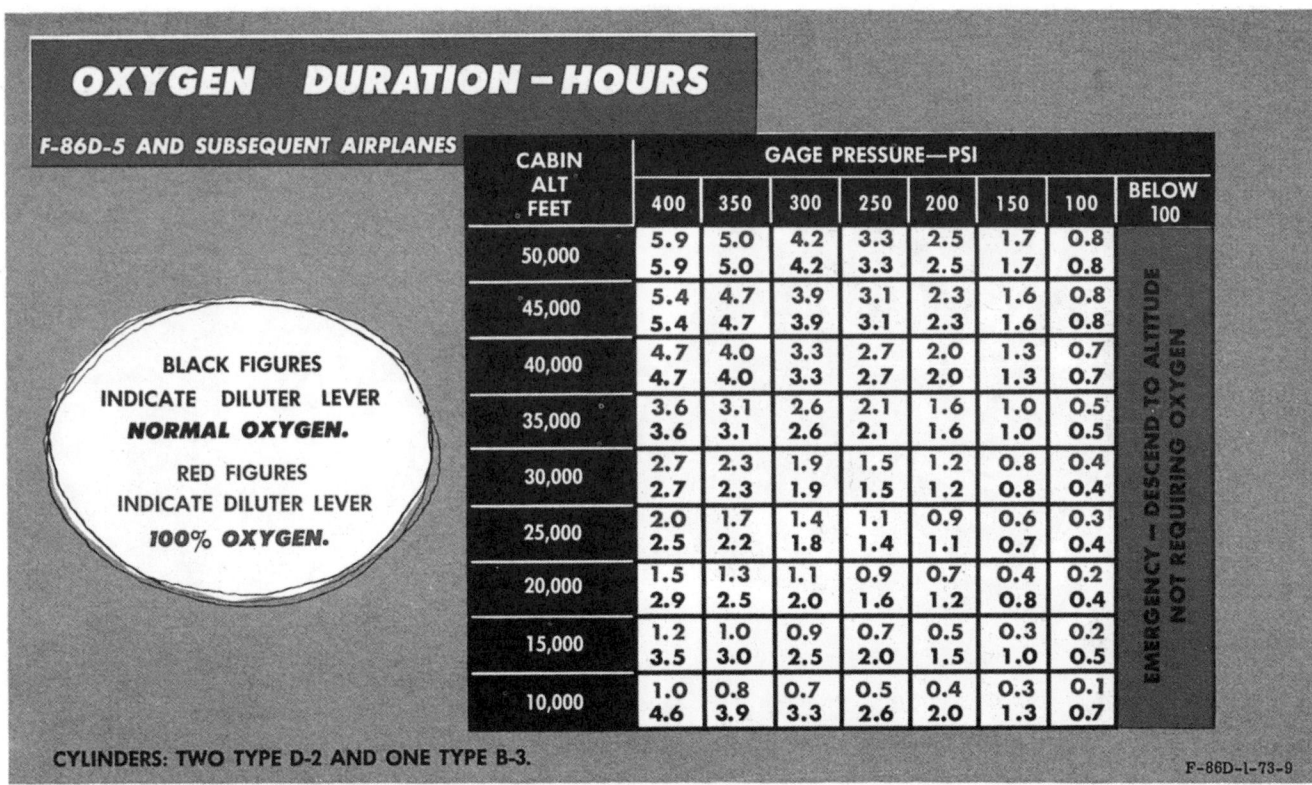

Figure 4-10

again, so that the rate of oxygen usage may appear to be slower than normal. A rapid fall in oxygen pressure while the airplane is in level flight, or while it is descending, is not ordinarily due to falling temperature. When this happens, leakage or loss of oxygen must be suspected.

Oxygen System Warning Light.

An oxygen system warning light (4, figure 1-4; 10, figure 1-5) is provided in the left side (lower right side on F-86D-30 Airplanes) of the instrument panel and is powered by the primary bus. When the warning light switch is moved to ON, the light comes on and becomes bright or blinking bright within 15 seconds. It remains bright if there is no oxygen flow or if there is a continuous flow through the regulator. However, if there is a continuous flow, the light may dim within 10 seconds and then return to bright within 60 seconds and remain bright or blinking bright. If the pilot has the mask on, the warning light becomes dim within 10 seconds when normal breathing causes proper oxygen flow through the regulator. With the flow induced by a normal breathing cycle, the warning light continues to be dim. However, any departure from proper operation that subsequently causes oxygen flow to cease or to flow from the regulator in a continuous stream provides a constant or blinking bright light.

Note
The action of the warning light system is based on a normal breathing rate. Too fast or too slow a breathing rate may result in erratic warning light indications.

OXYGEN SYSTEM PREFLIGHT CHECK.

Before take-off, the oxygen system should be checked as follows:

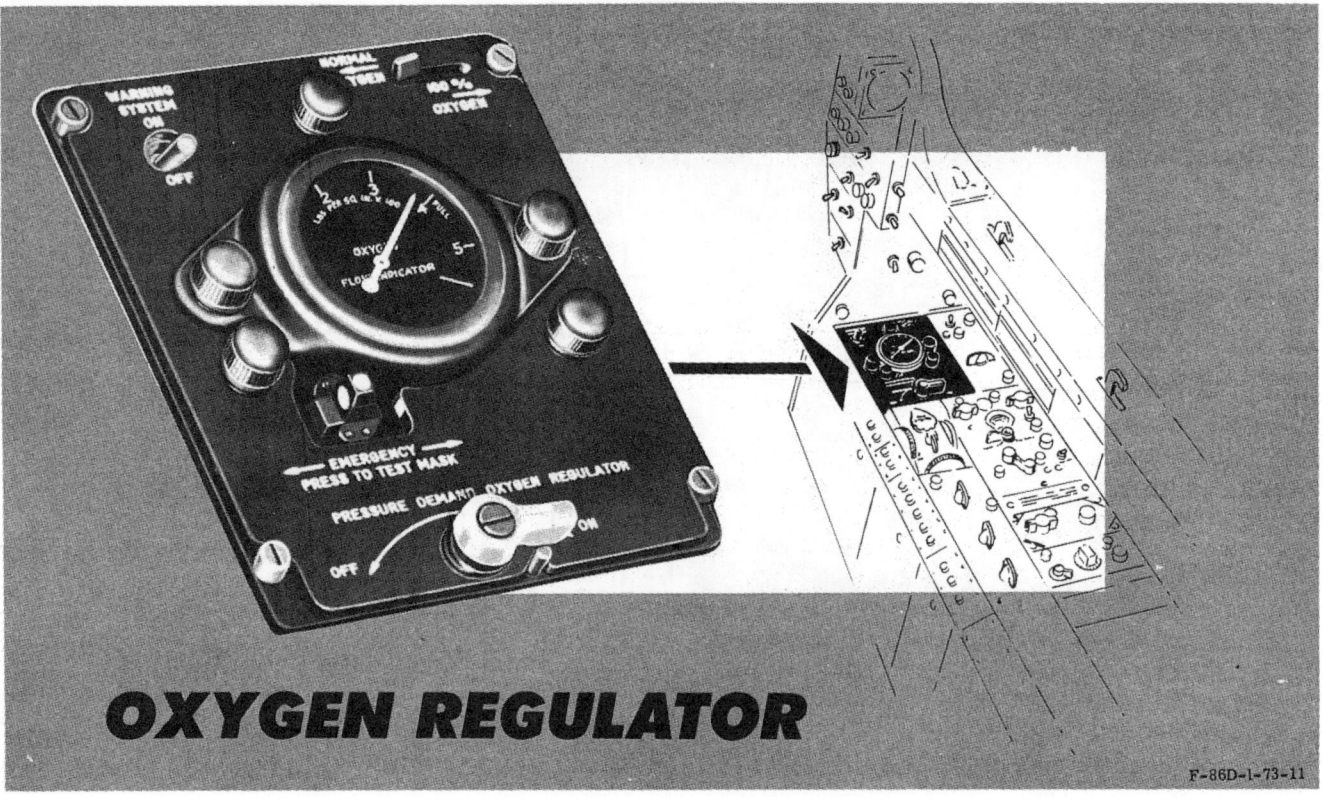

Figure 4-11

Note

- This test procedure applies only to an initial preflight check of the system. In-flight tests or repeated tests made within short periods may produce false or misleading indications.
- Above 30,000 feet, you may sometimes notice a vibration, or wheezing sound, in the pressure-demand mask. This condition does not indicate a malfunction and can be overlooked.

1. Check that personal leads are properly mated at ejection seat fitting. Note oxygen pressure gage indication (400 psi minimum). See figure 4-12 for oxygen hose hookup.

2. Check oxygen regulator with the diluter lever first at the NORMAL OXYGEN position and then at the 100% OXYGEN position as follows: Remove mask and blow gently into end of the oxygen regulator hose as during normal exhalation. There should be resistance to blowing. Little or no resistance to blowing indicates a leak or faulty operation.

3. Place oxygen regulator warning light switch in ON position. Warning light should give a bright (steady or blinking) light. Move emergency toggle from center to left or right position. The warning light should change from a bright light to a dim glow and back to bright. Return emergency toggle to center (off) position.

4. With regulator supply valve ON, oxygen mask connected to regulator, and diluter lever in 100% OXYGEN position, breathe normally into mask and conduct the following checks:

  a. Observe blinker for proper operation. Warning light should change from a bright to a dim glow.

  b. Deflect emergency toggle to right or left. A positive pressure should be supplied to mask. Return emergency toggle to center position.

  c. Depress emergency toggle straight in. A positive pressure should result within the mask. Hold breath to determine whether there is leakage around mask. Release emergency toggle; positive pressure should cease.

5. Return diluter lever to NORMAL OXYGEN.

OXYGEN SYSTEM NORMAL OPERATION.

1. Before each flight, be sure oxygen pressure gage reads at least 400 psi. If pressure is below this minimum, have the oxygen system charged to capacity before take-off.

2. Oxygen regulator diluter lever NORMAL OXYGEN.

3. Oxygen regulator supply lever ON.

4. Oxygen regulator warning light switch ON.

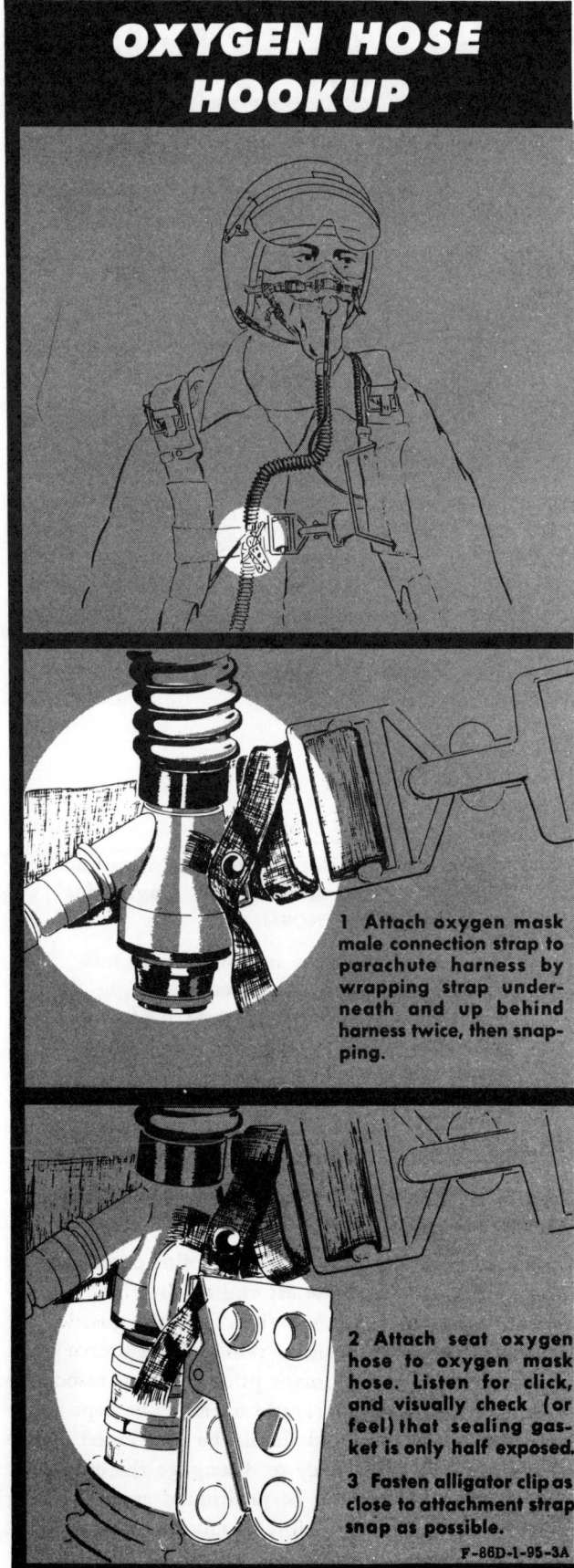

Figure 4-12

OXYGEN SYSTEM EMERGENCY OPERATION.

With development of anoxia symptoms, proceed as follows:

1. Oxygen regulator diluter lever 100% OXYGEN.

2. Push oxygen regulator emergency toggle lever either way from center. If oxygen regulator becomes inoperative, pull ball handle on H-2 emergency oxygen bail-out bottle and descend to a cockpit altitude below 10,000 feet as soon as possible.

AUTOMATIC PILOT.*

The F-5 automatic pilot is an electronic flight control equipped with an automatic horizontal tail trim unit. This automatic pilot will hold the airplane on any preselected course that may be desired, change the course at will with a coordinated turn, or maintain the airplane laterally level and in any desired angle or climb or dive up to 40 degrees from level flight. Automatic control starts in the gyro and amplifier control unit, which includes ac-powered directional and vertical gyros as references. The directional gyro establishes a reference for the azimuth heading of the airplane; the vertical gyro establishes a flight reference about the lateral and longitudinal axis of the airplane. The automatic horizontal tail trim unit automatically operates the horizontal tail trim actuator to maintain the airplane in proper longitudinal trim while the automatic pilot is engaged. The horizontal trim portion of the normal trim switch on the control stick is inoperative while the automatic pilot is engaged, to prevent manual operation of the horizontal tail trim in opposition to the automatic function. Disengaging the automatic pilot will automatically restore the horizontal tail trim function to the normal trim switch. The automatic pilot can be overpowered at any time or can be immediately disengaged by use of the automatic pilot release switch on the control stick or the automatic pilot engaging switch on the flight controller. If the automatic pilot is engaged during a wing-level dive or climb, the airplane will continue on course in the dive or climb. However, if the automatic pilot is engaged while the airplane is in a level, climbing, or diving turn, the wings will return to about level attitude. On some airplanes† and those changed by T. O., an automatic approach coupler is installed. The automatic pilot uses signals from the automatic approach coupler to guide the airplane during instrument approaches on the radio beams received from the instrument landing transmitters. The automatic approach coupler equipment is controlled by engage buttons on the automatic approach coupler controller on the vertical panel forward of the right console. Indicator

---

*Removed from TF-86D Airplanes
†F-86D-1 Airplane AF54-477 and F-86D-30 and later airplanes

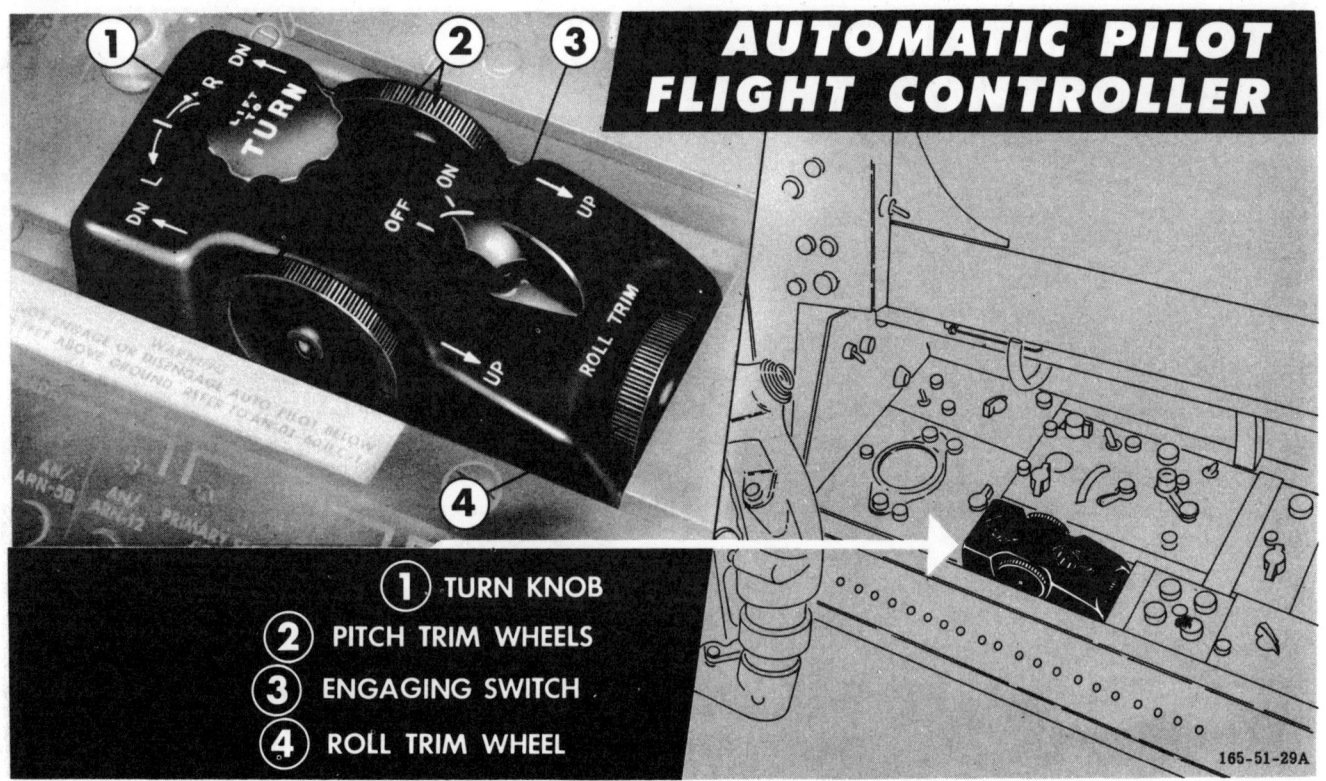

Figure 4-13

lights, incorporated in the engage buttons, come on to show when the localizer and glide path channels are engaged. When the airplane approaches the localizer beam, the localizer engage button is pressed. When the center of the localizer beam is approached, the automatic pilot automatically turns the airplane into the localizer beam and establishes a heading coincident with the beam center. When the glide path beam center is reached, the glide path engage button is depressed. The automatic pilot then automatically noses the airplane down until the flight path coincides with the center of the glide path beam. The automatic pilot automatically compensates the airplane for normal crosswind conditions. Since no automatic flare-out feature is incorporated, the automatic approach system must be turned off just before touchdown, or sooner if desired, and the landing completed manually. As the automatic approach coupler can be engaged only while the automatic pilot is engaged, disengaging the automatic pilot automatically turns the approach coupler off. However, if it is desired to accomplish a go-around on automatic pilot, the automatic approach coupler can be turned off without disengaging the automatic pilot, by lifting the turn knob on the flight controller out of the detent position and dropping it back again into the detent position. All automatic pilot controls are powered from the gyro busses.

Note

- The automatic pilot automatic trim will not function unless the alternate longitudinal trim switch is at NORM.
- Maximum use of the autopilot on all missions is recommended, because flight familiarization and repeated practice improve proficiency and instill confidence in the equipment.

AUTOMATIC PILOT CONTROLS AND INDICATORS.*

Automatic Pilot Power Switch (F-86D-20 Airplane AF51-3044 and All Later Airplanes).

A guarded two-position automatic pilot power switch (10, figure 1-9) is on the aft end of the right circuit-breaker panel. Moving the switch from the guarded ON position to the OFF position removes the source of ac and dc power to the automatic pilot gyros and associated equipment. This switch should normally be kept in the guarded ON position and should be positioned at OFF only in case of emergency to disengage the automatic pilot. Should the switch be positioned at OFF during flight, it will not be possible to engage the automatic pilot until about 3 minutes after the switch has been returned to the ON position. On airplanes with control system tie-in (CSTI) installed, there is a three-position

*Removed from TF-86D Airplanes

switch, CSTI, OFF, and CSTI & AUTOPILOT, and the switch guard is removed. [Refer to "Control Surface Tie-in System (CSTI)," in this section.]

Automatic Pilot Release Switch.

An automatic pilot release switch is on the control stick (figure 1-23), just below the stick grip. The switch is actuated by squeezing the grip that covers it. Actuation of the switch disengages the automatic pilot and causes the automatic pilot engaging switch on the flight controller to return automatically to the OFF position.

Automatic Pilot Flight Controller.

All flight control functions of the automatic pilot are centered in the flight controller (figure 4-13), on the right console. The flight controller incorporates the engaging switch, the roll trim wheel, the pitch trim wheels, and the turn knob.

Engaging Switch.
The automatic pilot engaging switch (figure 4-13) is a rotary switch with an OFF and an ON position. Placing the switch at ON electrically connects the automatic pilot to the flight control system. The switch is automatically locked in the OFF position until a time delay of 3 minutes has elapsed from the time the power is supplied to the primary bus, or whenever the turn knob is not in the neutral detent position.

Pitch Trim Wheels.
The pitch trim wheels (figure 4-13) control the nose-up or nose-down position of the airplane. If the pitch trim wheels are rotated aft for nose-up trim or forward for nose-down trim, the airplane will maintain the selected attitude. The pitch trim is limited to a climb or dive angle of about 40 degrees.

Roll Trim Wheel.
The roll trim wheel (figure 4-13) controls the lateral trim of the airplane. If the roll trim wheel is rotated clockwise for right wing down or counterclockwise for left wing down, the airplane will maintain the selected roll attitude. The roll trim is limited to about 10 degrees left wing or right wing down.

Turn Knob.
The turn knob (figure 4-13), marked "LIFT TO TURN," must be lifted before it can be turned to the right or left. When the knob is lifted out of neutral detent and turned to right or left, the airplane will make a coordinated turn in the corresponding direction. The angular rotation of the turn knob will govern the bank angle in the turn up to maximum of about 50 degrees. The azimuth heading at the end of the turn will be the actual heading of the airplane at the instant the turn knob is returned to its neutral detent position.

Note

It will be necessary to introduce appropriate pitch trim corrections with the pitch trim wheels on the flight controller if it is desired to maintain altitude during, or at the completion of, a turn maneuver.

Automatic Approach Coupler Controller.

The automatic approach coupler controls are grouped on the approach coupler controller (figure 4-14), on the vertical panel forward of the right console. The controller incorporates three combination push-button and indicator light switches, marked "LOCALIZER," "GLIDE PATH," and "ALTITUDE," and an altitude "OFF" push-button switch. The localizer and glide path switches are used to engage the automatic approach coupler to the automatic pilot. Pressing the altitude switch (not connected at present) will engage a barometric pressure control to the automatic pilot, which will automatically maintain the airplane at the specific altitude at which it was engaged. The altitude "OFF" switch (not connected at present) is used to disengage the altitude control.

Localizer Engage Button and Indicator Light.
A combination push-button switch and indicator light, marked "LOCALIZER," is provided on the automatic approach coupler controller (figure 4-14) to connect the localizer receiver signals to the automatic pilot. As the airplane approaches the localizer beam, depressing the localizer button allows the automatic pilot to use the proper maneuvering signals from the localizer receiver and automatically turn the airplane to intercept and establish a heading along the center of the localizer beam. Illumination of the indicator light, within the engage button, shows that the localizer channel is connected to the automatic pilot.

Glide Path Engage Button and Indicator Light.
A combination push-button switch and indicator light, marked "GLIDE PATH" and located on the automatic approach coupler controller (figure 4-14), is used to connect the glide path receiver signals to the automatic pilot as the airplane reaches the center of the glide path beam. Depressing the glide path button when the airplane reaches the center of the glide path beam connects the maneuvering signals from the glide path receiver to the automatic pilot, which uses these signals to nose the airplane down to intercept and establish a descent along the center of the glide path beam. A safety interlock prevents engagement of the glide path receiver to the automatic pilot until after the localizer signals are first connected to the automatic pilot. Illumination of the indicator light, within the engage button, shows that the glide path channel is connected to the automatic pilot.

Altitude Engage Button and Indicator Light.
A combination push-button and indicator light, marked "ALTITUDE" and located on the automatic approach coupler controller (figure 4-14), is used to maintain altitude control during automatic approaches. At present, this button is *not connected* and is therefore *inoperable*.

Altitude "OFF" Button.
The altitude "OFF" button, on the automatic approach coupler controller (figure

Section IV
T. O. 1F-86D-1

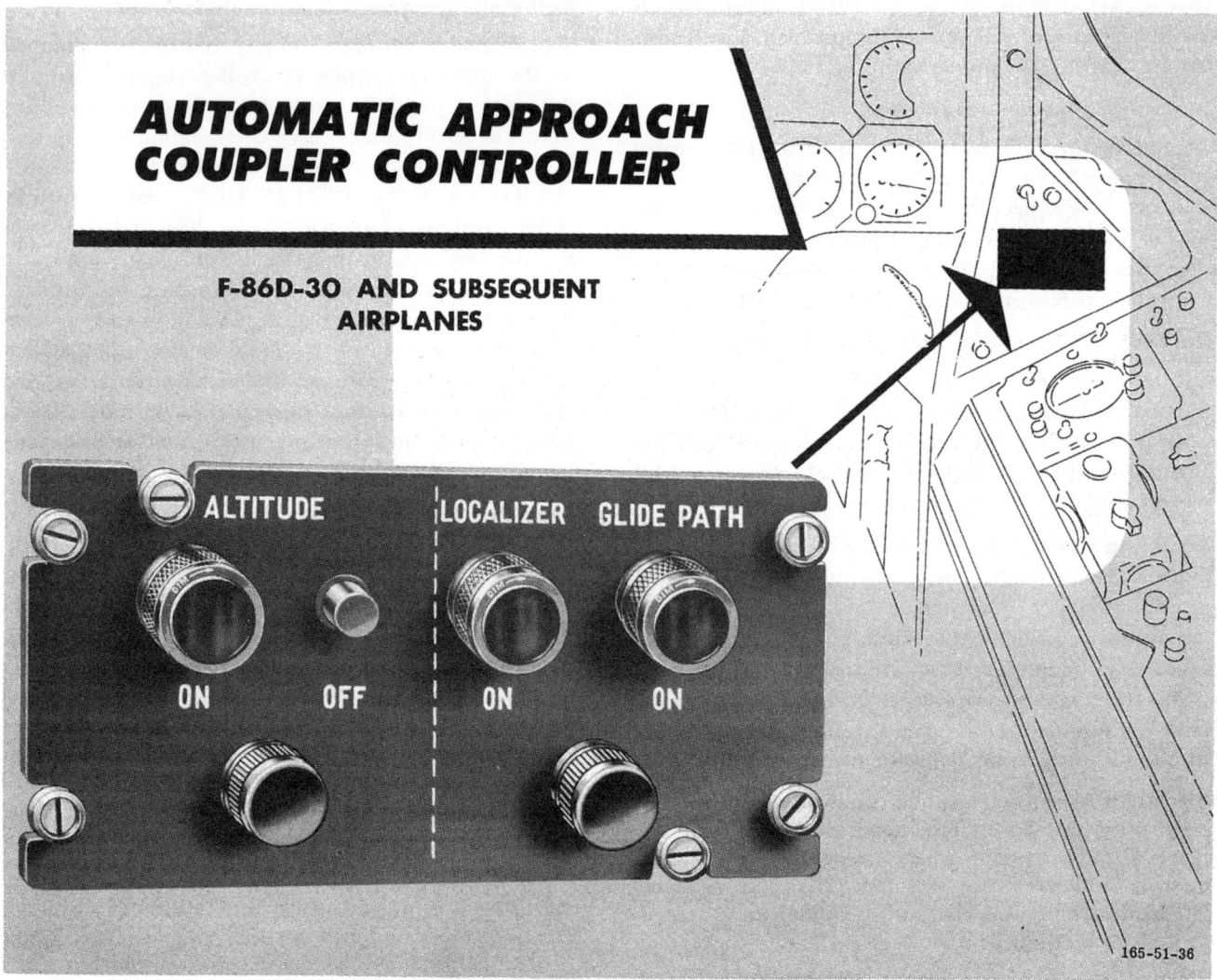

Figure 4-14

4-14), is used to disengage the altitude control. As the altitude control is not connected, this button is *not operable*.

Automatic Pilot Pitch Trim Indicator.

On late airplanes* and those changed by T. O., a pitch trim indicator (20, figure 1-4; 9, figure 1-5), on the upper left side of the instrument panel, shows the pitch trim of the airplane while it is operating on automatic pilot. Position of the needle allows the pilot to anticipate an airplane out-of-trim condition upon disengagement of the automatic pilot, if the automatic pitch trim should not function correctly. This indicator is powered by signals received from the automatic pilot horizontal tail servo and will operate only when the automatic pilot engaging switch is at ON. Needle displacement toward either "UP" or "DOWN" shows that the airplane is trimmed for that flight attitude.

F-86D-30 and later airplanes

4-26

AUTOMATIC PILOT NORMAL OPERATION.

Ground Tests.

The automatic pilot should be ground-checked before each flight as follows:

1. With flight controls in neutral and turn knob in the neutral detent, turn engaging switch to ON.

Note

Engaging switch is automatically locked OFF until primary bus has been energized for about 3 minutes.

2. Rotate roll trim wheel in each direction and check control stick for corresponding movement. Return roll trim wheel to neutral position by rotating it as required to streamline ailerons.

3. Lift turn knob out of neutral detent; turn knob in each direction and check control stick for corresponding movement. Rudder pedals will momentarily move to

coordinate with control stick. Return turn knob to neutral detent. Control stick will return to neutral, but rudder pedals will not.

Note

On F-86D-10 through F-86D-30 Airplanes, the rudder pedals will not move during positioning of the turn knob, because of the method of automatic pilot rudder servo tie-in.

4. Rotate pitch trim wheels in each direction and check control stick for corresponding movement. Return control stick to neutral, using pitch trim wheels.

5. On airplanes equipped with automatic approach coupler, perform the following:

    a. With instrument approach radio receivers on (refer to "Glide Path and Localizer Receivers"), press localizer engage button and see that indicator light comes on. Control stick should move to show turn in direction of deflection of localizer needle on course indicator (approach indicator on F-86D-1 through F-86D-30 Airplanes).

    b. Depress glide path engage button and see that indicator light comes on. Control stick should move back for an upward deflection of the glide path needle.

    c. Lift turn knob on flight controller to disengage automatic approach coupler from automatic pilot. See that localizer and glide path indicator lights go out.

6. Recheck roll and pitch trim wheels for neutral setting.

7. Squeeze release switch on control stick to disengage automatic pilot. Engaging switch on flight controller should return to OFF. Manually check flight controls for correct operation and freedom of movement.

In-flight Operation.

1. Manually trim airplane for wing-level flight on desired course and pitch attitude.

2. Turn engaging switch to ON.

When automatic pilot is being engaged, hold control stick firmly to prevent any abrupt resultant maneuver that may occur should automatic pilot not function properly.

Note

• Failure to return roll trim wheel to neutral before take-off can cause the airplane to roll suddenly either right or left to an extreme of 10 degrees when the automatic pilot is engaged.

• Engaging switch cannot be turned ON unless turn knob is in the neutral detent.

• There are no indices to be lined up before automatic pilot engagement.

3. Adjust roll trim wheel as necessary to maintain wings level.

4. Perform turns and changes in pitch attitude as desired by operation of appropriate controls on flight controller. Climbing or diving turns can be accomplished by simultaneous use of pitch trim wheels and the turn knob. It is recommended that the autopilot be engaged during IFR conditions, to assist the pilot in retaining the desired flight attitude. If the autopilot is engaged while the pilot still has valid attitude indication from the flight instruments, it may preclude difficulties arising as a result of losing such indication.

Note

Use of the autopilot for recovery from unusual flight attitudes is not recommended. While successful recovery is likely in most instances, certain critical attitudes, airspeeds, and altitudes make such a procedure inadvisable.

Maintain close supervision of the automatic pilot, particularly below 5000 feet, to reduce effect should automatic pilot not function correctly.

Note

Any time binding and/or jerky control operation is experienced, the automatic pilot power switch should be moved to OFF to eliminate this problem.

5. When automatic pilot run is completed, squeeze release switch on control stick to disengage automatic pilot, or turn engaging switch on flight controller to OFF. On F-86D-30 and later airplanes, the pitch trim indicator may be checked for proper alignment. Observation of a misalignment allows the pilot to anticipate a respective airplane out-of-trim condition upon disengagement of the automatic pilot.

When automatic pilot is being disengaged, hold control stick firmly to prevent any abrupt maneuver that may occur should the automatic pilot not function properly.

Automatic Approach Operation.

Familiarity with ILAS beam is necessary in order to properly make an acceptable automatic approach.

During automatic approach, the airplane will follow a course shown by the course indicator* (approach indicator†). On airplanes equipped with an automatic approach coupler, an automatic approach may be accomplished as follows:

1. Turn on instrument approach radio receivers according to directions in this section.

Note

The power switch on the instrument approach† or vhf navigation* radio panel must be ON and frequency selector set to the desired channel about 20 minutes before arrival at destination.

2. With automatic pilot turn knob in neutral detent, turn automatic pilot engaging switch ON.

CAUTION

When automatic pilot is being engaged, hold control stick firmly to prevent any abrupt resultant maneuver that may occur should automatic pilot not function properly.

3. Approach localizer beam heading at the specific minimum approach altitude, or any altitude above the minimum so long as it is well below the glide path beam, and at a maximum airspeed of 180 to 200 knots IAS. Intercept localizer beam at any angle up to 90 degrees of the beam heading (smaller intercept angles give less overshoot and are preferable) and not less than 10 miles from the runway (transmitter station). The greater the intercept angle, the greater must be the distance of beam intercept from the runway. Entry into the beam should be at a minimum of 15 miles from the end of the runway when the intercept angle is 90 degrees.

4. When the localizer needle on the course indicator (approach indicator on F-86D-1 through F-86D-30 Airplanes) starts a steady movement toward center (between one and two dots needle deflection), depress localizer button on approach coupler controller. The indicator light will come on when the approach coupler is engaged. Maintain altitude during turn-on and until glide path is intercepted, by introducing necessary pitch corrections using pitch trim wheels on flight controller.

Note

When the airplane rolls into a bank during automatic turn-on to the localizer, the nose will drop. Introduce nose-up trim by using pitch trim wheels on flight controller to hold level flight. When the airplane rolls out of a bank on the localizer beam, the airplane will climb. Introduce nose-down trim in the same manner to hold level flight.

5. After airplane has automatically turned and is stabilized on center of beam heading (vertical needle centered), and before glide path needle starts its downward movement, lower landing gear and flaps (below 185 knots IAS) and extend speed brakes as desired.

Note

- When flaps are lowered, the airplane will start to climb immediately. Introduce nose-down trim, using pitch trim wheels and flight controller to hold level flight.
- A more stable glide path control is obtained if full flaps are used.

6. Reduce and stabilize airspeed to 160 knots IAS before intercepting glide path. Power settings should be the same as for a normal approach pattern.

7. When glide path needle on course indicator (approach indicator on F-86D-1 through F-86D-30 Airplanes) reaches mid-position, depress glide path button. The indicator light will come on when approach coupler is engaged.

Note

It is permissible to use the pitch trim wheels to assist the approach coupler if it should be necessary to correct for a large glide path error signal in a relatively short time.

8. During descent on glide path, changes in airspeed, power, and configuration should be held at a minimum to minimize deviations from glide path beam.

9. Automatic pilot pitch trim indicator on F-86D-30 and later airplanes may be checked for proper alignment. This allows the pilot to anticipate an airplane out-of-trim condition upon disengagement of the automatic pilot, should the automatic pitch trim not function correctly.

10. Just before touchdown, or sooner if desired, squeeze automatic pilot override switch on control stick (disengaging automatic pilot and automatic approach coupler) and complete landing manually.

CAUTION

When automatic pilot is being disengaged, hold control stick firmly to prevent any abrupt maneuver that may occur should the automatic pilot not function properly.

Note

- If it is necessary for an automatic go-around, the automatic approach coupler may be

---

*F-86D-35 and later airplanes
†F-86D-1 through F-86D-30 Airplanes

disengaged from the automatic pilot by lifting the automatic pilot turn knob in the detent position and dropping it again. This leaves the automatic pilot in control, and a go-around may be made on automatic pilot. If a manual go-around is desired, squeeze automatic pilot override switch on control stick or turn engaging switch on automatic pilot to OFF, to remove both automatic approach coupler and automatic pilot from control of airplane.

- Complete failure of instrument approach equipment will cause the airplane to continue at the attitude previously maintained at time of equipment failure.

AUTOMATIC PILOT EMERGENCY OPERATION.

In any emergency, the automatic pilot may be disengaged by either the control stick release switch or the flight controller. If the switches do not function, electrical power to the system may be removed by moving the autopilot power switch from ON to OFF. The switch is on the aft end of the right circuit-breaker panel. The autopilot can be overpowered when engaged, and the stick forces will not be excessively high. Rudder forces, however, may require maximum pilot effort.

AUTOMATIC PILOT EMERGENCY DISCONNECT.

Binding and/or jerky control operation can be caused by malfunction of either the flight control system or the autopilot system. It is possible for the autopilot system to become partially engaged with the flight controller switch in the OFF position. Therefore, to eliminate the possibility of autopilot system malfunction when abnormal control operation occurs, one of the following actions, listed in order of preference, should be taken:

1. Place guarded autopilot power switch at OFF.
2. Pull autopilot circuit breaker on left circuit-breaker panel.
3. Remove autopilot ac fuse on left fuse panel.

NAVIGATION EQUIPMENT.
STAND-BY COMPASS.

Refer to "Instruments" in Section I.

RADIO COMPASS.

Refer to "Communication and Associated Electronic Equipment" in this section.

SLAVED GYRO MAGNETIC COMPASS.

The slaved gyro magnetic compass (12, figure 1-5) is basically a directional gyro that is automatically kept on the magnetic heading of the airplane by a flux valve in the left wing, inboard of the tip. The flux valve "senses" the south-north flow of the earth's magnetic flux and shows magnetic heading without northerly turning error, oscillation, or swinging. On F-86D-1 through F-86D-30 Airplanes, the magnetic heading is shown on the zero reader compass card by the white heading pointer. On F-86D-35 and later airplanes, the magnetic heading is shown by the needle on a separate slaved gyro magnetic compass indicator that replaces the zero reader indicator. Electrical power for the slaved gyro magnetic compass is provided only when dc power and 400-cycle, three-phase ac power is available.

Note

On late airplanes,* should either the ac or the dc power supply fail, the slaved gyro magnetic compass system is automatically disconnected from all electrical power.

The gyro is energized when external power or generator power is applied to the airplane, and is on a fast slaving cycle for the first 2 to 3 minutes of operation, during which it should align with the magnetic heading. The gyro then begins a slow slaving cycle. On some airplanes,† a switch is provided to energize the fast slaving circuit for faster recovery during flight.

Note

After the gyro reaches operating speed, the needle should be checked against the stand-by compass indication to make sure it does not show a 180-degree ambiguity. If such ambiguity exists, the slaved gyro magnetic compass is not operating properly.

A knob on the lower left of the zero reader indicator (slaved gyro magnetic compass indicator on some airplanes†) permits the compass card to be rotated to a preselected heading. Indicator readings will be incorrect if the airplane exceeds 85 degrees of climb or dive or if it banks left or right more than 85 degrees.

Slaved Gyro Magnetic Compass Fast Slaving Switch.

On some airplanes† and airplanes changed by T. O., a fast slaving cycle of the slaved gyro magnetic compass can be selected by means of a push-button switch (7, figure 1-4; 18, figure 1-5) on the instrument panel. Momentary actuation of the switch interrupts dc power to the slaved gyro. This power interruption

---

*F-86D-60 Airplane AF53-1007 and all later airplanes
†F-86D-35 and later airplanes

automatically de-energizes the slow slaving cycle and engages the fast slaving cycle, as during an initial start, permitting faster gyro recovery to the true heading.

Do not hold fast slaving switch depressed over 2 seconds, and allow a minimum of 10 minutes between depressions of the switch. Excessive use can damage the slaving torque motor.

ARMAMENT.*

The airplane is equipped with a hydraulically operated rocket package containing twenty-four 2.75-inch rockets. The package is in the under portion of the fuselage and is automatically extended and retracted for rocket firing. The fire control computer automatically triggers the firing circuit, which lowers the rocket package, and then commences firing rockets. This sequence requires ½ second. Two-tenths of a second is required to fire 24 rockets, after which the package is retracted, in 3.3 seconds. Thus, the total firing sequence requires 4 seconds for a complete cycle. The entire rocket package can be jettisoned in an emergency. If any firing malfunction occurs, the package will remain extended and can be retracted in the air by either of the following methods: (1) placing the armament master switch at CAMERA (PKG ONLY†), placing the rocket-firing switch at MANUAL, and depressing the trigger; or (2) placing the armament master switch at OFF and the rocket package override switch at UP. The

*Removed from TF-86D Airplanes

†F-86D-40 Airplane AF52-3848 and all later airplanes

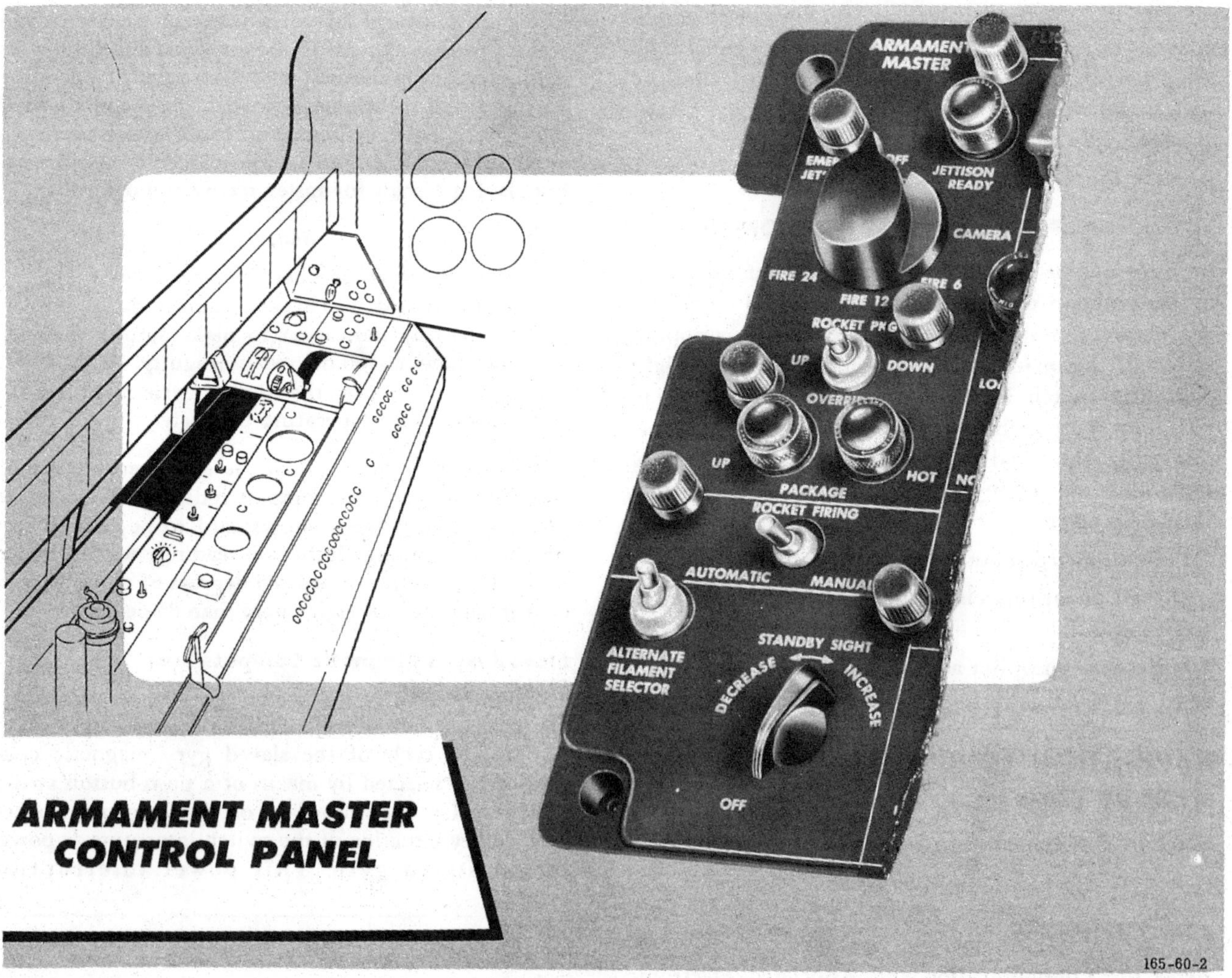

ARMAMENT MASTER CONTROL PANEL

Figure 4-15

rockets can be fired automatically or manually through the fire control system. For manual rocket firing, an N-9, N-9-1, or MK VIII (used interchangeably) fixed-reticle gun sight with reflector glass removed projects the reticle image onto the armor glass for sighting purposes. A camera, which operates automatically in conjunction with rocket firing, is mounted in the left wing leading edge next to the fuselage. On some airplanes,* a switch is provided to control camera lens opening. On late airplanes,† the wing-mounted camera is not installed.

Note

If utility hydraulic system pressure on F-86D-10 and later airplanes momentarily falls below 1500 psi, a pressure priority valve will cut out the portion of the system powering the rocket package in an effort to sustain a system pressure of 1500 psi.

ARMAMENT CONTROLS.

Rocket-firing Switch.

A two-position rocket-firing switch is on the armament master control panel (figure 4-15) on the left console, aft of the throttle. Power for this switch is derived from the secondary bus. The switch has an AUTOMATIC position for automatic firing and a MANUAL position for manual firing.

Armament Master Switch.

A rotary, seven-position armament master switch is on the armament master control panel. (See figure 4-15.) The switch is powered from the secondary bus, except for the EMERG. JET'S'N position, which gets power directly from the battery. The switch positions are OFF, JETTISON READY, CAMERA, FIRE 6, FIRE 12, FIRE 24, and EMERG. JET'S'N. On late airplanes,† the wing-mounted camera is not installed and the CAMERA position nomenclature is changed to PKG ONLY. On these airplanes, selection of this position (CAMERA on early airplanes) allows the rocket package to cycle open and closed when the trigger is held depressed, if the weight of the airplane is not on the landing gear and if the rocket-firing switch is in MANUAL position. Turning the switch to rocket selector positions selects the number of rockets to be fired with one depression of the trigger. Raising the knob enables the switch to be turned to EMERG. JET'S'N. This action immediately jettisons the rocket package, if the weight of the airplane is not on the landing gear. The normal position

Warning

To prevent inadvertent release of drop tanks and/or rocket package, do not depress trigger when armament master switch is being moved.

for the armament master switch during take-off and landing is OFF. Turning the switch to the JET'S'N. READY position at any time after take-off permits the rocket package and drop tanks to be jettisoned when the tank-rocket jettison button on the control stick is depressed. With the switch at CAMERA and with the rocket-firing switch in MANUAL position, the camera operates as long as the trigger is pressed and continues to operate for a period of time after the trigger is released, depending on the camera overrun adjustments (0 to 3 seconds if an N-9 camera is used, or from 0 to 5 seconds if an N-6 camera is used). This action of the camera is accompanied by one complete cycle of rocket package operation. If the trigger is released before the package is completely extended, the package remains down until the trigger is again depressed. Release of the trigger while the package is retracting immediately causes the package to extend and remain extended. The trigger should be held depressed until the rocket-package-up indicator light comes on. (Armament master switch must be at CAMERA.)

Camera and Rocket-firing Trigger.

A trigger on the control stick (figure 1-23) has two stages of travel easily discernible through trigger feel. The first stage of trigger travel is not used. The second stage of trigger travel, or fully depressed trigger

---

*F-86D-40 Airplanes AF52-3598 through -3847
†F-86D-40 Airplane AF52-3848 and all later airplanes

position, actuates the gun camera and causes operation of the rocket package. For automatic rocket firing, the trigger is fully depressed at the first radarscope indication that 20 seconds or less remains until firing time. The trigger must be held down throughout the firing run until breakaway. When the rocket-firing switch is at MANUAL and the armament master switch is at a rocket selector position for firing, the fully depressed position of the trigger actuates the gun camera, causes the rocket package to be extended, fires the selected rockets, and causes the rocket package to retract. The camera will cease operation within 0 to 3 seconds on an N-9 camera (0 to 5 seconds on an N-6 camera) after the trigger is released, depending on the camera overrun adjustment. Only momentary use of the trigger is necessary for manual firing, and the trigger must be released before the firing cycle can be repeated. Power for the trigger comes from the secondary bus. On late airplanes,* the wing-mounted camera is not installed.

Note

Before flight, check that rocket temperature correction factor has been set on rocket temperature potentiometer, in nose section right side.

Rocket Package Override Switch.

The automatic extension or retraction of the rocket package can be overridden by an override switch on the armament master control panel (figure 4-15) below the armament master switch. The rocket package override switch has three positions: UP, DOWN, and an unmarked neutral off position. This switch is powered from the battery bus.

Tank-Rocket Jettison Button.

A tank-rocket jettison button is provided on the control stick. (See figure 1-23.) Power for this switch comes from the secondary bus. When the armament master switch is at JETTISON READY, pressing the tank-rocket jettison button jettisons the rocket package and drop tanks.

CAUTION

With the armament master switch at JETTISON READY, the drop tanks will be jettisoned either on the ground or in the air when the tank-rocket jettison button is depressed. The rocket package can be jettisoned only when the airplane is airborne.

---

*F-86D-40 Airplane AF52-3848 and all later airplanes

Rocket External Loading Switch.

A three-position rocket-ground-loading switch, powered by the secondary bus, is under an access door on the lower left side of the nose section, just aft of the nose gear. This switch has three positions: EXTEND, NORMAL, and RETRACT (spring-loaded from the RETRACT to the NORMAL position), and is used for ground operation of the rocket pod.

Rocket Pod External Jettisoning Switch.

A rocket pod external jettisoning switch, for releasing the rocket pod while the airplane is on the ground, is under an access door on the lower left side of the nose section, just aft of the nose gear. This switch is powered by the secondary bus and has two positions, NORMAL and JETTISON. The switch is guarded in the NORMAL position.

Camera Lens Switch (F-86D-40 Airplanes AF52-3598 Through -3847).

A rotary switch, on the left console and having BRIGHT, HAZY, and DULL positions, is provided to adjust lens opening of the camera. Positioning the switch at the desired setting adjusts the camera lens opening for the existing conditions.

ARMAMENT INDICATORS.

Rocket-package-up Indicator Light.

Whenever the rocket package is up and locked, a green light to the left of the override switch on the armament master control panel (figure 4-15) will come on, provided the armament master switch is at any position except OFF, EMERG. JET'S'N, or CAMERA. This light derives its power from the secondary bus.

Hot-rocket-package Warning Light.

An amber warning light, on the armament master control panel (figure 4-15) next to the package-up indicator light, will come on whenever the trigger is depressed for firing rockets. The light will stay on if any of the selected rockets do not fire or if the rocket package fails to retract for any other reason. If the rocket package is jettisoned, the light will go out. This indicator is powered from the secondary bus.

Jettison-ready Indicator Light.

An amber light, on the armament master control panel (figure 4-15) above the armament master switch, comes on whenever the armament master switch is moved to JETTISON READY and remains on until the armament master switch is moved to another position. The jettison-ready indicator light is a push-to-test type light and is powered from the secondary bus.

Warning

Radar ground checks must not be made within 50 feet of operations involving fuel or other inflammable liquids. Tests indicate that electrical energy from radar equipment may ground through steel tools, common pencils, etc, causing ignition of fuel vapors.

F-86D-1-0-22

FIRE CONTROL SYSTEM.*

An all-weather rocket-firing control system is incorporated to provide position information that enables the pilot to locate an air-borne target, maneuver the airplane to launch an attack, and accurately fire rockets. The electronic fire control system operates automatically to fire rockets at the proper release point while the trigger is held depressed and if the rocket-firing switch is in AUTOMATIC position. However, a selected number of rockets (6, 12, or 24) may be fired manually by momentarily depressing the trigger for each firing cycle. The radarscope (flight indicator) (30, figure 1-4; 28, figure 1-5), in the center of the instrument panel, furnishes the pilot with a visual presentation of the interception. Because of the classified nature of this equipment (E-3 on some F-86D-1 Airplanes† and E-4 on all other airplanes), only elementary information on it is supplied in this publication. In case failure of the electronic rocket-firing control system occurs, the stand-by sight can be used. (Refer to "Stand-by Sight" in this section.) On late airplanes‡ and airplanes changed by T. O., a radarscope camera connector plug is installed just above the lower edge and behind the right side of the instrument panel. A decal, "RADARSCOPE CAMERA CONNECTOR," next to the plug also identifies it. A radarscope camera may be installed. The purpose of this camera is to record the attack phase of the rocket-firing mission and to provide a visual record for study as a training aid. Early airplanes§ were delivered with an elevation bias in the fire control system computer. This was to preclude the possibility of scoring hits on target aircraft during training missions. Late airplanes¶ were delivered with the elevation bias in the fire control system computer connected in the combat position. A placard is mounted on the forward instrument panel. One side reads: "THIS AIRCRAFT IS EQUIPPED WITH ELEVATION BIAS INCORPORATED IN THE FIRE CONTROL SYSTEM." The other side reads: "THE FIRE CONTROL COMPUTER IN THIS AIRPLANE IS CONNECTED FOR COMBAT USE." The fire control system should be checked each time a replacement is made, to determine whether elevation bias is in or out, and whether the placard is installed accordingly. On late airplanes** and those changed by T. O., a magnetic tape recorder is installed in conjunction with the E-4 fire control system. This unit automatically records the attack phase of the intercept from lock-on to pull-out. The tape recordings are reproducible after each flight or as necessary for the purpose of studying pilot technique as a training aid.

RADAR AND ROCKET-FIRING SYSTEM CONTROLS.

There are three primary locations of the rocket-firing system controls. A radar power control panel is forward of the throttle. On F-86D-1 Airplanes, a scope presentation intensity control panel is in the lower left corner of the instrument panel, and an antenna hand control is mounted below and to the left of the radarscope. (See figure 4-16.) On F-86D-5 and later airplanes, the scope presentation intensity control panel is midway on the right console, and the antenna hand control is midway and inboard on the left console, just aft of the throttle. (See figure 4-17.) Both the E-3 system and the E-4 system are powered from monitored bus No. 3 and depend upon availability of ac power.

---

*Removed from TF-86D Airplanes
†F-86D-1 Airplanes AF50-455, -457, -458, -459, and -472
‡F-86D-30 Airplane AF51-6070 and all later airplanes

§F-86D-1 through F-86D-30 Airplanes and F-86D-35 Airplanes AF51-6145 through -6262 and -8274 through -8395
¶F-86D-35 Airplane AF51-8396 and all later airplanes
**F-86D-55 and later airplanes

Section IV T. O. 1F-86D-1

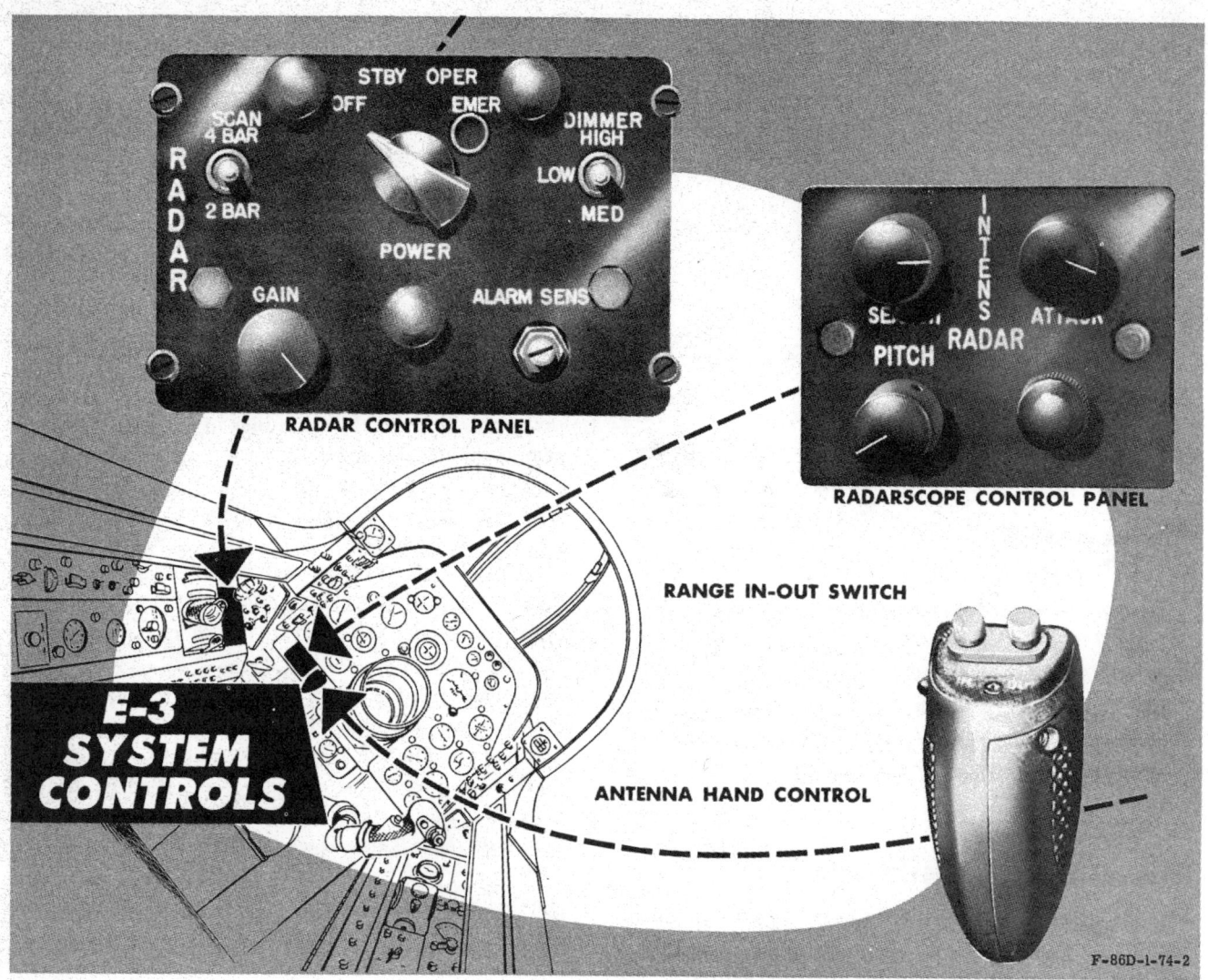

Figure 4-16

Radar Control Panel.

Master Power Switch. The master power switch, on the radar control panel (figure 4-17), is a rotary-type switch that controls electrical power to the fire control system. It has four positions: DISCONN (OFF on E-3 fire control system), STBY, OPER, and EMER. The DISCONN (or OFF) position is used only when it is desired to disconnect power to the system or in case of a failure or malfunction. To select the DISCONN (or OFF) position, the pilot must raise the switch; this releases a lock and enables the switch to rotate. With the switch in the STBY position, power is applied to the system to allow for a warm-up period of about 4½ minutes (3½ minutes on the E-3 fire control system) before the switch is positioned at OPER. It also offers a means of discontinuing operation while the system remains in a stand-by condition for immediate use. The OPER position permits system operation after a protective time delay of about 4½ minutes (3½ minutes on E-3 fire control system) or immediately if the switch has been in STBY for a minimum of 4½ minutes (3½ minutes on E-3 fire control system). The switch may be positioned directly to OPER; however, the system is still protected by the time delay. The EMER position is used only for an emergency situation that requires immediate use of the radar without benefit of the warm-up time delay. To select the EMER position, it is necessary to raise the switch; this releases a lock and allows the switch to rotate. (The lock is depressed and rotated to EMER on the E-3 fire control system.)

CAUTION

- A 4½-minute (3½-minute on E-3 fire control system) warm-up period is required before taxi or take-off, to permit the radar gyro to acquire enough speed to prevent damage to the suspension points.

4-34

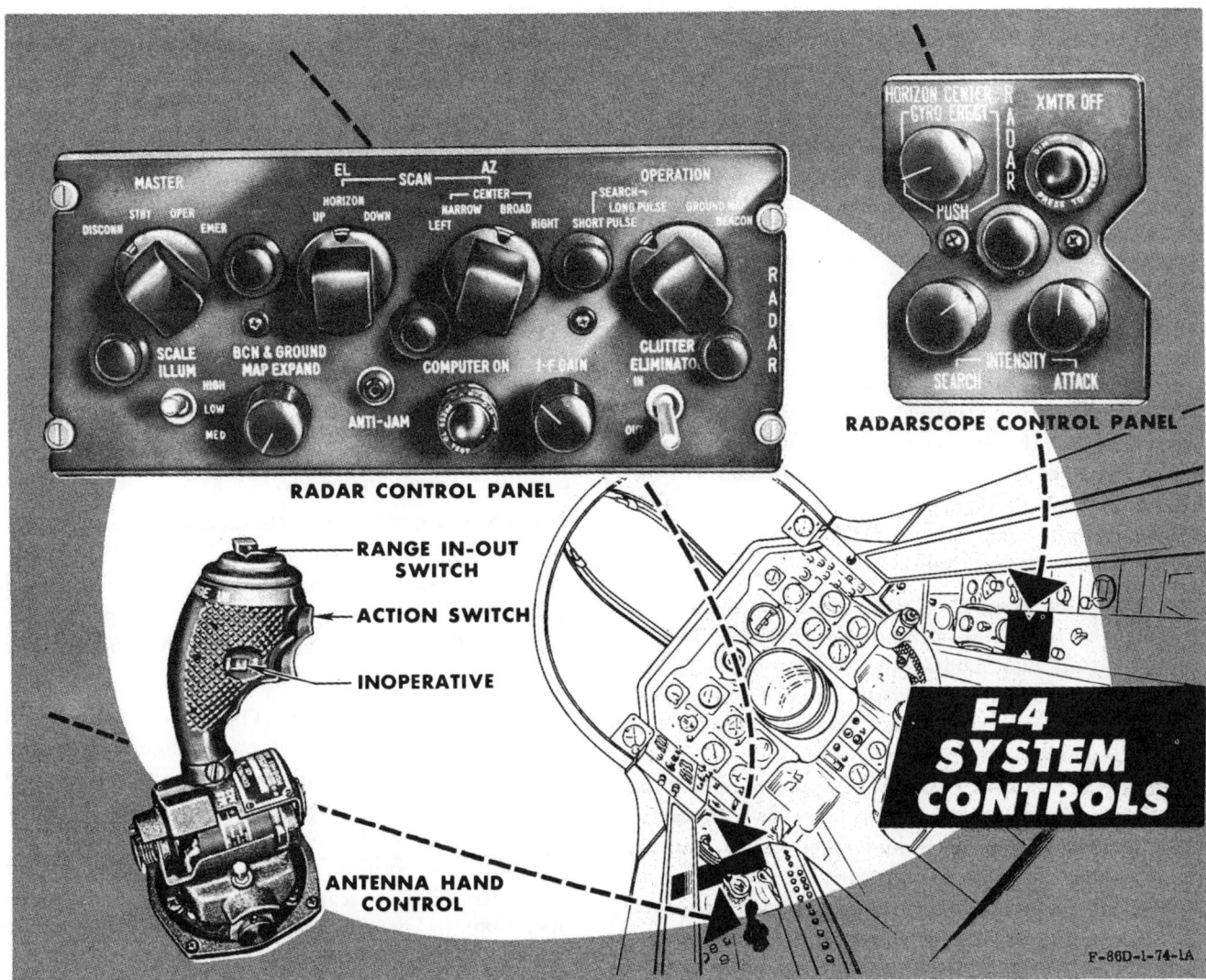

Figure 4-17

- The DISCONN (or OFF) position should not be used while the airplane is performing flight maneuvers or landing, unless 3½ minutes is allowed in level flight for the roll-and-pitch gyro to come to a stop, thus preventing damage to the suspension points.

"EL SCAN" Switch. The "EL SCAN" switch of the E-4 fire control system provides means for tilting the antenna radiation pattern up or down. This rotary-type switch, on the radar control panel (figure 4-17), is continuous from UP to DOWN, with a detent in the HORIZON position. During search operation with the switch in the HORIZON position, the antenna sweeps an area covering about 3 degrees above and 3 degrees below the horizon. During ground map and beacon interrogation with the switch set at HORIZON, the antenna sweeps an area about 6 degrees in height, centered 6 degrees below the horizon. When the switch is in the UP position with the airplane in level flight, the upper sweep of the antenna is 33.5 degrees above the horizon; with the switch in the DOWN position, the lower sweep of the antenna is 13.5 degrees below the horizon. The UP and DOWN positions of the "EL SCAN" switch provide variable, rather than preset, scanning positions. Rotation of the switch adjusts the scanning area to the elevation desired for best coverage. On the E-3 fire control system, the "SCAN" switch (figure 4-16) provides a two-bar or a four-bar selection. With the switch in the 2 BAR position, the antenna scans a 10-degree sector of ±5 degrees from the horizontal; with the switch in the 4 BAR position, the antenna scans a 30-degree sector of ±15 degrees from the horizontal.

"AZ SCAN" Switch. The E-4 fire control system "AZ SCAN" switch, to the right of the "EL SCAN" switch on the radar control panel (figure 4-17), is a four-position rotary switch, labeled "NARROW,"

"BROAD," "LEFT," and "RIGHT." It provides a maximum radar azimuth coverage of 64 degrees left and right of center in the BROAD position and a minimum of 36.5 degrees left and right of center in the NARROW position. Selection of the LEFT position gives an azimuth coverage of 64 degrees left and 6.5 degrees right. With the switch in the RIGHT position, the antenna sweeps an area of 64 degrees right and 6.5 degrees left. When the "AZ SCAN" switch is placed in the BROAD position, the antenna completes one scan pattern cycle in about 3½ seconds. With the switch in either of the three other positions, a scan pattern cycle is completed in about 2 seconds. When the elevation and azimuth controls are used correctly, the antenna will search any area in front of the airplane, above and below the horizon. On the E-3 fire control system, azimuth scan is 50 degrees on either side of center with the "SCAN" switch in either the 2 BAR or 4 BAR position.

"OPERATION" Switch.* Three operational modes are initiated with the four-position rotary "OPERATION" switch on the radar control panel (figure 4-17), to the right of the azimuth scan control. The positions for the three modes are SEARCH, GROUND MAP, and BEACON. In the search mode, a choice of two presentations is offered, LONG PULSE or SHORT PULSE. When the switch is in the LONG PULSE position, maximum power is used over a longer period to give maximum target detection ranges up to 30 nautical miles; the SHORT PULSE position provides a short pulse of higher pulse-repetition frequency for better echo returns at short range. With the switch in the GROUND MAP position, the antenna searches the terrain below and ahead of the airplane to a maximum range of 200 nautical miles. With the switch in the BEACON position, radar beacon code numbers appear on the scope as a series of horizontal bars positioned to show relative range and bearing. These assist the pilot in locating and identifying his position with respect to the beacon station. The beacon mode also has a maximum range of 200 nautical miles.

"SCALE ILLUM" Switch.* The "SCALE ILLUM" switch, on the radar control panel (figure 4-17), has HIGH, LOW, and MED positions. It controls the intensity of the lights illuminating the scales on the radarscope.

"BCN & GROUND MAP EXPAND" Control Knob.* The "BCN & GROUND MAP EXPAND" control knob is on the radar control panel. (See figure 4-17.) During ground map operation, depressing the switch permits expansion of any 20-mile zone of the range sweep trace selected by the pilot to cover the entire scope display. This allows a more detailed presentation. During beacon operation, positioning the range marker strobe just below the lowest marker of the beacon return signal and depressing the "BCN & GROUND MAP EXPAND" knob, causes the beacon indications to be expanded, and the coding can be more easily interpreted.

"ANTI-JAM" Switch.* Operation of the "ANTI-JAM" push-button switch, on the radar control panel (figure 4-17), varies the frequency of the radar transmitter-receiver to counteract jamming or other interference. The switch is operative only in systems employing a radar transmitter-receiver with a tunable magnetron. To operate, hold button depressed until jamming is eliminated.

"COMPUTER ON" Light.* On some airplanes, a "COMPUTER ON" light is installed on the radar control panel (figure 4-17) to the right of the "ANTI-JAM" switch. The light shows when the computer is operating. The "COMPUTER ON" light comes on after the 4½-minute warm-up delay, showing that the computer is ready to operate.

"COMPUTER OFF" Light.* On some airplanes, a "COMPUTER OFF" light replaces the "COMPUTER ON" light and comes on when the master switch is turned on. At the end of the 4½-minute warm-up period, the "COMPUTER OFF" light goes out, showing that the computer is ready for operation.

"I-F GAIN" Control Knob. This rotary-type control knob, on the radar control panel (figures 4-16 and 4-17), governs the amplification of signal returns by adjusting the sensitivity of the radar receiver. For fire control operation, the control should be turned to the full clockwise position. It may be necessary to adjust the control during search, ground map, and beacon operation, and in cases where jamming or clutter is evident. Small adjustments may provide a clearer presentation on the radarscope and eliminate inherent instability in the radar response from different reflecting surfaces.

"CLUTTER ELIMINATOR" Switch.* This two-position switch, labeled "IN" and "OUT," is on the radar control panel, (See figure 4-17.) In automatic search operation, the "CLUTTER ELIMINATOR" switch may be used to eliminate long, formless trains of cloud, ground, or sea return echoes to improve the radarscope presentation.

Radarscope Control Panel.

The radarscope control panel (figures 4-16 and 4-17) is on the right console panel. It is flush-mounted and has three control knobs and one indicator light. These are the "HORIZON CENTER GYRO ERECT" control knob ("PITCH" control knob on the E-3 fire control system), "XMTR OFF" indicator light (reduced-power indicator light on E-3 fire control system), and two intensity control knobs, "SEARCH" and "ATTACK." Lighting of this panel is controlled by the instrument panel light dimmer switch. (See figure 4-8.)

*****E-4 fire control system**

"HORIZON CENTER GYRO ERECT" Control Knob ("PITCH" Control Knob on E-3 Fire Control System). This control knob (figures 4-16 and 4-17) is used when the artificial horizon on the radarscope fails to show the true attitude of the airplane. At times, as a result of high-G maneuvers that occur over a prolonged period, the artificial horizon on the scope develops an alignment error of several degrees and may be corrected by depressing the horizon adjustment knob on the radarscope control panel when in straight-and-level flight. Rotating the knob raises or lowers the horizon on the scope until the indication correctly shows the airplane attitude. Depressing the control knob provides fast erection of the roll and pitch; however, the horizon line may move off the scope or be distorted momentarily when the adjustment knob is depressed. This phenomenon takes only a few seconds.

"XMTR OFF" Indicator Light.* Illumination of this light (figure 4-17) shows that an overload has occurred in the transmitter and that the system is no longer transmitting radar energy. Often, this light comes on because of an overload of short duration. If the master power switch is momentarily positioned to STBY, then turned back to OPER, use of the radar may be regained. Also, an overload may exist in one mode of operation and not in another; therefore, beacon and ground map modes may be inoperable because of overload, whereas search modes will operate satisfactorily.

Reduced-power Indicator Light.† Illumination of this light (figure 4-16) shows an overload in the transmitter and a power reduction of 10% or more. Often these overloads are of short duration and the use of the radar may be regained by positioning the master power switch momentarily to STBY, then back to OPER.

Intensity Control Knobs. Intensity of the attack and search presentations may be varied by rotation of the "ATTACK" and "SEARCH" control knobs on the radarscope control panel. (See figures 4-16 and 4-17.) Rotation of the "SEARCH" control knob varies the contrast between the target presentation and the background; rotating the "ATTACK" control knob increases or decreases the intensity of the rest of the display on the radarscope.

Antenna Hand Control.

The antenna hand control for the E-4 fire control system (figure 4-17), mounted aft of the throttle quadrant, is used when manual control of the radar antenna is desired. Antenna hand control movement has the same effect on antenna action as control stick movement does on airplane controls, forward-and-back action for vertical movement of the antenna and side-to-side action for lateral movement of the antenna. On the top of the control is a range in-out switch. The front part of the hand control incorporates an action switch for placing the antenna in manual search. When the antenna hand control is momentarily moved to the full aft position, a limit switch, in the base of the antenna hand control, returns the antenna to automatic search from either manual search or radar track operation. The range in-out switch provides the pilot with a means of positioning the range gate marker over the selected target on the range trace to effect a lock-on. The switch is a five-position, rocker-type switch, actuated by depressing with the left thumb. When the action switch on the front of the antenna hand control is depressed, the range gate marker (a small blip) appears at the 5-mile position on the range trace. Depressing the range in-out switch to the first or second detent position moves the range gate marker up or down the range trace. With the switch in the first detent, the range gate marker stops the radar set and locks it on the first target on the range trace that it comes to. If the radar locks on an undesired target, momentary depression of the range in-out switch to the second detent causes the range gate marker to jump past this undesired target. (To automatically lock on the next target it comes to, the switch must be returned to the first detent.) If the pilot wants to pass through several targets before locking on his selected target, the switch should be held fully depressed until the desired target is reached. Then, when the range in-out switch is released to the first detent or neutral position, the radar set will automatically lock on the selected target and the scope will display the tracking phase of operation. The action switch is a spring-loaded, trigger-type switch on the front of the antenna hand control. (See figure 4-17.) Depressing this switch enables the pilot to manually position the radar antenna to "searchlight" any desired area in front of the airplane. If the action switch is in the normal position, movement of the antenna hand control will have no effect on the antenna. Release of the action switch is necessary after range lock-on in order to get an attack presentation and a track lock-on. The E-3 fire control system antenna hand control, at the lower left corner of the instrument panel (figure 4-16), incorporates two separate buttons on the top of the handgrip. These buttons are actuated with the left thumb to move the range gate marker in and out on the scope. An action switch is on the front of the antenna hand control for placing the antenna in manual search. Targets may be by-passed by holding both the action switch and the range in-out button fully depressed. A lock-on is achieved by placing the range gate marker over the target blip and releasing the action switch.

---

*E-4 fire control system

†E-3 fire control system

RADARSCOPE DISPLAY

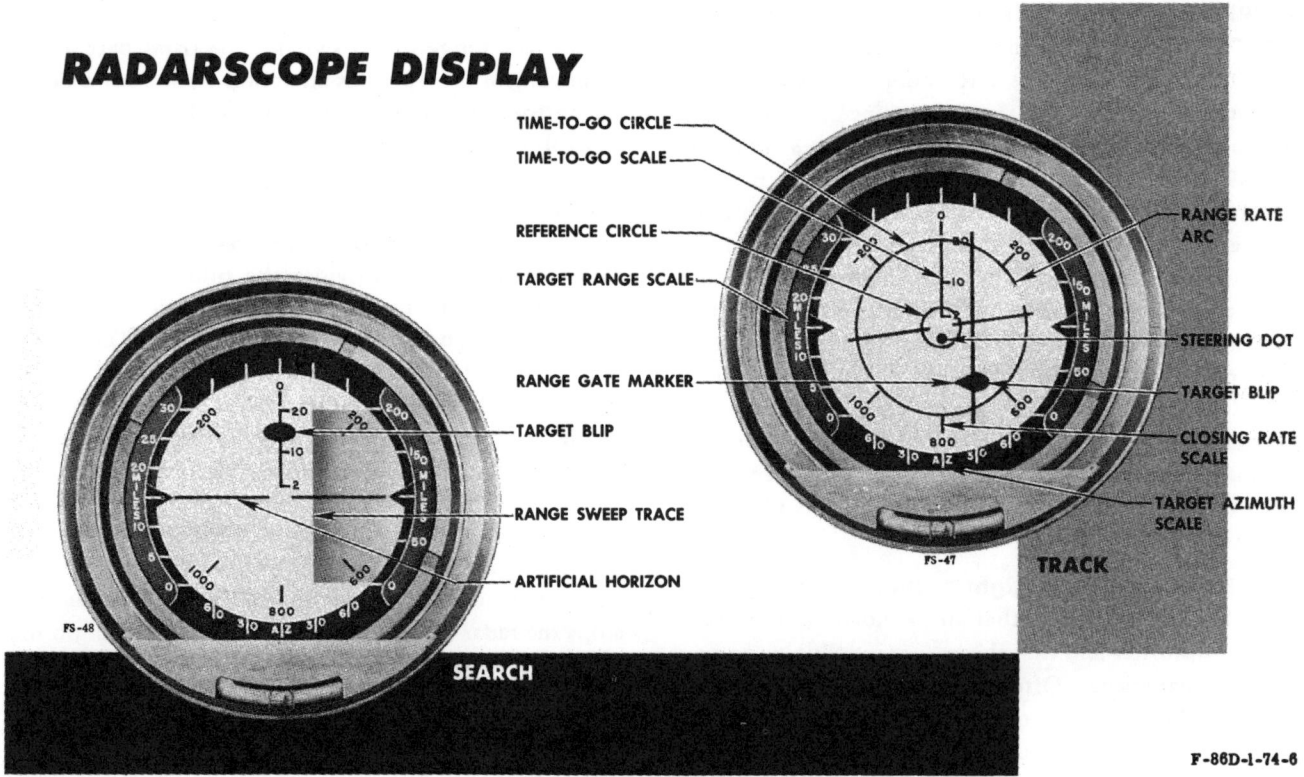

Figure 4-18

RADARSCOPE PRESENTATION.

Azimuth Scale.

Short vertical lines at the top and bottom of the scope face show 30-degree intervals on either side of center to +60 degrees and −60 degrees and provide azimuth reference during search display. The symbol "AZ" is engraved below the bottom series of lines at the zero degree or dead-ahead position. The azimuth scale is lighted during all modes of operation except automatic track.

Range Scales.

These scales consist of short horizontal lines along the right and left edges of the scope and show the range of the search display in nautical miles. The left scale, used during automatic search, manual search, and automatic track, is calibrated in 5-nautical-mile intervals from zero to 30 miles maximum range. On the E-4 fire control system, the right scale, used during beacon and ground map, is calibrated in 50-nautical-mile intervals from zero to 200 miles maximum range.

Artificial Horizon Reference.

There is a V-shaped mark at each side of the horizontal diameter of the tube face. These marks determine the roll and pitch attitude of the artificial horizon during flight.

Time-to-go Scale.

Illuminated during automatic track operation, this scale is calibrated at 2, 10, and 20 seconds on a vertical line extending upward above the center of the scope. The scale provides a time reference for the time-to-go circle.

Range Rate Scale.

Closing rates to a maximum of 1000 knots, calibrated from the 12 o'clock position in a clockwise direction, and opening rates to a maximum of 200 knots read in a counterclockwise direction are provided by the range rate scale on the face of the scope. Closing and opening rates are read from the range rate arc as it closes toward the center of the scope.

Range Rate Arc.

The range rate or relative speed between interceptor and target is shown by a small blanked segment of the time-to-go circle. Closing or opening range rates may be read directly from the range rate scale. With a zero range rate, the segment is at the 12 o'clock position.

Reference Circle.

The reference circle is a circular trace centered in the attack display. Basically it serves as the position reference for the steering dot. It also shows the particular phase of automatic track in which the system is operating. In Phase I, the reference circle has a diameter of one inch. In Phase II, the diameter is ¼ inch. At the start of Phase III, the circle collapses to a ¼-inch horizontal line.

Steering Dot.

A bright spot on the scope display is the primary reference for pilot guidance. It is displaced from the center of the reference circle during the attack display in proportion to the angle that the airplane deviates from the computed course. When centered in the reference circle, the steering dot shows that the airplane is on the computed attack course.

Pull-out Warning Signal.

The pull-out warning signal, which appears at the instant of rocket firing, is a large "X" centered on the screen. The pull-out warning also appears as a collision-warning symbol when the time to go is less than 4½ seconds and the computed relative rocket travel is less than 260 yards. In this instance, no rocket-firing signals are initiated by the computer.

Range Gate Marker.

This element, a ⅛-inch horizontal blip, appears on the range trace as soon as the action switch on the antenna control is depressed, and remains throughout manual search and automatic track operation. The marker on the range trace is first at the 5-mile position. The range in-out switch on the antenna control is used to move the marker in or out in range. The marker can be made to move either slowly or rapidly, depending upon whether the switch is partially depressed or fully depressed.

NORMAL OPERATION OF E-3 AND E-4 FIRE CONTROL SYSTEMS.

Note

- Radar tracking and rocket firing should be accomplished at speeds above .78 Mach number to ensure accurate fire control system computing. At speeds below .78 Mach number, the angle-of-attack output for the computer becomes fixed and therefore does not give accurate elevation steering information.

- If an attack presentation on the radarscope is to be obtained, the rocket-firing switch on the armament control panel must be in the AUTOMATIC position.

- Rockets cannot be fired if the nose gear and nose gear doors are not up and locked or if the rocket package is not fully extended.

Preoperational Check.

1. Radar and inverter circuit breakers in.
2. Check rocket-package-up indicator light on.
3. Alternator switch ON.
4. Set rocket-firing switch to AUTOMATIC for automatic firing.
5. Set master armament switch as desired.

Before Radar Warm-up Is Completed.

A 4½-minute (3½-minute on E-3 fire control system) warm-up period is required before taxi or take-off, to permit the radar gyro to acquire enough speed to prevent damage to the suspension points.

1. Set master power switch to STBY.
2. Set "EL SCAN" switch to HORIZON.*
3. Set "AZ SCAN" switch to BROAD.*
4. Set "OPERATION" switch to SHORT PULSE.*
5. Set "CLUTTER ELIMINATOR" switch to OUT.*
6. Turn "I-F GAIN" control knob fully clockwise.
7. Set "SCALE ILLUM" switch as desired.
8. Depress "XMTR OFF" indicator light (reduced-power light on E-3 fire control system) to check bulb.

After Warm-up Is Completed.

1. Set master power switch to OPER.
2. Observe appearance of range sweep trace and artificial horizon.
3. Turn "I-F GAIN" control knob fully counterclockwise.
4. Reduce search intensity until range sweep trace is just barely visible.
5. Restore I-F gain, turn "I-F GAIN" control knob fully clockwise.
6. Reduce attack intensity for best legibility of artificial horizon.
7. Depress "COMPUTER ON" light ("COMPUTER OFF" light on some airplanes) to test bulb.
8. Yaw damper switch ON.

AUTOMATIC SEARCH.

On the E-4 fire control system, during automatic search, the antenna automatically scans any one of several sectors ahead of the airplane in a rectangular scan pattern,

---

*E-4 fire control system

determined by the settings on the radar set controls. Target information is supplied to the pilot on the radarscope. A range trace sweeps back and forth across the indicator, "painting" the area in front of the airplane on the face of the radarscope. Targets are represented by blips whose relative positions, reading from the bottom of the scope upward, give target range, and whose deviation from the centerline of the scope give target azimuth. Scales engraved on the radarscope permit the pilot to determine target range and azimuth. On the E-3 fire control system, during automatic search, the antenna automatically scans either of two sectors ahead of the airplane in a rectangular pattern determined by the position of the "SCAN" selector switch on the radar control panel, and antenna position is indicated by lights on the radarscope. In automatic search operation, proceed as follows:

1. Direct airplane into interception area, according to plans of tactical mission.

2. At approach of interception area, with E-4 fire control system installed, adjust settings of "EL SCAN" and "AZ SCAN" controls to facilitate searching zone relative to anticipated position of target.

Note

If approximate altitude of target is unknown, use "AZ SCAN" and "EL SCAN" controls to the fullest extent on E-4 fire control system to obtain maximum space coverage. When target is detected, adjust "EL SCAN" control for desired elevation angle.

3. Watch search display on radarscope as target range approaches 15 miles. The target will appear as a bright blip.

4. Monitor target position closely to determine range and azimuth data.

5. To place system in manual search, depress action switch on antenna hand control.

MANUAL SEARCH.

After the pilot selects a target, he takes over manual control of the antenna by depressing the action switch on the front of the antenna hand control. He then manipulates this control to place the range sweep trace over the blip representing the target he has selected. The range-gate marker, which normally appears at the 5-mile mark on the range sweep trace, is then moved up or down on the range sweep trace by the left or right side of the range in-out switch. When the range-gate marker, on the E-4 fire control system, is moved to cover the target blip on the scope, the radar automatically locks on the target selected; when the action switch is released, the radar goes into automatic track operation. On the E-3 fire control system, there is no automatic lock-on feature; however, the radar goes into automatic track operation when the action switch is released. In manual search operation, proceed as follows:

1. Manipulate antenna hand control so that position of range-sweep trace on radarscope indicator coincides with azimuth position of target.

2. "Spotlight" target by moving antenna hand control backward and forward until target blip appears brightest.

3. Depress IN or OUT side of range in-out switch to first detent position to move range-gate marker to indicated target range.

4. Release action switch. The attack display will appear on the radarscope; then the radar will automatically track the target.

AUTOMATIC TRACK.

Phase I. Phase I of the automatic track operation is that part of the attack operation from lock-on until 20 seconds to go. Phase I enables the pilot to make the maneuvers necessary to bring the airplane onto the lead-collision course. Only approximate steering is necessary, and the pilot need only keep the steering dot within the one-inch reference circle. If extreme maneuvers are called for, they should be made in Phase I and performed as easily as possible.

Phase II. The beginning of Phase II is defined as 20 seconds to go, the time at which the time-to-go circle begins to shrink. Phase II enables the pilot to perform the more precise steering that is necessary as the airplane approaches the target. During this phase, the pilot is required to steer so as to keep the steering dot centered within the ¼-inch reference circle.

Phase III. If the system goes into Phase III operation, the reference circle flattens into a ¼-inch horizontal line at 4½ seconds to go. Phase III enables the pilot to perform the most precise steering possible during the final stages of side attacks. Rocket firing and the appearance of the pull-out warning signal occur at the instant when there is the greatest probability of scoring a hit on the target. During Phase III, the time of firing depends essentially upon three factors: (1) the point of intersection of target and attacking aircraft paths; (2) the time until the target reaches the intersection; (3) the time required for the rockets to travel to the intersection. At 2½ seconds to go, the circuits in the firing section of the computer are readied, and when the computer calculates that the target and the rockets will arrive at the intersection simultaneously, electrical firing signals are initiated. Just before the firing signals, the computer initiates an electrical signal to lower the rocket pod. In Phase III, the computer compensates

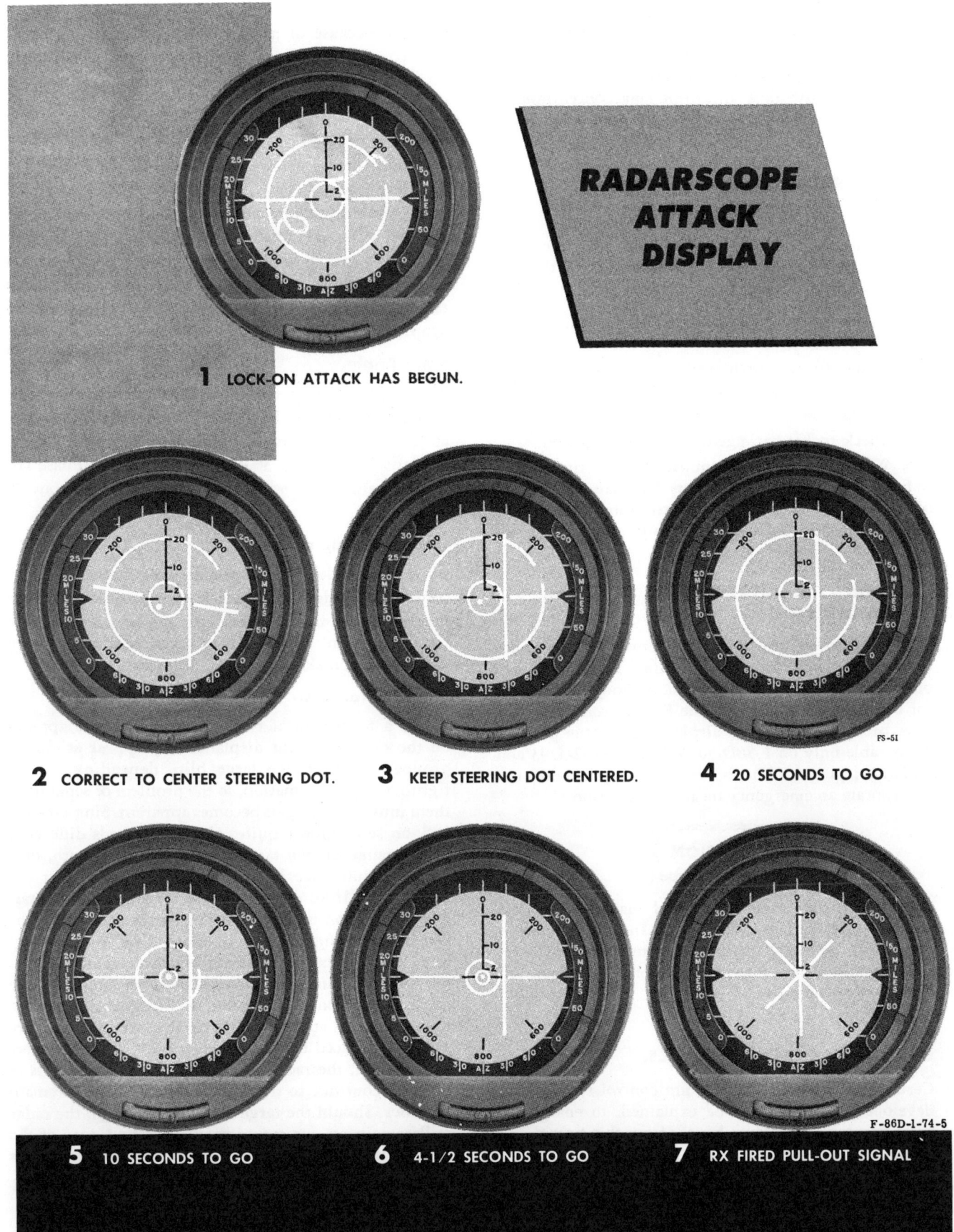

Figure 4-19

for an azimuth steering error by recalculation of the problem based on the new conditions brought about by the error. Azimuth excursion of the steering dot shows bank angle only; thus the pilot may concentrate on vertical steering and keeping the airplane wings level.

MANUAL ROCKET-FIRING OPERATION.

Note

Rockets cannot be fired if the nose gear and nose gear doors are not up and locked or if the rocket package is not fully extended.

1. Stand-by sight rheostat on, with brilliance adjusted as desired.
2. Rocket-firing switch MANUAL.
3. Turn armament master switch to desired rocket selector position.
4. Check rocket-package-up indicator light on.
5. When on target, momentarily depress trigger fully to fire selected number of rockets. Each later depression of the trigger will cause the selected number of rockets to be fired until the package is empty.

EMERGENCY OPERATION OF E-4 FIRE CONTROL SYSTEM.*

The EMER position of the master power switch places the equipment in emergency operation about 45 seconds after the system is turned on. Although provisions for emergency operation of the E-4 fire control system have been installed on all airplanes, the EMER position is operable only on F-86D-50 Airplane AF52-4203 and all later airplanes. (The E-3 fire control system does not incorporate an emergency means of operation.)

Do not use EMER position of master power switch except in emergencies. Indiscriminate use of the EMER position to shorten the normal 4½-minute delay period will probably damage units of the system.

OPERATIONAL CHARACTERISTICS.

Certain characteristics of the fire control system have developed which should be explained, to enable the pilot to receive maximum benefit from this system.

Rocket Drop.

If the rockets are launched in a horizontal direction (angle of attack of zero degrees), they will drop a short distance because of gravity before hitting the target. The computer allows for this drop by computing an attack course which passes above the target path by the amount of the drop.

Angle of Attack.

If the rockets are launched in an upward direction (positive angle of attack), they will rise above the attack course before weather-cocking into the air stream. This effectively reduces the distance of rocket drop from airplane to target. The computer considers both factors and computes an attack course which passes above the target path by a distance less than the normal rocket drop.

Bank Angle.

The airplane wings should be within about 10 degrees of horizontal during Phase III. If they are not, the probability of scoring a hit is reduced. For example: if the airplane remains in a 30-degree bank during Phase III, the probability of scoring a hit is reduced about 25 percent.

Undesired Echoes.

At low altitudes over mountainous terrain or water, continuous undesired echoes known as ground clutter may produce images on the scope. These images may induce lock-on; however, they are generally extensive and diffused, making them readily identifiable.

Multiple Targets.

When a formation of two or more airplanes appears on the radarscope, the airplanes may appear as closely grouped blips or one large blip, depending on the tightness of the formation, so the problem of separating them into single targets becomes apparent. Single-target lock-on separation requires about 100 yards difference in the range of two targets at the same azimuth, or a 4-degree difference in azimuth of two targets at the same range. If an elongated blip representing two targets appears on the scope, it is possible to lock on one end of the elongated blip by moving the range sweep trace onto the extreme end of the blip desired, and then moving the range-gate marker into position on the trace. A lock-on should occur if the targets are more than 4 degrees apart in azimuth. If the two targets are so closely spaced that the radar cannot distinguish between them, the radar will lock on the two targets as one and continue to track both as long as they remain together. Should the targets separate enough, the radar will remain on one target, generally the larger of the two, or if they are of the same size, the lock-on occurs on the nearer target.

Altitude Mark.

Radar echoes from the ground will appear on the scope as a narrow horizontal line, known as the altitude mark. When the distance from the interceptor to the target

---

*E-4 fire control system

is equal to the distance from the interceptor to the ground, the echoes from the ground and the target will appear at the same position on the scope display. When this happens, the radar can lock on either the target or the altitude mark. If the radar locks onto the altitude mark, the range circle closing rate segment goes to zero and the steering dot becomes erratic. The pilot must then maintain his course while he again locks his radar on the target. With a little experience, the pilot can anticipate the lock on the altitude mark and can quickly relock on the target by use of the range in-out switch alone after the target has passed through the altitude mark.

Attack Geometry.

The use of air-to-air rockets has permitted a change in the type of an attack employed by a fighter-type airplane. For the fighter equipped with guns, a curved pursuit course is used because the guns must be on target at least several seconds to ensure enough hits for a kill. The interceptor armed with rockets makes use of an essentially straight-line course, since the full armament load can be fired in roughly two tenths of a second. Thus, the interceptor flies a lead collision course which allows for distance of rocket travel relative to interceptor. The fire control system computer furnishes the necessary steering data for the pilot to fly this lead collision course and automatically fires the rockets at the split second required for a hit. The interceptor makes this straight-line run-in on target regardless of whether he is on a beam approach or stern approach. It is recommended that near-beam approaches be made and that GCI and the interceptor pilots train to this end. The beam attack provides the largest target profile, thus increasing the hit probability. Figure 4-20 illustrates a stern attack and a beam attack.

Distance of Closest Approach—During Attack.

In flying the lead collision course, it must be remembered that the interceptor is carrying the rockets to a firing point where the rockets will be fired on a true collision course with the target, thus allowing the rockets to travel several hundred yards ahead of the interceptor. This means that the target will cross in front of the interceptor at the time of impact. This distance of relative rocket run is about 500 yards. The actual clearance then depends on the relationship of the interceptor and target courses and the ratio of their respective speeds. Figure 4-21 assumes that the interceptor is making a 90-degree beam attack and the ratio of interceptor speed to the target speed is 3 to 1. The distance of closest approach is about 150 yards. This, of course, is true only when the interceptor continues on the firing course; if you break off at the pull-out signal, the interceptor will miss the target by a larger distance.

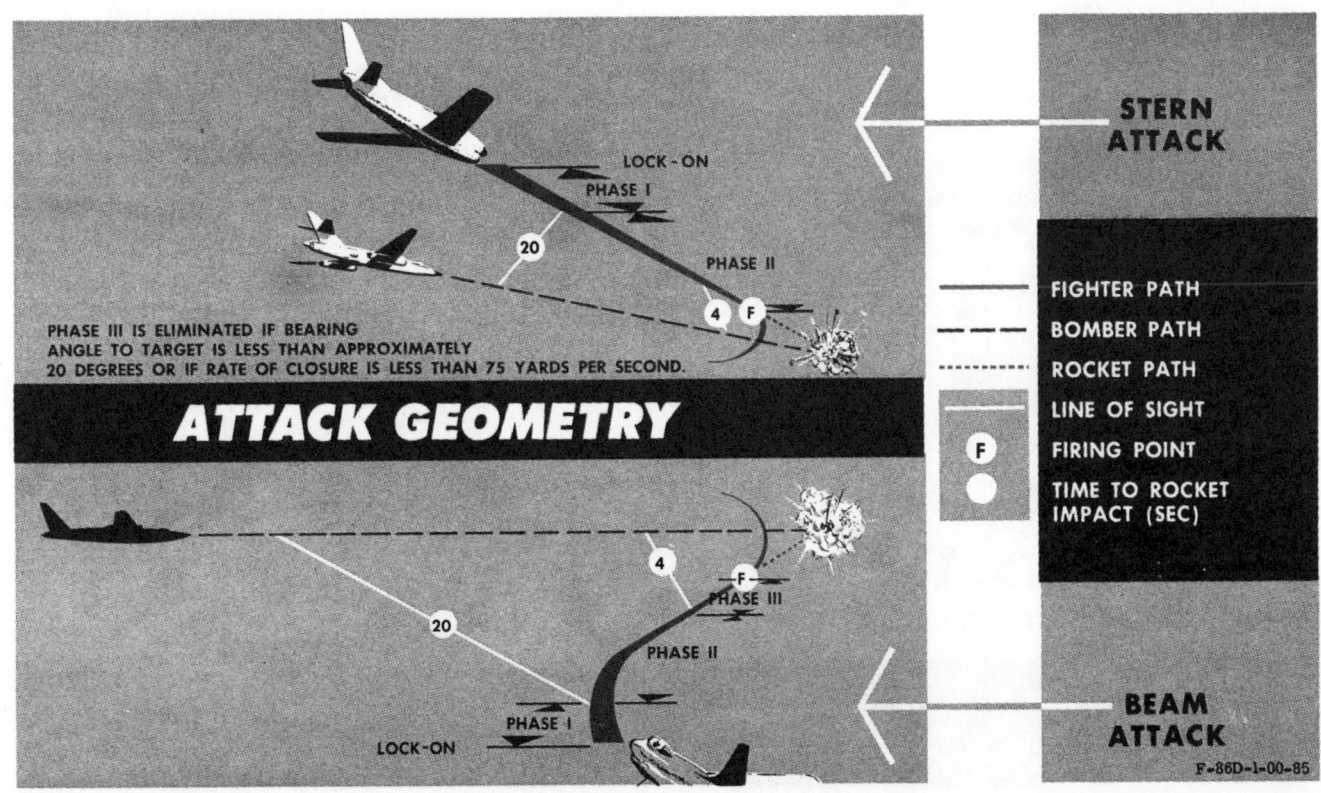

Figure 4-20

Section IV T. O. 1F-86D-1

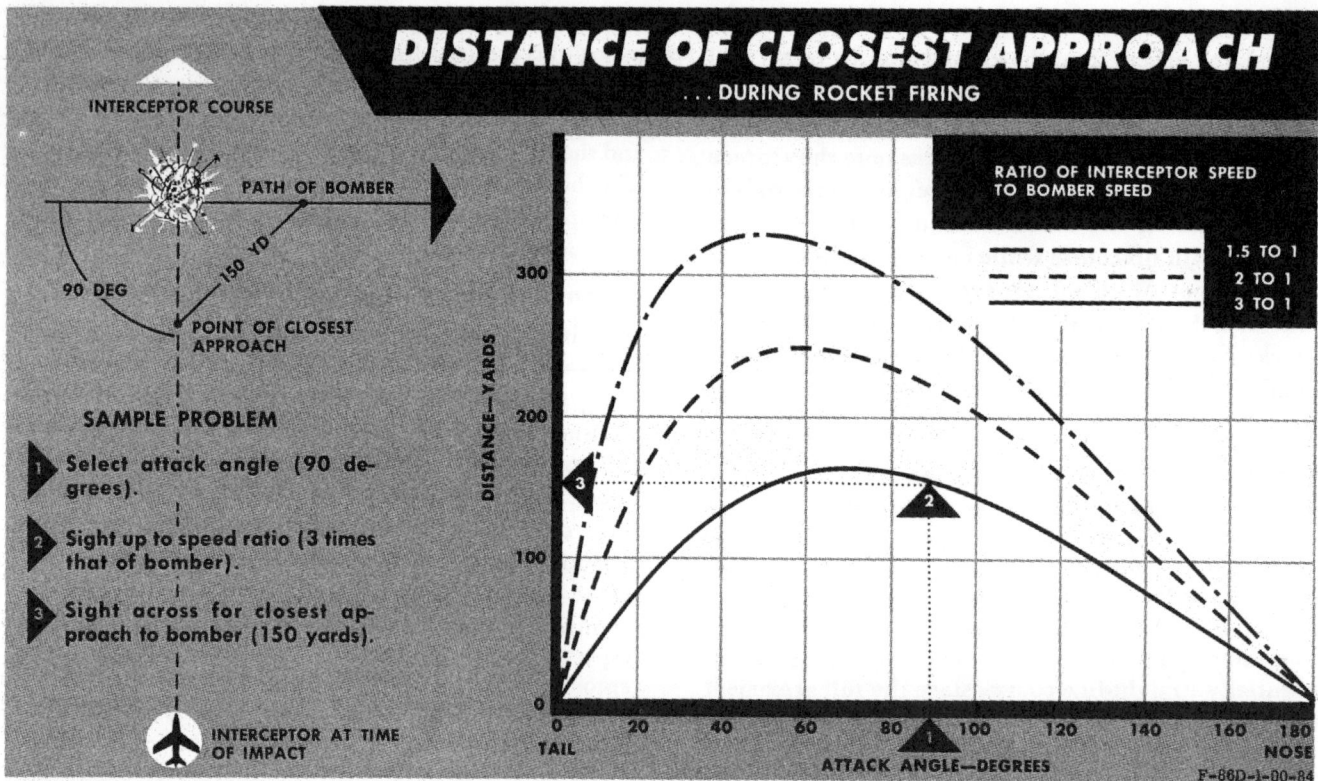

Figure 4-21

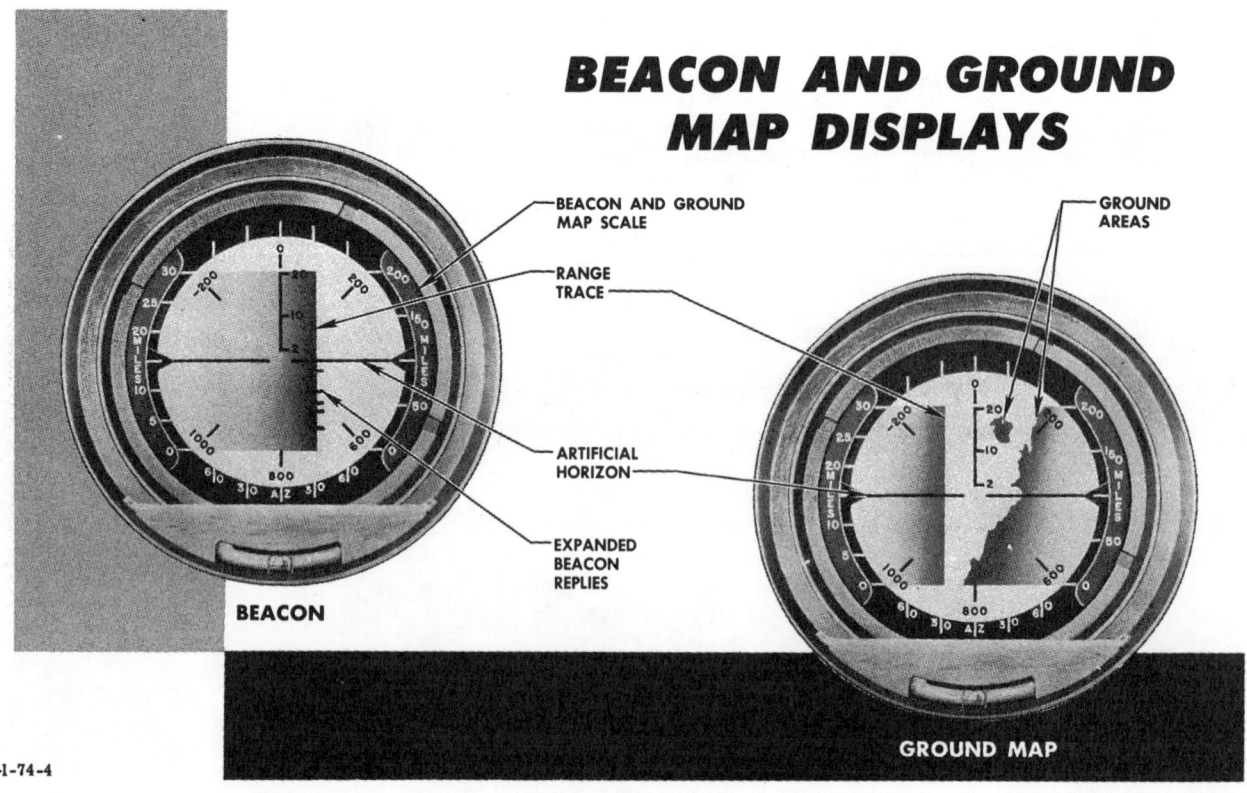

Figure 4-22

GROUND MAP OPERATION.*

Ground map function may be used for navigation purposes by properly setting the switches on the radar control panel. (See figure 4-17.) During ground map operation, the antenna scans a selected area ahead of the airplane and projects the ground return on the radarscope. During ground map operation, range is shown on the right side of the scope from a distance of 0 to 200 nautical miles in front of the airplane. Any 20-mile sector of the scope presentation (beyond 5 miles) may be expanded for easier interpretation by use of the "BCN & GROUND MAP EXPAND" control knob. The strobe line on the scope, indicated by a marker on the range trace, should be moved up just below the area to be expanded, by rotation of the "BCN & GROUND MAP EXPAND" control knob. When the control knob is depressed, the 20-mile zone selected is expanded to cover the entire area of the scope.

BEACON OPERATION.*

With the controls on the radar control panel (figure 4-17) set for beacon operation, radar beacons may be used as an aid in navigation. Radar beacon signals will appear on the radarscope indicator as short horizontal bars. Range to the station and azimuth location may be read from the scales on the right and bottom side of the indicator. The bottom bar represents the range to the station. The presentation may be expanded for easier operation by use of the "BCN & GROUND MAP EXPAND" control knob as in ground map operation. Depressing the knob with the strobe marker below the bottom mark of the beacon return will expand the bars for easier reading of the coded reply to identify the radar station.

SHUTDOWN PROCEDURE.

For shutdown of fire control system, turn radar power and armament master switches OFF.

CAUTION

To avoid damage to the radar gyro, turn radar off at least 6 minutes before landing, to allow enough time for gyro rotation to stop. If a landing is made, taxi to the line before shutting radar off.

EMERGENCY OPERATION OF ROCKET PACKAGE.

Hot-rocket Package.

If the amber hot-rocket-package warning light remains on after rockets are fired, indicating that one or more rockets have failed to fire and rocket package is still extended, either jettison rocket package or turn armament master switch OFF and, after a safe interval (about 3 minutes), retract rocket package by moving rocket package override switch to UP. The amber warning light will go out whether package is jettisoned or manually retracted. If the rocket package is manually retracted, the remaining rockets may be selected and fired by either procedure 1 or procedure 2; however, if the armament master switch has been turned OFF, any previously selected rockets cannot be fired.

1. Turn armament master switch to previously set position and pull trigger once for each remaining group of rockets.

2. Turn armament master switch to FIRE 24 position and squeeze trigger once, thereby salvoing all remaining rockets.

3. If, after completion of step 1 or 2, hot-rocket-package warning light is still on, jettison or retract package as described.

Jettisoning Rocket Package.

To jettison rocket package, turn armament master switch to EMERG. JET'S'N. To jettison rocket package and drop tanks simultaneously, turn armament master switch to JETTISON READY and press tank-rocket jettison button.

STAND-BY SIGHT.

An N-9-1, N-9, or Mark VIII fixed-reticle gun sight is provided for use during manual rocket firing. The reticle is projected onto the armor glass. The stand-by sight is mounted forward of the instrument panel in the cockpit.

Stand-by Sight Rheostat.

On F-86D-1 Airplanes, a rheostat (11, figure 1-6) for the stand-by sight is mounted on the stand-by sight control panel, on the left console forward of the throttle quadrant. On F-86D-5 and later airplanes, the rheostat for the stand-by sight is on the left aft console on the armament master control panel. (See figure 4-15.) When moved from OFF toward INCREASE or DECREASE, the rheostat turns on and regulates the brilliance of the reticle image projected on the armor glass. This control is powered from the secondary bus.

Alternate Filament Selector Switch.

On F-86D-1 Airplanes, a two-position alternate filament selector switch (10, figure 1-6) is on the stand-by sight control panel on the left console forward of the throttle. On F-86D-5 and later airplanes, this switch is on the armament master control panel. (See figure 4-15.) This switch, powered from the secondary bus, may be moved to select an alternate filament if the first fails to illuminate the reticle image.

---

*E-4 fire control system

CONTROL SURFACE TIE-IN CONTROL PANEL

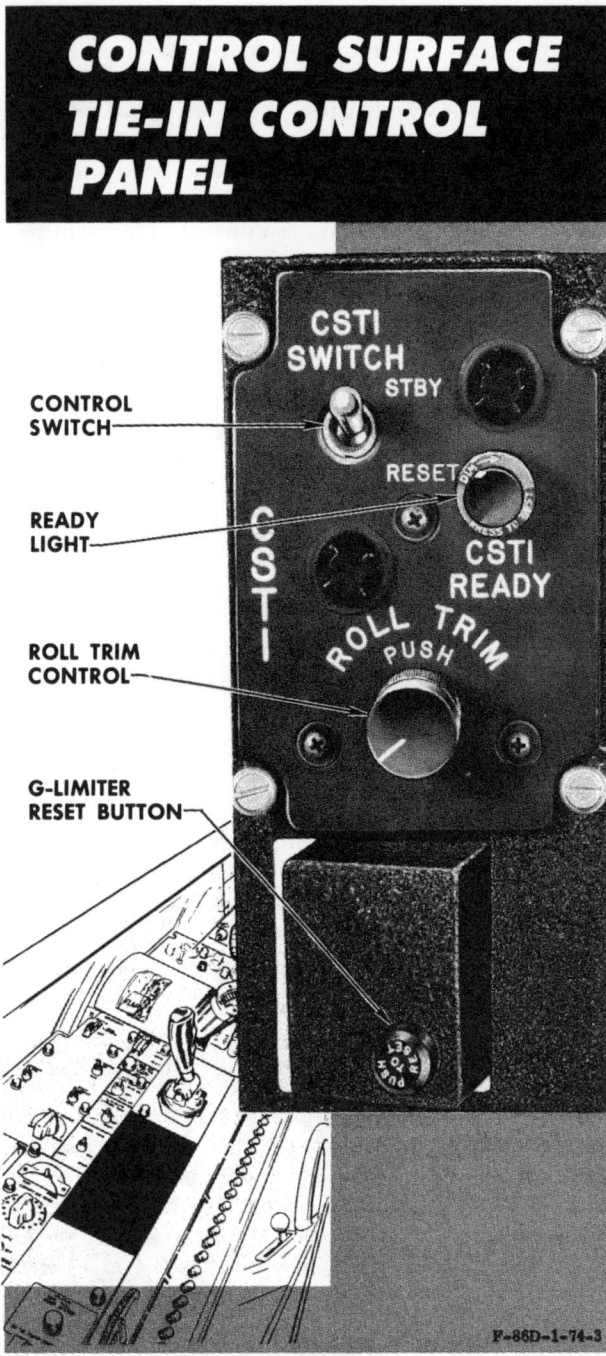

Figure 4-23

CONTROL SURFACE TIE-IN SYSTEM (CSTI).*

On late airplanes,† provisions are made for the installation of a control surface tie-in system. During the attack phase of the interception, this system has an electrical tie-in of the E-4 fire control system with the automatic pilot horizontal stabilizer and aileron servo actuators. This allows the CSTI system to control the airplane from signals received from the fire control computer and transmitted through the CSTI to the servo actuators. The CSTI will control the airplane throughout the attack phase until the pull-out signal appears on the radarscope, or until lock-on is broken. The CSTI system will properly track the target and fire the rockets at the correct time and range, with no further action on the part of the pilot.

CSTI CONTROLS AND INDICATOR.

When CSTI is installed in the airplane, the operation is controlled at the option of the pilot by use of the controls on the CSTI control panel (figure 4-23), on the left console aft of the antenna hand control. These controls receive their power from the E-4 fire control system when the E-4 master switch is in the STBY or OPER position. Power is also furnished from the gyro bus to the servo actuators during operation.

"CSTI & AUTOPILOT" Power Switch.

A three-position switch, powered by the gyro bus, is on the aft end of the right circuit-breaker panel. The switch positions are CSTI, OFF, and CSTI & AUTOPILOT. With the switch in CSTI & AUTOPILOT, power is available to the CSTI and the automatic pilot control panels. The CSTI position on the switch is for ground test purposes only.

"CSTI SWITCH."

The "CSTI SWITCH" is a two-position switch, spring-loaded to the STBY position and having a momentary contact at the RESET position. With switch in the STBY position, the CSTI is not in operation. Momentarily positioning the switch to RESET places the system in operation provided the "CSTI & AUTOPILOT" switch has been positioned at CSTI & AUTOPILOT.

Roll Trim Control.

A rotary-type push-to-turn roll trim switch is on the CSTI control panel. This control permits the pilot to make necessary trim corrections before lock-on, to properly trim the airplane for CSTI operation.

CAUTION

Do not use normal airplane trim system while CSTI is in operation. Structural G-limits may be exceeded when CSTI is disengaged if the airplane has been retrimmed after the lock-on.

"CSTI READY" Light.

A push-to-test light, labeled "CSTI READY," comes on when the CSTI is controlling the airplane flight path.

---

*Removed from TF-86D Airplanes
†F-86D-55 and later airplanes

CSTI G-limiter.

If the CSTI G-limits are exceeded during an attack, the G-limiter, on the aft end of the CSTI control panel, will disengage the CSTI. To regain CSTI operation, push G-limit reset button and move "CSTI SWITCH" to RESET before another attack is made.

CSTI OPERATION.

With E-4 fire control system in operation and "CSTI & AUTOPILOT" power switch positioned at CSTI & AUTOPILOT, perform the following procedure *before lock-on occurs:*

1. Manually trim airplane to hands-off flight with stick trim button.

2. Level radarscope horizon.

3. Move "CSTI SWITCH" from STBY to RESET and observe "CSTI READY" light on.

Note

If light fails to come on, push G-limiter reset button and again move "CSTI SWITCH" from STBY to RESET.

4. Depress roll trim knob and trim ailerons to zero roll attitude. *Do not use stick trim button after CSTI trim is completed.*

Note

- Occasionally, as the roll trim knob is pressed, a sharp aileron roll may be experienced, as the trim action is very sensitive and requires fine adjustments. This is a normal function and should be trimmed out by slow, smooth roll trim knob adjustment.

- When a target signal is received and a lock-on accomplished, the CSTI is automatically engaged after a 4-second time delay. From this point to the pull-out signal, the CSTI is in control of the airplane. It is recommended that a hands-off procedure be used to prevent overriding the controls during the balance of the attack phase.

- With CSTI in operation, the rockets fire automatically, after which the pull-out warning appears on the radarscope and the CSTI is disengaged, requiring the pilot to assume control and continue the recovery. If another attack is desired, the "CSTI SWITCH" must be recycled to regain the "CSTI READY" light.

- At any time during the attack phase, lock-on can be broken by squeezing the "AUTOMATIC PILOT RELEASE" switch, on the control stick.

MISCELLANEOUS EQUIPMENT.

ANTI-G SUIT PROVISIONS.

An air pressure outlet connection on the front of the pilot's seat provides for attachment of the air pressure intake tube of the pilot's anti-G suit. Air pressure for inflation of the anti-G suit bladders comes from the engine compressor section and through the air cooling radiator. An anti-G suit pressure regulator valve (2, figure 1-6; 2, figure 1-7) on the left aft console, marked "HI" and "LO," functions at a predetermined number of G, depending on the selected setting. Acceleration above about 1.75 G (HI or LO setting) causes the valve to open, inflating the anti-G suit. For each additional 1 G acceleration force, a corresponding one psi (LO setting) or 1.5 psi (HI setting) air pressure is exerted in the anti-G suit. A button on top of the valve can be manually depressed to inflate the suit momentarily when desired, for the purpose of lessening fatigue during prolonged flight.

MAP CASE.

The map case (3, figures 1-6 and 1-7) is on the aft left console. Some airplanes have two cases installed on the sides of the ejection seat for storage of instrument flight charts. (See figure 1-29.)

CHECK LIST.

The pilot's check lists are on the inboard face of the cockpit ledge (left side) above the left console.

REAR-VISION MIRROR.

An adjustable, rear-vision mirror is attached to the upper inner surface of the canopy, just aft of the canopy bow.

PROTECTIVE COVERS.

Removable covers include wing and horizontal stabilizer covers, a cockpit and forward fuselage cover, and an engine compartment cover. An intake duct plug and cover for the tail pipe, and a pitot tube cover are also provided.

The air intake duct plug and tail pipe cover should not be installed until the engine has cooled, to prevent formation of excessive moisture.

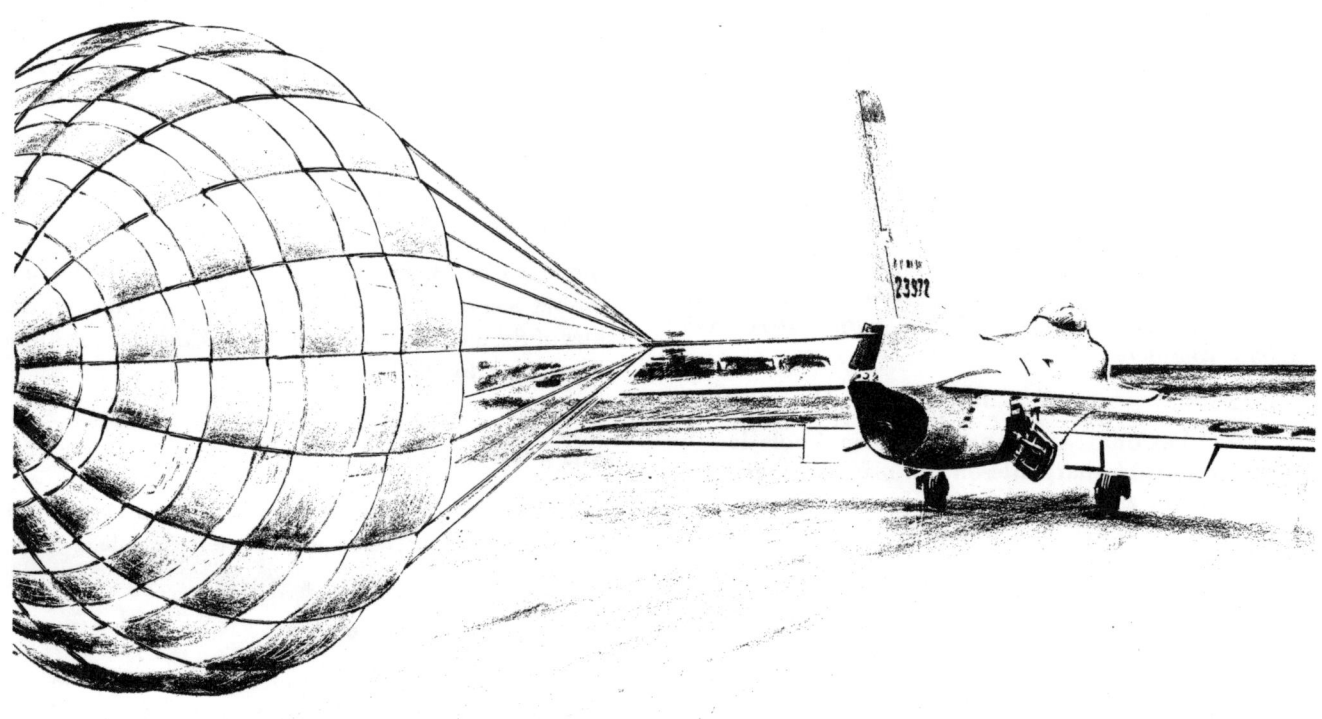

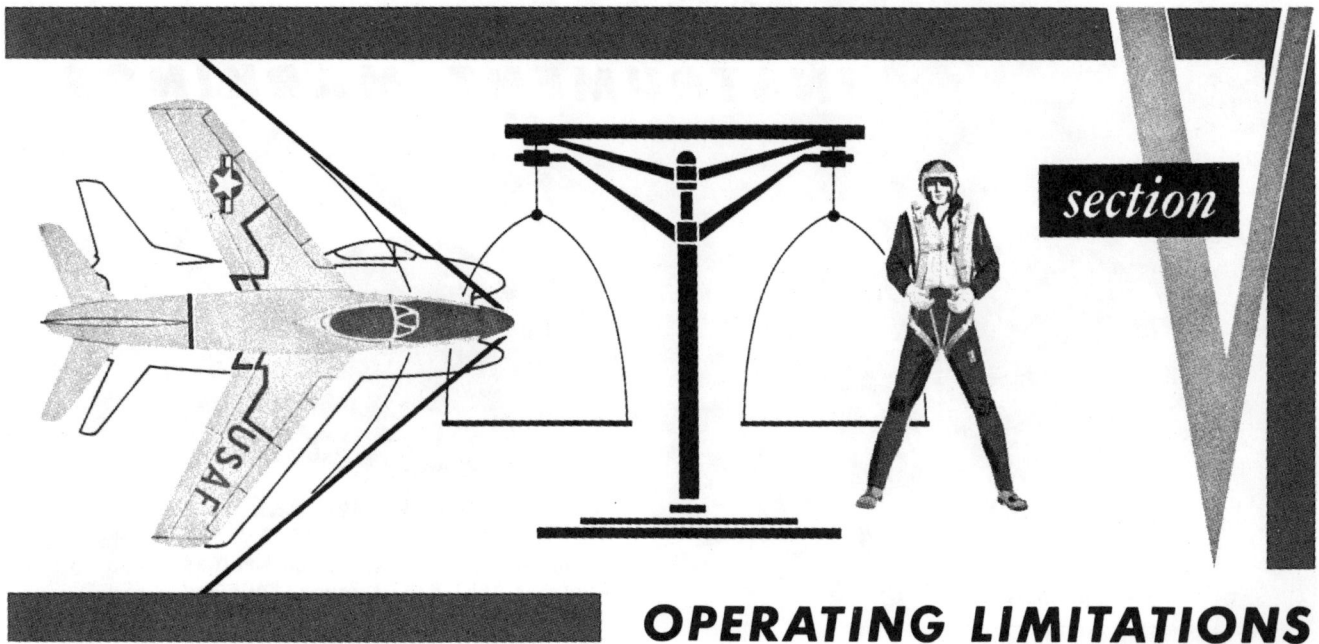

section V
OPERATING LIMITATIONS

TABLE OF CONTENTS	PAGE		PAGE
Instruments Markings	5-1	Rocket-firing Limitation	5-6
Engine Limitations	5-1	Acceleration Limitations	5-6
Airspeed Limitations	5-4	Center-of-Gravity Limitations	5-6
Prohibited Maneuvers	5-5	Weight Limitations	5-6

INSTRUMENT MARKINGS.

The limitation markings as shown on the instruments (figure 5-1) and noted in the captions are not necessarily repeated in the text of this or other sections.

ENGINE LIMITATIONS.

All normal engine limitations are shown in figure 5-1.

AFTERBURNER LIMITATIONS.

Afterburner operation is prohibited temporarily until such time as T. O. 1F-86D-519 is accomplished. Afterburner operation is permitted only on late airplanes* and those changed by T. O. 2J-J47-293 to incorporate the mechanical stop in the afterburner fuel control valve. (DD Form 781 should show if noncompliance of the T. O. exists.)

ENGINE OVERSPEED.

All engine overspeeds of more than 104% rpm, with or without an overtemperature condition, necessitate engine removal and overhaul.

ENGINE EXHAUST TEMPERATURE.

Engine Start.

During engine starts up to idle rpm (within 2 minutes), exhaust temperatures of 950°C or above for 2 seconds or more constitute overtemperature operation.

Engine Operation.

For all engine operation (except starting), exhaust temperatures of 690°C to 750°C for 40 seconds or more temperatures of 750°C to 800°C for 10 seconds or more and temperatures above 800°C for 2 seconds or more constitute overtemperature operation.

Note
The duration and degree of all overtemperature must be entered in the DD Form 781.

---

*F-86D-35 Airplanes AF51-8397 through -8406 and -8419 through -8505, and F-86D-40 and later airplanes

INSTRUMENT MARKINGS

OIL PRESSURE
- 12 psi minimum
- 12-45 psi continuous
- 50 psi maximum

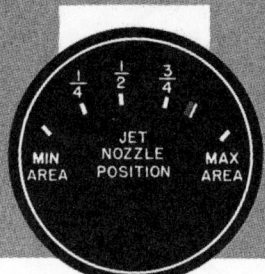

VARIABLE-NOZZLE
- 3/4 plus 10 degrees open maximum*

The red radial is not installed on F-86D-35 Airplanes AF51-8397 through -8406 and -8419 through -8505, F-86D-40 and subsequent airplanes, and those changed by T.O. 2J-J47-293, 294, and -311 ("flattop" fuel schedule).

HYDRAULIC PRESSURE

	UTILITY HYDRAULIC SYSTEM / FLIGHT CONTROL NORMAL HYDRAULIC SYSTEM	FLIGHT CONTROL ALTERNATE HYDRAULIC SYSTEM
650-2550 psi	Malfunction within system— unit operation sluggish	Normal only if system is engaged and controls operating
2550-3200 psi	Normal when systems are in operation.*	Normal when controls are not in use
3200 psi	Maximum	Maximum when NOT using emergency override handle for alternate system operation
3200-4000 psi	Engine-driven pump compensator failure	Normal only if emergency override handle is pulled

*For static (no-flow) conditions, gage pressure should be 2900 to 3200 psi.

FUEL PRESSURE
- 40 psi minimum
- 40-400 psi continuous
- 500 psi maximum

F-86D-1 AIRPLANES

FUEL PRESSURE
- 40 psi minimum
- 40-400 psi continuous
- 600 psi maximum

F-86D-5 THROUGH F-86D-35 AIRPLANES

Figure 5-1

BASED ON ALL GRADES OF FUEL

TACHOMETER

- ▬ 75% minimum cruise
- ▬ 75%-100% continuous
- ▬ 100% maximum

EXHAUST TEMPERATURE

- ▬ 150°C — minimum
- ▬ 150°C-635°C (655°C) continuous
- ▬ 685°C — maximum at Maximum Power (20 min limit)
- ▬ 685°C — maximum at Military Power (30 min limit)
- ▬ 950°C — maximum starting engine or afterburner, or acceleration only

AIRSPEED
NO EXTERNAL LOAD

- ▬ 610 knots max or speed where wing roll becomes excessive
- ▬ 185 knots IAS gear-down limit airspeed

(195 knots IAS flap-down limit airspeed)

NOTE
WITH DROP TANKS INSTALLED, AIRSPEED LIMITS ARE:
Types I and III
Below 15,000 ft   555 knots or .9 Mach number, whichever is less
Above 15,000 ft   same as with no external load
Types II and IV
500 knots IAS or .9 Mach number, whichever is less

ACCELEROMETER

- ▬ 5.6 G max with no external load
- ▬ 5.0 G max with Types I and III 120-gallon drop tanks (4.0 G max with Types II and IV 120-gallon drop tanks)
- ▬ -2.0 G max for all configurations

Max G allowable for operation of rocket package above 560 knots is 3.5 G.

ENGINE EXHAUST TEMPERATURE (DESCENT).

On airplanes equipped with J47-GE-17 or -17B engines, the following minimum exhaust temperatures must be observed during any descent:

- At any altitude, when using Normal Rated Thrust or below, maintain 300°C minimum during descent.
- Above 25,000 feet altitude, when using Maximum or Military Thrust, maintain 600°C for about 2 minutes. After about 2 minutes at 600°C or when descending through 25,000 feet altitude, the throttle may be retarded further to maintain a minimum of 300°C for the remainder of the descent.
- At or below 25,000 feet altitude, retard throttle to maintain a minimum of 300°C throughout descent.

AIRSPEED LIMITATIONS.

LANDING GEAR LOWERING SPEEDS.

Limit airspeed for landing gear lowering is 185 knots IAS. If the landing gear is lowered at speeds above this value, the air loads may damage the fairing, doors, or operating mechanism.

WING FLAP LOWERING SPEED.

The limiting airspeed for lowering of the wing flaps is 195 knots IAS. If the wing flaps are lowered above this limiting airspeed, the fairing or operating mechanisms may be damaged.

LANDING LIGHT LOWERING SPEED.

The landing light is designed to be lowered after the landing gear is extended. The limit airspeed for lowering the landing light is 185 knots IAS.

CANOPY OPENING SPEED.

The canopy is not to be opened in flight. On the ground, while taxiing, the canopy may be operated at airspeeds

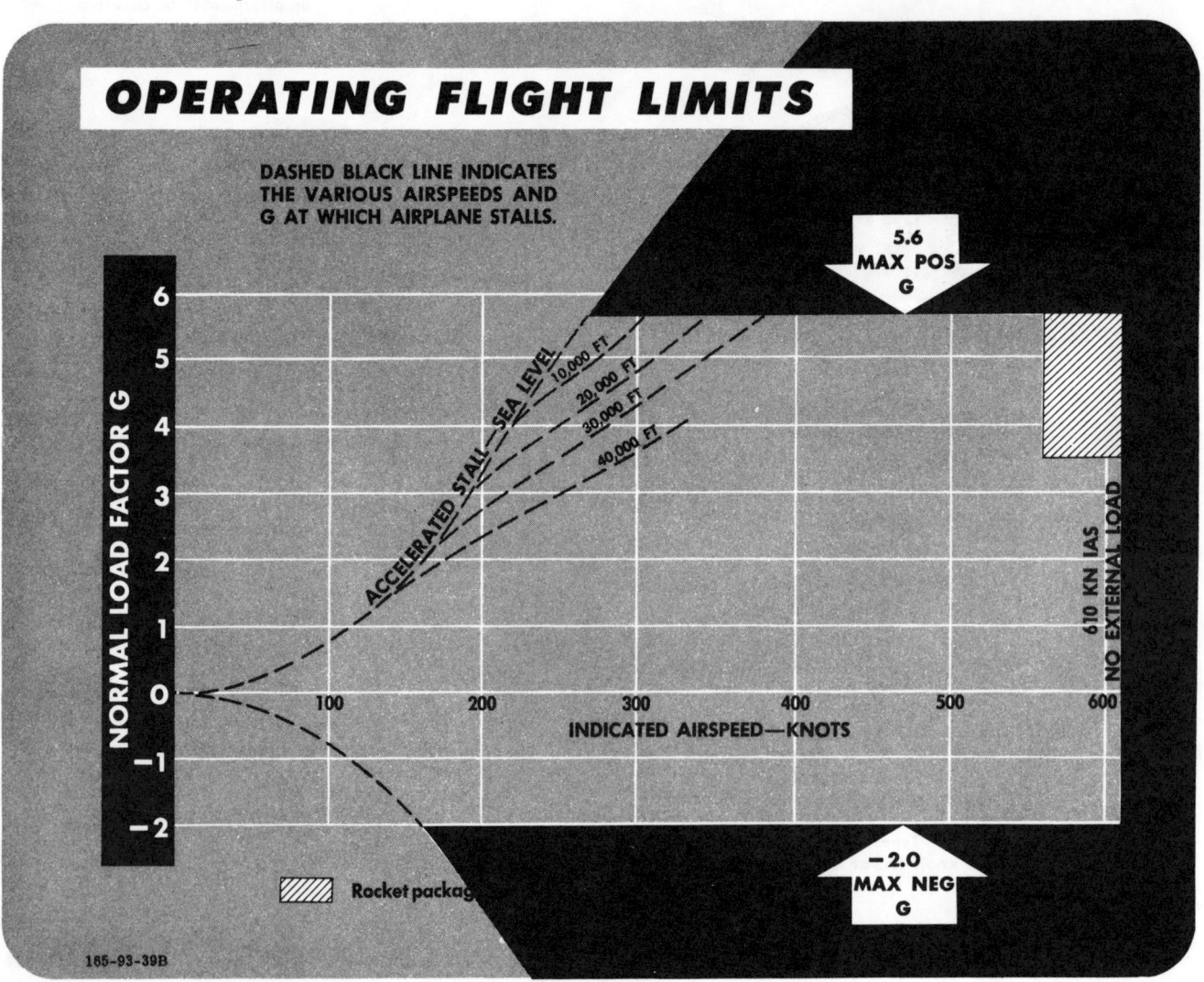

Figure 5-2

not exceeding 50 knots IAS. If canopy is operated at airspeeds above this value, damage to canopy and canopy operating mechanism will result.

ROCKET PACKAGE OPERATION SPEED.

Rocket package operation under normal conditions imposes no airspeed limitations. However, at airspeeds above 560 knots IAS, the rocket package must not be operated during normal accelerations greater than 3.5 G.

DROP TANK RELEASE SPEED.

The drop tank release limits for all types (I, II, III, and IV) of tanks are as follows (maximum airspeed and G-limitations must be observed):

Full tanks . . . . . drop at any speed.
Empty or
partially full . . . drop at any speed above 220 knots IAS.

Note

- All drops should be made from straight-and-level (1 G) attitude.
- In an emergency, drops may be made under any flight condition within the airspeed limitations.

DRAG CHUTE OPERATING SPEED.

The drag chute is designed to be deployed at speeds of 150 knots IAS or below and *only after touchdown*. The drag chute is automatically released from the airplane if deployed at speeds above about 160 knots IAS. If the chute is deployed at speeds above 150 knots IAS, the breakaway fitting tension element must be visually inspected before further flight and replaced if found deformed. The drag chute should not be deployed in a 90-degree cross wind which exceeds 20 knots nor in a 45-degree cross wind which exceeds 30 knots, except in an emergency. Flight tests have shown that a properly packed chute has the least compartment pull-out resistance and will deploy at speeds as low as 60 knots IAS in about 4 seconds. However, to ensure consistent and proper operation, it is recommended that the chute be deployed above 75 knots IAS.

Note

Although the drag chute is not designed for in-flight use, it will not adversely affect the airplane flight characteristics if it is inadvertently deployed just before touchdown and the proper flare-out has been initiated.

MAXIMUM ALLOWABLE AIRSPEED.

No External Load.

No Mach number limitation is imposed on the airplane with no external load. However, the airspeed limitation at any altitude is 610 knots IAS, or airspeed where wing roll becomes excessive.

External Drop Tanks Installed.

For maximum allowable airspeeds with 120-gallon external drop tanks installed, see figure 5-1.

PROHIBITED MANEUVERS.

INVERTED FLIGHT.

Inverted flying, or any maneuver resulting in negative acceleration, must not be performed with the afterburner operating.

Note
*Inverted flight with afterburner operating is prohibited. Inverted flight without the afterburner operating must be limited to **10 seconds duration**, as there is no means of ensuring a continuous flow of fuel or oil in this attitude.*

INTENTIONAL SPINS.

With 120-gallon external drop tanks installed, intentional spins are prohibited.

PILOT-INDUCED OSCILLATION.

All pilot-induced oscillations ("porpoising") must be reported in DD Form 781.

OTHER MANEUVERS.

Snap rolls or any other snap maneuvers are prohibited at all times. Aerobatics are prohibited when external drop tanks are installed and contain fuel. When Types II or IV 120-gallon external drop tanks are installed and are empty, rate of roll is limited to 90 degrees per second.

ROCKET-FIRING LIMITATION.

Do not fire MK II 2.75-inch rockets above 20,000 feet, except in an emergency. Below 20,000 feet, not more than six MK II 2.75-inch rockets may be fired per salvo.

Firing of MK II rockets above 20,000 feet could cause engine compressor stall and flame-out.

ACCELERATION LIMITATIONS.

MAXIMUM ACCELERATION.

For maximum allowable G for symmetrical (no-roll) pull-outs, see figure 5-1. The operating flight limit diagram (figure 5-2) graphically illustrates symmetrical (no-roll) G-limits with no external load. Maximum allowable positive G for rolling pull-outs with no external load is 3.7 G. Maximum allowable positive G for rolling pull-outs with 120-gallon external drop tanks installed is 3.3 G. Maximum allowable negative G during rolls is −1.0 G in any configuration.

ENGINE.

If the engine has been subjected to a load factor in excess of 10 G, it must be removed and a special inspection performed.

CENTER-OF-GRAVITY LIMITATIONS.

The center-of-gravity position of the airplane is chiefly affected by the distribution of the fuel load carried and by whether or not the 2.75-inch rockets are aboard. External 120-gallon drop tanks do not greatly change the airplane center of gravity, although the airplane weight is increased. Since there is no in-flight control of CG position other than the normal expenditure of rockets and release of external loads, major factors affecting CG position must be checked before flight. Refer to Handbook of Weight and Balance Data, T. O. 1-1B-40.

WEIGHT LIMITATIONS.

The design of the airplane prevents the possibility of overloading; therefore, there are no weight limitations to be watched so long as standard drop tanks are carried. The normal gross weight for take-off with rockets and no external load is about 18,760 pounds. If a hard landing is made with the airplane near take-off gross weight, the airplane should be inspected for signs of structural damage before the next flight.

section VI

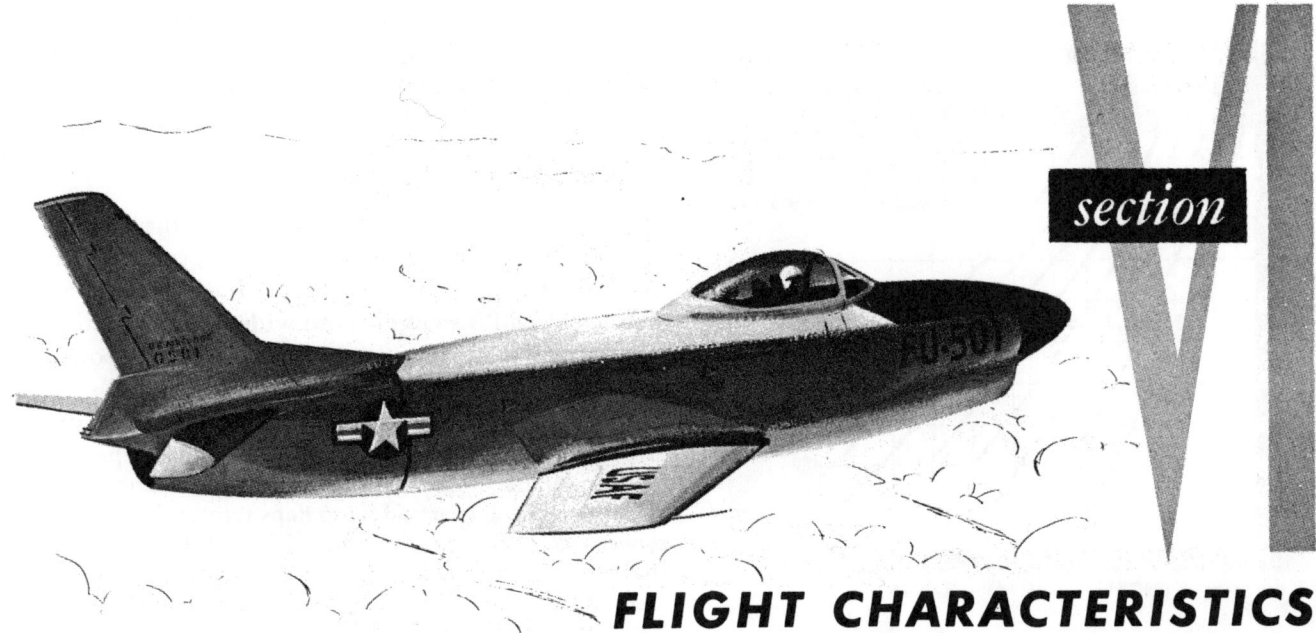

FLIGHT CHARACTERISTICS

TABLE OF CONTENTS	PAGE		PAGE
Mach Number	6-1	Diving	6-19
Stalls	6-1	Take-off Distances	6-21
Spins	6-4	Effects of Gusts	6-21
Flight Controls	6-7	Rocket Package	6-22
Level-flight Characteristics	6-12	Ferry Operations	6-22
Climb Characteristics	6-14	Flight With Drop Tanks	6-23
Maneuvering-flight Characteristics	6-15	Vortex Generators	6-23

GENERAL.

Note

The information in this section applies only to the airplane with no external load, unless otherwise noted.

The stability and control characteristics of the airplane are excellent throughout its entire speed range. These characteristics are made possible by incorporation of the controllable horizontal tail as the primary longitudinal control and the adoption of the completely hydraulic flight control system. Use of this type control system provides comfortable stick forces and superior handling qualities, particularly in regions of high Mach numbers. Wing slats and speed brakes are provided to further improve flight control.

MACH NUMBER.

Note

Mach number represents a percentage of the speed of sound. For example, if you are flying at Mach .75 at any altitude, your speed is 75 percent of the speed of sound at that altitude.

For easier association, the speeds in this section are given in terms of Mach number rather than indicated airspeeds. In order to relate a flight characteristic to airspeed, you would need to know a different airspeed at which that characteristic occurred for every altitude. However, if a flight characteristic is related to Mach number, the flight characteristic will occur at the same Mach number at any altitude and will vary only in intensity, depending upon the altitude. At low altitude, the indicated airspeed for a given Mach number will be higher than at high altitude, and, hence, pressures on the airplane will be greater than at high altitude. Therefore, you will notice that, although the same handling characteristics will occur at the same Mach number at any altitude, the effect on the airplane and on the controls will be more pronounced, and possibly limiting, at low altitude. A Mach number chart (figure 6-1) illustrates the variation of airspeed with altitude for given Mach numbers.

STALLS.

Stall characteristics of the airplane are typical for a swept-wing fighter, which has a higher angle of attack

6-1

Section VI — T. O. 1F-86D-1

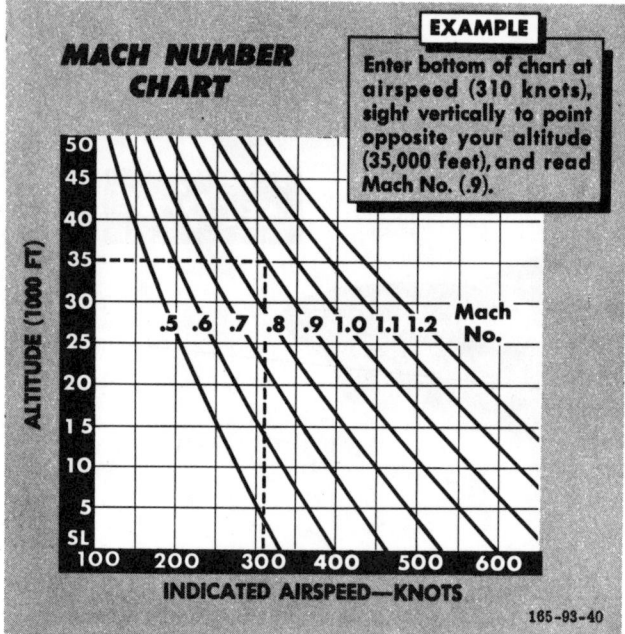

Figure 6-1

at the stall point than straight-wing fighters. There is no severe rolling or yawing tendency, and positive aileron control is available through the stall and during recovery. The airplane has good stall warning characteristics in all attitudes. Entry into the stall speed range is shown by a medium to heavy general air-frame buffet, depending upon the configuration and the G-load imposed.

UNACCELERATED STALLS.

Unaccelerated stalls (stalls at 1 G), with the landing gear and wing flaps down and power off, are preceded by stall warning in the form of mild airframe buffet. The actual stall is straight ahead with a slight pitching motion. Stalls in the same configuration with power on have the same stall warning, but power-on stalls are not recommended with the afterburner on since the airplane attains a very nose-high attitude accompanied by considerable pitch, roll, and yaw. Unaccelerated stalls with the landing gear and wing flaps retracted and with power on or off occur at speeds of 5 to 10 knots higher than those with the landing gear and wing flaps down. The stall warning is a light airframe buffet, which becomes heavier just before the stall. The nose drops through the horizon and the airplane may roll in either direction.

ACCELERATED STALLS.

Accelerated stalls (stalls at more than 1 G) are sometimes referred to as high-speed stalls because they occur

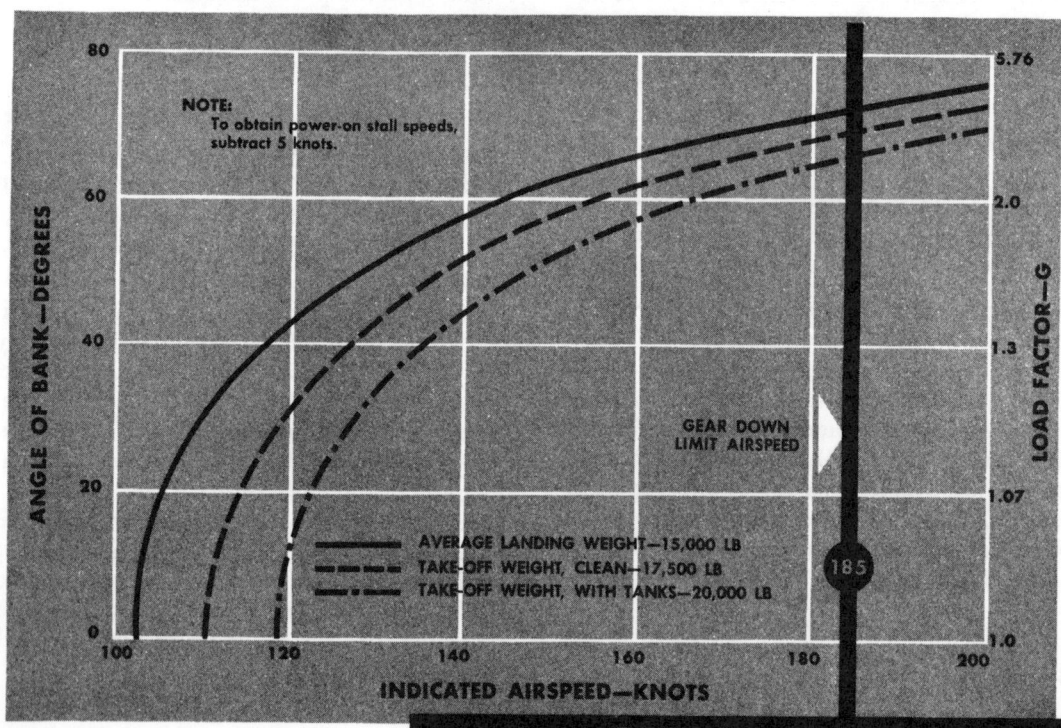

Figure 6-2

above the unaccelerated stall speeds. Applying G on an airplane raises its stalling speed; for example, the application of 2 G doubles the weight of the airplane and wing lift is not always sufficient to support this weight. All accelerated stalls are preceded by heavy buffet and the higher the stall speed the heavier the buffet.

Low-speed Accelerated Stalls.

Low-speed accelerated stalls, in any configuration with power on or off, provide adequate stall warning with a medium to heavy airframe buffet. Accelerated stalls at low speeds usually occur when too tight a turn is made. At the stall, the nose drops out of a turn. When warned of an approaching stall, you can avoid stalling the airplane by releasing back pressure on the stick. The effect of the angle of bank upon accelerated stall speeds is shown in figure 6-2 for 15,000, 17,500, and 20,000 pounds. The curve for a 20,000-pound airplane represents the take-off weight with drop tanks, and the 15,000-pound curve represents average weight on an approach at completion of a flight. The 17,500-pound curve represents take-off clean or maneuvering weight with the drop tanks. The stall speeds shown are based on landing gear and wing flaps down or up with power off. As the engine thrust is increased, the stall speed will be slightly decreased at a given angle of bank. As the speed is decreased during approach, the amount of bank angle or G-load that can be imposed before stalling also decreases. For example, using figure 6-2, during a final approach at 140 knots IAS weighing 15,000 pounds, a stall will not occur until an angle of bank of 58 degrees and 1.8 G are imposed on the airplane. Therefore, considerable maneuvering can be accomplished in the traffic pattern without stalling. For an additional example, suppose you must land immediately after take-off with a maximum gross weight of 20,000 pounds. At the recommended final approach speed of 160 knots IAS for the 20,000-pound weight, stall will occur at an angle of bank of 57 degrees and 1.7 G, allowing good maneuverability.

High-speed Accelerated Stalls.

WARNING

An accelerated, high-speed stall at low altitude can damage the airplane or cause you to black out and possibly lose control.

As the airplane approaches a high-speed stall, there will be considerable airplane buffet. Depending on the

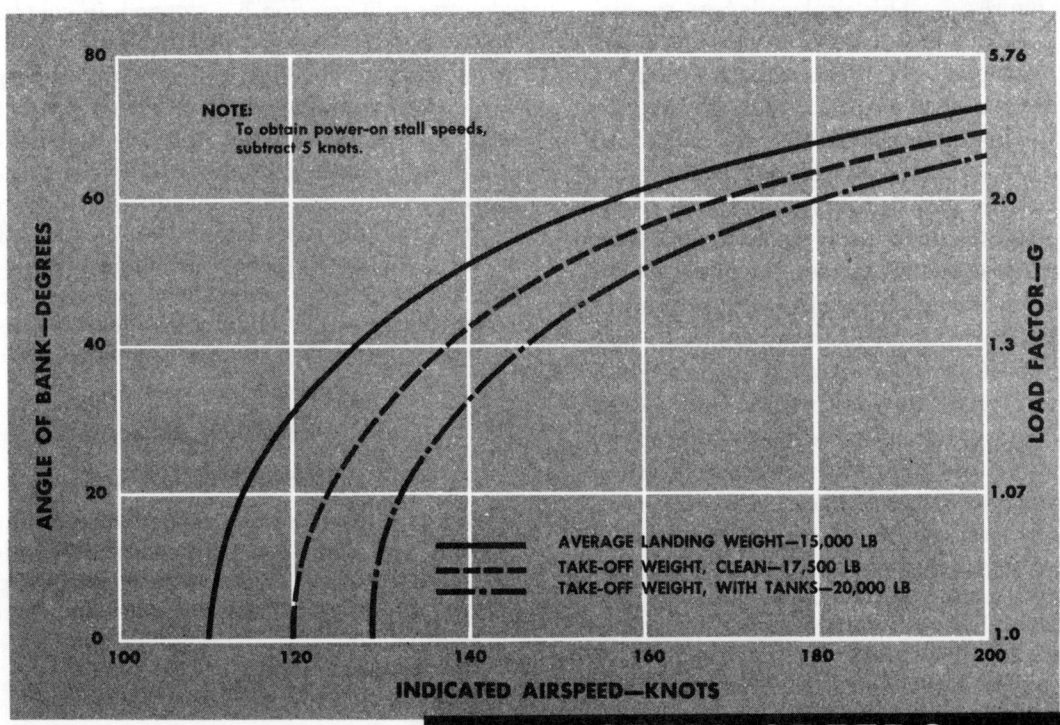

STALL SPEEDS
(IDLE POWER—GEAR AND FLAPS UP)

violence of the maneuver, the actual stall may be accompanied by G-overshoot and wing drop accompanied by heavy buffet. When you are approaching a high-speed stall, take the buffet as a warning and be prepared to relax stick back pressure or use push force to avoid the stall. See figure 5-2 for G at which accelerated stalls occur.

STALL RECOVERY.

Stall recovery is made in the normal manner by applying forward stick and increasing power. If the landing gear or wing flaps are down, care should be exercised to avoid exceeding the landing gear or wing flaps down airspeed limit during the recovery.

PRACTICE STALL.

Practice stalls should be executed at any altitude above 10,000 feet. Normally, altitude loss during practice stall and recovery is only 1000 feet.

SPINS.

NORMAL SPINS.

This airplane has satisfactory spin characteristics regardless of the type of spin entry or configuration of the airplane. (See figure 6-3.) This airplane is hard to spin, and must be "kicked" into an intentional spin. Accidental or intentional spins have the same type of entries. As the airplane enters into a spin, the nose drops down through the horizon to nearly vertical, reaching a dive angle of 50 to 75 degrees about one-half way through the first turn of the spin. During the first half of this turn, the airplane begins its spin rotation gradually; but as the nose drops steeply, the rotation rate speeds up to a point where you sense the airplane suddenly whipping down to the vertical. At the completion of about the first half turn of the spin, the rapid rate of rotation decreases almost as suddenly as it began; as the second half of the turn progresses, the nose pitches up and the spin rotation slows to a point where it appears to stop. At this point the nose will come almost up to the horizon with the wings level, and the first turn of the spin is complete. On the average, 8 seconds will be required to complete the first turn with a loss in altitude of 500 or 600 feet. As the airplane rolls into the second turn of the spin, it follows the same pattern of an increased rate of spin rotation as the airplane pitches down and a slowing rotation accompanied by the nose rising toward the horizon again as the second turn is completed. However, the second as well as any continuing turns are characterized by the airplane pitching down steeper to the 80- or 90-degree dive angle at about the half turn point, and by a smaller amount of pitch-up of the nose toward the horizon as each turn is completed. By the completion of the third or fourth turn, the nose is only coming up to within 50 or 60 degrees of the horizon in contrast to the return of within 10 to 15 degrees during the first turn. Each turn of spin is completed about a second quicker than the preceding turn until a minimum of about 3 seconds is reached. Altitude losses during later turns require 1000 feet per turn on the average. The airplane spins faster to the right than to the left, but requires less altitude to complete. In addition to the greater altitude loss in left-hand spins, the airplane has a tendency to pitch down steeper while rotating in this direction. Use of aileron in the spin is not recommended. Aileron against the spin increases buffet, and slightly increases the pitch-down angles. The outstanding characteristics of using aileron against the spin is that it slows recovery time by doubling the ordinary 3 seconds required to stop rotation. Wind tunnel tests have revealed that if full ailerons are held against the spin when one slat is jammed closed, recovery cannot be made until the ailerons are neutralized. Using aileron with the spin does not delay recovery but it may cause the airplane to spin slightly faster with some increase in altitude loss. Speed brakes have no noticeable effect upon spin characteristics. Spinning with power on (from 2 G turn with 80% rpm) is characterized by lesser pitch-down angles and by a 45-degree nose-down attitude after spin rotation has stopped, in contrast to the 90-degree dive during power-off recovery. However, the advantage of having a much shallower angle with power on to complete recovery is offset by the fact that speed increases so rapidly, that just as much or more altitude is lost in comparison to the 90-degree, power-off recovery completion. If you inadvertently spin with the landing gear and wing flaps down, the airspeed during recovery will exceed placard limits. Retract the landing gear and wing flaps immediately to avoid structural damage. Spins in the landing configuration are characterized by slightly less altitude loss during the first turn.

WARNING

Spins with drop tanks installed are prohibited. If a spin is inadvertently entered when drop tanks are installed, use normal recovery procedure. If spin does not stop immediately, jettison drop tanks and repeat normal recovery procedure.

NONOSCILLATORY SPINS.

You may encounter a different kind of spin, a nonoscillatory-type, in which the normal rise and fall of the

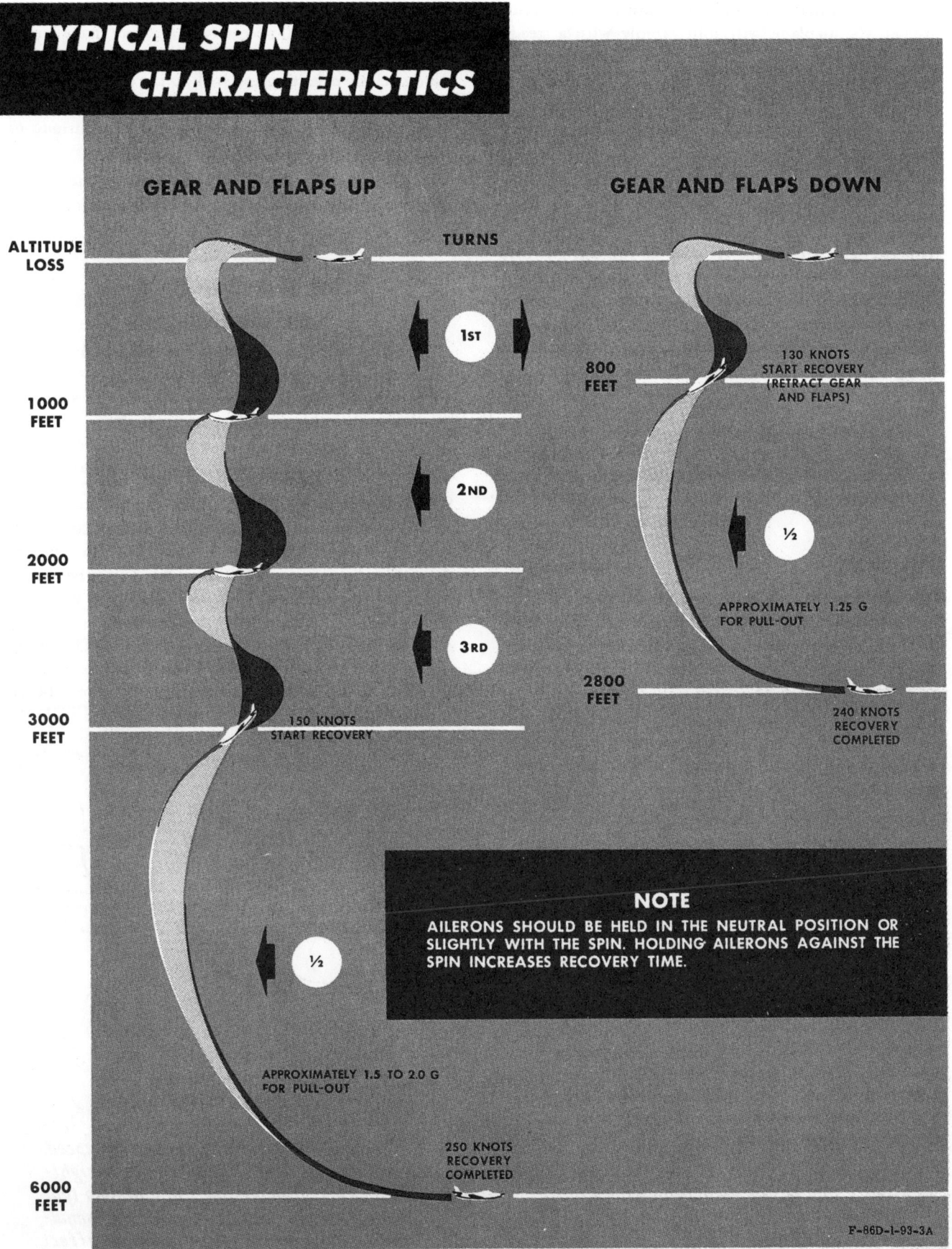

Figure 6-3

nose of the airplane through each turn does not occur. Instead, the airplane will spin rapidly with a steady pitch angle. The nonoscillatory spin can be encountered when the outboard or inboard ends of the slats stick closed while the other ends rack open. These spins usually require more turns for recovery after recovery controls are applied.

INVERTED SPINS.

Inverted spins are characterized by a roll upright into a 45-degree dive attitude about every three fourths of a turn and are followed by a roll again into the inverted position. Each turn takes about 6 seconds. Recovery can be initiated at any time by neutralizing the controls and dropping the nose as the airplane rolls upright.

Note

Flame-outs can occur during an inverted spin, because of interrupted flow of fuel to the engine while the airplane is in the inverted position.

SPIN RECOVERY.

This airplane has excellent spin recovery characteristics in that rotation can be quickly stopped in about one-half turn, using normal recovery techniques. In addition to the rapid spin recovery characteristics, using normal procedure, the airplane will recover from a spin itself, once you release the controls. It will require about two turns to recover "hands off," and naturally is not recommended at low altitudes. To recover from a spin, proceed as follows:

1. Retard throttle to IDLE upon spin entry to prevent excessive altitude loss.

2. Apply full opposite rudder followed immediately by neutralizing the stick.

WARNING

- Do not hold stick back during recovery, as this may cause a spin in the opposite direction when the turn is stopped.
- Hold ailerons neutral during all spin recoveries, since recovery may be delayed by improper use of ailerons.
- If slats are assymetrical (one slat jammed closed), spin recovery will be prevented if full ailerons are held against the spin.

3. If the spin is nonoscillatory (as shown by failure of the nose of the airplane to rise and fall through each turn), maintain standard recovery control for a minimum of three turns, if necessary. Make sure that ailerons are neutral and that you have neutral or slightly forward stick by orienting the stick to the cockpit visually—do not depend on stick force for this orientation. If the airplane still does not respond properly, continue to hold recovery controls and apply power.

4. After spin rotation has been stopped, neutralize rudder and regain flying speed before opening speed brakes or starting pull-out.

WARNING

Failure to hold nose down to regain flying speed before opening speed brakes or beginning pull-out may cause the airplane to stall and snap into a secondary spin. However, full-forward stick is not recommended, because an excessively steep recovery attitude may result.

Spin recovery is completed about one-half turn after recovery control is initiated. As recovery control is applied, the spin speeds up momentarily just before the airplane stops rotating. Therefore, do not be misled into thinking your recovery technique is ineffective. Flight tests show that speed brakes have no adverse effect on the spin characteristics or recovery. Therefore, if the speed brakes are open when a spin is entered, complete recovery with them open, if desired, being sure to hold forward stick to allow airspeed to build up above stall speed.

Warning

If airplane snaps out of a turn at any speed, enters a spin from a low-speed straight-ahead stall, or enters any form of spin-type maneuver, apply opposite rudder and simultaneously neutralize the stick to effect immediate recovery.

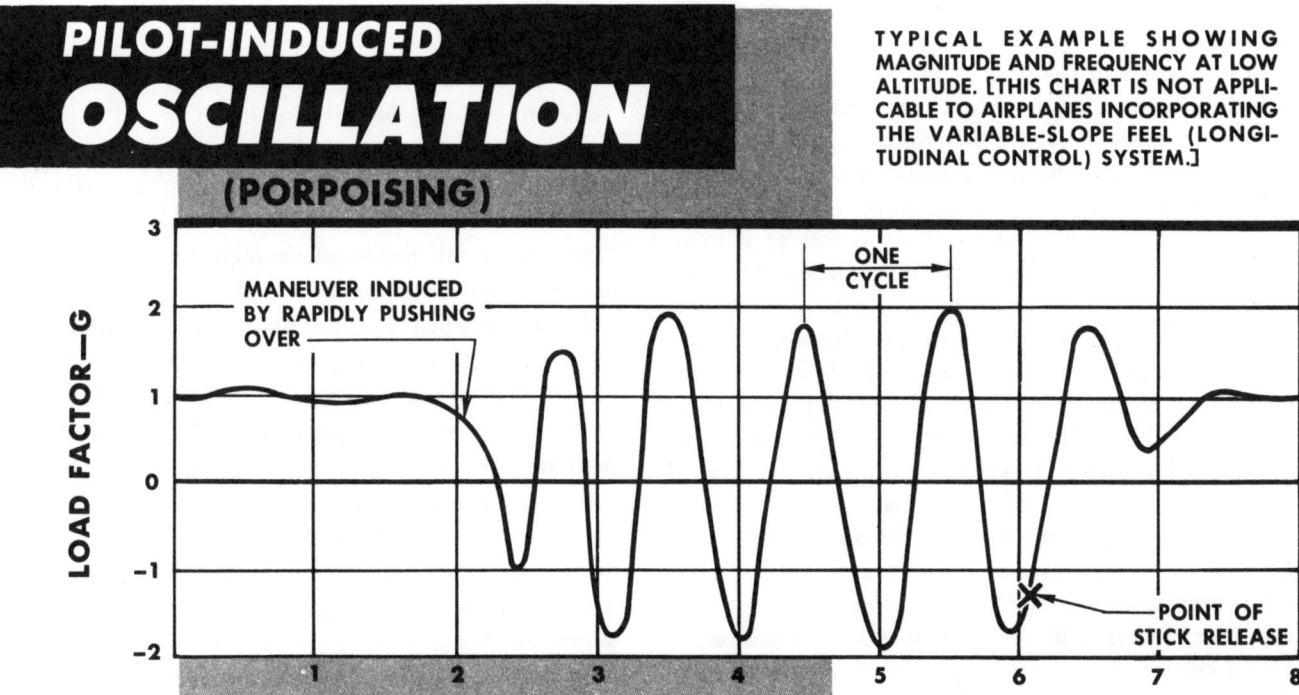

Figure 6-4

WARNING

Do not trim into a turn, since the stick may not return to neutral if the controls are released for recovery.

Note

If altitude permits, you can recover from a spin by releasing the controls completely—spin rotation should cease within one to two turns.

FLIGHT CONTROLS.

CONTROLLABLE HORIZONTAL TAIL.

The controllable horizontal tail provides extremely effective longitudinal control because of the increased movable surface area and improved surface effectiveness. Therefore, use of this control requires considerably less applied pilot force in maneuvering flight than a conventional stabilizer-elevator configuration. Similarly, the amount of stick travel required to perform a given maneuver is reduced. This control improvement is most noticeable at high speeds at low altitudes, and care should be exercised to avoid application of excessive G by overcontrolling. This means that until you gain enough experience to anticipate the approximate response of the airplane, you should not attempt close-formation flight or large, abrupt stabilizer motions.

Pilot-induced Oscillation (Porpoising).*

Occasionally, you may induce an overcontrol maneuver that consists of a rapid up-and-down pitching or porpoising motion. Usually, the tendency is to induce this maneuver at altitudes below 20,000 feet and between Mach .8 and .9. The lower the altitude, the easier the oscillation may be induced. When the porpoising occurs, it usually is induced by pushing over to about zero or negative G too rapidly, or trying to correct rapidly for any trim change such as caused by a gust, speed brake operation, rapid throttle operation, or cutting the afterburner off or on. It usually begins from forces applied in the push direction. The resulting maneuver is a rapid pitching oscillation between negative and positive G, the magnitude of which depends on how rapidly and how much corrective control you attempt to apply. A typical example of the magnitude and frequency of the G encountered during one of these maneuvers is shown in figure 6-4. The oscillating maneuver is basically caused by the combination of ap-

*F-86D-1 through F-86D-45 Airplanes not changed by T. O.

plied stick force, stick displacement, and the inherently fast response of the airplane. You inadvertently give a series of boosts to the stick at just the right instant to sustain the oscillation. These inadvertently applied boosts are made worse by the effects of the G on you, throwing your weight up and down as well as fore and aft at just the right time to sustain the oscillation through inadvertent stick movements. This maneuver is generally encountered only by pilots with less than 10 hours total time in the airplane, or those who have not flown for some time. As your hours in the airplane increase, corrective control movements will become smooth, and rarely, if ever, will you encounter this porpoising condition. A light grip on the control stick is favorable for avoiding this condition, as is keeping the seat belt tight. If the seat belt is loose when you encounter the porpoising, you will be thrown violently up and down in the cockpit, further aggravating the maneuver. During low-level, high-speed passes, it is also advisable to keep the shoulder harness tight. Should you encounter this oscillating condition, you can do several things to stop it. The quickest way to damp the oscillation is to release the stick. The number of oscillations which the airplane will make after the release of the stick depends on the magnitude of the positive and negative G being reached in the maneuver. For a mild porpoising condition, the airplane will damp in about one cycle; for a severe case of porpoising, it will damp in about three cycles. Each cycle takes approximately one second as shown in figure 6-4. Another method to stop the oscillation is to make a slow, positive pull-out to about 3 G, trying to maintain a steady back pressure or pull force on the stick. The oscillations will not damp out quite as fast for the positive pull-up method as for the stick release method, but they will damp out. *Do not attempt to stop the oscillations by attempting to push the stick fore and aft in opposition to the airplane motion. This will only make the condition worse, since the motion is too rapid for you to estimate correctly and apply rapid corrections.* It is more important to remember that while the porpoising is startling to you, no damage to the airplane has occurred in more than a hundred such maneuvers purposely flight-tested.

The following recommendations may be used to avoid porpoising:

1. During your first five flights in this airplane, do not exceed Mach .8 below 20,000 feet altitude.

2. Carry the equivalent weight of 24 rockets in the rocket package during the first five flights, to provide more-forward center-of-gravity positions. More-forward center-of-gravity positions decrease the tendency to encounter the porpoising conditions.

3. Keep seat belt tight at all times.

4. Practice applying corrective control movements smoothly.

5. Do not fly close formation until you have had sufficient training in this airplane.

AILERON CONTROL.

The rate of roll produced through use of the ailerons is very high. Extreme caution should be exercised in aileron use until you are thoroughly familiar with aileron effectiveness. Figure 6-5 shows the maximum rate of roll of the airplane at 10,000 and 30,000 feet throughout its entire speed range. Note that at high altitude, aileron effectiveness is reduced at high Mach numbers (.8 to .95) because of compressibility effects and then returns until the maximum aileron power output is reached at Mach 1. At low altitudes, the loads on the ailerons become very high and the maximum aileron power is reached at a much lower Mach number (about .78), sharply reducing the rate of roll above Mach .9, to a point where aileron control power is very low. The hazard of low aileron control power at low altitude and high Mach number should be recognized, and a reduction in speed should be made to satisfactorily control this condition. The maximum aileron power output is a safety factor to prevent possible damage to the structure when extremely high loads are placed on the aileron.

RUDDER CONTROL.

Rudder control is satisfactory and very effective at low and intermediate airspeeds. Very little rudder action is necessary to execute all normal maneuvers. Sufficient control is provided to trim the airplane to straight-wing and level flight and to make coordinated turns properly. At high airspeeds, the increasing rudder deflections required for sideslips, and the corresponding increase in pedal forces, show that rudder effectiveness is decreasing. This is a normal phenomenon due to the occurrence of shock waves on the vertical tail in the transonic Mach number range. The effect of shock wave formation results in boundary layer separation and an increased wake effect, decreasing the effectiveness of the control surface. However, very little sideslip control is normally needed for coordinating into high-speed turns. As the speed decreases, it is noticeable that more rudder is required for coordinating turns. In this respect the airplane is similar to all conventional fighter-type aircraft. Small amounts of rudder may also be required to counteract trim changes due to power at high speeds. On airplanes equipped with the power rudder control, lower rudder pedal forces will

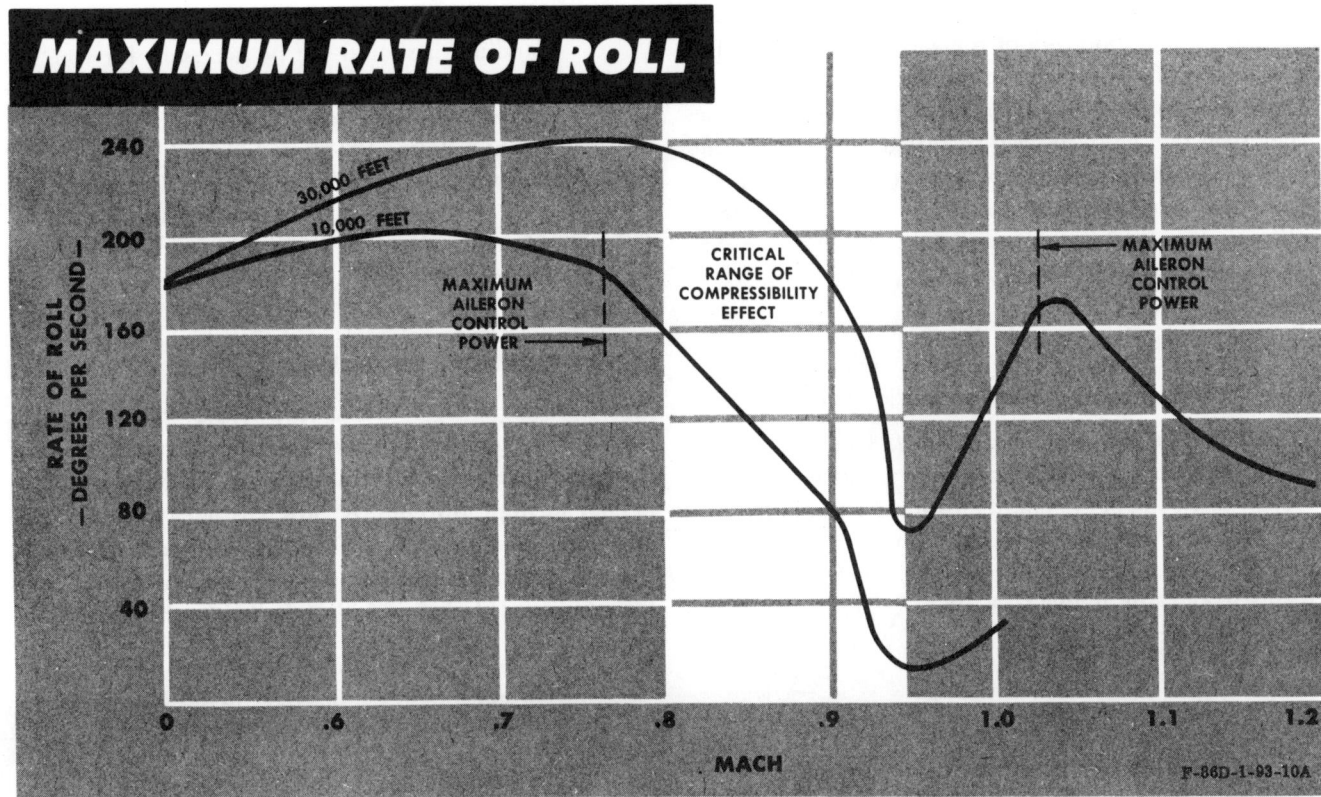

Figure 6-5

be experienced in flight up to the maximum output of the rudder hydraulic system. Beyond this point, rudder pedal forces increase in the same proportion as with the manual rudder system and are considered quite high. Normally, high forces are not encountered, except when you are trying to counteract directional trim changes associated with wing drop, which occurs at high Mach numbers. The rudder does not provide enough control to counteract wing drop, although it aids in correcting for it. A "rudder buzz," which is a small-amplitude, high-frequency buffet on the rudder, is felt through the rudder pedals on the manual and the power rudder system from about .97 to 1.05 Mach number. Also, at Mach number of about .98, a phenomenon termed "rudder kick" is noticeable. This is caused by a fluctuating wake behind the shock wave on the vertical tail. It is noticeable when you are trying to hold zero yaw or when you are making rudder angle changes. As a pedal force is applied, the rudder may move rapidly in the direction the force was applied, overshooting the intended deflection. The angular change of the rudder during which rudder kick occurs is about ±3 degrees. This condition is not dangerous unless aggravated by a loose rudder trim tab.

FLIGHT TRIM CHARACTERISTICS.

No trim tabs are provided on the horizontal tail or ailerons. These surfaces are trimmed by changing the no-load (neutral) position of the stick. Rudder trim is obtained by an electrically actuated trim tab. However, as a rudder trim tab is not provided on airplanes equipped with hydraulically powered rudder,* rudder trim on these airplanes is obtained by changing the no-load (neutral) position of the rudder pedals. The pitching action that normally occurs during operation of the rocket package, or speed brakes,† is automatically corrected by an electrically operated pitch corrector actuator: thus, little or no corrective action is necessary by the pilot. The actuator repositions the horizontal tail without changing control stick position. On airplanes not equipped with automatic pitch correction for speed brakes,‡ a slight, easily controlled, nose-up pitch will be noticed when the speed brakes are extended; correspondingly, a slight nose-down pitch will be noticed when speed brakes are retracted. Opening the speed brakes without correcting the resulting pitch-up with stick action, results in a maximum of about 1½ additional G being imposed on the airplane. On late airplanes§ and airplanes changed by

---

*F-86D-10 through F-86D-30 Airplanes
†F-86D-1 through F-86D-25 Airplanes

‡F-86D-30 and later airplanes
§F-86D-50 and later airplanes

T. O., the longitudinal trim characteristics are improved by incorporation of the variable-slope feel control system. This new system markedly reduces the trim lag at all speeds, giving immediate pilot trim response. The trim rate has also been increased; however, in the high-speed range, it will not be as noticeable as in the low-speed range. For example, in the landing condition, the trim rate has been approximately doubled over that of the original trim system.

Note

- Trim should not be used to reduce stick forces to zero during aerobatic maneuvers.
- During the first two or three landings in airplanes that incorporate the variable-slope feel control system, trim should be applied with care. The increased trim rate, at slow flight, may result in a nose-up pitch, which may cause undue concern.
- Because of the lighter stick forces during landing, it should not be necessary for you to apply continuous nose-up trim during the landing approach. Trimming for level flight at 150 to 180 knots IAS will give comfortable stick forces (maximum of 20 pounds pull as compared to 50 pounds pull on the original control system) for the complete landing sequence.

YAW DAMPER OPERATION.

Improvement in dynamic directional stability is obtained by use of the yaw damper, to make a more effective and efficient rocket-firing platform, particularly at high altitudes. At low altitudes and high airspeeds, the inherent dynamic directional stability is satisfactory, and damper action is not necessary. It is recommended that it be used during the search and

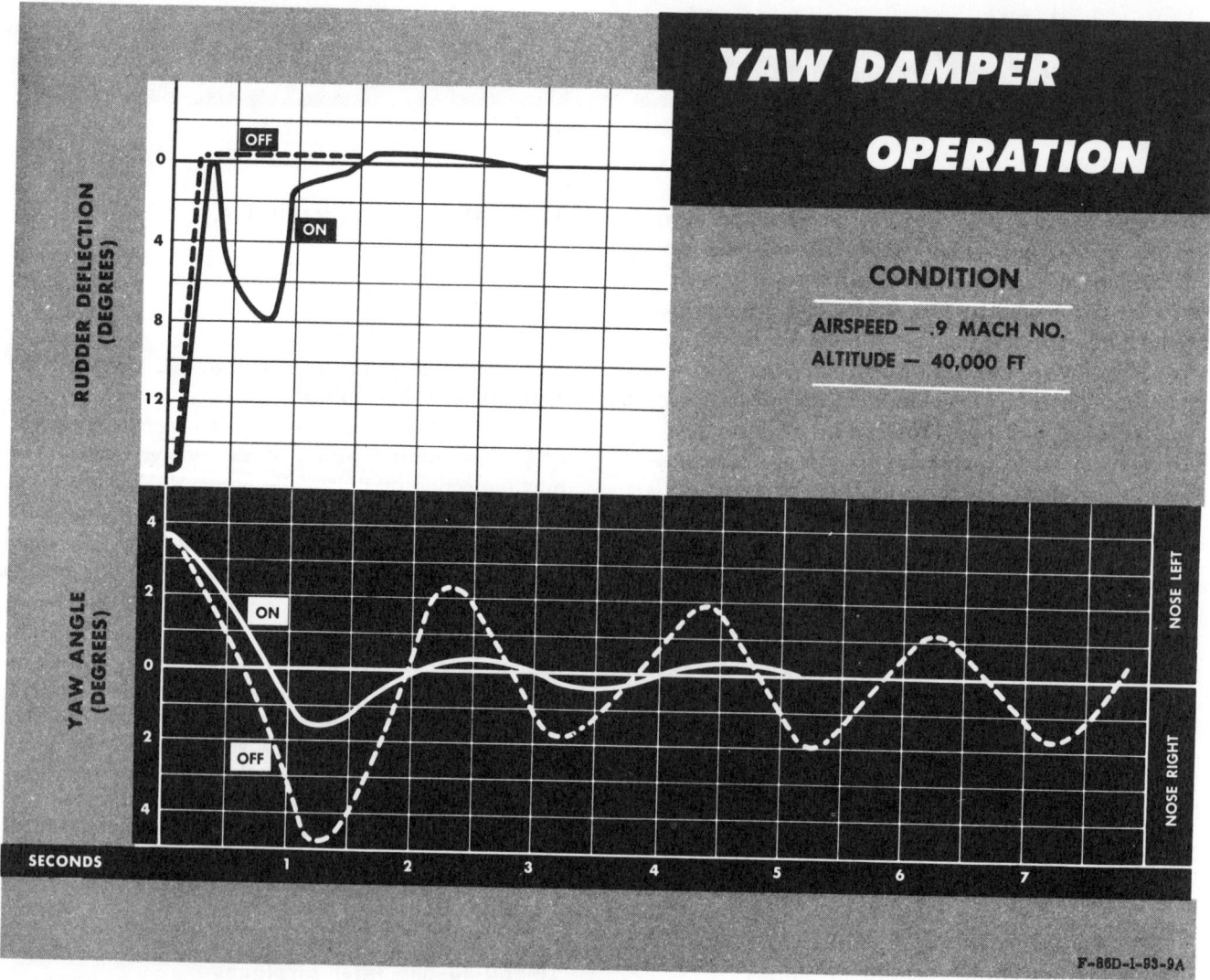

Figure 6-6

tracking phases of the attack, to obtain maximum hit probabilities. However, to avoid forgetting to turn the yaw damper on, it is suggested that it be turned on during the climb to altitude. The yaw damper consists of a rate gyro, a "washout" circuit, and a servomechanism. The rate gyro senses turning rate, which is then fed through the washout circuit to the servomechanism, which moves the rudder in such a way as to decrease airplane yaw oscillations. While the yawing oscillation may be of such a small degree that you will not be able to visually detect it, it could reduce the kill probability considerably, unless the yaw damper was turned on. This yawing motion could be induced by your applying any correction during tracking, either by rudder or aileron deflections. This corrective rudder is in a direction to resist the yawing motion of the airplane. The washout circuit eliminates any effect of the yaw damper, once a steady rate of turn is established. This action prevents the yaw damper from opposing pilot control during steady turns. Thus the yaw damper will only operate when the turning rate is building up or decreasing. Figure 6-6 illustrates the improvement in the dynamic direction characteristics. The difference in damping time is shown by the two curves which show airplane response to a release from a steady sideslip with the yaw damper "on" and "off." These particular data, taken at an altitude of 40,000 feet and Mach .9, are typical of high-altitude directional characteristics. From these data, it can be seen that the yaw damper is an essential device to make this airplane a more effective and efficient rocket-firing platform. During an entry into a turn, when a turning rate is being built up, the rudder will kick back if your feet are on the rudder pedals, since rudder action is in such a direction as to resist rapid direction changes. It is recommended that your feet remain on the rudder pedals, but do not resist the yaw damper action. The magnitude of this kickback force is about 50 percent of the force that you apply. In the event of a damper failure, the maximum override force required to hold the rudder control is 180 pounds, which can be easily controlled until the yaw damper is turned off. The yaw damper should be turned "off" during pre-traffic-pattern check. Specific operational characteristics applicable for the manual rudder and powered rudder are given in the following paragraphs.

MANUAL RUDDER OPERATION (F-86D-1, F-86D-5, AND F-86D-35 AND LATER AIRPLANES, AND THOSE CHANGED BY T. O.).

During normal damper operation in straight-and-level flight, pilot override rudder pedal forces will vary from 0 to 90 pounds. The magnitude of force required will depend upon the flight condition and the air turbulence. It is recommended that your feet remain on the pedals, but avoid interfering with the damper operation, as your force will decrease the damper effectiveness. In a turning maneuver, damper action will last ½ second or less. Within this time, the override force can build up to 180 pounds at the pedals. For this reason, it is recommended that the damper be inoperative during landing procedures. In the event of a yaw damper hard-over failure (electrical short), the maximum override force required to obtain rudder control would be 180 pounds at the pedals until the yaw damper is turned off. This type of yaw damper failure is not of sufficient magnitude to cause any structural damage to the airplane even if you do nothing to keep the airplane from yawing.

POWER RUDDER OPERATION (F-86D-10 THROUGH F-86D-30 AIRPLANES).

Override forces during straight-and-level flight will vary from 0 to 90 pounds, depending upon the flight condition encountered. The force required will be greater during high dynamic pressure conditions (i.e., low altitude and high speed) and rough air. Pedal motion is unaffected during damper operation in the power rudder configuration. As in the manual installation, it is recommended that the damper be inoperative during a landing condition. In the event of a yaw damper hard-over failure, the maximum override force required to obtain rudder control would be about 90 pounds maximum at the pedals until the yaw damper is turned off. No airplane structural damage can occur from this type of failure even though nothing is done to prevent the yaw.

SPEED BRAKES.

Deceleration.

At any time that deceleration is desired, speed brakes may be used without objectionable buffeting. In a pullout, you can effect recovery with minimum loss of altitude by first opening speed brakes and then pulling out at maximum permissible G. Since turning radius increases with speed, a very effective method of tightening a turn is to decrease the speed as desired by opening the speed brakes. Use speed brakes as necessary to tighten your turn, and then close them again before too much speed is lost.

Tactical Maneuvers.

Speed brakes may be used to an advantage during tactical maneuvers whenever steep angles of approach are desired.

SLAT OPERATION.

Leading edge wing slats are installed to improve lateral handling characteristics at low airspeeds and to reduce the stalling speed. Whether open or closed, they do not appreciably change the handling qualities of the airplane. The slats are fully automatic and operate as a function of airspeed and attitude of the airplane, being full open at low speeds and full closed at cruising speeds and high speeds. For normal slat operation, on deceleration, the slats will begin to open at about 180 knots IAS and be fully opened at 160 knots IAS. On normal accelerations, the slats will begin closing at about 160 knots IAS and fully close at 180 to 200 knots IAS.

LEVEL-FLIGHT CHARACTERISTICS.

LOW SPEED.

The stalling characteristics and handling qualities at low speed are very good. They are quite similar to those of a straight-wing fighter airplane, the only exception being that a higher angle of attack is required for take-off and landing, which is typical for a swept-wing airplane. When the afterburner is used, a much faster acceleration will be apparent because of the increased thrust. The rate of roll is very high, and aileron control is effective down through the stall. Since the airplane has a high wing loading, a somewhat higher rate of descent will be noticed at any given approach airspeed. Figure 6-7 shows the recommended speeds for take-off, approach, and touchdown and the stall speeds for the entire weight range with the landing gear and wing flaps down. Recommended take-off speeds for minimum ground roll are about 10 per cent greater than the power-off stall speeds. Using afterburner power, the airplane is 17 knots above stall speed at take-off accelerating at a rate of 4 to 5 knots per second. The recommended approach speeds are the indicated airspeeds to obtain the maximum glide distance with flaps and gear down. The recommended final approach speed is 140 knots for a normal landing with 1000 pounds of fuel or less remaining as noted in figure 2-6. If a landing is necessary immediately after take-off at maximum take-off weight (with drop tanks), the final approach should be made at 160 knots. As a rule of thumb, the approach speed should be increased 5 knots for each additional 1000 pounds of fuel remaining, using 140 knots as a base point. For example, if 3000 pounds of fuel remain, this is 2000 pounds more than for a normal landing; therefore, 10 knots should be added to 140 knots, giving an approach speed of 150 knots IAS. Because of the high wing loading, the airplane has a fairly high rate of sink at low speed; therefore, caution should be exercised not to allow the airspeed to get too low, since sufficient airspeed will not be available to flare for touchdown.

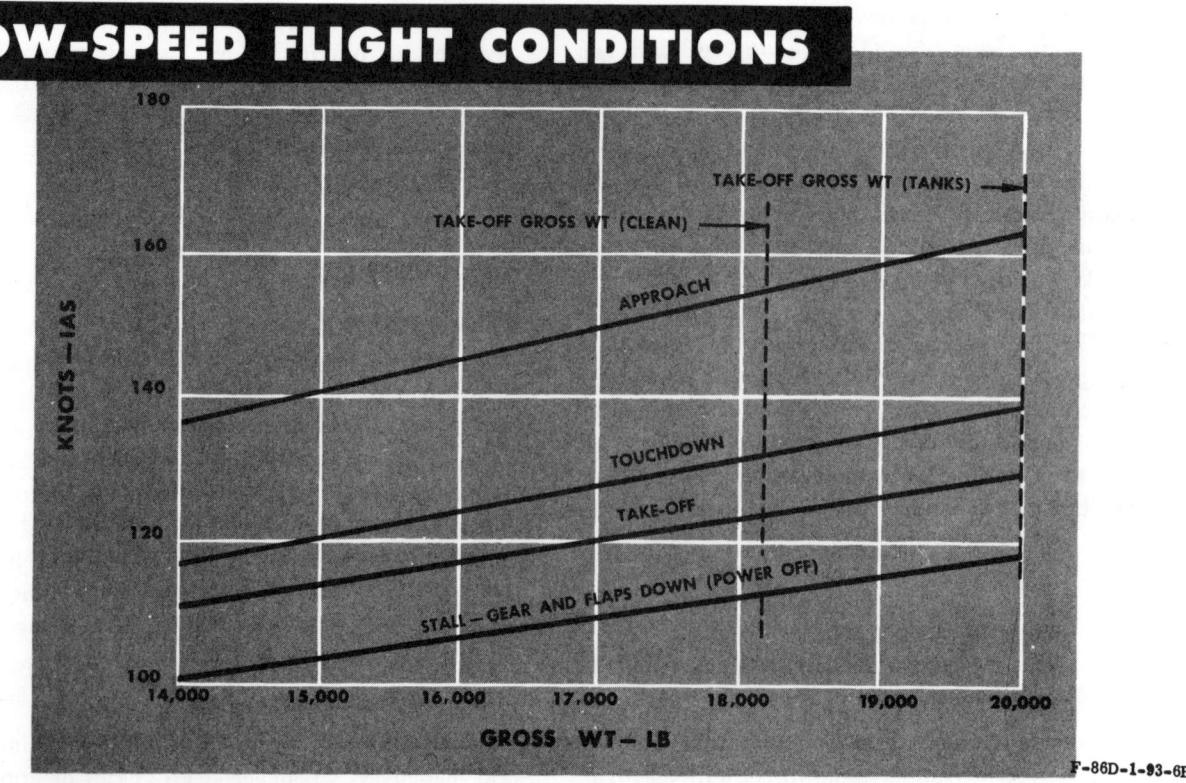

Figure 6-7

This will result in an extremely hard landing unless it is anticipated and is avoided by an application of power. For best landing results, power approaches with a simultaneous flare and power cut are recommended. The recommended touchdown speeds are about 17 percent above power-off stall speeds and are set up to give a reasonable flare from approach speed to permit a normal landing without touching down too hard.

CRUISE SPEED.

At medium to high speeds, maximum lift capabilities of the airplane, thrust-drag ratio, handling characteristics, and control effectiveness are excellent. These qualities ensure good maneuverability and combat performance. The controllable horizontal tail is very effective in the cruise Mach number range; until you have become accustomed to it, the fast response of the airplane to small stick movements may cause you to feel that the airplane is too sensitive. Thus, it is advisable to become thoroughly familiar with the airplane before attempting close formation flight.

HIGH SPEED.

This airplane is capable of speeds into the transonic speed range. Figure 6-8 shows the maximum level-flight Mach number capabilities of a clean airplane and an airplane carrying 120-gallon drop tanks, using Military and Maximum Thrust. Certain portions of the drop tank Maximum Thrust curve exceed the placard limit. (Refer to Section V.) These Mach numbers represent level-flight stabilized speeds. The airplane is easily controlled through the transonic speed range to the maximum capabilities of the airplane. Stability and control are essentially unaffected up to about Mach .95. However, you may notice a reduction in the rate of stick force change between Mach .8 and .9 when flying at one G. As the speed is increased above Mach .9, the

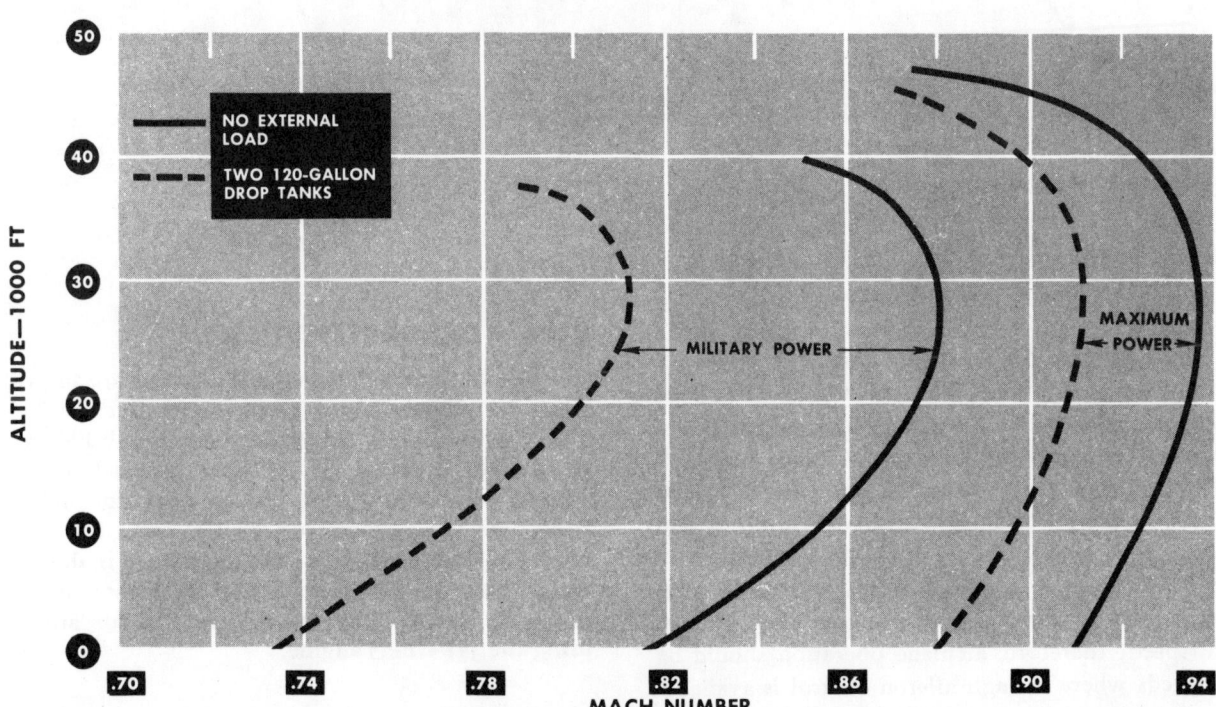

NOTE:
Airplane (no external load)—16,000 lb; Airplane (drop tanks)—17,000 lb.
With Types I and III drop tanks and using afterburner, limit airspeed of 555 knots IAS or .9 Mach No., whichever is lower, must be observed.
With Types II and IV drop tanks and using afterburner, limit airspeed of 500 knots IAS or .9 Mach No., whichever is lower, must be observed.

Figure 6-8

CLIMB PERFORMANCE

MAXIMUM POWER

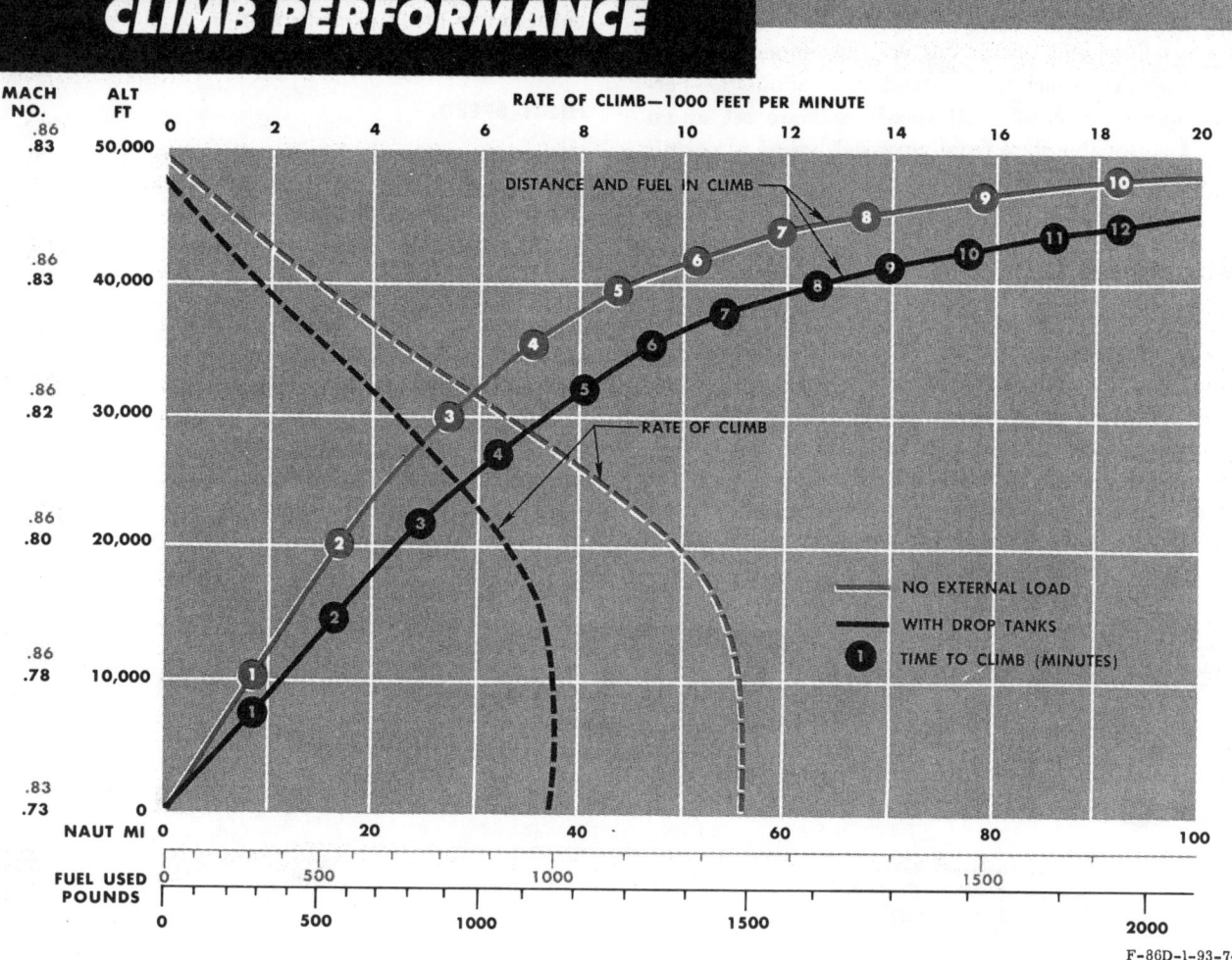

Figure 6-9

stick push forces will steadily increase (airplane "tucks up," showing positive stability), but will never become uncomfortably high. The controllable horizontal tail is very effective at high indicated airspeeds and particularly between Mach .8 and .9. Since pilot feel is achieved through a spring bungee, the resultant effect of these trim changes is relatively mild, in that stabilizer stick forces increase only about 20 pounds in the "tuck-up" region. At low altitudes, progressive wing heaviness may develop on some airplanes with increasing airspeed; therefore, airplane operation should be at airspeeds where enough aileron control is available to control this characteristic. If an uncontrollable wing heaviness or wing drop is encountered, slow up by making a gentle pull-up, by opening speed brakes, or by reducing power. On most airplanes, the maximum level-flight speed is below the speed where wing drop is encountered. Rate of roll is high for fighter-type airplanes, particularly in the combat Mach number range.

CLIMB CHARACTERISTICS.

The climb characteristics of this airplane are shown in figure 6-9. Climb data is given for take-off weights of 18,250 pounds clean and 20,000 pounds with 120-gallon drop tanks installed. In all cases, the fuel used (or weight reduction) during ground operation, take-off, and climb is accounted for. Fuel allowed for ground operation and accelerating to climb speed is about 600 to 800 pounds. Anticipate a slightly higher fuel consumption during afterburner operation for airplanes using the J47-GE-33 engine.

CLIMB SPEEDS.

The climb speed schedules (figure 6-9) are shown in terms of Mach number. A Mach number schedule is considered much more desirable to follow and easier to remember, permitting easier attainment of a well-stabilized climb. The proper technique to accelerate to best climb speed after take-off is to hold level-flight at

MILITARY POWER

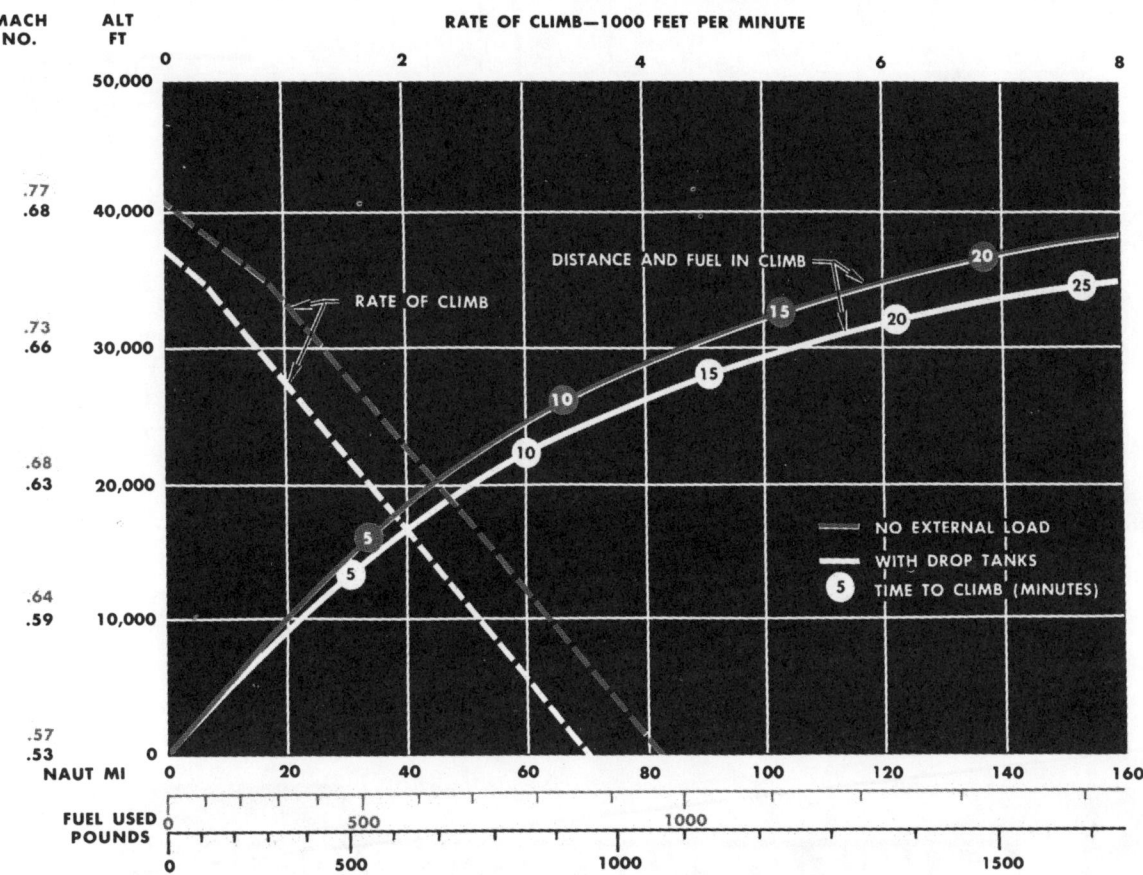

the lowest practical altitude and start the transition into the climb about .03 Mach number below the desired climb schedule (.06 for Maximum Thrust clean), picking up the stabilized climb schedule about 5000 to 10,000 feet above the ground. This transition is shown on the climb speed chart.

TIME TO CLIMB.

These climb schedules (figure 6-9) have been determined to give the shortest time to any altitude for Maximum Thrust and the longest range for Military Thrust. Time required to accelerate to climb speed from brake release at take-off and time required to accelerate from climb speed at end altitude to combat speed have been considered in these climb schedules. If minimum time to altitude is the primary objective, a Maximum Thrust climb should be used. If the consideration is maximum range, a Military Thrust climb should be used.

MANEUVERING-FLIGHT CHARACTERISTICS.
MANEUVERABILITY.

At all Mach numbers and airspeeds, maneuvers may be accomplished with relative ease. The flight capabilities achieved through use of the swept wing, the horizontal tail as the direct longitudinal control, and the completely hydraulic flight control system are especially noticed during maneuvers at high Mach numbers. Very little rudder action is necessary in performing maneuvers. Stick forces during maneuvering flight (figure 6-10) are moderate and relatively uniform over the entire speed and altitude range. The stick force required to pull G does not decrease at high altitudes and at low indicated airspeeds. Instead, there is a slight increase in stick force required to pull G as the indicated airspeed is decreased. This occurs because the artificial feel system is based on stabilizer deflection alone, rather than on stabilizer deflection and indicated airspeed.

Section VI
T. O. 1F-86D-1

MANEUVERING STICK FORCES

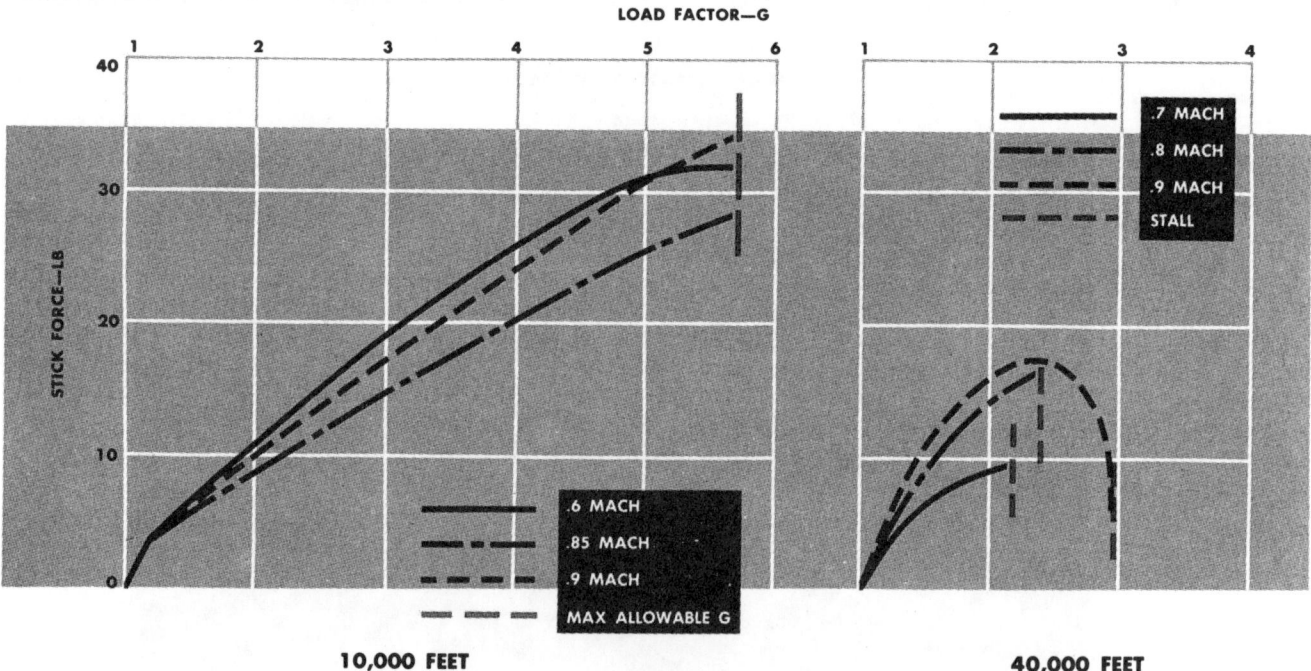

Figure 6-10

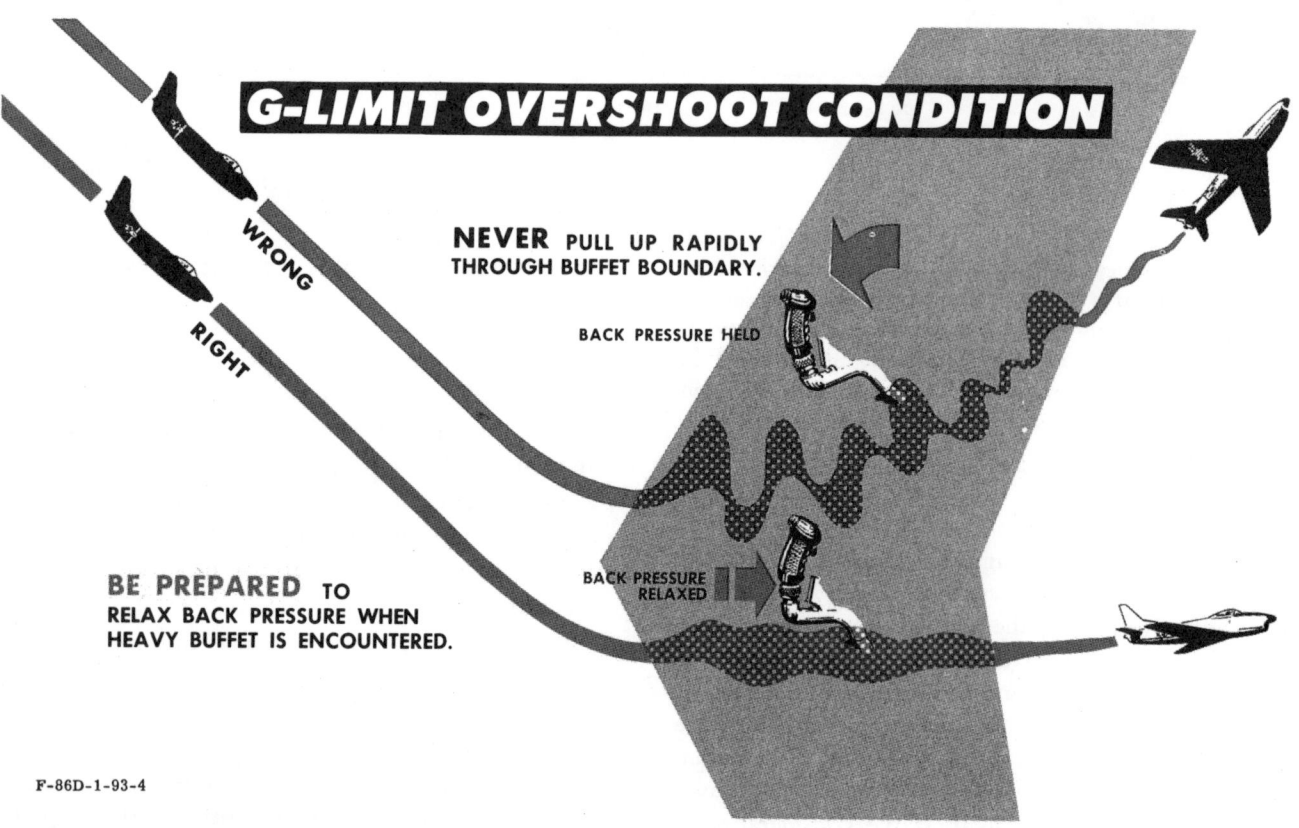

Figure 6-11

6-16

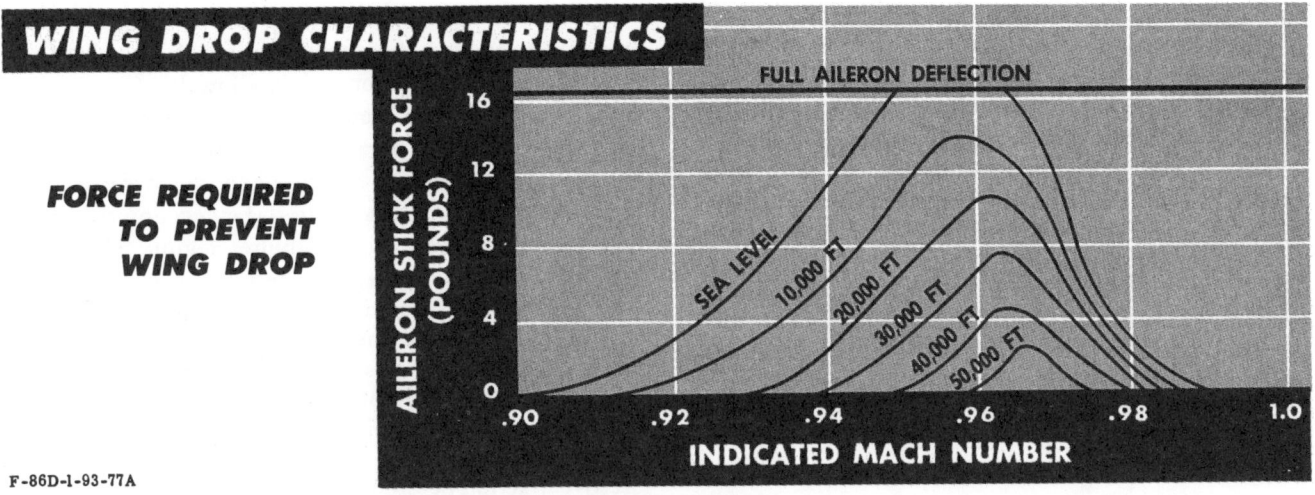

Figure 6-12

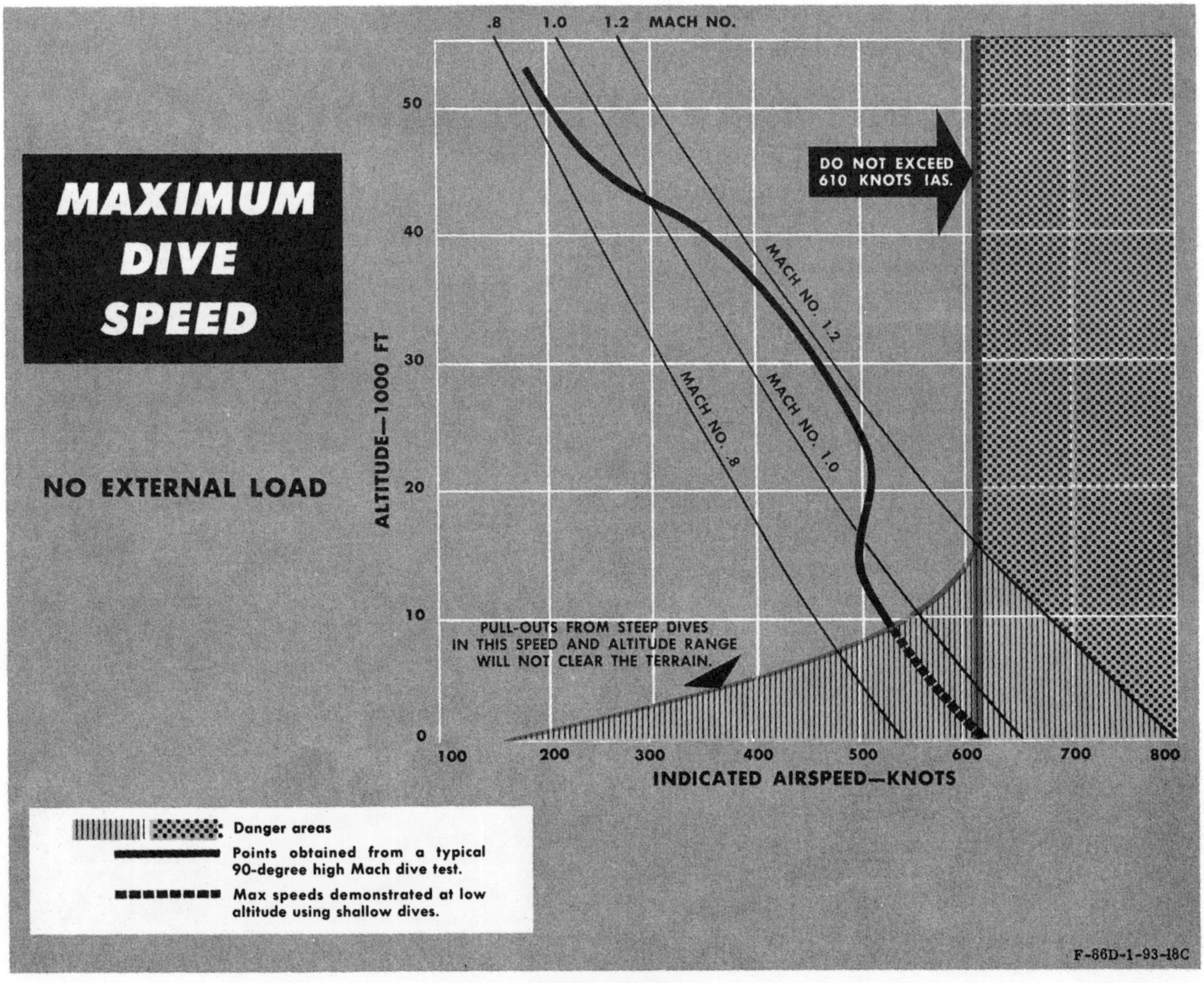

Figure 6-13

This may seem unnatural at first, but you will soon become accustomed to this type of variation. You will find that the reduced stick forces and increased maneuverability resulting at high Mach numbers and high indicated airspeeds greatly improve the tactical capabilities of the airplane. The increase in stick force required to pull G at high altitudes effectively results in a more stable and comfortable airplane to fly at altitudes where most airplanes become very "sloppy." At high altitudes during pull-ups into the buffet region, or at intermediate altitudes and low Mach numbers, you may notice a slight decrease in stick force just before the stall. This characteristic is particularly noticeable at high altitudes near Mach .9. This condition is termed "dig-in."

G-LIMIT OVERSHOOT.

When G is increased to a certain value above the G at which buffet begins, the airplane will feel less stable in pitch and may dig in. As the airplane digs in, thus tending to increase G automatically, the intended G — and in some cases the maximum allowable G — may be exceeded. This condition is termed "overshoot." This overshoot is caused by a basic instability characteristic of the airplane which exists when the wing is near stall. Overshoot is most likely to be encountered when the airplane is well into the buffet region. Therefore, the start of general airplane buffet is a warning that you are approaching the overshoot region. Although overshoot can cause the maximum allowable G-limit to be exceeded and possibly damage the airplane, the control power available, because of the completely hydraulic flight control system and the one-piece horizontal tail, enables you to apply immediate and effective recovery action before the airplane exceeds the G-limit. Since the buffet boundary automatically accounts for changes in altitude, Mach number, and gross weight, use the buffet region as a sign of possible overshoot conditions. Always remember that the airplane

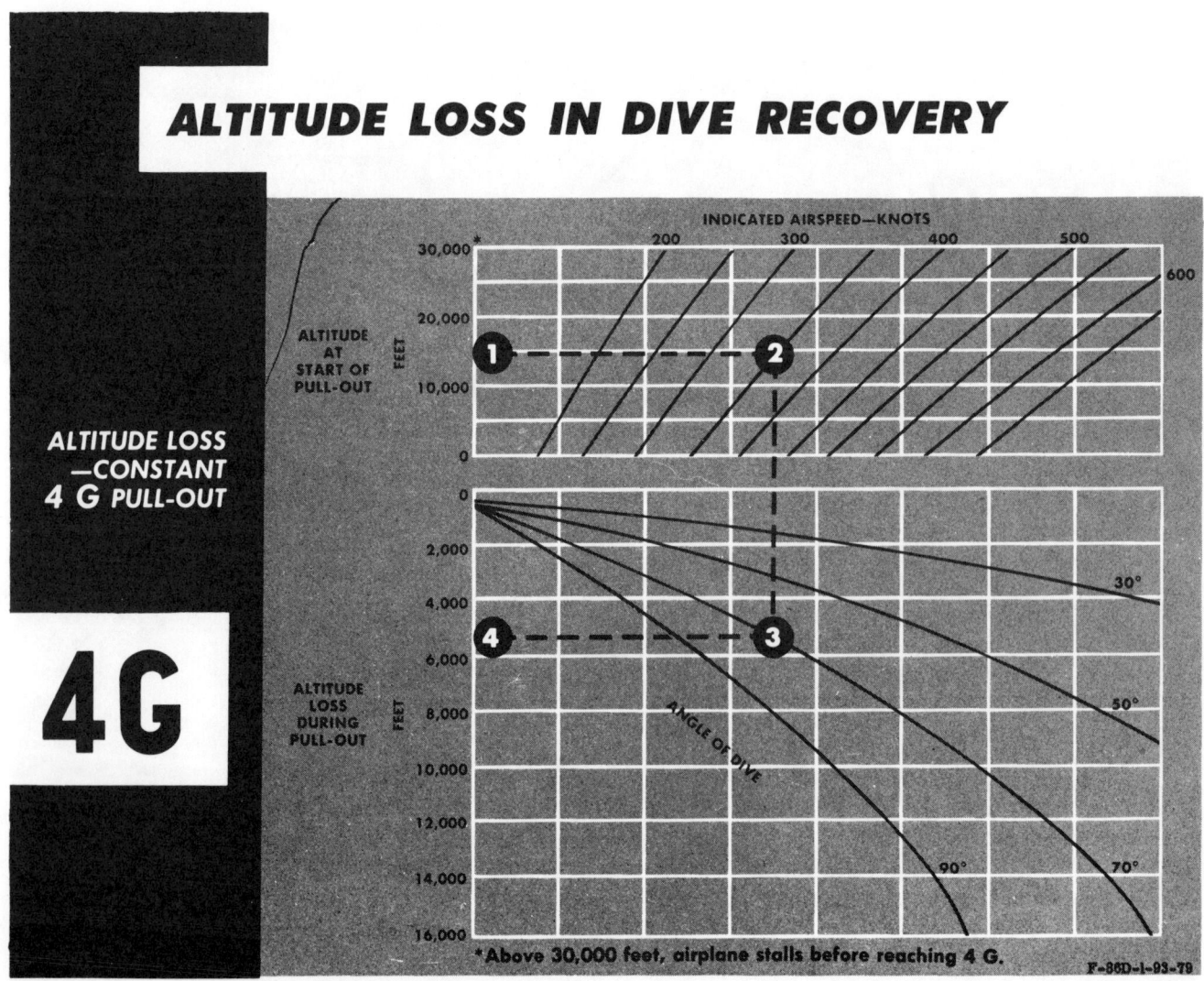

Figure 6-14

is limited to 5.6 G clean and 5.0 G with drop tanks installed. When encountering the buffet boundary, slow your rate of pull-up and be prepared to apply immediate recovery control to prevent overshoot and possible damage to the airplane. (See figure 6-11.)

DIVING.

DIVES.

In high Mach number dives and maneuvers, airplane stability and handling qualities are very good. It is in this speed range that the advantage of using the horizontal tail as the primary longitudinal control are most apparent. The stick forces remain at a comfortable level, and the airplane is easily controlled at all Mach numbers. In the transonic speed range between Mach .96 and 1.0, a wing drop and a slight yawing characteristic are encountered. The wing drop is a rather abrupt roll but may be controlled by application of corrective aileron and rudder. The airplane handles very smoothly with no uncontrollable or erratic motions up to maximum possible dive speeds. The severity of the wing drop is greater at low altitudes than at high altitudes. This is shown by figure 6-12, which presents stick force to control the wing drop for various altitudes.

FLIGHT TEST DIVES.

During the flight testing of this airplane, many high Mach number dives were conducted. A sample of these dives is shown in figure 6-13 for a 90-degree dive, using Maximum Thrust. For example, the highest true Mach number obtained was 1.17 Mach number shown between 35,000 and 30,000 feet with the dive started from service ceiling. No undesirable flight characteristics are encountered during high Mach dives other than wing drop which is easily corrected. The speeds

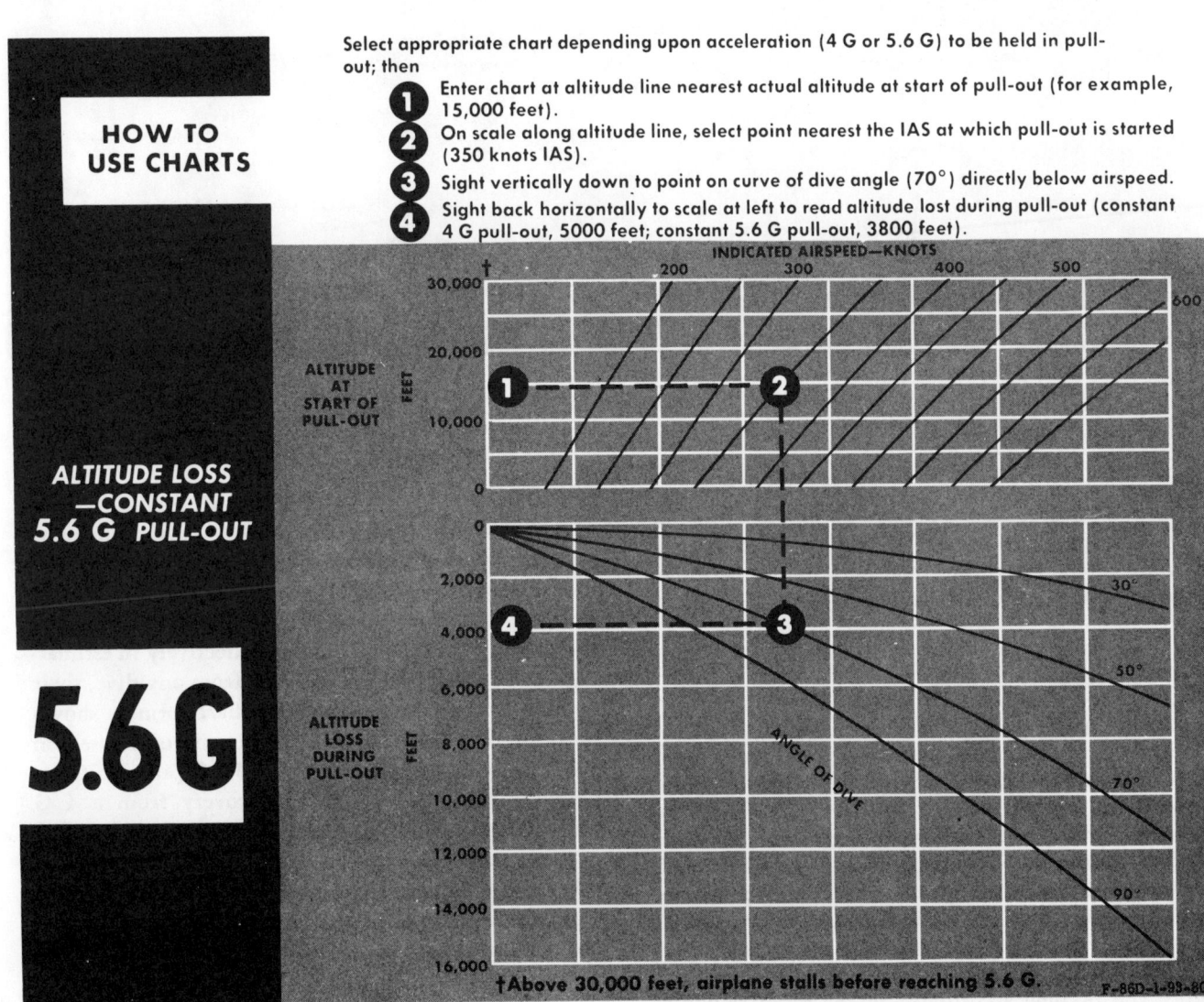

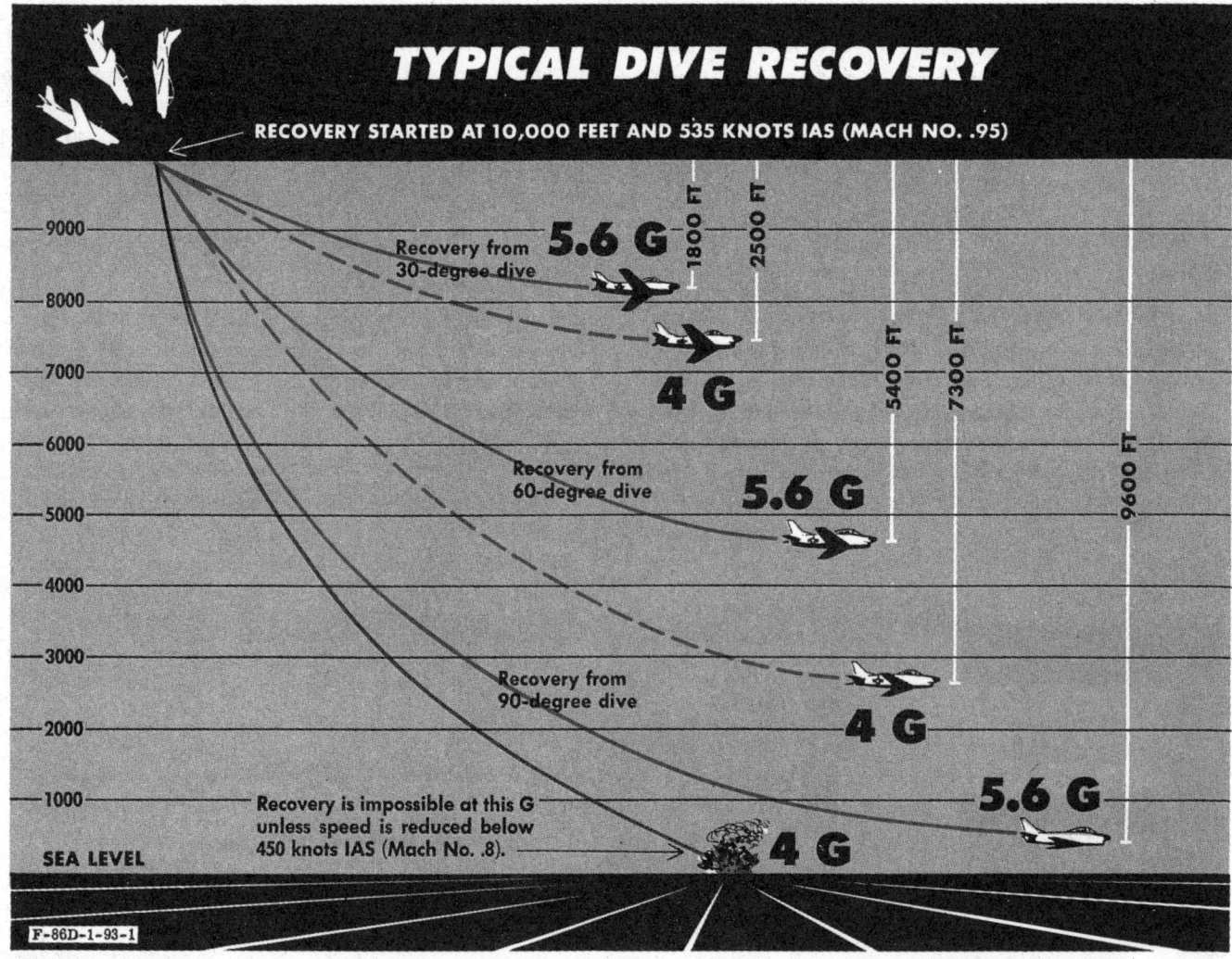

Figure 6-15

shown in figure 6-13 below 15,000 feet were not obtained at 90-degree dives. Mach numbers attained in this range are lower because of reduced dive angles, the more severe wing drop tendency, and the altitude required to perform a safe pull-out.

DIVE RECOVERY.

Dive recovery (figure 6-15) is accomplished by application of necessary stick back pressure to effect the desired pull-out. Speed brakes may be used if desired to reduce airspeed during pull-outs. Stabilizer stick forces to accomplish pull-outs are satisfactory and do not increase rapidly. During pull-outs from dives or in accelerated turns, the stabilizer develops sufficient control power to enable the maximum allowable G or stall to be reached throughout the speed and altitude range. Take care that you do not damage the airplane by overcontrol before you become accustomed to the rapid response of the airplane to control stick movement.

Altitude Loss in Dive Recovery.

The altitude lost during dive recovery is determined by four interdependent factors: (1) angle of dive, (2) altitude at start of pull-out, (3) airspeed at start of pull-out, and (4) the G maintained during pull-out. Because these factors must be considered collectively in estimating altitude required for recovery from any dive, their relationship is best presented in chart form as shown in figure 6-14. Note that one of the charts is based on a 4 G pull-out, and the other on a 5.6 G pull-out. Compare the altitude lost during recovery from a 4 G pull-out with that lost during recovery from a 5.6 G pull-out; also compare the effects of variations in the other three factors. Remember that a value obtained from either chart is the altitude lost during recovery — not the altitude at which recovery is completed. Therefore, in planning maneuvers that involve dives, consider first the altitude of the terrain and then use the charts to determine the altitude at which recovery must be started for pull-out with adequate terrain clearance. In using the charts, you should allow for the fact that, without considerable experience in this airplane, you cannot determine exactly what your dive angle and speed are going to be at the start of the pull-out. If you come out of a split "S" or other high-speed maneuver in a near-vertical dive, speed builds up rapidly. Therefore, until you know the airplane well, go into the chart at the highest speed and dive angle you might expect to reach after completing your maneuvers. If, for instance, you are in a 90-degree dive at an airspeed above Mach .8 and you wait until 10,000 feet to start your pull-out, you would have to make a 5.6 G pull-out; a 4 G pull-out would not clear the terrain. (See figure 6-15.) Maneuvers should be planned so that if they terminate in a near-vertical dive, the airplane may be pulled on through to a shallower dive angle before the speed becomes excessive or too low an altitude is reached.

Note

It is a good idea to memorize a few specific conditions from the dive charts so that you have a basis for judgments on pull-outs.

TAKE-OFF DISTANCES.

Figure 6-16 shows the take-off ground rolls required at sea level for various outside air temperatures. The optimum take-off technique is to allow the airplane to accelerate up to 115 knots IAS (120 knots IAS with 120-gallon drop tanks) before lifting the nose to the take-off attitude for a take-off speed of 125 knots (130 knots IAS tanks). Raising the nose to take-off attitude at the minimum nose wheel lift-off speed of 90 to 95 knots IAS will increase the take-off distances by 300 to 500 feet using Maximum Thrust. Using Military Thrust, take-off distances are increased 800 feet in clean airplanes and 1500 feet with airplanes carrying 120-gallon tanks. For take-offs above sea level, add 200 to 400 feet to the ground roll for each 1000 feet of elevation when using Maximum Thrust. For example, taking off on an 80°F day using Maximum Thrust and carrying 120-gallon drop tanks from a field whose elevation is 2000 feet would require 4000 feet of ground roll (3400 feet sea-level ground roll plus 300 feet for each 1000-foot increase in altitude to 2000 feet elevation).

EFFECTS OF GUSTS.

The gust load imposed on the airplane increases directly with the speed; if the speed is doubled, the gust load will double. At high speeds in extremely turbulent air, gust loads may be as high as 4 G. If the gusts occur during high-speed maneuvering flight, they can cause the limit load factor of the airplane to be exceeded. Therefore, if it is necessary to fly in turbulent

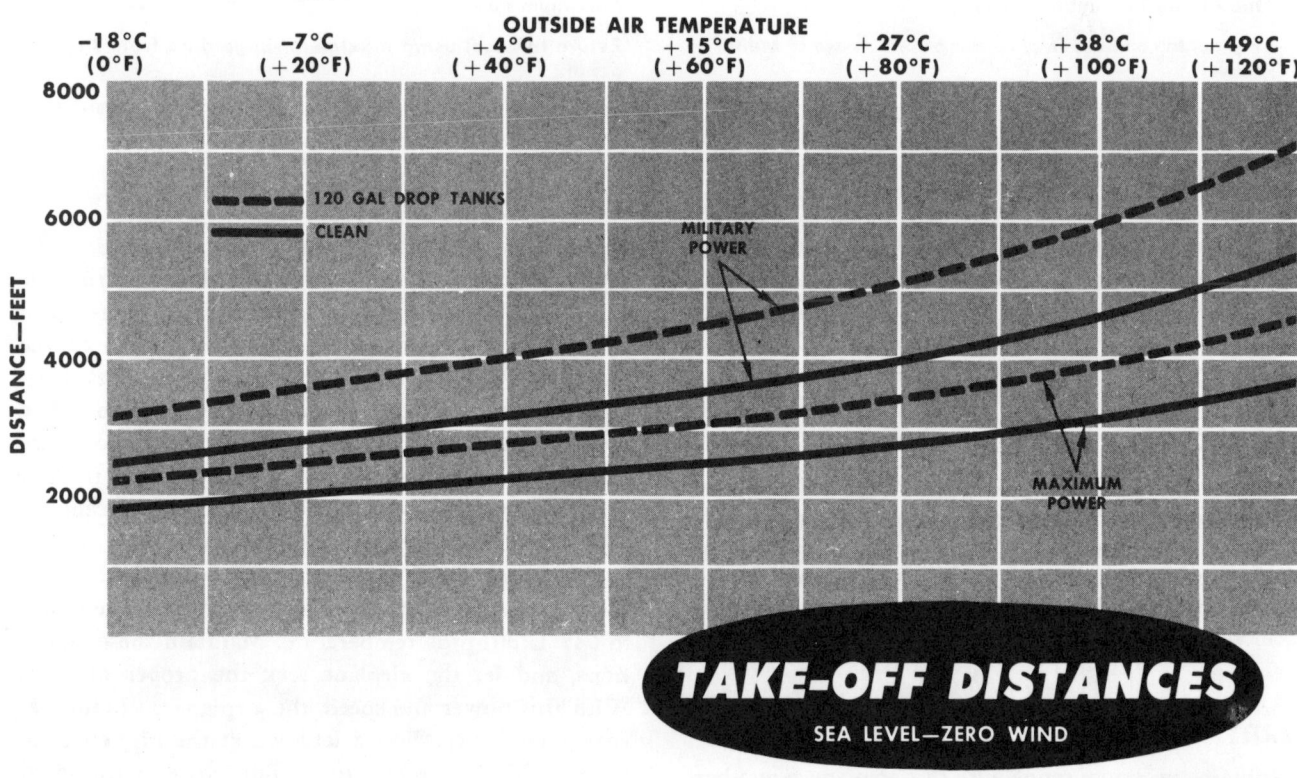

Figure 6-16

Section VI
T. O. 1F-86D-1

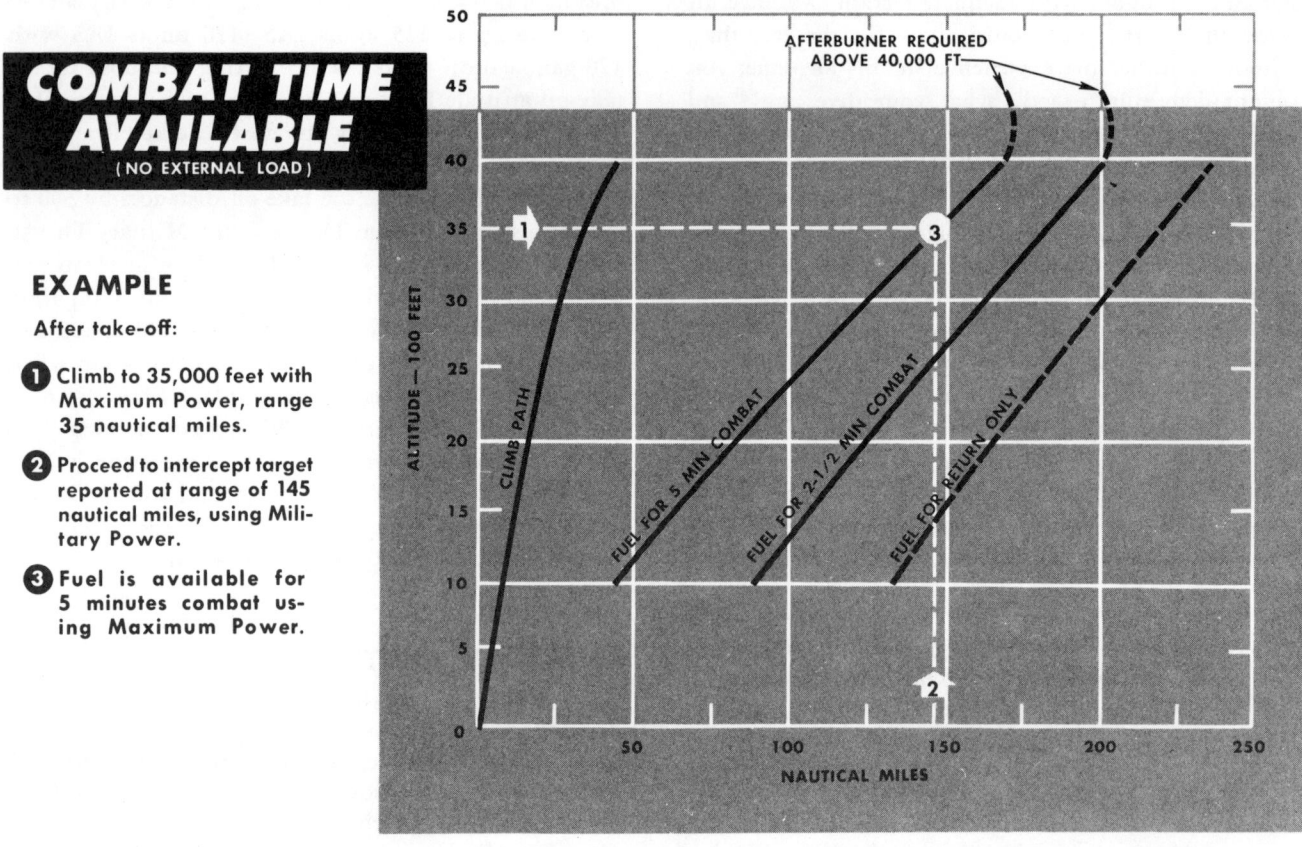

COMBAT TIME AVAILABLE
(NO EXTERNAL LOAD)

EXAMPLE

After take-off:

1 Climb to 35,000 feet with Maximum Power, range 35 nautical miles.

2 Proceed to intercept target reported at range of 145 nautical miles, using Military Power.

3 Fuel is available for 5 minutes combat using Maximum Power.

NOTE

Climb curve includes take-off and climb to desired altitude using Maximum Power.

Fly-out to combat range curves based on use of Military Power.

Five minute and 2-1/2 minute combat curves based on Maximum Power.

Return to base, using maximum range data from Appendix I.

Chart includes 10 percent fuel reserve of 400 pounds.

F-86D-1-93-5B

Figure 6-17

air, reduce your speed, and refrain from intentionally pulling more than 2G. (Refer to "Turbulence and Thunderstorms" in Section IX for a comfortable speed for penetrating an area of turbulent air.)

ROCKET PACKAGE.

As the rocket package is installed in the underside of the airplane, there are no changes in flight characteristics when rockets are carried. Therefore, no limiting Mach number or airspeed is required. However, the limitations on rocket package operation during normal accelerations are shown in Section V.

FERRY OPERATIONS.

To obtain maximum range with this airplane, a number of important techniques or flight conditions are necessary. The proper cruise technique is as follows: (1) Climb with Military Thrust to cruise altitude. The cruise altitude is defined as the altitude where the rate of climb is about 500 fpm. (This altitude rather than a fixed altitude is used because of variations in engine thrust between one engine and another.) (2) Level out and accelerate to the proper cruise Mach number, using Military Thrust. To aid in reaching the cruise Mach number sooner, it is recommended that the airplane be shallow-dived at 250 fpm rate of descent for about 500 feet of altitude. (3) Level out at the proper cruise speed (Mach .74 with tanks or Mach .83 for the clean configuration), and set up the engine power to 635°C tail-pipe temperature. Maintain these conditions, and let the airplane seek the proper altitude. With this power and speed, the airplane will climb as fuel is used. (4) Make a letdown at the highest comfortable Mach number, using idle power with speed brakes full open. Figure 6-18 shows a typical ferry range problem with the clean configuration, with two 120-

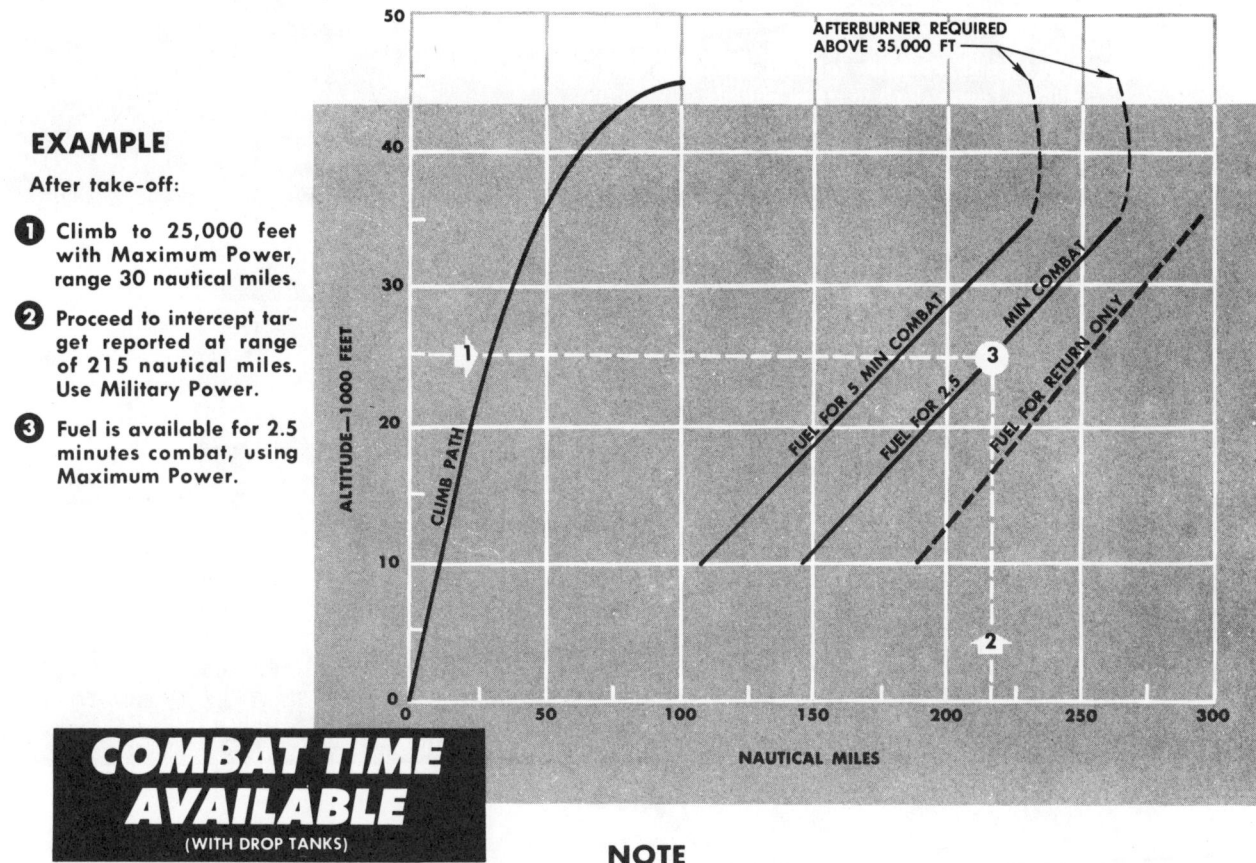

COMBAT TIME AVAILABLE (WITH DROP TANKS)

EXAMPLE

After take-off:

1. Climb to 25,000 feet with Maximum Power, range 30 nautical miles.
2. Proceed to intercept target reported at range of 215 nautical miles. Use Military Power.
3. Fuel is available for 2.5 minutes combat, using Maximum Power.

Climb curve includes take-off and climb to desired altitude, using Maximum Power.

Fly-out to combat range curves based on use of Military Power.

NOTE

Five-minute and 2.5-minute combat curves based on Maximum Power.

Return to base, using maximum range data from Appendix I.

Chart includes 10 percent fuel reserve of 550 pounds.

F-86D-1-93-78

gallon tanks carried the entire mission, and with the 120-gallon tanks dropped when empty. These ranges are obtained with 10 percent fuel remaining at landing (400 pounds clean configuration and 550 pounds when using 120-gallon tanks). For a further increase in range, a Military Thrust take-off could be used if runway conditions permitted, and an increase of 15 nautical miles would be realized. If 1000 pounds reserve is used at landing, the range shown would be reduced 140 nautical miles in the clean configuration, 90 nautical miles carrying tanks all the way, or 95 nautical miles dropping the tanks. These reductions with 1000 pounds fuel reserve give ranges of 385 nautical miles clean, 600 nautical miles carrying tanks all the way, and 700 nautical miles dropping tanks.

FLIGHT WITH DROP TANKS.

Flying characteristics are essentially unaffected by the installation of the 120-gallon drop tanks. Do not exceed airspeed limitations when drop tanks are installed. (See figure 5-1.) As a result of the increased drag and weight, take-off distances will naturally be greater and the rate of climb reduced.

VORTEX GENERATORS.

To minimize buffet caused by shock waves between Mach .81 and .92, a series of small vanes (figure 6-19) are installed on the underside of the horizontal tail and on the fuselage below the horizontal tail. Installation of these vanes eliminates the turbulent airflow which produces the buffet, and, with the elimination of the turbulent airflow, the airplane drag is also reduced. These vanes are termed "vortex generators," as they create small whirlpools of air, commonly called vortices. These vortices stir up the slow-moving air found close to the fuselage, thus allowing the smooth flow of air to continue farther aft on the fuselage before becoming turbulent.

Section VI
T. O. 1F-86D-1

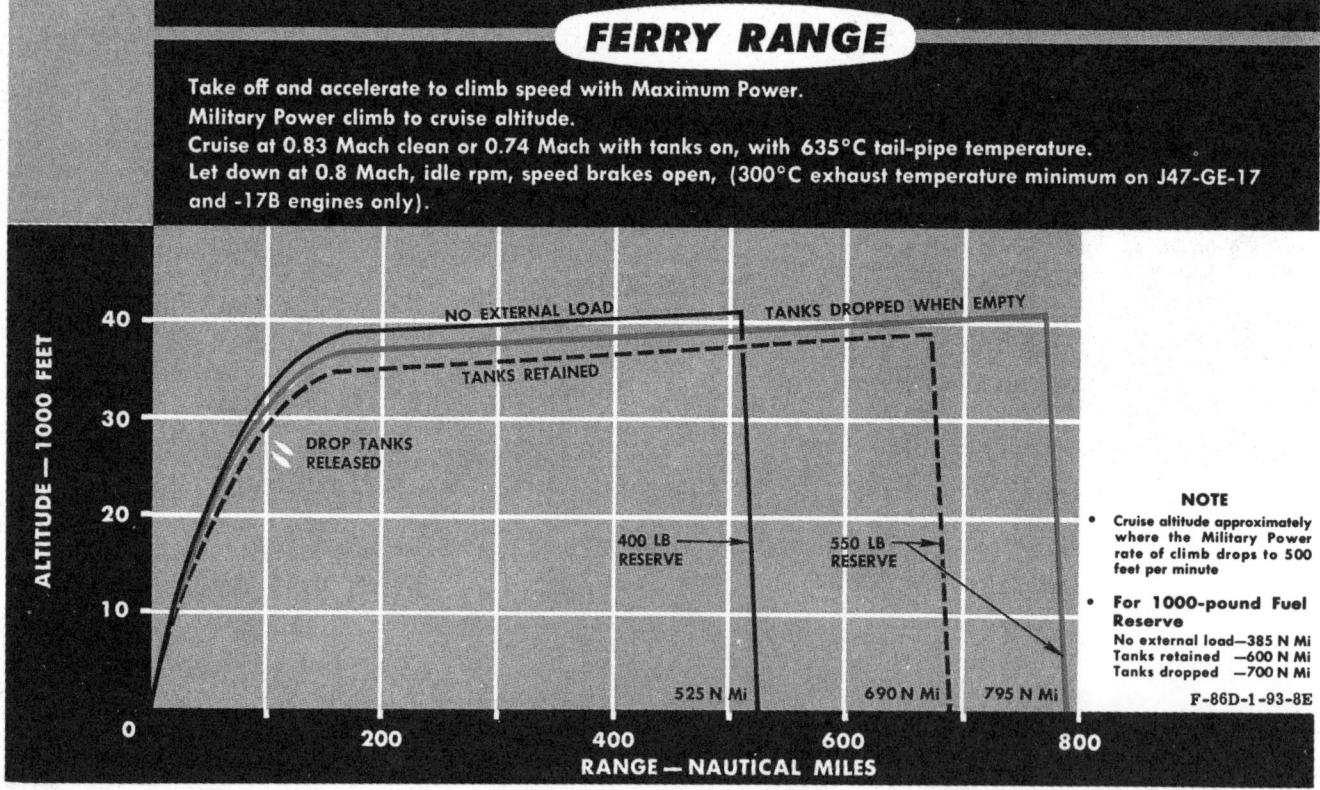

Figure 6-18

Figure 6-19

T. O. 1F-86D-1 Section VII

section VII

SYSTEMS OPERATION

F-86D-1-00-33A

TABLE OF CONTENTS	PAGE		PAGE
Electronic Engine Control	7-1	Exhaust Temperature Characteristics	7-10
Automatic Lockup System Characteristics	7-4	Inverter Change-over Characteristics	7-10
Engine Characteristics	7-5	Fuel System	7-11
Afterburner Characteristics	7-7	Hydraulic Systems	7-13
		Wing Flap Lever Operation	7-13
Emergency Fuel System	7-9	Landing Gear	7-14

ELECTRONIC ENGINE CONTROL.

The jet engine of this fighter-interceptor is controlled through an integrated electronic control from a single throttle. The throttle gives complete, correct control of engine fuel, variable-area nozzle, and afterburner fuel at all times. The control system (figure 7-1) is basically an engine speed and engine temperature regulator, in which variables are under control at all times. In relation to throttle position, the thrust selector sets engine speed, variable-nozzle area, and afterburner fuel flow and transmits these signals electrically to the amplifiers. The amplifiers also receive signals of engine speed, compressor inlet temperature, compressor discharge pressure, and turbine discharge temperature. The composite output of the amplifiers, resulting from the joining of these signals, controls the settings of the main fuel valve, the afterburner fuel valve, and the variable-area nozzle actuator. Outstanding features of this control system are strict control over engine speed and exhaust gas temperature throughout the operating range under all flight conditions; direct relationship between throttle position and engine thrust output; realization of near-optimum en-

gine conditions at each power setting; automatic ground starting; automatic engine and afterburner flame-out protection under all flight conditions; high rate of engine acceleration, automatically controlled; and freedom from compressor stall and engine overtemperature.

THRUST SELECTOR.

The thrust selector is in the left equipment bay. It converts throttle movement into electrical signals. There are three potentiometers within the thrust selector housing: one for engine speed signals, one for variable-nozzle position signals, and one for afterburner fuel scheduling signals. There are two types of thrust selectors presently in use. Both thrust selectors operate in the same manner and are interchangeable, the main difference being in the variable-nozzle position when at idle engine speed. With the throttle in the START IDLE position, the new thrust selector calls for a nozzle position of about three-fourths open instead of the one-half open position on the older type. In addition, throttle sensitivity is decreased at high power settings

7-1

Section VII

T. O. 1F-86D-1

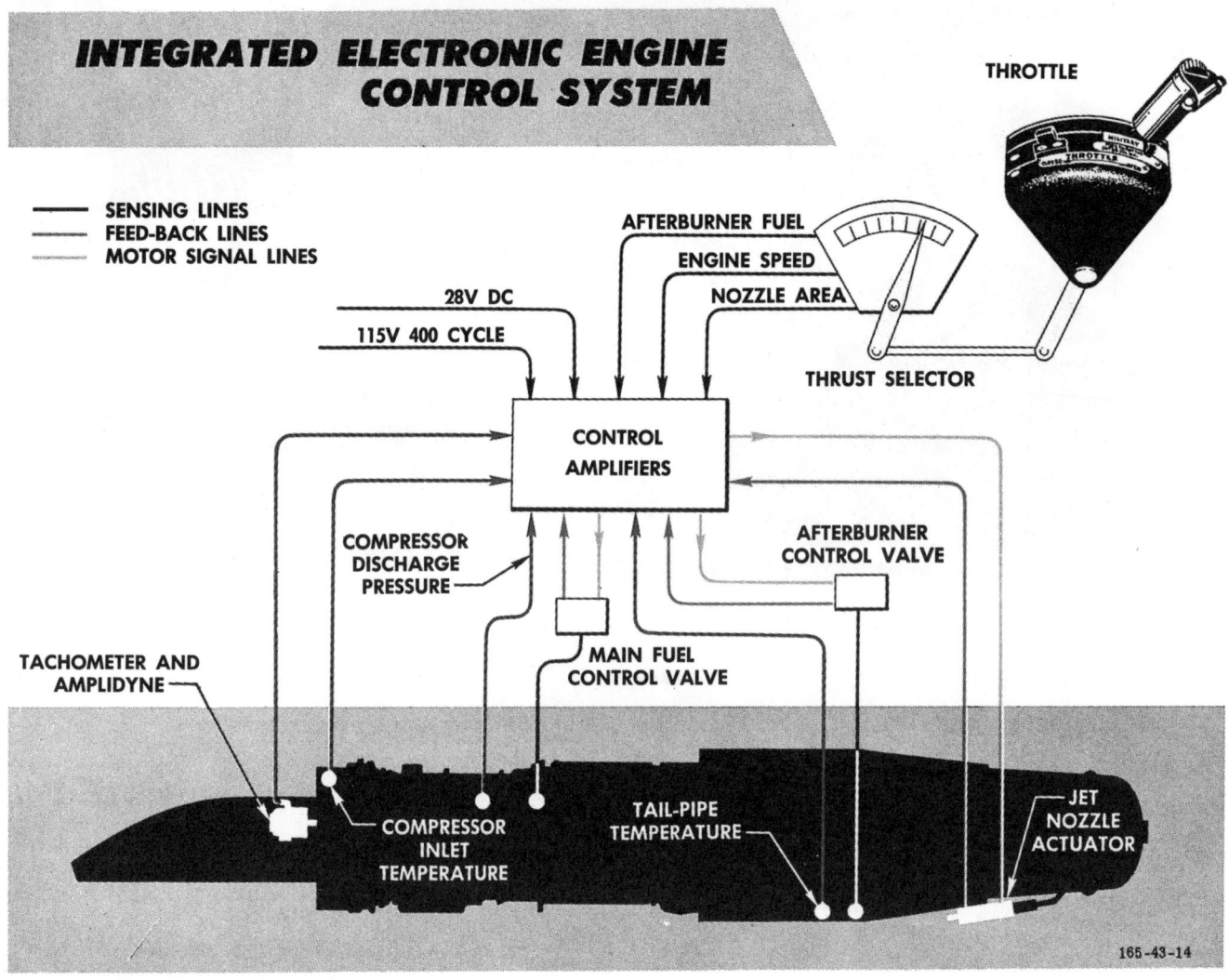

Figure 7-1

and increased at low power settings. Also, at high power settings, a given exhaust temperature can be selected easier, and the engine will maintain 100% rpm through a greater arc of throttle travel. At low power settings, engine rpm and thrust will respond more for a given throttle movement. This new thrust selector will also decrease acceleration time on throttle bursts from idle rpm, decrease thrust faster on a throttle chop, and give cooler engine shutdowns.

AUTOMATIC START CHARACTERISTICS.

The automatic starting system of the integrated electronic engine control has greatly simplified starting procedures and has virtually eliminated overtemperature

operation associated with jet-engine starting. If, however, a malfunction occurs during an automatic start, it is important that the pilot be familiar with the exhaust gas temperature and fuel pressure* (or fuel flow†) characteristics during ignition and acceleration to idle, so that proper action can be taken to prevent any possibility of later engine overtemperature operation. Full use of the automatic starting provisions of the electronic engine control by the contractor has proved the system to be very reliable. Exhaust gas temperature is a direct function of the amount of fuel being supplied to the engine, and the exhaust temperature indications will be very similar to the general pattern of the fuel flow. Pilot and crew chief familiarity with the starting fuel pressure and fuel flow pattern (figure 7-2) will make it obvious when an overtemperature condition will occur and allow enough time to retard the throttle to the CLOSED position to prevent an engine overtemperature condition. In case of a scramble, it may

*F-86D-1 through F-86D-35 Airplanes
†F-86D-40 and later airplanes

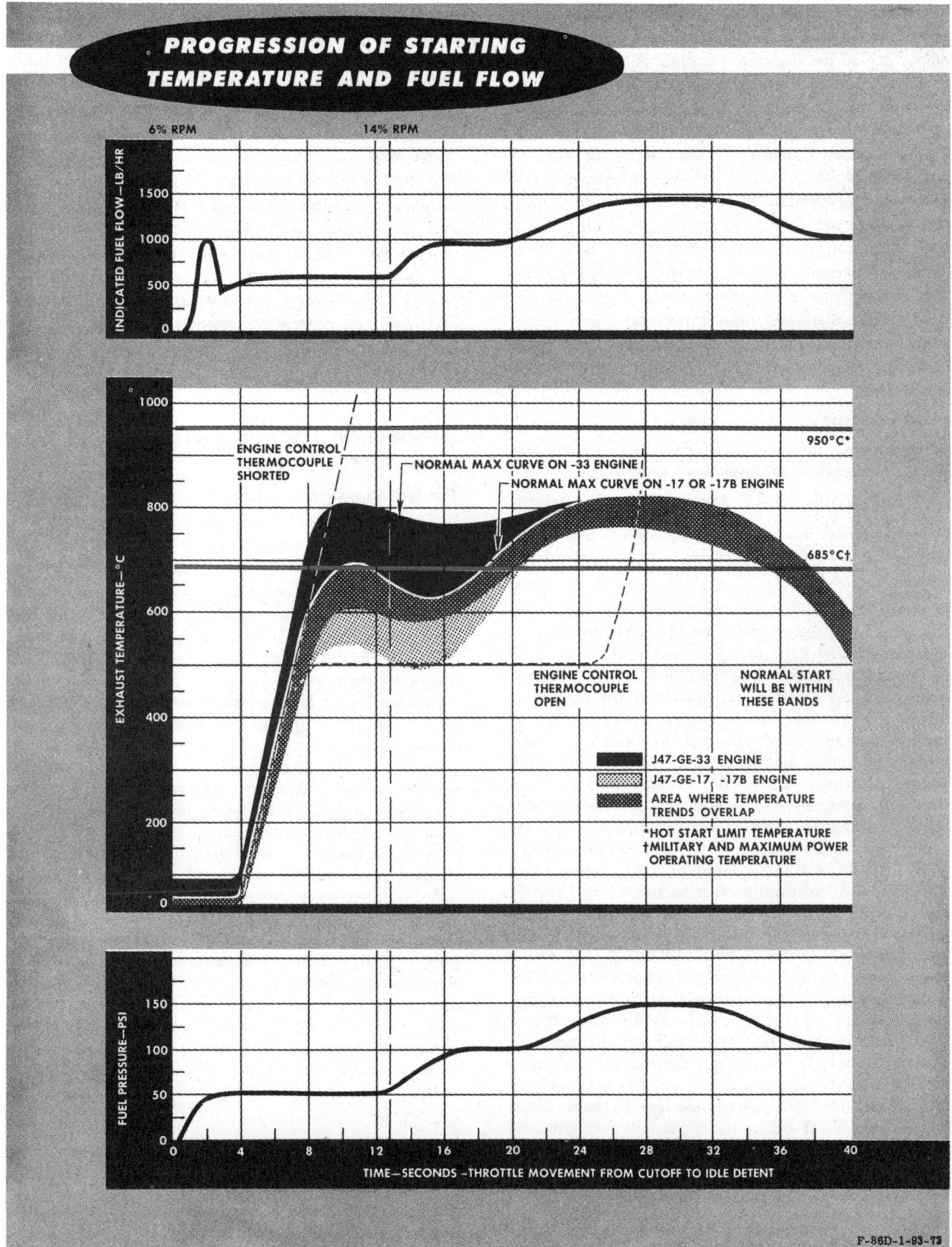

Figure 7-2

be necessary to make a start using the emergency start procedure, since it may not be feasible to wait the required period for amplifier warm-up. When conditions permit, or under ordinary circumstances, a start using the automatic starting system is recommended because starting is much easier and safer and less throttle manipulation is required to keep the exhaust gas temperatures within the required limits. Also, an automatic start will give an early indication of the operability of the engine control since inability to accomplish an automatic start indicates a control or fuel system failure. If an automatic start cannot be accomplished, it is recommended that the airplane not be flown until an investigation is made to isolate and replace the faulty part. There are three functional ground checks which the pilot can use to determine whether the electronic engine control is operating:

1. Automatic start capabilities.

2. Stall-free throttle bursts from idle to Military Thrust (emergency fuel switch in NORMAL).

3. Temperature control during afterburner lightup.

Omission of any one of these checks before take-off decreases the possibility of detecting improper engine control.

When the throttle is advanced directly to START IDLE at 6% rpm, fuel pressure* will build up to about 45 psi. On late airplanes† the fuel flow will build up to about 600 pounds per hour. (A characteristic of the fuel flowmeter indicating system is that when the throttle is moved to START IDLE, the fuel stopcock opening allows the fuel flow to rise very abruptly to about 900 to 1000 pounds per hour, and then rapidly fall to about 600 pounds per hour. This "blip" in the indicated fuel flow is momentary and should not be mistaken as a failure in the fuel control system.) When ignition occurs, exhaust temperature will rise and peak at about 600°C (700°C on the -33 engine). As engine speed increases, the fuel pressure* or fuel flow† will remain steady at 45 psi or 600 pounds per hour, and exhaust temperature will decline slightly. At about 14% rpm, fuel pressure* or fuel flow† will again rise rather sharply until it reaches a peak of about 100 psi or 950 pounds per hour. The exhaust temperature will increase correspondingly and peak at about 815°C. As engine rpm increases above 14%, the fuel flow will gradually climb to about 1500 pounds per hour and as the engine stabilizes at the idle rpm, the fuel flow and exhaust gas temperature will slowly decline to some lower value (about 100 psi or 1000 pounds per hour and 500°C). If cockpit indications during an automatic start depart from these trends (figure 7-2), shut down engine immediately by chopping throttle to OFF to prevent overtemperature. If the fuel pressure* or fuel flow† builds up too rapidly and does not level off at about 45 psi or 600 pounds per hour at 6% rpm, it is an indication of a *shorted thermocouple* or some other control system failure. Under this condition, exhaust temperature will rise at a rapid rate until 950°C is exceeded. Overtemperature caused by an *open thermocouple* is indicated by the fuel pressure* or fuel flow† and exhaust temperature remaining at the initial peak level until 14% rpm is exceeded, at which time the fuel pressure* or fuel flow† and exhaust temperature will increase very rapidly until 950°C temperature is exceeded. Knowledge of engine start characteristics will help to *anticipate* and *prevent* hot starts, and will help extend the engine service time to the normal engine overhaul time limit.

AUTOMATIC LOCKUP SYSTEM CHARACTERISTICS.

The lockup system was devised to immobilize the main fuel valve, afterburner fuel valve, and variable-area nozzle to prevent any erratic engine operation that may accompany an ac power supply loss or recovery. To further simplify pilot operating procedures during such an ac power supply loss, the lockup system was made to operate automatically. This permits full engine control to be maintained until an ac power supply failure is actually encountered. A voltage sensitometer unit, incorporated in the lockup system, senses voltage changes and, whenever ac voltage drops below about 92 volts, automatically locks the electronic engine controls in position. It also illuminates an amber light in the cockpit to show that the electronic engine controls are in the locked condition. When it is desirable to remain in lockup, during the critical take-off period or in anticipation of automatic unlocking, continue flying to a safe altitude and level off. When automatic unlocking occurs, a change in thrust may be expected. However, any power surges that may develop will be controlled electronically within the engine limits. If power readjustments are required when operating within the afterburner range while the engine control lockup indicator light is on, engine operation on the emergency fuel system must be manually selected by moving the emergency fuel switch to ON and the throttle must be retarded immediately from the afterburner range.

THREE-POSITION EMERGENCY FUEL SWITCH CHARACTERISTICS.

The automatic lockup system is made effective after a normal engine start when the three-position emergency fuel system switch is positioned at ON, then moved back to NORM without hesitating at TAKE OFF.

---

*F-86D-1 through F-86D-35 Airplanes
†F-86D-40 and later airplanes

It then remains operable during all normal operation whenever the emergency fuel system switch is positioned at either the TAKE OFF or the NORM position. If the ac power supply loss is momentary, the sensitometer maintains electronic engine controls in the locked condition until about 15 seconds after the ac voltage supply rises above about 98 volts. This 15-second interval, following an ac power supply build-up, is required so that the electronic engine control components can be rewarmed after an ac power failure. However, if the ac power supply is not re-established above about 98 volts, the electronic engine controls remain locked. It is important that power settings not be changed when operating on the main fuel system while the indicator light is on, as engine overtemperature and surging may result when lockup is removed. Manual release of automatic lockup can be accomplished by converting to operation on the emergency fuel system. Subsequent to manual unlocking, no attempt should be made to return to the main fuel system for operation while the engine control lockup indicator light is on, because while the emergency fuel switch is in the ON position, the controls are released from lockup. If the switch is returned to TAKE OFF or NORM position, the controls will lock up again in a position that may cause dangerous overtemperature or an rpm surge condition. A switch in the thrust selector at the 72-degree position (about ¾ throttle position) permits take-offs to be aborted if an automatic engine control lockup is encountered during the take-off roll. As the throttle is rapidly retarded to START IDLE, with the emergency fuel system switch at TAKE OFF, the 72-degree switch is actuated and de-energizes the main fuel system by-pass valve. This action opens the by-pass valve and permits the emergency fuel system to assume engine control; however, it does not unlock, or prevent locking of, the electronic engine controls. If throttle is not retarded as rapidly as possible, when an afterburner take-off is to be aborted, engine overspeeding results.

TWO-POSITION EMERGENCY FUEL SWITCH CHARACTERISTICS.

It is *not* necessary to "arm" the automatic lockup system after an engine start on airplanes with the two-position emergency fuel system switch, since lock-up protection is now provided during the engine start. If ac power loss occurs, the results will be the same as those described under the three-position emergency fuel system switch characteristics. If the lockup light comes on during the take-off roll and it is desired to abort the take-off, chop the throttle to the idle detent with enough effort to depress an idle detent plunger which actuates a detent switch and reverts engine control to the emergency fuel system (during lockup only). The emergency fuel system will then remain in control until the engine control lockup light goes out *and* until the emergency fuel system switch is cycled to ON and returned to NORM. It is necessary to manually reposition the exhaust nozzle when operating on the emergency fuel system during engine lockup. Positioning the emergency fuel system switch to ON during engine lockup does not unlock the exhaust nozzle on airplanes incorporating the two-position switch.

ENGINE CHARACTERISTICS.

ABNORMALLY SLOW ENGINE ACCELERATIONS.

At altitudes above 25,000 feet, if the fuel schedule of the electronic engine control has not been properly set, there will be a drop-off in maximum rpm and exhaust temperatures as altitude is increased. Should this condition exist, it is very likely that engine accelerations will be extremely slow. It is possible, however, to have abnormally slow accelerations without having a drop-off from maximum rpm. Both conditions are the result of improper fuel scheduling, but to different extents. When the conditions are extreme, the engine cannot accelerate to obtain 100% rpm at intermediate altitudes, and the airplane cannot climb to operational ceiling. These conditions can be corrected by proper ground adjustment procedures.

LACK OF RESPONSE TO THROTTLE MOVEMENT.

Actuation of the automatic lockup system is first evidenced by a lack of engine response to throttle movement and illumination of the lockup light. Should a condition arise where the engine fails to respond to a change in throttle position, it is probably caused by power failure either in the airplane electrical supply system or in the ac supply system, as shown by the engine control lockup indicator lights coming on. This condition could be caused by the failure of certain tubes in the electronic engine control amplifiers that control the main system and afterburner fuel valves. This lack of response to throttle movement is incorporated in an electronic engine control system as a safety device and shows a failure. Therefore, a failure of this type causes the system to remain locked in the position at which the electrical power failed. The obvious solution is to switch to the emergency fuel system. For example, if, during flight at 80% rpm, the throttle is advanced to MILITARY with no corresponding increase in rpm, first return the throttle to the previous position, or below; then switch to the emergency fuel system. Remember that severe engine transitions and compressor stall can occur during transfer to the emergency fuel system if the throttle has not been returned to the position that it was in when the main system failed, as the emergency fuel system takes into account only altitude, airplane speed, and throttle position.

COMPRESSOR STALL.

The integrated electronic engine control in this airplane has been designed to eliminate the possibility of compressor stall. The integrated electronic engine control properly and accurately provides fuel in the correct proportion to the engine under any rapid throttle advancement. *However, when an electronic engine control is improperly adjusted, when the emergency fuel system switch is inadvertently left in the* TAKE OFF *position, or when the emergency fuel system is in operation, a compressor stall may occur after any rapid advancement of the throttle.* Rapid throttle advancement injects more fuel into the combustion chambers than the engine can use for acceleration at the existing rpm. The burning of this additional fuel increases combustion pressures. Increase of these pressures creates a corresponding increase in the pressure against the compressor discharge air. This increase of pressure against the compressor discharge air results in a breakdown of airflow through the last stages of the compressor. This is known as a compressor stall. As a result of the stall, the mass airflow through the compressor is reduced, causing a reduction in the airflow through the turbine; thus, the energy available to the turbine wheel is decreased, causing loss in engine speed. If the engine is allowed to continue operation in a stalled condition, the temperature of the burning gases will increase until serious damage to the turbine section of the engine occurs, resulting in engine failure. A roaring, pulsating noise accompanies compressor stall and may precede any engine instrument indication of changing engine conditions. If the roaring noise is heard after a rapid engine acceleration, immediately retarding the throttle will eliminate the compressor stall. If exhaust temperature stabilizes at a normal value, the throttle should be readvanced slowly. Exhaust temperature rise should be normal during throttle advancement. However, if the temperature continues to drop after the throttle is retarded, flame-out has occurred and an air start should be attempted. (Refer to "Engine Air Start," Section III.) In addition to the roaring, pulsating noise, other indications of a compressor stall are a rapidly rising exhaust temperature, steady or decreasing rpm, a long flame from the tail pipe, loss of thrust, and heavy engine vibration. In general, injection of excessive fuel into the engine at altitudes below 25,000 feet tends to cause compressor stall. Above this altitude, flame-out usually results.

NORMAL ENGINE CHARACTERISTIC RESEMBLING COMPRESSOR STALL.

During acceleration from a very low power setting, as in a go-around from an aborted landing, the engine noise may change from a high-pitched whine to a low-pitched rumble, similar to that obtained in the first stage of compressor stall. As the throttle is advanced and the engine begins to accelerate through the low, inefficient operating rpm range, the fuel control valve supplies the engine with an excessive amount of fuel, which causes the exhaust temperature to rise rapidly. The rate of fuel injection is then reduced by the control valve, allowing the exhaust temperature to peak and then drop off slightly. As the engine speed increases into the intermediate and more efficient operating rpm range, the high-pitched whine decreases and the low-pitched rumble increases in intensity as the engine accelerates toward the desired rpm. As the higher operating rpm range is reached, the low-pitched rumble gradually decreases. When the desired rpm is reached, the exhaust temperature stabilizes at a lower value than that obtained during the acceleration. Engine noise then becomes steady. These phenomena are more noticeable at low altitude under low-ram flight conditions than at high altitude. The sound indications may be initially construed as symptoms of compressor stall. However, the only true indications of compressor stall or failure of engine to accelerate are the readings of the engine instruments. Compressor stall is characterized by rapid rise in exhaust temperature accompanied by a roaring noise and heavy vibration and followed by loss in engine speed.

FLAME-OUT.

Flame-out is just what the name implies and can occur during rapid accelerations or decelerations of the engine. *Acceleration* flame-out, like compressor stall, occurs when more fuel is injected into the combustion chambers than the engine can use for acceleration at the existing rpm. But, unlike the fuel-air mixture that causes compressor stall, this mixture is so excessively rich that it cannot burn, so the flame goes out. Flame-out during rapid engine *deceleration* will result whenever the amount of fuel injected into the combustion chambers is reduced to a level too low to sustain combustion at the existing rpm. Flame-outs are indicated by loss in thrust, drop in exhaust temperature, and possibly by a loud noise similar to engine backfire. During a partial flame-out, some of the combustion chambers may still maintain combustion if the exhaust temperature does not drop below 150°C. The throttle should be retarded to idle and readvanced slowly in an attempt to relight the other chambers. If exhaust temperature continues to decrease below 150°C, the flame-out is complete and an air start is necessary. During any rapid throttle movement above about 25,000 feet, flame-outs may occur if the electronic engine control does not function properly or is improperly scheduled, if the emergency fuel switch is inadvertently left in the TAKE OFF position, or if the emergency fuel system is in operation. A normal air start may be accomplished after a flame-out; however, caution should be exercised. The air start should be attempted as soon after a flame-out as possible. However, air starts are more readily attained below 40,000 feet.

ENGINE NOISE AND ROUGHNESS.

Thermal expansion and pressure surge occasionally occur in the pressurization system during flight, resulting in a number of abnormal sounds. Therefore, when any unusual noise appears, dump cabin pressure for a few minutes. If the noise continues, have the engine checked during shutdown after landing. During normal operation, the engine may seem to run rougher than other engines in jet-type airplanes. The reason is that it is equipped with an afterburner, which tends to make any normal vibration more apparent. The vibrations or roughness may tend to cause some concern until the pilot becomes familiar with the airplane and its characteristics. (Refer to "Afterburner Roughness," in this section.) Engine roughness may occur in flight, especially during operation at high powers above 15,000 feet. Usually this roughness can be eliminated by a change of rpm. However, if engine roughness occurs at all altitudes or engine speeds, it indicates some mechanical failure, and an immediate landing should be made.

TURBINE NOISE DURING SHUTDOWN.

The light scraping or squealing noise which may be heard during engine shutdown results from interference between the turbine buckets and turbine shroud. Contact of the two parts is due to the tendency of the shroud to shift and distort under varying temperature conditions, such as are induced by engine shutdown. The scraping, while undesirable, does not damage either part; however, in order to minimize it, idle the engine for at least 2 minutes at minimum temperature obtainable with the rpm at about 65% to 70% before shutdown after any high-power operation (either flight or ground). If, despite this precaution, heavy scraping does occur on shutdown, do not try to restart engine until turbine temperature has dropped enough to provide adequate clearance between the buckets and shroud, since a starting attempt might result in destruction of the starter. If a start must be made when interference is suspected, be particularly alert for engine response. If there is no audible indication of engine rotation, or if there is no response on the tachometer within a few seconds, depress the stop-starter button immediately.

SMOKE FROM TURBINE DURING SHUTDOWN.

White Smoke.

When the engine is shut down, fuel may accumulate in the turbine housing where heat of the turbine section of the engine causes the fuel to boil. (Although a turbine housing drain is provided, the drain may not prevent accumulations of some fuel.) Presence of this residual fuel in the engine will be shown by emission of fuel vapor or smoke from the tail pipe or inlet duct. Boiling fuel, indicated by appearance of white fuel vapor, does not damage the engine, but does create a hazard to personnel because of the possibility of ignition with explosive violence if the vapor is allowed to accumulate in the engine and fuselage. Therefore, all personnel should keep clear of tail pipe and intake duct for 15 minutes after shutdown and at all times when smoke or vapors issue from tail pipe.

Black Smoke.

The appearance of black smoke from the tail pipe after shutdown indicates burning fuel, which will damage the engine and should be cleared immediately as follows:

1. External power source connected to both receptacles.
2. Throttle closed.
3. Battery-starter switch momentarily at STARTER.
4. Allow engine to crank to about 9% rpm (one minute maximum); then depress stop-starter button and turn engine master switch OFF.

While following this procedure, keep in mind that the high current required for starting will burn out the starter in a matter of seconds if the engine doesn't turn over as soon as the starter is energized. If there is no audible indication of engine rotation or if there is no response on the tachometer within a few seconds, depress the stop-starter button immediately.

TACHOMETER INDICATION.

If a tachometer failure is shown by a drop in rpm, check oil pressure gage for a pressure indication, as both the tachometer and oil pump are driven from the same accessory drive. If loss of oil pressure is also shown, a landing should be made as soon as practicable.

AFTERBURNER CHARACTERISTICS.

AFTERBURNER BLOWOUT.

A severe loss of thrust while on afterburner usually means only an afterburner blowout. This can be caused by a rare combustion phenomenon which will probably occur only at extremely high altitude. Afterburner failure may also result from the failure of the afterburner air-turbine fuel pump, from the failure and closing of the afterburner air-turbine air-supply shutoff valve, from a negative-G maneuver, or from a control system failure. If the airplane is at a safe altitude when a failure occurs, the results are probably more bothersome than serious, as the automatic closing of the nozzle will restore full Military Thrust in about 2 seconds and any engine overspeed encountered will be controlled by the electronic engine control and by the hydraulic overspeed governor to prevent destructive overspeeding of the engine.

> **CAUTION**
>
> - If afterburner blowout occurs with less than 1300 pounds of fuel remaining, do not attempt further afterburner operation unless dictated by emergency or combat conditions.
> - This precaution does not constitute an operating limitation, but rather a measure for protection of the afterburner turbine-driven pump in the event of fuselage rear section tank transfer pump failure.

AFTERBURNER ROUGHNESS.

Reports of afterburner roughness at altitude have been received from pilots flying airplanes with the J47-GE-33 engine installed. This roughness, existing primarily at an altitude range of 25,000 to 35,000 feet, is exhibited to the pilot in the form of vibration on the rudder pedals and the control stick. Its frequency is not as high or constant as a bearing failure, and is felt in varying intensity between the altitudes quoted, reaching maximum intensity at a specific altitude. This afterburner roughness is the result of a poor spray pattern from the large-slot spray bars when the afterburner fuel pressure decreases (as fuel flow is decreased by increasing altitude) to a value approaching the cutout point of the afterburner fuel flow divider. This poor spray pattern causes partial and erratic burning of large-slot fuel in the afterburner. Flight tests, conducted with the aid of a simulated CDP (compressor discharge pressure) control in the cockpit, revealed that raising or lowering of the afterburner fuel schedule raised or lowered, respectively, the effective altitude of the roughness. Thus, the altitude at which the pilot feels afterburner roughness will be higher with the "flattop" fuel schedule than with the old, lower fuel schedule. If you should encounter engine roughness, remember the following points for properly diagnosing this afterburner roughness.

1. Afterburner roughness exists primarily at altitudes from 25,000 to 35,000 feet.

2. Intensity of afterburner roughness will reach maximum at a specific altitude and will diminish at either side of that altitude.

3. The frequency of the vibration felt on the stick and rudder pedals is not as high or constant as that of a bearing failure (133 cycles per second). The magnitude of the roughness will be more comparable to the tail buffet encountered with the drag chute aspirator than with the vibration accompanying either bearing or turbine wheel failure.

4. The roughness will not necessarily be accompanied by any noticeable change in engine instrument readings.

5. This condition will not contribute to activation of the fire-warning system.

6. Manufacturing and Air Force personnel agree that this roughness, although not desirable, is not a hazard.

ENGINE OVERSPEED DURING AFTERBURNER SHUTDOWN.

Emergency Fuel System Switch at NORM.

Excessive damping of the main fuel control valve by means of an improperly set stability adjustment could cause an overspeed condition when coming out of afterburning. If this adjustment is set too high, the main fuel valve will not reduce the fuel flow fast enough to prevent engine overspeeding before the nozzle has a chance to close. The amount of overspeeding will depend upon how far the control is out of adjustment. This condition can be minimized by retarding the throttle slowly whenever coming out of afterburner. This procedure permits the nozzle to close progressively while the engine is still using the gradually decreasing amount of afterburning. Thus, the nozzle will be nearly closed at the time the afterburner goes out. Protection against destructive engine overspeeding is still provided by the hydraulic overspeed governor.

Emergency Fuel System Switch at TAKE OFF. (Three-position Switch).

On some occasions, when the throttle is retarded out of the afterburner range with the emergency fuel system switch inadvertently left in the TAKE OFF position, engine overspeed is experienced. This condition usually occurs on hot days and is not considered undesirable, as the maximum overspeed usually experienced is about 102% rpm. This condition will be corrected as the variable nozzle adjusts itself to the Military Thrust position. Normally, when the throttle is retarded from the afterburner range, an immediate decrease in the back pressure on the turbine wheel occurs, which allows the engine to momentarily overspeed. The electronic engine control, sensing this overspeed, immediately starts to close the main fuel valve. This reduces fuel flow to prevent further overspeeding, until the variable nozzle can assume the correct position and allow the exhaust temperature and back pressure to build up. However, on a hot day, with the emergency fuel system switch at TAKE OFF, the emergency fuel system is in stand-by, with a fuel scheduling very close to that of the main fuel system. Thus, when the main fuel valve closes to prevent overspeed, the emergency fuel regulator restricts the amount of by-pass fuel from the main fuel system. (See figure 1-12.) This restriction then forces the by-pass fuel around the main fuel valve and into the engine, and therefore prevents reduction of the fuel flow. As this condition can occur only when the emergency fuel system switch is in the TAKE OFF position, positioning the switch to NORM before retarding the throttle from afterburner range will prevent its occurrence.

EMERGENCY FUEL SYSTEM.

EMERGENCY FUEL SYSTEM OPERATION.

During operation on this system, the scheduling of the emergency fuel regulator makes it necessary for the pilot to open the throttle farther to maintain a specified power setting than would be necessary during operation on the main fuel system. This is because the emergency fuel regulator scheduling is normally set lower than that of the main fuel system, to prevent overriding the main system while on stand-by. Therefore, while the engine is operating on the emergency fuel system, the lower portion of the throttle travel usually becomes less effective, and available power at full throttle is reduced as altitude is increased, varying considerably with altitude above 20,000 feet. Therefore, during operation on the emergency fuel system, it is necessary not only that all throttle movements be made cautiously, but also that the throttle be advanced farther than is necessary on the main fuel system for a specified power setting, the amount of advancement increasing with the altitude.

CAUTION

- If engine speed is inadvertently allowed to drop below 85% rpm before emergency fuel system switch is moved to the ON position, the throttle should be retarded to START IDLE before the switch is placed ON, to prevent an overtemperature condition.
- Extremely low engine rpm should be avoided, when operating on the emergency system, because of excessive slow acceleration characteristics from engine speeds below 40% rpm.

NONRECOVERY CHARACTERISTIC FOLLOWING AN EMERGENCY FUEL SYSTEM TEST (THREE-POSITION SWITCH).

On airplanes equipped with an old-type main fuel control valve, the inability of the engine to recover on the main fuel system following an emergency fuel system test is evidenced by failure of the engine rpm to fully recover to 100%. With the throttle at MILITARY stop and the emergency fuel system switch at TAKE OFF, depressing the emergency fuel system test button disables the main fuel system, causing the rpm to drop to the emergency fuel system value and the variable nozzle to go to the scheduled closed position. Releasing the test button returns engine control to the main fuel system, which locks the variable nozzle. The variable nozzle is locked in position whenever throttle position calls for more than 3% increase in rpm. Usually there is adequate fuel flow provided to accelerate the engine from emergency fuel system rpm to approximately 97% rpm with the variable nozzle locked closed. When 97% rpm is reached, the variable nozzle is automatically unlocked; and as it opens, it allows the engine to continue acceleration to full speed. Occasionally, after an emergency fuel system test, there is not enough fuel flow provided by the main fuel system schedule to enable the engine to accelerate to 97% rpm with the nozzle positioned to a minimum area. When this occurs, the rpm stabilizes, or "hangs up," at some lower value. In order to assist rpm to recover to 100% on the main fuel system, the emergency fuel system switch should be moved to NORM and the throttle retarded sufficiently to provide a throttle schedule within 3% of actual rpm, thus allowing the nozzle to open and enabling the rpm to increase. As the engine starts to accelerate, the throttle can then be readvanced. On other airplanes, recovery of rpm after an emergency fuel system check will not be affected by retarding the throttle. Because of the characteristics of the later-type main fuel control valve, it may take about 20 seconds before rpm begins to increase.

EMERGENCY FUEL SYSTEM OVERRIDING MAIN FUEL SYSTEM (THREE-POSITION SWITCH).

Any time ambient air temperature causes the emergency fuel regulator setting to approach that of the main fuel system, it is possible for the engine to gradually overspeed (above 100% rpm) during the initial climb after take-off. This is a result of the emergency fuel system overriding the main fuel system when the emergency fuel system switch is in the TAKE OFF position. Normally, the engine overspeed will not exceed 102% rpm; however, it should be noted that short periods of operation between 100% and 104% rpm will not damage the engine. When emergency fuel system override occurs, what appears to be a complete power loss will be experienced if the emergency fuel system switch is positioned to NORM, with the overspeed condition present. This power loss occurs because the main fuel system, on sensing the overspeed condition, has closed the main fuel valve in an attempt to bring the engine speed down to 100% rpm. The main fuel system returns the main fuel valve to its open position when the emergency fuel system switch is positioned at NORM. However, the time required is dependent on the rate of response of the main fuel system. The overriding of the main fuel system by the emergency fuel system may be caused by improper adjustment of the electronic engine control, accumulation of mechanical tolerances in the emergency fuel system under ram conditions, or an atmospheric temperature inversion resulting in excessive outside air temperature as altitude is increased. If the engine fuel systems are checked and found to be within acceptable limits, the overriding by the emergency fuel system is acceptable and corrective action should be taken by the pilot. Engine overspeeding to 104% rpm, when operating in afterburner, can be corrected after a safe altitude is reached, by moving the emergency fuel system switch to NORM and immediately retarding throttle from the afterburner range. The engine will respond on the main fuel system when the throttle is readvanced. If the engine overspeed condition stabilizes at about 102% rpm, climb may be continued without a power change. The altitude increase will cause the engine to return to 100% rpm. Wait 15 seconds after engine speed returns to 100% rpm before positioning emergency fuel system switch to NORM. The main fuel system will then take over engine control normally.

EXHAUST TEMPERATURE CHARACTERISTICS.

EXHAUST GAS THERMOCOUPLE CHARACTERISTICS.

The engine is equipped with a fast-responding, loop-type thermocouple in order that overtemperature conditions can be controlled as rapidly as possible. This thermocouple also permits optimum performance of the engine during accelerations and helps in the maintenance of steady thrust at Military Thrust.

SPEED AND EXHAUST TEMPERATURE FLUCTUATION.

Minor fluctuations of the engine speed or exhaust temperature can be caused by a number of factors. The stability adjustment, if set too high, will cause the engine to take an unusual length of time to stabilize at a new power setting, as called for by the throttle position. In this case, the engine responds normally up to some rpm or temperature close to the value desired; however, when that point is reached, the whole process slows down and the final stabilized value may not be reached until 5 to 20 seconds later. The stability adjustment, if set too low, will cause the control system to overshoot and undershoot, not too rapidly, but to the extent that it is apparent that some instability exists. In this case, the engine speed or exhaust temperature fluctuates, or hunts, in a manner similar to that which would be obtained with a slow-moving hydraulic engine control governor. The stability and transient temperature control may be adjusted to correct these fluctuations. More violent fluctuations would be cause for transferring to the emergency fuel system. On airplanes incorporating the three-position emergency fuel switch, the emergency fuel regulator may cause engine surges which occur when the switch is in the TAKE OFF position. The frequency of such surges is approximately one cycle per second.

CONTROL OF EXHAUST TEMPERATURE.

A variable-area nozzle is used on this engine to aid in maintaining exhaust temperature at the proper level, regardless of altitude or airspeed. The temperature depends upon the nozzle schedule adjustment, temperature control circuit, and thermocouple voltage. If, during a Military Thrust climb, the exhaust temperature falls off from 685°C (705°C*) to some lower value and the nozzle does not move to hold the exhaust temperature at 685°C (705°C*), the nozzle schedule settings are possibly at fault and should be checked. The variable-area nozzle should, within the limits of its range of operation, be able to correct any wandering of the exhaust temperature that is exhibited by most fixed-nozzle jet airplanes.

INVERTER CHANGE-OVER CHARACTERISTICS.

A both-inverters warning light (red) and a main inverter warning light (amber) are provided in the cockpit. The illumination of the main inverter warning light shows failure of the main inverter. Illumination of the both-inverters warning light is controlled by the ac bus and shows that both inverters are inoperative. As there is no single indication of secondary inverter condition, it may be checked on the ground during the inverter change-over check. On F-86D-1 through F-86D-50 Airplanes, positioning the inverter test switch at TEST fails the main inverter, which causes the main inverter light to come on, showing that the main inverter is inoperable. If the both-inverters warning light (red) remains out with the amber light on, the secondary inverter is, therefore, operable and has taken over the duties of the main inverter. Holding the inverter test switch at TEST will reinstate the main inverter and extinguish the main inverter warning light. During a ground check of the inverter change-over circuit or during flight after a main inverter failure, the both-inverters warning light (red) may come on momentarily. This momentary illumination of the both-inverters warning light must not be construed as failure of both inverters, as only steady illumination of the both-inverters warning light shows that inverters have failed. The length of momentary illumination, or flash, of the both-inverters warning light depends upon the position of the radar power switch. With the radar power switch in any position but OFF, the secondary inverter takes

---

*Airplanes not changed by T.O. 2J-J47-349

over immediately after a main inverter failure. This immediate change-over may result in a flicker or flash of the both-inverters warning light. When the radar power switch is at OFF, the secondary inverter is not operating; for this reason, when inverter change-over is called for, the time needed for change-over will be lengthened considerably because of the necessity of the secondary inverter to start operating and putting out ac power. Under this condition, therefore, the both-inverters warning light will come on and stay on for a short period of time until the secondary inverter can start operating and take over main inverter duties. This inverter change-over characteristic is very important to remember, as, in time of emergency, the momentary illumination of the both-inverters warning light might be construed as failure of both inverters instead of the time lag for the secondary inverter to take over. On F-86D-55 and later airplanes, and those changed by T.O., the inverter change-over feature is manual (switch must be positioned at SPARE) instead of automatic, and different characteristics are present when making the change-over. On these airplanes, failure of the inverter in use causes both the amber main inverter failure warning light *and* the red both-inverters failure warning light to come on. *This, however, does not show failure of both inverters.* When both lights come on, move inverter selector switch to SPARE. This causes the secondary inverter to drop the radar equipment, allowing secondary inverter power to become available for the ac-operated equipment. If the secondary inverter is operative, the amber main inverter failure warning light will remain on, but the red both-inverters failure warning light will go out when the switch is positioned at SPARE. If both lights remain on *when the switch is moved,* the secondary inverter has also failed.

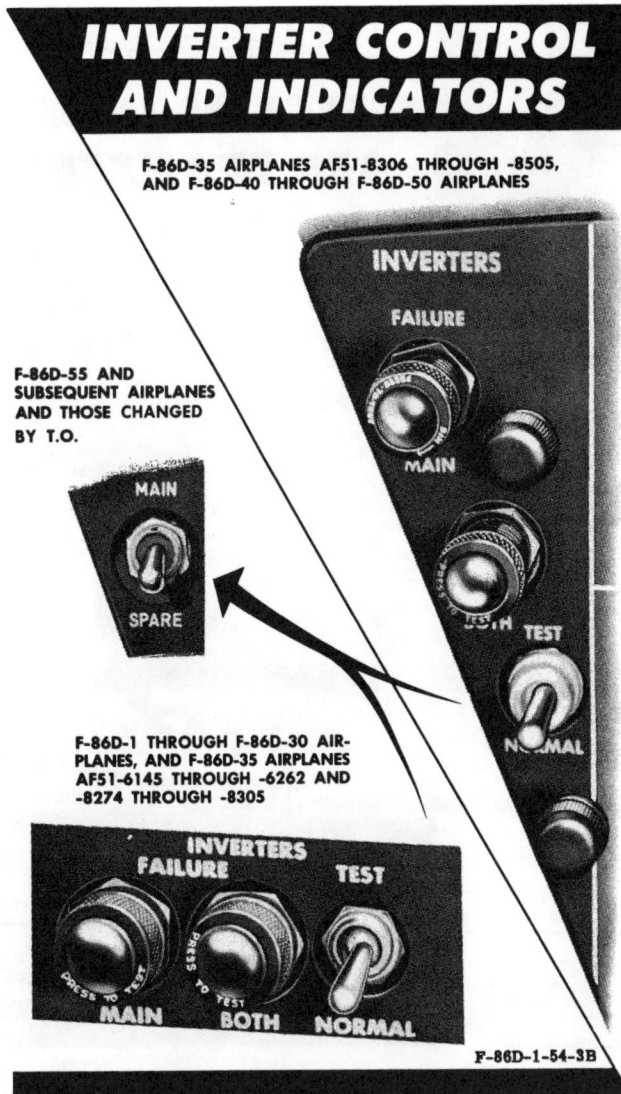

Figure 7-3

FUEL SYSTEM.

Operation of the fuel system is essentially automatic, requiring no action from the pilot during flight. However, it is essential that the pilot keep the following precautions in mind.

1. On airplanes incorporating a three-position emergency fuel system switch, place at NORM for all normal operation except take-off and initial climb. (If the two-position emergency fuel system switch is installed, the NORM position is to be used for *all* normal operation including take-off and initial climb.)

2. When drop tanks are carried, leave drop tank air pressure shutoff valve ON at all times during flight, to prevent possible collapse of drop tanks during rapid descents.

Note

Uneven feeding from the drop tanks does not affect the flight characteristics of the airplane.

FUEL SYSTEM OPERATION WITH INOPERATIVE AFT TRANSFER PUMP.

The fuel system provides for automatic fuel transfer from the aft fuselage tank by an electrically driven fuel transfer pump controlled by a fuel float switch. During engine operation with the aft fuselage tank transfer pump inoperative, fuel is transferred by gravity to the center wing fuel tank through the aft fuselage tank transfer line. (See figure 7-4.) Transfer of fuel continues until the fuel level in the aft fuselage tank drops below the level of the aft fuselage tank transfer line. Fuel is then drawn to the engine by the engine pump suction through the aft fuselage tank suction-feed outlet. However, a check valve incorporated in the suction-feed outlet prevents suction feed from the aft tank as long as there is fuel available at the fuel boost pump in the center wing tank. As a result, suction feed from the aft tank will not occur until all fuel in the center wing

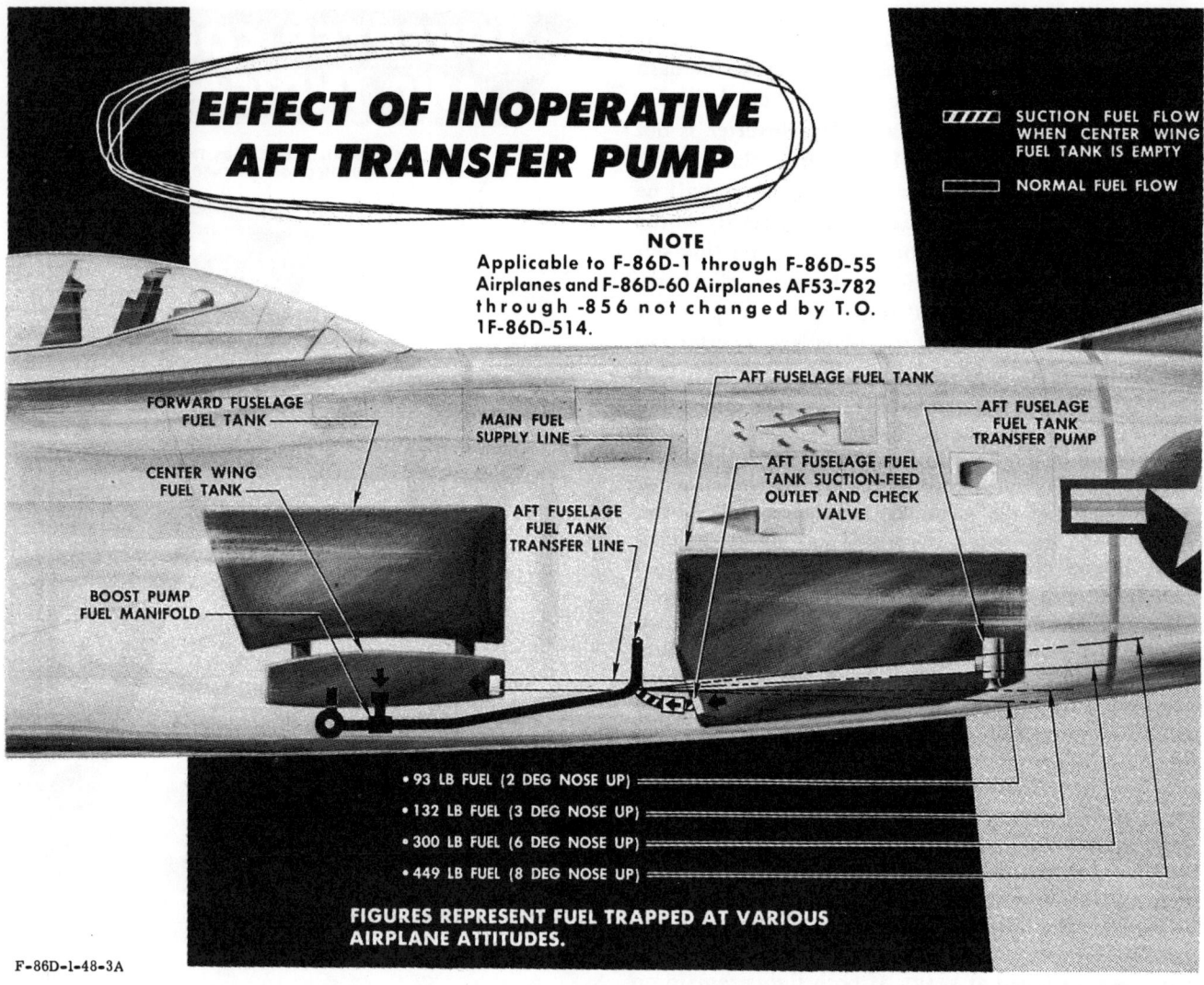

Figure 7-4

tank has been used. Figure 7-4 illustrates the amount of fuel that can be trapped in the aft fuselage tank at various flight attitudes with the transfer pump inoperative. It is obvious that any increased nose-up attitude will increase the amount of fuel trapped in the aft fuselage fuel tank. However, in-flight failure of the aft fuselage tank transfer circuit, float switch, or pump need not constitute a serious problem, provided excessive high angles of attack are avoided.

Note

- If fuel starvation is encountered, as shown by fuel pressure fluctuation and rpm drop-off on both the main and emergency fuel systems, try to regain rpm by lowering the nose, and land as soon as possible. Use increased power settings, if necessary, to maintain altitude at the decreased angle of attack.

- Afterburner operation with aft fuselage tank transfer pump inoperative will deplete the fuel in the center wing fuel tank faster than it can be replenished from the aft fuselage fuel tank by gravity feed. As a result, afterburner blowout can occur because of fuel starvation. If afterburner blowout occurs with less than 1300 pounds of fuel remaining, do not attempt further afterburner operation unless combat or emergency conditions dictate.

On late airplanes,* and airplanes changed by T. O. 1F-86D-514, the aft fuselage fuel tank feeding characteristics have been improved. (See figure 1-17.) The added features of this system preclude the possibility of trapping fuel in the aft tank, regardless of airplane attitude, thereby allowing all fuel to be available to the engine.

*F-86D-60 Airplane AF53-857 and all later airplanes

DUAL FUEL PUMP WARNING LIGHT CHARACTERISTICS.

The dual fuel pump warning light will be operable only on airplanes having the new type pressure differential switch installed. On all other airplanes, the light will be inoperable or removed, with a decal, "WARNING SYSTEM INOPERATIVE," mounted beside the light. If the warning light is installed, certain characteristics will be noted. As the engine master switch is placed at ON, the dual fuel pump warning light will come on, and as the throttle is advanced during engine start, the light will go off when the fuel pressure reaches about 50 psi or 600 to 700 pounds per hour fuel flow. If one element of the pump is inoperative, the switch will be unbalanced and the light will remain on. If this occurs, the engine should be shut down and the cause investigated. In flight and during normal engine operation, the fuel pump warning light should remain off; however, if the light does illuminate during flight, a landing should be made as soon as practicable.

HYDRAULIC SYSTEMS.

Check hydraulic systems periodically during flight as follows:

1. Hold pressure gage selector switch at UTILITY and read gage for proper utility system pressure.

2. Fly straight and level for 5 seconds and then, with gage selector switch at NORMAL, read pressure gage for flight control normal system pressure.

3. Without moving control stick and with gage selector switch at ALTER. (FLT. CONT. EMERG. on F-86D-1 Airplanes), read gage for flight control alternate system pressure.

On conventional flight control systems, intermediate rates and maximum rate of control movements were both directly proportional to pilot effort. In constant-pressure, irreversible hydraulic systems, such as on this airplane, the rate of control movement will vary with effort only until the actuator valve is completely open. Any additional effort by the pilot will not result in a further increase in rate of movement. Thus, the maximum rate obtainable is not determined as much by pilot effort as by the hydraulics and kinematics of the system. With a conventional system, almost any malfunction which could occur that would limit maximum rate of control movement would also be readily apparent at some lesser rate. It would be difficult for it to continue undetected. The same is not true of irreversible systems. Should there be some restriction in the rate of flow of hydraulic fluid in the irreversible system, it will not be apparent until an attempt is made to move the controls faster than the restriction will permit. Also, the rate of movement imposed by the restriction will be maximum regardless of pilot effort. Inability to lift the nose wheel during take-off can result if the stabilizer actuator control valves of the normal and alternate systems are not properly synchronized. If the valves are synchronized, available control valve displacement is reduced, resulting in a corresponding reduction in maximum rate of control movement. This reduced rate would obviously restrict airplane response. This same effect would occur if restriction in hydraulic flow were caused, for example, by improper attachment of quick-disconnect fittings. Experience shows that this reduction in rate of control movement can mislead the pilot and at the same time escape detection by maintenance personnel. Whether the pilot encounters or notices the malfunction depends upon individual technique and whether the pilot desires to move the controls at a rate faster than the malfunction would permit. It is during take-off and landing that full stick deflection is most often necessary. Should the stick fail to move at the normal rate, the pilot may apply greater than normal pressure and gain the impression that he had full stick deflection. Because of the short time involved and the surprise element, the pilot may have an erroneous impression of how far the stick moved. Since a ground check will show that full stick deflection occurs (ignoring the fact that it can be moved only at a slower than normal rate), the nature of the malfunction remains undetected. Another pilot using a slower technique and not having occasion to move the stick at rapid rates will not notice the failure.

During nose wheel lift-off on take-off, during misjudged and consequently late flare-out on landing, and in the technique of "feeling for the runway" a pilot may assume he is getting the desired stick deflection, whereas restriction of hydraulic fluid flow for any of the reasons mentioned may actually be limiting the rate and consequently the amount of immediate stick deflection. These examples are based on use of the horizontal stabilizer, but other difficulties could also result from similar malfunctions affecting aileron control. It is important to check rate of control surface movement before flight. If the rate is slower than normal, based on experience in other F-86D Airplanes, the previously described malfunction of the flight control system should be suspected.

WING FLAP LEVER OPERATION.

The original design use and purpose of the HOLD position of the flap lever was to allow varying degrees of flap extension to prevent "sink," if it should occur during high gross weight take-offs.

CAUTION

The flap actuating mechanism may be damaged if the flap handle is left in the HOLD position for an extended length of time.

After airspeed has built up enough for complete flap retraction, the flap lever should be moved to UP and left there until flaps are needed again. For landings, the flap lever is moved firmly to the full DOWN stop. The flap lever is built for normal usage and does not require special, gentle handling by the pilot during operation.

LANDING GEAR.

If the landing gear unsafe warning light comes on during flight, indicating an unsafe landing gear condition, airspeed should be reduced to below 185 knots IAS before cycling the gear. If the unsafe warning light does not go out after the gear is cycled several times, land as soon as practicable.

Section VIII
CREW DUTIES

Not applicable to this airplane

Section IX

ALL-WEATHER OPERATION

TABLE OF CONTENTS

	PAGE		PAGE
Instrument Flight Procedures	9-1	Night Flying	9-17
Ice and Rain	9-14	Cold-weather Procedures	9-17
Turbulence and Thunderstorms	9-15	Hot-weather and Desert Procedures	9-20

Except for some repetition necessary for emphasis or continuity of thought, this section contains only those procedures that differ from, or are in addition to, the normal operating procedures in Section II.

INSTRUMENT FLIGHT PROCEDURES

This airplane has satisfactory stability and excellent handling characteristics while being flown entirely by reference to instruments. The control feel is somewhat different at low speeds than at high speeds in that relatively large stick movements and somewhat greater stick forces are present, which will be absent in the higher speed ranges. Certain phases of instrument flight operations may result in overcontrolling and resulting pilot-induced oscillations, which should be dampened out by releasing the stick momentarily. Under absolutely no circumstances, except in the case of military necessity, should this plane be flown entirely by reference to instruments unless you are a qualified instrument pilot and a holder of the AF Form 8A (Green) or AF Form 8 (White) Instrument Certificate. The airplane is equipped with the latest radio navigational aids, a complete deicing system, and a zero reader that will enable you to fly in all kinds of weather with such ease and accuracy to approach the precision of an automatic pilot, which is also installed on the airplane. As certain phases of instrument flying may require delays in departures and additional time for approach procedures which are often made at low altitudes, the endurance factor is critical. Consult the appendix for flight planning information, and use particular care in planning an alternate and fuel consumption. It is necessary that your flight planning be accurate with special attention to the traffic density and the type of approaches available at your destination. The effect of a go-around on fuel reserve (because of a missed approach or traffic control emergencies) must be considered. You will be able to make low-frequency range, ADF, MDF, GCA, and ILAS approaches in this airplane. Omnirange approaches can be made in later airplanes.*

---

*F-86D-35 and later airplanes

BEFORE ENTERING AIRPLANE.

1. Remove pitot cover.
2. External power source—have connected.

ON ENTERING AIRPLANE.

1. Map case—check that Radio Facility Charts, "Pilot's Handbook—Jet," and other necessary publications are available in cockpit.
2. Zero reader selector switch* at FLIGHT INST.
3. Zero reader altitude control* at OFF.
4. Radar master switch at STBY.
5. Marker beacon light—push to test.
6. Altimeter—set on field elevation.
7. Zero reader heading selector*—check for erection and set to proper heading.
8. Slaved gyro magnetic compass†—check for stabilization of needle and check for 180-degree ambiguity against stand-by compass 3 to 4 minutes after power has been turned on.
9. Zero reader flight director*—set horizontal bar two dots fly-up.
10. Attitude indicator—check erection and retraction of warning "OFF" flag. Adjust reference airplane for level indication by aligning it with indices on the side of instrument face.
11. Rate-of-climb indicator—set at zero.
12. Inverters—test.
13. Surface anti-ice switch at OFF. Push to test overheat warning light.
14. Windshield and radome anti-ice switch OFF. Push to test overheat warning light.
15. Pitot heat switch ON. Check operation with crew chief.

WARNING

Warm-up time for the pitot heater is about one minute at 32°F. Allow sufficient heating time if taking off into freezing rain or other visible moisture with surface temperatures at or near freezing.

16. Engine inlet switch EXTEND SCREEN. (SCREEN IN on F-86D-1 Airplanes.)
17. Alternator switch‡ ON.
18. Yaw damper switch OFF.
19. Autopilot—check operation.

---

*F-86D-1 through F-86D-30 Airplanes
†F-86D-35 and later airplanes
‡F-86D-5 and later airplanes

20. Radio compass—check frequency alignment, antenna reception, manual loop rotation, and compass operation. Tune to low-frequency range or homer that serves field you are departing from, identify it, and turn function switch to COMP.
21. Command radio—check tower, approach control, GCI, GCA, and CAA radio frequencies.
22. Omni radio—check operation and set to first en route station.
23. ILAS receiver—select local channel and check for retraction of warning "OFF" flag.
24. IFF radar—STANDBY.

AFTER STARTING ENGINE.

1. Surface anti-ice—at about 70% rpm, have crew chief check operation.
2. Windshield and radome anti-ice—at idle power, have crew chief check air blast at windshield.

TAXIING.

1. Clock—set with tower time check.
2. Altimeter—check tower altimeter setting against your altimeter setting. Do not accept airplane for flight if altimeter is off ±75 feet.
3. Surface anti-icing switch—ON if required.

Note

With surface anti-icing system on, engine anti-icing is in operation and intake screens are automatically retracted.

4. Windshield and canopy defrost—INC or DEC as required.
5. Turn-and-bank indicator—check deflection of turn needle during taxi turns.
6. Radio compass—monitor relative bearings to selected station during taxi turns.
7. Approach indicator—check deflection of ILAS localizer needle, if instrument runway is crossed while taxiing.
8. Zero reader heading indicator*—check actual changes of heading against indicator while taxiing.
9. Slaved gyro magnetic compass†—check actual changes of heading against needle while taxiing.

BEFORE INSTRUMENT TAKE-OFF.

1. Line up visually with center line of runway.
2. Zero reader heading* selector—set to runway heading.
3. Slaved gyro magnetic compass†—rotate course index to align runway heading with top of dial.

4. Wing flap lever at DOWN.

5. Hold brakes and advance throttle to Maximum Thrust.

Note

Instrument take-offs can be made satisfactorily without the afterburner. However, the afterburner is strongly recommended to shorten take-off roll for very low visibility conditions or to aid acceleration with water or snow on the runway.

INSTRUMENT TAKE-OFF AND CLIMB.

1. Recheck all instruments quickly and release brakes.

2. Maintain heading, using nose wheel steering until rudder becomes effective at about 60 knots IAS. Maintain visual reference to runway if possible. If visual reference is lost or deteriorates to a point it becomes difficult to maintain your heading, go on instruments immediately, using your heading indicator as your primary instrument.

WARNING

Use of brakes for directional control lengthens runway roll and reduces acceleration during take-off. With the end of runway obscured, it is possible to use excessive distance to accelerate without realizing there is not enough runway remaining to take off.

3. Take off at normal VFR speeds.

4. Immediately establish an initial climb attitude on instruments with rate-of-climb indicator as primary instrument at 500 fpm.

5. Landing gear handle UP as soon as altimeter shows an increase in altitude.

6. Establish 160 knots IAS climb until a 1500 fpm climb is indicated; then retract wing flaps.

7. Holding 1500 fpm on the rate-of-climb indicator, accelerate to best VFR climbing speed.

WARNING

Care should be used in making turns and beginning accelerations to best climb speeds after take-off by taking into consideration terrain obstructions and minimum altitudes at the point of departure.

8. Engine inlet switch at RETRACT.

Note

When in areas of known or suspected icing conditions, use anti-ice systems to prevent ice formation.

INSTRUMENT CRUISING FLIGHT.

The airplane has excellent handling characteristics throughout its normal speed range if properly trimmed and flown by reference to the attitude flight instruments. However, at high speeds at low altitudes or in turbulent air, it is easy for you to overcontrol and induce oscillations (porpoising). This will not be experienced if the autopilot is used. The autopilot greatly simplifies the task of the all-weather pilot by enabling you to read charts and navigate without the responsibility of control of the airplane. If the zero reader is installed, the airplane can be controlled manually with the ease and proficiency that approaches the performance of the autopilot itself.

RADIO NAVIGATION EQUIPMENT.

In the earlier models of this airplane in which the zero reader is installed, the radio compass is the only radio equipment provided for en route navigation. Because this equipment is highly susceptible to precipitation and electrical static, its reliability at high altitudes is considerably reduced by thin overcasts, haze, and dust. For this reason, the automatic operation of the radio compass should not be relied on entirely to establish a fix. The signals of the low-frequency range station should be monitored at all times to ascertain that the station is still broadcasting and to verify station passage. With the function switch in the ANT. position, the antenna of the radio compass serves as a normal low-frequency receiver. Use of the loop will provide better reception during static conditions, but care should be taken to manually rotate the loop 90 degrees if you switch from the COMP position because of the fact the compass holds the loop in the null position. If reception becomes impossible, return the function switch to COMP and tune for maximum deflection of the tuning needle. Use dead-reckoning for primary navigation and use the radio compass only as a supporting aid. In later airplanes,* the installation of the vhf omnidirectional receiver enables you to navigate without interference from static or weather conditions.

JET PENETRATIONS.

Jet penetrations have been set up to provide a high-speed and high rate-of-descent letdown from cruising

---

*****F-86D-35 and later airplanes**

Section IX — T.O. 1F-86D-1

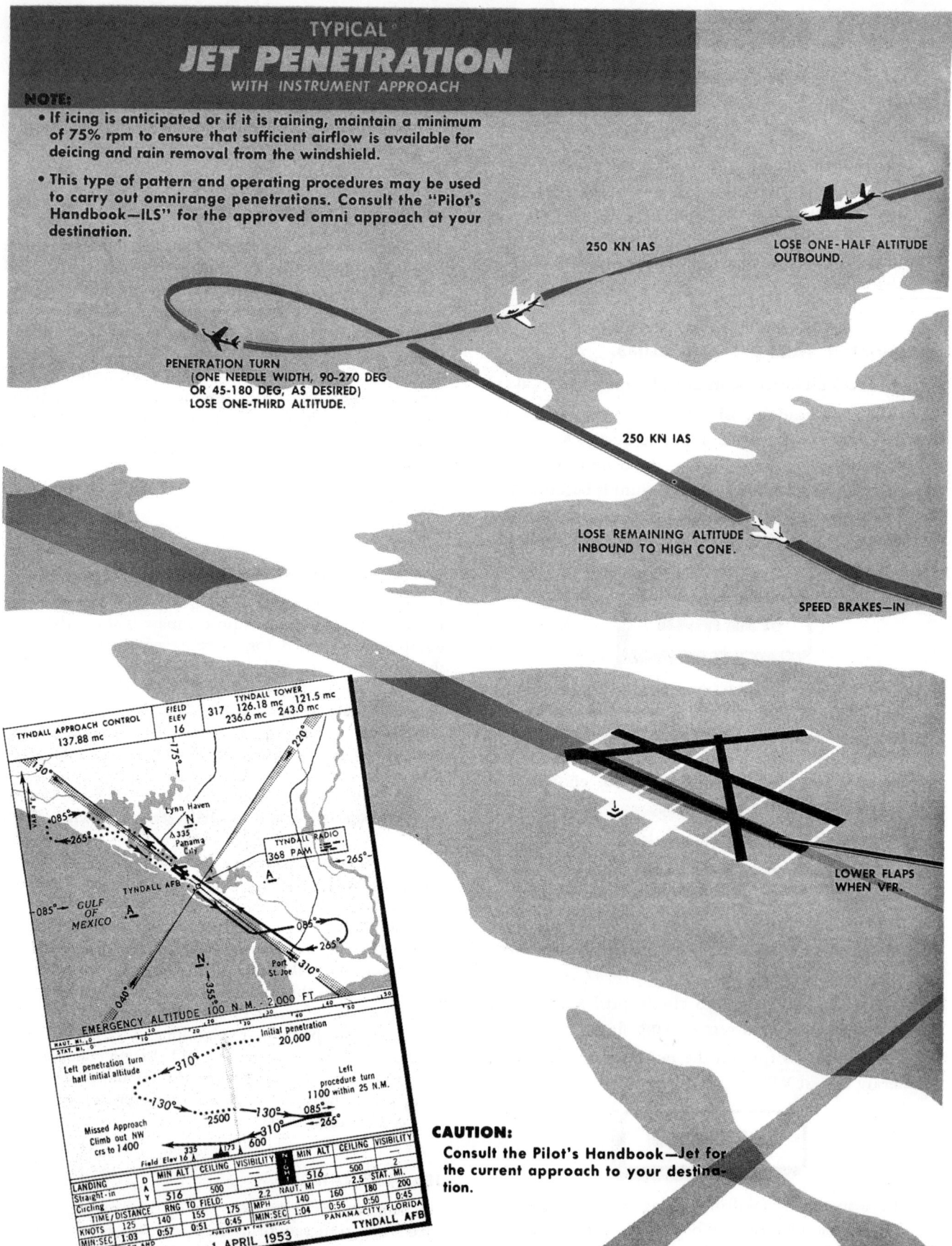

Figure 9-1

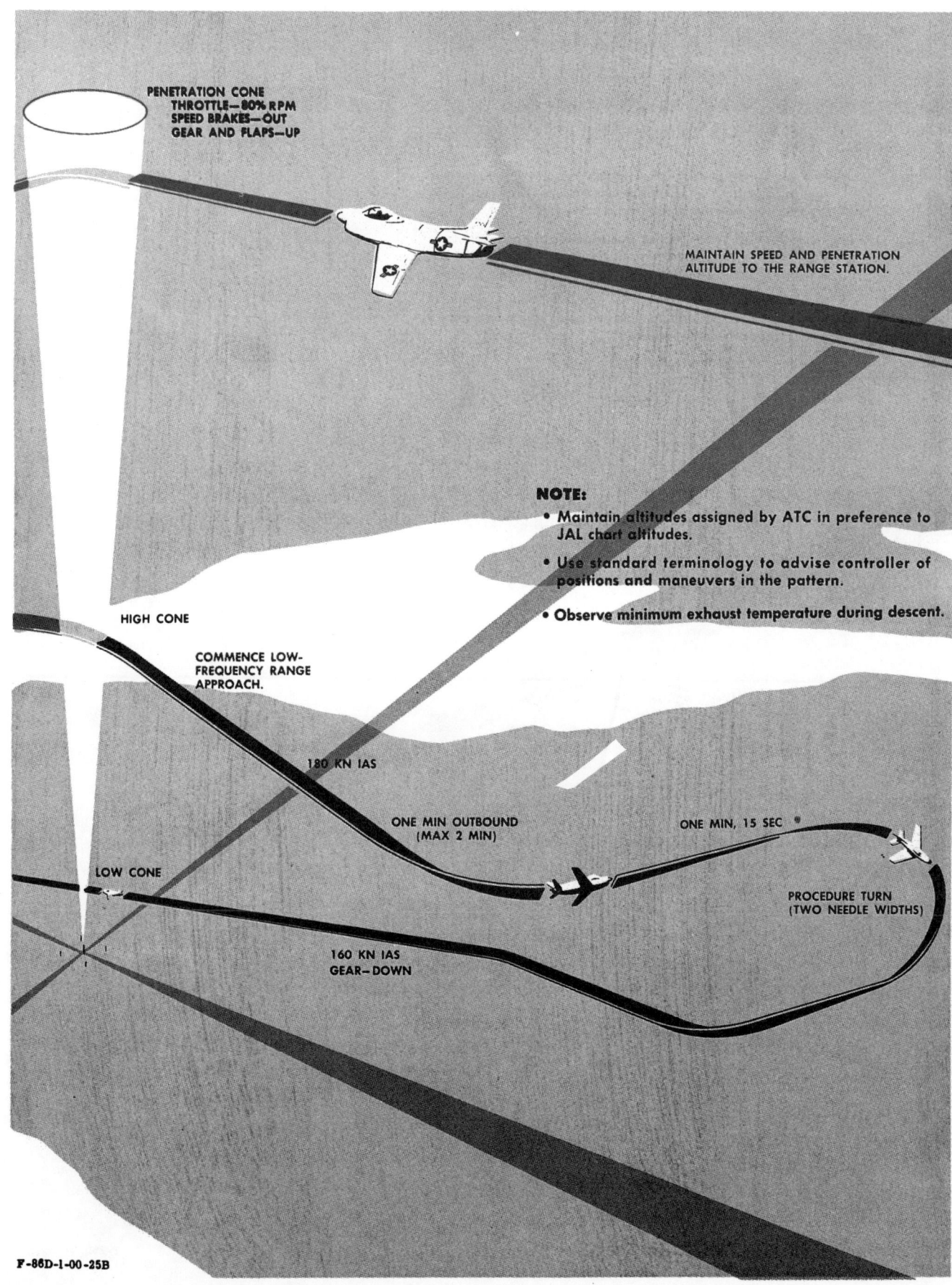

Section IX
T. O. 1F-86D-1

TYPICAL JET PENETRATION
WITH VFR APPROACH

MAINTAIN SPEED AND PENETRATION ALTITUDE TO THE RANGE STATION.

NOTE:
- If icing is anticipated or if it is raining, maintain a minimum of 75% rpm to ensure that sufficient airflow is available for deicing and rain removal from the windshield.
- This type of pattern and operating procedures may be used to carry out omnirange penetrations. Consult the Pilot's Handbook—ILS for the approved omni approach at your destination.
- If not contact when VFR minimums are reached, a controlled instrument approach must be made.

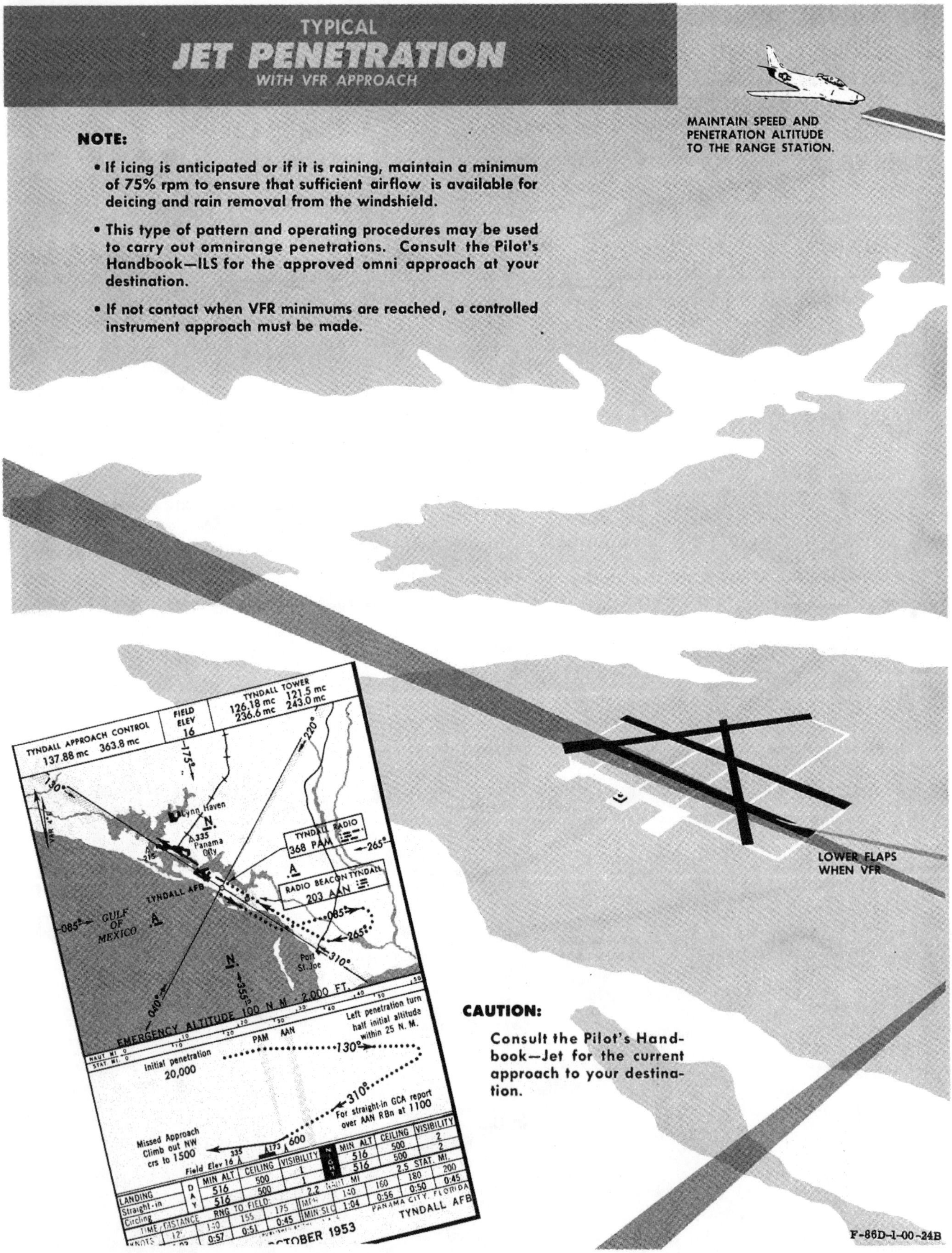

LOWER FLAPS WHEN VFR

CAUTION:
Consult the Pilot's Handbook—Jet for the current approach to your destination.

F-86D-1-00-24B

Figure 9-2

9-6

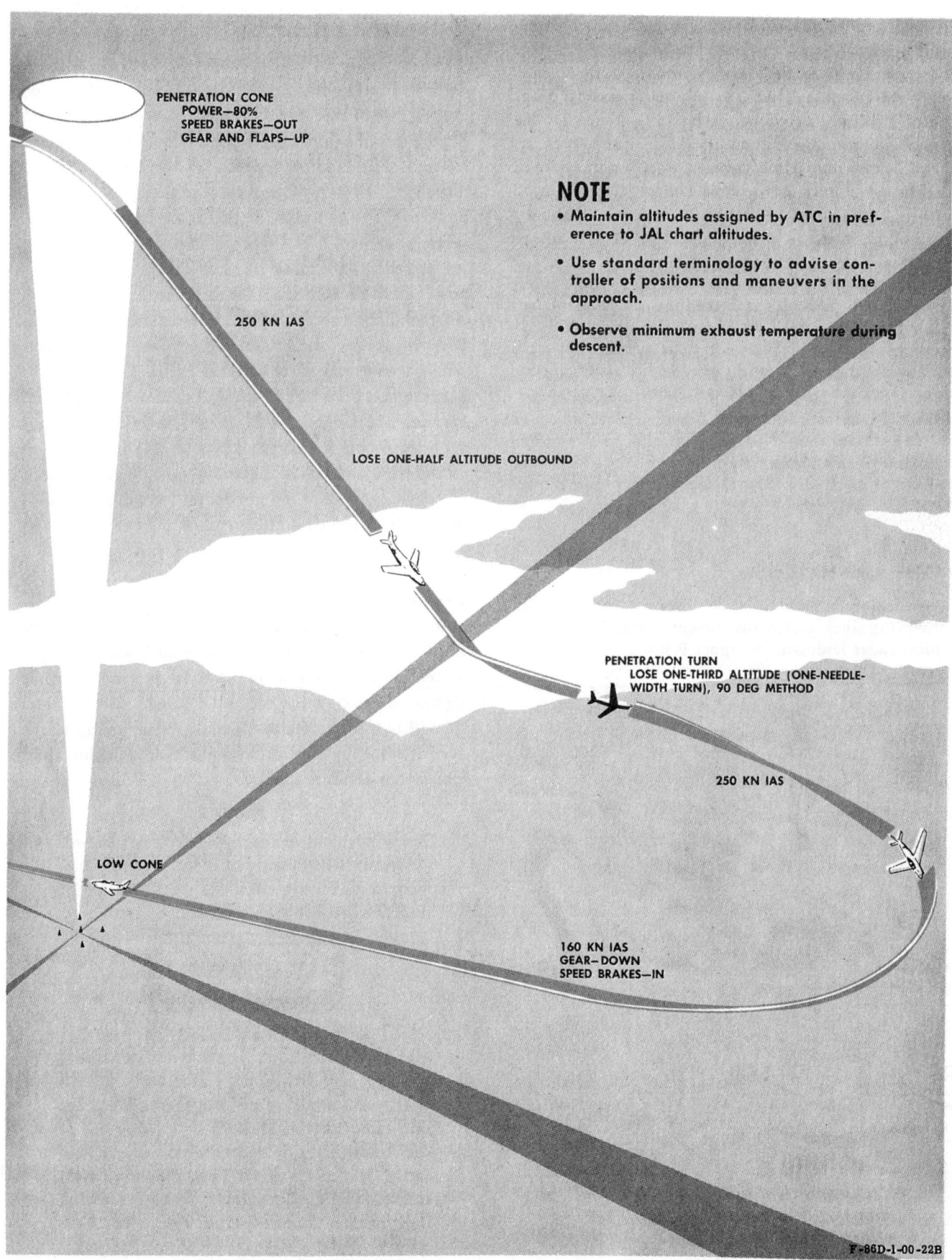

altitude to a point where VFR approach or an instrument approach (such as GCA, low-frequency range or ILAS) can be made. Penetration procedures for specific fields are given on JAL (jet approach and landing) charts. The Pilot's Handbook—Jet, in two parts for the eastern and western United States, has the JAL charts for all fields where jet penetration procedures have been established. Figure 9-1 shows a typical jet penetration with instrument approach, which is accomplished by beginning a letdown at the penetration cone (cruising altitude) on the heading specified in the JAL chart. The initial phase of the penetration is set up to avoid interference with altitudes occupied by other airplanes. After the high cone is crossed, a conventioned instrument approach is begun. A typical penetration with VFR approach is shown in figure 9-2. In such penetrations, if you are not VFR at low-cone altitude, an instrument approach must be made. The conditions set up in the JAL charts should be given careful consideration during flight planning. Availability of GCA, alternates, and operational problems in high-density traffic areas should be analyzed.

RADAR PENETRATIONS.

Radar letdowns with GCA landings are optimum for conserving fuel under instrument conditions. For a typical radar letdown, see figure 9-3.

Warning
It is imperative during descents that the altimeter be accurately read, with particular attention given to the **1000-** and **10,000-foot** pointers.

INSTRUMENT DESCENTS.

The best power setting for conservation of fuel during descents is START IDLE. However, 80% rpm will provide desired rate of descent and exhaust temperatures. Speed brakes should be opened, to limit airspeed and distance covered. The landing gear and wing flaps should be retracted. The autopilot is recommended for all types of instrument penetrations to enable you to maintain precision control over airspeed and pitch control during the descent. Descending turns on the autopilot present no problem because they are easily accomplished with the turn-knob control. Manual descents can be simplified with the use of the zero reader by one of two methods. Leaving the pitch attitude trim knob in zero position and using the horizontal needle as an artificial horizon, a full deflection of the needle will show about a 15-degree pitch change. The alternate method is to set the trim knob to the maximum nose down setting of 10 degrees and keep the horizontal bar centered. With this method, the dive angle can be increased by using a fly-up deflection. If icing conditions exist or are anticipated or if it is raining, maintain at least 75% rpm in descents to be assured that enough hot air will be available for deicing and rain removal. To aid in controlling air temperature to the windshield during a descent in rain (if rain removal air is used), ram air should be selected for cockpit cooling. Selecting ram air will reduce the temperature of the air going to the windshield, thus preventing windshield cracking from sudden temperature changes.

Note
The windshield and canopy defrost system provides sufficient heating of the transparent surfaces to effectively eliminate the formation of frost or fog during descent.

WARNING

When power is reduced below 75% rpm during an approach to the runway in a rainstorm, forward visibility will be obscured immediately, as hot air is no longer available for rain removal. Touch down by looking out of the windshield side panels, which will remain fairly clear at all times. Turn system off after touchdown if windshield overheat warning light has not illuminated. If light is on, leave system on and select ram air for cockpit cooling, which allows a gradual reduction of air temperature to windshield.

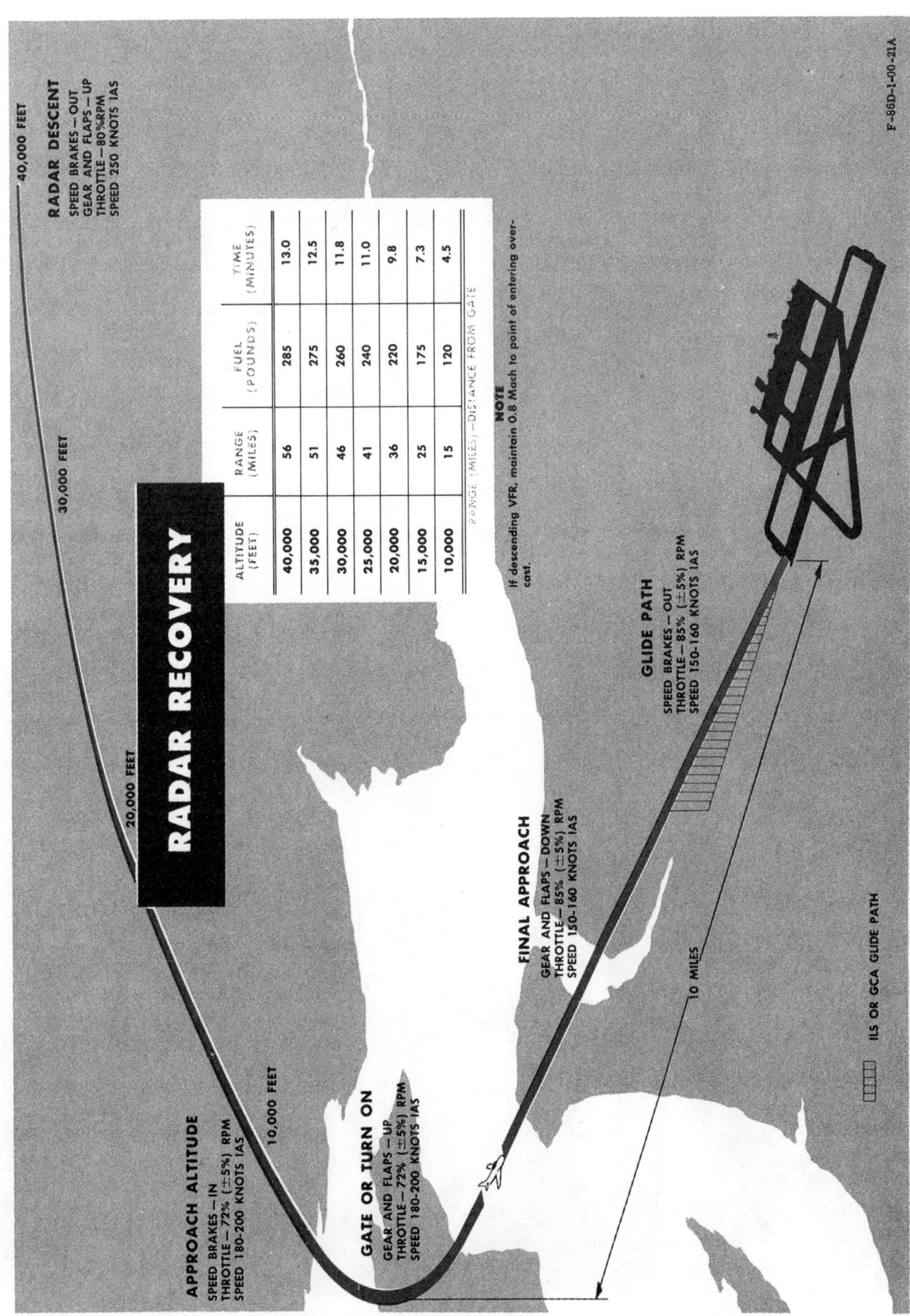

Figure 9-3

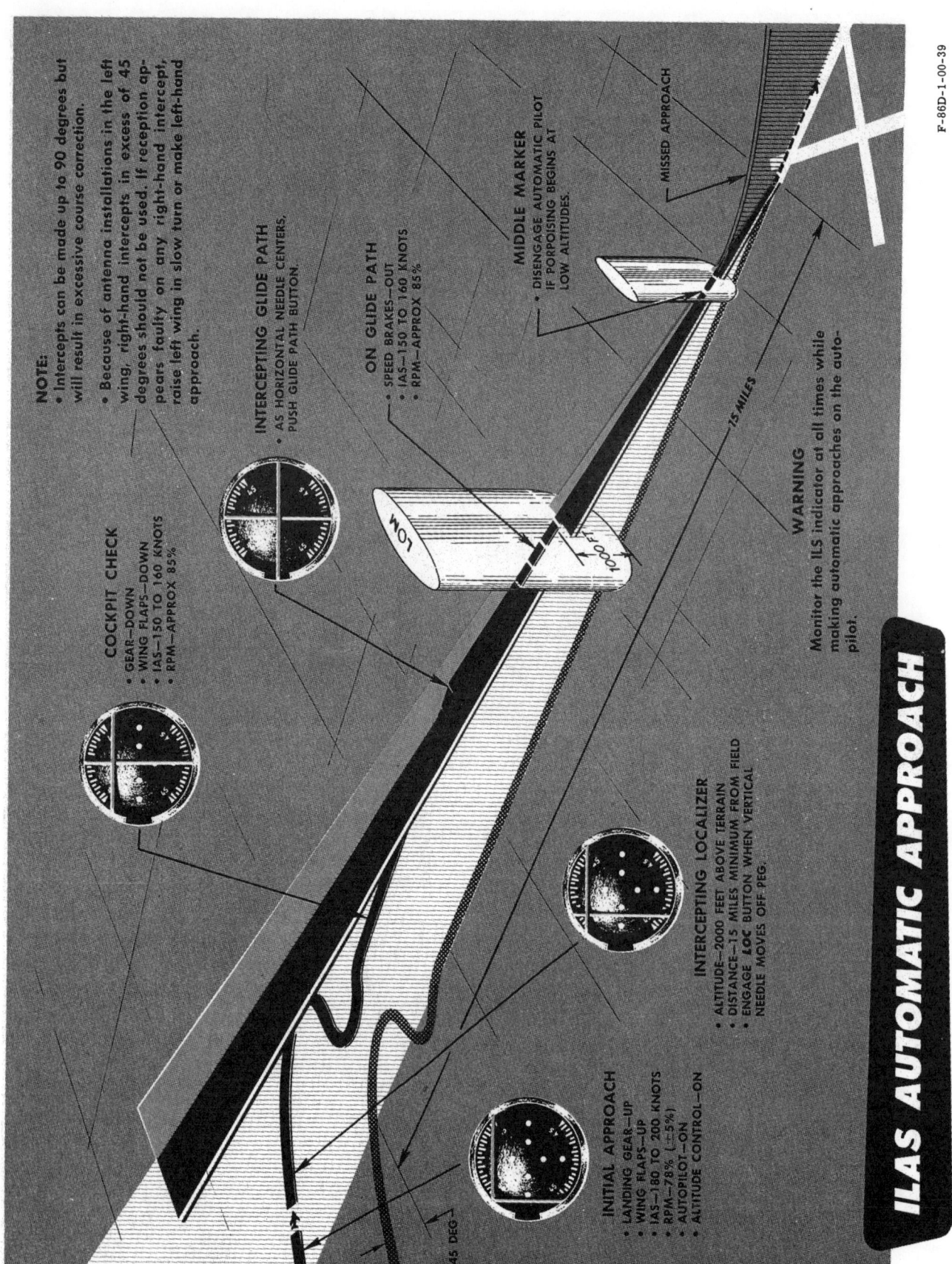

Figure 9-4

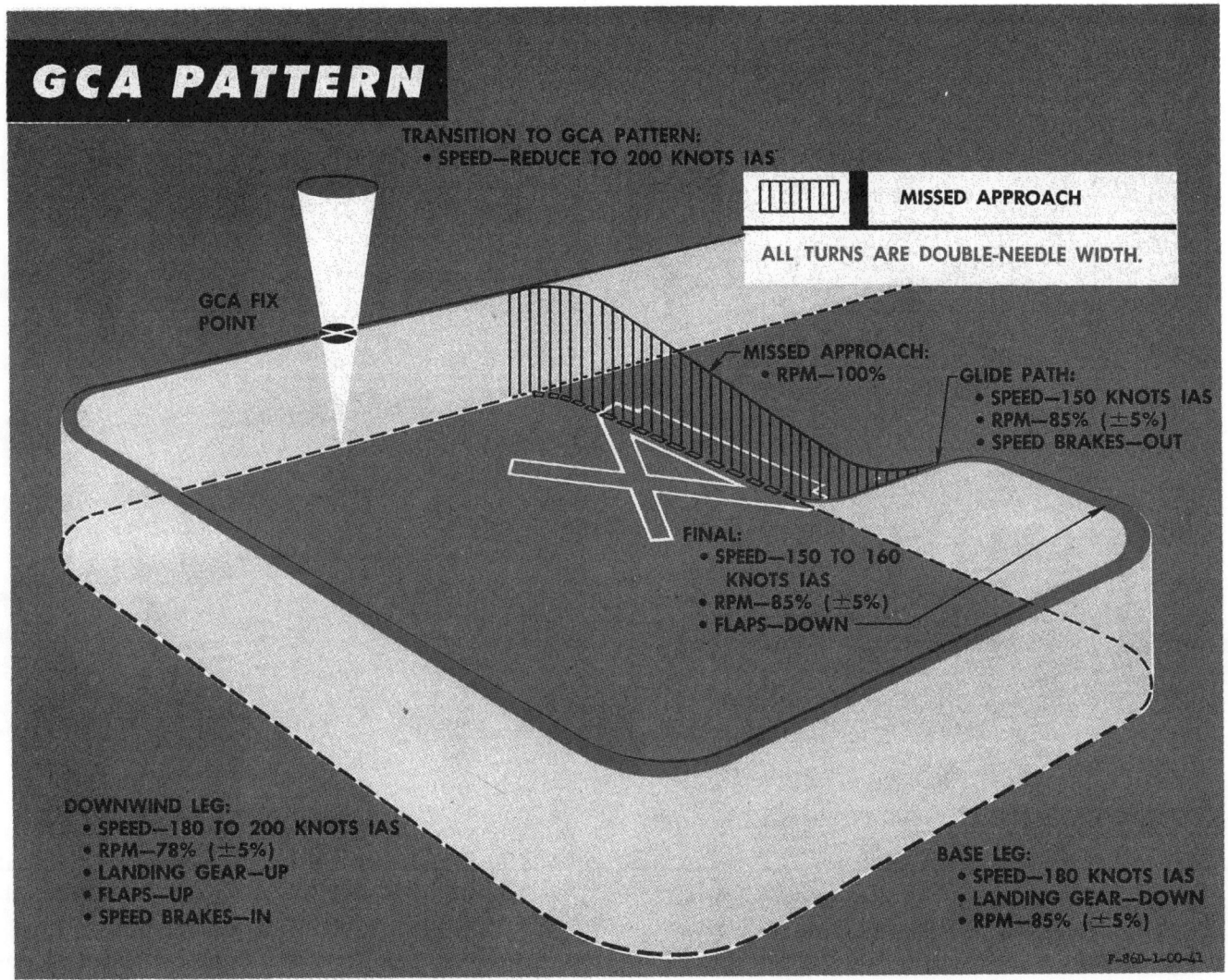

Figure 9-5

INSTRUMENT APPROACHES.

This airplane is equipped with radios and instruments, which will enable you to execute low-frequency range, ILAS, GCA, and ADF type approaches. Later models are equipped for omnirange approaches.* Flown with power settings from 75% to 85% rpm, power response to throttle movement is rapid and speed control is good at all times. Use of the deicing systems does not noticeably decrease available thrust, while use of windshield anti-icing increases forward visibility in rain. Runway stopping distances during landings out of low approaches are critical during rain or with ice on the runways. However, the drag chute will reduce these critical stopping distances considerably. You should use extreme caution by slowing the airplane to its correct speed as you approach touchdown, being careful to determine passage over the threshold lights at the same time. If you do not touch down at a normal speed immediately after crossing the threshold lights, execute a missed-approach and go-around. Once on the runway, drop the nose wheel and use maximum braking technique.

Low-frequency Range Approaches.

The normal low-frequency range approach as flown by conventional aircraft is seldom flown in this airplane. It will be flown as such if traffic control requires a standard jet penetration and you do not become VFR at the high cone. The low-frequency range approach procedure used by reciprocating engine airplanes may be used as part of a jet penetration with instrument approach, such as shown in figure 9-1. The range approach, in this case is begun after crossing the high cone. A jet penetration with VFR approach can be considered as combining the penetration and low-frequency range approach in one maneuver, such as in figure 9-2.

---

*F-86D-35 and later airplanes

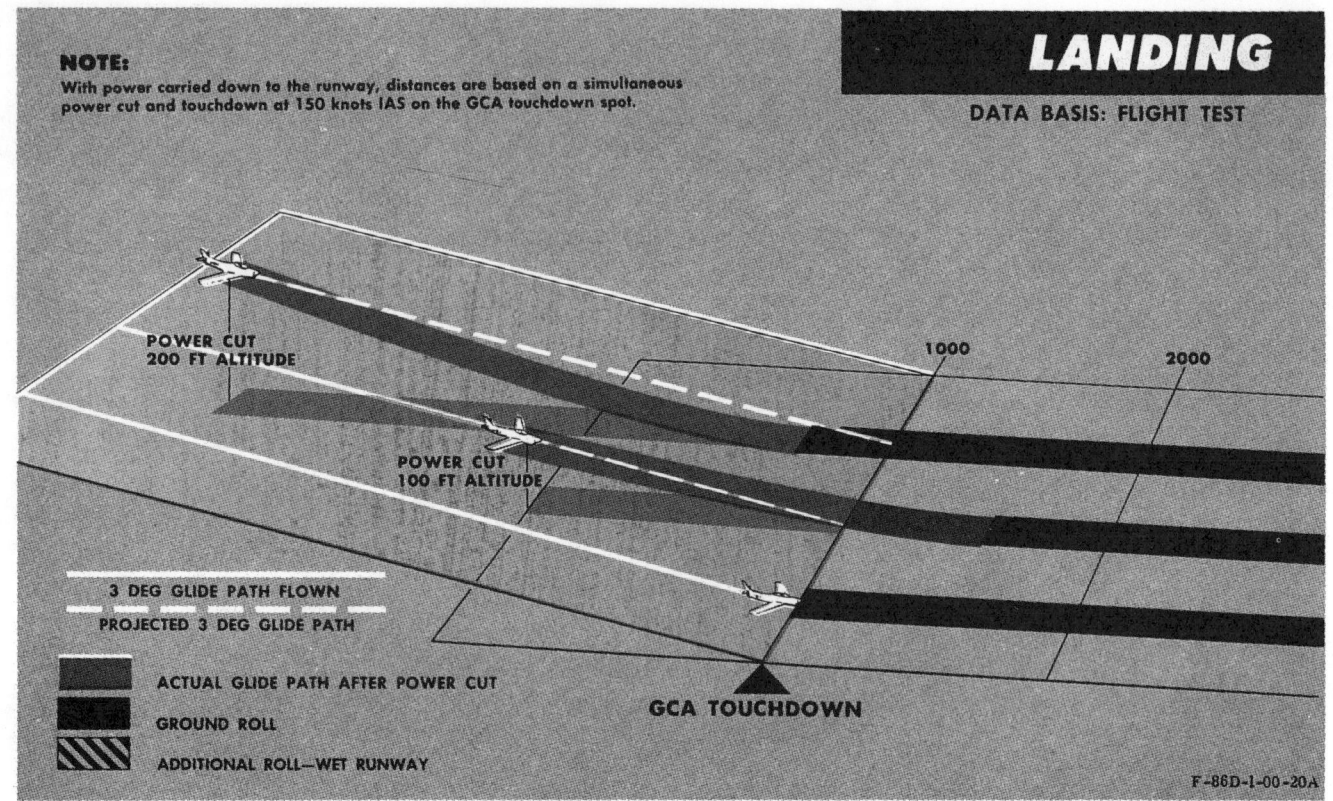

Figure 9-6

Ground-controlled Approaches.

Ground-controlled approaches can be successfully carried out in this airplane. However, the reduced reflecting surfaces of the clean design coupled with heavy precipitation can make it virtually impossible for the controllers to pick up your airplane during heavy rainstorms. The approaches can be satisfactorily carried out using the autopilot or the zero reader, but manual control flying attitude by reference to the flight instruments is considered more satisfactory. A typical approach is shown in figure 9-5. The runway distances required for a full stop landing, with power cuts at various altitudes, are shown in figure 9-6.

ILAS Approaches.

The instrument low approach system can be effectively used in this airplane whether it is flown manually or automatically. When you are using vhf frequencies and are not depending upon radar, heavy precipitation will not interfere with ILAS approaches. Where GCA is also available on the same runway, fly the ILAS approach and have GCA monitor you. This combination is considered the best setup for instrument approaches in minimum weather.

Automatic ILAS Approaches.

Automatic approaches are flown using the autopilot and approach coupler, which fly the airplane down the ILAS glide path and localizer course without any manual flight control by the pilot. A typical ILAS approach shown in figure 9-4 is flown as follows:

1. Before arrival over your last fix, study ILAS approach chart and visualize entire approach while firmly fixing headings and altitudes in your mind.

2. Set up your radio compass on outer compass locator or homer that will enable you to carry out transition to ILAS localizer course.

3. Tune vhf navigational receiver to ILAS frequency and identify it.

4. Initial approach to localizer should be flown with autopilot on. Altitude control, if installed, should be turned ON.

5. The preferable intercept is an angle of 60 degrees or less within a distance of 10 miles from the runway, and with a clean airplane at 180-200 knots IAS with 78% ($\pm 5\%$) rpm.

6. Closely monitor localizer needle to make sure alarm flag is retracted, and as needle moves to center of approach, lead turn onto the localizer course by one dot of needle deflection.

7. Push "LOCALIZER" button on approach coupler controller, and check for green light on, to show engagement.

8. Monitor approach indicator continuously to make sure that airplane is well established on localizer course.

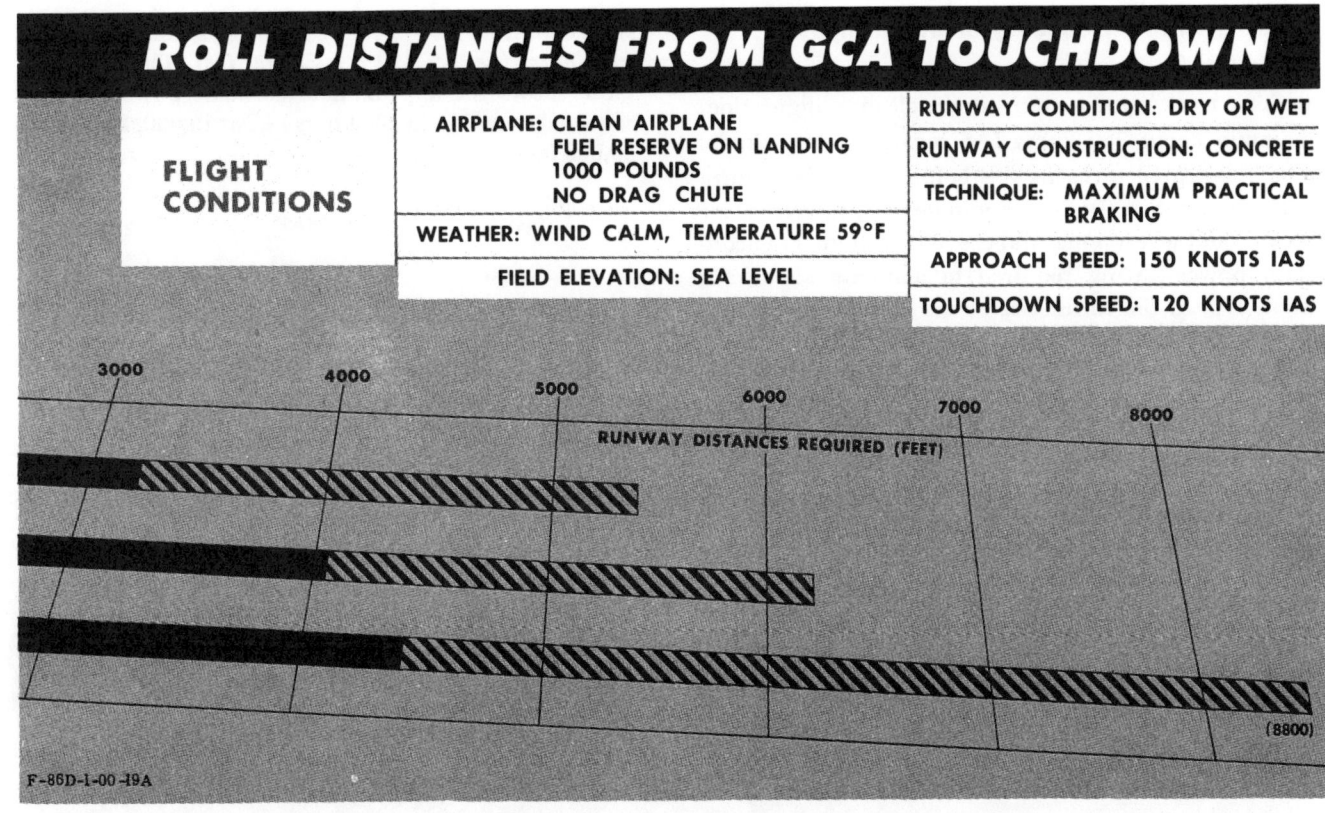

Note

Intercepting the localizer course at angles in excess of 45 degrees will make it difficult for the approach coupler signals to establish the airplane on course without several corrections. Entry angles in excess of 90 degrees will result in the airplane still correcting as the runway is approached.

9. When turn on is complete, perform landing cockpit check, reducing speed to 150-160 knots IAS at 85% (±5%) rpm with landing gear and wing flaps down.

10. Approaching glide path, push glide path button as horizontal needle moves down and reaches center of approach indicator.

11. Speed brake switch—OUT. Return switch to neutral after extension.

12. Assume manual control when definitely VFR or when glide path porpoising occurs by raising turn knob on the flight controller or squeezing automatic pilot release switch on the stick. Automatic control should be effective down to 200 feet altitude.

13. Execute missed approach upon reaching ILAS minimums by disengaging approach coupler and pulling up manually.

Manual ILAS Approaches With Zero Reader.

Manual approaches using the zero reader differ only in that the zero reader must be set up to enable you to correctly fly the localizer and glide path manually.

1. Set localizer heading on heading indicator.

2. Set zero reader selector control to RIGHT (blue). If flying backside of ILAS, set selector control to LEFT (blue).

3. Approaching glide path, turn zero reader selector switch to APPROACH.

4. Keep zero reader needles centered, and monitor approach indicator.

5. Execute missed approach by setting pitch trim knob to fly up, and selector switch to FLIGHT INST., which will enable you to assume a safe climb out.

Missed-approach Go-around.

1. Throttle—100% rpm. Afterburner can be used in an emergency, but ordinary use is not advised because of high fuel consumption.

2. Speed brake switch—IN. Return switch to neutral after full retraction.

3. Landing gear handle—UP.

4. Wing flap lever—UP at 160 knots IAS.

5. Execute missed-approach procedure on chart or as directed.

Section IX
T. O. 1F-86D-1

Holding-on Low-frequency or Omniranges.

For holding over radio range or omni stations or fixes in "race track" type patterns in the clean configuration, maintain about 200 knots IAS regardless of altitude. The 180-degree turns in the holding pattern require more power than the 2- or 3-minute legs; therefore, for maximum fuel economy and ease of handling, hold constant power setting required to maintain about 200 knots IAS in the turns. Use of the autopilot is recommended for holding. *The optimum altitude for holding, consistent with satisfactory handling characteristics and maximum fuel economy, is 30,000 feet.* The following table shows the approximate constant power settings required to maintain 200 knots IAS at 10,000, 20,000 and 30,000 feet:

ALTITUDE (feet)	KNOTS (IAS)	POWER (% rpm)
10,000	200	85
20,000	200	85
30,000	200	97

ICE AND RAIN

When flying on instruments, the possibility of engine or airfoil icing is often present. However, this airplane will normally operate above serious icing levels, and its high performance makes it possible to fly out of dangerous icing altitudes. If the airplane does ice up, remember the two most serious aspects. First, engine ice can result in serious engine damage. Second, regardless of amount, airfoil ice destroys lift and creates drag. This in turn raises stalling speeds abnormally high, requiring careful airspeed control on landing.

ENGINE ICING.

WARNING

Because of the features of the electronic engine controls, there has been no positive way established for detecting engine icing by reference to the engine instruments during operation on the main fuel system. Use of airplane anti-ice equipment is recommended when flying in areas of known icing.

WING ICING.

Even in the most severe icing conditions, simultaneous operation of all anti-icing systems will keep all heated surfaces clear of ice without noticeable loss of engine thrust. The surface anti-icing system is very effective in deicing the airplane, if ice is allowed to accumulate on wings and tail. *However, the purpose of the anti-icing systems is to prevent formation of ice rather than to dispose of ice already formed.* Therefore, use all anti-icing systems continuously whenever conditions show there is a possibility of icing. Maintain a minimum of 75% rpm to allow the system to operate at full efficiency.

WARNING

- Ice around the leading edges of the air inlet duct, the accessory cover, the inlet screens, and around the engine compressor inlet can be extremely hazardous. Also, if windshield and radome heat is not used in icing conditions, it is possible for a considerable amount of ice to accumulate on the radome. Therefore, operation of the surface anti-icing system is recommended when in icing conditions.

- If any well-formed ice formation erodes or melts off and blows back into the intake duct and compressor section, possible engine damage may occur. Therefore, it is unsafe to fly in icing conditions unless all of the anti-icing systems are in operation.

USE OF ANTI-ICE SYSTEMS.

Place the engine inlet switch in the ACCESSORY COVER position as a precautionary measure during all flights in weather regardless of icing probability. (Refer to "Anti-icing and Defrosting Systems," Section IV.)

All systems may be used simultaneously during take-off and instrument approaches without noticeable loss in thrust. Therefore, if taking off in conditions of freezing rain or severe icing, all systems should be operated. Wing leading edge anti-icing is not at maximum efficiency below approximately 180 knots IAS clean, and approximately 160 knots IAS in the landing configuration, because the leading edge slats will be partially or fully opened.

TURBULENCE AND THUNDERSTORMS

Thunderstorm flying demands considerable instrument experience and should not be intentionally undertaken unless you are a well-qualified pilot. However, thunderstorm penetrations can safely be flown by experienced pilots using modern equipment and the recommended procedures.

> **CAUTION**
>
> If at all possible, avoid flight through a thunderstorm to prevent hail damage to the airplane. The plastic radome can be seriously damaged to the point of disintegration by the impact of hail and heavy rain. However, many routine flight operations require a certain amount of thunderstorm flying because it is not always possible to avoid storm areas. Especially at night, it is often impossible to detect individual storms and find the in-between clear areas.

Constant throttle setting, constant pitch attitude, and light stick forces are the keys to flying this airplane in turbulent air. The power setting and pitch attitude required for the recommended penetration airspeed should be established before entering the storm. Avoid making abrupt pitch corrections when the nose pitches up or down in strong drafts or gusts. Avoid chasing the airspeed indicator because the readings are unreliable during pressure changes within the storm cell and have been known to go to zero during thunderstorm penetration. Fly by pitch attitude reference, and airspeed and altitude will remain constant regardless of readings. "Half-the-battle" of a thunderstorm penetration is mental preparation. Prepare yourself mentally for the worst, ride the storm, and let your good judgment and instrument flight ability get you through. Specific instructions for preparing to enter a thunderstorm and flying through it are given in the following paragraphs:

BEFORE TAKE-OFF.

Perform the following before take-off when flight through a thunderstorm is anticipated:

1. Make a thorough analysis of the general weather situation to determine thunderstorm areas, and prepare a flight plan that will avoid these areas whenever possible.

2. Be sure to check the flight instruments, navigation equipment, pitot heater, interior lighting, and anti-icing equipment.

APPROACHING THE STORM.

It is imperative that you prepare the airplane before entering a zone of turbulent air. If the storm cannot be seen, its proximity may be detected by radio crash static. Prepare the airplane as follows:

1. Adjust throttle as necessary to obtain a safe penetration speed.

2. Pitot heater switch—ON.

3. Surface anti-ice switch—ON.

4. Engine inlet switch—ANTI-ICE on F-86D-1 Airplanes; ACCESSORY COVER on F-86D-5 and later airplanes.

5. Windshield and radome anti-ice system—ON.

6. Safety belt tight *(this is very important)*.

7. Shoulder harness locked.

8. Turn radio volume down during severe crash static conditions.

9. At night, turn cockpit lights to full intensity to minimize blinding effect of lightning. On F-86D-25 and later airplanes, turn on thunderstorm lights.

Note
Make every effort to avoid looking up from the instrument panel at lightning flashes. The blinding effect of lightning can be reduced by lowering the seat.

10. Use the radarscope to pick "soft" spots.

Note
Do not lower gear or wing flaps, as they decrease the aerodynamic efficiency of the airplane.

IN THE STORM.

While flying through the storm, observe the following:

1. Maintain power setting and pitch attitude established before entering storm. Do not chase airspeed indicator, since this will result in extreme attitudes. If a sudden gust should be encountered while in a nose-high attitude, a stall might result. Use as little horizontal tail control as possible to minimize the possibility of inducing "porpoising" which might, together with gust effect, overstress the airplane.

2. Devote all attention to flying airplane.

3. Expect turbulence, precipitation, and lightning. Do not allow these conditions to cause undue concern.

4. *Maintain attitude.* Concentrate principally on holding a level attitude by reference to the attitude indicator.

5. Maintain original heading. Do not make any turns unless absolutely necessary.

6. Don't chase altimeter. It may be in error because of differential barometric pressure within the storm. An indicated gain or loss of several thousand feet should be expected. Make allowance for this error in determining minimum safe altitude.

Note
A comfortable penetration speed for entering a zone of turbulent air is 250 knots IAS.

NIGHT FLYING

There are no specific techniques for flying this airplane at night which differ from those required for daylight operation.

WARNING

Be alert when landing light is on, to avoid following light beam into ground.

COLD-WEATHER PROCEDURES

Icing conditions are covered under "Ice and Rain" in this section. While still a factor for successful cold-weather operation, generally cold-weather postflight preparation is not as critical in jet-powered airplane operation as in reciprocating-engine airplane operation, because there is no need for oil dilution, etc. To expedite preflight inspection and ensure satisfactory flight during cold-weather operation, adhere to the normal operating procedures outlined in Section II, with the following additions and exceptions.

BEFORE ENTERING COCKPIT.

1. At temperatures below −26°C (−15°F), have preheat used in cockpit and on canopy seal.

2. Check entire airplane for freedom from frost, snow, and ice. Check that all light snow, ice, or frost is removed. Do not permit ground crew to chip or scrape away ice, as this may damage airplane.

WARNING

The collection of snow, frost, and ice on the airplane surfaces constitutes one of the major flight hazards in low-temperature operation and can result in the loss of lift and treacherous stalling characteristics.

3. Be sure that wing slats move freely and that they can be closed manually.

> **CAUTION**

Slat retaining straps are provided to hold wing slats in a closed position during preheating of flight surfaces. Check that these straps are removed before flight.

4. Make sure shock struts and actuating cylinders are clear of ice and dirt.

5. Check oil cooler drain and fuel tank drain cocks for ice and for drain condensate.

6. Inspect pitot tube, fuel tank vent, and oil tank vent, and have any ice removed.

7. Check fuel system for proper fuel.

Note

JP-4 fuel (Specification MIL-F-5624), or gasoline (Specification MIL-F-5572) if JP-4 fuel is not available, should be used at all temperatures below −18°C (0°F) to provide satisfactory low-temperature engine starts.

8. Inspect lower portion of engine compressor section for evidence of ice formation on forward stator and rotor blades. If accumulation of ice can be seen or is suspected in the area of the compressor or turbine sections, check engine for freedom of rotation.

Note

External heat must be applied to forward section of engine to remove ice. Engine should be started as soon as possible after heating, to prevent moisture from refreezing.

9. Be sure that an external power source of 28.5 volts at 1200 amperes surge and a continuous current of 500 amperes is available for starting. Have preheat used on engine accessory section. If necessary, ground heating equipment can be connected to the engine air intake duct, cockpit air conditioning and pressurization system, rocket package, or tail-pipe nozzle.

WARM-UP AND GROUND CHECK.

1. Check to ensure that emergency fuel regulator and variable nozzle are adjusted in accordance with cold-weather requirements. (See figure 2-4.)

Note

In extremely cold weather, it may not be possible to close variable nozzle enough to maintain rated exhaust temperature under all flight conditions.

Warning

This airplane is not equipped with parking brakes. Use firmly anchored wheel chocks for engine run-ups. Make sure the airplane is tied down securely before attempting a full-power run-up. During low outside air temperatures, the thrust developed at all engine speeds is noticeably greater.

F-86D-1-0-8

2. Turn on cockpit air conditioning system and windshield and canopy defrosting system as required, immediately after engine start.

> **CAUTION**

Make sure all instruments have been sufficiently warmed up to ensure normal operation. Check for sluggish instruments during taxiing.

TAXIING.

1. Avoid taxiing in deep snow, as taxiing and steering are extremely difficult and frozen brakes are likely to result.

2. To conserve battery life while taxiing at low engine speeds, use only essential electrical equipment.

3. Increase space between airplanes while taxiing at subfreezing temperatures, to ensure safe stopping distance and to prevent icing of airplane surfaces by melted snow and ice in the jet blast of a preceding airplane.

4. Minimize taxi time to conserve fuel and reduce amount of ice fog generated by jet engines.

BEFORE TAKE-OFF.

1. Make normal full-power check if on a dry, clear runway; however, if take-off is started on ice or snow,

make check during the initial part of the take-off roll. Do not attempt to hold the brakes while the engine is accelerating and the take-off roll is beginning, as you are likely to lose control of the airplane if one wheel begins to slide ahead of the other.

2. Turn pitot heater switch ON.

3. Retract engine inlet screens whenever take-off is to be made into known, or possible, icing conditions.

AFTER TAKE-OFF.

1. After take-off from a wet snow- or slush-covered field, operate brakes several times to expel wet snow or slush, and operate landing gear and wing flaps through several complete cycles to prevent their freezing in retracted position. (Expect considerably slower operation of the landing gear in cold weather, due to stiffening of all lubricants.)

Do not exceed the landing gear and wing flap down limit airspeed during the operation.

2. Check instruments. At extremely low outside air temperatures, instruments should be sufficiently warmed up to ensure reliable operation.

DURING FLIGHT.

1. Use cockpit air conditioning system as desired.

2. Use anti-icing and defrosting systems continuously whenever conditions indicate possible icing.

Care should be taken when flying in known icing conditions with the slats open, as ice removal is very slow at or around the slats.

DESCENT.

1. Operate windshield and canopy defrost system to clear windshield armor glass of frost usually formed during rapid descent from altitude.

Note

The windshield and canopy defrost system provides sufficient heating of the transparent surfaces to effectively eliminate the formation of frost or fog during descent.

2. Check engine operating temperatures during descents and in traffic pattern, as low temperatures are common at low altitudes because of frequent temperature inversions.

3. If icing conditions exist, use at least 75% rpm, which is required to operate the deicing system.

APPROACH.

1. Make normal pattern and landing, but allow for flatter glide due to increased thrust caused by extremely low surrounding air temperatures.

2. Pump brake pedals several times to free any accumulated ice.

AFTER LANDING.

1. Deploy drag chute below 150 knots IAS.

The drag chute should not be deployed in 90-degree cross winds exceeding 20 knots or in 45-degree cross winds exceeding 30 knots because of weather cocking tendencies of the airplane with the chute deployed.

- In an emergency, however, the drag chute may be deployed during cross-wind landing to provide fast decelerations, but only after the nose wheel is on the ground; then jettison the chute as soon as practical if excessive yaw develops. Be prepared to use brakes, rudder, and/or nose wheel steering to maintain directional control. (On wet or icy runways, brakes and nose wheel steering are relatively ineffective.)

- Caution should be used if possible, to be sure that the drag chute will clear other airplanes if it becomes necessary to jettison the chute to maintain control after touchdown.

2. If snow and ice tires are installed on airplane, apply brakes intermittently and carefully to keep treads from filling and glazing over.

Note

Hard braking on icy or wet runways may result in dangerous skidding or fishtailing.

3. If conditions permit, taxi with enough rpm to cut in the generator, as low temperatures decrease battery output.

4. Turn pitot heater switch OFF.

| CAUTION |

The drag chute should be jettisoned before taxiing downwind in winds exceeding 15 knots because of the possibility of the chute collapsing and risers burning by contact on hot areas of exhaust nozzle.

STOPPING ENGINE.

The engine is stopped in the normal manner. Since JP-4 fuel or gasoline is used, it is unnecessary to drain fuel tanks and lines.

BEFORE LEAVING AIRPLANE.

1. If it is not snowing or raining, leave canopy partly open to allow circulation within cockpit, to prevent canopy cracking from differential contraction, and to decrease windshield and canopy frosting.

2. Check that protective covers are installed on canopy and pitot head. Allow 15 minutes after engine shutdown before installing intake and exhaust duct covers.

3. Whenever possible, leave airplane parked with full fuel tanks. Every effort should be made during servicing to prevent moisture from entering the fuel system.

4. Check that batteries are removed when airplane is parked outside at temperatures below −29°C (−20°F) for more than 4 hours.

HOT-WEATHER AND DESERT PROCEDURES

BEFORE TAKE-OFF.

The emergency fuel regulator is set to give 96% rpm on a 100°F day, and does not compensate for temperature changes. If the emergency fuel system is turned on at maximum rpm when temperature is above 100°F, the engine may overspeed.

| CAUTION |

If the airplane is based at a field where normal temperature range is above 100°F, the emergency regulator should be reset as soon as possible to give the 100°F day setting (figure 2-4) at the maximum outside air temperature.

If the emergency regulator has been reset, the normal preflight fuel control system tests may be performed and the normal take-off procedure may be followed. If outside air temperatures are excessively high and the emergency fuel regulator has not been reset to the higher outside air temperature, test the fuel control system as follows:

1. With emergency fuel system switch at NORM, advance throttle to 80% to 85% rpm and move emergency fuel system switch to ON. A slight increase in engine speed verifies that the emergency regulator is controlling fuel flow and is set for a lower temperature. Return emergency fuel system switch to NORM.

| CAUTION |

No other fuel control system test should be performed at outside air temperatures of more than 100°F because of possible engine overspeed on the emergency regulator.

On airplanes with the three-position emergency fuel system switch, when the outside air temperatures are excessively high and the emergency fuel regulator has not been reset to the higher outside air temperature, a take-off may be accomplished if the emergency fuel system switch is first positioned at ON momentarily. Then, without hesitating at TAKE OFF, move switch to NORM in order to use the automatic lockup system features during take-off.

WARNING

- Do not position emergency fuel system switch to TAKE OFF or ON at engine speeds near 100% rpm. This may result in overspeed.

- With the emergency fuel system switch at NORM, the emergency regulator cannot take over the fuel control. Consequently, if the main fuel control valve fails, the throttle must be immediately retarded to START IDLE and the emergency fuel system switch placed ON to prevent engine failure. The throttle must then be cautiously advanced to obtain the desired power.

Note

Do not attempt to take off in a sandstorm or dust storm. Park the airplane cross-wind and shut down engine to prevent sand or dirt from damaging engine.

TAKE-OFF.

The increase in required take-off distances commonly associated with hot-weather operation of any airplane is even greater when the airplane is powered by jet engines. (See figures A-3 and A-4 for take-off distances at various temperatures.)

AFTER TAKE-OFF AND DURING CLIMB.

On airplanes with the three-position emergency fuel switch installed, during hot-weather operation, the engine may overspeed during the climb after take-off. This overspeed is gradual and is a result of the emergency fuel system overriding the main fuel system, when the emergency fuel system switch is in the TAKE OFF position. If the emergency fuel system switch is positioned to NORM with the overspeed condition present, what appears to be a complete power loss will occur. (Refer to Section VII for further information.) If engine overspeed tends to exceed 104% rpm during climb after take-off, while operating in afterburner range with the emergency fuel system switch at TAKE OFF, perform the following:

1. Move emergency fuel system switch to NORM.

2. Immediately and rapidly retard throttle to below MILITARY stop.

Note

When emergency fuel system switch is positioned to NORM, a loss in power results. For this reason, the throttle must be retarded rapidly from the afterburner range.

3. Readvance throttle to desired setting. Engine will respond on the main fuel system.

If engine overspeed stabilizes at about 102% rpm, the climb may be continued without any power change being made. As altitude is increased, the engine speed will return to 100% rpm. However, before the emergency fuel system switch is positioned to NORM, the engine must be allowed to remain stabilized at 100% rpm for about 15 seconds.

BEFORE LEAVING AIRPLANE.

1. If sand or dust is not blowing, leave canopy slightly open to permit air circulation within cockpit.

2. Check that protective covers are installed on pitot head, canopy, and intake and exhaust ducts.

T. O. 1F-86D-1

Reproduction for non-military use of the information or illustrations contained in this publication is not permitted without specific approval of the issuing service (BuAer or USAF). The policy for use of Classified Publications is established for the Air Force in AFR 205-1 and for the Navy in Navy Regulations, Article 1509.

LIST OF EFFECTIVE PAGES

INSERT LATEST REVISED PAGES. DESTROY SUPERSEDED PAGES.

NOTE: The portion of the text affected by the current revision is indicated by a vertical line in the outer margins of the page.

This publication consists of the following pages:

Page No.	Date of Latest Issue
i through iv	18 May 1956
1-1 through 1-60	18 May 1956
2-1 through 2-38	18 May 1956
3-1 through 3-24	18 May 1956
4-1 through 4-48	18 May 1956
5-1 through 5-6	18 May 1956
6-1 through 6-24	18 May 1956
7-1 through 7-14	18 May 1956
9-1 through 9-22	18 May 1956
A-1 through A-50	18 May 1956
Index-1 through Index-8	18 May 1956

*The asterisk indicates pages revised, added or deleted by the current revision.

ADDITIONAL COPIES OF THIS PUBLICATION MAY BE OBTAINED AS FOLLOWS:

USAF ACTIVITIES.—In accordance with Technical Order No. 00-5-2.
NAVY ACTIVITIES.—Submit request to nearest supply point listed below, using form NavAer-140; NASD, Philadelphia, Pa.; NAS, Alameda, Calif.; NAS, Jacksonville, Fla.; NAS, Norfolk, Va.; NAS, San Diego, Calif.; NAS, Seattle, Wash.; ASD, NSC, Guam.
For listing of available material and details of distribution, see Naval Aeronautics Publications Index NavAer 00-500.

Appendix I

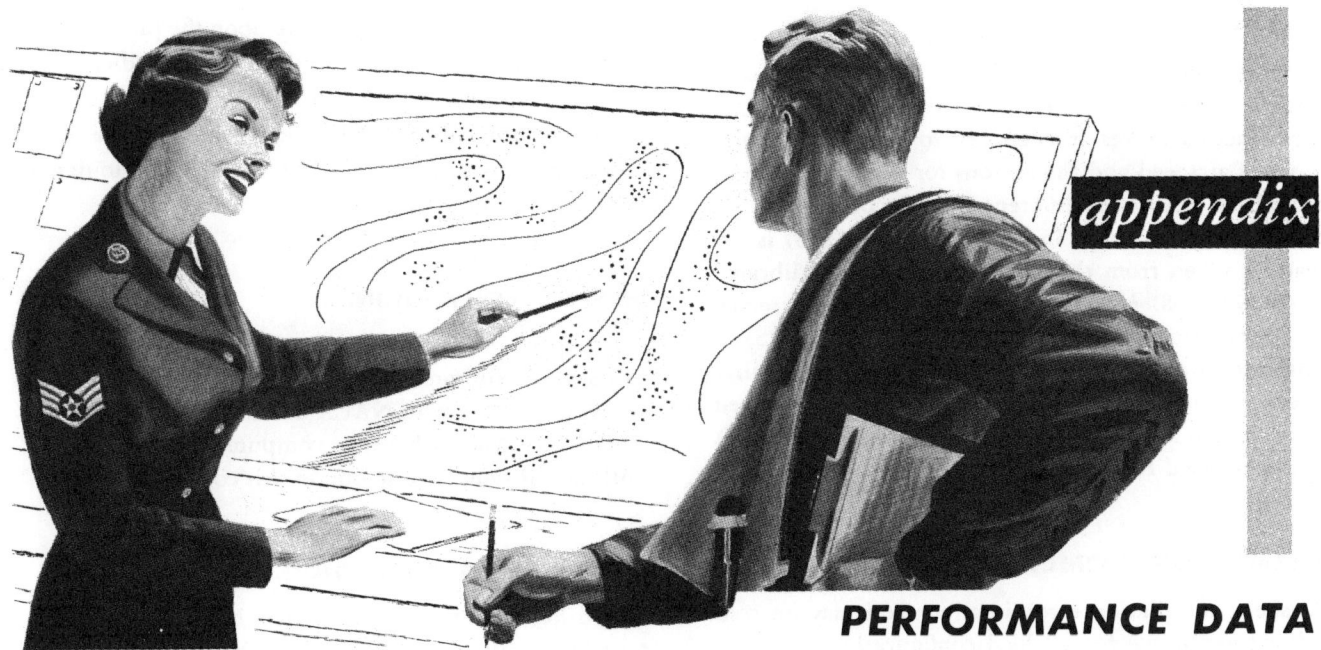

PERFORMANCE DATA

F-86D-1-00-77

TABLE OF CONTENTS	PAGE
Discussion of Charts	A-1
Compressibility Correction	A-2
Airspeed Conversion	A-3
Take-off Distances	A-18
Take-off Acceleration	A-20
Refusal Speeds	A-21
Profile Charts (Clean Configuration)	
Climb Profile	A-22
Mission Profile	A-23
Intercept Profile	A-24
Optimum Return Profile	A-25
Maximum Endurance Profile	A-26
Optimum Maximum Endurance Profile	A-27

	PAGE
Profile Charts (Two 120-gallon Drop Tanks)	
Climb Profile	A-28
Mission Profile	A-29
Intercept Profile	A-30
Optimum Return Profile	A-31
Maximum Endurance Profile	A-32
Optimum Maximum Endurance Profile	A-33
Combat Allowance	A-34
Descent Graphs	A-36
Landing Distances	A-38
Climb Graphs	A-40
Nautical Miles Per Pound of Fuel Graphs	A-46

INTRODUCTION.

The flight performance charts in this section provide the pilot with data for flight planning purposes. Two types of charts are included: (1) Profile-type charts for maximum range, endurance, and Maximum Continuous Thrust operation, and (2) graphical charts for take-off, climb, nautical miles per pound of fuel, descents, and landings. The profile-type charts are a supplement to the graphical data and help flight planning by reducing the computations that must be made. These charts are based on the recommended climb and cruise settings shown on the profile for the particular load configuration of the airplane. This type of presentation gives a direct indication of the fuel and time required to cover a given distance, if the recommended settings are maintained. For cruise at Mach numbers other than those given on the profile charts, the graphical charts should be used for flight planning. A decrease in weight has been accounted for as fuel is consumed. The graphical charts supply cruise performance data throughout the operating speed range of the airplane. For flight planning where accurate results are necessary, the graphical data should be used. All charts are based on NACA Standard Day conditions. Airplanes equipped with J47-GE-33 engines have an improved Maximum Thrust climb performance. A note on each Maximum Thrust climb chart shows the percent changes which must be incorporated in the time, fuel, and distance to climb with the -33 engine. Other performance is the same as for airplanes with J47-GE-17 or -17B engines.

AIRSPEED CORRECTIONS.

Several mechanical and physical factors must be considered to obtain true ground speed. The influence of these factors makes it necessary to recognize several types of airspeed and the reasons for the conversion of each. Each airspeed is different from the other and each has its own definition. Indicated airspeed (IAS) is the reading taken from the airspeed indicator. Calibrated airspeed (CAS) is indicated airspeed (IAS) corrected for installation effects. Equivalent airspeed (EAS) is calibrated airspeed (CAS) corrected for compressibility effects. True airspeed (TAS) is equivalent airspeed corrected for atmospheric density. True ground speed is TAS corrected for wind.

INSTALLATION CORRECTION.

Airspeed installation error is minor and may be considered negligible for all load configurations.

COMPRESSIBILITY CORRECTION.

Equivalent airspeed (EAS) is calibrated airspeed (CAS) corrected for compressibility effects. Though the difference between EAS and CAS is negligible at low speeds and low altitudes, impact pressure upon the pitot tube at high speeds increases, causing the airspeed indicator to show values above normal. The correction factors shown in the compressibility correction table (figure A-1) should be subtracted from calibrated airspeed to determine equivalent airspeed.

AIRSPEED CONVERSION.

An airspeed conversion graph (figure A-2) is provided to convert calibrated airspeed (CAS) directly to true airspeed (TAS) on an NACA Standard Day. The Type AN5834-1 dead-reckoning computer (formerly the E6B) also may be used to obtain this conversion.

MACH NUMBER CORRECTION.

The difference between indicated Mach number and *true* Mach number at all speeds is negligible.

TAKE-OFF DISTANCES.

Ground-run distances and total distances to clear a 50-foot obstacle with Maximum and Military Thrust are plotted in the take-off distance graphs (figures A-3 and

COMPRESSIBILITY CORRECTION

SUBTRACT CORRECTION FROM CALIBRATED AIRSPEED
TO OBTAIN EQUIVALENT AIRSPEED

PRESSURE ALTITUDE	CAS—KNOTS									
	150	200	250	300	350	400	450	500	550	600
5,000	0	0	1	2	2	3	5	6	8	10
10,000	0	1	2	3	5	7	10	13	17	21
15,000	1	2	3	5	8	12	16	21	27	
20,000	1	3	5	8	12	17	23	31		
25,000	2	4	7	11	17	24	32			
30,000	2	5	9	15	23	32				
35,000	3	7	12	20	29					
40,000	4	9	16	25						

Figure A-1

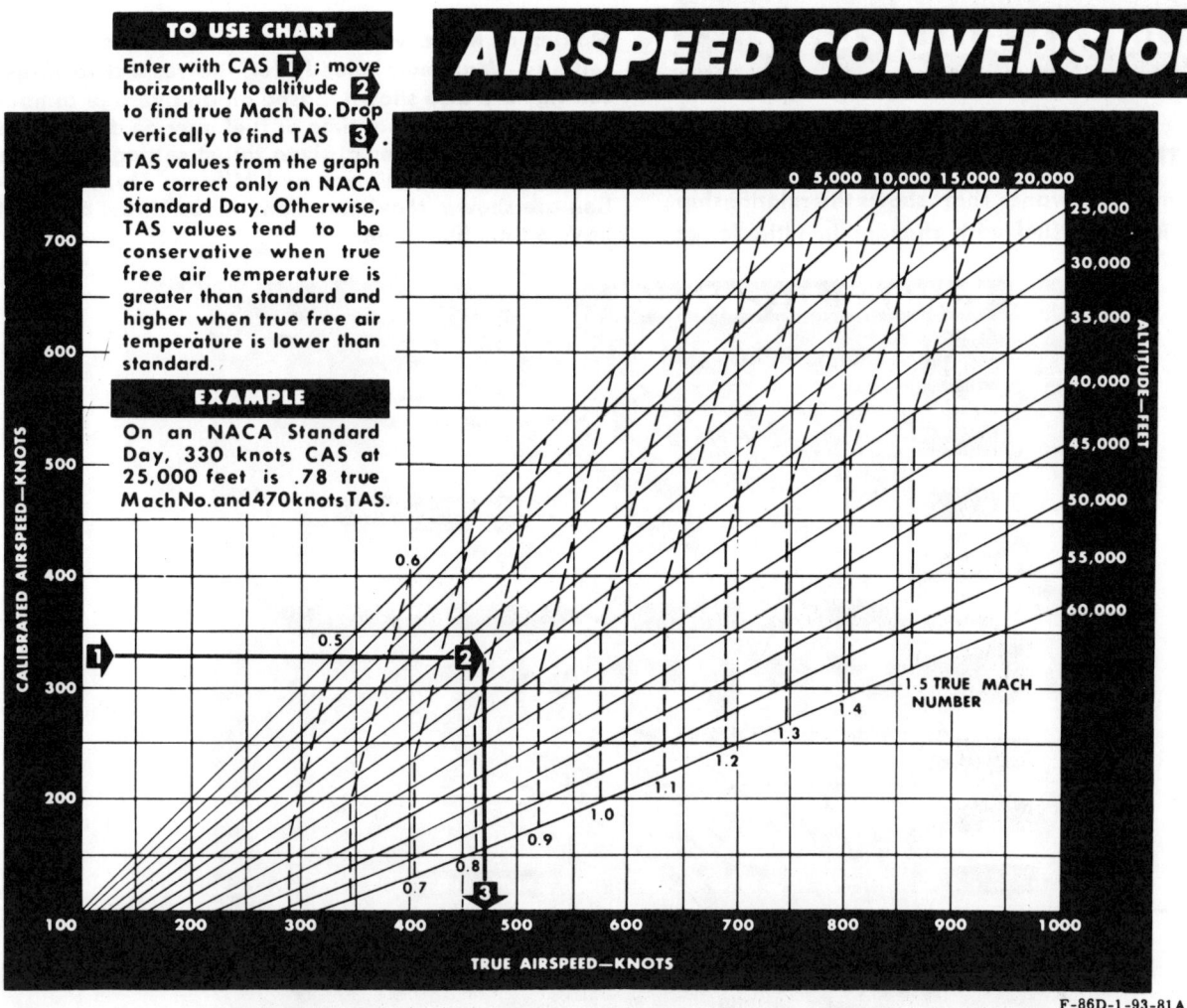

Figure A-2

A-4). The distances shown are for normal take-off technique on a dry, hard-surface runway. The following variables are incorporated: temperature, −10°C through 60°C; pressure altitude, sea level through 6000 feet; gross weight, 16,000 through 22,000 pounds; and head winds, −20 through 40 knots. These graphs may be used for any configuration if the gross weight at take-off is considered. The indicated airspeeds (IAS) for take-off are shown on the gross weight lines. Use of the graphs is explained by a sample problem on each.

TAKE-OFF ACCELERATION.

The take-off acceleration chart (figure A-5) gives the ground roll distance required to accelerate to any desired indicated airspeed using Maximum Thrust. Also, check-point speeds may be determined for desired ground roll distances and for existing take-off conditions (gross weight, surface air temperature, pressure altitude, and relative wind speed).

REFUSAL SPEEDS.

The highest indicated airspeed at which a take-off can be safely aborted is called the *REFUSAL SPEED*. This is obtained from the refusal speed chart (figure A-6) for the existing take-off conditions and runway length. The refusal speed chart is based on a Maximum Thrust acceleration to the refusal speed followed by normal braking to a stop on a dry, hard-surface runway without drag chute or speed brakes. Drag chute and/or speed brakes reduce the distance required to stop and should be used if possible. The ground roll distance required to accelerate to refusal speed can be found on the take-off acceleration chart (figure A-5). Use of the charts is explained by a sample problem on each.

COMBAT ALLOWANCE

DESCRIPTION

The Combat Allowance chart shows the relationship between time and fuel with changes in altitude, at Maximum, Military, and Maximum Continuous Thrust settings. Maximum speeds for the respective thrust settings are also shown, based on an average combat gross weight. Combat time or fuel may be determined from these charts for a given thrust setting. The time limitations for Maximum and Military Thrust operation are shown. Maximum Continuous Thrust does not have a time limitation.

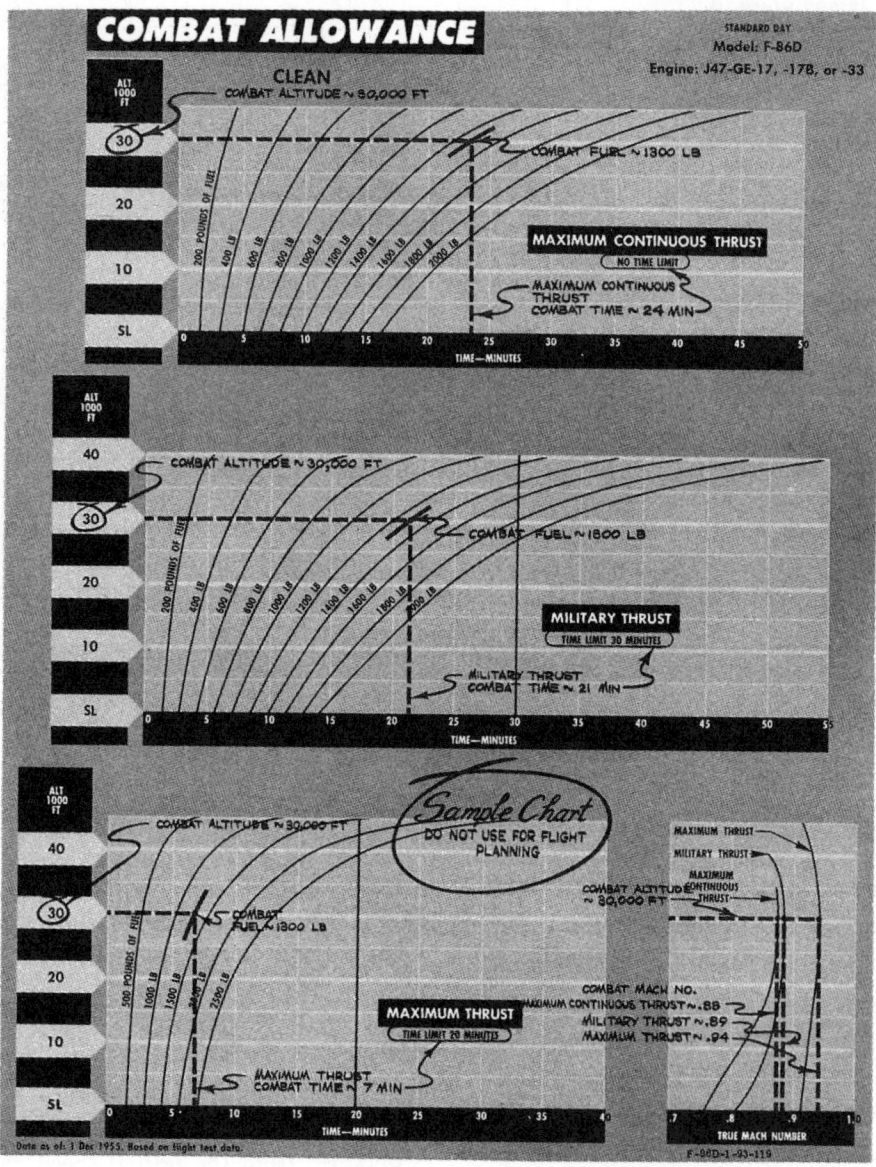

USE

Enter the chart at the combat altitude and the fuel quantity to be used for combat to obtain the time available. Enter at the altitude and time available for combat to obtain the fuel required.

Using the example shown for the clean configuration, obtain the time available for a combat fuel allowance of 1300 pounds at 30,000 feet, using Maximum, Military, and Maximum Continuous Thrust. Also obtain the maximum level-flight Mach number for the altitude and thrust setting.

	TIME AVAILABLE	MACH NO.
Maximum Thrust	7.0 min	.94
Military Thrust	21.0 min	.89
Max Cont Thrust	24.0 min	.88

CLIMB PROFILE

DESCRIPTION

The climb profile charts give time required, distance traveled, and fuel used (based on the recommended climb speed schedule) for a Military Thrust climb from sea level for several gross weights. The reduction in weight due to fuel used during climb is taken into account. Approximate climb data for climbs between two specific altitudes may be obtained from these profile charts, but it is recommended that the graphical climb charts be used for such in-flight climb data.

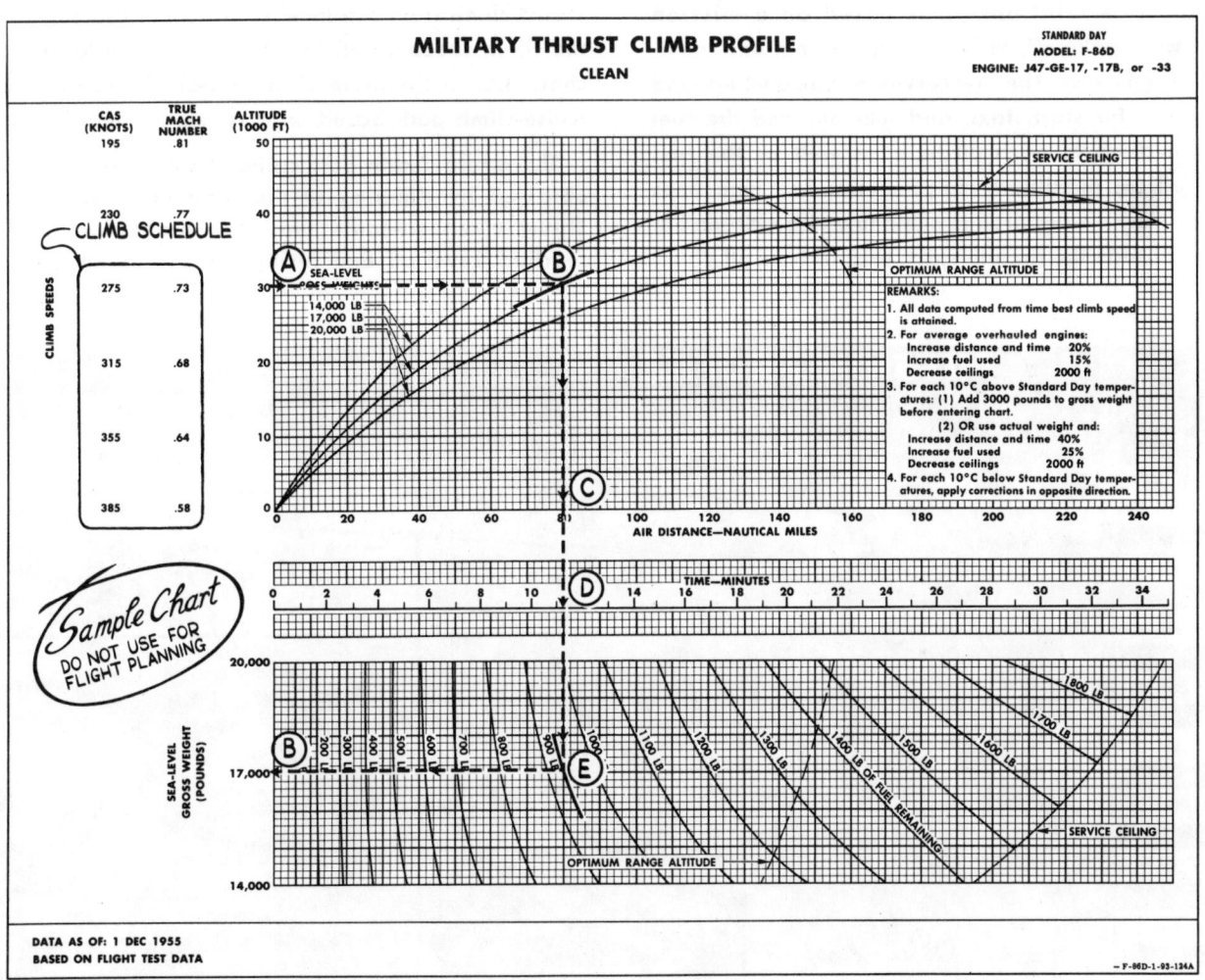

USE

Enter the chart at the altitude at end of climb and the gross weight at start of climb (sea level). From this point, read the distance traveled and time required to climb. To obtain the fuel used during climb, project the point down to the sea-level gross weight in the lower portion of the chart and interpolate for fuel used. The gross weight at the end of climb is the sea-level gross weight minus fuel required to climb.

The example shown is for a Military Thrust climb from sea level to 30,000 feet with a gross weight of 17,000 pounds in the clean configuration.

A	is altitude at end of climb	30,000 ft
B	is gross weight at start of climb (sea level)	17,000 lb
C	is distance traveled in climb	81 n mi
D	is time required to climb	11.5 min
E	is fuel used during climb	940 lb
B minus E	is gross weight at end of climb	16,060 lb

Appendix I T. O. 1F-86D-1

MISSION PROFILE

DESCRIPTION

These charts give the time, fuel, distance, and altitude relationship to maximum range for no-wind conditions. This relationship is based on a mission sequence of take-off, Military Thrust climb, and maximum range cruise. The fuel curves include a 600-pound allowance for start, taxi, and take-off, and the fuel used in climb to each altitude, as well as the fuel required for maximum range cruise. The time lines include the time required to climb to cruise altitude but do not include the time to start, taxi, or take off.

The line labeled "Initial Climb Path" shows the distance traveled and time consumed during the Military Thrust climb from sea level to cruising altitude, using the climb speed schedule tabulated at the left of the chart. The continuation of the initial climb path is the cruise-climb path based on a constant Mach number.

The approximate best cruise-climb altitude can be obtained by climbing at the recommended Military Thrust climb schedule until the proper altitude is reached. Level off and set up the power setting and

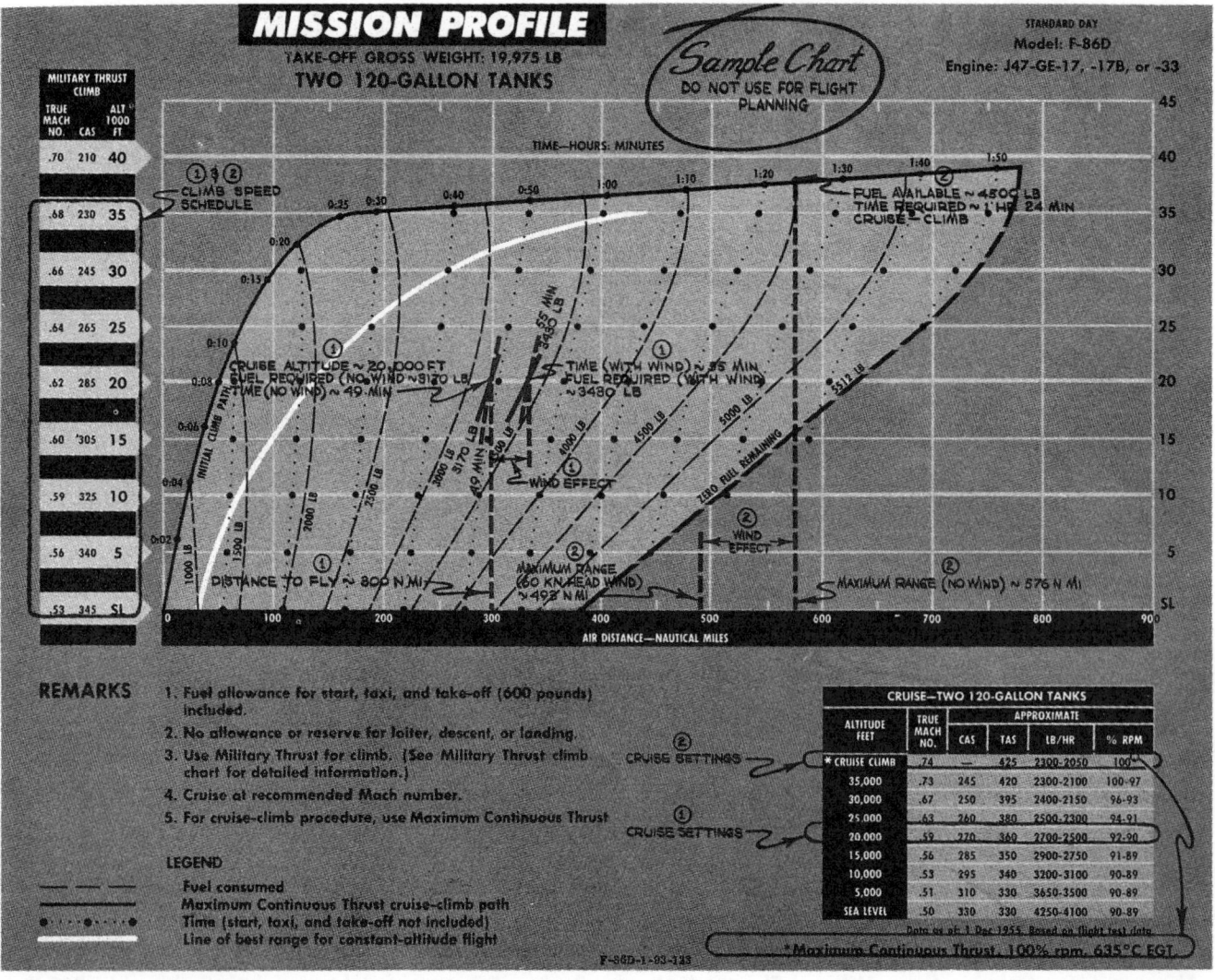

A-6

Mach number given for cruise-climb procedure; the airplane automatically seeks the cruise-climb altitude for its particular gross weight. Maintain the initial throttle setting throughout the remainder of cruise-climb. For cruise at a constant altitude, set up the recommended Mach number at the intersection of the climb path and the cruise altitude. As the flight progresses, the power setting must be decreased gradually as fuel is consumed, to maintain the recommended Mach number.

As an aid to preflight planning, a line of best range for constant-altitude flight appears on the chart (white dashed line). *This curve is not a flight path*, but a plot of best cruise altitude against distance. For distances greater than those covered by the curve, use cruise-climb procedure for maximum range.

A cruise table gives recommended Mach numbers and approximate operating conditions for both cruise-climb procedure and for cruise at constant altitude. (Cruise-at-constant-altitude data is given for each 5000 feet.)

USE

The chart may be entered with one or more of the four range factors: time, fuel, distance, and altitude. By entering the chart with the known factors, the others may readily be determined. This is for a no-wind condition.

To determine wind effect upon time, fuel, and distance, compute the average true airspeed (distance ÷ time) no wind, and apply wind to TAS to obtain ground speed (G.S.). Then compute the time with wind (distance ÷ G.S.). Re-enter the profile at the cruising altitude and the computed time with wind to determine the fuel required with wind.

Sample Problem 1.

From the example shown, find the fuel required, time, necessary speed, and power setting to cruise 300 nautical miles at 20,000 feet with a head wind of 40 knots in the two 120-gallon tank configuration.

- a. Enter at 300 nautical miles and 20,000 feet to obtain fuel required (no wind) .... 3170 lb
- b. Time (no wind) .... 49 min (0.82 hr)
- c. Average TAS (300 ÷ 0.82) .... 366 kn
- d. Apply wind to obtain G.S. (366 − 40) .... 326 kn
- e. Calculate time with 40-knot wind (300 ÷ 326) .... 55 min (0.92 hr)
- f. Re-enter at cruise altitude at the time with wind. Fuel required with wind .... 3430 lb
- g. Tabular cruise speed .... .59 Mach No.
- h. Tabular cruise power setting (% rpm) .... 92% to 90% rpm
(Power setting decreases with gross weight.)

Note that if this flight had been made at 32,000 feet cruising altitude (reference, the line of best range at 300 nautical miles), the time and fuel required would have been less.

Sample Problem 2.

Determine the maximum distance flyable, using the two 120-gallon tank configuration with 4500 pounds of fuel and a 60-knot head wind.

(Hint: Use line of best range for constant-altitude flight to determine maximum range.)

- a. Enter at 4500 pounds of fuel and obtain maximum air distance at cruise-climb (no wind) .... 576 n mi
- b. Time (no wind) .... 1 hr 24 min (1.4 hr)
- c. Calculate average TAS (576 ÷ 1.4) .... 412 kn
- d. Apply wind to obtain G.S. (412 − 60) .... 352 kn
- e. Calculate distance with wind (1.4 × 352) .... 493 n mi
- f. Tabular cruise-climb speed .... .74 Mach No.
- g. Tabular cruise power setting (% rpm) .... 100% rpm 635°C egt

INTERCEPT PROFILE

DESCRIPTION

The intercept profile is used to obtain the fuel necessary to fly to a given distance and altitude in a minimum amount of time, using a Maximum Thrust climb to altitude and Normal Thrust (Maximum Continuous) for cruise. The intercept profile is similar to the mission profile in use; however, the intercept profile should be restricted to flights where time is the important factor, while the mission profile is employed for maximum range flights.

A cruise table gives approximate operating conditions along with the true Mach numbers for both cruise-climb procedure and for cruise at constant altitude (cruise-at-constant-altitude data is given for each 5000 feet).

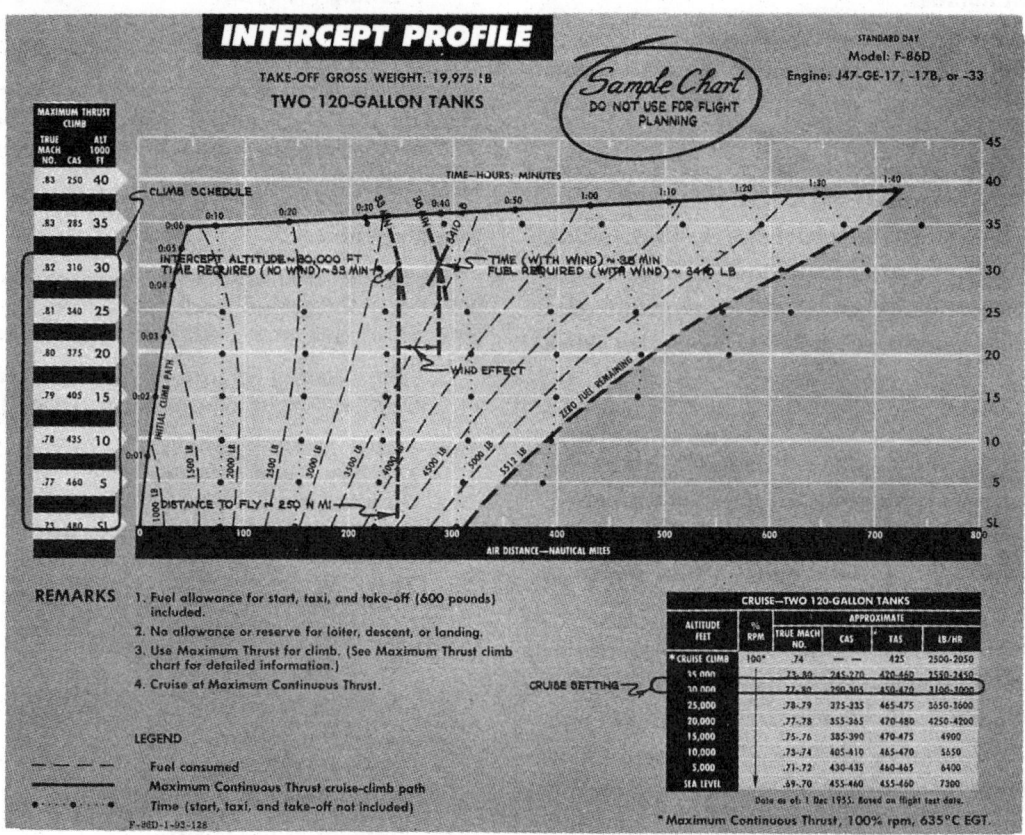

USE

Like the mission profile, the chart may be entered with one or more of the four range factors: time, fuel, distance, and altitude. By entering the chart with the known factors, the others may readily be determined. This is for a no-wind condition.

To determine wind effect upon time, fuel, and distance, compute the average true airspeed (distance ÷ time), no wind, and apply wind to TAS to obtain ground speed (G.S.). Re-enter the profile at the cruising altitude and the computed time with wind to determine the fuel required with wind.

Using the example shown, find the time and fuel required to reach a point of interception 250 nautical miles away at an altitude of 30,000 feet with a head wind to 60 knots in the two 120-gallon tank configuration.

a. Enter at 250 nautical miles and 30,000 feet to determine the time required (no wind) .... 33 min

b. Average TAS (250 ÷ 0.55) .... 454 kn

c. Apply wind to obtain G.S. (454 − 60) .... 394 kn

d. Calculate time with 60-knot head wind (250 ÷ 394) .... 38 min

e. Re-enter at cruise altitude at the time with wind. Fuel required with wind .... 3410 lb

f. Tabular cruise speed .... .77 to .80 Mach No.

g. Tabular cruise power setting (% rpm) .... 100% rpm, 635°C egt

A-8

OPTIMUM RETURN PROFILE

DESCRIPTION

These profiles show the minimum fuel required for maximum distance (no wind) based on an optimum flight path from any starting point within the range of the airplane configuration. The flight path required is indicated by the different shaded areas and the notes relative to them.

The cruise altitude giving maximum distance appears on the profile as the "line of best range for constant-altitude flight." The maximum distance using cruise-climb procedure is shown as the "line of best range for cruise-climb flight." The intersection of the cruise-climb line and the constant-altitude line determines whether the return will be made at a constant altitude or at cruise-climb. Climb path guide lines and lines of constant fuel are added for interpolation. The fuel lines are based on a Military Thrust climb to, and recommended cruise at, the optimum altitude. The Military Thrust climb speed schedule and recommended cruise settings are tabulated on each chart. <u>No fuel reserve for descent and landing has been included.</u> The time shown at the optimum altitude is cruise time only; it does not include time required for climb to optimum altitude or any allowance for descent, loiter, or landing.

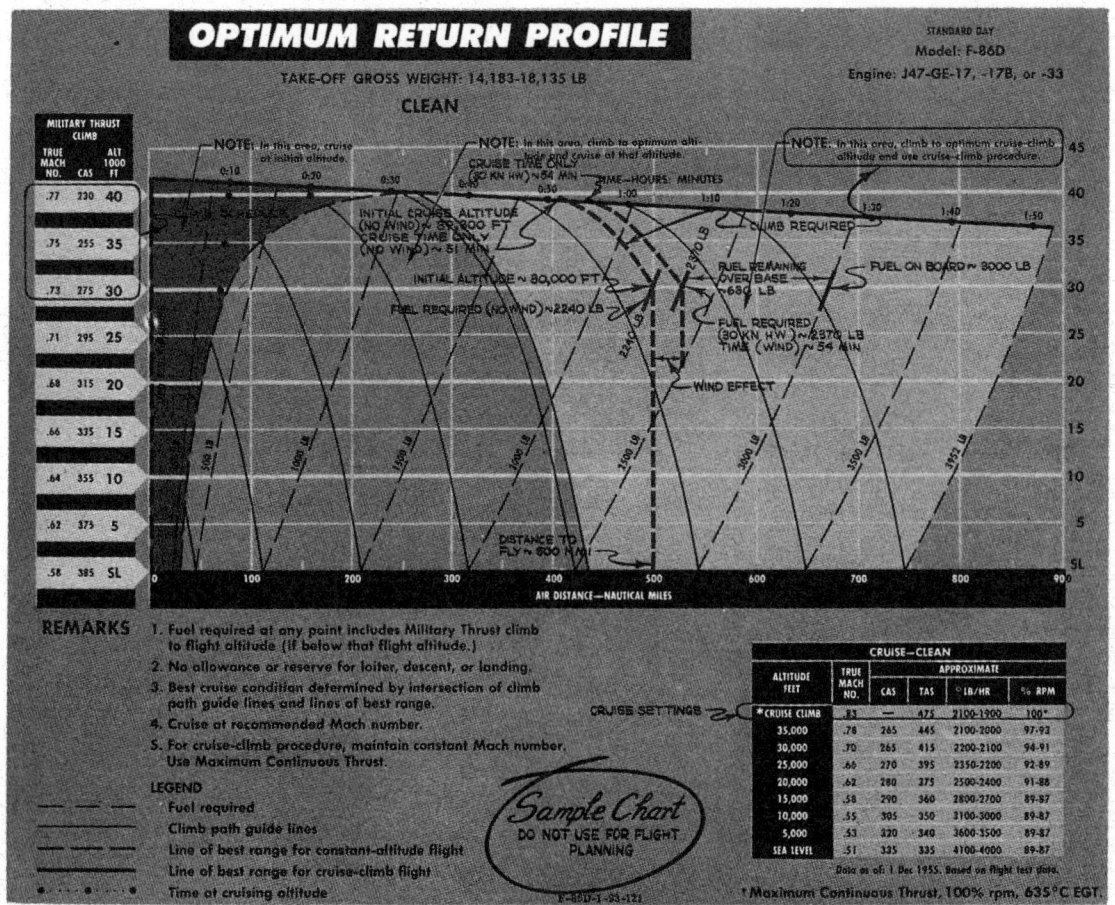

USE

The chart may be entered at the initial altitude with either the fuel on board (to determine the distance available) or with the distance to be flown (to determine the fuel required). The shaded area in which the initial point falls establishes the cruising procedure to be used, as stated in the note relative to the area.

The total time required to fly the distance is the time at cruise altitude (obtain from profile), plus the time required to climb (obtained from the graphical Military Thrust climb chart). To simplify the calculation of distance and/or fuel with wind, however, the time to climb may be omitted and the profile cruise time used to determine the average return speed. If greater accuracy is desired, the graphical data should be used.

The effect of wind must be applied to obtain the actual fuel and time to fly the distance. A close approximation can be obtained by considering the head or tail wind for the time required to complete the flight (neglecting the difference in wind at the lower altitudes since comparatively little time is spent in the climb phase).

From the example shown, determine the fuel and time required to return to a base 500 nautical miles away. The airplane is at 30,000 feet with 3000 pounds of fuel on board in the clean configuration (gross weight 17,183 pounds). A 30-knot head wind is assumed.

a. Enter profile at 500 nautical miles and 30,000 feet to establish starting point. Fuel required (no wind) .... 2240 lb
(In this area, note that a climb is required and a cruise-climb procedure is followed.)

b. By following the climb guide lines, the initial cruise altitude is .... 39,300 ft

c. Cruise time*
(no wind) .... 51 min (0.85 hr)

d. Average TAS
(500 ÷ 0.85) .... 588 kn

e. Average ground speed
(588 − 30) .... 558 kn

f. Time with wind
(500 ÷ 558) .... 54 min (0.90 hr)

g. Air distance traveled
(588 × 0.90 hr)
(d × f) .... 529 nautical air miles

h. Re-enter the profile at the air distance (g) and move to the initial altitude (30,000 feet) to obtain the fuel required with wind .... 2370 lb
(Use the flight path originally determined for no wind.)

i. Fuel remaining over base at altitude
(3000 − 2370) .... 630 lb

Note: It is recommended that sufficient reserve be considered for a normal landing operation when determining maximum distance obtainable; unless, however, an emergency condition prevails.

*Greater accuracy can be obtained by considering the time to climb, which is obtained from the Military Thrust climb chart.

MAXIMUM ENDURANCE PROFILE

DESCRIPTION

These profiles show the maximum time available for the fuel on board when loitering at a constant altitude. The recommended calibrated airspeed (CAS) and the approximate operating conditions are tabulated on each chart for several fuel quantities.

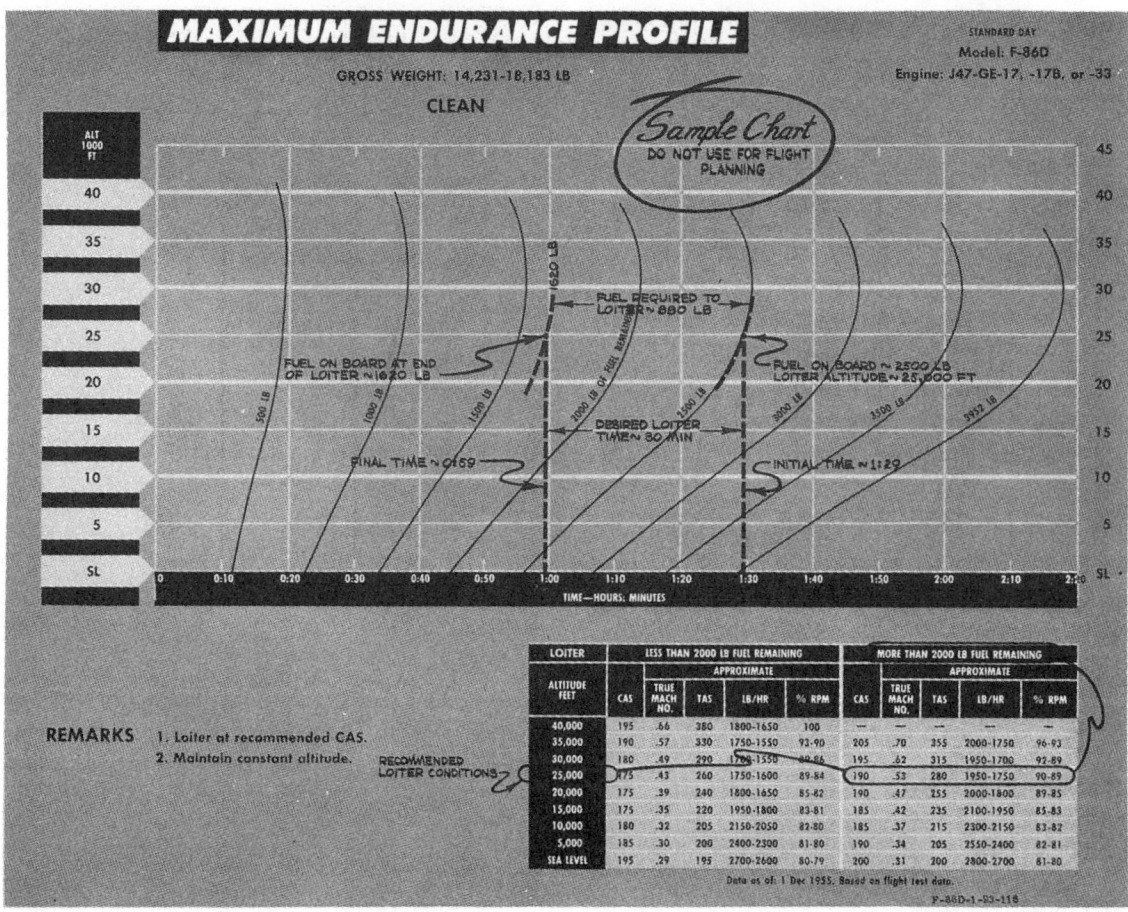

USE

To determine the time available for a given amount of fuel, enter the chart at the amount of fuel on board at the start of loiter and the flight altitude; note the initial time. Re-enter the chart at the amount of fuel on board at the end of the endurance flight (initial fuel on board less fuel to be used) and read the final time. The difference between the initial and final time is the time available to loiter at constant altitude.

To obtain the fuel required to loiter a given time, enter the chart at the amount of fuel on board at the start of loiter and flight altitude; note the initial time. Re-enter the chart at the time at the end of loiter (initial time less time to loiter) and read final fuel on board. The difference between the initial and final fuel on board is the fuel required to loiter.

From the example shown, determine the fuel required to loiter at 25,000 feet with clean airplane for 30 minutes. The fuel on board at start of loiter is 2500 pounds (gross weight 16,731 pounds).

a. Initial time at 2500 pounds and 25,000 feet .... 1 hr 29 min

b. Final time (1:29 — 0:30) .... 59 min

c. Fuel on board at end of loiter (0:59 at 25,000 feet) .... 1620 lb

d. Fuel required to loiter (2500 — 1620) .... 880 lb

e. Recommended loiter (CAS) .... 190 kn

OPTIMUM MAXIMUM ENDURANCE PROFILE

DESCRIPTION

These profiles give the maximum time in the air for the fuel remaining, based on an optimum flight path, from any starting altitude. The flight path required is indicated by the different shaded areas and the notes relative to them. Time and fuel lines shown are based on a Maximum Continuous Thrust climb to best endurance altitude, loiter at the altitude, and recommended descent to sea level (no reserve for landing). The climb speed schedule is tabulated at the left of the chart; the loiter speed schedule is tabulated below the chart.

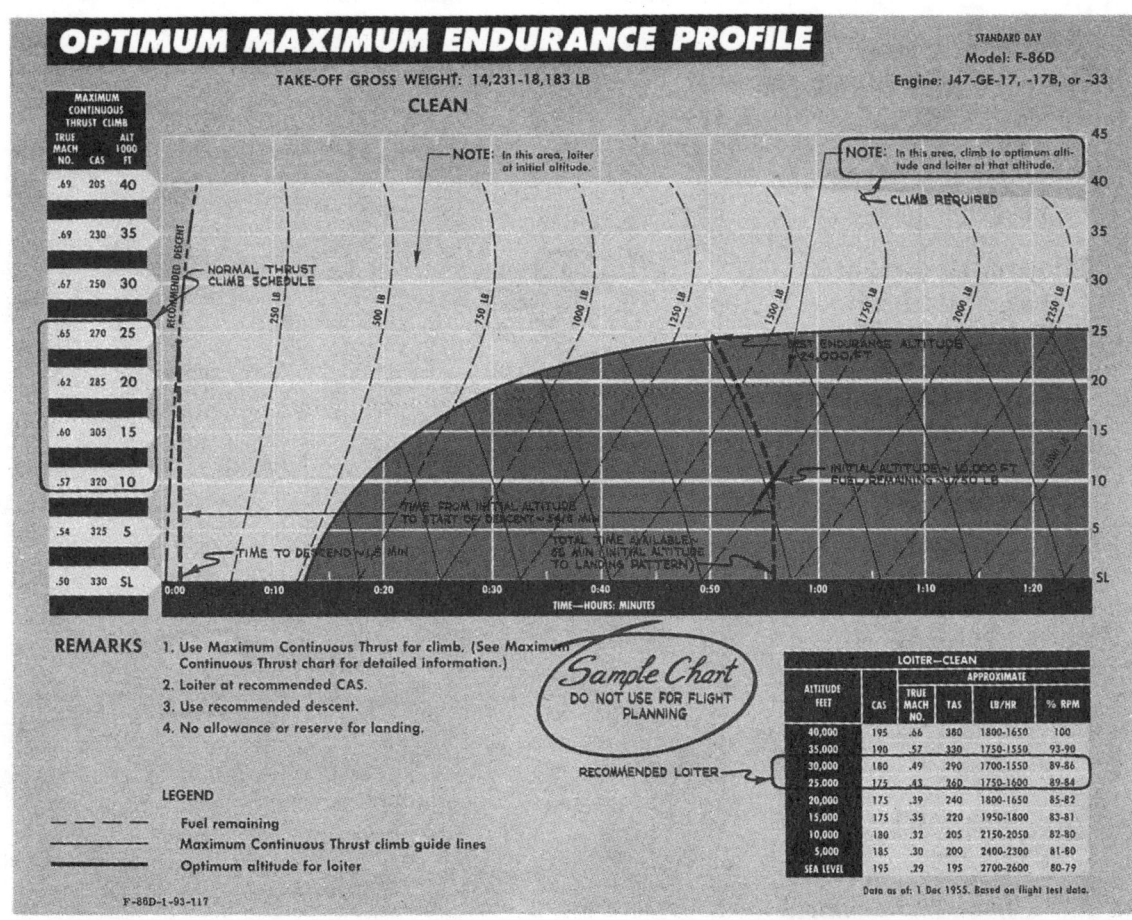

USE

The chart may be entered at the initial altitude with either the fuel remaining (to determine the time available) or the time desired (to determine the fuel requirement). The shaded area in which the initial point falls establishes the flight path to be used, as stated in the note relative to the area.

From the example shown, determine the time available and necessary flight path to remain aloft with 1750 pounds of fuel remaining at 10,000 feet in the clean configuration.

- a. Enter profile at 10,000 feet and 1750 pounds of fuel remaining to establish starting point. Total time available .... 56 min
- b. In this area, note that a climb is required.
- c. By following the climb guide lines, the best endurance altitude is .... 24,000 ft
- d. Descent time from 24,000 feet to sea level .... 1.5 min
- e. Elapsed time from start of climb to start of descent (0:56 − 0:015) .... 54.5 min

Suppose a reserve of 500 pounds of fuel had been desired for landing; then enter the profile at 1250 pounds of fuel (1750 − 500) and proceed as outlined in steps a. through e.

Time available .... 35 min

Endurance altitude .... 21,000 ft

Descent time .... 1.3 min

Elapsed time .... 33.7 min

CLIMB GRAPHICAL

DESCRIPTION

Climb charts for Maximum, Military, and Maximum Continuous Thrust operation, based on a recommended climb speed schedule, are shown for each configuration. Time and distance are plotted against gross weight with guide lines to show the reduction in gross weight during climb due to the fuel used. Service ceiling (100 fpm), combat ceiling (500 fpm), and optimum range altitude (constant Mach cruise-climb) are superimposed on the graph.

EXAMPLE:

- Ⓐw is initial gross weight (16,550 LB)
- Ⓐh is initial altitude (15,000 FT)
- Ⓐd is initial distance (29 Naut. Miles)
- Ⓐt is initial time (4.0 Min.)
- Ⓑh is final altitude (40,000 FT)
- Ⓑd is final distance (180 Naut. Miles)
- Ⓑt is final time (25.3 Min.)
- Ⓑw is final gross weight (15,500 LB)
- Ⓐw minus Ⓑw is fuel used (1050 LB)
- Ⓑd minus Ⓐd is distance traveled (151 Naut. Miles)
- Ⓑt minus Ⓐt is time to climb (21.3 Min.)

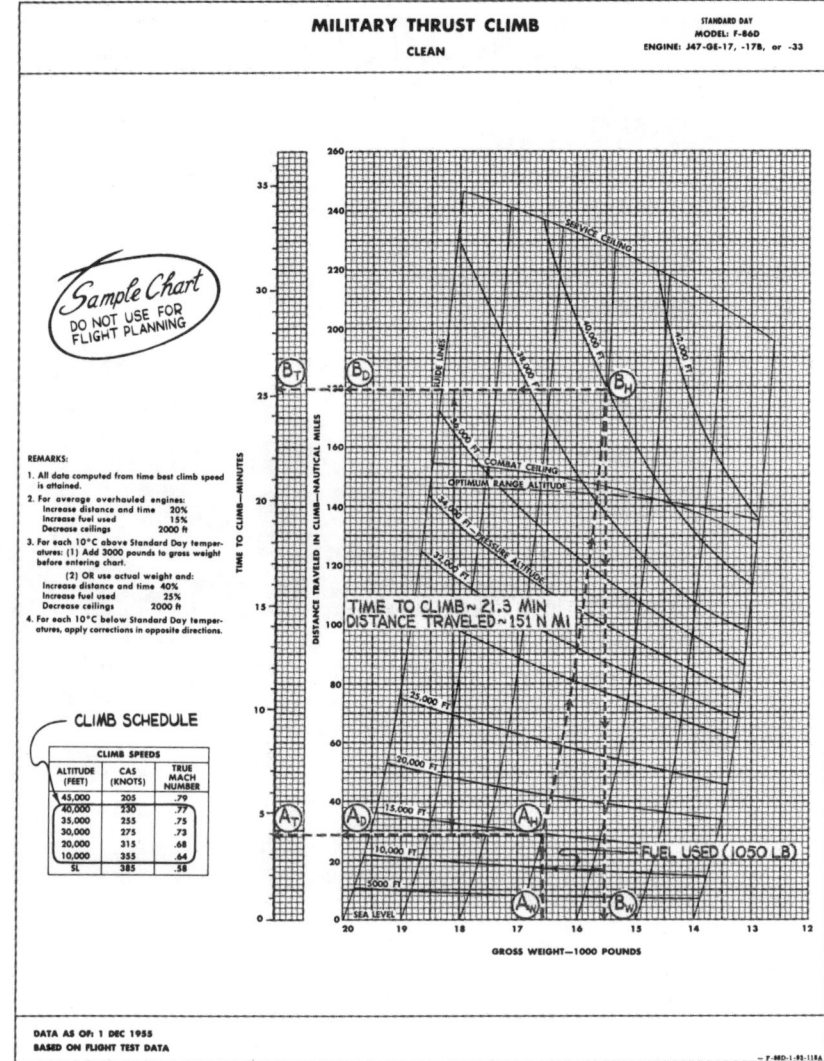

USE

To obtain the climb data desired, enter the proper climb chart at the gross weight and altitude at start of climb. Note the time and distance at this point. From this initial altitude point, trace a curve parallel to the guide lines until it intersects the desired altitude at end of climb. Note the time, distance, and gross weight at this intersection. The difference between the initial and final time is the time required to climb. The difference between initial and final values for distance and for gross weight gives, respectively, the distance traveled and fuel used to climb. Since time and distance are zero at sea level, the time required and distance traveled may be read directly for climbs starting at sea level. Fuel used, however, must still be determined by the difference in gross weights.

The effect of temperature on time, fuel, and distance to climb is accounted for by using a corrected gross weight at start of climb (increased at temperatures above standard; decreased at temperatures below standard). Instructions for temperature correction are given on each climb chart.

The example shows the fuel used, distance traveled, and time to climb from 15,000 feet to 40,000 feet, using Military Thrust, clean airplane, with an initial gross weight of 16,550 pounds at start of climb.

DESCENTS.

The descent charts are based on the use of speed brakes to provide high rates of descent with idle power to minimize fuel consumption. Distance, time, fuel consumed, and rate of descent are shown in figures A-21 and A-22. Descent speed schedules are also included.

LANDING DISTANCES.

Distances, ground and total to clear a 50-foot obstacle, with or without the aid of the drag chute are shown in figures A-23 and A-24. In both graphs, the distances are computed for the speed brakes extended and full flaps. The following conditions are also considered: dry, hard-surface runway; temperature, −10°C through 60°C; pressure altitude, sea level through 6000 feet; gross weight, 14,000 through 20,000 pounds; and head winds, 0 through 60 knots. The recommended indicated airspeeds for the approach, over a 50-foot obstacle, and touchdown are listed on the graph. Use of the graphs is explained by a sample problem on each.

NAUTICAL MILES PER POUND OF FUEL.

Cruise data (zero wind) throughout the speed range from maximum endurance to Military Thrust are shown on the nautical miles per pound of fuel graphs (figures A-31 through A-35). Several weights for each configuration are given at altitudes of sea level, 15,000, 25,000, 35,000, and 40,000 feet. Each graph includes specific range (nautical miles per pound), fuel flow, and power settings (% rpm). Also included are curves of recommended cruise Mach number, maximum endurance, and Normal and Military Thrust. Specific range is plotted against Mach number, with subscales of calibrated airspeed (CAS) and true airspeed (TAS). Cruising range is the product of specific range multiplied by fuel amount. Large fuel amounts should be divided into several smaller quantities. The smaller the amount of fuel used in the calculations, the greater the accuracy of the range.

To obtain the cruising range for a given amount of fuel, use the following steps. (If several fuel amounts are used, repeat the steps for each. The sum of the individual ranges is the total cruising range.) For greatest accuracy in determining cruising range, consider small amounts of fuel at a time rather than the total fuel available. Then, the total cruising range is the sum of the individual ranges obtained for each amount of fuel considered.

 a. Select the proper graph for the airplane configuration and altitude.

 b. Determine the average weight of the airplane for the amount of fuel being considered.

 c. Enter the graph at this average weight and the desired Mach number, or desired power setting (% rpm), to obtain specific range (nautical miles per 1000 pounds of fuel).

 d. To obtain the cruising range, multiply the specific range by the amount of fuel (pounds ÷ 1000).

 e. Interpolate the approximate fuel flow and power setting (% rpm) at the Mach number and average weight.

When there is a wind to be considered, multiply the specific range found in step c. by the range factor (ground speed divided by true airspeed) to obtain the specific range for wind. Proceed with steps d. and e. to complete the problem.

For temperatures other than Standard Day, apply the corrections shown on each graph to true airspeed and fuel flow. Do not change the nautical miles per pound of fuel, Mach number, or power setting (% rpm).

SUMMARY.

Check your flight plan during the actual flight to determine whatever deviations exist. These deviations may be applied to the reserve expected at the destination. The most important factors to consider are:

 a. Fuel used during start, taxi, and take-off. (The mission and intercept profiles allow 600 pounds for this phase.)

 b. Wind effect.

 c. Deviation from the recommended climb schedule.

 d. Deviation from the recommended cruise settings.

 e. Variation in engine performance.

 f. Navigational errors, formation flight, and fuel actually aboard at take-off.

Appendix I

SAMPLE PROBLEM.

This sample problem combines the use of the charts and graphs in this section to plan a mission.

An intercept mission is to be flown using two 120-gallon drop tanks which are to be dropped before combat.

Prepare a flight plan based on the following data:

   a. Distance to combat area..........................200 naut mi
   b. Assigned altitudes
      Inbound to combat
      (constant altitude) ....30,000 ft
      Outbound from combat
      (cruise-climb) ....38,500 ft
      and above
   c. Combat—35,000 feet
      (Military Thrust) ....10 min
   d. Combat—35,000 feet
      (Maximum Thrust) .... 5 min
   e. Weather (assume Standard Day
      temperature throughout) ....CAVU
     Winds aloft
      Inbound (30,000 feet) ....30 kn head wind
      Outbound (35,000 feet
      and above) ....45 kn tail wind
     Field elevation ....1500 ft
   f. Airplane gross weight
      Basic (includes trapped oil
      and internal fuel, and
      miscellaneous equipment) ....13,599 lb
      Pilot .... 200 lb
      Two 120-gallon drop tanks
      (empty weight) .... 232 lb
      Rockets (24) .... 432 lb
      Maximum usable fuel (internal)
      and drop tanks (848 gallons) .... 5,512 lb
      Total gross weight ....19,975 lb

TAKE-OFF.

Obtain the take-off distance from the maximum thrust take-off distance graph, figure A-3. (Standard Day temperature at 1500 feet is 12°C.) Use zero wind.

    Ground roll distance (19,975 pounds)........3250 ft
    Total take-off distance over
    50-foot obstacle ....4900 ft
    Take-off speed (IAS) .... 134 kn

INBOUND TO COMBAT.

The inbound leg may be determined directly from the intercept profile chart for two 120-gallon drop tanks, figure A-15. The profile includes a 600-pound fuel allowance for start, taxi, and take-off, as well as the fuel required to climb and cruise at 30,000 feet.

   a. Distance ....200 naut mi
   b. Fuel required (no wind) from profile..........2830 lb
   c. Time (no wind) from profile ....26 min
   d. Average TAS (a ÷ c) ....461 kn
   e. Ground speed (d − 30 kn) ....431 kn
   f. Time with wind (a ÷ e) ....28 min
   g. Fuel required (with wind)
      from profile ....2930 lb
   h. Cruise speed (30,000 ft) .... .77 Mach no
   i. Cruise Normal Thrust
      power setting ....100% rpm
   j. Military Thrust climb speed
      schedule .... (See figure A-7.)
   k. Gross weight at end of cruise
      (drop tanks released at end of
      cruise) 19,975 pounds minus (g)
      minus 232 lb ....16,813 lb

CLIMB.

Military Thrust climb to combat altitude (35,000 feet), zero distance traveled. (Use Military Thrust climb graph, clean, figure A-7.)

    Gross weight at start of climb
    from 30,000 feet ....16,813 lb
    Gross weight at end of climb to
    35,000 feet ....16,560 lb
    Fuel used to climb (26,350 pounds minus
    25,970 pounds) ....253 lb
    Time required to climb ....5 min
    Military Thrust climb speed
    and power schedules........................ (See figure A-7.)

COMBAT ALLOWANCE.

From the combat allowance chart (clean), obtain the fuel required for combat at 35,000 feet.

    Combat, Military Thrust
    (10 minutes) .... 500 lb
    Combat—Maximum Thrust
    (5 minutes) .... 770 lb
      Total combat fuel ....1270 lb
    Gross weight at end of combat
    16,560 pounds minus 1270 pounds
    (combat fuel) minus 432 pounds
    (rockets) ....14,858 lb

Determine the fuel remaining at end of combat.
    Take-off climb and cruise............................ 2930 lb
    Climb to combat altitude .... 253 lb
    Combat .... 1270 lb
      Total fuel used ....4453 lb
    Fuel remaining (5512 pounds minus
    4453 pounds) ....1059 lb

OUTBOUND FROM COMBAT (RETURN).

Assume return is started 200 nautical miles from base at an altitude of 35,000 feet. Enter the optimum return profile for the clean configuration (figure A-10) at the distance from base, and determine the fuel required and reserve with the existing tail wind.

    a. Distance ....200 naut mi
    b. Fuel required (no wind) ....880 lb
    c. Recommended cruise altitude
       (constant) ....38,500 ft
    d. Cruise time (no wind) ....21 min
    e. Time to climb* (Military
       Thrust, clean) 35,000 feet to
       38,500 feet, gross weight
       14,858 pounds ....3 min
    f. Total time, no wind (d + e) ....24 min
    g. Average TAS (a ÷ f) ....500 kn
    h. Average ground speed (g + 45) ....545 kn
    i. Total time, wind (a ÷ h) ....22 min
    j. Air distance with wind (g × i) ....184 naut mi
    k. Fuel required (wind) ....800 lb
    l. Cruise speed (38,500 ft) ....80 Mach no.
    m. Power setting ....(See figure A-10.)
    n. Reserve over base at 38,500 feet
       (1059 pounds minus k) ....259 lb

DESCENT.

Obtain the fuel required to descend to base from the descent graph—clean configuration.

    Recommended descent (38,500 feet)................25 lb
    Time to descend ....2 min
    Speed schedule, using idle power and
    speed brakes extended....................(See figure A-21.)
    Fuel reserve for landing
    (259 pounds minus 25 pounds) ....234 lb
    Airplane gross weight for landing..............14,033 lb

LANDING.

Obtain the landing distance from the landing distance graph (with drag chute deployed), figure A-23. Use 1500 feet, 12°C, and no wind.

    Ground roll distance ....1700 ft
    Total distance over 50-foot obstacle..............3000 ft
    Approach speed (IAS) .... 136 kn
    50-foot obstacle speed (IAS) .... 121 kn
    Touchdown speed (IAS) .... 116 kn

The sum of all the time required gives
the time from take-off to landing....................1 hr 12 min

---

*Calculation of time to climb is not necessary unless an accurate time history is required. (See use of optimum return profile.)

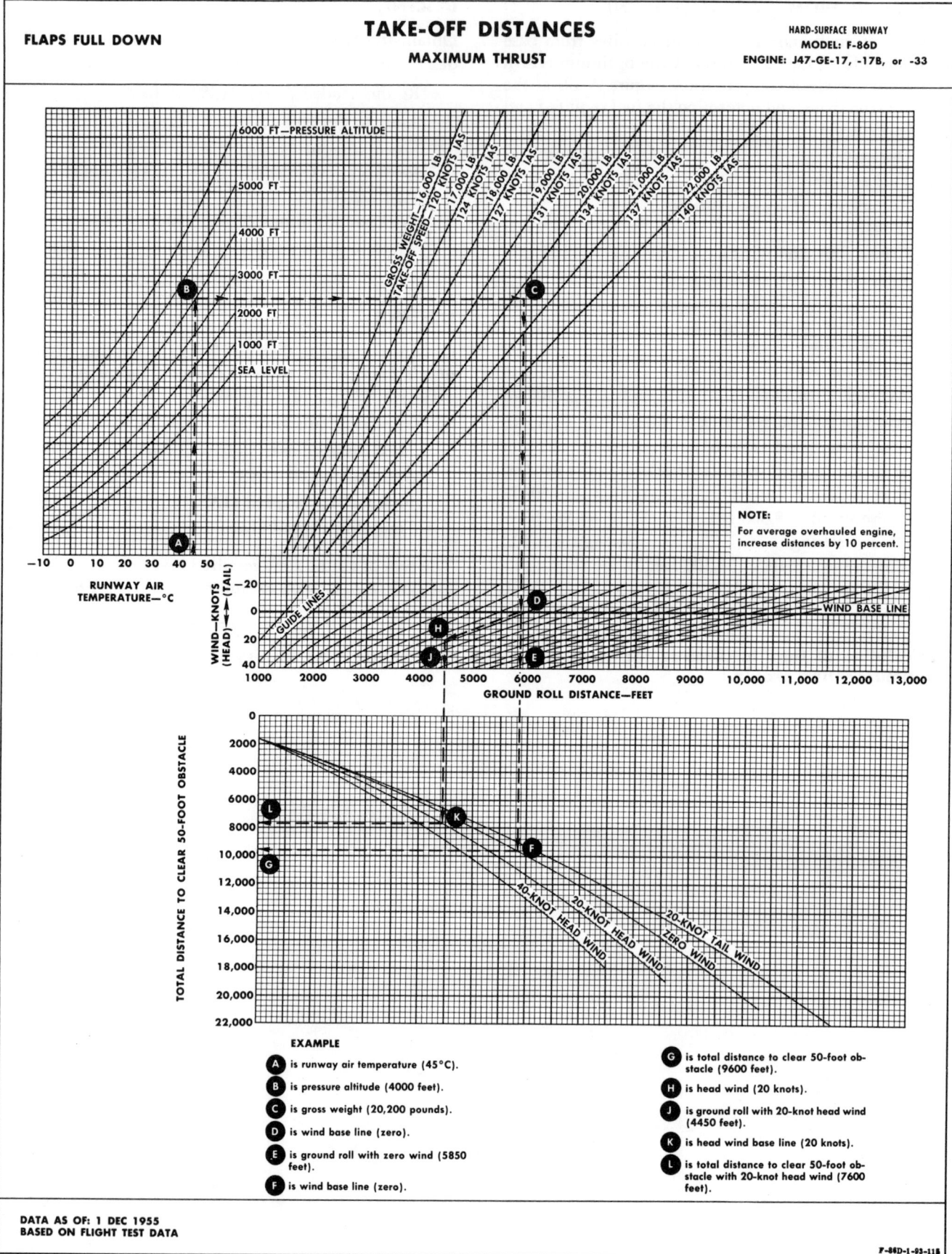

Figure A-3

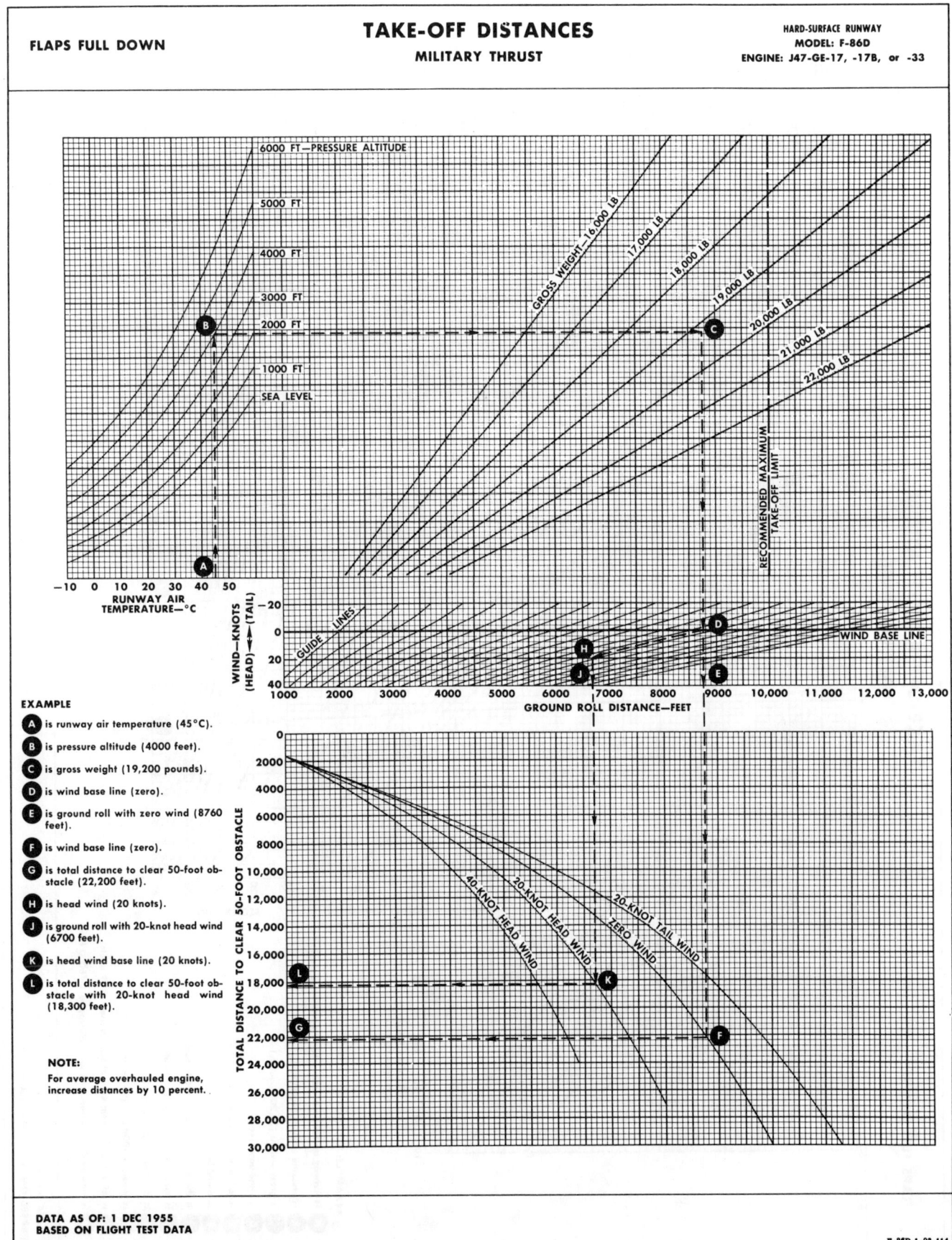

Figure A-4

Appendix I

T. O. 1F-86D-1

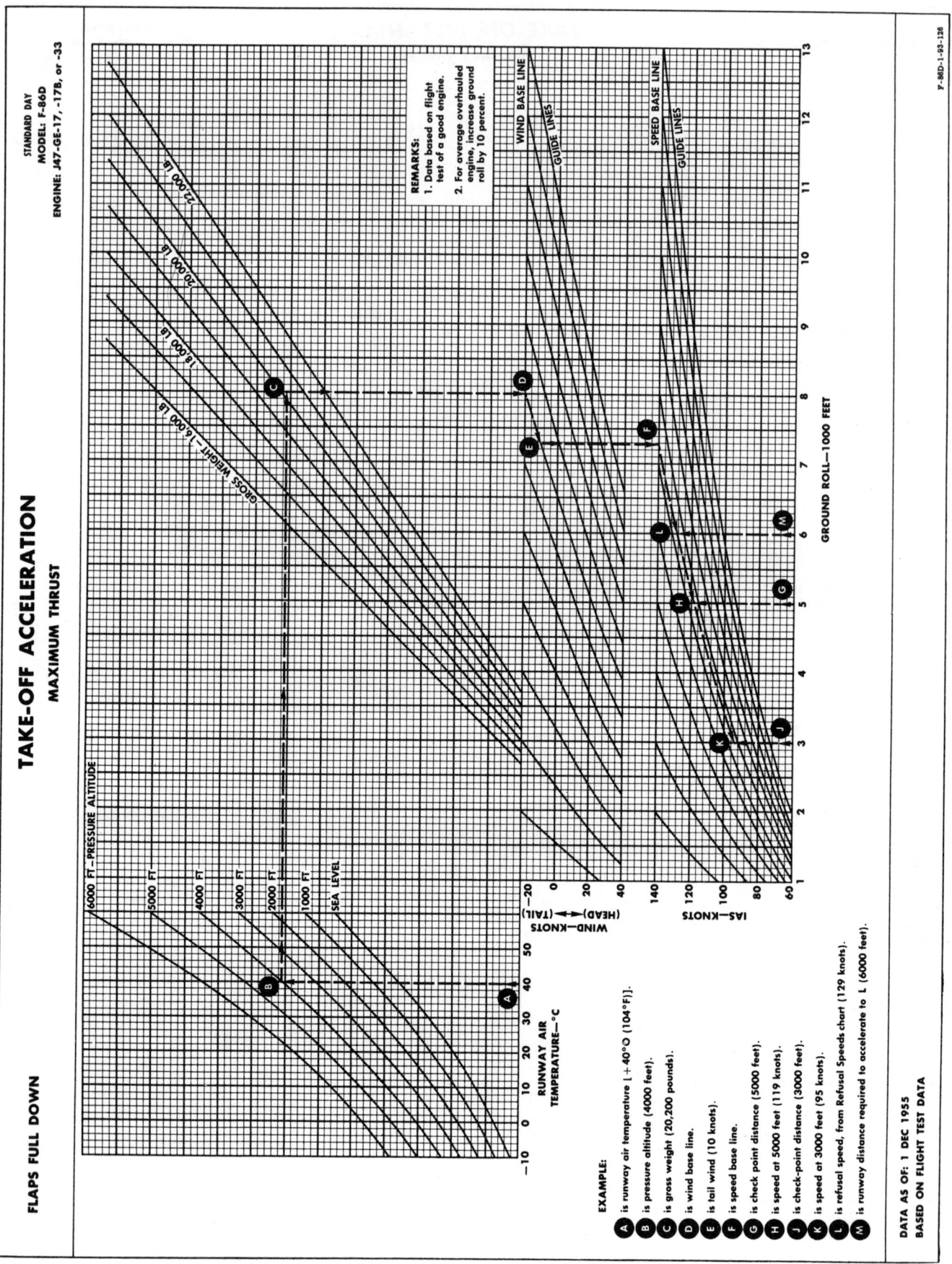

Figure A-5

A-20

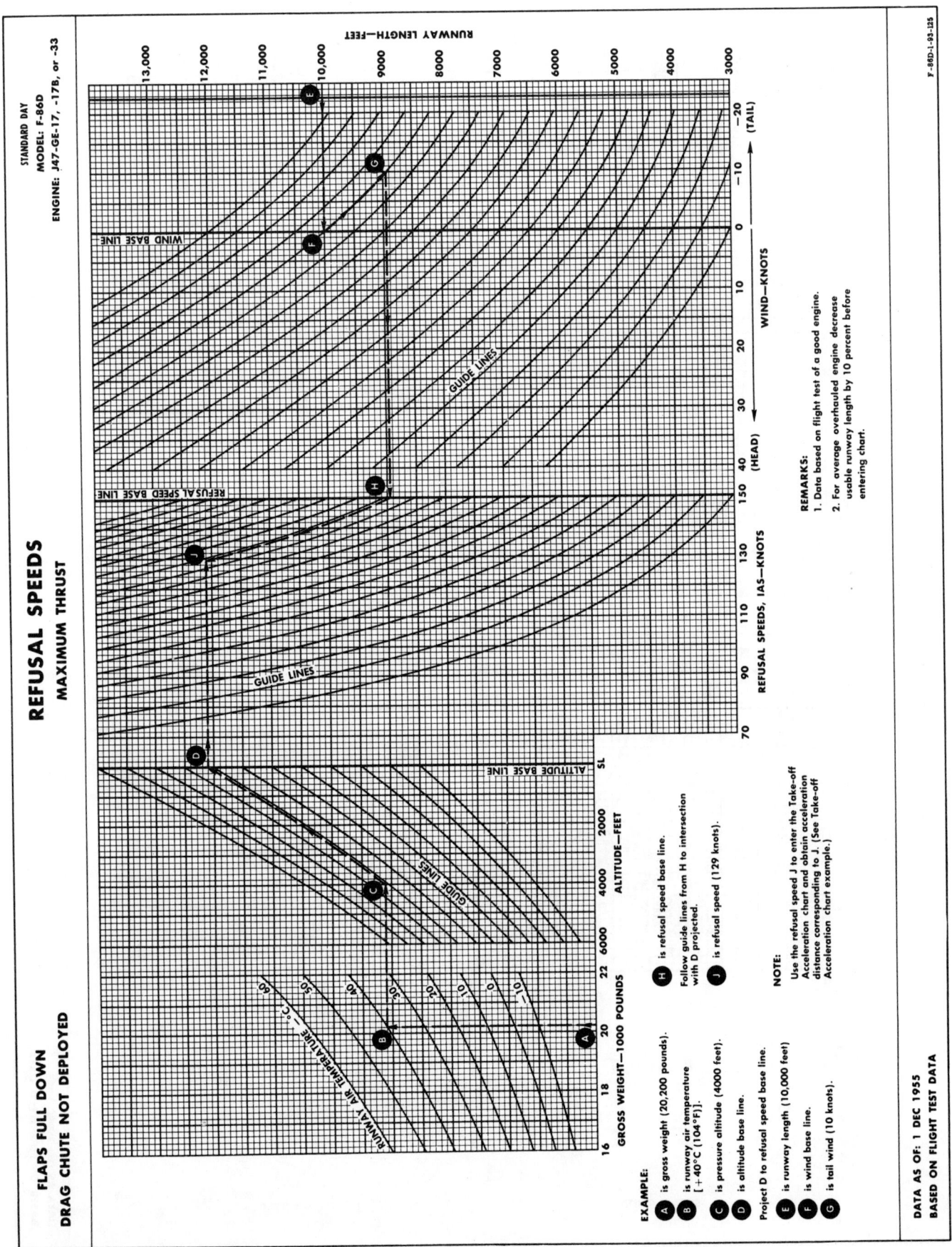

Figure A-6

Appendix I

T.O. 1F-86D-1

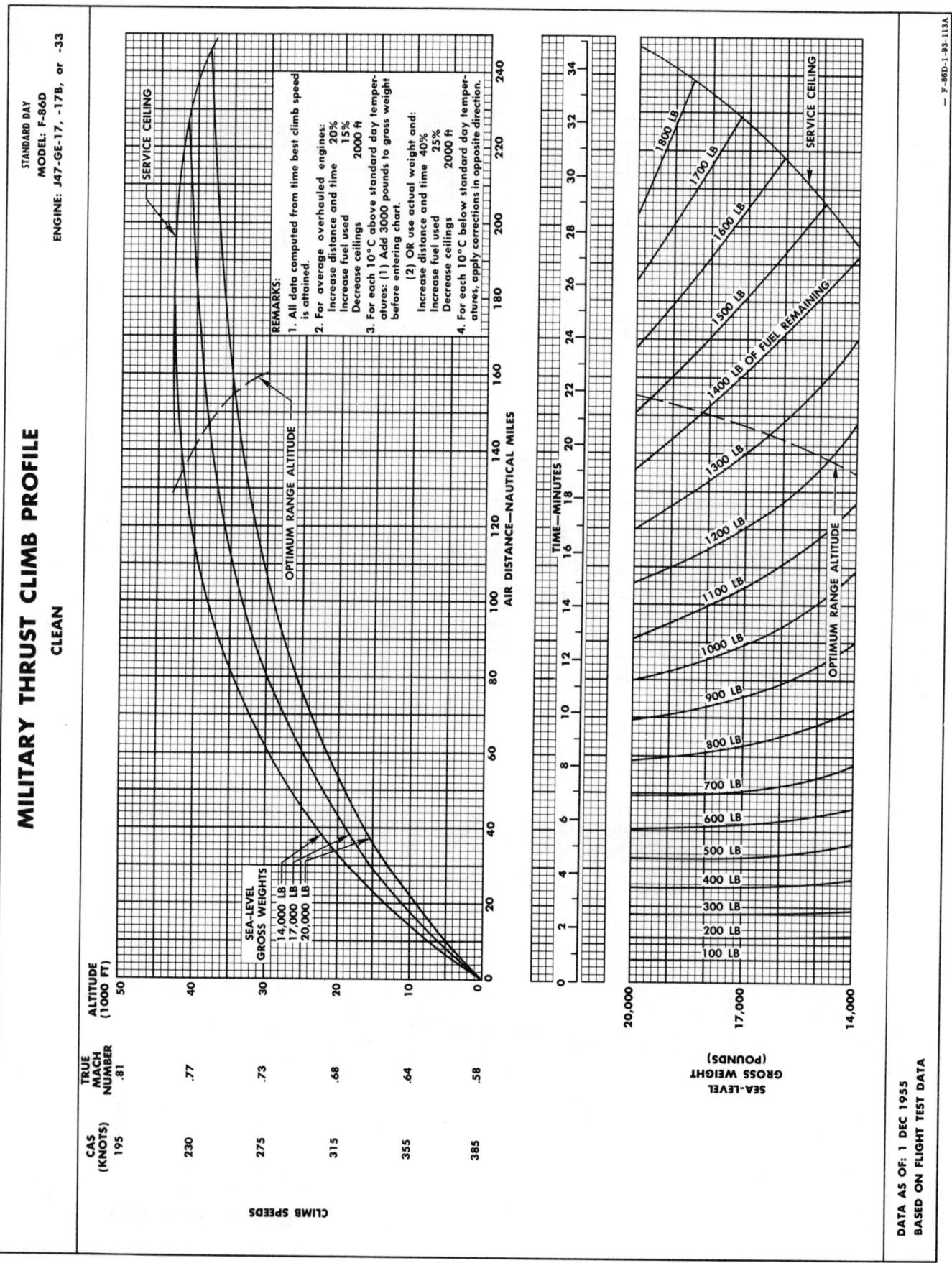

Figure A-7

A-22

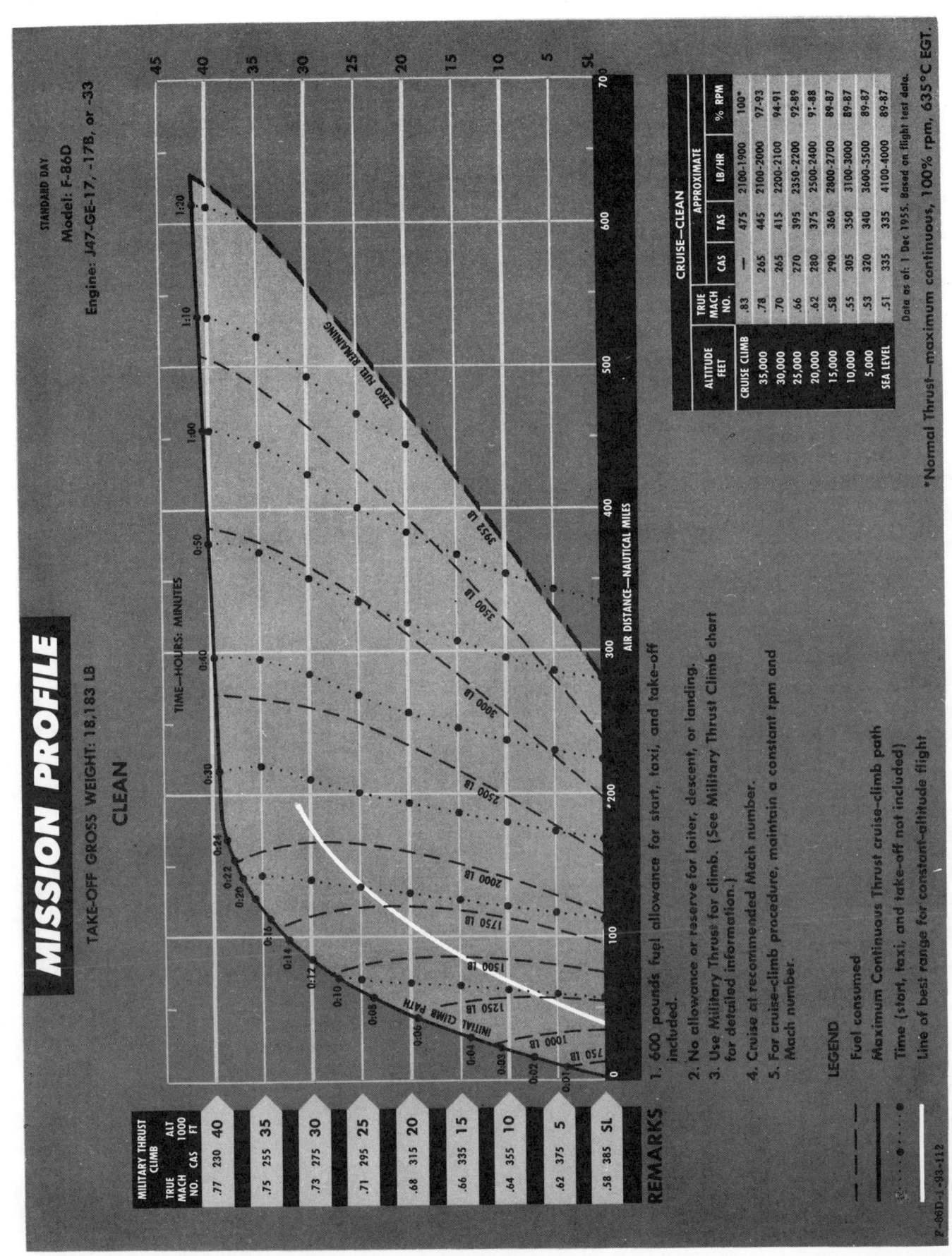

Figure A-8

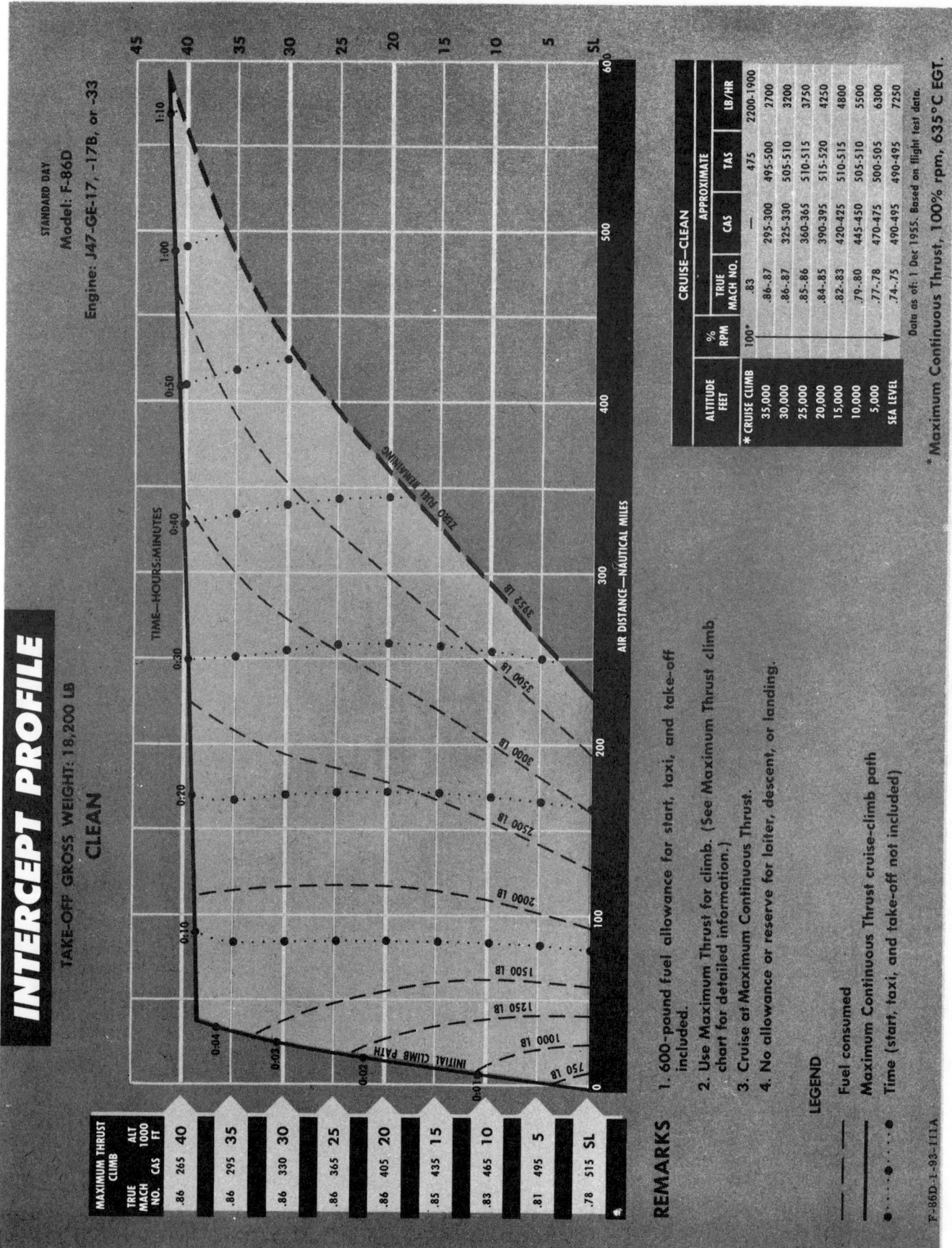

Figure A-9

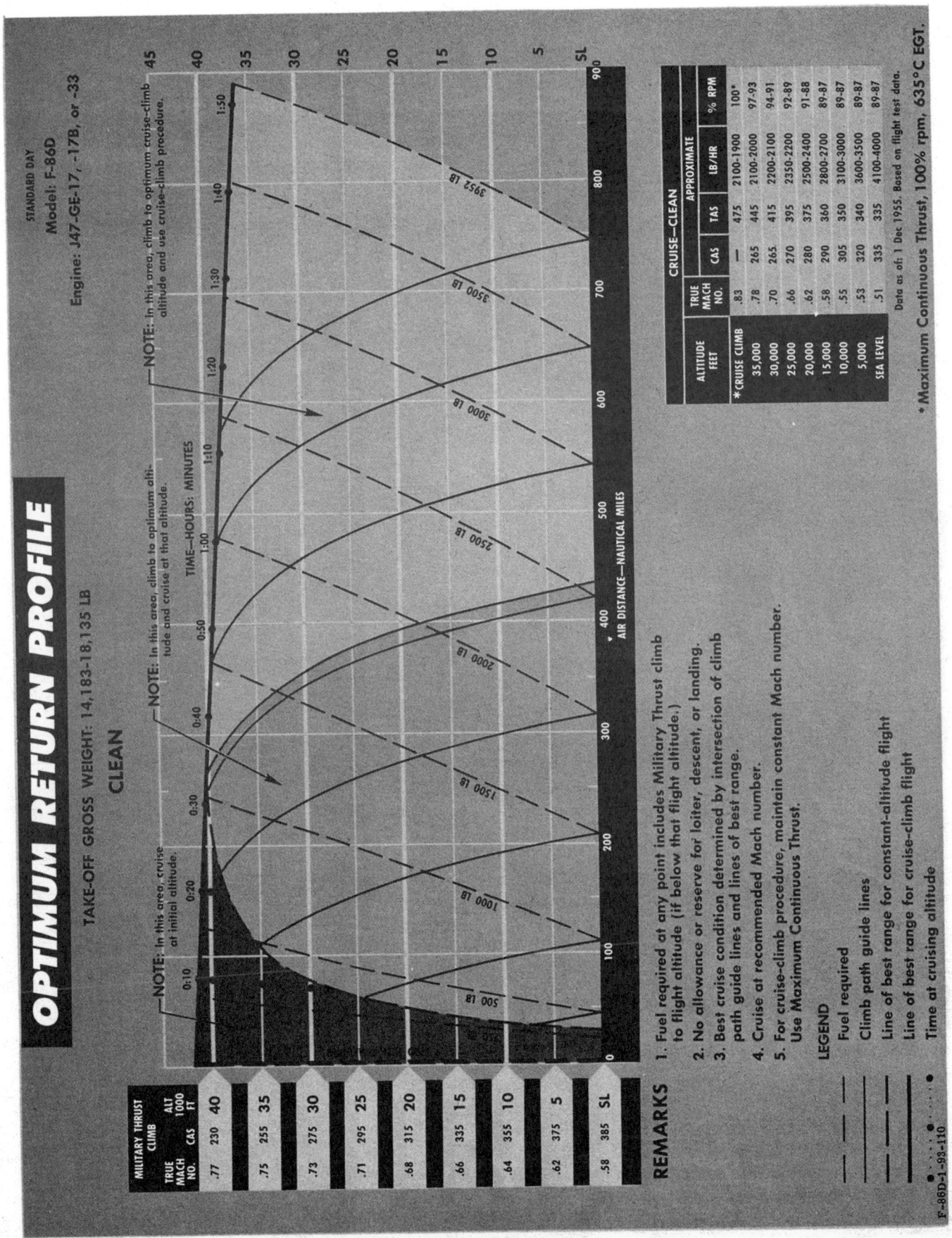
Figure A-10

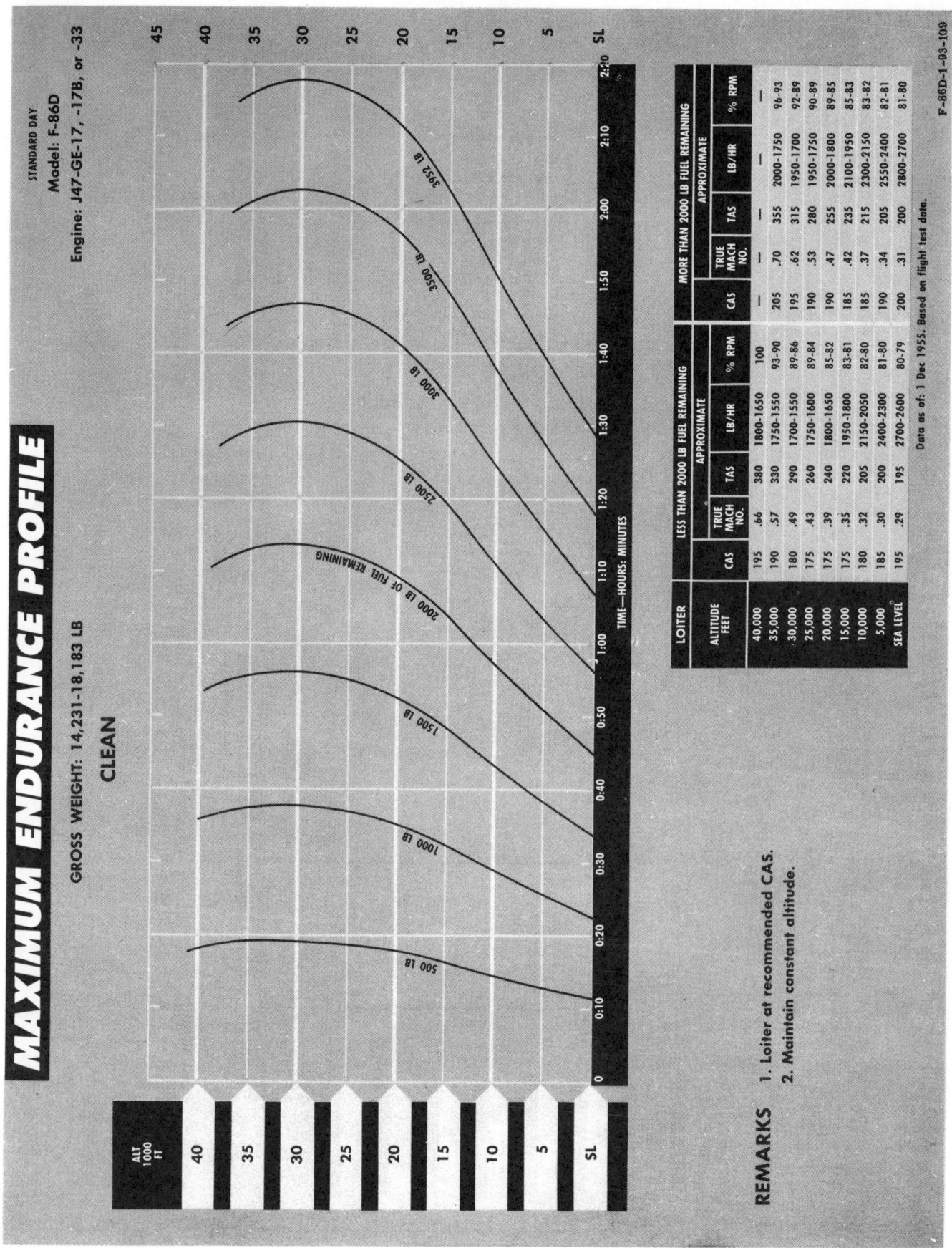

Figure A-11

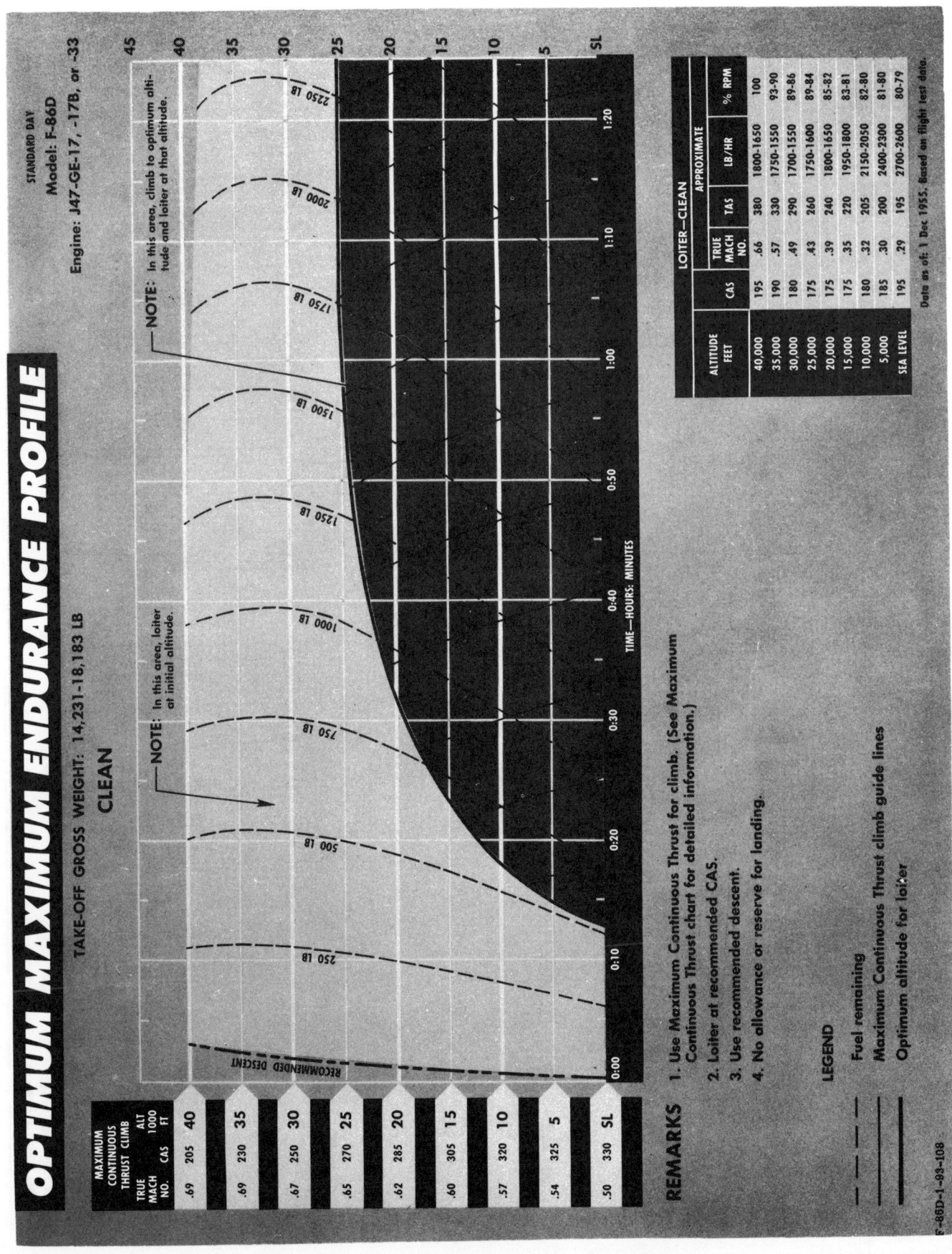

Figure A-12

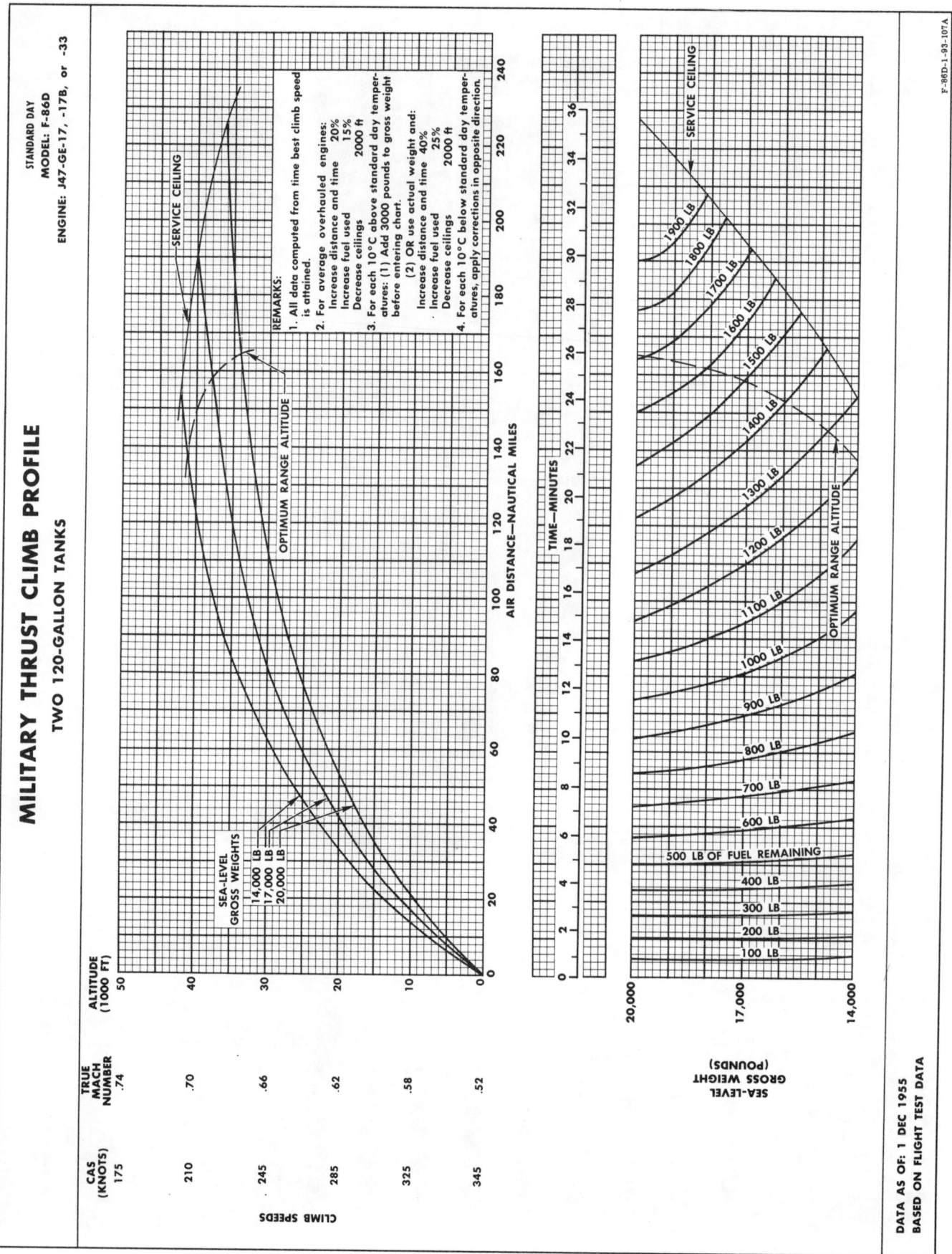

Figure A-13

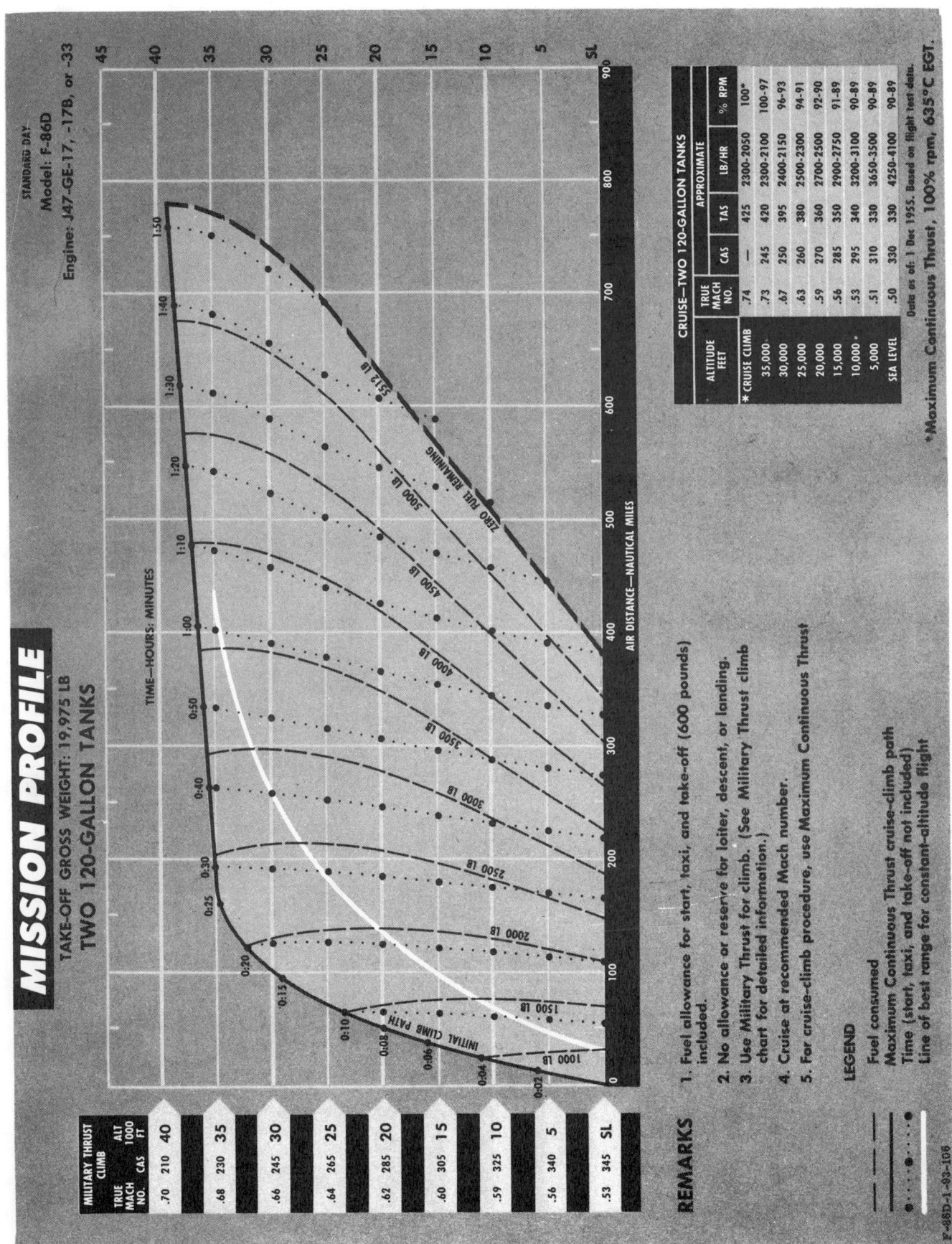

Figure A-14

Appendix I
T. O. 1F-86D-1

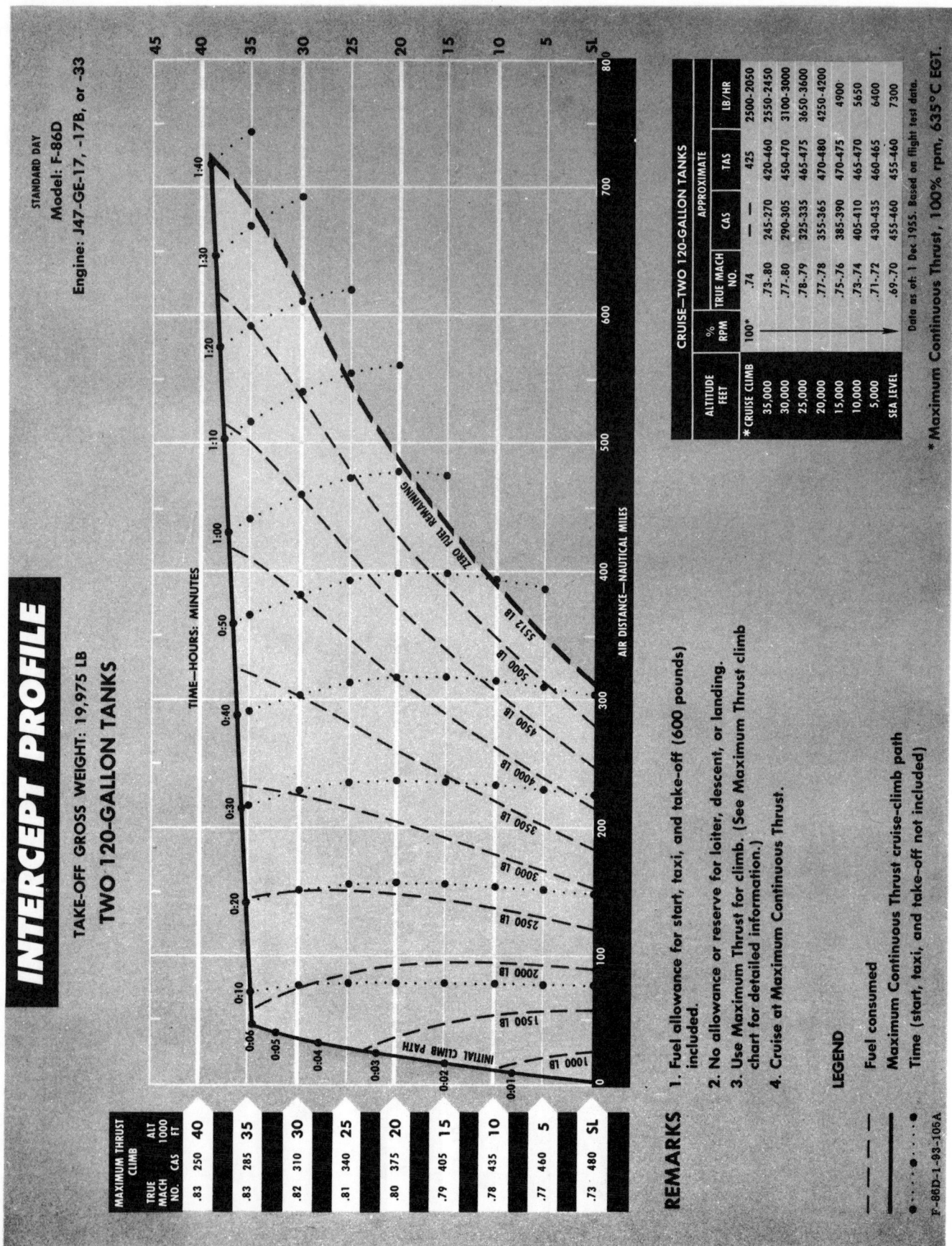

Figure A-15

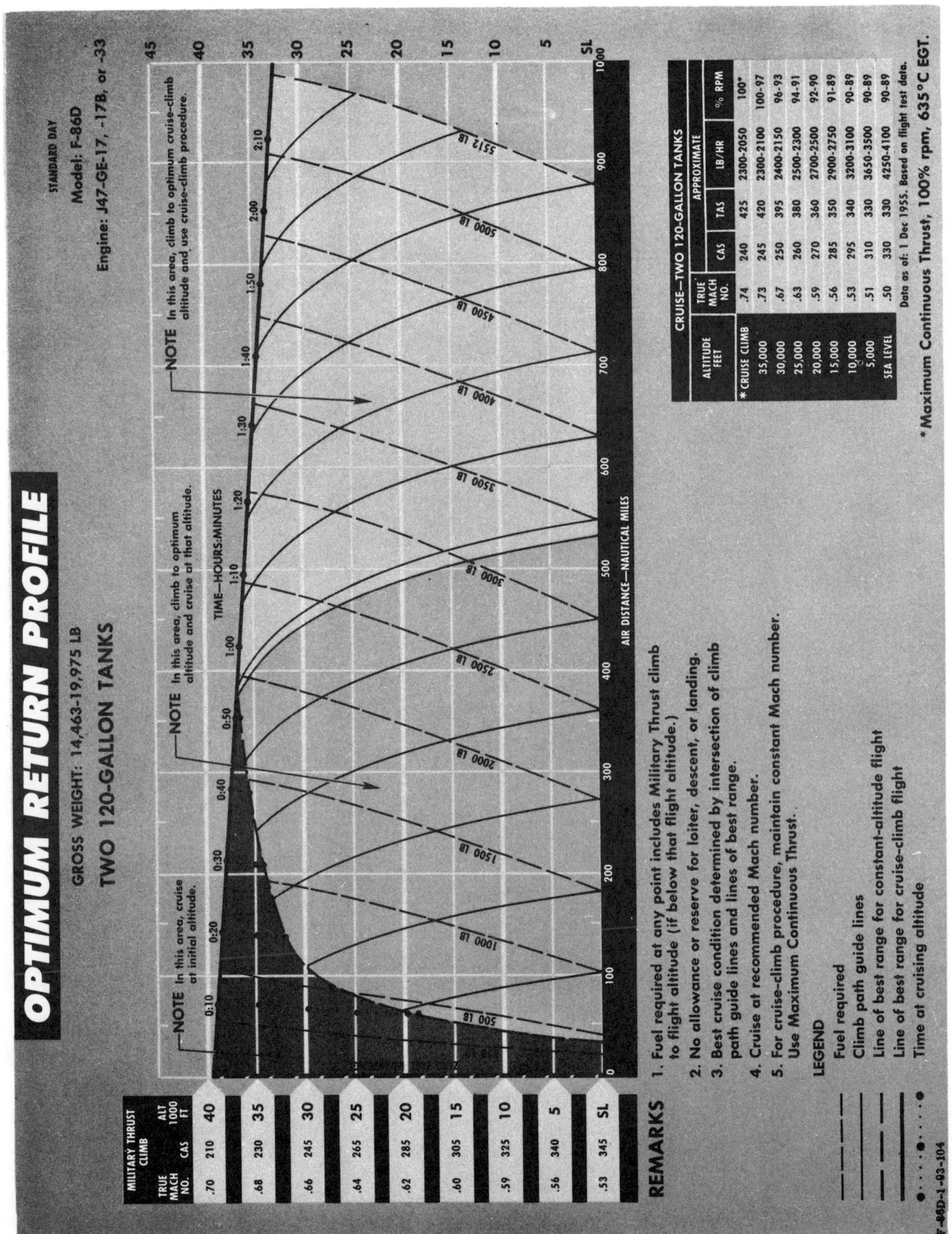

Figure A-16

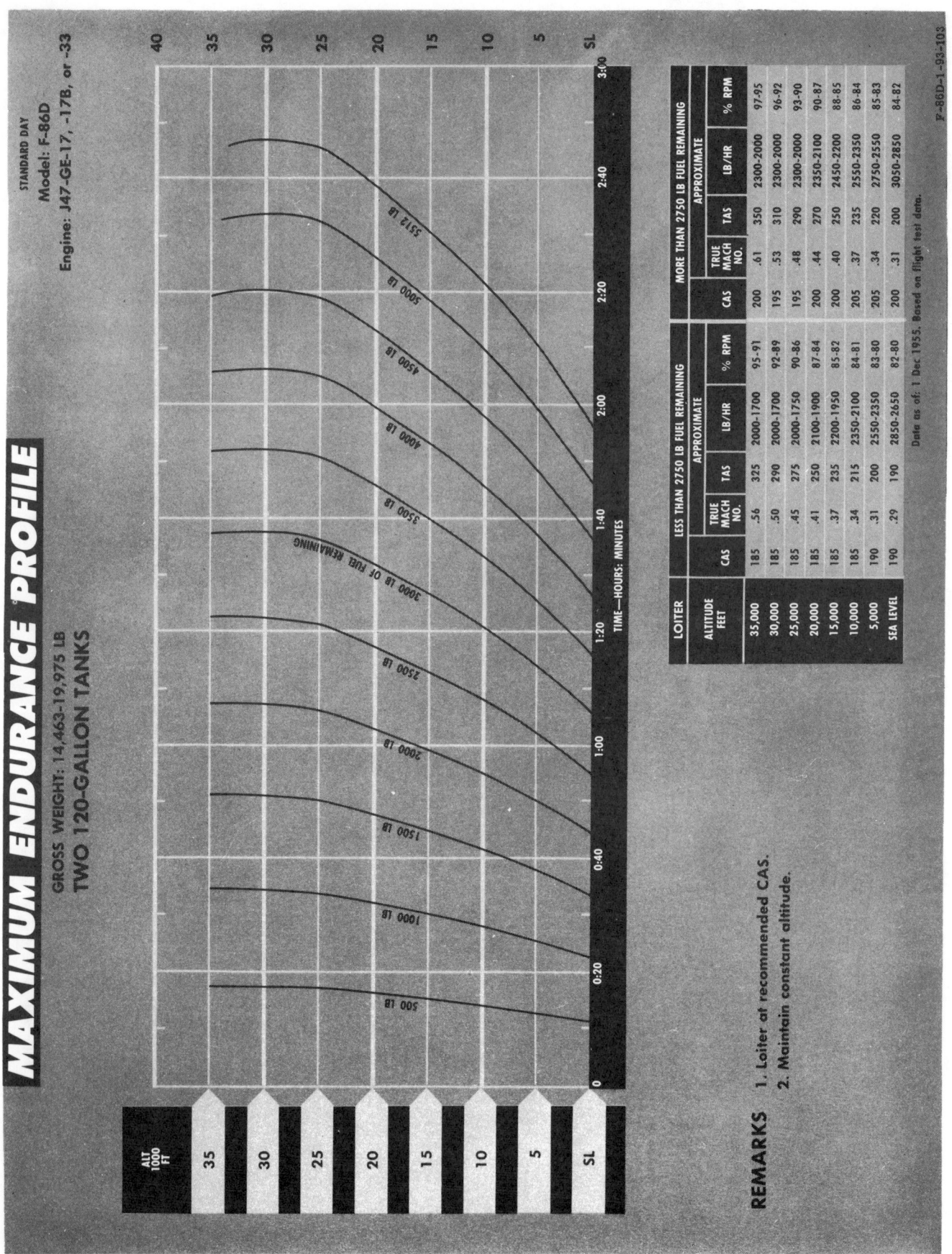

Figure A-17

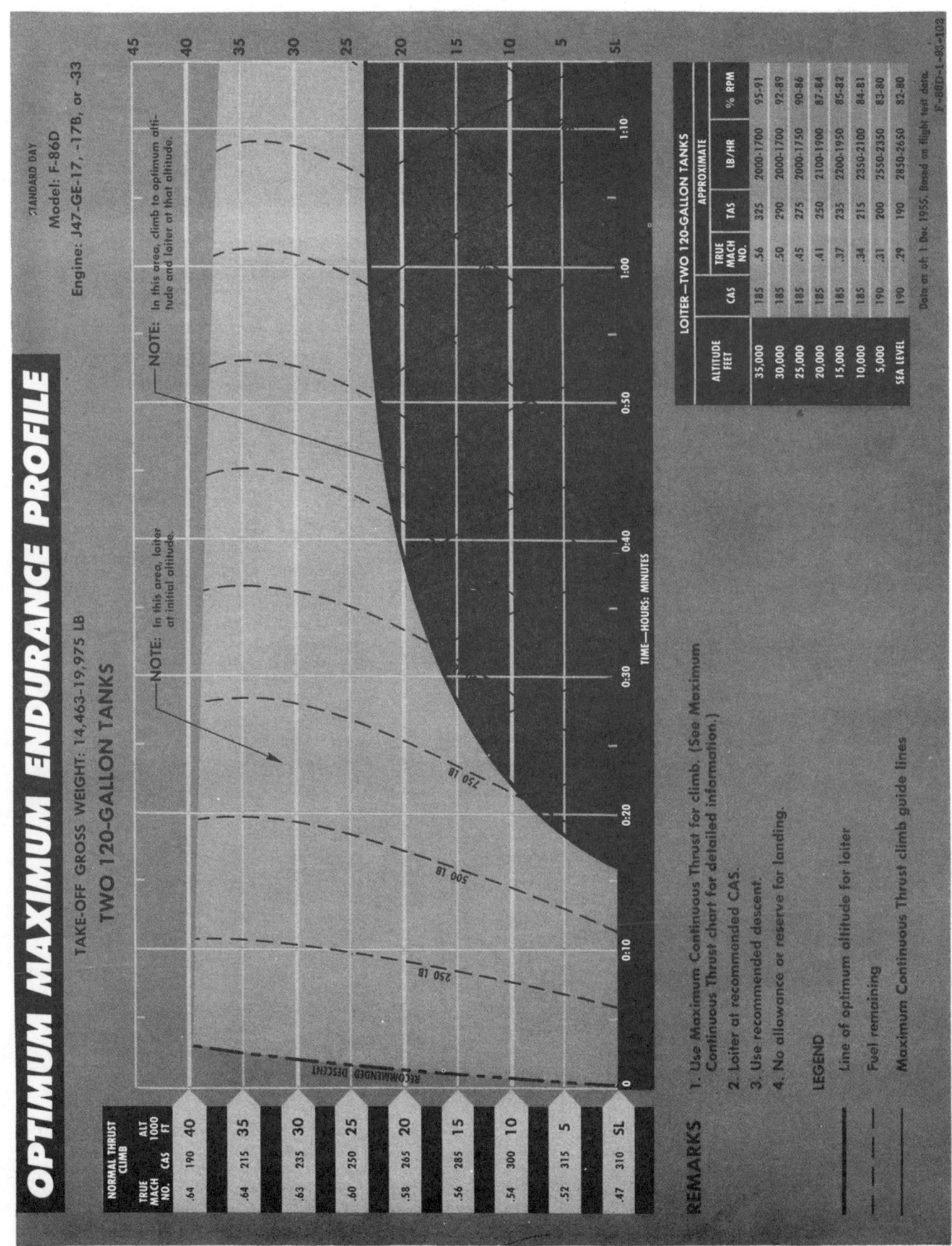

Figure A-18

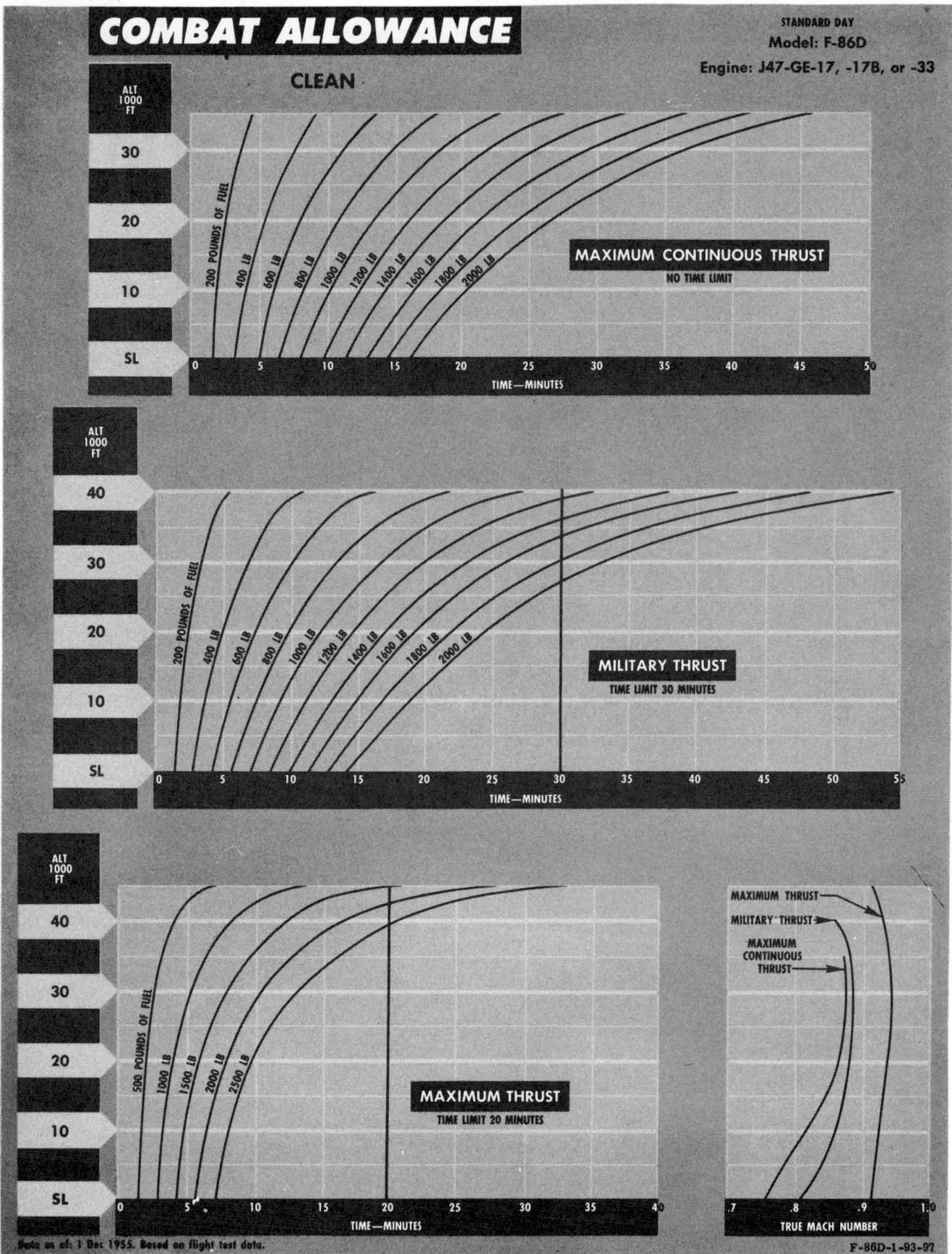

Figure A-19

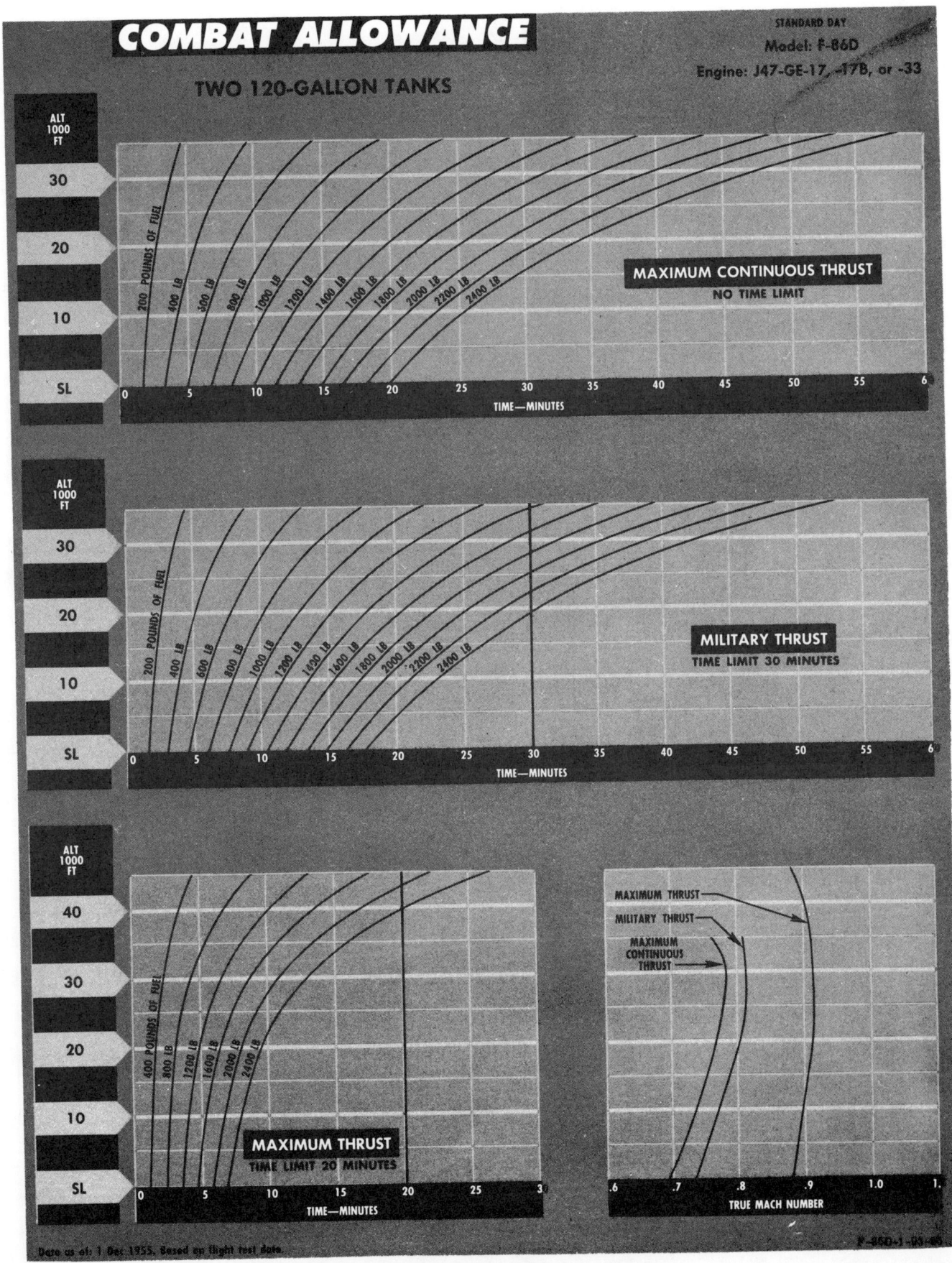

Figure A-20

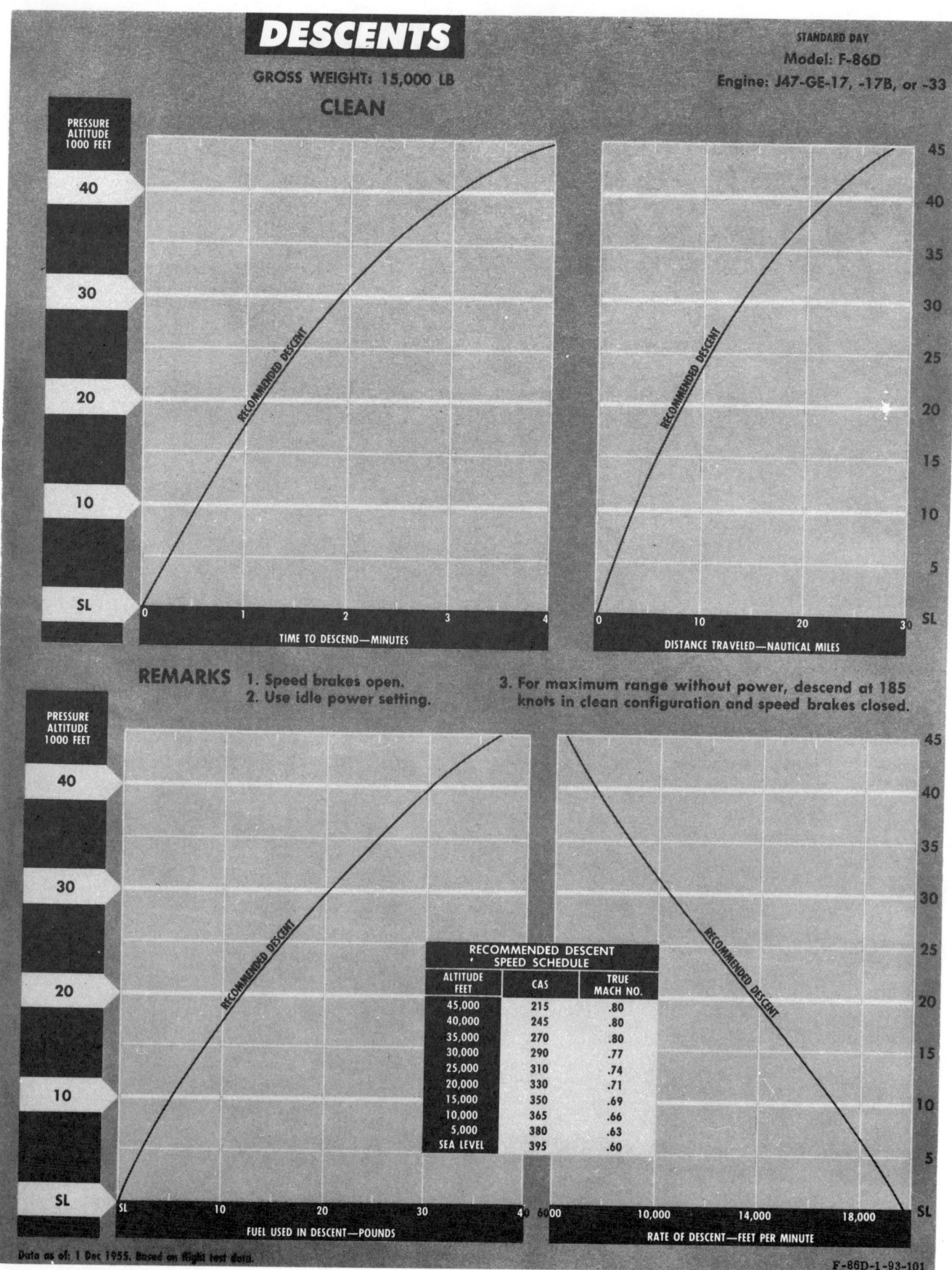

Figure A-21

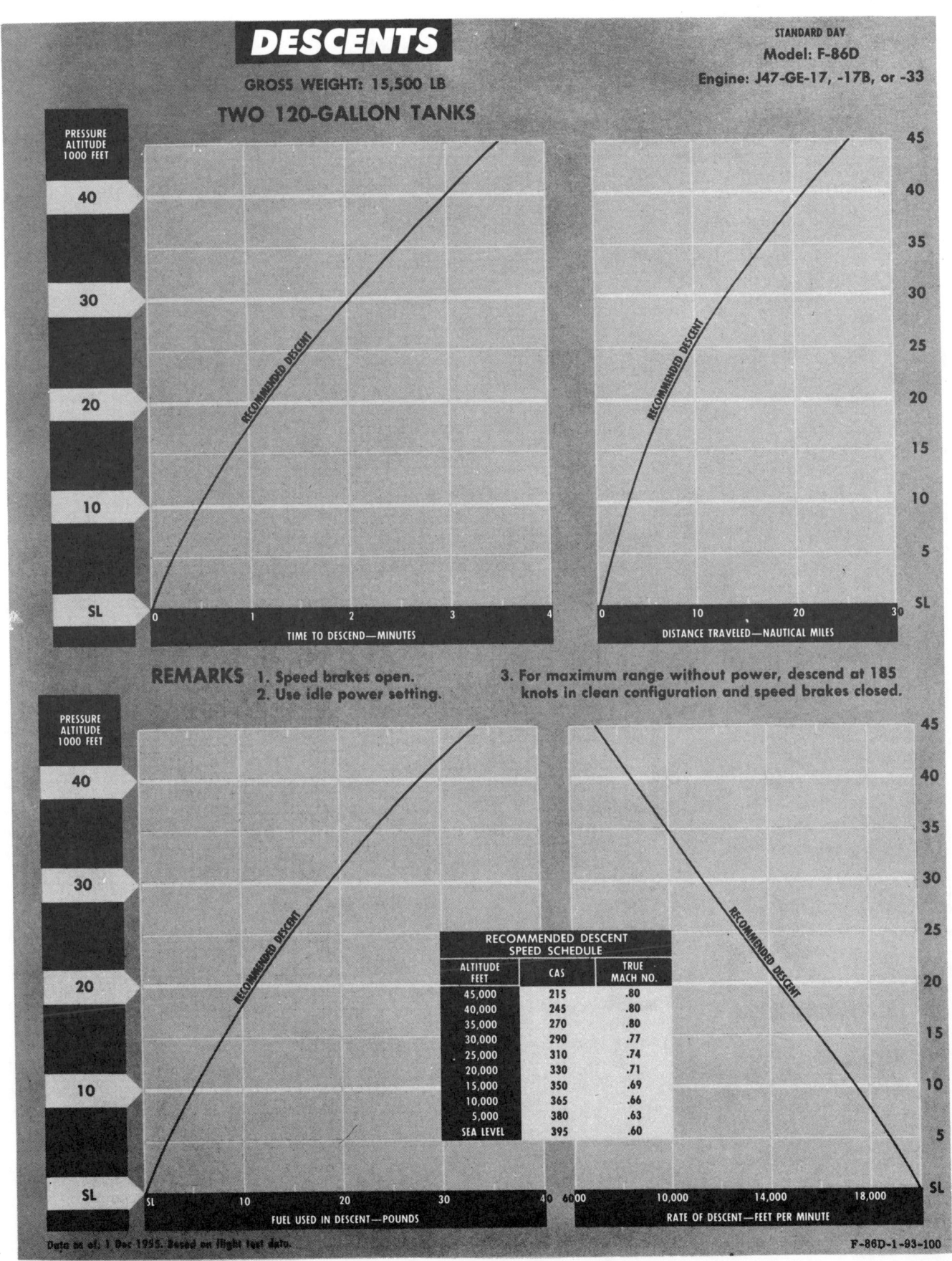

Figure A-22

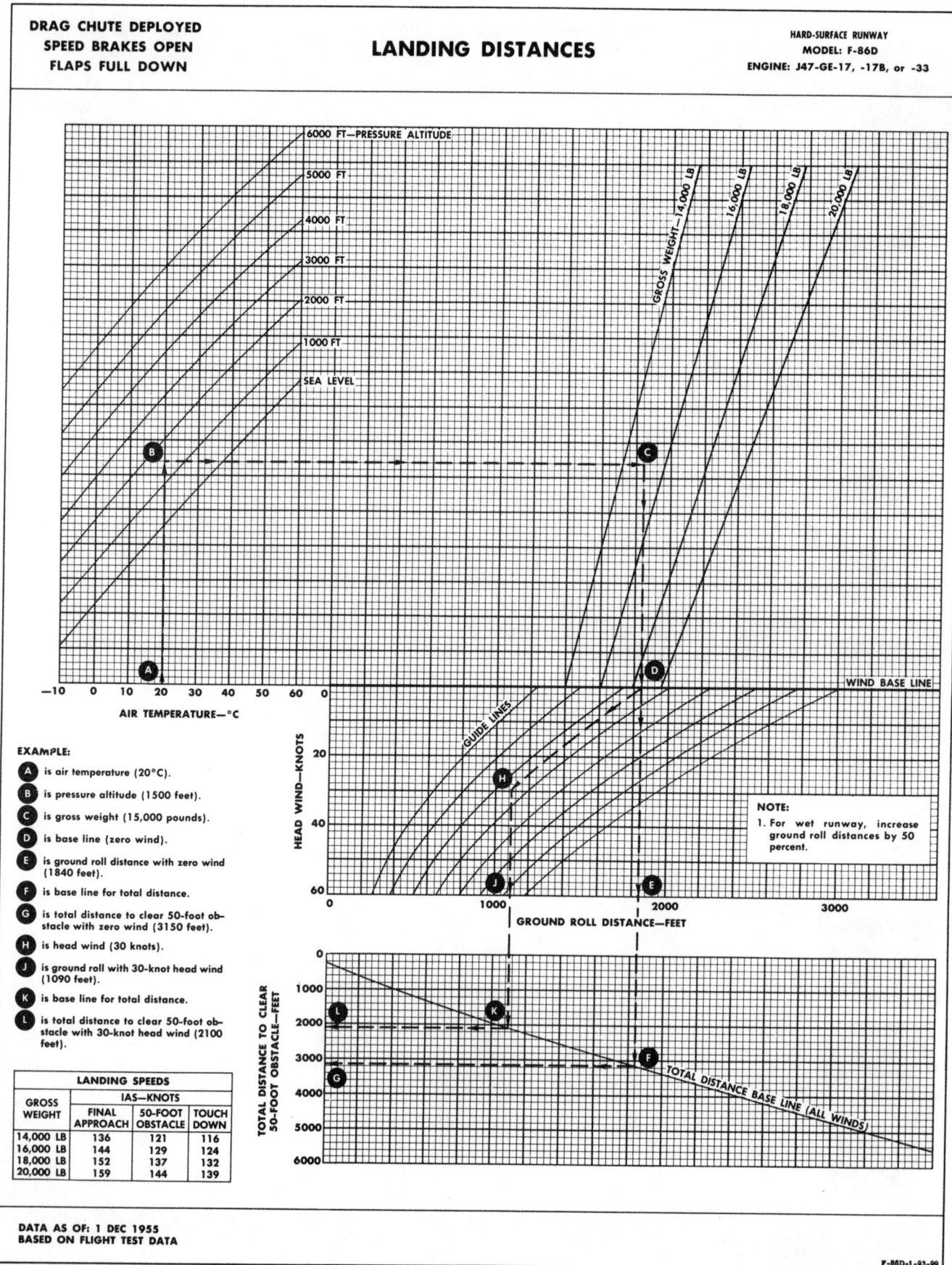

Figure A-23

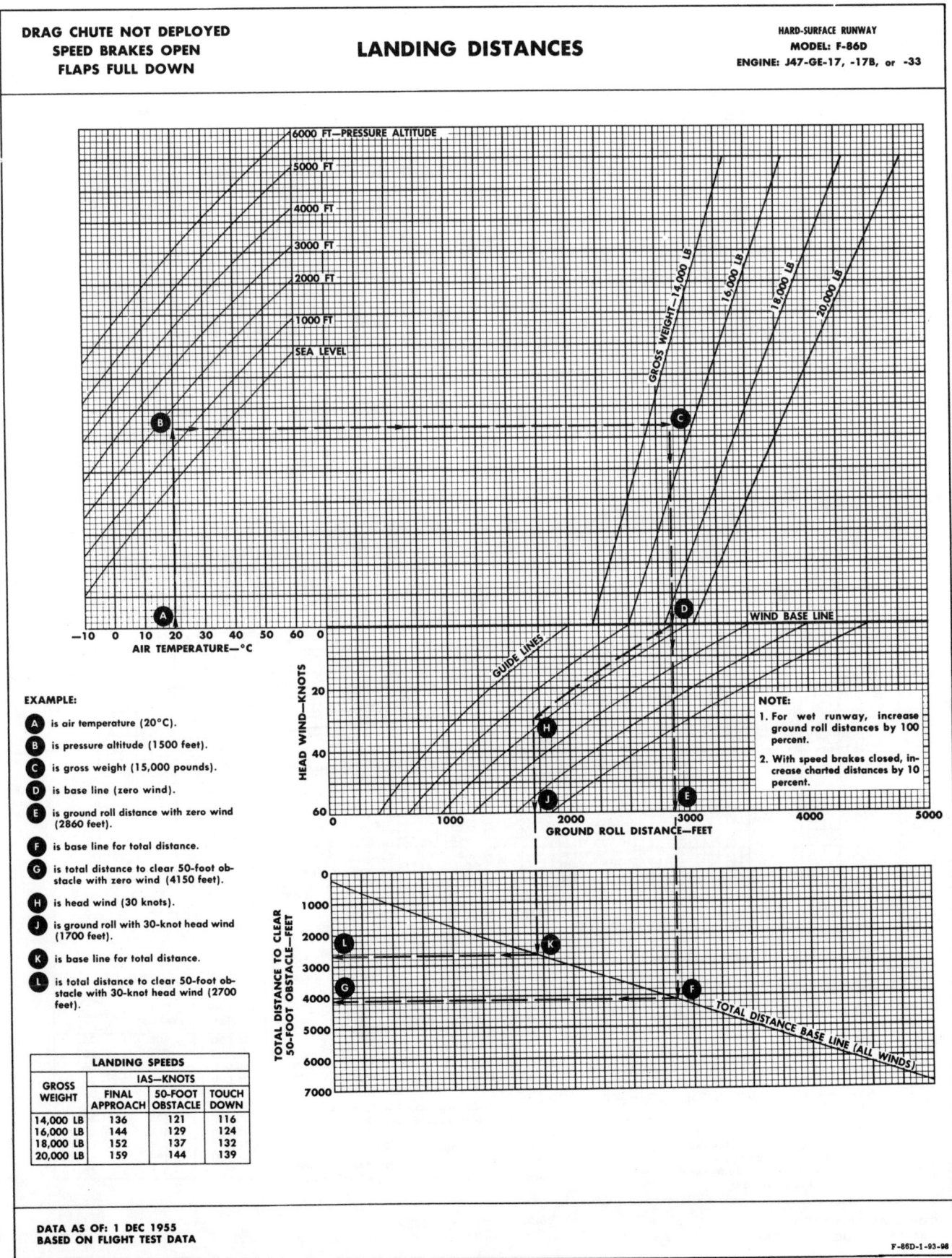

Figure A-24

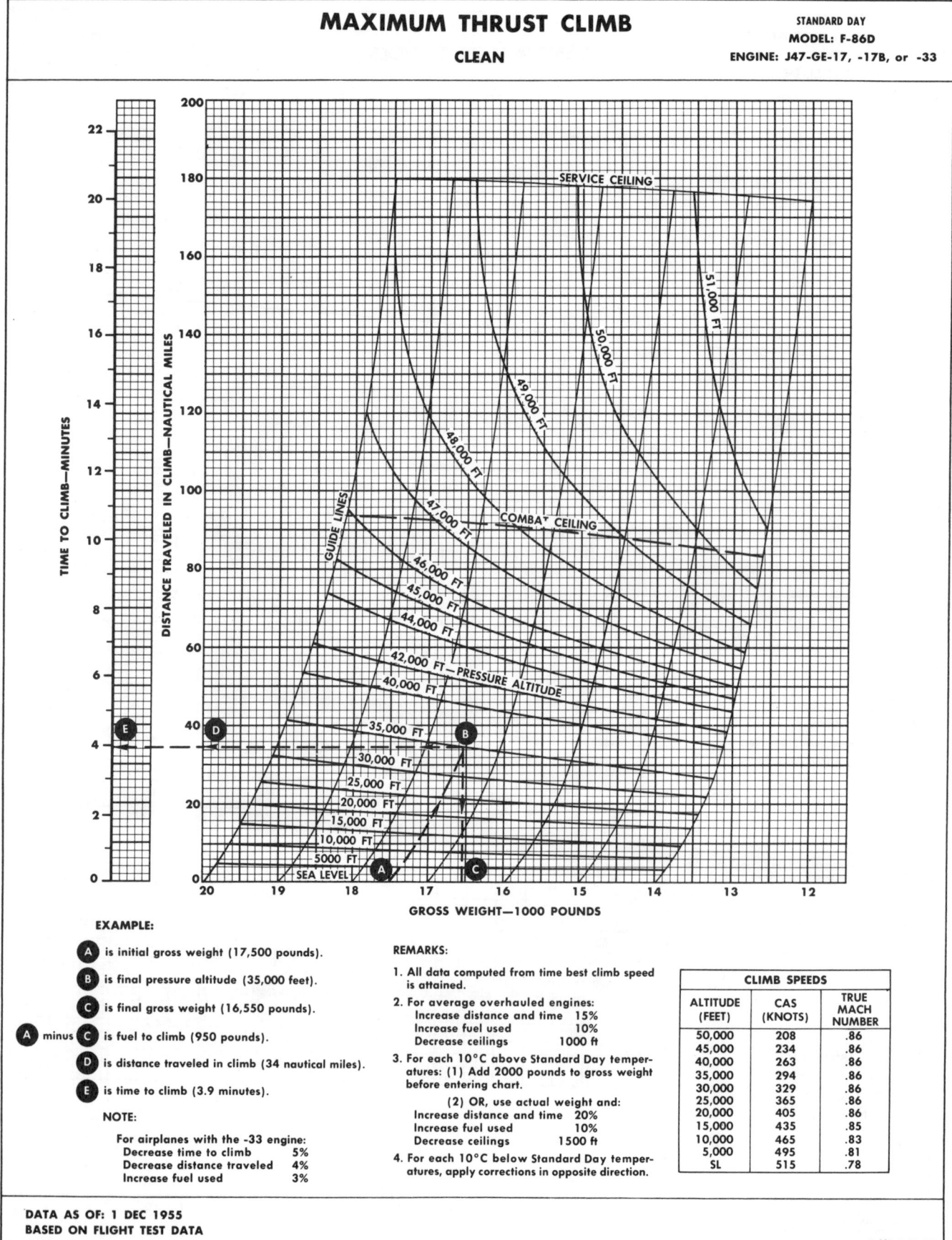

Figure A-25

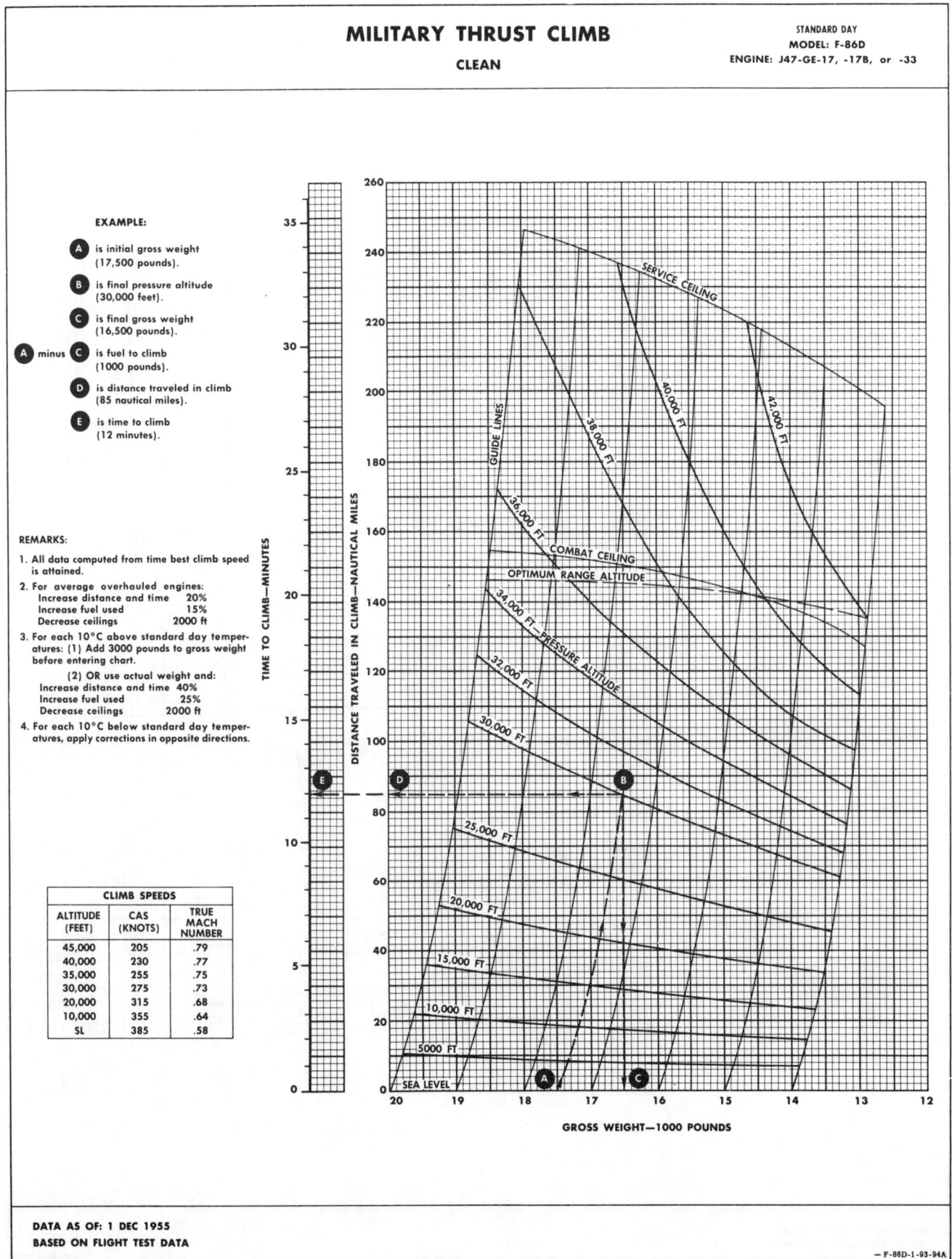

Figure A-26

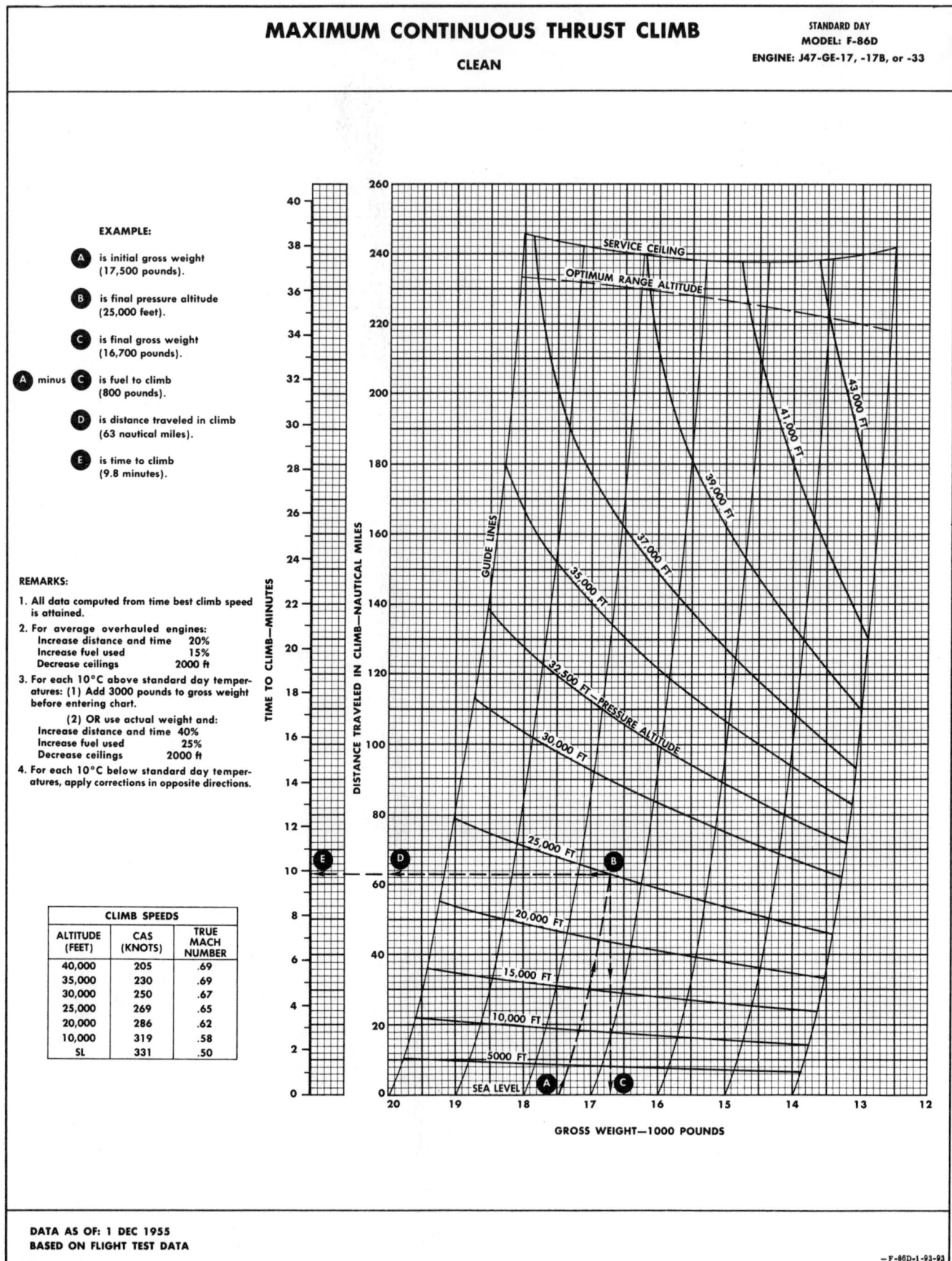

Figure A-27

MAXIMUM THRUST CLIMB

TWO 120-GALLON TANKS

STANDARD DAY
MODEL: F-86D
ENGINE: J47-GE-17, -17B, or -33

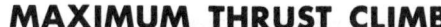

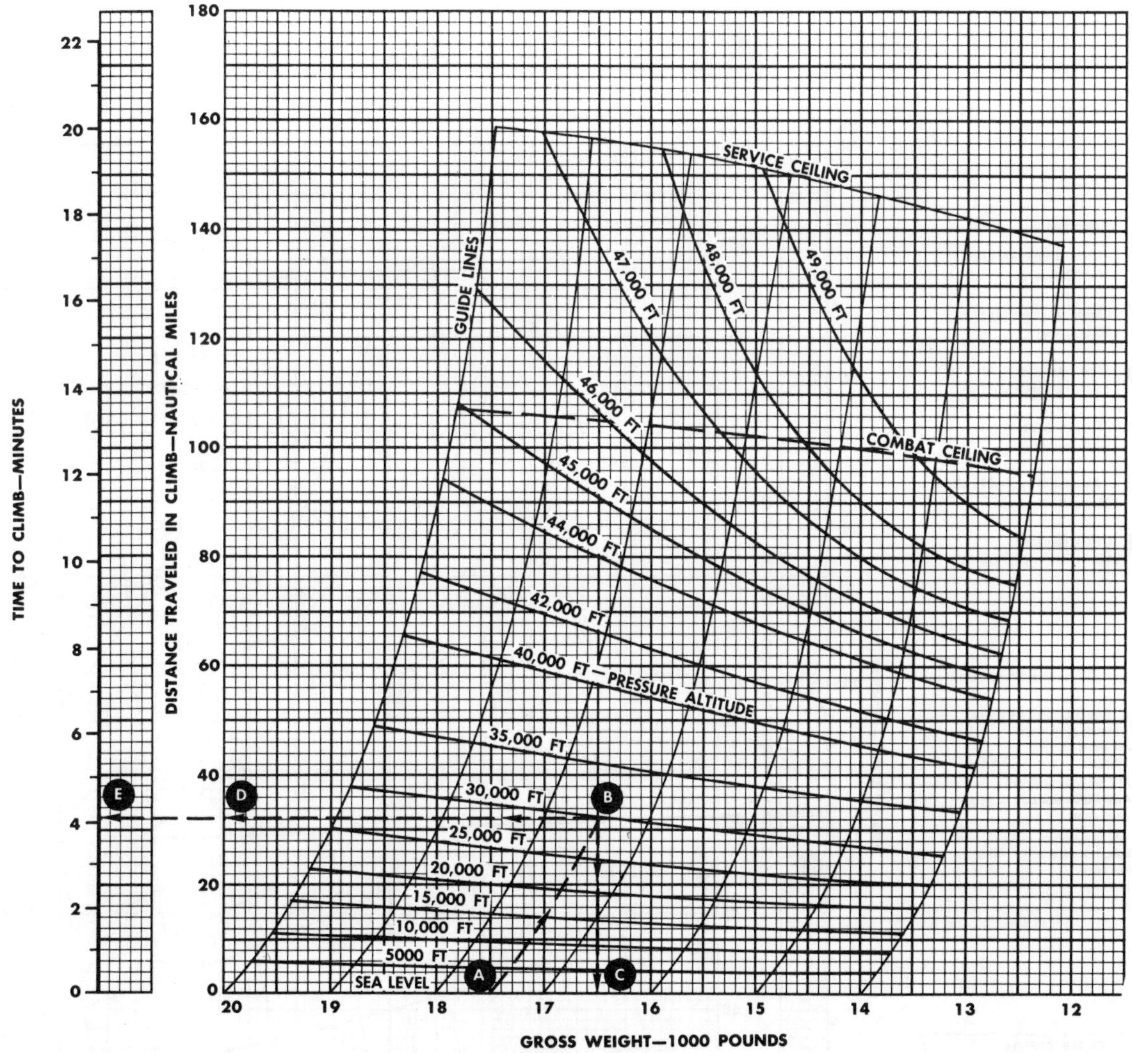

EXAMPLE:

- (A) is initial gross weight (17,500 pounds).
- (B) is final pressure altitude (30,000 feet).
- (C) is final gross weight (16,500 pounds).
- (A) minus (C) is fuel to climb (1000 pounds).
- (D) is distance traveled in climb (32 nautical miles).
- (E) is time to climb (4.1 minutes).

NOTE:

For airplanes with the -33 engine:
Decrease time to climb 5%
Decrease distance traveled 4%
Increase fuel used 3%

REMARKS:

1. All data computed from time best climb speed is attained.
2. For average overhauled engines:
   Increase distance and time 15%
   Increase fuel used 10%
   Decrease ceilings 1000 ft
3. For each 10°C above Standard Day temperatures: (1) Add 2000 pounds to gross weight before entering chart.
   (2) OR, use actual weight and:
   Increase distance and time 20%
   Increase fuel used 10%
   Decrease ceilings 1500 ft
4. For each 10°C below Standard Day temperatures, apply corrections in opposite direction.

CLIMB SPEEDS		
ALTITUDE (FEET)	CAS (KNOTS)	TRUE MACH NUMBER
50,000	200	.83
45,000	225	83
40,000	252	.83
35,000	283	.83
30,000	312	.82
20,000	373	.80
10,000	436	.78
SL	482	.73

DATA AS OF: 1 DEC 1955
BASED ON FLIGHT TEST DATA

— F-86D-1-93-92A

Figure A-28

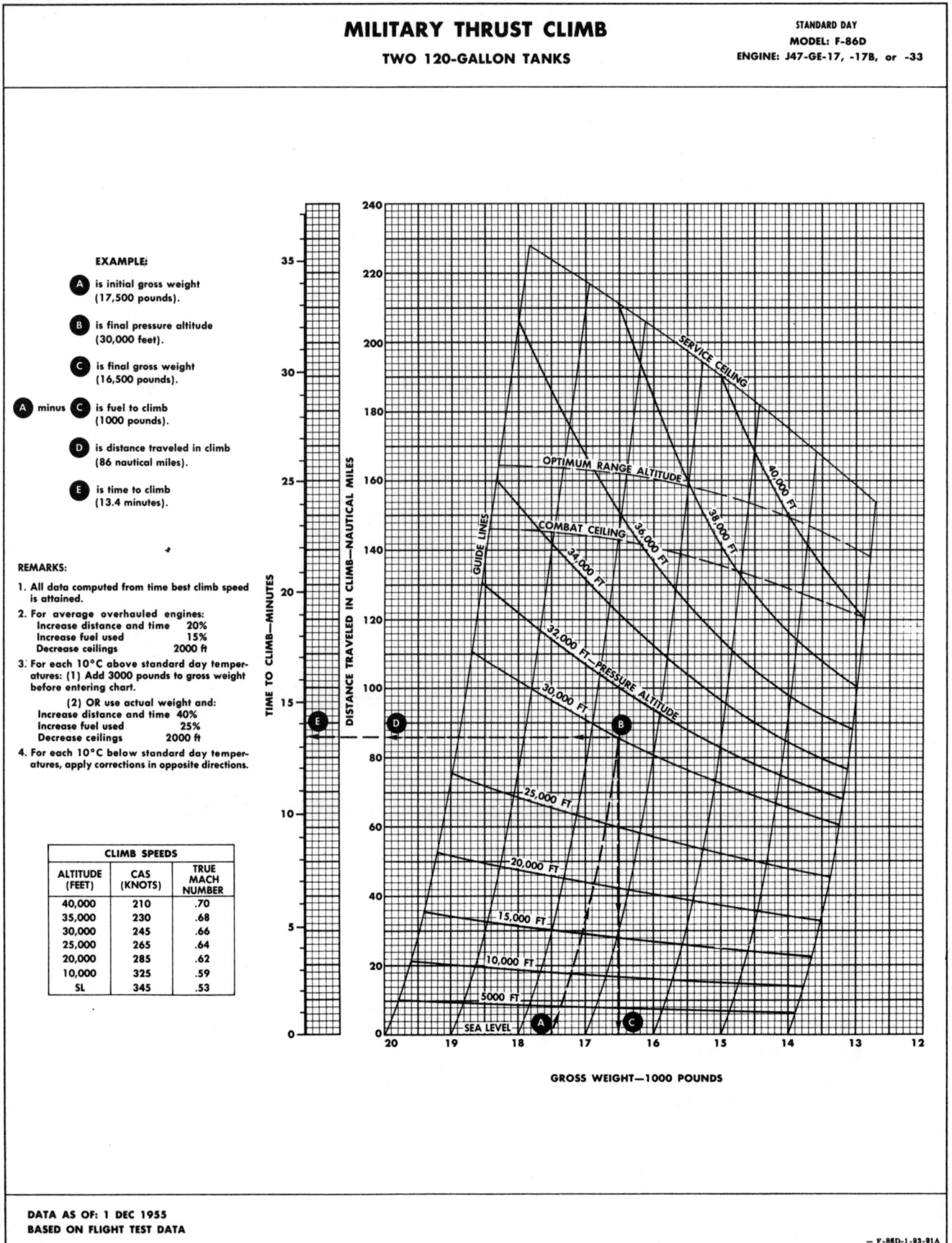

Figure A-29

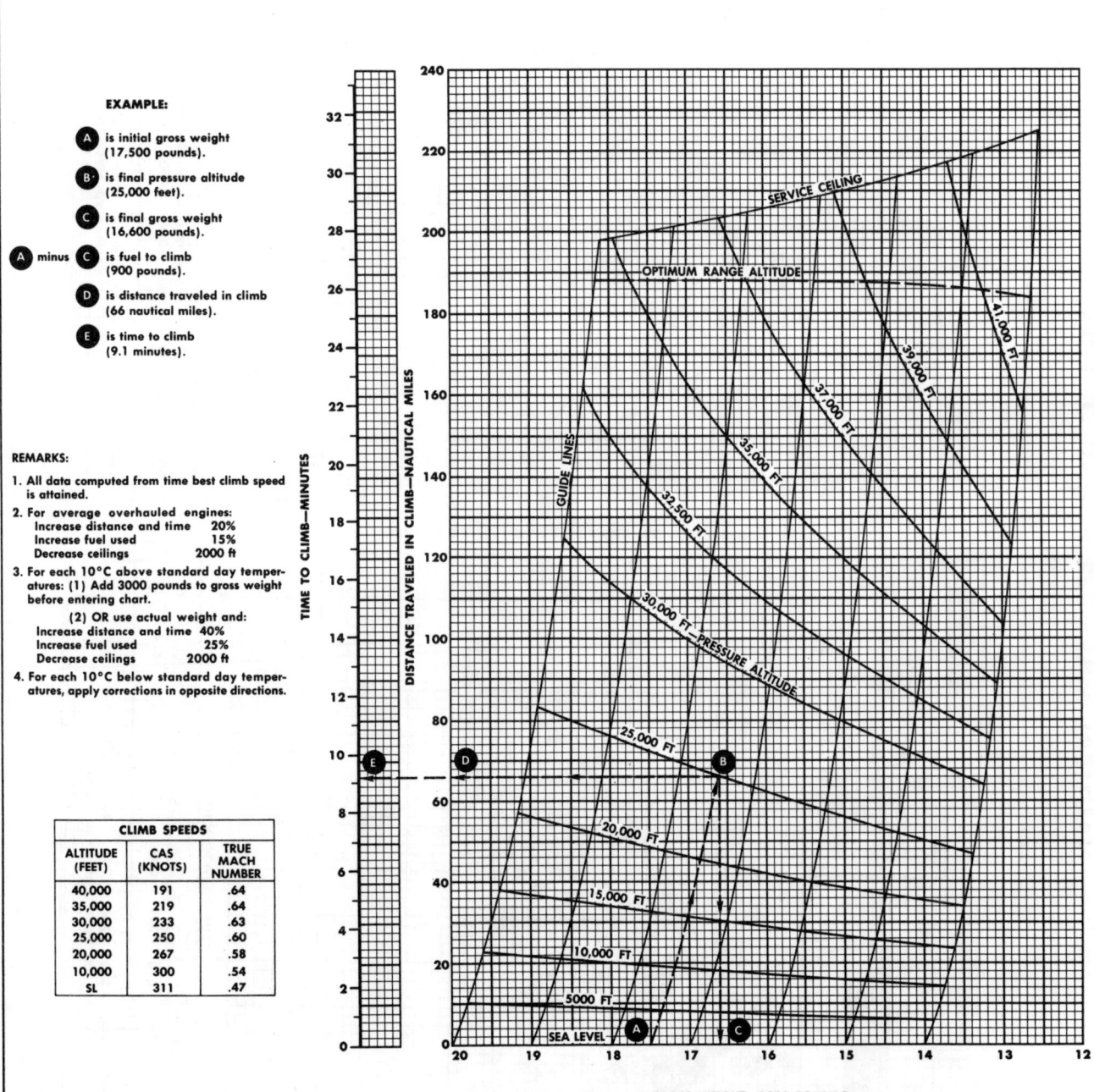

Figure A-30

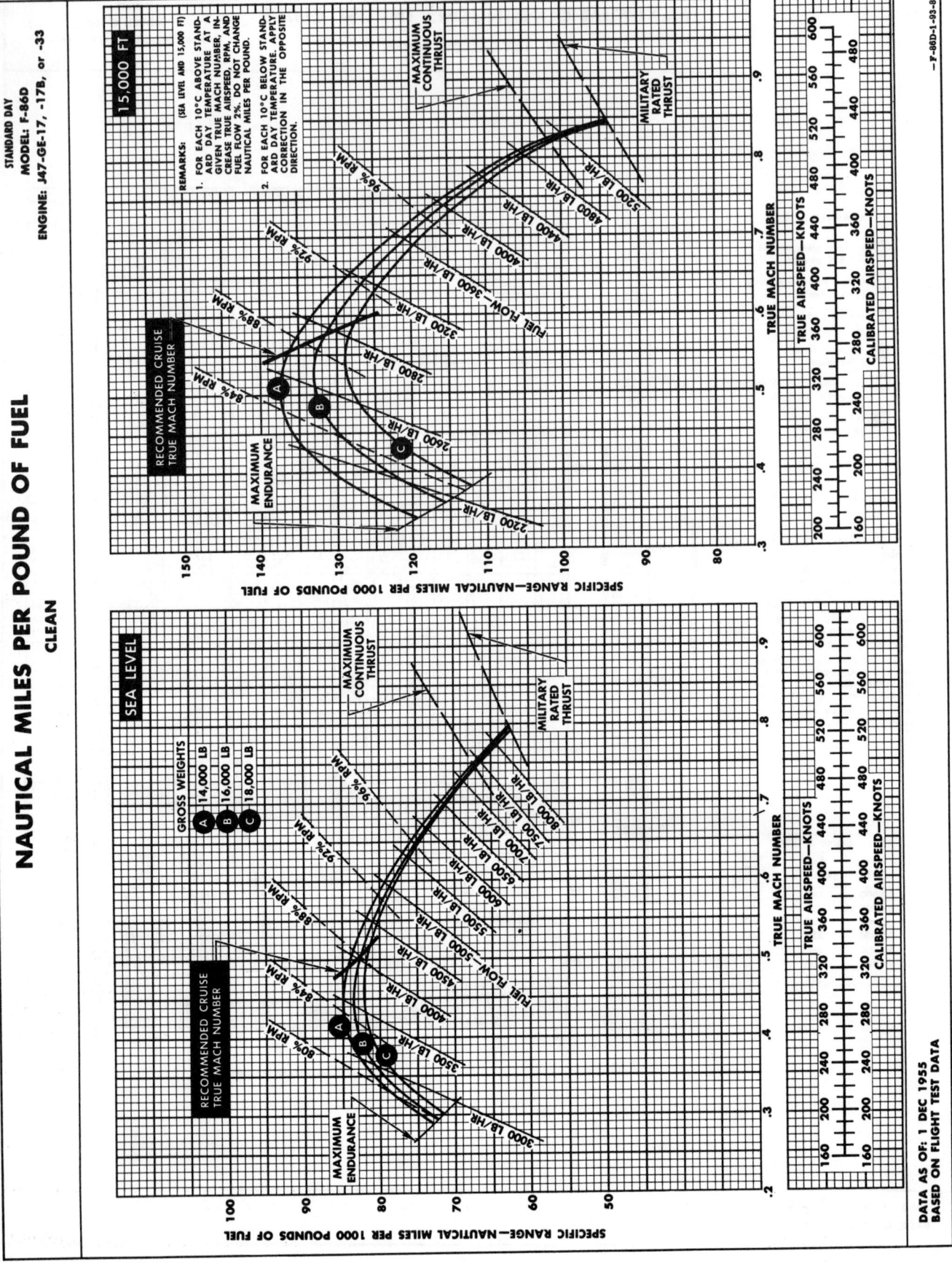

Figure A-31

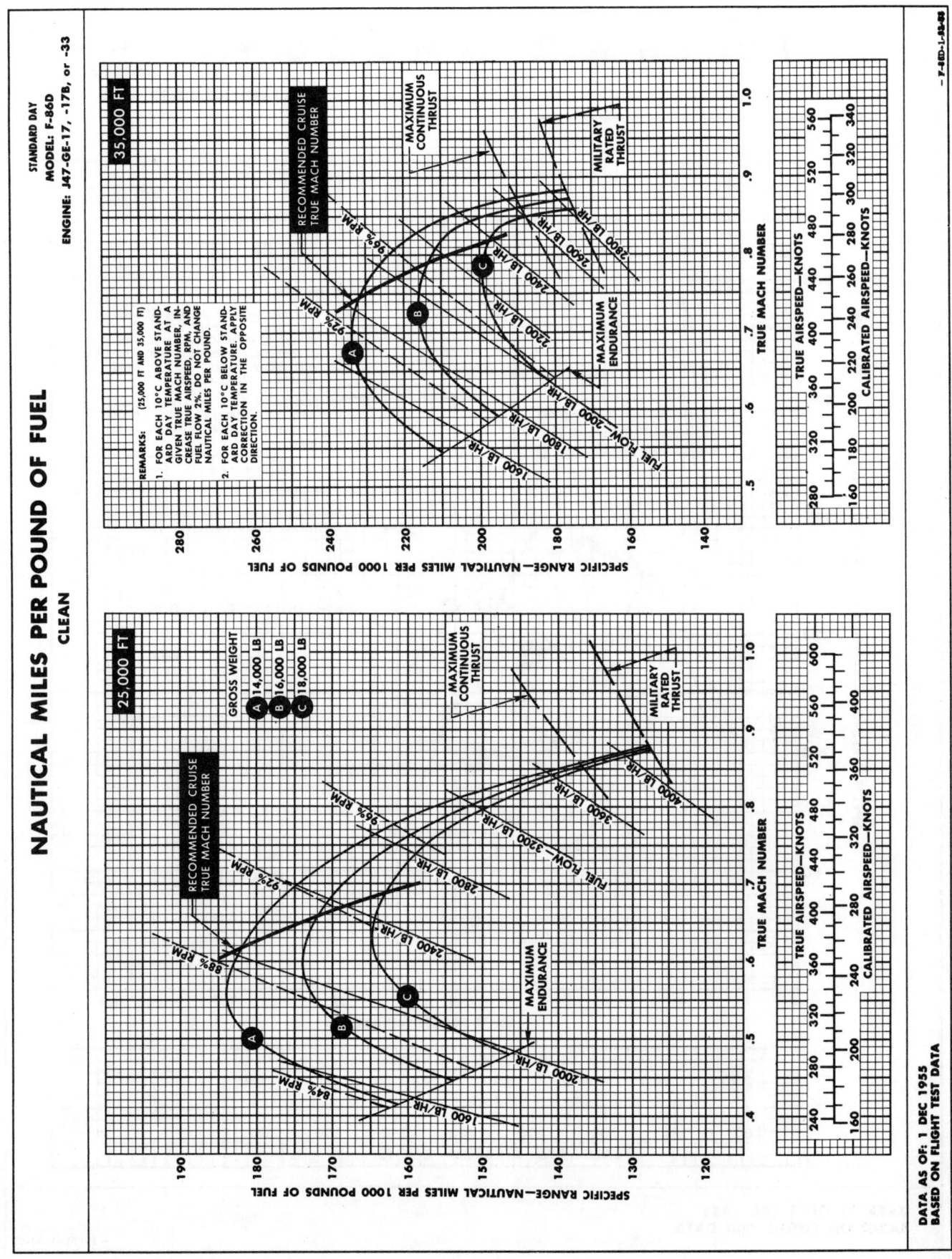

Figure A-32

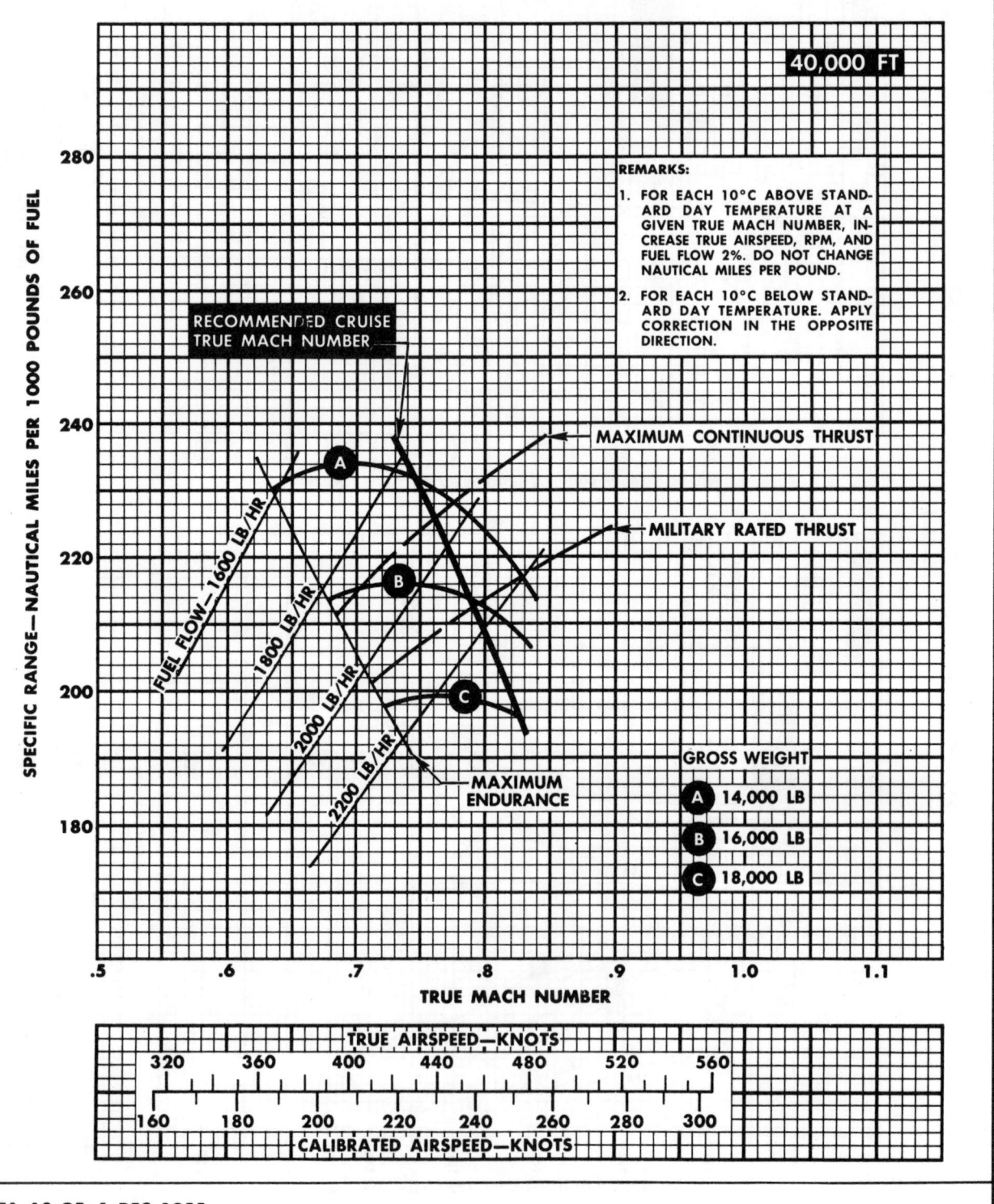

Figure A-33

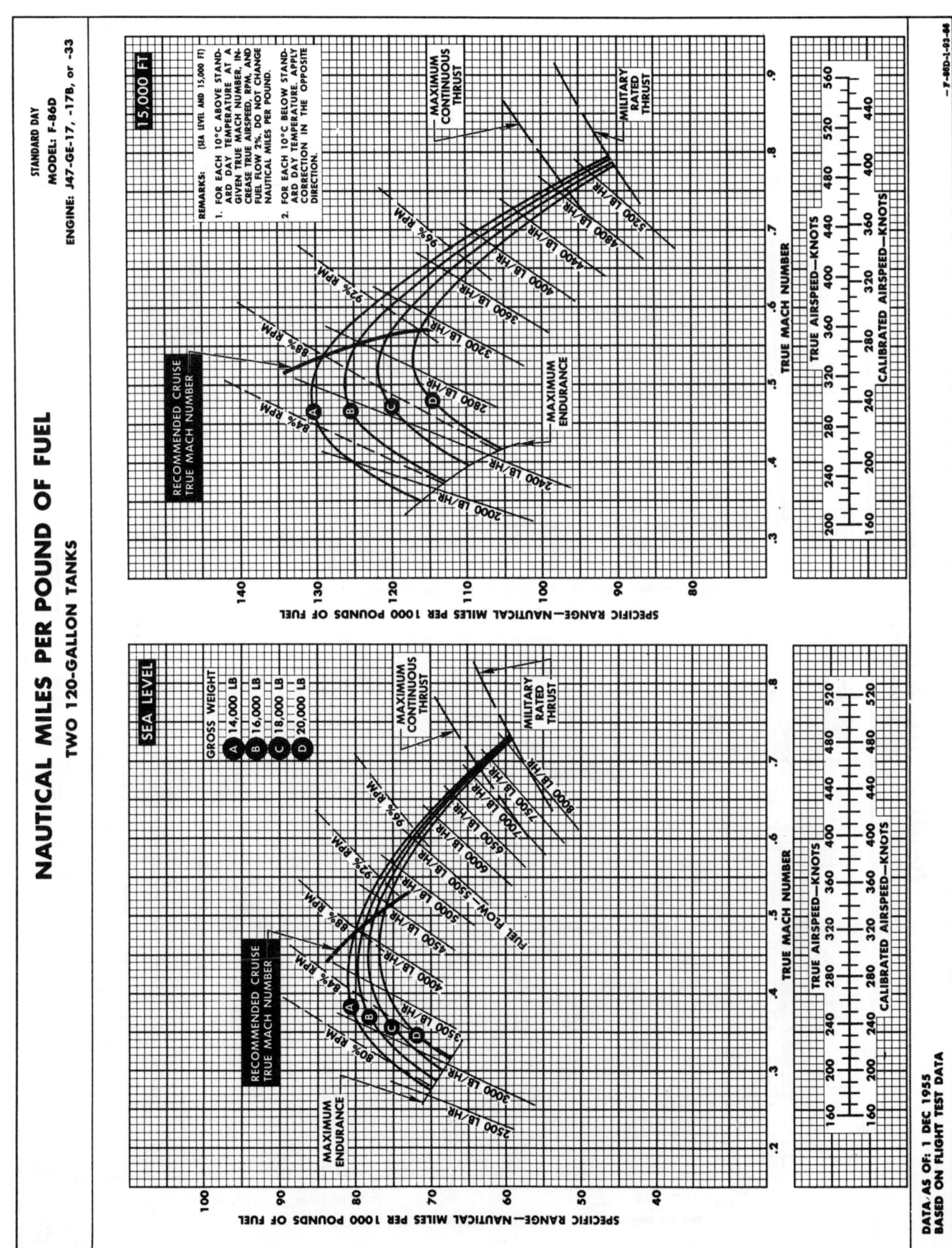

Figure A-34

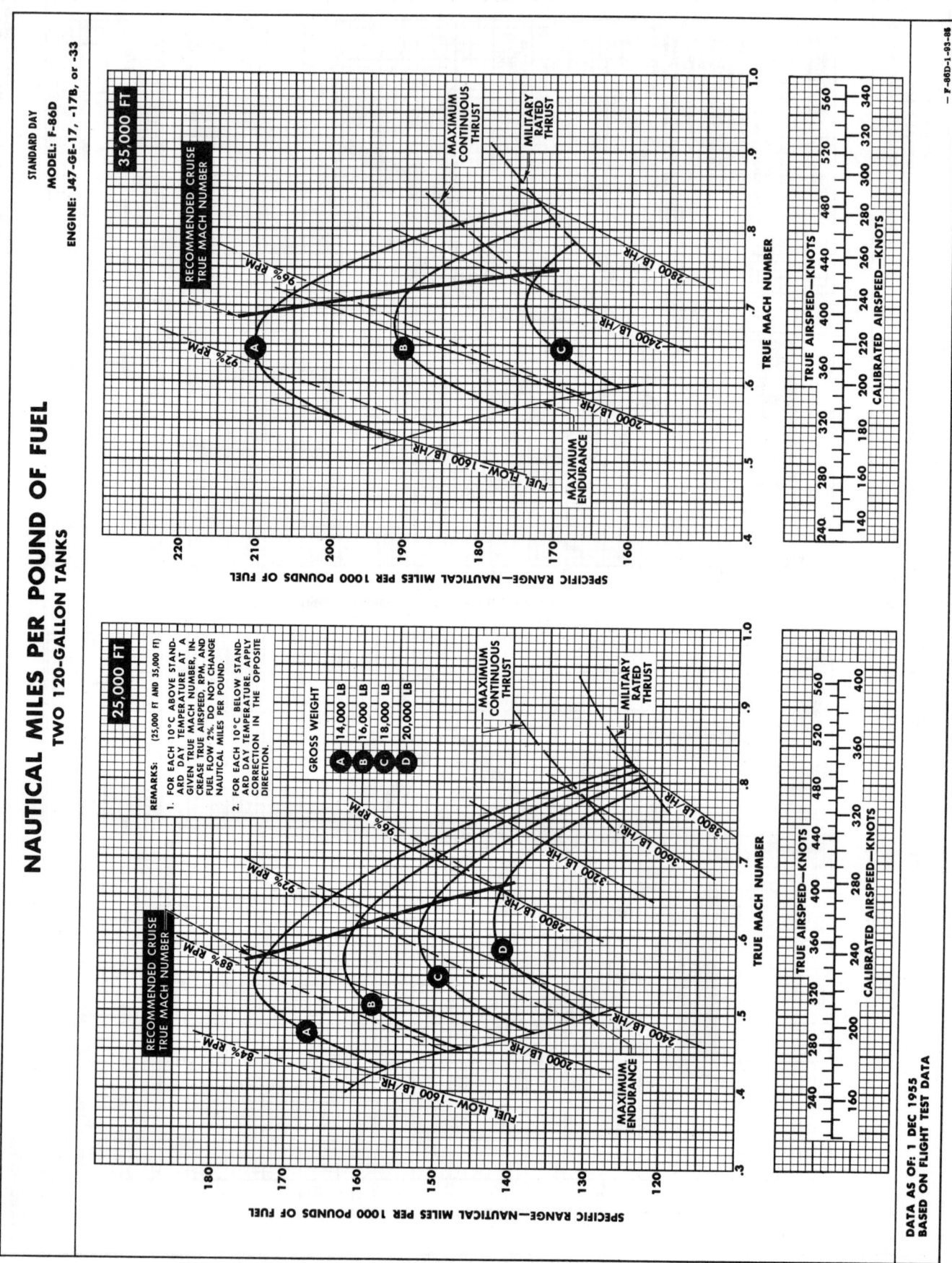

Figure A-35

INDEX

Acceleration Limitations—Armament

ALPHABETICAL index

PAGE NUMBERS IN BOLDFACE DENOTE ILLUSTRATIONS

A

Acceleration Limitations	5-6
Accelerometer	1-50
switch, light	4-19
Accumulator Air Pressure Gages, Flight Control Alternate System	1-44
Afterburner System	1-24
blowout, afterburner	7-7
engine overspeed during afterburner shutdown	7-8
failure	3-15
loss of afterburning during climb-out	3-15
loss of afterburning during flight	3-15
loss of afterburning during take-off	3-15
shutoff failure	3-15
limitations	5-1
operation during flight	2-19
roughness, afterburner	7-8
switch, shutoff	1-26
After Landing	2-24
cold-weather procedure	9-19
After Take-off	2-18
cold-weather procedure	9-19
hot-weather and desert procedure	9-21
Ailerons	1-38
flight characteristics	6-8, 6-9
normal trim failure	3-23
Air Conditioning and Pressurization System, Cockpit	4-1, 4-2
altimeter, cockpit	4-6
controls	4-1, 4-4
lever, manual ram-air	4-4
lever, ventilation air	4-5
rheostat, air temperature	4-4
switch, air temperature	4-4
switch, cockpit air	4-1
switch, pressure selector	4-5
normal operation	4-6
panel, control	4-4
pressure schedule	4-5
pressurization system emergency operation	4-6

Air Inlet, Engine	1-24
switch	1-24, 4-8
Airspeed Corrections	A-2, A-2, A-3
Airspeed Indicator	1-50
Airspeed Limitations	5-4
Air Start, Engine	3-5, **3-6**
Air Start Switch	1-22
Alternator	1-34
switch	1-36
Alternator External Power Receptacle	1-34, **1-35**
Altimeter	1-50
Altimeter, Cockpit	4-6
Antenna Hand Control	4-34, 4-35, 4-37
Antennas, Radio and Radar	**4-12**
Anti-G Suit Provisions	4-47
Anti-icing Systems	4-2, 4-7
controls	4-7
emergency operation	4-9
overheating of windshield and radome anti-icing system	4-9
overheating of surface anti-icing system	4-10
light, surface anti-ice overheat warning	4-8
light, windshield and radome anti-ice overheat warning	4-8
normal operation	4-9
rain removal system	4-9
switch, engine inlet	4-8
switch, pitot heat	4-8
switch, radome anti-ice	4-8
switch, surface anti-ice	4-8
switch, windshield and radome anti-ice	4-8
switch, windshield anti-ice	4-8
use of	9-15
Approach	**2-22**
cold-weather procedure	9-19
instrument approaches	9-4, 9-6, 9-10, 9-11, **9-11**
go-around, missed-approach	9-13
ground-controlled approaches	9-11, 9-12, **9-12**
holding	9-14
ILAS approaches	9-10, 9-12, 9-13
low-frequency range approaches	9-4, 9-6, 9-11
Armament	1-4, 4-30
also see Fire Control System	
controls	4-31
button, tank-rocket jettison	4-32
switch, armament master	4-31
switch, camera lens	4-32
switch, rocket external loading	4-32
switch, rocket-firing	4-31
switch, rocket package override	4-32
switch, rocket pod external jettisoning	4-32
trigger, camera and rocket-firing	4-31
indicators	4-32
light, hot-rocket package warning	4-32
light, jettison-ready indicator	4-32
light, rocket-package-up indicator	4-32

Index-1

INDEX
Armrests, Seat—Climb

PAGE NUMBERS IN BOLDFACE DENOTE ILLUSTRATIONS

panel, master control **4-30**
rocket-firing limitations 5-6
rocket package:
   emergency jettison in flight 3-23
   flight characteristics 6-22
   operation speed 5-5
Armrests, Seat 1-57
Artificial Feel System, Flight Control 1-39, **1-39**
   failure 3-23
Attitude Indicator 1-51
Automatic Pilot 4-23
   controls 4-24
     controller, automatic approach coupler 4-25, **4-26**
       button, altitude "OFF" 4-25
       button and indicator light, altitude engage 4-25
       button and indicator light, glide path engage 4-25
       button and indicator light, localizer engage 4-25
     controller, flight **4-24**, 4-25
       knob, turn 4-25
       switch, engaging 4-25
       wheel, roll trim 4-25
       wheels, pitch trim 4-25
     switch, power 4-24
     switch, release 4-25
   emergency disconnect 4-29
   emergency operation 4-29
   indicator, pitch trim 4-26
   normal operation 4-26

B

Battery 1-31
   switch, battery-starter 1-23
Before Entering Airplane
   cold-weather procedure 9-17
   instrument flight procedure 9-2
Before Leaving Airplane 2-26
   cold-weather procedure 9-20
   hot-weather and desert procedure 9-21
Before Take-off
   airplane check 2-14
   cold-weather procedure 9-18
   engine check 2-13, **2-14**
   hot-weather and desert procedure 9-20
   instrument flight procedure 9-2
   thunderstorm flying 9-16
Belt, Automatic-opening Safety 1-56, **1-57**
   lanyard, automatic parachute arming 1-57
Block Number Designations 1-4
Booster Pumps, Fuel 1-27
Brake System 1-49
Buttons, Control
   see applicable system

C

Camera
   see Armament
Canopy 1-52
   buttons (external), operating 1-53
   check 2-2
   ejector 1-54, **1-55**
   handle, external emergency release 1-53
   handle, lock 1-54
   light, unsafe warning 1-55
   loss of 3-12
   opening speed 5-4
   pins, ground and maintenance safety 1-52
   release, emergency 1-54
   seal 1-53
   switch 1-53
Canopy Defrost Lever 4-6
Center-of-Gravity Limitations 5-6
Charts A-1
   airspeed correction A-2, **A-2**, A-3
   climb graphs A-14
     clean:
       Maximum Continuous Thrust A-42
       Maximum Thrust A-40
       Military Thrust A-41

     tanks, two 120-gallon:
       Maximum Continuous Thrust A-45
       Maximum Thrust A-43
       Military Thrust A-44
   climb profiles A-5
     clean:
       Military Thrust A-22
     tanks, two 120-gallon:
       Military Thrust A-28
   combat allowance A-4
     clean A-34
     tanks, two 120-gallon A-35
   descent A-15
     clean A-36
     tanks, two 120-gallon A-37
   fuel quantity data 1-30
   instrument markings 5-1, 5-2
   intercept profiles A-8
     clean A-24
     tanks, two 120-gallon A-30
   landing distances A-15
     drag chute deployed A-38
     without drag chute A-39
   Mach number 6-1, **6-2**
   maximum endurance profiles A-12
     clean A-26
     tanks, two 120-gallon A-32
   mission profiles A-6
     clean A-23
     tanks, two 120-gallon A-29
   nautical miles per pound of fuel A-15
     clean .... A-46—A-48
     tanks, two 120-gallon A-49, A-50
   operating flight limits 5-4
   optimum maximum endurance profiles A-13
     clean A-27
     tanks, two 120-gallon A-33
   optimum return profiles A-10
     clean A-25
     tanks, two 120-gallon A-31
   oxygen duration 4-20, 4-21
   refusal speeds A-3, A-21
   stall speeds 6-2
   take-off acceleration A-3, A-20
   take-off distances A-2
     Maximum Thrust, full flaps A-18
     Military Thrust, full flaps A-19
Check List 4-47
Check List, Condensed 2-27
Checks
   airplane check, preflight 2-14
   automatic pilot ground tests 4-26
   before leaving airplane 2-26
   canopy and ejection seat 2-2
   engine check, preflight 2-13, **2-14**
   exterior inspection 2-2, **2-3**
     before exterior inspection 2-2
   ground tests 2-10
     cold-weather procedure 9-18
   interior check 2-4
   oxygen system preflight check 4-21
   pre-traffic-pattern check 2-20
   traffic-pattern check 2-21, **2-22**
   weight and balance 2-1
Circuit Breakers 1-31
Climb 2-19
   characteristics 6-14, **6-14**
   climb graphs A-14
     clean:
       Maximum Continuous Thrust A-42
       Maximum Thrust A-40
       Military Thrust A-41
     tanks, two 120-gallon:
       Maximum Continuous Thrust A-45
       Maximum Thrust A-43
       Military Thrust A-44
   climb profiles A-5
     clean:
       Military Thrust A-22
     tanks, two 120-gallon:
       Military Thrust A-28

T. O. 1F-86D-1 INDEX
Cockpit—Emergency Procedures

PAGE NUMBERS IN BOLDFACE DENOTE ILLUSTRATIONS

hot-weather and desert procedure 9-21
instrument climb 9-3
loss of afterburning during climb-out 3-15
main fuel control system failure during climb 3-18
Cockpit ....**1-6—1-11**
emergency entrance **3-13**
entrance 2-1, **2-2**
smoke or fumes, elimination of 3-10
Cockpit Air Conditioning and Pressurization System
see Air Conditioning and Pressurization System, Cockpit
Cockpit Altimeter 4-6
Cockpit Defrosting System 4-6
lever 4-6
operation 4-9
Code Indicator Light 4-18
Code Switch and Code Selector Switch, Master 4-17
Cold-weather Procedures 9-17
Combat Allowance A-4
clean **A-34**
tanks, two 120-gallon **A-35**
Combat Time Available **6-22**
Communication and Associated Electronic Equipment 4-10, **4-11**
antenna location, radio and radar **4-12**
command radio, AN/ARC-27 uhf 4-10
command radio, AN/ARC-34 uhf 4-10
compass, AN/ARN-6 radio 4-14
identification radar, AN/APX-6 4-14
identification radar, AN/APX-25 4-15
marker beacon radio, AN/ARN-12 4-16
panels, radio control **4-13**
receiver, AN/ARN-14 omnidirectional 4-15
receivers, glide path and localizer 4-15, 4-16
zero reader 4-16
controls, indicator 4-17
switch unit, selector 4-17
Compass, AN/ARN-6 Radio **4-11**, 4-14
Compass, Slaved Gyro Magnetic 4-29
switch, fast slaving 4-29
Compass, Stand-by 1-51
switch, light 4-19
Compressor Stall 7-6
Console Panel and Floodlight Rheostat and Selector Switch 4-19
Controller, Automatic Approach Coupler 4-25, **4-26**
Controller, Automatic Pilot Flight **4-24**, 4-25
Controls
see applicable system
Control Surfaces
see Flight Control System
Control Surface Tie-in System (CSTI) 4-46
controls 4-46
control, roll trim 4-46
G-limiter 4-47
switch, "CSTI" 4-46
switch, "CSTI & AUTOPILOT" power 4-46
light, "CSTI READY" 4-46
operation 4-47
panel, control **4-46**
Covers, Protective 4-47
Crash Barrier, Engaging 3-12
Cross-wind Landing 2-23
Cross-wind Take-off 2-17

D

Defrosting System, Cockpit 4-6
lever, windshield and canopy defrost 4-6
operation 4-9
rheostat, pressure suit face mask heater 4-7
Descent 2-20
charts A-15
clean **A-36**
tanks, two 120-gallon **A-37**
cold-weather procedure 9-19
exhaust temperature limitations 5-4
instrument descents 9-8
Dimensions, Airplane 1-4
Ditching 3-14
Diving **6-17**, **6-18**, 6-19, **6-20**
flight test dives 6-19
recovery **6-18**, 6-20, **6-20**
Drag Chute System 1-49
handle 1-50
indicator, door latch safe 1-50
operating speed 5-5
Drop Tanks
see Fuel System

E

Ejection 3-14, **3-16**
also see Seat, Ejection
failure of seat to eject 3-15
Electrical Power Supply System 1-30, **1-32**
ac power distribution 1-34
alternator 1-34
fuses, ac 1-36
lights, inverter failure warning 1-36
receptacle, alternator external power 1-34, **1-35**
receptacle, inverter external power 1-35, **1-35**
switch, alternator 1-36
switch, inverter selector 1-36
switch, inverter test 1-36
dc power distribution 1-31
circuit breakers 1-31
lights, generator warning 1-34
loadmeters 1-34
receptacles, external power 1-31
rheostats, generator voltage regulator 1-34
switch, battery-starter 1-23
switches, generator 1-34
switch, voltmeter selector 1-34
voltmeter 1-34
emergency operation 3-19
fire 3-10
generator failure 3-19
inverter change-over characteristics 7-10, **7-11**
inverter failure 3-21
Electronic Engine Control 1-14
lockup system, automatic 1-20
light, indicator 1-20
operation 7-1, **7-2**
automatic start 7-2, **7-3**
thrust selector 7-1
Electronic Equipment
see Communication and Associated Electronic Equipment
Emergency Fuel System 1-14
button, test 1-19
emergency fuel regulator check **2-13**
operation 7-9
start on 2-10
switch, three-position 1-18
characteristics 7-4, 7-8, 7-9
switch, two-position 1-19
characteristics 7-5, 7-8, 7-9
Emergency Handle, Flight Control 1-44
Emergency Jettison Handle, Drop Tank 1-27
Emergency Procedures 3-1
afterburner failure 3-15
loss of afterburning during climb-out 3-15
loss of afterburning during flight 3-15
loss of afterburning during take-off 3-15
shutoff failure 3-15
artificial feel system failure, flight control 3-23
automatic pilot emergency disconnect 4-29
automatic pilot emergency operation 4-29
canopy, loss of 3-12
ditching 3-14
drop tank emergency jettison in flight 3-23
E-4 fire control system emergency operation 4-42
ejection 3-14, **3-16**
failure of seat to eject 3-15
electrical system emergency operation 3-19
generator failure 3-19
inverter failure 3-21
engine failure 3-1
air start 3-5, **3-6**
during flight 3-3

Index-3

INDEX
Emergency Release—Fire Control System

PAGE NUMBERS IN BOLDFACE DENOTE ILLUSTRATIONS

during take-off:
    after leaving ground 3-2
    before leaving ground 3-2
  forced landing, simulated **3-4**, 3-8
  landing with engine inoperative **3-4**, 3-6
  maximum glide **3-3**, 3-6
  overspeed during take-off 3-1
entrance, emergency **3-13**
fire 3-8
  electrical fire 3-10
  engine fire:
    after shutdown 3-10
    during flight 3-9
    during starting 3-9
    during take-off 3-9
  fire-warning circuits 3-8
fuel control system failure, main 3-18
  during flight 3-19
  during take-off and climb 3-18
  transfer pump failure 3-19
hydraulic system failure, flight control 3-22
landing emergencies 3-10
  any one gear up or unlocked 3-11
  barrier, engaging runway 3-12
  belly landing 3-10
  landing with flat tire 3-12
landing gear emergency operation 3-22
  emergency lowering **3-23**
  emergency retraction 3-22
oxygen system emergency operation 4-23
pressurization system emergency operation 4-6
rocket package emergency operation 4-45
  emergency jettison in flight 3-23
  hot-rocket package 4-45
  jettisoning rocket package 4-45
smoke or fumes, elimination of 3-10
trim failure, aileron normal 3-23
trim failure, horizontal tail normal 3-23
variable-area nozzle automatic control failure 3-18
Emergency Release, Canopy 1-54
Emergency Release Handle, External Canopy 1-53
Emergency Release Handle, Landing Gear 1-47
Emergency Retract Button, Landing Gear 1-46
Emergency Toggle Lever, Oxygen Regulator 4-20
Engine 1-5, 1-15
  also see Afterburner System
  acceleration limitations 5-6
  anti-icing system 4-2, 4-7, **4-7**
    switch, inlet 4-8
  electronic control 1-14
    operation 7-1, **7-2**
      automatic start characteristics 7-2, **7-3**
      thrust selector 7-1
  exhaust temperature 5-1
    characteristics 7-10
  failure 3-1
    air start 3-5, **3-6**
    during flight 3-3
    during take-off:
      after leaving ground 3-2
      before leaving ground 3-2
    forced landing, simulated 3-8
    landing with engine inoperative **3-4**, 3-6
    maximum glide **3-3**, 3-6
    overspeed during take-off 3-1
  fire 3-8
    after shutdown 3-10
    during flight 3-9
    during starting 3-9
    during take-off 3-9
  fire-warning system 1-52
  "flattop fuel schedule" 1-14
  fuel control system 1-14, 1-16
    button, emergency fuel system test 1-19
    emergency fuel regulator check **2-13**
    emergency system operation 7-9
    failure, main system 3-18
    light, dual fuel pump warning 1-19
    light, emergency fuel system indicator 1-19
    switch, emergency fuel system 1-18, 1-19

switch, engine master 1-18
throttle (power control) 1-18, **1-18**
icing 9-14
ignition system 1-22
  switch, air start 1-22, **1-23**
indicators 1-24
  flowmeter, fuel 1-24
  gage, exhaust temperature 1-24
  gage, fuel pressure 1-24
  gage, oil pressure 1-24
  tachometer 1-24
inlet, engine air 1-24
  switch, inlet 1-24, 4-8
limitations 5-1, **5-2**
lockup system, electronic control automatic 1-20
  ground tests 2-10
  light, engine control lockup indicator 1-20
  operation 7-4
nozzle, variable-area 1-21, **1-21**
  failure, automatic control 3-18
  indicator 1-22
  switch 1-21
operation 7-5
  accelerations, slow 7-5
  compressor stall 7-6
  flame-out 7-6
  ground operation 2-10
  lack of response to throttle movement 7-5
  noise and roughness 7-7
  preflight check **2-13**, 2-14
  smoke from turbine during shutdown 7-7
  starting 2-6, **2-8**
    instrument flight procedure after starting 9-2
  stopping 2-24
    cold-weather procedure 9-20
  tachometer indication 7-7
overspeed 5-1
starter system 1-23
  button, stop-starter 1-24
  switch, battery-starter 1-23
Entrance 2-1, **2-2**
  emergency entrance **3-13**
Exhaust Temperature Gage 1-24
Exterior Inspection 2-2, **2-3**
  before exterior inspection 2-2
External Power Receptacle, Alternator 1-34, **1-35**
External Power Receptacle, Inverter 1-34, **1-35**
External Power Receptacles, DC 1-31

F

Ferry Operations 6-22, **6-24**
Fire 3-8
  electrical 3-10
  engine 3-9, 3-10
    light, aft fire-warning 3-9
    light, forward fire-warning 3-9
Fire Control System 4-33
  automatic search 4-39
  automatic track 4-40
  beacon operation 4-44, 4-45
  controls, radar and rocket-firing system **4-33**, **4-34**, **4-35**
    control, antenna hand **4-34**, **4-35**, 4-37
    panel, radar control 4-34, **4-34**, **4-35**
      knob, "BCN & GROUND MAP EXPAND" control 4-36
      knob, "I-F GAIN" control 4-36
      light, "COMPUTER OFF" 4-36
      light, "COMPUTER ON" 4-36
      switch, "ANTI-JAM" 4-36
      switch, "AZ SCAN" 4-35
      switch, "CLUTTER ELIMINATOR" 4-36
      switch, "EL SCAN" 4-35
      switch, master power 4-34
      switch, "OPERATION" 4-36
      switch, "SCALE ILLUM" 4-36
    panel, radarscope control **4-34**, **4-35**, 4-36
      knob, "HORIZON CENTER GYRO ERECT" control 4-37
      knob, "PITCH" control 4-37
      knobs, intensity control 4-37

Index-4

INDEX

Fire-warning System—Instruments

PAGE NUMBERS IN BOLDFACE DENOTE ILLUSTRATIONS

light, reduced-power indicator	4-37
light, "XMTR OFF" indicator	4-37
emergency operation of E-4 fire control system	4-42
ground map operation	**4-44**, 4-45
manual search	4-40
normal operation	4-39, **4-41**
operational characteristics	4-42, **4-43**, **4-44**
radarscope presentation	4-38, **4-38**
rocket-firing operation, manual	4-42
rocket package emergency operation	4-45
hot-rocket package	4-45
jettisoning rocket package	4-45
shutdown procedure	4-45
sight, stand-by	4-45
rheostat	4-45
switch, alternate filament selector	4-45
Fire-warning System, Engine	1-52
Flame-out	7-6
Flap System, Wing	1-45
lever	1-45
operation	7-13
lowering speed	5-4
Flasher Switch, Exterior Lighting	4-17
Flight Characteristics	6-1
Flight Controller, Automatic Pilot	4-24, **4-25**
Flight Control System	1-38
aileron flight characteristics	**6-8**, **6-9**
aileron normal trim failure	3-23
artificial feel system	1-39, **1-39**
failure	3-23
controls	1-39
control stick	1-39, **1-40**
lock, control	1-40
pedals, rudder	1-39
switch, alternate lateral trim	1-40
switch, alternate longitudinal trim	1-40
switch, normal trim	1-40
switch, rudder trim	1-41
switch, yaw damper	1-41
flight characteristics	6-7
horizontal tail flight characteristics	**6-7**, **6-7**
horizontal tail normal trim failure	3-23
hydraulic systems	1-42, **1-43**
alternate hydraulic system	1-42
failure	3-22
fluid specification	**1-58**
gage, pressure	1-38
switch, selector	1-38
gages, alternate system accumulator air pressure	1-44
ground tests	2-10
handle, flight control emergency	1-44
light, alternate system indicator	1-44
normal hydraulic system	1-42
operation	7-13
rudder control system	1-42
switch, flight control	1-44
light, take-off (trim) position indicator	1-41
panel, control	1-41
rudder flight characteristics	6-8
rudder operation	6-11
trim characteristics, flight	6-9
variable-slope feel system	1-38, **1-39**
yaw damper	1-39
operation	**6-10**, **6-10**
Forced Landing (Dead Engine)	**3-4**, 3-6
Forced Landing, Simulated	3-8
Fuel Control System, Engine	
see Engine	
Fuel Flowmeter	1-24
Fuel Pressure Gage	1-24
Fuel System	**1-26**, **1-28**, **1-29**
controls	1-27
button, drop tank jettison	1-27
button, tank-rocket jettison	4-32
handle, drop tank emergency jettison	1-27
switch, engine master	1-18
throttle	1-18
valve, drop tank air pressure shutoff	1-27
fuel quantity data	**1-30**
fuel specification	**1-58**
gage, fuel quantity	1-30
switch, test	1-30
operation	7-11, **7-12**
dual fuel pump warning light characteristics	7-13
with inoperative aft transfer pump	7-11
pumps, booster	1-27
tanks, drop	1-27
emergency jettison in flight	3-23
flight characteristics	6-23
maximum allowable airspeeds when tanks installed	5-2, 5-5
release speed	5-5
transfer pump failure	3-19
Fumes, Elimination of	3-10
Fuselage Light Dimmer Switch	4-17
Fuses, AC	1-36

G

Gages	
see applicable system	
Generator	
see Electrical Power Supply System	
Generators, Vortex	**6-23**, **6-24**
Glide Path and Localizer Receivers	4-11, 4-15, 4-16
G-limit Overshoot	**6-16**, 6-18
Go-around	2-24, **2-25**
Go-around, Missed-approach	9-13
Ground-controlled Approaches	9-11, 9-12, **9-12**
Ground Operation, Engine	2-10
Ground Tests	2-10
automatic pilot	4-26
cold-weather procedure	9-18
Gust, Effects of	6-21

H

Handles	
see applicable system	
Heavy-weight Landing	2-23
Horizontal Tail	1-38
flight characteristics	**6-7**, **6-7**
normal trim failure	3-23
Hot-weather Procedure	9-20
Hydraulic Power Supply System, Utility	1-36, **1-37**
fluid specification	**1-58**
ground tests	2-10
indicators	1-38
gage, fluid quantity	1-38
gage, pressure	1-38
switch, selector	1-38
operation	7-13
Hydraulic Systems, Flight Control	
see Flight Control Systems	

I

Ice and Rain	9-14
anti-ice systems, use of	9-15
engine	9-14
wing	9-14
Identification Radar, AN/APX-6	4-11, 4-14
Identification Radar, AN/APX-25	4-15
Ignition System	1-22
switch, air start	1-22, **1-23**
switch, engine master	1-18
ILAS Approaches	9-10, 9-11
Indicators	
see applicable system	
Instrument Descents	9-8
penetrations, jet	9-3, **9-4**, **9-6**
penetrations, radar	9-8, **9-9**
Instrument Flight Procedures	9-1
Instrument Panel Light Rheostats	4-19
Instruments	1-50
also see applicable system	
accelerometer	1-50
altimeter, cockpit	1-50, **1-51**
compass, slaved gyro magnetic	4-29
switch, fast slaving	4-29
compass, stand-by	1-51
indicator, airspeed	1-50

Index-5

PAGE NUMBERS IN BOLDFACE DENOTE ILLUSTRATIONS

indicator, attitude	1-51
indicator, turn-and-bank	1-52
Machmeter	1-50
markings	**5-1, 5-2**
pitot-static boom	1-50
subpanels	1-12
Intercept Profiles	A-8
clean	**A-24**
tanks, two 120-gallon	**A-30**
Interior Check	2-4
Inverters	
see Electrical Power Supply System	

J

Jettison Button, Drop Tank	1-27
Jettison Handle, Drop Tank Emergency	1-27

K

Knobs, Control
see applicable system

L

Landing	2-21, **2-22**
after landing	2-24
cold-weather procedure	9-19
cross-wind landing	2-23
distances	A-15
drag chute deployed	**A-38**
without drag chute	**A-39**
emergencies	3-10
any one gear up or unlocked	3-11
belly landing	3-10
barrier, engaging runway	3-12
with flat tire	3-12
forced landing, simulated	3-8
heavy-weight landing	2-23
minimum-run landing	2-23
normal landing	2-21, **2-22**
with engine inoperative	3-4, 3-6
Landing and Taxi Light Switch	4-17
Landing Gear System	1-46
button, emergency retract	1-46
emergency operation	3-22
emergency lowering	**3-23**
emergency retraction	3-22
handle	1-46
handle, emergency release	1-47
indicators	1-47
lock, nose gear ground safety	1-46, **1-46**
lowering speeds	5-4
operation	7-14
panel, control	**1-48**
switch, door ground control	1-47
Landing Light Lowering Speed	5-4
Level-flight Characteristics	6-12, **6-12, 6-13**
Levers	
see applicable system	
Lighting Equipment	4-17
exterior lighting	4-17
light, code indicator	4-18
switch, code selector	4-17
switch, exterior lighting flasher	4-17
switch, fuselage light dimmer	4-17
switch, landing and taxi	4-17
switch, master code	4-17
switch, position light dimmer	4-17
interior lighting	4-18
rheostat, console panel and floodlight	4-19
rheostat, instrument panel floodlight	4-19
rheostat, instrument panel light	4-19
rheostat, thunderstorm light	4-19
switch, compass and accelerometer light	4-19
switch, console panel and floodlight selector	4-19
panels, control	**4-18**
Lights, Indicator	
see applicable system	
Limitations, Operating	5-1, **5-2**, 5-4

Loadmeters	1-34
Localizer Receivers	4-11, 4-15, **4-16**
Locks	
canopy	1-54
flight control	1-40
nose gear ground safety	1-46, **1-46**
shoulder harness	1-60
Lockup System, Electronic Engine Control Automatic	1-20
ground tests	2-10
light, indicator	1-20
operation	7-4

M

Machmeter	1-50
Mach Number	6-1, **6-2**
correction	A-2
Main Differences Table	1-5, **1-5**
Maneuvering-flight Characteristics	6-15, **6-16**
Maneuvers, Prohibited	5-5
Map Case	4-47
Marker Beacon Radio, AN/ARN-12	4-11, **4-16**
Maximum Endurance Profiles	A-12
clean	**A-26**
tanks, two 120-gallon	**A-32**
Maximum Endurance Profiles, Optimum	A-13
clean	**A-27**
tanks, two 120-gallon	**A-33**
Maximum Glide	3-3, **3-6**
Minimum-run Landing	2-23
Minimum-run Take-off	2-17
Mirror, Rear-vision	4-47
Missed-approach Go-around	9-13
Mission Profiles	A-6
clean	**A-23**
tanks, two 120-gallon	**A-29**

N

Nautical Miles Per Pound of Fuel Graphs	A-15
clean	**A-46—A-48**
tanks, two 120-gallon	**A-49, A-50**
Navigation Equipment	4-29
compass, radio	4-11, 4-14
compass, slaved gyro magnetic	4-29
switch, compass fast slaving	4-29
compass, stand-by	1-51
instrument flight procedure	9-3
Night Flying	9-17
Nose Gear Ground Safety Lock	1-46, **1-46**
Nose Wheel Steering System	1-48
button, engaging	1-49
pin, release	1-48
Nozzle, Variable-area	1-21, **1-21**
failure, automatic control	3-18
indicator, position	1-22
switch	1-21

O

Oil Pressure Gage	1-24
Oil System	1-26
oil specification	1-58
Omnidirectional Receiver, AN/ARN-14	4-11, 4-15
On Entering Airplane, Instrument Flight Procedure	9-2
Optimum Maximum Endurance Profiles	A-13
clean	**A-27**
tanks, two 120-gallon	**A-33**
Optimum Return Profiles	A-10
clean	**A-25**
tanks, two 120-gallon	**A-31**
Oxygen System	4-19
controls	4-19
lever, regulator diluter	4-19
lever, regulator emergency toggle	4-20
lever, regulator supply	4-20
switch, regulator warning light	4-20
duration charts	4-20, **4-21**
emergency operation	4-23
hose hookup, oxygen	4-23

PAGE NUMBERS IN BOLDFACE DENOTE ILLUSTRATIONS

indicators 4-20
    light, warning 4-21
    pressure gage and flow indicator 4-20
normal operation 4-22
preflight check 4-21
regulator 4-22

P

Panels, Control
    see applicable system
Penetrations, Jet 9-3, **9-4, 9-6**
Penetrations, Radar **9-8, 9-9**
Pitch Trim Indicator, Automatic Pilot 4-26
Pitot Heat Switch 4-8
Pitot-Static Boom 1-50
Porpoising 6-7, **6-7**
Preflight Checks 2-2
    airplane check 2-14
    canopy and ejection seat check 2-2
    engine check 2-13, 2-14
    exterior inspection 2-2, **2-3**
        before exterior inspection 2-2
    ground tests 2-10
        automatic pilot ground tests 4-26
        cold-weather procedure 9-18
    interior check 2-4
    oxygen system check 4-21
    weight and balance 2-1
Pressure Gage and Flow Indicator, Oxygen 4-20
Pressure Gage, Hydraulic System 1-38
Pressure Suit Face Mask Heater Rheostat 4-7
Pressurization, Radar 4-6
Pressurization System, Cockpit
    see Air Conditioning and Pressurization System, Cockpit
Pre-traffic-pattern Check 2-20
Prohibited Maneuvers 5-5
Protective Covers 4-47
Pump Failure, Transfer 3-19
Pumps, Fuel Booster 1-27

R

Radar, AN/APX-6 Identification 4-11, 4-14
Radar, AN/APX-25 Identification 4-15
Radar and Rocket-firing System Controls ... 4-33, **4-34, 4-35**
    control, antenna hand 4-37
    panel, radar control 4-34
    panel, radarscope control 4-36
Radar Pressurization 4-6
Radarscope Control Panel **4-34, 4-35, 4-36**
Radarscope Presentation 4-38, **4-38**
Radio, AN/ARC-27 UHF 4-10, 4-11
Radio, AN/ARC-34 UHF Command 4-10, 4-11
Radio, AN/ARN-12 Marker Beacon 4-11, 4-16
Radio Compass, AN/ARN-6 .... 4-11, 4-14
Radio Navigation Equipment 9-3
Radome Anti-icing System 4-2, 4-6, **4-7**
    light, overheat warning 4-8
    normal operation 4-9
    overheating 4-9
    switch 4-8
Rain Removal System 4-9
Rear-vision Mirror 4-47
Receiver, AN/ARN-14 Omnidirectional 4-11, 4-15
Receivers, Glide Path and Localizer 4-11, 4-15, 4-16
Receptacle, Alternator External Power 1-34, **1-35**
Receptacle, Inverter External Power 1-34, **1-35**
Receptacles, DC External Power 1-31
Refusal Speeds **A-3, A-21**
Regulators
    see applicable system
Rheostats
    see applicable system
Rocket System
    see: Armament
        Fire Control System
Rudder 1-38
    control system 1-42
    flight characteristics 6-8

lock, control 1-40
operation 6-11
pedals 1-39
switch, trim 1-41

S

Safety Pins, Canopy Ground and Maintenance ... 1-52
Safety Pins, Seat Ground and Maintenance 1-56
Seat, Ejection 1-55
    armrests 1-57
    belt, automatic-opening safety 1-56, **1-57**
        lanyard, automatic parachute arming ... **1-57**
    check 2-2
    ejector **1-54, 1-55**
    handle, shoulder-harness lock 1-60
    lever, vertical adjustment 1-60
    operation 3-16
    pins, ground and maintenance safety 1-56
    trigger, catapult 1-57, 1-60
Selectors
    see applicable system
Servicing Diagram **1-58**
Shoulder-harness Lock Handle 1-60
Sight, Stand-by 4-45
    rheostat 4-45
    switch, alternate filament selector 4-45
Slats, Wing 1-44
    operation 6-12
Smoke or Fumes, Elimination of 3-10
Speed Brake System 1-45
    flight characteristics 6-11
    switch 1-45
Spins 5-5, 6-4, **6-5**
    inverted spins 6-6
    nonoscillatory spins 6-4
    normal spins 6-4
    recovery 6-6
Stalls 6-1, **6-2**
    accelerated stalls 6-2
    practice stalls 6-4
    recovery 6-4
    unaccelerated stalls 6-2
Stand-by Compass 1-51
    switch, light 4-19
Starter System 1-23
    button, stop-starter 1-24
    switch, battery-starter 1-23
Starting Engine 2-6, **2-8**
    automatic start 2-7, 7-2, **7-3**
    exhaust temperature limitations 5-4
    instrument flight procedure after starting ... 9-2
    start on emergency fuel system 2-10
Status of the Airplane 2-1
Steering System, Nose Wheel 1-48
    button, engaging 1-49
    pin, release 1-48
Stopping Engine 2-24
    cold-weather procedure 9-20
    fire after shutdown 3-10
    smoke from turbine during shutdown 7-7
    turbine noise during shutdown 7-7
Surface Anti-icing System 4-2, 4-7, **4-7**
    light, overheat warning 4-8
    operation 4-9
    overheating 4-10
    switch 4-8
Switches
    see applicable system

T

Tachometer 1-24
    indication 7-7
Take-off 2-16
    also see: After Take-off
            Before Take-off
    acceleration **A-3, A-20**
    cross-wind take-off 2-17
    distances 6-21, **6-21, A-2**
        Maximum Thrust, full flaps **A-18**
        Military Thrust, full flaps **A-19**

Take-off (Trim)—Zero Reader

PAGE NUMBERS IN BOLDFACE DENOTE ILLUSTRATIONS

engine failure during take-off 3-2
engine fire during take-off 3-9
engine overspeed during take-off 3-1
hot-weather and desert procedure 9-21
instrument take-off 9-3
inverter failure during take-off roll 3-21
loss of afterburning during take-off 3-15
main fuel control system failure during take-off 3-18
minimum-run take-off 2-17
normal take-off 2-16
take-off speeds, effect of **2-17**
Take-off (Trim) Position Indicator Light 1-41
Taxiing 2-12
  cold-weather procedure 9-18
  instrument flight procedure 9-2
Throttle (Power Control) 1-18
  grip **1-18**
Thrust Selector Operation 7-1
Thunderstorm Flying 9-15
Thunderstorm Light Rheostat 4-19
Traffic-pattern Check 2-21, **2-22**
Trigger, Camera and Rocket-firing 4-31
Trigger, Seat Catapult 1-57, 1-60
Trim Switches
  see Flight Control System
Trim Tab 1-38
  flight characteristics 6-9
Turn-and-Bank Indicator 1-52

V

Valves
  see applicable system
Variable-area Nozzle 1-21, **1-21**
  indicator, position 1-22
  switch 1-21
Variable-slope Feel System 1-38, **1-39**
Voltmeter 1-34
  switch, selector 1-34
Vortex Generators 6-23, **6-24**

W

Warm-up and Ground Check 9-18

Warning Lights
  canopy unsafe 1-55
  dual fuel pump 1-19
    characteristics 7-13
  generator 1-34
  hot-rocket-package 4-32
  inverter failure 1-36
  oxygen system 4-21
  surface anti-ice overheat 4-8
  windshield and radome anti-ice overheat 4-8
Warning Light Switch, Oxygen Regulator 4-20
Weight 1-4
  limitations 5-6
  weight and balance 2-1
Windshield Anti-icing System **4-2, 4-6, 4-7**
  light, overheat warning 4-8
  normal operation 4-9
  overheating 4-9
  switch 4-8
Windshield Defrosting System 4-6
  lever 4-6
  operation 4-9
Wing Flap System 1-45
  lever 1-45
    operation 7-13
  lowering speed 5-4
Wing Icing 9-14
Wing Slats 1-44
  operation 6-12

Y

Yaw Damper 1-39
  operation 6-10, **6-10**
  switch 1-41

Z

Zero Reader **4-11**, 4-16
  controls, indicator 4-17
  manual ILAS approaches 9-13
  switch unit, selector 4-17

Index-8